# ASPECTS OF RABBINIC THEOLOGY

BY SOLOMON SCHECHTER

*Introduction to New Edition*
*by* LOUIS FINKELSTEIN

SCHOCKEN BOOKS

NEW YORK

*First* SCHOCKEN PAPERBACK *edition 1961*

10 9 8 7 6   82 83 84 85

*Library of Congress Catalog Card No. 61-14919*

*Manufactured in the United States of America*

ISBN 0-8052-0015-0

To

LOUIS MARSHALL, ESQUIRE

JEW AND AMERICAN

# *Introduction to New Edition*

## *by* LOUIS FINKELSTEIN

Solomon Schechter's main contribution to Jewish theology is perhaps his rediscovery that to be fully understood it must be experienced emotionally; it must be felt as well as "known." The emotional reactions evoked by the concept of the Kingdom of God, of the Messiah, of the Revelation, are as much part of the doctrines, as the propositions themselves regarding them.

Schechter felt that he could better penetrate Talmudic thought because he was reared in a world which it dominated. Rabbinic theology was the mother tongue, so to speak, of the East European community where he was born. Talmudic doctrines underlay both the conscious and many unconscious decisions of individuals and groups in that region. Although his native Rumania in the second half of the nineteenth century bore little resemblance economically, sociologically, politically, and culturally to Judea, Galilee, and Babylonia of Rabbinic times, so far as the Jews were concerned, spiritually not much had really altered. The aspirations of the people, especially of the intellectual elite, had remained the same—the highest possible perfection in the art and science of life; respect for learning, piety, and good deeds; the conviction that no matter how difficult man's fate on earth, mortal life was eminently worthwhile if it led to the true life of the hereafter.

The home, the school, the synagogue, and the organized community were all based on these premises, expressed far more clearly in the existence and influence of these institutions, than in verbal propositions. The Prayer Book, largely composed under the Persian domination of the Near East twenty-three centuries earlier, reflected both the beliefs and the strivings of these Jews of Eastern Europe in the nineteenth century, as well as those of the Judea where it emerged.

In this rejuvenated ancient world, reestablished on European soil and persisting almost until our own time, leading figures usually, and lesser figures frequently, made their life decisions in a frame of reference of eternity. In that society, one might, without arousing comment, deliberately choose poverty for oneself and one's children in order to inherit the world to come. The spirit of man was far more real than his body; mastery of Torah and compliance with its *dicta* far more urgent and important than success in any aspect of mortal life. The kingdom of God was at once distantly future and immediately present. It was distant in the sense that the vast majority of mankind lived outside it. It was present in the sense that one spent almost all one's life within it. Every Jew "accepted" each day "the yoke of the Kingdom of Heaven," and a moment later prayed that this Kingdom might through a miracle be realized on earth in the future.

The belief that the Torah was the revealed word of

God could scarcely be challenged by those who spent most of their waking hours mastering its intricacies and discovering its joys. To suppose that the Torah did not emanate from God (no matter what metaphors might be employed to describe His method of communication with His chosen prophets) was far more unrealistic than to suppose that the material Universe had just "happened," and far more incredible.

This society had no need for a systematic theology based on verbalized assumptions and theories of contemporary science, and built up with logical precision and coherence. The verbalized doctrines to which one appealed in moments of particular temptation or distress were valid independently of their logical relationship to one another. The concepts were real, and the propositions true, because without them life, as it was lived, made no sense.

Inconsistent maxims could equally be accepted as true, relating doubtless to different situations. Inconsistent theological propositions did not have to be reconciled; their validity as propositions was not really important. What was significant was their pedagogical value and their poetical meaning, expressing the underlying premises on which all of life's decisions were based.

Theological maxims and assertions were either footnotes, documenting ideas expressed in righteous living, or parenthetical statements, making symbolic actions clearer than they could otherwise be to the untutored mind.

Thus Schechter's early milieu was intellectually and spiritually far closer to that of the Talmudists of the age of Hillel and Rabbi Akiba, than to that of Rab Saadia Gaon and Maimonides. These later immortal scholars had lived in the midst of the highly developed Moslem science and philosophy of the Middle Ages and were inevitably exposed to alien theological, ethical, and religious ideas, both verbalized and systematized and, because of this, profoundly attractive to many Jews. Therefore these Jewish teachers, and many others like them, had struggled hard to impose on Rabbinic Judaism a form analogous in symmetry and system to that confronting Jews in the dominant religion.

The same forces played a similar role in Western Europe in the eighteenth and nineteenth centuries, producing a literature of philosophy, historical research, and religious polemic which, while not rising to the high intellectual and spiritual levels of Rab Saadia Gaon and Maimonides, was by no means insignificant. The level of the general culture of Eastern Europe, the almost complete separation of Jew from Gentile in the social and intellectual life, and the dynamic energy of the great Rabbinic academies, which in that region succeeded the earlier schools of the great commentators and super-commentators on the Bible and Talmud, made such efforts superfluous in such countries as Rumania, Russia, Poland, and Lithuania.

Out of this rejuvenated Talmudic world, Solomon Schechter moved to the West—in the first instance to Vienna. He had gone there not in search of a better livelihood, for an emigrant student was sure to encounter much suffering and self-denial. Nor did he seek "emancipation" from ritual: Rabbinic knowledge and compulsion to study had throughout his youth provided him with intellectual and spiritual nourishment. Like others who had heard of the wisdom of the West, he yearned to master it, and thus to understand better the wisdom of Judaism as incorporated in the Talmud and later writings. Rumania was at the time far behind both Austria and Lithuania in depth of Jewish studies; and an eager student might well seek the opportunity to commune with the great scholars of the West, to discover how with their superior equipment they approached the Talmud.

Arriving in Vienna, Schechter traversed not only many miles, but also many centuries. In this world new to him, not only in Vienna but ultimately in Britain, he observed and studied that from which he had emerged. Child of two worlds, he could be critical of both, as he sought to integrate that which was most creative and beneficial in both.

He discovered that his native Rumania had not really fulfilled the standards of the Talmud. The energetic striving of the great Talmudic heroes for knowledge of the good life, their power to translate their insights into immortal words, their ability to compose prayers which could be recited centuries later with passion, had given way to slothful reliance on these inherited treasures. Jewish Rumania in the latter half of the nineteenth century was a pale reflection, but not a replica, of

Yabneh or Usha or Sura or Pumbedita. Something had passed out of Judaism, even in this Eastern world which superficially seemed so pervaded with the tradition.

On the other hand, Schechter never seems to have overcome his wonder at the struggle of so many brilliant minds in Western Judaism to force into alien form the theological and ethical concepts of Rabbinic Judaism, and to substitute for living, vital Judaism a reconstruction which transformed it into a series of ponderous volumes and unappreciated dogmas.

Schechter does not seem to have drawn the inference that the Rabbinic theological system is really part of its juristic system which, like all other juristic systems, has a logic of its own, quite different from that of Aristotle. As Schechter himself suggests, opposing theological traditions had not given concern to the individual Jew of earlier days because he had not supposed that Judaism was a "system" of belief but, rather, of conduct. Action, based largely on impulse (which can never become a logical system, for it arises from a variety of human needs), is never free of apparent logical contradiction, and cannot be forced into a Procrustean bed of rational propositions. Hence Schechter was not even much attracted to the philosophical efforts of Maimonides, his predecessors, and his followers. These scholars had written philosophical books, valuable in themselves and sometimes illuminating through insights into the Talmud, but generally based on interpretation and re-interpretation. To understand Maimonides' *Guide for the Perplexed,* one obviously had to study it; to understand the Talmud, one turned to its major commentaries, particularly those of Rashi and the Tosafot, and to the Code of Maimonides himself.

To the extent that its origin was simply human, Judaism was a "system" only in the sense that the Common Law or the Roman Law might be a system, or a language might have a grammatical structure. The human mind, being what it is, generally approaches the problems to which it addresses itself with preconceptions which impose a certain type of unity and coherence upon its creations. Shakespeare and Milton are in a certain way unified wholes; the literary critic can discover in their respective works a type of organic and biological coherence demonstrating the unity of their origin. He soon discovers when a play or part of a play ascribed to Shakespeare is not really his; not being a schizophrenic, Shakespeare's work had characteristic traits and a development natural to it. What is true of the artist applies also to the judge, the painter, the architect, the sculptor, and to man generally.

Judaism differs from the creation of specific individuals because it took form under many conditions, in many centuries, and in a variety of countries. Inherent logical unity can be forced on Judaism only at the cost of distortion.

Perhaps Schechter failed to associate the nature of Jewish theology with the nature of its Law because he despaired of the effort to transmit to the Western world the meaning of Rabbinic law for those engrossed in it.

With some expectation of being understood, if vaguely, he could hope to bring scholars outside Judaism some appreciation of the theological insights of the Talmud and its associated writings. He could describe the life and activity of great Talmudists—Nahmanides, R. Elijah Gaon of Wilna, or R. Joseph Caro of Saphed—and show how each was psychologically consistent. But how could he communicate the joy, the creativeness, the sense of order in life under the Law? How was he to explain a religion which expects each adherent to develop judicial qualities? How was he to give an outsider the sense of world responsibility felt by a sensitive Rabbinic Jew concerning a simple gesture? For each Jew the world seemed always to be hanging in balance, between good and evil, between creation and destruction. To decide wrongly was to imperil more than his own personal salvation, it was to imperil mankind. An error in addressing an invitation, the Talmud holds, was the immediate cause of the destruction of Jerusalem: the person invited in error was embarrassed and infuriated, and became a Roman informer against the Jews. A garment of many colors, given by Jacob to his favorite son, led to an incredible crime, with equally incredible consequences for future generations who, in the last analysis, have had to pay the penalty for the transgressions of their ancestors.

Yet life has to be lived; decisions have to be reached; errors are inevitably made; and somehow the world survives. This then is the real miracle of existence—at each moment God intervenes to transform the results of man's bad judgment into creative forces. Yet while to quote Schechter, "one should leave a little bit to God" and avoid morbidity, nevertheless one should seek to avoid error, for avoidable error is a truly heinous wrong.

To explain the complicated structure of Judaism, as more than a system of theology, or of law, or of ethics, or of all combined, would have taxed even the genius of Schechter. To have tried to compress any satisfactory explanation into a single volume was impossible. Schechter therefore satisfied himself with a book called "Some Aspects of Rabbinic Theology," indicating that he was presenting neither a complete system nor a thoroughgoing analysis of the nature of Judaism.

Yet a careful reading suggests clearly the nature of the faith he is describing.

In Rabbinic Judaism study is more than a method of worship, although it is also that. Study is more than a means of acquiring information about the tradition, although it is surely that. Study is a method of developing sensitivity to the moral element in complex issues: to analyze the nature of these issues, to discover the arguments pro and con any specific decision, and to master the art and science of presenting these arguments to one's mind and heart, so that one's decision will be based on mature analysis and awareness of ethical alternatives.

It is not always easy to reconstruct the nature of the argument which must have passed through the mind of the ancient Rabbinic Sages, even after the fact. (Yet without study of the process through which they arrived at their decisions, how is one to learn how to behave in the perplexities and complications of life?)

Jesus found that the Pharisees in Judea tithed spelt for the benefit of priests, Levites, and the poor. In his native Galilee this was not done, and he could not but suppose that the Judean Pharisees were indulging in super-piety, intended to impress with their devoutness visitors from other parts of Palestine. How could he, or anyone else outside the Talmudic academies, know that the question whether spelt was to be tithed was the subject of disagreement between Shammaites and Hillelites? The former, generally the wealthier group, used spelt only as animal food, not subject to tithing. The latter, retaining traditions of the poorer sections of Jerusalem, used the spelt for their own food, and therefore had to tithe it. Galilee was dominated by Shammaitic thought; Judea by that of the Hillelites. One not immersed in the Law might well be astonished that the Judaite landowners, who had far smaller farms than the Galilean, should practice a type of charity unknown among their wealthier brethren. But the Judaites really had no choice. If spelt was human food, it had to be shared with others.

The issue is interesting because it illustrates a curious paradox. The Shammaites, who were not only the wealthier aristocratic group but also included many priests, tended to be more rigorous in interpretation of the ritual than their Hillelite brethren. And surely

Hillelite scholars might well have sought some means of relief from the burden of a ten percent tax for their followers, reduced to eat food elsewhere considered fit only for beasts. But the right (as well as the duty) of the poor to be givers as well as receivers was of profound importance to the Hillelites. The commandment to be charitable was not limited to those who had much but extended also to those who had little, because the sense of giving was even more important to Man than his need for food.

On the other hand, the Shammaite scholar might well retort that it was not fitting to offer poor men food otherwise given only to beasts. That is in general why produce used for animal feed was not tithed, and for the Shammaites what applied to other animal foods applied also to spelt. If the poor, the Levite, or the priest could not obtain sufficient food for his needs from the grain customarily used by human beings, he would have to be supported by charity. The obligation of the community could not be satisfied with spelt whose very use was an insult.

This argument, applying to whole geographical districts and large sections of the population, had been developed in ancient academies, perhaps in early pre-Rabbinic times. Its analysis by the student, trying to understand why Shammaites and Hillelites should disagree in such a matter, and why each group should take the position it did, is intended (from the Hillelite point of view) to make him sensitive to the underlying issue

—the recognition that Man needs more than food to live; that frequently physical hunger is less important than spiritual hunger.

Analysis of this issue is, of course, far simpler than the highly technical arguments that fill the pages of the Talmud and its commentaries. Sometimes it is extremely difficult to uncover the moral issue at stake; sometimes the technicalities of the legal, juristic debate even seem to conceal the real issues. A reader of an English translation of the Talmud will encounter great difficulty in any effort to understand what the ancient scholars were talking about and why they spent so much time talking about it.

But the ancient academicians remarked that often sinful men, attracted to study of the Torah either through hope of glory or through curiosity, or for want of something else to do, emerged from the discipline righteous and saintly.

If Schechter's thesis is correct, that to be understood theological doctrines have to be experienced (i.e., felt emotionally as well as learned intellectually) is it not certain that a method by which a whole people was to be called to righteousness has to be experienced in order to be appreciated? And how difficult it would have been even for Schechter to communicate to the English reader through words the nature of the Rabbinic commitment to the study of Torah as a means for dealing with man's problem of moral perceptivity.

Schechter briefly refers to this profounder and more comprehensive concept of Torah at the close of the chapter dealing with "The Law as Personified in Literature." "The Torah," he says, "was simply the manifestation of God's will, revealed to us for our good—the pedagogue, as the Rabbis expressed it, who educates God's creatures. *The occupation with the Torah was, according to the Rabbis, less calculated to produce schoolmen and jurists than saints and devout spirits."* To document this thesis, Schechter quotes the beautiful paean honoring study of Torah, composed by R. Meir and found in the opening passage of *Perek Kinyan Torah.*

The view that inquiry into the nature and requirements of Torah is more than a human need, being a cosmic process, is even more difficult to communicate to the uninitiate. Doubtless that is why Schechter did not include in his book any discussion of the fundamental Rabbinic concept of the Academy on High. The belief that study of the Torah is one of the Deity's main concerns, and that God Himself is each day expanding the scope and insight of Torah, engaging in this labor in association with the souls of the saints who have departed mortal life, is a theological metaphor; but for the Rabbinic scholars the metaphor represented reality—the profoundest of all realities.

That the Torah is at once perfect and perpetually incomplete; that like the Universe itself it was created to be a process, rather than a system—a method of inquiry into the right, rather than a codified collection of answers; that to discover possible situations with which it might deal and to analyze their moral implications in the light of its teachings is to share the labor of Divinity—these are inherent elements of Rabbinic thought, dominating the manner of life it recommends.

Joy in the Law is therefore more than joy in the fulfilment of the commandments; it is also joy in the discovery of new ones relating to situations never before explicitly formulated.

Perhaps no concept in Judaism is more alien to the current trends of thought; and yet perhaps none is more relevant to the problems Judaism and the world faces in our time. In an era of rapid change the student of Torah will find himself confronted daily with issues to which answers may well be sought in Torah; but for which the search must be strenuous, laborious, indefatigable, and persistent. "Do not," Rabbi Tarfon urged his disciples, "turn away from labor which has no end." The study of Torah, as conceived by most Rabbis of the Talmud, is such a labor; and whatever else one may be willing to abandon, that study must be recognized as of paramount importance.

The Jewish Theological Seminary of America
June, 1961

# PREFACE*

This volume represents no philosophic exposition of the body of doctrine of the Synagogue, nor does it offer a description of its system of ethics. Both the philosophy of the Synagogue and its ethics have been treated in various works by competent scholars belonging to different schools of thought. The main aim of such works is, however, as it would seem, interpretation, more often re-interpretation. The object of the following pages is a different one. The task I set myself was to give a presentation of Rabbinic opinion on a number of theological topics as offered by the Rabbinic literature, and forming an integral part of the religious consciousness of the bulk of the nation or "Catholic Israel."

Keeping this end in view, I considered it advisable not to intrude too much interpretation or paraphrase upon the Rabbis. I let them have their own say in their own words, and even their own phraseology, so far as the English idiom allowed. My work consisted in gathering the materials distributed all over the wide domain of Rabbinic literature, classifying, sifting, and arranging them, and also in ascertaining clearly and stating in simple, direct terms the doctrines and theological concepts that they involved, in such a manner as to convey to the student a clear

* Abridged from the original edition of 1909

notion of the Rabbinic opinion of the doctrine under discussion. In cases where opinion differed, the varying views were produced, and so were inconsistencies pointed out, stating, however, when there was sufficient authority for doing so, what the prevailing opinion in the Synagogue was. Where such authority was lacking, it was assumed that the Synagogue allowed both opinions to stand, neither opinion containing the whole truth, and being in need of qualifications by the opposite opinion.

As really representative of such opinion, we can only take into account the Talmudic and the recognised Midrashic literature, or the "great Midrashim." This literature covers, as stated elsewhere, many centuries, and was produced in widely differing climes amid varying surroundings and ever-changing conditions, and was interrupted several times by great national catastrophes and by the rise of all sorts of sects and schisms.

Notwithstanding, however, all these excrescences which historic events contributed towards certain beliefs and the necessary mutations and changes of aspects involved in them, it should be noted that Rabbinic literature is, as far as doctrine and dogma are concerned, more distinguished by the consensus of opinion than by its dissensions. On the whole, it may safely be maintained that there is little in the dogmatic teachings of the Palestinian authorities of the first and second centuries to which, for instance, R. Ashi of the fifth and even R. Sherira of the tenth century, both leaders of Rabbinic opinion in Babylon, would have refused their consent, though the emphasis put on the one or the other doctrine may have differed widely as a result of changed conditions and surroundings.

It was in view of this fact that I did not consider it necessary to provide the quotations given from the Talmud and the Midrash with the date of their authors, assuming that as long as there is no evidence that they are in contradiction to some older or even contemporary opinion they may be regarded as expressive of the general opinion of the Synagogue. Such a treatment of the subject was, I thought, the more justified as it did not lie within the scope of this work to furnish the student with a history of Rabbinic theology, but rather, as already indicated, to give some comprehensive view of a group of theological subjects as thought out and taught by the Synagogue.

It is one of the most interesting of religious phenomena to observe the essential unity that the Synagogue maintained, despite all antagonistic influences. Dispersed among the nations, without a national centre, without a synod to formulate its principles, or any secular power to enforce its decrees, the Synagogue found its home and harmony in the heart of a loyal and consecrated Israel.

It is this body of Israel in which the unity of the Synagogue was and is still incorporate that I called occasionally as witness in some cases of religious sentiment wholly unknown to the outsider. I may as well state here that it was my knowledge of this Israel which gave the first impulse to these essays.

In conclusion, I wish to thank Dr. Alexander Marx, Professor of History in the Jewish Theological Seminary of America, who prepared the list of Abbreviations for me. I am also indebted to Mr. Joseph B. Abrahams, Clerk of the Seminary office, who was always at my call during the progress of this work. I can further hardly express sufficiently my obligations to my friend Rabbi Charles Isaiah Hoffman, of Newark, N.J., for his painstaking reading of the proofs and for ever so many helpful suggestions, by which this volume has profited. And last, but not least, I have to record my special obligations to my friend, Miss Henrietta Szold, who likewise read the proof, and made many a valuable suggestion. I am particularly grateful to her for the excellent Index she has prepared to this work, which will, I am convinced, be appreciated by every reader of this volume.

S. S.

# CONTENTS

*Introduction to New Edition by Louis Finkelstein*

*Preface*

| CHAPTER | | PAGE |
|---|---|---|
| I. | INTRODUCTORY | 1 |
| II. | GOD AND THE WORLD | 21 |
| III. | GOD AND ISRAEL | 46 |
| IV. | ELECTION OF ISRAEL | 57 |
| V. | THE KINGDOM OF GOD (INVISIBLE) | 65 |
| VI. | THE VISIBLE KINGDOM (UNIVERSAL) | 80 |
| VII. | THE KINGDOM OF GOD (NATIONAL) | 97 |
| VIII. | THE "LAW" | 116 |
| IX. | THE LAW AS PERSONIFIED IN THE LITERATURE | 127 |
| X. | THE TORAH IN ITS ASPECT OF LAW (MIZWOTH) | 138 |
| XI. | THE JOY OF THE LAW | 148 |
| XII. | THE ZACHUTH OF THE FATHERS. IMPUTED RIGHTEOUSNESS AND IMPUTED SIN | 170 |
| XIII. | THE LAW OF HOLINESS AND THE LAW OF GOODNESS | 199 |
| XIV. | SIN AS REBELLION | 219 |
| XV. | THE EVIL YEZER: THE SOURCE OF REBELLION | 242 |
| XVI. | MAN'S VICTORY BY THE GRACE OF GOD, OVER THE EVIL YEZER CREATED BY GOD | 264 |
| XVII. | FORGIVENESS AND RECONCILIATION WITH GOD | 293 |

| CHAPTER | | PAGE |
|---|---|---|
| XVIII. | Repentance: Means of Reconciliation | 313 |
| | Additions and Corrections | 345 |
| | List of Abbreviations and Books not quoted with Full Title | 349 |
| | Index | 353 |

# ASPECTS OF RABBINIC THEOLOGY

# I

## INTRODUCTORY

My object in choosing the title "Some Aspects of Rabbinic Theology" is to indicate that from the following chapters there must not be expected either finality or completeness. Nor will there be made any attempt in the following pages at that precise and systematic treatment which we are rightly accustomed to claim in other fields of scientific inquiry. I have often marvelled at the certainty and confidence with which Jewish legalism, Jewish transcendentalism, Jewish self-righteousness, are delineated in our theological manuals and histories of religion; but I have never been able to emulate either quality. I have rather found, when approaching the subject a little closer, that the peculiar mode of old Jewish thought, as well as the unsatisfactory state of the documents in which this thought is preserved, "are against the certain," and urge upon the student caution and sobriety. In these introductory paragraphs I shall try to give some notion of the difficulties that lie before us.

To begin with the difficulties attaching to the unsatisfactory state of Rabbinic documents. A prominent theologian has, when referring to the Rabbis, declared that one has only to study the Mishnah to see that it was not moral or spiritual subjects which engrossed their attention, but the characteristic hair-splitting about ceremonial trifles. There is an appearance of truth in this statement. The Mishnah, which was *compiled* about the beginning of the third century of the C.E., consists of sixty-one (or sixty-three) tractates, of which only one, known by the title of "The Chapters of the Fathers," deals with moral and spiritual matters in the narrower sense of these terms. Still this is not the whole truth, for there are also other tractates, occupying about one-third of the whole Mishnah, which deal with the civil law, the procedure of the criminal courts, the regulation of inheritance, laws regarding property, the administration of oaths, marriage, and divorce. All these topics, and many similar ones relating to public justice and the welfare of the community as the Rabbis understood it, are certainly not to be branded as ceremonial trifles; and if the kingdom of God on earth means something more than the mystical languor of the individual, it is difficult to see on what ground they can be excluded from the sphere of religion. But, apart from this consideration —for it seems that theologians are not yet agreed in their answer to the question whether it is this world, with all its wants and complications, which should be the subject for redemption, or the individual soul, with its real and imaginary longings — there runs, parallel with this Mishnah, a vast literature, known under the name of Agadah, scattered over a multitude of Talmudical and Midrashic works, the earliest of which were compiled even before or about the time of the Mishnah, and the latest of which, while going down as far as the tenth or even the eleventh century, still include many ancient elements of Rabbinic thought. In these *compilations* it will be found that the minds of the so-called triflers were engrossed also with such subjects as God, and man's relation to God; as righteousness and sin, and the origin of evil; as suffering and repentance and immortality; as the election of Israel, Messianic aspirations, and with many other cognate subjects lying well within the moral and spiritual sphere, and no less interesting to the theologian than to the philosopher.

It is these Talmudic and Midrashic works, to which I should like to add at once the older Jewish liturgy, which will be one of the main sources of the material for the following chapters. Now I do not want to enter here into bibliographical details, which may be found in any good history of Jewish literature. But it may have been noticed that I spoke of "compilations"; and here a difficulty comes in. For a compilation presupposes the existence of other works, of which the compiler makes use. Thus there must have been some Rabbinic work or works composed long before our Mishnah, and perhaps as early as

30 C.E.[1] This work, or collection, would clearly have provided a better means for a true understanding of the period when Rabbinism was still in an earlier stage of its formation, than our present Mishnah of 200 C.E. Is it not just possible that many a theological feature, characteristic of the earlier Rabbis, found no place in the Mishnah, either because of its special design or through the carelessness or fancy of its compiler, or through some dogmatic consideration unknown to us? Is it not likely that the teaching of the Apostle Paul, the antinomian consequences of which became so manifest during the second century, brought about a growing prejudice against all allegoric explanations of the Scriptures,[2] or that the authorities refused to give them a prominent place in the Mishnah, which was intended by its compiler to become the great depository of the Oral Law? But whatever the cause, the effect is that we are almost entirely deprived of any real contemporary evidence from the most important period in the history of Rabbinic theology. The Psalms of Solomon may, for want of a better title, be characterized as the Psalms of the Pharisees; but to derive from them a Rabbinic theology is simply absurd. They have not

[1] See D. Hoffmann, *Magazin für die Wissenschaft des Judenthums* (Berlin), 8, p. 170.

[2] See the ל״ב מדות of R. Eleazar b. Jose of Galilee, where we read that the *Mashal* (allegoric interpretation) was only used in the Prophets and in the Hagiographa, "but the words of the Torah and commandments thou must not interpret them as *Mashal*." Cf. Bacher, *Terminologie*, I 122.

left the least trace in Jewish literature, and it is most probable that none of the great authorities we are acquainted with in the Talmud had ever read a single line of them, or even had heard their name. The same is the case with other Apocryphal and Apocalyptic works, for which Rabbinism is often made responsible. However strange it may seem, the fact remains that whilst these writings left a lasting impress on Christianity, they contributed — with the exception, perhaps, of the Book of Ecclesiasticus — little or nothing towards the formation of Rabbinic thought. The Rabbis were either wholly ignorant of their very existence, or stigmatised them as fabulous, or "external" (a milder expression in some cases for heretical), and thus allowed them to exert no permanent influence upon Judaism.

Passing from the Mishnah to the Talmud proper (the Gemara) and to the Midrash, the same fact meets us again. They, too, are only compilations, and from the defects of this, their fundamental quality, we frequently suffer.

There is, for instance, the interesting subject of miracles, which plays such an important part in the history of every religion. Despite the various attempts made by semi-rationalists to minimise their significance, the frequent occurrence of miracles will always remain, both for believers and sceptics, one of the most important tests of the religion in question; to the former as a sign of its superhuman nature, to the latter as a proof of its doubtful origin. The student is accordingly anxious to see whether the miraculous formed an essential element of Rabbinic Judaism. Nor are we quite disappointed when we turn over the pages of the Talmud with this purpose in view. There is hardly any miracle recorded in the Bible for which a parallel might not be found in the Rabbinic literature. The greatest part of the third chapter of the Tractate Taanith, called also the "Chapter of the Saints," is devoted to specimens of supernatural acts performed by various Rabbis. But miracles can only be explained by more miracles, by regular epidemics of miracles. The whole period which saw them must become the psychological phenomenon to be explained, rather than the miracle-workers themselves. But of the Rabbinical miracles we could judge with far greater accuracy if, instead of the few specimens still preserved to us, we were in possession of all those stories and legends which once circulated about the saints of Israel in their respective periods.[1]

Another problem which a fuller knowledge of these ancient times might have helped us to solve is this: With what purpose were these miracles worked, and what were they meant to prove? We are told in I Corinthians (I 22), that "the Jews ask for signs as the Greeks seek for wisdom." As a fact, however, in the whole of Rabbinic literature, there is not one single instance on record that a Rabbi was ever asked by his

[1] About the probability that there may have existed other collections of such stories, see Rapoport, *Bikkure Haittim*, I2 78 79.

colleagues to demonstrate the soundness of his doctrine, or the truth of a disputed Halachic case, by performing a miracle. Only once do we hear of a Rabbi who had recourse to miracles for the purpose of showing that his conception of a certain Halachah was the right one. And in this solitary instance the majority declined to accept the miraculous intervention as a demonstration of truth, and decided against the Rabbi who appealed to it.[1] Nor, indeed, were such supernatural gifts claimed for *all* Rabbis. Whilst many learned Rabbis are said to have "been accustomed to wonders," not a single miracle is reported for instance of the great Hillel, or his colleague, Shammai, both of whom exercised such an important influence on Rabbinic Judaism. On the other hand, we find that such men, as, for instance, Choni Hammaagel,[2] whose prayers were much sought after in times of drought, or R. Chaninah b. Dosa, whose prayers were often solicited in cases of illness,[3] left almost no mark on Jewish thought, the former being known only by the wondrous legends circulating about him, the latter being represented in the whole Talmud only by one or two moral sayings.[4] "Signs," then, must have been as little required from the Jewish Rabbi as from the Greek sophist. But if this was the case, we are actually left in darkness about

[1] See *Baba Mezia*, 59 *b*.

[2] *Taanith*, 24 *b*; cp. *Jer. Taanith*, 64 *a*, 64 *b*.

[3] See *Berachoth*, 33 *a*, and *Jer. Berachoth*, 10 *b*.

[4] *Aboth*, 3 9. See Bacher, *Ag. Tan.* I 288, p. 2.

the importance of miracles and their meaning as a religious factor in those early times. Our chances of clearing up such obscure but important points would naturally be much greater if some fresh documents could be discovered.

As another instance of the damage wrought by the loss of those older documents, I will allude only here to the well-known controversy between the school of Shammai and the school of Hillel regarding the question whether it had not been better for man not to have been created. The controversy is said to have lasted for two years and a half. Its final issue or verdict was that, as we have been created, the best thing for us to do is to be watchful over our conduct.[1] This is all that tradition (or the compiler) chose to give us about this lengthy dispute; but we do not hear a single word as to the causes which led to it, or the reasons advanced by the litigant parties for their various opinions. Were they metaphysical, or empirical, or simply based, as is so often the case, on different conceptions of the passages in the Scripture germane to the dispute?[2] We feel the more cause for regret when we recollect that the members of these schools were the contemporaries of the Apostles; when Jerusalem, as it seems, was boiling over with theology, and its market-places

[1] *Erubin*, 13 *b*.

[2] For other controversies of a theological nature between the same schools, see *Gen. R.*, 12 14, *Rosh Hashanah*, 16 *b*; *Chagigah*, 12 *a*; *P. K.* 61 *b*. Cf. Bacher, *Ag. Tan.*, I 14.

and synagogues were preparing metaphysics and theosophies to employ the mind of posterity for thousands of years. What did the Rabbis think of all these aspirations and inspirations, or did they remain quite untouched by the influences of their surroundings? Is it not possible that a complete account of such a controversy as I have just mentioned, which probably formed neither an isolated nor an unprecedented event, would have furnished us with just the information of which now we are so sorely in need?

In the Jewish liturgy we meet with similar difficulties. It is a source which has till now been comparatively neglected. Still, its contents are of the greatest importance for the study of Jewish theology; not only on account of the material it furnishes us, but also for the aid it gives us in our control over the Talmud. For the latter is a work which can never be used without proper discretion. Like many another great book of an encyclopædic character, the Talmud has been aptly described as a work "full of the seeds of all things." But not all things are religion, nor is all religion Judaism. Certain ideas of foreign religions have found their way into this fenceless work, but they have never become an integral part of Jewish thought. Others again represent only the isolated opinions of this or that individual, in flagrant contradiction to the religious consciousness of Catholic Israel; whilst others again, especially those relating to proselytes or the Gentiles, were in many cases only of a transitory character, suggested by the necessities or even the passions of the moment, but were never intended to be taught as doctrine. In like manner the exaltation, by sectarians, of one special doctrine at the cost of essential principles of the faith led at times by way of reaction to an apparent repudiation of the implied heresy; whilst the synagogue, through its interpreters, recognised the true nature of this apparent repudiation and continued to give the objectionable doctrine its proper place and proportion among the accepted teachings of Judaism.[1] Some test or tests as to the real theological value of a Talmudic saying will, therefore, always be necessary in making use of the old Rabbinic literature as a source of theology. The Jewish liturgy, which was from earliest times jealously guarded against

[1] See Weiss דו״ד 1 287 and Joel's *Blicke*, 2 170, seq. As an illustration we refer here to the well-known objection to the explanation of certain laws (Lev. 22 28 and Deut. 22 6 and 7) on the mere principle of mercy, "for he (who does so) declares the attributes (or the laws dictated by such attributes) of the Holy One, blessed be he, mercy, whilst they are only commands" מפני שעושה של הקבّה רחמים ואינן אלא גזירות. See *Mishnah Berachoth*, 5 3; *Megillah*, 4 9; *Jer. Berachoth*, 9 *c* and B. T. *Berachoth*, 33 *b*, text and commentaries. Cf. also Bacher, *Ag. Am.*, 3 728. All these authorities, however, were set aside by the synagogue which continued the tradition of Pseudo-Jonathan to Lev. 22 28 (see Berliner, *Targum*, 2 85) and never hesitated to explain such laws on the principle of mercy. See *Gen. R.*, 75 13; Deut. R., 6 1; *Tan. B.*, 3 48 *a*. Cf. also *Gen. R.*, 33 3, where with reference to Ps. 145 9 the words occur שהן מדותיו הוא מרחם. As to mediæval authorities for the *paitan* Kalir, see Buber's note to *P. K.*, 98 *b*. Cf. also Nachmanides Commentary to Deut., 22 6 and 7, and the reference there to Maimonides. See also ילקוט יצחק by Isaac Zaler, Warsaw, 1895, 3 59 *a* and *b* and 5 45 *b* and 46 *a*.

heresy,[1] and which in its essentials always was under the control of the synagogue at large, may fairly be regarded as such a test. Now there is no reason to doubt that in its broad outlines this liturgy — as far as the Prayer Book is concerned — has its origin in the earliest Tannaitic times, whilst certain portions date from the pre-Christian era, but it is at present so overgrown with additions and interpolations, that the original contents are hardly discernible from the constant accretions of succeeding ages. The Talmud, and even the Mishnah, occasionally quote some ancient liturgical passages, and these might prove useful in helping us to fix their date.[2] But, unfortunately, it was not thought necessary to give these quotations in full. They are only cited by the word with which they begin, so that we are left in uncertainty as to the exact contents of the *whole* prayer, and have only guesses to rely on.

Even more embarrassing than these textual difficulties are those defects which are inherent in the peculiar nature of old Rabbinic thought. A great English writer has remarked "that the true health of a man is to have a soul without being aware of it; to be disposed of by impulses which he does not criticise."

[1] See I. Elbogen, *Geschichte des Achtzehngebets*, Breslau, 1903, 34, note 4.

[2] See *Mishnah Tamid*, 5 1. *Pesachim*, 118 *a*. Cf. Landshut הגיון לב to the שמונה עשרה, and Elbogen, as quoted above. See also Schechter's notes to *The Wisdom of Ben Sira* (edited by S. Schechter and C. Taylor), to XXXVI 17 *c* (p. 60) and LI 12 *c* (p. 66), and *J. Q. R.* 10[3], p. 654.

In a similar way the old Rabbis seem to have thought that the true health of a religion is to have a theology without being aware of it; and thus they hardly evei made — nor could they make — any attempt towards working their theology into a formal system, or giving us a full exposition of it. With God as a reality, Revelation as a fact, the Torah as a rule of life, and the hope of Redemption as a most vivid expectation, they felt no need for formulating their dogmas into a creed, which, as was once remarked by a great theologian, is repeated not because we believe, but that we may believe. What they had of theology, they enunciated spasmodically or "by impulses." Sometimes it found its expression in prayer "when their heart cried unto God"; at others in sermons or exhortations, when they wanted to emphasise an endangered principle, or to protest against an intruding heresy. The sick-bed of a friend, or public distress, also offered an opportunity for some theological remark on the question of suffering or penance. But impulses are uncertain, incoherent, and even contradictory, and thus not always trustworthy. The preacher, for instance, would dwell more on the mercy of God, or on the special claims of Israel, when his people were oppressed, persecuted, and in want of consolation; whilst in times of ease and comfort he would accentuate the wrath of God awaiting the sinner, and his severity at the day of judgement. He would magnify faith when men's actions were lacking in inward motive, but he would urge the claim of works when the Law had been declared to be the strength of sin. When the Law was in danger he would appeal to Lev. 27 43, "Those are the commandments which the Lord commanded Moses," and infer that these laws, and no others, were to be observed forever, and that no subsequent prophet might add to them.[1] At another time he would have no objection to introduce new festivals, *e.g.* the Lighting of the Chanukah Candles, and even declare them to be distinct commands of God,[2] so long as they were, as it seemed to him, within the spirit of the Law. He would not scruple to give the ideal man his due, to speak of him as forming the throne of God,[3] or to invest him with pre-mundane existence;[4] but he would watch jealously that he did not become, as it were, a second god, or arrogate to himself a divine worship. I shall have frequent occasion to point out such apparent or actual contradictions.

The Rabbis, moreover, show a carelessness and sluggishness in the application of theological principles which must be most astonishing to certain minds

1 See *T. K.* 115 *d.*

2 *Shabbath*, 23 *d.* See also *Jer. Sukkah*, 53 *d.*

3 See *Gen. R.* 47 6.

4 See *Gen. R.* 1 1 about the pre-mundane existence of the *name* of the Messiah. Cf. *ibid.* 2 4, about the soul of the Messiah. *Ibid.* 8 4 mention is made of the souls of the righteous with whom God took counsel when he was going to create the world. See also *PRE.* 3, text and commentary. Cf. also Joel, *Blicke*, 2 181 and *S. E.* 160, text and notes, and below, p. 70. See also Dr. L. Ginzberg, "*Die Haggada bei den Kirchenvätern*," p. 4, note 1.

which seem to mistake merciless logic for God-given truths. For example, it is said: "He who believes in the faithful shepherd is as if he believes in the word of him whose will has called the world into existence." . . . "Great was the merit of the faith which Israel put in God; for it was by the merit of this faith that the Holy Spirit came over them, and they said *Shirah* to God, as it is said, 'And they believed in the Lord and his servant Moses. Then sang Moses and the children of Israel this song unto the Lord.'"[1] . . . Again, "Our father, Abraham, came into the possession of this world and the world hereafter only by the merit of his faith."[2] Of R. Jose it is recorded that he said: "If thou art desirous to know the reward awaiting the righteous, thou mayest infer it from Adam the First, for whose single transgression he and all his posterity were punished with death; all the more then shall the good action of a man confer bliss upon him, and justify him and his posterity to the end of all generations."[3] Another Rabbi tells us that by the close contact of the serpent with Eve, he left in her a taint which infected all her seed, but from which the Israelites were freed when they stood before Mount Sinai, for there they came into immediate contact with the divine presence.[4]

[1] *Mechilta* (ed. Friedmann), 33 *a*. By *Shirah* שירה is meant the Song of Moses (Exod. 15).

[2] *Mechilta*, *ibid.*

[3] *T. K.* 27 *a*. Cf. Delitzsch, *Hebrew Translation of the Romans* (Leipzig, 1870), p. 82.

[4] *Jebamoth*, 103 *b*.

To the professional theologian, it is certainly distressing to find that such sayings, which would have made the fortune of any ancient Alexandrian theosophist or modern Hegelian of the right wing, were never properly utilised by the Rabbis, and "theologically fructified," nor ever allowed to be carried to what appears to the scholastic mind as their legitimate consequences. The faithful shepherd and the bliss-conferring righteous were never admitted into the Rabbinic pantheon; the concession made to the patriarch was never extended to his posterity, faith only modifying and vivifying works, but not superseding them, and even the direct contact with the Deity, which the fact of being present at the Revelation of Sinai offered to every Israelite, were conceived of only as the beginning of a new life, with new duties and obligations.

This indifference to logic and insensibility to theological consistency seems to be a vice from which not even the later successors of the Rabbis — the commentators of the Talmud — emancipated themselves entirely. I give one example: We read, in the name of R. Akiba, "Everything is foreseen; freedom of choice is given. And the world is judged by grace, and yet *all is according to the amount of work.*" This is the usual reading. But some of the best Mss. have the words, "And *not* according to the amount of work."[1] The difference

[1] See Dr. Taylor's *Sayings of the Jewish Fathers*, Appendix 152. I add here Ms. Oxford Heb., c. 17. Parma, 802, 975. See *Machzor*

between the two readings being so enormous, we should naturally expect from the commentators some long dissertation about the doctrines of justification by grace or works. But nothing of the sort happens. They fail to realise the import of the difference, and pass it over with a few slight remarks of verbal explanation. Perhaps they were conscious that neither reading ought to be accepted as decisive, each of them being in need of some qualification implied in the other.

It will, therefore, suggest itself that any attempt at an orderly and complete system of Rabbinic theology is an impossible task; for not only are our materials scanty and insufficient for such a purpose, but, when handling those fragments which have come down to us, we must always be careful not to labour them too much, or to "fill them with meaning" which their author could never have intended them to bear, against which all his other teachings and his whole life form one long, emphatic protest, or to spin from the harmless repetition by a Rabbi of a gnostic saying or some Alexandrinic theorem the importance of which he never understood, a regular system of Rabbinic theology. All that these fragments can offer us are some aspects of the theology of the Rabbis, which may again be modified by other aspects, giving us another side of the same sub-

*Vitri*, pp. 514, 515. Compare also *Die Responsen des R. Meschullam ben Kalonymos*, by Dr. Joel Müller (Berlin, 1893), p. 11, note 19. See below p. 306.

ject. What we can obtain resembles rather a complicated arrangement of theological checks and balances than anything which the modern divine would deign to call a consistent "scheme of salvation." Still, I am inclined to think that a religion which has been in "working order" for so many centuries — which contains so little of what we call theology, and the little theology of which possesses so few fixities (whilst even these partake more of the nature of experienced realities than of logically demonstrated dogmas) — that this religion forms so unique and interesting a phenomenon as to deserve a more thorough treatment than it has hitherto received. It is not to be dismissed with a few general phrases, only tending to prove its inferiority.

This brings me to one other introductory point which I wish to suggest by the word *Aspects*. Aspects, as we know, vary with the attitude we take. My attitude is a Jewish one. This does not, I hope, imply either an apology for the Rabbis, or a polemic tendency against their antagonists. Judaism does not give as its *raison d'être* the shortcomings of any of the other great creeds of the civilised world. Judaism, even Rabbinic Judaism, was there before either Christianity or Mohammedanism was called into existence. It need not, therefore, attack them, though it has occasionally been compelled to take protective measures when they have threatened it with destruction. But what I want to indicate and even to emphasise is, that my attitude towards Rabbinic theology is necessarily different from that taken by most commentators on the Pauline Epistles. I speak advisedly of the commentators on Paul; for the Apostle himself I do not profess to understand. Harnack makes somewhere the remark that in the first two centuries of Christianity no man understood Paul except that heathen-Christian Marcion, and he misunderstood him. Layman as I am, it would be presumptuous on my part to say how far succeeding centuries advanced beyond Marcion. But one thing is quite clear even to every student, and this is that a curious alternative is always haunting our exegesis of the Epistles. Either the theology of the Rabbis must be wrong, its conception of God debasing, its leading motives materialistic and coarse, and its teachers lacking in enthusiasm and spirituality, or the Apostle to the Gentiles is quite unintelligible. I need not face this alternative, and may thus be able to arrive at results utterly at variance with those to be found in our theological manuals and introductions to the New Testament.

The question as to how far the theology of the Rabbis could be brought into harmony with the theology of our age is a matter of apologetics, and does not exactly fall within the province of these essays. With a little of the skill so often displayed by the writers of the life and times of ancient heroes, particularly New Testament heroes, it would certainly not be an impossible task to draw such an ideal and noble picture of any of the great Rabbis, such as Hillel, R. Jochanan ben Sakkai, or R. Akiba, as would make us recognise a nineteenth-century altruist in them. Nor would it require much ingenuity to parade, for instance, R. Abuhah as an accomplished geologist, inasmuch as he maintained that before the creation of *our* world God was ever constructing and destroying worlds;[1] or again, to introduce as a perfect Hegelian that anonymous Rabbi who boldly declared that it was Israel's consciousness of God which was "the making of God":[2] or finally, to arrogate for R. Benaha the merit of having been the forerunner of Astruc, because he declared that the Pentateuch was delivered not as a complete work, but in a series of successive scrolls.[3] Indeed, the Rabbinic literature has already been described as a "wonderful mine of religious ideas from which it would be just as easy to draw up a manual for the most orthodox as to extract a vade-mecum for the most sceptical." But I have not the least desire to array the ancient Rabbis in the paraphernalia of modern fashion, and to put before the reader a mere theological masquerade, or to present the Talmud as a rationalistic production which only by some miracle escaped the vigilant eye of the authorities, who failed to recognise it as a heretical work and exclude it from the Synagogue. The "liberty of interpretation," in which so many theologians indulge, and which they even exalt as "Christian freedom," seems to me only another

[1] See *Gen. R.*, 9 2.

[2] See below, p. 24, note 2.

[3] See *Gittin*, 16 *a*.

word for the privilege to blunder, and to deceive oneself and others.

To show, however, that Rabbinic theology is, with the least modicum of interpretation or re-interpretation, equal to the highest aspirations of the religious man of various modes of thought, occasional illustrations have been given from the works of philosophers and mystics, thus proving the latent possibilities of its application by various schools in different ages. As to "modernity," it entirely depends whether there is still room in its programme for such conceptions as God, Revelation, Election, Sin, Retribution, Holiness, and similar theological ideas; or is it at present merely juggling with words to drop them at the first opportunity? If this latter be the case, it will certainly find no ally in Rabbinic theology, or for that matter, in any other theology.

## II

# GOD AND THE WORLD

AMONG the many strange statements by which the Jewish student is struck, when reading modern divinity works, there is none more puzzling to his mind than the assertion of the transcendentalism of the Rabbinic God, and his remoteness from man. A world of ingenuity is spent to prove that the absence of the mediatorial idea in Rabbinic Theology is a sign not of its acceptance of man's close communion with God, but of its failure to establish the missing link between heaven and earth. Sayings of a fantastic nature, as, for instance, when a Rabbi speaks of God's abode in heaven, with its various partitions;[1] epithets for God, such as Heaven or Supreme, which antique piety accepted for the purpose of avoiding the name of God "being uttered in idleness"; terms expressive of his providence and his sublime holiness, as the Holy One, blessed be he, the King, the Lord of the World,

[1] See Weber, *System der Altsynagogalen Palästinenischen Theologie* (Leipzig, 1880), pp. 158, 159. See B. Jacob, "*Im Namen Gottes*," p. 171. It is interesting that in the very passage in *Chagigah*, 5 *b*, where this sharp division between the inner and outer departments is given, it is also stated that in the latter God is mourning over the misfortunes of Israel.

or the Master of all Creation; Hellenistic phrases, which crept into Jewish literature, but which never received, in the mouth of a Rabbi, the significance which they had with an Alexandrine philosopher, or a Father of the Church,—are all brought forward to give evidence of the great distance which the Rabbinic Jew must have felt, and must feel, between himself and his God.

How strange all this to the Jewish student! Does the Jewish Prayer Book contain such passages as—"O our Father, merciful Father, ever compassionate, have mercy upon us. . . . Thou hast chosen us from all peoples and tongues, and hast brought us near unto thy great name forever in faithfulness, to thank thee and proclaim thy Unity in love; blessed art thou, O God, who hast chosen thy people Israel, in love":[1] or are they Christian interpolations from some unknown hand? Is the Jew taught to confess his sins daily in the following words: "Forgive us, our Father, for we have sinned; pardon us, our King, for we have transgressed . . . blessed art thou, our God, who art gracious and dost abundantly forgive":[2] or is this formula borrowed from a non-Jewish liturgy? Has the Jew ever heard his mother at the bedside of a sick relative, directing prayers to God, and appealing to him as "the beloved name, the gracious helper, the merciful Father, and

1 See *Daily Prayer Book*, edited and translated by the late Rev. S. Singer (1890), p. 40; Baer, עבודת ישראל, Rödelheim, 1868, p. 80.

2 See Singer, p. 46; Baer, p. 90.

the dear God": or was it some Christian neighbour to whom he was listening? Are the millions of worshippers in the synagogue addressing themselves directly to God, the king and creator of the universe, the Father in Heaven; or do they, in their thoughts, substitute for all these terms the Memra or the Logos, or some other abstraction, of which the writer of those prayers was unaware? For, according to what we are told by many theologians, God is too far off, the King of the Universe too cosmopolitan, and the Father in heaven too high for the mind of the Jew, and is thus an impossible object for worship. These are questions which readily suggest themselves when one, for instance, reads Weber's book, *System der Altsynagogalen Palästinensischen Theologie*, which has within the last decades become the chief source of information for the great majority of the writers on this subject. The thesis which Weber sets himself to prove through all his work is evidently that of the predominance of the legalistic element in Jewish theology, which was so overwhelming that it crushed even God under its oppressive burden, or, what is the same thing, removed him out of the world. Hence the strange arrangements of subjects in Weber's work, treating first of nomism (or legalism), then of the character of the oral law, the authority of the Rabbis, etc., and last of all, of the Jewish notion of God. The general impression conveyed by such a representation is that this Jewish God is not the God from whom the Torah has emanated, and on whom its authority rests, but that he is himself a feeble reflex of the law, improved occasionally by some prophetic notions, but jealously watched by the Rabbis lest he should come into too close contact with humanity.

This is very different from the impression which the Jewish student receives from a direct study of the sources. Quite the reverse! The student is overwhelmed by the conviction that the manifestation of God in Israel's history was still as vivid to the mind of the Rabbis and still as present as it was to the writer of Deuteronomy or the author of Psalm 78. "All souls," say the Rabbis, "even those which had still to be created, were present at the Revelation on Mount Sinai." [1] The freshness with which the Biblical stories are retold in the Agadic literature, the vivid way in which they are applied to the oppressed condition of Israel, the future hopes which are based on them, create the impression that to the Rabbis and their followers the Revelation at Sinai and all that it implies was to them not a mere reminiscence or tradition, but that, through their intense faith, they re-witnessed it in their own souls, so that it became to them a personal experience. Indeed, it is this witnessing, or rather re-witnessing, to revelation by which God is God; without it he could not be God.[2] People who

[1] *Exod. R.*, 28 6.

[2] See *P. K.*, 102 *b*, and *Sifre*, 144 *a*, with allusion to Is. 43 12. Cf. also Hoffmann's *Midrasch Tannaim*, 1 72, for more striking instances. The expression כביכול (as if it were possible to say so) is used in *Sifre*.

would doubt his existence and say, "There is no judgement and no judge," belong rather to the generation of the deluge, before God had entered so openly into relations with mankind.[1] To those who have experienced him through so many stages in their history, such doubt was simply impossible.

A God, however, who is mainly reached, not by metaphysical deductions, but, as was the case with the Rabbis, through the personal experience of his revelation and his continuous operations in the world, cannot possibly be removed from it, or be otherwise confined to any particular region. Such a locally limited conception of the deity could, according to the Rabbis, only be entertained by a newly fledged proselyte, who had not as yet emancipated himself from his polytheistic notions. To the Jew, God was at one and the same time above, beyond, and within the world, its soul and its life. "Jethro," say the Rabbis, "still believing that there was some substance in other gods, said, 'I know that the Lord is greater than all the gods' (Exod. 15 11). Naaman came nearer the truth (though still confining God to one part of the universe), for he said,

Cf. Bacher, *Terminologie*, I 78, for the etymology and a more precise explanation of this term. It may be remarked that in most cases this term כביכול is used by the Rabbis, when the anthropomorphism which they imply is carried *further* than that implied by the Bible. The instance which I have just cited from the *Pesikta* is a case in point. Cf. also the numerous instances given by Kohut in his *Aruch Completum*, s.v. יכל 2.

[1] See *Gen. R.*, 26 6 and *Pseudo-Jonathan*, *Gen.* 4 8.

'Now I know that there is no other God in all the earth, but in Israel' (2 Kings 5 15). Rahab (made even further progress, and) placed God both in heaven and earth, saying, 'For the Lord your God, he is God in heaven above and in earth beneath' (Josh. 2 11); but Moses made him fill all the space of the world (or universe), as it is said, 'The Lord he is God in the heaven above, and upon the earth beneath': there is none else (Deut. 4 39), which means that even the empty space is full of God." [1]

He is indeed to the Rabbis, as may be gathered from the various appellatives for God scattered over the Rabbinic literature, not only the Creator of the world, or "he who spake and the world existed," [2] but also the Father of the world,[3] the goodness (or the good one) of the world,[4] the light of the world [5] the life of the world,[6] the stay of the world [7] the eye of the world,[8] the only one of the world,[9] the ancient one of the world,[10] the righteous one of the world,[11] the master or the lord of the world,[12] and the space (*makom*)

1 *Deut. R.*, 2 27. cf. *Mechilta*, 59 *a*. Cf. *Tan. B.*, 4 15 *a*; *M.T.*, 19 8, 22 2, 62 8; cf. Bacher, *Ag. Am.*, I 182.

2 *Jer. Pesachim*, 18 *b*. Cf. Löw, *Gessammelte Schriften*, I 185, note 3.

3 *Midrash Prov.*, ch. 10.

4 *P. K.*, 161 *a*.

5 *Tan. B.*, 4 24 *b*.

6 *Tan.*, כי תשא, 24.

7 *Tan. B.*, 50 *b*.

8 *Gen. R.*, 42 2.

9 *Gen. R.*, 21 5.

10 *Yalkut* to *Chronicles*, section 1074, but the reading is rather doubtful. Cf. *Ruth R.*, 2 1, and commentaries.

11 *Yoma*, 37 *a*. Cf. *Yalkut* to *Prov.* § 346.

12 *Berachoth*, 4 *a*.

of the world.[1] In another place God is compared by a Rabbi to the soul "filling the whole world, as the soul fills the body,"[2] a comparison which may probably have suggested to later Jewish writers semi-pantheistic notions; as, for instance, when the author of the Song of the Unity says: "There is nothing but thy existence. Thou art alive, omnipotent, and none is be-

[1] *Gen. R.*, 68 9 and *P. R.* 104 *a*, and notes. Cf. E. Landau's essay *Die dem Raume entnommenen Synonyma für Gott in der Neuhebräischen Literatur* (Zürich, 1888), pp. 30 *seq.*, where the whole literature on the subject is put together: to which Bacher, *Ag. Tan.*, I 207, and Jacob, *Im Namen Gottes*, 119 may be added. According to the passage from the *Mechilta*, 52 *b*, given there by Bacher, מכאן לב״ד הגדול שהוא קרוי מקום it is the divine court of judgement which is called מקום. Cf. *Mechilta of R. Simon*, ed. Hoffmann, 81. See also Lewy, *Ein Wort über die Mechilta des R. Simon*, p. 9, note 4. See also *Midrash Temurah*, § 2. I believe, however, that in spite of all these authorities, that the older commentators of the Mechilta, explaining the passage to refer to the court or the Sanhedrin, were in the right, the reading of ב״ה in the *MHG* probably resting on some clerical error. The term is mainly indicative of God's ubiquity in the world and can best be translated by "Omnipresent." Cf. Taylor's *Sayings of the Jewish Fathers*, p. 53, note 42, though it is difficult to say with any certainty whether it is Jewish or Helenistic in its origin. On Landau's note 1, p. 40, it may be remarked that the text of Gemara in the *Mishnah Berachoth*, 5 1, has לאביהם שבשמים instead of מקום. Cf. Mishnah, *Rosh Hashana*, 4 8, ומשעבדים את לבם לאביהם שבשמים, where Mr. Lowe's ed., p. 62 *a*, reads ומכונים instead of ומשעבדים. Bishop Lightfoot's quotation (in his *Commentary to the Colossians*, p. 213) from בחיי on the *Pentateuch* (to Exod. 34 20), according to which God is also called בכורו של עולם, the "first-born of the world," is not to be found in the older Rabbinic literature, and seems to be only a later cabalistic term.

[2] See *Lev. R.*, 4 8.

sides thee. And before the All thou wast the All, and when the All became thou filledst the All." [1]

It is true that there are also other appellatives for God, placing him "above the world," as the heaven,[2] the height of the world,[3] and the high one.[4] Nor is it to be denied that there is a whole circle of legends mostly concentrated round the visions of Ezekiel, which give mystical descriptions of God's heavenly habitations. Here is an instance of the economy of the seventh heaven which is Araboth. It is with reference to Ps. 68 4: "'Sing unto God, sing praises to his name: extol him that rideth upon the Araboth (the heavens).' Araboth is the heaven, in which are righteousness and grace, the treasures of life, the treasures of peace and the treasures of bliss, and the souls of the righteous, and the souls and the spirits which are about to be created, and the dew with which the holy one, blessed be he, is to revive the dead . . . and there are the Ophanim, the Seraphim, and the holy Chayoth and the ministering angels and the throne of glory, and the king, the living God, high and exalted, rests above them, as it is said: 'Extol ye him that rideth upon the Araboth.'" [5] This passage, and a few others

[1] שיר היחוד, 3d day.

[2] See Rab. Dictionaries, sub. שמים. See also Schürer 2 : 539.

[3] *Tan.*, כי תשא, 27.

[4] See *Baba Bathra*, 134 *a*, and Rab. Dictionaries sub. גבוה. Cf. also Landau and Löw, about all these expressions.

[5] See *Chagigah*, 12 *b*, 13 *a*; and *P. R.*, 95 *b seq.* Cf. Ginzberg, *Die Haggada bei den Kirchenvätern*, p. 11.

of a similar character, dating perhaps from the first century, are developed later in the eighth and ninth centuries into an extensive mystical literature known under the name of Chapters of the Chambers,[1] which enlarge upon the topography of the heavens with great minuteness, besides giving very detailed descriptions of the various divisions of the ministering angels who dwell there, and their various functions, and producing even some of the hymns which are sung in heaven on particular occasions.

But first we must note that the fact of God's abiding in a heaven ever so high does not prevent him from being at the same time also on earth. "Thou art the Lord our God," runs the text of a prayer, which is still recited every day, "in heaven and *on earth*, and in the highest heavens of heavens";[2] whilst the fact of God's appearing to Moses in the bush is taken as a proof that there is no spot on earth be it ever so lowly which is devoid of the divine presence.[3] When a Rabbi was asked as to the seeming contradiction between Exod. 40 34, according to which the glory of God filled the tabernacle, and 1 Kings 8 27, in which it is said: "Behold, the heaven and heaven of heavens cannot contain thee," he answered, that the matter is to be compared to a cave by the shore of the sea; once the sea became stormy and inundated the land, when the cave filled

[1] פרקי היכלות existing in various versions, strongly reminding of the Book of Enoch and similar other Pseudoepigrapha.

[2] See *S. E.*, p. 118, and Introduction, p. 80.

[3] *P. K.*, 2 *b*.

with water, whilst the sea lost nothing of its contents; so the tabernacle became full of the glory of the divine presence, whilst neither heaven nor earth became empty of it.[1]

Secondly, and this is a point which cannot be sufficiently emphasised, that whatever mythologies and theosophies may be derived from the notion of heaven or height, on the one hand, or whatever pantheistic theories may be developed from the conception of the God-fulness of the universe, on the other hand, neither of these opposing tendencies were allowed to influence the theology of the Rabbis in any considerable degree.

Theirs was a personal God, and a personal God will always be accommodated by fancy and imagination with some sort of local habitation. The "Not-Ourselves" will always have to be placed somewhere else. Loftiness and height have always and will always suggest sublimity and exaltation, and thus they could not choose a more suitable habitation for the deity than the heavens, or the heaven of heavens. But theology proper, or religion, is not entirely made up of these elements. It does not suppress them, but with happy inconsistency, it does not choose to abide by their logical consequences.

Thus the very R. Simon b. Lakish, to whom we owe the Rabbinic version of the myth of the seven heavens, in the highest of which, as we have seen, the throne of glory is placed, declared the patriarchs (as models of

[1] *P. K.* 2 *b*; *P. R.*, 19 *a*. Cf. Bacher, *Ag. Tan.*, 2 27.

righteousness) to be the throne (or the chariot) of God; whilst his colleague and older contemporary, R. Jochanan, laid down the axiom, that every place where "thou findest the greatness of God mentioned, there thou findest also his humility"; and he further added illustrations from the Pentateuch, the Prophets, and the Hagiographa. The illustration from the latter is the very verse which partly suggested the legend of the seven heavens, namely the verse, "Extol ye him who rideth upon the Araboth"; being followed by the words, "A father of the fatherless, and a judge of the widows, is God in his holy habitation" (Psalm 78 5). Thus we may maintain safely that with the Rabbis distance does not imply aloofness or any interruption of God's communion with man. Notwithstanding all distance, "God is near in every kind of nearness."[1] For though the distance between heaven and earth is so infinitely great, yet "when a man comes to the synagogue and prays, God listens to him, for the petitioner is like a man who talks into the ear of his friend."[2] The same is the case with repentance, "the power of which is very great." Directly a man has a thought of repentance, it instantly reaches the throne of God.[3]

Something similar may be remarked of the conception of God's Kingship, forming, as we shall see in the sequence, an important feature of the theology of the Rabbis which undoubtedly contributed in some

[1] *Jer. Berachoth*, 13 *a*. [2] *Jer. Berachoth*, *ibid.*

[3] *P. R.*, 185 *a*. See also below, p. 335.

measure towards confining God to a *locale*, the elevation of which would not only suggest exaltation, but also convey to our mind a sense of security against all intrusion, so as to keep those below at a respectful distance. Yet this distance does not cause either remoteness and separation. These are only brought about by the evil actions of man. This we gather from such a passage as the following: It is with allusion to Ps. 18 12, "He made darkness his hiding-place, his pavilion round him." "This verse," it is explained, "David only said in the praise of the Holy One, blessed be he, he who is יה, ruling in the height . . . and he dwells in three hundred and ninety heavens . . . and in each of them there are ministering angels and Seraphim and Ophanim and Cherubim and Galgalim and a Throne of Glory. But thou must not wonder at this thing; for behold, the King of flesh and blood has many habitations, both for the warm and the cold (seasons), much more so the King who lives for eternity, to whom all belongs." But the author of this mystical passage winds up with the words, "When Israel performs the will of the Omnipresent, he dwells in the Araboth (the seventh heaven) and removeth not from his (world) in any way, but in the time of wrath he ascends on high and sits in the upper heavens.[1]

[1] See *D. E.* ch. 2. Cf. Friedmann נספחים 10, note 2, for parallels and the history of this passage. The word in brackets is given after an emendation of R. Elijah of Wilna. A good collection of comparisons

The fact is, that the nearness of God is determined by the conduct of man, and by his realisation of this nearness, that is, by his knowledge of God. "Thus taught the sages, Thy deeds will bring thee near (to God), and thy deeds will remove thee (from God). How so? If a man does ugly things his actions remove him from the divine presence, as it is said, 'Your sins have separated between you and your God' (Isa. 69 2). But if a man has done good deeds, they bring him near to the divine presence. . . . And it is upon man to know that a contrite and humble spirit is better than all the sacrifices (prescribed) in the Torah."[1] It is in conformity with this conception of the nearness of God that we read, "Before Abraham made God known to his creatures, he was only the God of the heaven; but afterwards he became (through Abraham's proselytising activity) also the God of the earth."[2] Hence the patriarchs are, as just quoted, the very throne of God,[3] whilst those, for instance, who speak untruth, are banished from his holy presence.[4] Indeed, "his main dwelling is among those below," and it is only sin and crime which cause God's removal to the upper regions.

between God and the King of flesh and blood, entering into such details as his throne, his palace, his legions, his court, his administering justice, etc., is to be found in *Die Königsgleichnisse des Midrasch*, by Dr. I. Ziegler (Breslau, 1903). See especially the Hebrew section of this book.

[1] *S. E.*, p. 104. Cf. also the reading in the old editions of תדב"א, ch. 18.

[2] *Gen. R.*, 59 8. [3] *Gen. R.*, 47 6. See below, p. 84.

[4] *Sanhedrin*, 102 *b*. *P. K.* 1 *a*. Cf. below, p. 223.

That such appellatives as space, or master of the world, are not meant to imply severance or remoteness, may be seen from the following instances: "Beloved are Israel, for they are called children of Space" (*makom*), as it is said: "Ye are children unto the Lord your God."[1] "He who helps Israel, is as if he would help space" (God).[2] "Israel (on the waters of Marah) was supplicating and praying to their Father in Heaven, as a son who implores his father, and a disciple who beseeches his master, saying unto him: Master of the world, we have sinned against thee, when we murmured on the sea."[3] Even the term *strength*, by which God is sometimes called,[4] occurs in such connections as: "When Israel does the will of God, power is added to strength."[5] In the Babylonian Talmud one of the most frequent appellations of God is "the merciful one," and it is worth noticing, that this term is mostly used in Halachic or casuistic discussions, which proves, by the way, how little in the mind of the Rabbis the Law was connected with hardness and chastisement. To them it was an effluence of God's mercy and goodness.[6]

1 *Aboth*, 3 18.

2 See *Sifre*, 22 *b*.

3 *Mechilta*, 45 *b*. See *Aruch*, s.v. גדר. See below, p. 336.

4 *Mechilta*, 48 *b*. *Shabbath*, 87 *b*.

5 See *P. K.*, 166 *a* and *b*. Cf. Kohut's *Aruch*, s.v. גאל. See below, p. 239.

6 See references of Kohut's *Aruch*, s.v. רחם. In *Tractate Pesachim* alone it occurs about forty-one times, but always in Halachic controversies.

Eager, however, as the Rabbis were to establish this communion between God and the world, they were always on their guard not to permit him to be lost in the world, or to be confused with man. Hence the marked tendency, both in the Targumim and in the Agadah, to explain away or to mitigate certain expressions in the Bible, investing the deity with corporeal qualities. The terms *Shechinah* and *Memra* in the former are well known, and have been treated of by various scholars.[1] As to the Agadah, we find the general rule applied to the Bible, that the Scriptures only intended "to make the ear listen to what it can hear"; or as it is elsewhere expressed, "to soothe the ear (so as to make it listen to) what it can hear," which might be taken as implying a tendency towards mitigating corporeal terms.[2] This tendency may also be detected in the interpretation of the Rabbis given in God's answer to Moses' question, "What is His name" (Exod. 3 13). "The Holy One, blessed be he, said to Moses, Thou wantest to know my name? I am called according to my deeds. When I judge the creatures I am named *Elohim*, when I wage war against the wicked I am named *Zebaoth*, when I suspend (the punishment of) the man's sins, I am named

[1] See Schürer, I 147, note 38, about the literature on this point. The term שכינה is very frequent in the *Talmud* and *Midrashim;* see Kohut's *Aruch*, s.v. שכן. Less frequent is דבור. Cf. Landau (as above), pp. 47 *seq.* and p. 53; Bacher, *Terminologie* 2 86.

[2] *A. R. N.*, I, c. 2, ל"ב מדות, § 14. See Reifmann, משיב דבר, p. 31; Bacher, *Terminologie*, I 8.

*El Shadai*, and when I have mercy with my world, I am named by the *tetragrammaton*."[1] The words, "The Lord is a man of war" (Exod. 15 3), are contrasted with (Hos. 11 9) "For I am God, and not man," and explained to mean that it is only for the love of Israel that God appears in such a capacity.[2] In another passage we read that the divine presence never came down, and Moses never went up to heaven, as it is said, "The heavens are the Lord's, and the earth hath he given to the children of men."[3]

This last passage is not only in contradiction with some of the quotations given in the foregoing pages, but is also directly opposed to another Agadic interpretation of this very verse from the Psalms, according to which the line drawn between heaven and earth was removed by the Revelation, when God came down on Mount Sinai (Exod. 19 19), and Moses was commanded to come up unto the Lord (*ibid.* 24 1).[4] This objection of the Rabbis — though only feebly expressed — to take the scriptural language in its literal sense must be attributed to a polemic tendency against rising sectarianism, which, laying too much stress on the corporeal terms in the Bible, did not rest satisfied with humanising the Deity, but even insisted on deifying man. To the former, that is, the humanising of the Deity and

[1] See *Exod. R.* 3 6.

[2] *Mechilta*, 38 *b*. See also below, p. 44, note 1.

[3] *Sukkah*, 5 *a*. See Bacher, *Ag. Tan.*, I 185.

[4] *Exod. R.*, 12 3.

endowing him with all the qualities and attributes which tend towards making God accessible to man, the Rabbis could not possibly object. A great number of scriptural passages, when considered in the light of Rabbinic interpretation, represent nothing else but a record of a sort of *Imitatio hominis* on the part of God. He acts as best man at the wedding of Adam and Eve;[1] he mourns over the world like a father over the death of his son when the sins of ten generations make its destruction by the deluge imminent;[2] he visits Abraham on his sick-bed;[3] he condoles with Isaac after the death of Abraham;[4] he "himself in his glory" is occupied in doing the last honours to Moses, who would otherwise have remained unburied, as no man knew his grave;[5] he teaches Torah to Israel, and to this very day he keeps school in heaven for those who died in their infancy;[6] he prays himself, and teaches Israel how to pray;[7] he argues with Abraham the case of Sodom and Gomorrah not only on equal terms, but tells him, If thou thinkest I acted unworthily, teach me and I will do so.[8] Like man he also feels, so to speak, embarrassed in the presence of the conceited and overbearing, and says, I and the proud cannot dwell in the same place.[9] Nay, it would seem that the

[1] *Gen. R.*, 8 8 13. Cf. Commentaries and *ibid.* 18 1.
[2] See *Gen. R.*, 27 4. [3] *Gen. R.*, 8 13. [4] *Gen. R.*, *ibid.*
[5] See *Gen. R.*, *ibid.*, and *Sota*, 9 *b*.
[6] *Exod. R.*, 28 5, and *Abodah Zarah*, 3 *b*.
[7] See *Berachoth*, 7 *a*, and *Rosh Hashanah*, 17 *b*.
[8] See *Tan. B.*, 1 46 *a*. [9] *Sotah*, 5 *b*.

Rabbis felt an actual delight in heaping human qualities upon God whenever opportunity is offered by Scripture. Thus, with reference to (Exod. 15 1) "I will sing unto the Lord," the Rabbis say, "I will praise him," that he is terrible, as it is said, "A great God, a mighty and a terrible" (Deut. 10 17). "I will praise him," that he is wealthy, as it is said, "The earth is the Lord's, and the fulness thereof" (Ps. 24 1). "I will praise him," that he is wise, as it is said, "For the Lord giveth wisdom: out of his mouth cometh knowledge and understanding" (Prov. 2 6). "I will praise him," that he is merciful, as it is said, "The Lord, the Lord God, is merciful and gracious" (Exod. 34 6). "I will praise him," that he is a judge, as it is said, "For the judgment is God's" (Deut. 1 17). "I will praise him," that he is faithful, as it is said, "Know therefore that the Lord thy God, he is God, the faithful God" (*ibid.* 7 9).[1]

What the Rabbis strongly objected to was the deification of man. Thus with reference to Exod. 6 and 7 1, God is represented by the Rabbis as having said to Moses, "Though I made thee a god to Pharaoh, thou must not become overbearing (and think thyself God); *I* am the Lord."[2] To Hiram, the Prince of Tyre, who said, "I am God; I sit in the seat of

[1] *Mechilta*, 35 *a*. Cf. *MHG.*, 677 *seq.*, about the seventy names of God, and note 12 to col. 681. Cf. also Saalfeld, *Das Hohelied Salomons*, p. 137.

[2] *Tan. B.*, 2, 13 *a*.

God" (Ezek. 28 2), God is supposed by the Rabbis to have answered, "Did Elijah, notwithstanding his reviving the dead, bringing rain, and making the fire to come down from heaven, ever make the claim to be a God?"[1] Both Pharaoh and the Prince of Tyre are, of course, only prototypes of persons deified in the times of the Rabbis, be it Roman emperors or Jewish Messiahs. And it was, as we may imagine, under the pressure of this controversy that the Rabbis availed themselves of any appellatives for God, as well as of any allegorical interpretation, that served as a check against this deification tendency.

It would, however, be a mistake to think that the Rabbis attached to appellatives for God, such as Shechinah, or Word, the same meaning which they have received in Hellenistic schools, or in the theology of the Fathers of the Church. Hallam somewhere quotes the shrewd remark of Montaigne, to the effect that we should try a man who says a wise thing, for we may often find that he does not understand it.

I am not quite certain as to the wisdom of the allegorical method and the various appellatives for God, some of which may perhaps have been of Hellenistic origin. But I am convinced that the Rabbis hardly understood the real significance and the inevitable consequences of their use.

Indeed, it soon must have become clear to the

[1] *Tan.*, בראשית, 7. Cf. Jellinek, *Beth Hammidrash*, 5, p. 111 and Introduction.

Rabbis that the allegorising method could be turned into a very dangerous weapon against the very principle which it was meant to defend. Not only was it largely used by the adversaries of the synagogue, as a means for justifying the abolition of the Law, but the terms which were accepted in order to weaken or nullify anthropomorphic expressions were afterwards hypostatised and invested with a semi-independent existence, or personified as the creatures of God. This will explain the fact that, along with the allegorising tendency, there is also a marked tendency in the opposite direction, insisting on the literal sense of the word of the Bible, and even exaggerating the corporeal terms.[1]

[1] See Weiss, דו״ד. I 111. Weber (pp. 153 and 179) makes a difference between the Targumim and the later Rabbinism. This theory is based chiefly on the assumption of the great antiquity of the former, which is still doubtful. A good essay on the various heresies which the Rabbis had to face, and which would, as I believe, throw much light on the inconsistencies of the Targumim and of the Rabbis concerning the question of anthropomorphism, is still a desideratum. That too much Targum only served to increase the danger, may be seen from the following extract from the *MHG.* (Ms.), to Exod. 24 10, ויראו את אלהי ישראל · אמ׳ ר׳ אליעזר כל המתרגם פיסוק בצורתו הרי זה בדאי · וכל המוסיף בו הרי זה מחרף ומגדף כגון שתרגם ויראו את אלהי ישראל וחזו ית אלהא דישראל הרי זה בדאי · שהקב״ה רואה ואינו נראה · תרגם וחזו ית יקר שכינת אלהא דישראל הרי זה מחרף ומגדף שהוא עושה כאן שלשה יקר ושכינה ואל. "R. Eliezer said: He who translates a verse (from the Bible) literally is a liar. He who adds to it commits blasphemy. For instance, if he translated (the above-quoted verse), *And they saw the God of Israel*, he spoke an untruth; for the Holy One, blessed be he, sees, but is not seen. But if he translated, *And they saw the glory of the Shechina of the God of Israel*, he commits blasphemy, for he makes *three* (a Trinity), namely,

We have unfortunately no sufficient data enabling us to form a real picture of this great theological struggle. What we perceive is rather confusion and perplexity.

The following fragment from a controversy between a Jew and a certain heretic will perhaps give us some idea of this confusion. We read in Exod. 24 1, "And unto Moses he said, Come up to the Lord." Said the heretic to the Rabbi, "If it was God who called Moses, it ought to be: And unto Moses he said, Come up *to me*." The Rabbi answers that by the word *he* is meant the angel Metatron who commanded Moses to ascend to God, the Rabbi identifying this angel, "whose name is like that of his master," with the angel spoken of in chapter 23 20, 21. What follows now is not quite clear, but we see the heretic claiming quite logically worship for Metatron (and perhaps also the power of forgiving sin), whilst the Rabbi retorts, "Faith in thy hands! We have not accepted him even as a messenger, as it is written, 'If thy presence

Glory, Shechina, and God." See *Das Fragmententargum* by M. Ginsburger, p. 43, where this rendering of Exod. 24 is to be found. See also *Kiddushin*, 49 *a*, and *Tosephta Megillah*, p. 228, and commentaries, and cf. Berliner *Targum*, 2, pp. 87 and 173. Our version proves that the objections were of a dogmatic nature. The fact that ר״א is introducing it makes me believe that the passage may have been in the פרקי דר״א (perhaps c. 45). In the older Jewish literature, the Christians are never introduced as Trinitarians. Instructive is also the fact that some Genizah fragments of the Passover Hagada have after the words לא על ידי שליח, the addition לא על ידי הדבר, אלא הקב״ה בעצמו. Cf. the phrase אנוס על פי הדבור. Cf. the Jewish Quarterly Review, vol. x (1897–8), p. 51.

go not (with us), carry us not up hence'" (Exod. 33 16). The heretic thus urges logical consistency and is ready to develop a whole theology from a doubtful interpretation ; the Rabbi is less logical, but merely insists upon the fact that Israel refused to give angels divine honours or divine prerogatives.[1]

The fact is that the Rabbis were a simple, naïve people, filled with a childlike scriptural faith, neither wanting nor bearing much analysis and interpretation. "Common sense," is somewhere aptly remarked, "tells us what is meant by the words 'My Lord and my God'; and a religious man upon his knees requires no commentator." More emphatically the same thought is expressed in the quaint answer of a mediæval Rabbi, who, when asked as to the meaning (philosophic or mystic) he was wont to give to his prayers, replied, "I pray with the meaning of this child."[2] Such simple people, however, were unequal to the task of meeting on the battlefield of speculation the champions of the Alexandrine schools. The *aperçu* stigmatising the Rabbis as the "virtuosi" of religion is well known and has in it some appearance of truth. A single letter, or a mere suffix or prefix, or a particle, would suffice for the Rabbis to derive therefrom, if not exactly a new custom or law, at least to give the latter

[1] See *Sanhedrin*, 38 *b*, and commentaries (also Edeles). The text is somewhat corrupt. Cf. Rabbinowicz, *Variæ Lectiones a. l.* and the commentary of R. Chananel *a. l.* Cf. Joel, *Blicke*, I 127; Bacher, *Ag. Am.*, 3 708, and Jacob, *Im Namen Gottes*, p. 41, n. 1.

[2] See *Responsa* of R. Isaac b. Shesheth, § 157.

some foundation in the Scriptures. But the *aperçu* would have more point and be more complete, if we would add that the antagonists of the Rabbis were just as expert "virtuosi" in dogmas and theosophies. What to the Rabbis was a simple adjective, a reverential expression, or a poetical metaphor, turned in the hands of the Hellenists into a new deity, an æon, or a distinct emanation. The Rabbis felt perplexed, and in their consternation and horror went, as we have seen, from one extreme to the other.[1]

The consternation felt by the Rabbis, at the thought of possible consequences, may perhaps be realised by the following passage with allusion to Exod. 19 2: "The Holy One, blessed be he, appeared to them on the (Red) Sea as a mighty warrior (Exod. 15 3) and revealed himself on Mount Sinai as a scribe teaching Torah, and was also visible to them in the days of Daniel, and as Elder teaching Torah (Dan. 7 9) he (therefore) said to them, 'Think not on account of these manifold appearances, there are many deities. I am the Lord thy God. The God of the Sea is the God of the Sinai.' The warning comes from God himself and shows the danger of the situation; indeed, it had become so threatening that even such innocent rhetorical exclamations as 'My God, my God, why hast thou forsaken me?' (Ps. 22 2) were apparently subject

[1] The difference between the Rabbi and the Hellenist in this respect may perhaps be reduced to this: The Rabbi may speak of the *Dibbur* or the *Memra*, but means God; the Hellenist may speak of God, but means the *Dibbur* or the *Memra*.

to misinterpretation, so that it was necessary to emphasise on this occasion, too, the God of the Red Sea is the God of the Revelation." [1]

Even more striking is the following Rabbinic homily on Exod. 3 7, "And the Lord said I have surely seen the affliction of my people": "God said to Moses, 'Thou seest only one sight, but I see two sights. Thou seest them coming to Mt. Sinai and receiving there my Torah; but I see also their making the golden calf. When I shall come to Sinai to give them the Torah, I will come down with my chariot of four *chayoth* (Ezek. 1 5-10), from which they will abstract one (of the four—the ox or the calf), by which they will provoke me.'" [2]

Amidst all these embarrassments, contradictions, confusions, and aberrations, however, the great principle of the Synagogue, that worship is due only to God, remained untouched. Into the liturgy none of the stranger appellations of God were admitted. "When man is in distress," says R. Judah, "he does not first call upon his patron, but seeks admittance to him through the medium of his servant or his agent;

[1] See *P. K.*, 109 *b*; *M. T.*, 22 16. אלי בים סוף אלי בסיני. Cf. *P. R.* 100 *b* and 101 *a*, and note 31 to the last page. See also *Tan. B.*, 2 40 *b*. Cf. *Kuzari*, ed. Cassel, 313, note 1.

[2] See *Exod. R.*, 3 2; 42 5, text and references given there in the commentaries. Cf. Ezek. 1 9 and 10; Ps. 106 19 and 20. See also Nachmanides to Exod. 18 1, who gives fuller and better readings of the passage in the Midrash. Cf. Bacher, *Ag. Pal.*, 1 43. About the notion that God came down from Mt. Sinai with the chariot, see *P.K.*, 107 *b*.

but it is different with God. Let no man in misfortune cry either unto Michael or Gabriel, but pray unto me (God), and I will answer him at once, as it is said: 'Whosoever shall call on the name of the Lord shall be delivered'" (Joel 3 5).[1] "Come and see," says another Rabbi, "that in the portions of the Scriptures treating of sacrifices, no other name of God is ever used than the Tetragrammaton. This is done so as not to give room for heretical interpretations," [2] which might claim divine worship for some other being. When the Rabbis fixed the rule, that no form of benediction is permissible in which the name of God does not occur,[3] they were probably guided by the same principle. At a certain period in history, when the heresy of the new sects was threatening to affect larger classes, the Rabbis even enforced the utterance of the Tetragrammaton in every benediction, lest there should be some misunderstanding to whom prayer is directed.[4]

[1] *Jer. Berachoth*, 13 *a*.

[2] See *Sifre*, 54 *a*. Cf. *T. K.*, 3 *c*. See Bacher, *Ag. Tan.* 1 422.

[3] *Berachoth*, 40 *b*.

[4] See *Tosephta Berachoth*, 9, ed. Schwartz, and notes (Graetz, *Geschichte*, 3 458). See also Jacob, *Im Namen Gottes*, p. 174.

## III

## GOD AND ISRAEL

We saw in the preceding chapter that neither the terms of space nor heaven as applied to God, nor the imaginary descriptions placing his particular abode on high, meant for the Rabbis remoteness from the world. Whatever the faults of the Rabbis were, consistency was not one of them. Neither speculation nor folklore was ever allowed to be converted into rigid dogma. As it was pointed out, when the Rabbis were taught by experience that certain terms meant for superficial proselytes only a reflex of their former deities, they not only abandoned them for a time, but substituted for them even the Tetragrammaton itself; a strong measure, taken in contradiction to ancient custom and tradition, and thus proving how anxious the Rabbis were that nothing should intervene between man and God.

We shall now proceed to show how still more intimate and close was the relation maintained and felt between God and Israel. He is their God, their father, their strength, their shepherd, their hope, their salvation, their safety; they are his people, his children, his first-born son, his treasure, dedicated to his name, which it is sacrilege to profane. In brief, there is not a single endearing epithet in the language, such as brother, sister, bride, mother, lamb, or eye, which is not, according to the Rabbis, applied by the Scriptures to express this intimate relation between God and his people.[1] God is even represented by the Rabbis as saying to Moses, "As much as thou canst exalt this nation (Israel) exalt it, for it is as if thou wert exalting me. Praise it as much as thou canst, glorify it as much as thou canst, for in them I will be glorified, as it is said, 'Thou art my servant, O Israel, in whom I will be glorified'" (Isa. 49 3).[2] "What is his (God's) name? *El* Shaddai, Zebaoth. What is the name of his son? Israel!"[3] Nay, more, though a king of flesh and blood would resent to hear one of his subjects arrogating his title (as Cæsar Augustus), the Holy One, blessed be he, himself confers on Israel the names by which he is himself distinguished, as wise, holy, the chosen ones, and does not even deny them the title of gods, as it is written, "I have said, Ye are gods" (Ps. 82 6).[4]

This intimacy of relationship is reciprocal. "He (God) needs us even as we need him" was a fa-

[1] This feature is so strongly represented in the Rabbinic literature that I must satisfy myself with a few general references. See *T. K.*, 44 *c*; *Mechilta*, 28 *a*, 29 *b*, 41 *b*, 43 *b*, 44 *a*, 57 *a*, 62 *b*; *P. K.*, 1 *a*, 1 *b*, 4 *a*, 4 *b*, 47 *a*, 47 *b*, 50 *a*, 104 *a*, 157 *a*; *Gen. R.*, 81; *Exod. R.*, 15, 20, 27, 33, 52; *Lev. R.*, 2. See also *Sifre*, 68 *a*, בני אברהם יצחק ויעקב שנקראו אחים ... וכל לשון חבה. The various Midrashim as well as the Targum to the Song of Songs is permeated by the same tendency. Cf. Elbogen, *Religionsanchauungen der Pharisäer*, p. 60 *seq.*

[2] *Lev. R.*, 2 5.

[3] See *P. R.*, 15 *a*. Cf. *P. K.*, 4 *b*.

[4] See *M. T.*, 21 2; *Exod. R.*, 8 1.

vourite axiom with certain mystics. In the language of the Rabbis we should express the same sentiment thus, "One God through Israel, and one Israel through God. They are his selected people, and he is their selected portion."[1] "God is the help and the support of all mankind, but still more of Israel." "They recognised in him the King, and he recognised in them the masters of the world. . . . Israel declares (his unity) in the words, 'Hear, O Israel: The Lord our God, the Lord is *one*' (Deut. 6 4); and the holy spirit (or word of God) proclaims their election (in the words), 'And who is like thy people Israel, a nation that is *one* (or alone) in the earth'" (1 Chron. 17 21).[2] "He glorified them when he said, 'Israel is my son, even my first-born,' whilst they sang a song unto him in Egypt."[3] Israel brought him down by their praise (from all the seven heavens to earth, as it is said, "And let them make me a sanctuary, that I may dwell among them") (Exod. 25 9), and he lifted them by his praise above [to the heaven], as it is said, "That the Lord thy God will set thee on high above" (Deut. 28 1).[4] "Blessed be his (God's) name for ever," exclaims a Rabbi, enthusiastically, "who left those above and chose those below to dwell in the Tabernacle because of his love of Israel."[5] Indeed, the Holy One, blessed

[1] *Sifre*, 134 *b*.

[2] See *Mechilta*, 36 *b*; *Chagigah*, 3 *a*, 3 *b*, and parallels. Cf. Bacher, *Ag. Tan.*, 1 235, and Levy, *Talmud. Wörterbuch*, s. אמירה, 2, and חטיבה.

[3] *Mechilta*, 35 *b*.

[4] See *Cant., R.*, 5 16.

[5] *Tan. B.*, 3 8 *a*. Cf. *Tan. B.*, 2 47 *a* and *b*.

be he, says to Israel, you are my flock and I am the shepherd, make a hut for the shepherd that he come and provide for you; you are the vineyard and I am the watcher, make a tent for the watcher that he guards you; you are the children and I am the father, — it is a glory for the father when he is with his children and a glory for the children when they are with their father; make therefore a house for the father that he comes and dwells with his children.[1]

Israel bears in common with the angels such names as gods, holy ones, children (of God). But God loves Israel more than the angels. Israel's prayer being more acceptable to him than the song of the angels, whilst the righteous in Israel are in closer contact with the Deity than the angels, and are consulted by them as to "what God hath wrought." [2]

[1] *Exod. R.*, 33 3.

[2] See *Chullin* 91 *b*. *Yalkut* I § 890 (quotation from the *Yelamdenu*). *Yalkut to Prov.*, § 951, and *Shabbath* 8 d. Cf. also Friedmann, נספחים, p. 47, to which more passages of a similar nature can be added. It should, however, be remarked that the rationalistic school rather objected to this teaching of the inferiority of angels. Cf. Schmiedel's *Studien über . . . Religionsphilosophie*, p. 70 *seq.*, and p. 78 *seq.* Cf. also R. Meir ibn Gabbai's עבודת הקדש, the ten first chapters of the section תכלית. In general, the belief in angels was fairly maintained by Rabbinism throughout all its history, although it was only David Bilia (fourteenth century) who raised it to the importance of a dogma. Cf. Schechter, *Studies in Judaism*, p. 203. For opposing tendencies in comparatively early times, see *Exod. R.*, 17 5, ועבר ה׳ לנגוף את מצרים י״א ע״י מלאך וי״א הקב״ה בעצמו. See also מהרז״ו to this passage. Naturally, it was subject in the course of history to all sorts of interpretations, qualifications, and modifications. Cf. Professor

Again, "He who rises up against Israel rises up against God; hence the cause of Israel is the cause of God; their ally is also his." [1] For God suffers with them in their suffering and is with them in their distress.[2] Their subjection implies his subjection,[3] and his presence accompanies them through their various captivities among the Gentiles.[4] Therefore their redemption is his redemption,[5] their joy is his joy,[6] their salvation his salvation,[7] and their light his light.[8]

Their cause is indeed so closely identified with God's cause that on the occasion of the great historical crisis at the Red Sea, God is supposed rather to resent the lengthy prayer of Moses, and says unto him, "Wherefore criest thou to me? (Exod. 14 15). I need no asking for my children, as it is said, 'Wilt thou ask me concerning my children?'" (Isa. 45 11).[9] The recognition of this fatherhood is all that God wants from Israel. "All the wonders and mighty deeds

Blau's article *Angelology*. Occasionally, the authorities would have to enter their protest against such excesses as invocations addressed to the angels soliciting their intercession. See *Kerem Chemed*, 9 141 *seq.*, and Zunz, *Synagogale Poesie*, p. 148 *seq.*

1 *Mechilta*, 39 *a*, 39 *b*; *Sifre*, 29 *b* and parallels.

2 *P. K.*, 47 *a*. By Israel is also meant the individual. See *Mechilta*, 17 *a*, 119 *b*, אין לי אלא צרת ציבור צרת יחיד מנין, etc., *S. E.*, p. 89. Cf. *Sabbath*, 12 *b*.

3 *Mechilta*, 16 *a*.

4 *Sifre*, 62 *b*; *P. K.*, 113 *b*. Cf. Bacher, *Ag. Tan.*, I 283, note 2.

5 *Mechilta*, 16 *a*.

6 *Ibid.*, 56 *a*.

7 *Lev. R.*, 9 3.

8 See *P. K.*, 144 *b*.

9 See *Mechilta*, 30 *a*. Cf. *Num. R.*, 21.

which I have done for you," says God unto Israel, "were not performed with the purpose of being rewarded (by you), but that you honour me like children and call me your father."[1] The filial relationship suffers no interference, whether for good or evil, of a third person between Israel and God. Israel loves him and loves his house, no man indeed knowing the love which is between Israel and their Maker. And so does the Holy One, blessed be he, love them. He wants to hear Israel's voice (as expressed in prayer), and is anxious for them to listen unto his voice.[2] According to another explanation (of Exod. 14 15), Moses was given to understand that there was no need for his prayers, the Holy One by his intimate relation to Israel being almost himself in distress.[3]

This paternal relation, according to the great majority of the Rabbis, is unconditional. Israel will be

[1] *Exod. R.*, 32 5. [2] *M. T.*, 116 1.

[3] *Mechilta*, 29 *b*, in the name of R. חנינה בן חלניסי. Some parallel to this strong confidence in the identity of Israel's cause and God's may be found in various utterances of Luther, as, "Know that God so takes thee to himself, that thy enemies are his enemies"; or, "He who despises me despises God"; or, "God suffers and is despised and persecuted in us." And when anxiously waiting for news from the Diet at Augsburg, "I know," he was overheard saying, or rather praying, "that thou art our father and our God; I am certain, therefore, that thou art about to destroy the persecutors of thy children. If thou doest this not, then our danger is thine too. This business is wholly thine. We come to it under compulsion. Thou, therefore, defend." See the preface of the Bishop of Durham (p. xi) to the volume, *Lombard Street in Lent*. See also Mr. Beard in his *Hibbert Lectures*, p. 87.

chastised for its sins, even more severely than other nations for theirs; but this is only another proof of God's fatherly love. For it was only through suffering that Israel obtained the greatest gifts from heaven,[1] and what is still more important to note is, that it was affliction which "reconciled and attached the son to the father (Israel to God)."[2] "The Israelites are God's children even when full of blemishes," and the words, "A seed of evildoers, children that are corrupt" (Isa. 1 4), are cited as a proof that even corruption cannot entirely destroy the natural relation between father and child.[3] Indeed, when Isaiah received the call, "the Holy One, blessed be he, said unto him, 'Isaiah! my children are troublesome and rebellious. If thou dost take upon thyself to be insulted and beaten by my children thou wilt be sent as my messenger, not otherwise!' Isaiah answered, 'Yes, on this condition. As it is said, "I gave my back to smiters and my cheeks to them that plucked off the hair (Isa. 50 6)," I am not even worthy to carry messages to thy children.'"[4] But Elijah, the Rabbis say, who in his zeal denounced Israel, saying, "I have been very jealous for the Lord God of hosts; because the children of Israel have forsaken thy covenant, thrown down thine altars, and slain thy prophets with the sword" (1 Kings 19 14),

[1] See *Berachoth*, 5 *a*, and *Exod. R.*, 1 1.

[2] *Sifre*, 73 *b*. Cf. *M. T.*, 96.

[3] *Sifre*, 133 *a*, 133 *b*.

[4] *Lev. R.*, 10 2 and references. Cf. also *Exod. R.*, 7 8, regarding the call of Moses and Aaron.

was dismissed with the answer, "I have no desire in thy prophecy"; and his prophetic office was transferred to the milder Elisha, the son of Shaphat, who was anointed in Elijah's place (19 16). Likewise is the Prophet Hosea rebuked for his refraining from praying for Israel, God saying unto him, They are my beloved ones, the sons of my beloved ones, the sons of Abraham, Isaac, and Jacob. For this is indeed the glory of both patriarchs and prophets, that they are prepared to give themselves (as an atoning sacrifice) for Israel; as, for instance, Moses, who said in case God would not forgive the sin of Israel, "Blot me, I pray thee, out of thy book which thou hast written" (Exod. 23 32). Jeremiah, however, who proved himself just as jealous for the glory of the son (Israel) as for the glory of the father (God), saying as he did, "We have transgressed and have rebelled: thou hast not pardoned" (Lam. 3 42) (thus though confessing Israel's guilt, still reproaching God, so to speak, for his declining to forgive), was rewarded by the continuation of his gift of prophecy, as it is said, "And *he adds* besides unto them many like words" (Jer. 36 32).[1] And, it is on the strength of this view of childship that some of the prophets pleaded with God on behalf of Israel. "Behold," they said to the Holy One, blessed be he, "thou sayest (because of their transgressions) they are not any longer thy children,

[1] See *Mechilta*, 2 *a*. See also *Pesachim*, 87 *a* and *S. E. Z.*, p. 187, text and notes.

but they are recognisable by their countenances as it is said, 'All that see them shall acknowledge them that they are the seed, which the Lord has blessed' (Is. 61 9). As it is the way of the Father to be merciful with his children though they sin, so thou wilt have mercy with them (notwithstanding their relapses). This is (the meaning of the verse): 'But now, O Lord, thou art our father. . . . Be not wroth very sore, O Lord, neither remember iniquity forever'" (Isa. 64 8, 9).[1] Indeed, God says, after you (Israel) stood on the mount of Sinai and received the Torah and I wrote of you that I love you; and since I loved you, how could I hate you (considering that I loved you as children)?[2]

The only opponent to the view of the majority regarding the paternal relation is R. Judah, who limits it to the time when Israel acts as children should act.[3] When R. Akiba, in a time of great distress, opened the public service with the formula, "Our father, our king, we have sinned against thee; our father, our king, forgive us," he only expressed the view of the great majority, that Israel may claim their filial privileges even if they have sinned.[4] The formula of the daily confession, "Forgive us, O our Father, for we have sinned," points in the same direction. In fact, the

[1] *Exod R.*, 46 4.

[2] See *Exod. R.*, 32 2. Cf. Commentaries *a. l.*

[3] *Sifre*, 133 *a* and *b*. Cf. also 94 *a* and *Kiddushin*, 36 *a*.

[4] *Taanith*, 26 *b*. See Rabbinowitz, *Variae Lectiones*, *a. l.*, and Baer, p. 119, text and commentary. Cf. Löw, *Gesammelte Schriften*, I 181.

term "Father," or "Our Father, who is in heaven," or "My Father, who is in heaven," is one of the most frequent in the Jewish Prayer Book and the subsequent liturgy. The latter seems to have been a favourite expression with the Tanna of the school of Elijah, who very often introduces his comments on the Bible (a mixture of homiletics and prayer) with the words, "My Father in heaven, may thy great name be blessed for all eternity, and mayest thou have delight in thy people Israel."[1] Another consequence of this fatherly relation is that Israel feels a certain ease and delight in the fulfilment of the Law which to slaves is burdensome and perplexing. For "the son who serves his father serves him with joy, saying, 'Even if I do not entirely succeed (in carrying out his commandments), yet, as a loving father, he will not be angry with me'; whilst the Gentile slave is always afraid lest he may commit some fault, and therefore serves God in a condition of anxiety and confusion."[2] Indeed, when Israel feels uneasy because of their having to stand in judge-

[1] See *S. E.*, pp. 51, 53, 83, 89, 100, 110, 115, 121. The formula אבי שבשמים occurs on p. 112 eight times. Cf. Friedmann's Introduction, p. 80.

[2] *Tan.* נח, 19. Israel's relation to God seems only then to assume the aspect of slavery, when the whole nation is determined to apostatise. Then God enforces his mastership over them by the right of possession. This seems to me the meaning of the rather obscure passage in *Exod. R.*, 24, 1, ד״א אם אביך למה קנך. Cf. *ibid.* 3, § 6, where a distinction is made between the individual and the greater number of Israel, to the former free action being left; this contains undoubtedly a deep historical truth. See also *Sifre*, 112 *b*.

ment before God, the angels say unto them, "Fear ye not the judgement. . . . Know ye not him? He is your next of kin, he is your brother, but what is more, he is your father."[1]

[1] *M. T.*, 118 10.

# IV

## ELECTION OF ISRAEL

THE quotations in the preceding chapter will suffice to show the confidence with the Rabbis felt in the especially intimate relations existing between God and Israel. This renders it necessary to make here some reference to the doctrine of Israel's election by God, which in fact is only another term for this special relation between the two. "To love means in fact, to choose or to elect." The doctrine has found no place in Maimonides' Thirteen Articles of the Creed, but still even a cursory perusal of Bible and Talmud leaves no doubt that the notion of the election always maintained in Jewish consciousness the character of at least an unformulated dogma.[1]

The Rabbinic belief in the election of Israel finds, perhaps, its clearest expression in a prayer which begins as follows: "Thou hast chosen us from all peoples; thou hast loved us and taken pleasure in us, and hast exalted us above all tongues; thou hast sanctified us by thy commandments and brought us near unto thy service; O our King, thou hast called us by thy great and holy name." These words, which

[1] See Weiss, דו"ד, 3 801. Cf. Kaufmann, *J. Q. R.*, 2 442.

still breathe a certain scriptural air, are based, as may be easily seen, on the Biblical passages of Deut. 10 15, 14 2; Ps. 149 2; and Jer. 14 27.[1] There was thus hardly any necessity for the Rabbis to give any reasons for their belief in this doctrine, resting as it does on ample Biblical authority; though, as it would seem, they were not quite unconscious of the difficulties which such a doctrine involves. Thus Moses is represented by them as asking God: "Why out of all the seventy nations of the world dost thou give me instructions only about Israel?" the commandments of the Torah being mostly addressed to the "children of Israel" (*e.g.* Exod. 3 15, 31 30, 33 5, Lev. 24 2);[2] whilst in another place we read, with reference to Deut. 7 7, that God says to Israel, "Not because you are greater than other nations did I choose you, nor because you obey my injunctions more than the nations; for they (the nations) follow my commandments, even though they were not bidden to do it, and also magnify my name more than you, as it is said, 'From the rising of the sun, even unto the going down of the same, my name is great among the Gentiles'" (Mal. 1 11).[3] The answers given to these and similar ques-

[1] See Singer, p. 227, and Baer, p. 247. This is the introductory prayer to the original liturgy for the festivals. In olden times the morning prayer for Sabbaths began with the same prayer. See Zunz, *Die Ritus*, p. 13. The benediction over the sanctification cup on festivals opens with a similar formula.

[2] See *P. K.*, 16 *a seq.* and *Lev. R.*, 2 4.

[3] *Tan.*, עקב, 2. See also *Tan. B.*, 5 9 *a*.

tions are various. According to some Rabbis, Israel's election was, as it would seem, predestined before the creation of the world (just as was the name of the Messiah), and sanctified unto the name of God even before the universe was called into existence.[1] Israel was there before the world was created and is still existing now and will continue to exist in the future (by reason of its attachment to God).[2] "The matter is to be compared to a king who was desiring to build; but when he was digging for the purpose of laying the foundations, he found only swamps and mire. At last he hit on a rock, when he said, 'Here I will build.' So, too, when God was about to create the world, he foresaw the sinful generation of Enosh (when man began to profane the name of the Lord), and the wicked generations of the deluge (which said unto God, 'Depart from us'), and he said, 'How shall I create the world whilst these generations are certain to provoke me (by their crimes and sins)?' But when he perceived that Abraham would one day arise, he said, 'Behold, I have found the *petra* on which to build and base the world.'" The patriarch Abraham is called the rock (Isa. 51 1.2); and so Israel are called the rocks (Num. 33 9).[3] They are an obstinate race and their faith in God is not a shifting one, and, as a later author expresses it, if you leave them no

[1] See *Gen. R.*, 1 4 and *S. E.*, p. 160. [2] See *Tan.*, נח, 12.

[3] *Yelamdenu* quoted by the Yalkut, *Num.*, § 766. Cf. *Exod. R.*, 15 17. See also below, p. 173.

alternative but apostasy or crucifixion, they are certain to prefer the latter.[1] "Hence the thought of Israel's creation preceded the creation of the world." According to other Rabbis, Israel's claim to the election is because they declared God as king on the Red Sea, and they said, "The Lord shall reign for ever and ever" (Exod. 15 18). According to others again, it was on account of their having accepted the yoke of his kingdom on Mount Sinai.[2] Why did the Holy One, blessed be he, choose Israel? Because all the other nations declared the Torah unfit and refused to accept it, whilst Israel agreed and chose God and his Torah.[3] Another opinion maintains that it was because of Israel's humbleness and meekness that they were found worthy of becoming the chosen people.[4] This may perhaps be connected with the view expressed that God's reason for the election of Israel was the fact that they are the persecuted ones, all the great Biblical characters such as Abraham, Isaac, Jacob, Moses, David, having been oppressed and especially chosen by God.[5] From another place it would seem that it is the holiness of Israel which made them worthy of the election.[6] It is worth noting, however, that the passage in which the reason of Israel's meekness is advanced concludes with the reminder that God

[1] See *Exod. R.*, 42 9. Cf. Nachmanides to *Deut.* 7 7, and see also Friedmann, הציון, p. 12.

[2] See *P. K.*, 16 *b* and 17 *a* and parallels.

[3] *Num. R.*, 14 10. [4] *Tan. B.*, 5 9 *a*. [5] See *Lev. R.*, 27 6.

[6] See *Sifre*, 94 *a* (§ 97), but the meaning is not quite clear.

says, "My soul volunteered to love them, though they are not worthy of it," quoting as a proof from the Scriptures the verse, "I will love them freely" (Hos. 14 5).[1] This suggests that even those Rabbis who tried to establish Israel's special claim on their exceptional merits were not altogether unconscious of the insufficiency of the reason of works in this respect, and therefore had also recourse to the love of God, which is not given as a reward, but is offered freely. When an old Roman matron challenged R. Jose (b. Chalafta) with the words, "Whomsoever your God likes he brings near unto him (elects)," the Rabbi answered her that God indeed knows whom to select: in him whom he sees good deeds he chooses him and brings him near unto him.[2] But the great majority of the Rabbis are silent about merits, and attribute the election to a mere act of grace (or love) on the part of God. And he is represented as having answered Moses' question cited above, "I give these instructions about Israel (and not about the nations) because they are beloved unto me more than all other nations; for they are my peculiar treasure, and upon them I did set my love, and them I have chosen."[3] "Praised be the Omnipresent" (*makom*), exclaims the Tanna of the school of Elijah, "blessed be he, who chose Israel from among all the

[1] *Tan. B.*, 5 9 *a*.

[2] See *Midrash Shemuel B.*, 8 2, and *Num. R.*, 3 2, text and commentaries.

[3] *Tan.*, כי תשא, 8.

nations, and made them verily his own, and called them children and servants unto his name . . . and all this because of the love with which he loved them, and the joy with which he rejoiced in them."[1]

It must, however, be noted that this doctrine of election — and it is difficult to see how any revealed religion can dispense with it — was not quite of so exclusive a nature as is commonly imagined. For it is only the privilege of the first-born which the Rabbis claim for Israel, that they are the first in God's kingdom, not the exclusion of other nations. A God "who had faith in the world when he created it,"[2] who mourned over its moral decay, which compelled him to punish it with the deluge, as a father mourns over the death of his son,[3] and who, but for their sins, longed to make his abode among its inhabitants,[4] is not to be supposed to have entirely given up all relations with the great majority of mankind, or to have ceased to take any concern in their well-being. "Though his goodness, loving-kindness, and mercy are with Israel, his right hand is always stretched forward to receive *all* those who come into the world, . . . as it is said, 'Unto me every knee shall bow, every tongue shall swear'" (Isa. 45 23). For this confession from the Gentiles the Holy One is waiting.[5] In fact, it did not

[1] See *S. E.*, p. 129 and p. 127. Cf. *Tan. B.*, 4 9 *a.*

[2] *Sifre*, 132 *b.*

[3] *Gen. R.*, 27 4. Cf. *Sanhedrin*, 108 *a.* See also above, p. 37.

[4] *P. R.*, 27 *b* and parallels.

[5] See *Mechilta*, 38 *b.* Cf. *M. T.*, 100 1.

escape the composers of the Liturgy that the same prophet by whom they established their claim to election called God "the King of the Gentiles" (Jer. 10 7), and on this the Rabbis remark that God said to the prophet, "Thou callest me the King of the Gentiles. Am I not also the King of Israel?"[1] The seeming difference again between "I am the Lord, the God of *all* flesh" (Jer. 32 27), and "the Lord of hosts, *the God of Israel*" (ver. 15), or between the verse "Three times in the year all thy males shall appear before *the Lord God*" (Exod. 23 17) and another passage enjoining the same law, but where God is called "the Lord God, the God *of Israel*" (34 23), is explained by the Rabbis to indicate the double relation of God to the world in general, and to Israel in particular. He is the Lord of all nations, while his name is especially attached to Israel.[2] Of more importance is the interpretation given to Deut. 6 4, "Hear, O Israel," etc.

[1] *M. T.*, 93 1.

[2] See *Mechilta*, 102 *a*, and *Sifre*, 73 *a*. The text is in a rather corrupt state. I have partly followed here the text of the *MHG.*, which on Exod. 34 24 reads : את פני האדון אדון אני על כל באי עולם · יכול אף אתה כיוצא בהן ת״ל אלהי ישראל יכול עליך בלבד ת״ל את פני האדון ה׳ · הא כיצד אלוה אני על כל באי עולם ושמי יחול עליך. Friedmann's suggestion (in *Mechilta*, *ibid.*, note 156) that the original explanation was in כי תשא (not משפטים) is thus confirmed, though, of course, the *Mechilta* of the compiler of the *MHG.* is not the same as ours. In Deut. 6 4, the same Ms. has כיוצא כו אמר ה׳ צבאות אלהי ישראל מה אני צריך והלא כבר נאמר הנה אני ה׳ אלהי כל בשר *both* verses taken from Jeremiah. Cf. Introduction to *Ruth R.*, 1 1. Cf. *Mechilta*, of R. Simon, p. 164.

(the *Shema*), which runs as follows: "He is *our* God by making his name particularly attached to us; but he is also the one God of *all* mankind. He is *our* God in this world, he will be the only God in the world to come, as it is said, And the Lord shall be King over all the earth; in that day there shall be one Lord, and his name one" (Zech. 14 9).[1] For, "in this world, the creatures, through the insinuations of the evil inclination, have divided themselves into various tongues, but in the world to come they will agree with one consent to call only on his name, as it is said, 'For then I will restore to the people a pure language, that they may all call upon the name of the Lord, to serve him with one consent'" (Zeph. 3 9).[2] Thus the *Shema* not only contains a metaphysical statement (about the unity of God), but expresses a hope and belief — for everything connected with this verse has a certain dogmatic value — in the ultimate universal kingdom of God.[3]

[1] See *Mechilta* and *Sifre*, *ibid.* I follow the reading of the לקח טוב to Deut. 6 4, which seems to me to be the best one, and is also supported by quotations in Mss. Cf. the commentaries of Rashi, Ibn Ezra, Nachmanides, and Bachye on this verse. See also *Mechilta*, 44 *a*, text and note 20.

[2] *Tan.*, נח, 19, and *Tan. B.*, I 28 *b*, the source of which is the *Sifre*. See Rashi's commentary, just referred to, where also the verse in Zephaniah is cited.

[3] See *Rosh Hashanah*, 32 *b.*, and *Tosefta*, *ibid.* 213, that the *Shema* is taken by the consent of the majority as implying מלכות. Cf. also below, p. 96, note 2, and p. 133, note 2.

## V

# THE KINGDOM OF GOD (INVISIBLE)

THE concluding words of the last chapter, "The kingdom of God," derived from the *Shema*, have brought us to a theological doctrine described by some Rabbis as the very "Truth (or essence) of the Torah,"[1] or as another Rabbi called it, "The 'weighty' law." The typical expressions in the Bible, "I am the Lord your God," or "I am the Lord," are also thought by the Rabbis to suggest the idea of the kingship.[2] It is at once the centre and the circumference of Rabbinic divinity. God is king and hence claiming authority; the king is God, and therefore the manifestation and assertion of this authority are the subject of Israel's prayers and solicitations. The conception has, of course, its origin in the Bible, in which God appears so often as a king with his various attributes, but it is the Rabbinic literature where we first meet with the term "kingdom of heaven," a term, as it seems, less expressive of an accomplished fact than of an undefined

[1] See *Megillah*, 16 *b*, and the commentary of R. Chananel to that passage as reproduced by the *Tosafoth*, in *Gittin*, 6 *b*, and *Menachoth*, 32 *b*, which is accepted in the text here. Cf. Kohut, *Aruch*, s.v. אמת.

[2] See *Mechilta of R. Simon*, p. 30, and *Sifre*, 19 *b*.

and indefinable ideal, and hence capable of a wider interpretation and of varying aspects.

For our present purpose it will be best to view it from its two larger aspects, the invisible kingdom and the visible kingdom.

The invisible kingdom is mainly spiritual, expressive of a certain attitude of mind, and possessing a more individual character. "He who is desirous to receive upon himself the yoke of the kingdom of heaven let him first prepare his body,[1] wash his hands, lay his *Tephilin* (phylacteries), read the *Shema*, and say his prayers." Should he happen to be on a journey, then, for the purpose of receiving the yoke of the kingdom, he must "stop still and direct his heart to heaven in awe, trembling, and devotion, and (in the thought) of unifying the Name, and so read the *Shema*"; after which he may say the rest of the prayers on his way.[2] The worshipper is even bidden to dwell so long in his devotional attitude of mind when uttering the words "only one" (אחד) as to declare God king in all the four corners of the world.[3] Communion with God by means of prayer through the removal of all intruding elements between man and his Maker, and through the implicit acceptance of God's unity as well as an un-

[1] *Berachoth*, 14 *b*, 15 *a*. The cleansing here has nothing to do with priestly ablutions; it means simply to prepare oneself in such a way as to be able to concentrate all one's mind during the prayer without any disturbance. Cf. *Jer. Berachoth*, 4 *c*.

[2] *Tan.* לך לך, 1. Cf. *Tan. B.*, 1 29 *a*, text and notes.

[3] *Berachoth*, 13 *b*.

conditional surrender of mind and heart to his holy will, which the love of God expressed in the *Shema* implies, this is what is understood by the receiving of the kingdom of God. "What is the section of the Law where there is to be found the acceptance of the kingdom of heaven" to the exclusion of the worship of idols? ask the Rabbis. The answer given is, "This is the *Shema*."[1] But under the word *idols* are included all other beings besides God. "Some nations confess their allegiance to Michael, others to Gabriel; but Israel chose only the Lord: as it is said, 'The Lord is my portion, saith my soul' (Lam. 3 24). This is the meaning of 'Hear, O Israel,'" etc.[2] The *Shema* also implies the exclusion of any human mediator, Israel desiring, whether on earth or in heaven, none but God.[3] It is in this sense that the scriptural words, "there is none else beside thee" (Deut. 4 35), and "The Lord, he is God, in heaven above and the earth beneath, there is none else" (Deut. 4 39), are declared to imply kingship.[4]

What love of God means we learn from the interpretation given to the words, "And thou shalt love the Lord with all thy heart, with all thy soul, and with all thy might" (Deut. 6 5). "Love God with all thy desires, even the evil *Yezer* (that is to say,

[1] *Sifre*, 34 *b* קיבול מ״ש ומיעט בה ע״ז. Cf. *Berachoth*, 13 *a*, and *Deut. R.*, 2 31, ואיזהו מלכות שמים ה׳ אלהינו ה׳ אחד. See also *Sifre*, 80 *a*, that this division of the *Shema* addresses itself to the individual, ליחיד.

[2] *Deut. R.*, 2 34.

[3] *Deut. R.*, *ibid.*, § 33. Cf. *Ag. Ber.*, ch. 27.

[4] *Rosh Hashanah*, 32 *b*.

make thy earthly passions and fleshly desires instrumental in the service of God), so that there may be no corner in thy heart divided against God." Again, "Love him with thy heart's last drop of blood, and be prepared to give up thy soul for God, if he requires it. Love him under all conditions, both in times of bliss and happiness, and in times of distress and misfortune.[1] For every measure he metes out to thee, praise and thank him exceedingly."[2] In a similar way the words, "To love the Lord your God" (Deut. 11 13), are explained to mean, "Say not, I will study the Torah with the purpose of being called Sage or Rabbi, or to acquire fortune, or to be rewarded for it in the world to come; but do it for the sake of thy love to God, though the glory will come in the end."[3] It is especially the love of self that is incompatible with the love of God or with the real belief in the unity. On this point the mediæval philosophers and mystics dwell with special emphasis, of which the following may serve as specimens: R. Bachye Ibn Bakudah, in his "Duties of the Heart": "The things detrimental to the (belief) in the Unity are manifold. . . . Among them is the disguised polytheism (or providing God with a companion), as, for instance, the religious hypocrisy of various kinds (being in reality worship of

[1] *Sifre*, 73 *a*. Cf. *Berachoth*, 61 *b* and parallels.

[2] *Mishnah Berachoth*, 9 5.

[3] *Sifre*, 79 *b*, to be supplemented and corrected by the parallel, 84 *b*. Cf. *Nedarim*, 62 *a*. See also Nachmanides' *Commentary to the Pentateuch* to Deut. 6 5. See also below, p. 162.

man instead of worship of God) or when man combines with the worship of God the devotion to his own gain, as it is said, 'There shall be no strange God in thee' (Ps. 81 10), on which our teachers remarked that it meant the strange god in the very body of man. . . ."[1] R. Meir Ibn Gabbai (born 1420), in commenting on Deut. 11 13, rightly remarks, "It is clear from these words that he who serves God with any personal object in view loves none but himself, the Most High having no share in his service; whilst the original design was that man should perform his religious duties only for God's sake, which alone means the establishing of the Unity of the Great Name both in action and in thought. . . . It is the man with such a purpose (aiming towards bringing about the perfect unity to the exclusion of all thought of self) who is called the lover of God."[2] Furthermore, R. Moses Chayim Luzzatto, a mystic of the seventeenth century, when speaking of the function of love in religion, says: "The meaning of this love is that man should be longing and yearning after the nearness of him (God), blessed be he, and striving to reach his holiness (in the same manner) as he would pursue any object for which he feels a strong passion. He should feel that bliss and delight in mentioning his name, in uttering his praises and in occupying himself with the words of the Torah which a lover feels towards the wife of his youth, or the father towards his only

[1] See חובות הלבבות שער היחוד פ״י.

[2] עבודת הקדש, Section יחוד ch. 28.

son, finding delight in merely holding converse about them. . . . The man who loves his Maker with a real love requires no persuasion and inducement for his service. On the contrary, his heart will (on its own account) attract him to it. . . . This is indeed the degree (in the service of God) to be desired, to which our earlier saints, the saints of the Most High, attained to, as King David said, 'As the heart panteth after the water brooks, so panteth my soul after thee, O God. My soul thirsteth for God, for the living God,' and as the prophet said, 'The desire of our soul is to thy name and to the remembrance of thee' (Is. 26 8). This love must not be a love 'depending on something,' that is, that man should not love God as his benefactor, making him rich and prosperous, but it must be like the love of a son to his father, a real natural love . . . as it is said, 'Is he not thy father who has bought thee?'"[1]

"Her yoke is a golden ornament," said Jesus, the son of Sirach, of Wisdom He considered it as a thing "glorious," and invited mankind to put their necks under her yoke. The Rabbis likewise looked upon the yoke of the kingdom of God and the yoke of the Torah as the badge of real freedom. "And if thou hast brought thy neck under the yoke of the Torah she will watch over thee," in both worlds.[2] The yoke of this kingdom was not felt as a burden. If the Rabbis

[1] See Luzzatto, מסילת ישרים, Warsaw, 1884, p. 27 *b*.

[2] See Ecclus. 6 30, 51 17, and 26 *b* (Hebrew), and cf. *Kinyan Torah* 2; *Erubin*, 54 *a*; and *M. T.*, 2 11.

had any dread, it was lest it might be removed from them. "I shall not hearken unto you," said one of them to his disciples, who on a certain joyous occasion wanted him to avail himself of his legal privilege, and omit the saying of the *Shema;* "I will not remove from myself the yoke of the kingdom of heaven even for a single moment."[1] Even to be under the wrath of this yoke is a bliss. When one Rabbi quoted the verse from Ezekiel, "As I live, saith the Lord God, surely with a mighty hand, and with a stretched-out arm, and with fury poured out, will I be king over you" (20 33), his colleague answered to the effect, Let the merciful continue his wrath with us, and redeem (and reign over us against our will).[2] What the typical Rabbi longed for was that sublime moment when the daily professions of a long life might be confirmed by act. When R. Akiba, who died the death of a martyr, was in the hands of his torturers, he joyfully "received upon himself the yoke of the kingdom of heaven (by reciting the *Shema*). When asked why he did so, he answered, 'All my life I have recited this verse ('And thou shalt love,' etc.), and have longed for the hour when I could fulfil it. I loved him with all my heart, I loved him with all my fortunes. Now I have the opportunity to love him with all my soul. Therefore I repeat this verse in joyfulness.' And thus he died."[3]

[1] *Mishnah, Berachoth,* 2 5. Cf. Rabbinowicz, *Varia Lectiones a. l.*

[2] *Sanhedrin,* 105 *a.* Cf. Rashi, *a. l.*

[3] See *Jer. Berachoth,* 14 *b.* מיתדין means probably tortured, and has to be supplied by the parallel from Babli, *Berachoth,* 61 *b.*

There is no indication of despair in Akiba's death, but also no thought of a crown of martyrdom awaiting him for this glorious act.[1] He simply fulfils a commandment of love, and he rejoices in fulfilling it. It is "a love unto death,"[2] suffering no separation. "Though God," says Israel, "brings me into distress and embitters me, he shall lie betwixt my breasts,"[3] and to be always in contact with the object of his love is Israel's constant prayer. "Unite our hearts," runs an old Rabbinic prayer, "to fear thy name; remove us from all thou hatest, and bring us near to all thou lovest, and be merciful unto us for thy name's sake."[4] Even fear is only another expression with them for love. "I feared in my joy, I rejoiced in my fear, and my love prevailed over all."[5]

Still more distinctly, though not more emphatically, is this thought of the constant union with God and the constant love of God expressed in the later Jewish authors, with whom it takes a certain mystical turn. "What is the essence of love to God?" says R. Bachye

[1] The words in *Aboth.*, 4 7, "Make not (of the Torah) a crown," are explained by R. Samuel de Ozedo, to mean the crown of the saints in the after-life; any thought of reward, whether material or spiritual, whether in this world or in the next, being unworthy of the real worshipper of God. It may, of course, be questioned whether this was the real meaning of the Tanna's saying; but it is highly characteristic of the feelings of the Talmudical Jew in this respect.

[2] *Mechilta*, 37 *a*.

[3] See *Shabbath*, 88 *b*, on the interpretation of Song of Songs I 13. Cf. *Cant. R.* to this verse.

[4] *Jer. Berachoth*, 7 *d*.

[5] See *S. E.*, p. 3.

Ibn Bakudah mentioned above. "It is the longing of the soul for an immediate union with him, to be absorbed in his superior light. For the soul, being a simple spiritual substance, is naturally attracted towards spiritual beings. And when she becomes aware of any being that could give her added strength and light, she devises means how to reach it, and clings to it in her thought . . . longing and desiring after it. This is the aim of her love. . . . And when the soul has realised God's omnipotence and his greatness, she prostrates herself in dread before his greatness and glory, and remains in this state till she receives his assurance, when her fear and anxiety cease. Then she drinks of the cup of love to God. She has no other occupation than his service, no other thought than of him, no other intent than the accomplishment of his will, and no other utterance than his praise. If he deal kindly with her she will thank him, if he bring affliction on her she will submit willingly, and her trust in God and her love of God will always increase. So it was told of one of the saints that he used to rise up in the night and say: My God, thou hast brought upon me starvation and penury. Into the depth of darkness thou hast driven me, and thy might and strength hast thou taught me. But even if they burn me in fire, only the more will I love thee and rejoice in thee. For so said the prophet, 'And thou shalt love thy God with all thy heart.'"[1]

[1] חובות הלבבות שער אהבת ה׳ פ״א. Of one of the exiles from Spain — who was exposed by the captain of the vessel, in which he

R. Eliezer of Worms writes to the effect: The meaning of this love is that the soul is full of the love of God and attached by the bonds of love in joyfulness and gladness of the heart. He is not one who serves his Master under compulsion. His love is burning in his heart urging him to serve God, and he rejoices so much to accomplish the will of the Creator even if they would seek to prevent him from it. . . . He does not serve him for his own profit or for his own glory. He says to himself, "How, was I chosen and created to be a servant to the King of Glory, I, who am despised and rejected of men, I, who am to-day here and to-morrow in the grave?" When the soul sinks in the depths of awe, the spark of the love of the heart breaks out in flames and the inward joy increases . . . the men of divine wisdom think with joy of the heart of accomplishing the will of their Creator, of doing all his commandments with all their hearts. Such lovers think not of the pleasures of the world, nor are they concerned in the idle pastimes of their wives and families. They desire only to accomplish the will of God and to lead others to righteousness, to sanctify his name and to deliver up his soul for the sake of his love as Abraham

had fled with his family, on a deserted island—something similar is reported. When his wife died from exhaustion, and his two children perished by famine, and he himself was in a fainting state, he exclaimed: "O Lord of the world, great are the afflictions thou hast brought upon me, tempting me to leave the faith. But thou knowest that I shall not solve thy covenant (with us) until death," שארית ישראל פכ״ג.

did. . . . They exalt not themselves, they speak no idle word, they see not the face of woman, they hear their reproach and answer not. All their thoughts are with their God. They sing sweet songs to him, and their whole frame of mind is glowing in the fire of their love to him.[1] An anonymous author (probably about the same period) says, "Those who believe that works are the main thing are mistaken. The most important matter is the heart. Work and words are only intended as preparatory actions to the devotion of the heart. The essence of all the commandments is to love God with all the heart. The glorious ones (*i.e.* the angels) fulfil none of the 613 commandments. They have neither mouth nor tongue, and yet they are absorbed in the glory of God by means of thought."[2] R. Meir Ibn Gabbai (quoted above) expresses the same thought in words to the effect: The love of the Only Name forms the highest attainment (in the scale) of the service of the Sanctuary. For the perfect adoration worship demanded of the true worshipper is the service of the Unity, that is, the unification of the glorious and the Only Name. But the essence of Love is the true Unity, and the true Unity is what is termed Love. . . . And behold, the soul comes into the body from the abode

[1] See R. Eliezer of Worms, רוקח שורש האהבה and ספר החסידים, Parma, § 300. The book רוקח is a casuistic book on questions of the Law. See also Dr. Güdemann, *Culturgeschichte*, I 160.

[2] Communicated by Dr. Güdemann, *Culturgeschichte*, I 160, from a Munich Ms., ספר החיים, emanating, as it seems, from the Franco-German school.

of Love and Unity, therefore she is longing for their realisation and by loving the Beloved One (God), she maintains the heavenly relations as if they had never been interrupted through this earthly existence.[1]

These instances, which could be multiplied by numerous other extracts from the later devotional literature and hymnology, suffice to show that there are enough individualistic elements in Judaism to satisfy all the longings of the religionist whose bent lies towards mysticism. And just as every Israelite "could always pour out his private griefs and joys before him who fashioneth the hearts," so was he able to satisfy his longing for perfect communion with his God (who is 'nigh to all them who call upon him') by means of simple love, without the aid of any forcible means.

It must, however, be remarked that this satisfying the needs of anybody and everybody is not the highest aim which Judaism set before itself. Altogether, one might venture to express the opinion that the now fashionable test of determining the worth of a religion by its capability to supply the various demands of the great market of the believers has something low and mercenary about it. Nothing less than a good old honest heathen pantheon would satisfy the crazes and cravings of our present pampered humanity, with its pagan reminiscences, its metaphysical confusion of

[1] עבודת הקודש, Section יחוד ch. 28. והאהבה עניינה היחוד האמיתי והיחוד האמיתי הוא הנקרא אהבה.

languages and theological idiosyncrasies. True religion is above these demands. It is not a Jack-of-all-trades, meaning monotheism to the philosopher, pluralism to the crowd, some mysterious Nothing to the agnostic, Pantheism to the poet, service of man to the hero-worshipper. Its mission is just as much to teach the world that there *are* false gods as to bring it nearer to the true one. Abraham, the friend of God, who was destined to become the first winner of souls, began his career, according to the legend, with breaking idols, and it is his particular glory to have been in opposition to the whole world.[1] Judaism means to convert the world, not to convert itself. It will not die in order *not* to live. It disdains a victory by defeating itself in giving up its essential doctrines and its most vital teaching. It has confidence in the world; it hopes, it prays, and waits patiently for the great day when the world will be ripe for its acceptance.

Nor is the individual — the pet of modern theology — with his heartburnings and mystical longings, of such importance that Judaism can spend its whole strength on him. De Wette was certainly guilty of a gross exaggeration when he maintained "that all mysticism tends to a more refined lust, to a feasting upon the feelings" — something like our conceited culture dandy, who is eaten up with the admiration of his vague denials and half-hearted affirmations. For undoubtedly

[1] See *Gen. R.*, 38 13, and 42 8 (the explanations of R. Judah to העברי); cf. Beer, *Leben Abrahams*, p. 8 *seq.*

every religion can boast of saintly mystics who did much good service to their own creed and to the world at large. Indeed, no creed worthy of the name could or would ever dispense with that sprinkling of mystics representing the deeper elements of saintliness and religious delicacy. But they were of little use either to themselves or to the world when they emancipated themselves from the control of the law. For it cannot be denied that the mystic has not always shown himself very trustworthy in his mission. Instead of being absorbed by God, he has absorbed God in himself. His tendency towards antinomianism, and to regard law and works as beneath him, is also a sad historic fact. But the worst feature about him is his egoism, the kingdom of God within him never passing beyond the limits of his insignificant self, who is the exclusive object of his own devotions. The Rabbis often speak of the reward awaiting the righteous after their death as consisting, not in material pleasures, but in feeding on, or revelling in, the divine glory.[1] But such a vision "of the blissfulness of the spirit" is wisely confined to the next world, when the Great Sabbath will break upon us, when all things will be at rest. In this world, "the world of activity," the righteous have no such peace; they have to labour and to suffer with their fellow-creatures; and even such a sublime quietism as revelling in God may, without strong control, too easily degenerate into a sort of religious epicureanism. It

[1] See *Berachoth*, 17 *a* and parallels.

would seem as though it were with an eye to such "idle spirituality," that with reference to Deut. 6 5, "And thou shalt love the Lord thy God with all thy heart," the Rabbis make the remark, "I know not in which way they should love the Holy One, blessed be he," therefore the Scripture continues, "And these words which I command thee this day, shall be in thine heart" (Deut. 6 6), which means, "Place these words upon thy heart, for through them thou wilt learn to know the Holy One, blessed be he, and cleave unto his ways."[1] And "these ways," as we shall see, concern this world. The best control is thus to work towards establishing the visible kingdom of God in the present world. This, the highest goal religion can strive to reach, Judaism never lost sight of. It always remained the cherished burden of its most ardent prayers and the object of its dearest hopes.

[1] See *Sifre*, 74 *a*.

## VI

## THE VISIBLE KINGDOM (UNIVERSAL)

THE visible kingdom may be viewed from two aspects, national and universal. An attempt will be made to give the outlines of these Aspects as they are to be traced in Rabbinic literature.

"Before God created the world," we read in the Chapters of R. Eliezer, "there was none but God and his great name." The great name is the tetragrammaton, the name expressive of his being, the "I am." All other names, or rather attributes, such as Lord, Almighty, Judge, Merciful, indicative of his relation to the world and its government, had naturally no meaning before the world was created. The act of creation again is a manifestation of God's holy will and goodness; but it requires a responsive goodness on the part of those whom he intends to create. For "whatever the Holy One, blessed be he, created in his world, he created but for his glory, for it is said, Every one that is called by my name: for I have created him for my glory. I have formed him; yea, I have made him (Is. 43 7), and again it is said, The Lord shall reign for ever and ever (Exod. 15 18)." "The Lord has made everything for himself" (Prov. 16 4), and heaven and earth, angels and planets, waters and herbs and trees and birds and beasts, all join in the great chorus of praise to God. But the attribute of kingship apparently does not come into full operation before the creation of man. Hence, "when the Holy One, blessed be he, consulted the Torah as to the creation of the world, she answered, 'Master of the world (to be created), if there be no host, over whom will the king reign, and if there be no peoples praising him, where is the glory of the king?' The Lord of the world heard the answer, and it pleased him." [1]

To effect this object, the angels already in existence did not suffice. "When God had created the world," one of the later Midrashim records, "he produced on the second day the angels with their natural inclination to do good, and an absolute inability to commit sin. On the following days he created the beasts with their exclusively animal desires. But he was pleased with neither of these extremes. 'If the angels follow my will,' said God, 'it is only on account of their inability to act in the opposite direction. I shall, therefore, create man, who will be a combination of both angel and beast, so that he will be able to follow either the good or the evil inclination.'" [2] His evil deeds will

[1] See *P. R. E.*, ch. 3. The thought of the world, and especially man, having been created for God's glory, is very common in Jewish literature. Cf. *A. R. N.*, 67 *b*, text and notes at the end; *Tan.* בראשית, 1; *Exod. R.* 17: 1 and *M. T.*, 148 5.

[2] Quoted in the סמ"ק, § 53. Cf. *Tan. B.*, Introduction, 76 *b*. Cf. below, p. 261, note 1.

place him below the level of the brutes, whilst his noble aspirations will raise him above the angels.

In short, it is not slaves, heaven-born though they may be, that can make the kingdom glorious. God wants to reign over free agents, and it is their obedience which he desires to obtain. Man becomes thus the centre of creation, for he is the only object in which the kingship could come into full expression. Hence it is, as it would seem, that on the sixth day, after God had finished all his work, including man, that God became king over the world.[1]

Adam the First invites the whole creation over which he is master "to clothe God with majesty and strength," and to declare him King, and he and all the other beings join in the song, "The Lord reigneth, he is clothed with majesty," which forms now the substance of the 93d Psalm.[2] God can now rejoice in his world. This is the world inhabited by man, and when he viewed it, as it appeared before him in all its innocence and beauty, he exclaimed, "My world, O that thou wouldst always look as graceful as thou lookest now." "Beautiful is the world," a Rabbi exclaims, "blessed be the Omnipresent who shaped it and created it by his word. Blessed art thou (world) in which the Holy One, blessed be he, is king."[3]

[1] See *Rosh Hashanah*, 31 *a*, assuming, of course, that the words ומלך עליה on the second day came into the text by a clerical error. Cf. Rabbinowicz, *Variae Lectiones*, *al.* *A. R. N.*, Appendix 76 *b*, and the Mishna, ed. Lowe, 191 *a*. [2] *P. R. E.*, ch. 11.

[3] *Gen. R.*, 9 4. See also *Exod. R.*, 15 22. Cf. also *Num. R.*, 10 1, that God longed to create the world.

This state of gracefulness did not last long. The free agent abused his liberty, and sin came into the world, disfiguring both man and the scene of his activity. Rebellion against God was characteristic of the generations that followed. Their besetting sin, especially that of the generation of the Deluge, which had to be wiped out from the face of the earth, was that they said, "There is no judge in the world," it being "an automaton."[1] They were the reverse of the faithful of later generations, that proclaimed God's government and kingship in the world every day.[2] They maintained that the world was forsaken by God, and said unto God, "Depart from us, for we desire not the knowledge of thy ways" (Job 21 14).[3] The name of God was profaned by its transfer to abominations (or idols), and violence and vice became the order of the day.[4] By these sins God was removed from the world in which he longed to fix his abode, and the reign of righteousness and justice ceased. The world was thus thrown into a chaotic state of darkness for twenty generations, from Adam to Abraham, all of them continuing to provoke God.[5] With Abraham the light returned,[6] for he was the first to call God master (אדון), a name which declares God to be the Ruler of the

[1] *A. R. N.*, 47 *b* and parallels. *M. T.*, 1 21.

[2] See *M. T. ibid.*

[3] See *Sanhedrin*, 108 *a*. Cf. also *P. R. E.*, ch. 24, with special reference to the generation of Nimrod, who threw off the yoke of heaven.

[4] See *Mechilta*, 67 *b*. See also *Pseudo-Jonathan*, Gen. 4 26.

[5] See *Aboth*, 5 1, and commentaries. [6] See *Gen. R.*, 3 8.

world, and concerned in the actions of men.[1] Abraham was also the first great missionary in the world, the friend of God, who makes him beloved by his creatures, and wins souls for him, bidding them, even as he bade his children, to keep the way of the Lord, to do righteousness and judgement.[2] It was by this activity that Abraham brought God again nearer to the world;[3] or, as the Rabbis express it in another passage, which we already had occasion to quote: Before Abraham made God known to his creatures he had been only the God (or the king of the heavens), but since Abraham came (and commenced his proselytising activity) he has become also the God and the King of the earth;[4] Jacob also is supposed by the Rabbis to have taught his children before his death the ways of God, whereupon they received the yoke of the kingdom of heaven.[5] Hence the patriarchs (as models and propagators of righteousness) became, as mentioned above, the very throne of God, his kingdom being based upon mankind's knowledge of him, and their realisation of his nearness.[6]

But the throne of God is not secure as long as the recognition of the kingship is only the possession of a few individuals. At the very time when the patriarch

[1] *Berachoth*, 7 *b*. See Edeles' Commentary to the passage.

[2] See *Sifre*, 73 *a* and parallels.

[3] *P. K.*, 1 *b*, and *P. R.*, 18 *b*.

[4] *Sifre*, 134 *b*, where the word מלך occurs.

[5] See *Num. R.*, 2 8. See also *Gen. R.*, 93 8 and parallels.

[6] See above, p. 33.

was teaching righteousness, there were the entire communities of Sodom and Gomorrah committed to idolatry and the basest vices,[1] whilst in the age of Moses, Pharaoh said, "Who is the Lord that I should obey his voice?"[2] The kingship is therefore uncertain until there was called into existence a whole people "which knows God," is sanctified unto his name, and devoted to the proclamation of his unity.[3] "If my people," God says to the angels, "decline to proclaim me as King upon earth, my kingdom ceases also in heaven." Hence Israel says unto God, "Though thou wast from eternity the same ere the world was created, and the same since the world has been created, yet thy throne was not established and thou wast not known; but in the hour when we stood by the Red Sea, and recited a song before thee, thy kingdom became firmly established and thy throne was firmly set."[4] The establishment of the kingdom is indicated in the eighteenth verse of the Song (*Shirah*), where it is said, "The Lord shall be king for ever and ever." But even more vital proofs of their readiness to enter into the kingdom, Israel gave on the day of "the glorious meeting" on Mount Sinai, when they answered in one voice, "All that the Lord hath said we will do, and be obedient" (Exod. 24. 7).[5] This unconditional surrender to the will of God in-

[1] *Sanhedrin*, 108 *a* and parallels.

[2] See Maimonides' *Mishneh Torah*, הלכות עכו״ם פ״א ה״ו, which seems to be a paraphrase of some Midrash. Cf. *Num. R.*, 2 6.

[3] See *Agadath Shir Hashirim*, pp. 11, 53.

[4] See *Exod. R.*, 23 1.

[5] See *P. K.*, 17 *a*.

vested Israel, according to the Rabbis, with a special beauty and grace.[1] And by the manifestation of the knowledge of God through the act of the revelation the world resumes its native gracefulness, which makes it again heaven-like, whilst God finds more delight in men than in angels.[2]

There is a remarkable passage in the Mechilta, in which Israel is strongly censured because in the song at the Red Sea, instead of using the present tense, ה׳ מֶלֶךְ, "God *is* King," they said ה׳ ימלוך, "God *shall be* King," thus deferring the establishment of the kingdom to an indefinite future.[3] Israel had accordingly some sort of foreboding of the evil times to come, a foreboding which was amply justified by the course of history. Israel soon rebelled against the kingdom. There was the rebellious act of the Golden Calf, which took place on the very spot where the kingdom was proclaimed, and which was followed by other acts of

[1] See *Midrash Agadah*, ed. B. 171 *a*. Cf. the Targum to Song of Songs, 7 7.

[2] See *Exod. R.*, 51 8, and parallels.

[3] See *Mechilta*, 44 *a*, in the name of R. Jose of Galilee. The text in the editions is corrupt. In the *M. H. G.* it runs: ה׳ ימלוך לעולם ועד ׳ ר׳ יוסי אומ׳ אלו אמרו ישראל ה׳ מלך עולם ועד לא שלטה בהם אומה ומלכות אלא ה׳ ימלוך לעולם ועד לעתיד לבוא ׳ מפני מה כי בא סום פרעה מלמד שאף פרעה בכלל ׳ וישב עליהם את מי הים ׳ עליהם שב ׳ אבל עמך וצאן מרעיתך ונחלתך בני אברהם אוהבך זרע יצחק ידידך משפחת יעקב בכורך ׳ גפן שהסעת ממצרים וכנה שנטעה ימינך ׳ ובני ישראל הלכו ביבשה בתוך הים. Cf. Targum Onkelos to this verse, whose paraphrase may have been intended to avoid the difficulty felt by R. Jose. Cf., however, Nachmanides' commentary to this verse and his reference to Onkelos.

rebellion against God.[1] "In the days of Joshua b. Nun, Israel received upon themselves the kingdom of heaven in love . . . and their reward was that God regarded them as pupils in the house of their teacher and children gathered round the table of their father, and he apportioned to them a blessing."[2] Then came again continual relapses, and the sons of Eli were called בני בליעל, the sons of Belial, — men who threw off the yoke of God[3] and denied the kingdom of heaven,[4] but "in the times of the prophet Samuel, Israel (again) received upon themselves the kingdom of heaven in fear . . . and their reward was that God came down from the upper heavens, the place of his glory . . . and abode with them during the battle (with the Philistines), and apportioned to them a blessing."[5] After David came the decay, and Solomon is described as one who threw off the yoke of God.[6] The division of the ten tribes under Jeroboam was also regarded as a rebellion against the kingdom of God. The Rabbis interpreted 2 Samuel 20. 1, as if the original reading had been איש לאלהיו ישראל, "Every man *to his gods*, O Israel" (instead of to his *tents*).[7] Even the princes

[1] See *Num. R.*, 7 2. [2] *S. E.*, p. 86. [3] See *Sifre*, 93 *b*.

[4] See *Yalkut to Shemuel*, § 86, and *Midrash Shemuel*, B. p. 31 *b*, from which the passage in question was taken. The marginal reference to *T. K.* (39 *d*) refers only to the first lines of the passage, which Schöttgen (1149) confused. See *Eccles. R.*, 1 18.

[5] *S. E.*, p. 86. [6] *Num. R.*, 4 10.

[7] The rebellion of the Belial Sheba, the son of Bichri, is only a prelude to that effected by Jeroboam. See *Midrash Shemuel*, B. ch. 42 *b*, § 4, and notes, and *Mechilta*, 39 *a*, כיוצא בו אין לנו חלק בדוד, etc.

of Judah at a later time "broke the yoke of the Holy One, blessed be he, and took upon themselves the yoke of the King of Flesh and Blood." The phrase, "broke" or "removed" the yoke, is not uncommon in Rabbinic literature, and has a theological meaning. The passage just cited refers probably to some deification of Roman emperors by Jewish apostates, and not exactly to a political revolt.[1]

Yet, notwithstanding all these relapses, one great end was achieved, and this was, that there existed a whole people who did once select God as their king. Over the people as a whole, as already hinted, God asserts his right to maintain his kingdom. Thus the Rabbis interpret Ezekiel 20 33, "Without your consent and against your will I (God) shall be King over you;" and when the elders of Israel remonstrate, "We are now among the Gentiles, and have therefore no reason for not throwing off the yoke of his kingdom," the Holy One answers, "This shall not come to pass, for I will send my prophets, who will lead you back under my wings."[2] The right of possession is thus enforced by an inner process, the prophets being a part of the people; and so there will always be among them a remnant which will remain true to their mission of preaching the kingdom. The remnant is naturally small in number, but

[1] See *A. R. N.*, 36 *b*. See, however, Bacher, *Ag. Tan.*, I 58, note 1, and the reference there to Weiss ד"דו. Cf. *Beth Talmud*, 2, 333–334.

[2] See *T. K.*, 112 *b*. Cf. *Sanhedrin*, 105 *a* and parallels. Cf. also *Exod. R.*, 3 2, and above, p. 55, note 2.

is sufficient to keep the idea of the kingdom alive. "God saw," say the Rabbis, "that the righteous were sparse; he therefore planted them in (or distributed them over) all generations, as it is said (2 Samuel 1 8), 'For the pillars of the earth are the Lord's, and he has set the world upon them.'" The pillars, according to the Rabbinical explanation, are the righteous, who, by the fact of their being devoted to the Lord, form the foundation of the spiritual world.[1]

We will now try to sum up in some clearer way the results to which the preceding statements mostly consisting of Rabbinical quotations, may lead us. We learn first that the kingdom of God is in *this world.* In the next world, if we understand by it the heavens, or any other sphere where angels and ethereal souls dwell, there is no object in the kingdom. The term "kingdom of heaven" must therefore be taken in the sense in which heaven is equivalent to God, not locally, as if the kingdom were located in the celestial spheres. The term מלכות שדי in the Prayer Book,[2] the kingdom of the Almighty, may be safely regarded as a synonym of מלכות שמים.

This kingdom again is established on earth by man's consciousness that God is near to him; whilst nearness

[1] *Yoma*, 38 *b*.

[2] Beginning על כן נקוה, see below, p. 94. Cf. *A. R. N.*, 36 *b*, where he speaks of עולו של הקב"ה, instead of which certain Mss. have all עול שמים. The mystical literature, it should be noted, speaks of angels "taking upon themselves the yoke of the kingdom of heaven." See Singer, p. 38 and Baer, p. 132.

of God to man means the knowledge of God's ways to do righteousness and judgement. In other words, it is the sense of duty and responsibility to the heavenly king who is concerned in and superintends our actions. "Behold thou art fair, my love," says God to Israel, "you are fair through the giving of alms and performing acts of loving-kindness; you (Israel) are my lovers and friends when you walk in my ways. As the Omnipresent is merciful and gracious, long-suffering and abundant in goodness, so be ye . . . feeding the hungry, giving drink to the thirsty, clothing the naked, ransoming the captives, and marrying the orphans. . . . They will behold the Right One, which is the Holy One, blessed be he, as it is said, 'A God of truth and without iniquity, just and Right is he'" (Deut. 32 4).[1] "The hill of the Lord," and "the tabernacle of God" in the Psalms, in which only the workers of righteousness and the pure-hearted shall abide, are kingdoms of God in miniature.

The idea of the kingdom may thus be conceived as ethical (not exactly eschatological) and it was in this sense perhaps that the Rabbis considered the patriarchs and the prophets as the preachers of the kingdom. It is not even exactly identical with the law or the Torah. Why do we read, ask the Rabbis, first the *Shema* (*i.e.* Deut. 6. 4-9), and afterwards the section Deut. 11 13, commencing with the words, "And it shall come to pass if ye will hearken diligently unto my command-

[1] See *Agadath Shir Hashirim*, p. 18, and p. 61.

ments"? This is done, say the Rabbis, to the end that we may receive upon ourselves first the yoke of the kingdom and afterwards the yoke of the commandments.[1] The law is thus only a necessary consequence of the kingdom, but not identical with it.[2]

Indeed, the Torah itself indicates its relation to the Kingdom; for the Rabbis say in allusion to Deut. 32 29, "Had Israel looked properly into the words of the Torah that were revealed to them, no nation would have ever gained dominion over them. And what did she (the Torah) say unto them? Receive upon yourselves the yoke of the kingdom of my name; outweigh each other in the fear of heaven, and let your conduct

[1] *Berachoth*, 13 *a*.

[2] In this connection reference may be had to the following Midrashic passage alluding to Zech. 99: "Rejoice greatly, O daughter of Zion, . . . behold thy King is coming unto thee. . . ." God says to Israel: "Ye righteous of the world, the words of the Torah are important for me; ye were attached to the Torah, but did not hope for my kingdom. I take an oath that with regard to those who hope for my kingdom I shall myself bear witness for their good. . . . These are the mourners over Zion who are humble in spirit, who hear their offence and answer not, and never claim merit for themselves." Lector Friedmann, in his commentary on the Pesikta, perceives in this very obscure passage the emphatic expression of the importance of the kingdom, which is more universal than the words of the Torah; the latter having only the aim of preparing mankind for the kingdom. See *P. R.*, 159 *a*, text and notes (especially note 23). To me it seems that the passage has probably to be taken in the sense of the text communicated from Friedmann's נספחים, below, p. 292. There are, also, very grave doubts as to the age and character of all these *Messianic Pesiktoth*. See Friedmann's interesting note, *ibid.*, p. 164 *a*, 164 *b*, though he defends their genuineness.

be mutual loving-kindness."[1] Among the features of the kingdom, the fear of God and the love of one's neighbor are thus found to be prominent.

Nor, again, is the kingdom of God political. The patriarchs in the mind of the Rabbis did not figure prominently as worldly princes, but as teachers of the kingdom.[2] The idea of theocracy as opposed to any other form of government was quite foreign to the Rabbis. There is not the slightest hint in the whole Rabbinic literature that the Rabbis gave any preference to a hierarchy with an ecclesiastical head who pretends to be the vice-regent of God, over a secular prince who derives his authority from the divine right of his dynasty.[3] Every authority, according to the creed of the Rabbis, was appointed by heaven;[4] but they had also the sad experience that each in its turn rebelled against heaven. The high priests, Menelaus and Alcimus, were just as wicked and as ready to betray their nation and their

[1] *Sifre*, 138 *a*. Perhaps we ought to read שמים instead of שמי. Cf. also *S. E.*, p. 143: "And thus said the Holy One, blessed be he, My beloved children, do I miss anything (which you could give me)? I want nothing but that you love each other, respect each other, and that no sin or ugly thing be found among you."

[2] There are some legends in which Abraham appears in the capacity of a prince, cf. *Gen. R.*, 42 5, but, it is not as a ruler, but as a teacher, that he figures mostly in Rabbinic literature.

[3] See Renan, *Hibbert Lectures*, p. 107, who has some apt remarks on this point, but which are at the same time greatly disfigured by his mania of generalising on Semitic religions.

[4] See *Berachoth*, 58 *a*. With regard to Rome in particular, see *Abodah Zarah*, 17 *a*, שאומה זו המליכוה מן השמים.

God as the laymen, Herod and Archelaus, who owed their throne to Roman machinations.

If, then, the kingdom of God was thus originally intended to be in the midst of men and for men at large (as represented by Adam), if its first preachers were, like Abraham, ex-heathens, who addressed themselves to heathens, if, again, the essence of their preaching was righteousness and justice, and if, lastly, the kingdom does not mean a hierarchy, but any form of government conducted on the principles of righteousness, holiness, justice, and charitableness, then we may safely maintain that the kingdom of God, as taught by Judaism in one of its aspects, is universal in its aims.

Hence the universal tone generally prevalent in all the kingship prayers (מלכיות). The foremost among these are the concluding lines of the kingship benediction recited on the New Year, running thus: "Our God and God of our fathers, reign thou in thy glory over the whole universe, and be exalted above all the earth in thine honour, and shine forth in the splendour and excellence of thy might, upon all the inhabitants of thy world, that whatsoever hath been made may know that thou hast made it, and whatsoever hath been created may understand that thou hast created it, and whatsoever hath breath in its nostrils, may say, the Lord God of Israel is King, and his dominion ruleth over all. . . . O purify our hearts to serve thee in truth, for thou art God in truth, and thy word is truth, and endureth forever. Blessed art thou, O Lord,

King over all the earth, who sanctifiest Israel and the Day of Memorial."[1] A later variation of this benediction, forming now a part both of the kingship prayers and of the daily prayer, is the passage referred to above, expressing the hope of Israel for the future, in the following exalted language: "We therefore hope in thee, O Lord our God, that we may speedily behold the glory of thy might, when thou wilt remove the abominations from the earth, and the idols will be utterly cut off, when the world will be perfected under the kingdom of the Almighty, and all the children of flesh will call upon thy name, when thou wilt turn unto thyself all the wicked of the earth. Let all the inhabitants of the world perceive and know that unto thee every knee must bow, every tongue must swear. Before thee, O Lord our God, let them bow and fall; and unto thy glorious name let them give honour; let them all accept the yoke of thy kingdom, and do thou reign over them speedily, and for ever and ever. For the kingdom is thine, and to all eternity thou wilt reign in glory; as it is written in thy Torah, the Lord shall reign for ever and ever."[2] One of the evening benedictions in the German ritual, which probably formed once the whole of the evening prayer, concludes with the following passages: "Our God who art in heaven, assert the unity of thy name, and

[1] See Singer, p. 249, and Baer, p. 399.

[2] Singer, pp. 76 and 247, and Baer, *ibid.*, pp. 132 and 398. See above, p. 89.

establish thy kingdom continually, and reign over us for ever and ever. May our eyes behold, our hearts rejoice, and our souls be glad in thy true salvation, when it shall be said unto Zion, Thy God reigneth. The Lord reigneth: the Lord hath reigned; the Lord shall reign for ever and ever: for the kingdom is thine, and to everlasting thou wilt reign in glory; for we have no king but thee. Blessed art thou, O Lord, the King, who constantly in his glory will reign over us and over all his works for ever and ever."[1] The Kaddish (the "Sanctification"), again, which is recited several times a day, in every synagogue, commences with the words: "Magnified and sanctified be his great Name in the world which he hath created according to his will. And may he establish his kingdom during your life and during your days,"[2] etc. A variation of it is the prayer sung before the reading of the law on the Sabbath, after the declaration of the unity by the *Shema* and other verses, "Magnified and hallowed . . . be the name of the King of Kings of Kings, the Holy One, blessed be he, in the worlds which he hath created, — this world and the world to come."[3] The magnifying of God's name, as a consequence, both of his Unity and of his Kingship, finds also expression in the first line of an ancient prayer

[1] Cf. Singer, p. 101; Baer, p. 169.

[2] Baer, *ibid.*, p. 129. See Singer, p. 75.

[3] See Baer, p. 224. Cf. Mueller, *Masechet Soferim*, ch. 25, and p. 196. See also Singer, p. 146.

known to the Geonim: "Our King, our God, assert the unity of thy name in thy world, assert the unity of thy kingdom in thy world."[1] In this connection it is worth noting that citations from the Scriptures embodied in the Kingship Benediction conclude with the verse from Deut. 6 4, "Hear, O Israel," etc., which proves again the close relation between the doctrine of the Unity and that of God's universal Kingdom,[2] which belief is among others well illustrated by the words of R. Bachye Ibn Chalwah, who says: "And it is well known that the real Unity (will only be realised in the days of the Messiah, for in the times of subjection of Israel) the signs of the Unity are not discernible (the worship of mankind being distributed among many unworthy objects), so that the denying of the truth is constantly in the increase. But with the advent of the Messiah all the nations will turn to one creed, and the world will be perfected under the Kingdom of the Almighty, all of them agreeing to worship the name and to call upon the name of God. Then only will the unity of God become common in the mouth of all the nations. This is the promise the prophet made for the future: "And the Lord shall be King over all the earth: in that day shall the Lord be One and his name One."[3]

[1] See *Seder Rab Amram*, p. 9 *a*.

[2] Baer, *ibid.*, p. 399, and cf. above, p. 64, note 3.

[3] כד הקמח, end of the chapter יחוד.

## VII

## THE KINGDOM OF GOD (NATIONAL)

THE Kingship Prayer, just cited, is introduced by another group of prayers relating also to the kingdom of heaven, but containing at the same time emphatic references to Israel's connection with it. These prayers have for their burden the speedy advent of the day in which all creatures will form one single band to do God's will with a perfect heart, when righteousness will triumph, and the pious and the saints will rejoice; but also when God will give glory to his people, joys to his land, gladness to his city, and a clear shining light unto his Messiah, the son of Jesse. They conclude with the words, "And thou, O Lord, shalt reign, thou alone over all thy works on Mount Zion, the dwelling place of thy glory, and in Jerusalem, thy holy city, as it is written in thy Holy words, 'The Lord shall reign for ever, thy God of Zion, unto all generations. Praise ye the Lord'" (Ps. 146 10). The prayer of the Geonim also continues with the words, "Build thy house, establish thy Temple, bring near thy Messiah, and rejoice thy congregation." Indeed, the credit is given to Israel that they suppress the *Evil Yezer*, declare his (God's) unity, and proclaim him as king every day, and wait for his kingdom, and hope to see the building of his Temple, and say every day, "The Lord doth build up Jerusalem: he gathereth together the outcasts of Israel" (Ps. 147 2).[1] The idea of the kingdom is accordingly often so closely connected with the redemption of Israel from the exile, the advent of the Messiah, and the restoration of the Temple, as to be inseparable from it. This is its national aspect. "Israel are the people for whose sake (or *Zachuth*) the world was created; and it is on them that the world was based." Israel, again, as we have seen, are the people, who, by their glorious acts at the Red Sea, and especially by their readiness at Mount Sinai to receive the yoke of the kingdom, became the very pillars of the throne. To add here another passage of the same nature, the saying of R. Simon may be given, who expresses the idea in very bold language. Speaking of the supports of the world, and Israel's part in them, he says: "As long as Israel is united into one league (that is, making bold front against any heresy denying the unity or the supremacy of God), the kingdom in heaven is maintained by them; whilst Israel's falling off from God shakes the throne to its very foundation in heaven."[2] The banishment of Israel from the holy land has the same consequence.

[1] See Singer, p. 239 *seq.*; Baer, p. 395 *seq.*; *Seder R. Amram*, 9 *a*; Friedmann, נספחים, p. 56.

[2] See Exod. R. 38 4. See also *Midrash Shemuel*, B. 5, 11 and references. Cf. Bacher, *Ag. Tan.* 2 140, note 1. See also above, p. 85.

Thus said the congregation of Israel before the Holy One, blessed be he, "Is there a king without a throne; is there a king without a crown; is there a king without a palace? 'How long wilt thou forget me, O Lord?'" (Ps. 13 2).[1] Jerusalem, which the Prophet (Jer. 3 17) called the throne of the Lord, becomes identified with it; and Amalek, who destroyed the holy city, is guilty of rebellion against God and his kingdom.[2] Therefore neither the throne of God nor his holy name is perfect (that is to say, fully revealed) as long as the children of the Amalekites exist in the world.[3] And just as Israel are the bearers of the name of God, so the Amalekites are the representatives of idolatry and every base thing antagonistic to God, so that R. Eleazar of Modyim thinks that the existence of the one necessarily involves the destruction of the other. "When will the name of the Amalekites be wiped out?" he exclaims. "Not before both the idols and their worshippers cease to exist, when God will be alone in the world and his kingdom established for ever and ever."[4] These passages, to which many more of a similar nature might be added, are the more calculated to give to the kingdom of heaven a national aspect, when we remember that Amalek is only another name for his ancestor Esau, who is the father of Edom, who is but a prototype for Rome. With this kingdom, represented in Jewish

[1] *M T.*, 13 1. [2] *P. K.*, 28 *a*.

[3] *P. K.*, 29 *a*, *P. R.*, 51 *a* and parallels.

[4] *Mechilta*, 56 *a*, 56 *b*. Cf. M. T. 97: 1 and 99: 1.

literature by the fourth beast of the vision of Daniel,[1] Israel according to the Rabbis is at deadly feud, a feud which began before its ancestors even perceived that the light of the world is perpetually carried on by their descendants, and will only be brought to an end with history itself.[2] The contest over the birthright is indicative of the struggle for supremacy between Israel and Rome. It would seem even as if Israel despairs of asserting the claims of his acquired birthright, and concedes this world to Esau. "Two worlds there are," Jacob says unto Esau, "this world and the world to come. In this world there is eating and drinking, but in the next world there are the righteous, who with crowns on their heads revel in the glory of the divine presence. Choose as first-born the world which pleases thee. Esau chose this world."[3] Jacob's promise to join his brother at Seir meant that meeting in the distant future, when the Messiah of Israel will appear and the Holy One will make his kingdom shine forth over Israel, as it is said (Obadiah 21): "And saviours shall come up on Mount Zion to judge the mount of Esau; and the kingdom shall be the Lord's."[4]

[1] See *Lev. R.*, 13 5 and parallels. Valuable information on this point is to be found in Senior Sachs's edition of the *Carmina Sancta Solomonis Ibn Gabirol*, pp. 70–100. Cf. also Zunz, *Synagogale Poesie*, p. 437 *seq.* See also A. Epstein, *Beiträge zur jüdischen Alterthumskunde*, p. 35.

[2] *Gen. R.*, 61, §§ 6, 7, 9.

[3] See Friedmann, נספחים, 26 *b* and *P. K.*, 59 *b*.

[4] *Gen. R.*, 78 and parallels.

Thus the kingdom of heaven stands in opposition to the kingdom of Rome, and becomes connected with the kingdom of Israel, and it is in conformity with this sentiment that a Rabbi, picturing the glorious spring, in which the budding of Israel's redemption will first be perceived, exclaims: "The time has arrived when the reign of the wicked will break down and Israel will be redeemed; the time has come for the extermination of the kingdom of wickedness; the time has come for the revelation of the kingdom of heaven, and the voice of the Messiah is heard in our land." [1]

This is only a specimen of dozens of interpretations of the same nature, round which a whole world of myths and legend grew up, in which the chiliastic element, with all its excesses, was strongly emphasised. They fluctuate and change with the great historical events and the varying influences by which they were suggested.[2] But there are also fixed elements in them

[1] See *P. K.*, 50 *a*, and *P. R.*, 75 *a*, text and notes.

[2] Dr. Joseph Klausner's *Die messianischen Vorstellungen im Zeitalter der Tannaiten* is very instructive, though not all his results seem to me acceptable. See also Dr. Julius H. Greenstone's *The Messiah Idea in Jewish History*, which gives also references to the latest literature on the subject, including the Rev. Dr. R. H. Charles' *Eschatology*. On the whole I think that R. Isaac Abarbanel's noble משמיע ישועה contains still the best presentation of the Rabbinic belief in the Messiah, as entertained by the great majority of Rabbinic Jews. (See especially in his fourteen articles, עיקרים.) The statement by some moderns, to the effect that Rabbinism did not hold the belief in a personal Messiah essential, is unscientific and needs no refutation for those who are acquainted with the literature.

which are to be found in the Rabbinic literature of almost every age and date. These are: —

1. The faith that the Messiah, a descendant of the house of David, will restore the kingdom of Israel, which under his sceptre will extend over the whole world. 2. The notion that a last terrible battle will take place with the enemies of God (or of Israel), who will strive against the establishment of the kingdom, and who will finally be destroyed. "When will the Lord be King for ever and ever? When the heathen — that is, the Romans — will have perished out of the land."[1] 3. The belief that the establishment of this new kingdom will be followed by the spiritual hegemony of Israel, when all the nations will accept the belief in the unity of God, acknowledge his kingdom, and seek instruction from his law. 4. The conviction that it will be an age of material happiness as well as spiritual bliss for all those who are included in the kingdom,[2] when further death will disappear and the dead will revive.

[1] See *M. T.*, 10 7.

[2] It should however be noticed that the authorities are not quite in agreement as to the date of resurrection, not all of them making it a condition of the Messianic times. Rabbi Hillel's (fl. 3^d century) statement, "Israel has no hope for a Messiah" (*Sanhedrin* 99^a), is entirely isolated. It should further be noticed that in some sources the kingdom of the Messiah is to a certain extent a preparation for the time when God himself will reign. Indeed, all the versions of the well-known Midrash of the Ten Kings after the Messiah, the kingdom comes back to his first master, that is God, who was the first King after the creation of the world. The only place where the kingdom of Mes-

The two ideas of the kingdom of heaven, over which God reigns, and the kingdom of Israel, in which the Messiah holds the sceptre, became thus almost identical.

This identification has both narrowed, and to some extent even materialised, the notion of the kingdom. On the other hand, it also enriched it with certain features investing it with that amount of substance and reality which are most necessary, if an idea is not to become meaningless and lifeless. It is just this danger to which ideas are exposed in the process of their spiritualisation. That "the letter killeth, but the spirit giveth life," is a truth of which Judaism, which did depart very often from the letter, was as conscious as any other religion. Zerachya ben Shealtiel, in his Commentary to Job[1] 2 14, goes even so far as to say: "Should I explain this chapter according to its letter, I should be a heretic, because I would have to make such concessions to Satan's powers as are inconsistent with the belief in the Unity. I shall therefore interpret it according to the spirit of philosophy." But, unfortunately, there is also an evil spirit which sometimes possesses itself of an idea and reduces it to a mere

siah is identified with that of God is Pugio Fidei, by Raymundus, p. 397; but there is good reason to suppose that the text of Raymundus was tampered with for controversial purposes. See the literature on this point in the *Expositor*, vol. 7, 3d series, p. 108. Neubauer's remarks there are far from convincing. See also Cassel in his Commentary to Esther, p. 263, where he gives a reference to the New Testament, 1 Corinthians 15 23–28.

[1] Published in the תקות אנוש, a collection of commentaries to Job, by Schwartz.

phantasm. The history of theology is greatly haunted by these unclean spirits. The best guard against them is to provide the idea with some definiteness and reality in which we can perceive the evidence of the spirit.

This was the service rendered by the connection of the kingdom of Israel with the kingdom of God. It fixed the kingdom *in this world.* It had, of course, to be deferred to some indefinite period, but still its *locale* remained in our globe, not unknown regions in another world. It was extended from the individual to a whole nation, placing a whole people into its service and training it for this end, thus making the idea of the kingdom visible and tangible. A whole commonwealth, with all its institutions, civil and ecclesiastical, becomes part and parcel of the kingdom of God. The Lord has made all things for himself, for the glory of his kingdom, which includes all creation. But Israel understood their duty to the extent of giving in time of persecution their very lives rather than transgress the slightest law, as such a transgression at such a time involved the sin of profaning the Holy Name, and may be taken as a sign of apostasy or betrayal of the kingdom. For they are indeed the very legions of the kingdom.[1]

By this fact, it is true, the kingdom of God becomes greatly nationalised. But even in this case it loses nothing of its spiritual features. For even in its

[1] See *Tosephta Shabbath*, p. 134; *Agadath Shir Hashirim*, p. 34. See also above, p. 81, note 1.

identification with the nation, Israel is only the depository of the kingdom, not the exclusive possessor of it. The idea of the kingdom is the palladium of the nation. According to some, it is the secret which has come down to them from the patriarchs;[1] according to others, the holy mystery of the angels overheard by Moses, which Israel continually proclaims.[2] It has to be emphasised in every prayer and benediction,[3] whilst the main distinction of the most solemn prayers of the year on the New Year's Day consists, as we have seen, in a detailed proclamation of the kingdom of God in all stages of history, past, present, and future. "Before we appeal to his mercy," teach the Rabbis, "and before we pray for redemption, we must first make him King over us."[4] We must also remember that Israel is not a nation in the common sense of the word. To the Rabbis, at least, it is not a nation by virtue of race or of certain peculiar political combinations. As R. Saadya expressed it, כי אומתינו איננה אומה אם כי בתורותיה ("Because our nation is only a nation by reason of its Torah").[5] The brutal Torah-less nationalism promulgated in certain quarters, would have been to the Rabbis just as hateful as the suicidal Torah-less universalism preached in other quarters. And if we could imagine for a moment Israel giving up its allegiance

[1] See *Sifre*, 72 *b*, and the very instructive notes by the editor.

[2] *Deut. R.*, 2.

[3] See *Berachoth*, 12 *a*.

[4] See *Sifre*, 19 *b*, and *Rosh Hashanah*, 16 *a*. See also whole extract from the liturgy at the end of ch. 5.

[5] אמונות ודעות, 3 : 7.

to God, its Torah and its divine institutions, the Rabbis would be the first to sign its death-warrant as a nation. The prophecy (Isa. 44 5), "Another shall subscribe with his hands unto the Lord," means, according to the Rabbis, the sinners who return unto him from their evil ways, whilst the words, "And surname himself by the name of Israel," are explained to be proselytes who leave the heathen world to join Israel.[1] It is then by these means of repentance and proselytism that the kingdom of heaven, even in its connection with Israel, expands into the universal kingdom to which sinners and Gentiles are invited. It becomes a sort of spiritual imperialism with the necessary accompaniment of the doctrine of the "Open Door" through which the whole of humanity might pass into the kingdom. "Open ye gates that the righteous people (*Goi*) which keepeth the truth may enter in" (Isa. 26 2). It is not said that the Priests or the Levites or the Israelites may enter, but *Goi* (Gentile). "Behold even one of other nations who fulfils (the laws of) the Torah is (as good) as the very high priest."[2]

The antagonism between the kingdom of God and the kingdom of Rome, which is brought about by the connection of the former with that of Israel, suggests also a most important truth: *Bad government is incompatible with the kingdom of God.* As already pointed

[1] *Mechilta*, 95 *b* and parallels.

[2] *T. K.*, 86 *b*, taking the word גוי in the sense of heathen, non-Jew, and stranger. See also below, p. 133.

out above, it is not the *form* of the Roman Government to which objection is taken, but its methods of administration and its oppressive rule. It is true that they tried "to render unto Cæsar the things that were Cæsar's, and unto God the things that were God's." Thus they interpreted the words in Ecclesiastes 8 2: "I counsel thee, keep the king's commandments and *that* in regard of the oath of God," in the following way: "I take an oath from you, not to rebel against the (Roman) Government, even if its decrees against you should be most oppressive; for you have to keep the king's commands. But if you are bidden to deny God and give up the Torah, then obey no more." And they proceed to illustrate it by the example of Hananiah, Mishael, and Azariah, who are made to say to Nebuchadnezzar, "Thou art our king in matters concerning duties and taxes, but in things divine thy authority ceases, and therefore 'we will not serve thy gods, nor worship the golden image which thou hast put up.'"[1] But compromises forced upon them by the political circumstances of the time must not be regarded as desirable ideals or real doctrine. Apart from the question as to the exact definition of things falling within the respective provinces of Cæsar and of God — a question which, after eighteen hundred years' discussion, is still unsettled — there can be little doubt that the Rabbis looked with dismay upon a government which derived its authority from the deification of

[1] See *Tan.*, נח, 10, and *Lev. R.*, 33 6. Cf. *Num. R.*, 14 6.

might, whereof the emperor was the incarnate principle. Edom recognises no superior authority, saying, "Whom have I in heaven?"[1] It represents iron (we would say blood and iron), a metal which was excluded from the tabernacle, the abode of the divine peace,[2] whilst its king of flesh and blood, whom Edom flatters in its ovations as being mighty, wise, powerful, merciful, just, and faithful, has not a single one of all these virtues, and is even the very reverse of what they express.[3]

But besides these differences the Rabbis held the Roman Government to be thoroughly corrupt in its administration; Esau preaches justice and practises violence. Their judges commit the very crimes for which they condemn others. They pretend to punish crime, but are reconciled to it by bribery. Their motives are selfish, never drawing men near to them, except in their own interest and for their own advantage. As soon as they see a man in a state of prosperity, they devise means how to possess themselves of his goods. In a word, Esau is rapacious and violent, especially the procurators sent out to the provinces, where they rob and murder, and when they return to Rome pretend to feed the poor with the money they have collected.[4] Such a government was, according

[1] Lev. *R.*, 13 5. [2] See *Exod. R.*, 35 7. [3] *Mechilta*, 35 *a.*

[4] See *Lev. R.*, *ibid.*; *Aboth*, 2 8; *Exod. R.*, 31 11; *P. K.* 95 *b.* Interesting is a passage in Mommsen's *History of Rome*, 4, which shows that the Rabbis did not greatly exaggerate the cruelty of the Roman

to the Rabbis, incompatible with the kingdom of heaven, and therefore the mission of Israel was to destroy it.[1]

Another essential addition made to the kingdom of God by its connection with the kingdom of Israel is, as already indicated, the feature of material happiness. Popular fancy pictured it in gorgeous colours: The rivers will flow with wine and honey, the trees will grow bread and delicacies, whilst in certain districts springs will break forth which will prove cures for all sorts of diseases. Altogether, disease and suffering will cease, and those who come into the kingdom with bodily defects, such as blindness, deafness, and other blemishes, will be healed. Men will multiply in a way not at all agreeable to the laws of political economy, and will enjoy a very long life, if they will die at all. War will, of course, disappear, and warriors will look upon their weapons as a reproach and an offence. Even the rapacious beasts will lose their powers of doing injury, and will become peaceful and harmless.[2] Such are the details in which the Rabbis indulge in their descriptions

Government. "Any one who desires," says our greatest historian of Rome, "to fathom the depths to which men can sink in the criminal infliction, and in the no less criminal endurance of an inconceivable injustice, may gather together from the criminal records of this period the wrongs which Roman grandees could perpetuate, and Greeks, Syrians, and Phœnicians could suffer." Cf. Joel's *Blicke*, I. 109. How far matters improved under the emperors, at least with regard to the Jews, is still a question.

[1] *Berachoth*, 17 *a*. See Rabbinowicz, *Variae Lectiones*, *a.l.*

[2] See, for instance, *Kethuboth*, 111 *a*; *Shabbath*, 63 *a*; *Gen. R.*, 12 6; *M.H.G.*, 126 *seq.*; see also Klausner (as above, p. 101), p. 108 *seq.*

of the blissful times to come. We need not dwell upon them. There is much in them which is distasteful and childish. Still, when we look at the underlying idea, we shall find that it is not without its spiritual truth. The kingdom of God *is* inconsistent with a state of social misery, engendered through poverty and want. Not that Judaism looked upon poverty, as some author has suggested, as a moral vice. Nothing can be a greater mistake. The Rabbis were themselves mostly recruited from the artisan and labouring classes, and of some we know that they lived in the greatest want. Certain Rabbis have even maintained that there is no quality becoming Israel more than poverty, for it is a means of spiritual purification.[1] Still, they did not hide from themselves the terrible fact that abject poverty has its great demoralising dangers. It is one of the three things which make man transgress the law of his Maker.[2]

But even if poverty would not have this effect, it would be excluded from the kingdom of heaven, as involving pain and suffering. The poor man, they hold, is dead as an influence, and his whole life, depending upon his fellows, is a perpetual passing through the tortures of hell.[3] But it is a graceful world which God has created, and it must not be disfigured by misery and suffering. It must return to its perfect state when the visible kingdom is established. As we shall

[1] *Chagigah*, 9 *b*. [2] *Erubin*, 41 *b*.
[3] *Nedarim*, 7 *b*, and *Berachoth*, 6 *b*.

see in the sequence,[1] Judaism was certainly not wanting in theories, idealising suffering and trying to reconcile man with its existence. But, on the other hand, it did not recognise a chasm between flesh and spirit, the material and the spiritual world, so as to abandon entirely the one for the sake of the other. They are both the creatures of God, the body as well as the soul, and hence both the objects of his salvation.

To a certain Jewish mystic of the last century, R. Moses Loeb, of Sasow, the question was put by one of his disciples to the effect, "Why did God, in whom everything originates, create the quality of scepticism?" The master's answer was, "That thou mayest not let the poor starve, putting them off with the joys of the next world, or simply telling them to trust in God, who will help them, instead of supplying them with food."[2]

We venture to maintain with the mystic that a good dose of materialism is necessary for religion that we may not starve the world. It was by this that Judaism was preserved from the mistake of crying inward peace, when actually there was no peace; of speaking of inward liberty, when in truth this spiritual but spurious liberty only served as a means for persuading man to renounce his liberty altogether, confining the kingdom of God to a particular institution and handing over the world to the devil.

[1] See below, p. 309.

[2] See מעשה צדיקים, Lemberg, 1897, p. 39, which differs somewhat from the version I have heard often told, and which is given in the text.

This is not the place to enter into the charity system of the Rabbis, nor to enlarge upon the measures taken by them so as to make charity superfluous. But having touched upon the subject of poverty, a few general remarks will not be out of place. In that brilliant essay known under the title of *Ecce Homo*, we meet the following statement: "The ideal of the economist, the ideal of the Old Testament writers, does not appear to be Christ's. He feeds the poor, but it is not his great object to bring about a state of things in which the poorest shall be sure of a meal." But it was just this which was included in the ideal of the Rabbis. They were not satisfied with feeding the poor. Not only did they make the authorities of every community responsible for the poor, and would even stigmatise them as murderers if their negligence should lead to starvation and death;[1] but their great ideal was not to allow man to be poor, not to allow him to come down into the depths of poverty. They say, "Try to prevent it by teaching him a trade, or by occupying him in your house as a servant, or make him work with you as your partner."[2] Try all methods before you permit him to become an object of charity, which must degrade him, tender as our dealings with him may be.

Hence their violent protests against any sort of money speculation which must result in increasing

[1] See *B. T. Sotah*, 38 *b*, and *Jer. Sotah*, 23 *d*.

[2] See *T. K.*, 109 *b*, and Maimonides' *Mishneh Torah*, הלכות מתנות עניים פ״י ה״ז וה׳ י״ז. See also the older commentaries on *Aboth*, I 5.

poverty: Thou lendest him money on the security of his estate with the object of joining his field to thine, his house to thine, and thou flatterest thyself to become the heir of the land; be sure of a truth that many houses will be desolate.[1] Those again who increase the price of food by artificial means, who give false measure, who lend on usury, and keep back the corn from the market, are classed by the Rabbis with the blasphemers and hypocrites, and God will never forget their works.[2]

To the employers of workmen again they say: "This poor man ascends the highest scaffoldings, climbs the highest trees. For what does he expose himself to such dangers, if not for the purpose of earning his living? Be careful, therefore, not to oppress him in his wages, for it means his very life."[3] On the other hand, they relieved the workman from reciting certain prayers when they interfered with his duty to his master.[4]

From this consideration for the employer and the employed a whole set of laws emanate which try to regulate their mutual relations and duties. How far they would satisfy the modern economist I am unable to say. In general I should think that, excellent as they may have been for their own times, they would not

[1] See Introduction to Midrash to *Lament. R.*, 22, on Isa. 5 8.

[2] See *A. R. N.*, 43 *b*; *Baba Bathra*, 90 *a*.

[3] See *Sifre*, 123 *b*, and *B. Mezia*, and *Berachoth*, 16 *a*.

[4] *Berachoth*, 17 *a*.

quite answer to our altered conditions and ever varying problems. But this need not prevent us from perceiving, in any efforts to diminish poverty, a divine work to which they also contributed their share. For if the disappearance of poverty and suffering is a condition of the kingdom of the Messiah, or, in other words, of the kingdom of God, all wise social legislation in this respect must help towards its speedy advent.

It is this kingdom, as depicted in the preceding remarks in its larger features, with both its material and spiritual manifestations, that Israel is to express and establish. With this, it enters upon the stage of history. With its varying fortunes its own destiny is inseparably connected; and with Israel's final triumph, the kingdom will become fully effective. Or, as the Rabbis expressed it, it is only "with the redemption of Israel that the kingdom of heaven will be complete." Israel is the microcosm in which all the conditions of the kingdom are to find concrete expression. In the establishment of its institutions, in the reign of its law, in the peace and happiness of its people, the world would find the prototype and manifestation of these ideals in which universal holiness would be expressed. Not until these conditions were realised in Israel could like conditions obtain universally. The Rabbis have given expression to this correspondence of universalistic and national elements in the following statement: A solemn declaration has the Holy One, blessed be he, registered: I will not enter the heavenly Jerusalem until Israel shall come to the earthly Jerusalem. Thus Rabbinic Judaism does find a perfect consonance between Israel's establishment of the divine institutions in their full integrity in God's own land, and the triumph in all its glory of the kingdom of Heaven.[1]

[1] See *M. T.*, 99 1. See also *Taanith*, 5 *b*. The references speak of the oath.

## VIII

# THE "LAW"

THE Law derives its authority from the kingdom. For this, according to the Rabbis, is the meaning of the scriptural words, "I am the Lord thy God," or "The Lord your God," with which certain groups of laws are introduced (*e.g.* Exod. 22 2 and Lev. 18 2); that is, God makes his people conscious of the fact of his claims on them because of their having received his kingdom, saying unto them, "You have received my kingdom in love." "Aye" and "Aye" answers Israel, wherefore God says, "If you have received my kingdom, you receive now my decrees." [1]

Now the current notions about the Law or Torah are still so misleading that before entering upon the meaning and theological significance of the "decrees," a brief analysis of the term *Torah* seems most advisable. Even the hypothesis advanced by higher criticism, according to which it was just under the predominance of the Law that the Wisdom Literature was composed and most of the Psalms were written, had no effect on the general prejudice of theologians against the Torah. With a few exceptions our theo-

[1] *T. K.*, 85 *d*; *Mechilta*, 67 *a*, 67 *b*.

logians still enlarge upon the "Night of Legalism," from the darkness of which religion only emerges by a miracle supposed to have taken place about the year 30 of our era.[1]

An examination of the meaning of *Torah* and *Mizvoth* to the Jew will show that Legalism was neither the evil thing commonly imagined nor did it lead to the evil consequences assumed by our theologians. Nor has it ever constituted the whole religion of the Jew, as declared by most modern critics.

It must first be stated that the term *Law* or *Nomos* is not a correct rendering of the Hebrew word *Torah*. The legalistic element, which might rightly be called the Law, represents only one side of the Torah. To the Jew the word *Torah* means a teaching or an instruction of any kind. It may be either a general principle or a specific injunction, whether it be found in the Pentateuch or in other parts of the Scriptures, or even outside of the canon. The juxtaposition in which *Torah* and *Mizwoth*, Teaching and Commandments, are to be found in the Rabbinic literature, implies already that the former means something more than merely the Law.[2] Torah and Mitzvoth are a complement to each other, or, as a Rabbi expressed it, "they borrow from each other, as wisdom and understanding — charity and loving-

[1] See Mr. Israel Abrahams, *Jewish Quarterly Review*, 11 : 626–642. See also Schechter, *Studies in Judaism*, p. 219 *seq*.

[2] See, for instance, *Berachoth*, 31 *a*; *Makkoth*, 23 *a*; *Aboth*, 3 11.

kindness — the moon and the stars," but they are not identical.[1] To use the modern phraseology, to the Rabbinic Jew, Torah was both an institution and a faith. We shall treat them separately: first Torah, and then the Mitzvoth.

It is true that in Rabbinic literature the term *Torah* is often applied to the Pentateuch to the exclusion of the Prophets and the Hagiographa.[2] But this is chiefly for the purpose of classification. It is also true that to a certain extent the Pentateuch is put on a higher level than the Prophets — the prophetic vision of Moses having been, as the Rabbis avow, much clearer than that of his successors.[3] But we must not forget that for the superiority of the Torah, they had the scriptural authority of the Torah itself (Num. 12 6-8, Deut. 34 10), whilst on the other hand *they* could not find in the Prophets anything deprecatory of Moses' superior authority. They may, occasionally, have felt some contradictions between the Prophets and the Torah, but only in matters of detail, not in matters of principle.[4]

[1] See *Exod. R.*, 31 15.

[2] See, for instance, *Megillah*, 31 *a*; *Baba Bathra*, 13 *b*, and elsewhere.

[3] See *Jebamoth*, 49 *b*; *Lev. R.*, 1.

[4] See the well-known passages about Ezekiel in *Shabbath*, 13 *b*, and *Menachoth*, 45 *a*. The contradictions are there reconciled to the satisfaction of the Rabbis at least. See also below, p. 187. A contradiction which they did not try to reconcile was that between Isa. 6 1, "I saw the Lord sitting upon a throne," and Moses in Exod. 33 20, "For there shall no man see me, and live" (*Jebamoth*, 49 *b*). See

Of any real antagonism between Mosaism and "Leviticalism" and Prophetism, which modern criticism asserts to have brought to light, the Rabbis were absolutely unconscious. With the Rabbis, the Prophets formed only a complement or even a commentary to the Torah (a species of Agadah), which, indeed, needed explanation, as we shall see. Hence the *naïveté*, as we may almost call it, with which the Rabbis chose, for reading on the Day of Atonement, the 58th chapter of Isaiah — one of the most prophetic pieces of prophetism — as the accompanying lesson for the portion from the Pentateuch, Leviticus 16 — the most Levitical piece in Leviticalism.

But even the Pentateuch is no mere legal code, without edifying elements in it. The Book of Genesis, the greater part of Exodus, and even a part of Numbers are simple history, recording the past of humanity on its way to the kingdom, culminating in Israel's entering it on Mount Sinai, and their subsequent relapses. The Book of Deuteronomy, as the "Book containing the words of exhortation" (Tochachoth),[1] forms Israel's *Imitatio Dei*, consisting chiefly in goodness,[2] and supplying to Israel its confession of faith (in the *Shema*); whilst the Book of Leviticus — marvel

Jolowicz's *Himmelfahrt, etc., des Propheten Jesaiah*, p. 7, Leipzig, 1854. But it is significant that it is the wicked Manasseh who saw this contradiction.

[1] *Sifre*, 64 *a*.

[2] See *Sifre*, 74 *a*, 85 *a*; *Mechilta*, 37 *a* and parallels. See also below, p. 200.

upon marvel — first proclaims that principle of loving one's neighbour as one's self (Lev. 19 18) which believers call Christianity, unbelievers, Humanity.

The language of the Midrash would seem to imply that at a certain period there were people who held the narratives of the Bible in slight estimation, looking upon them as fictions (Piyutim) and useless stories. The Rabbis, however, reject such a thought with indignation. To them the whole of the Torah represented the word of God, dictated by the Holy Spirit, suggesting edifying lessons everywhere, and embodying even while it speaks of the past, a history of humanity written in advance.[1] "The Book of Generations of Adam," that is, the history of the Genesis, in which the dignity of man is indicated by the fact of his having been created in the image of God, teaches, according to Ben Azai, even a greater principle than that of Lev. 19, in which the law of loving one's neighbour as oneself is contained.[2] Another Rabbi deduces from the repetitions in Gen. 24 the theory that the conversation of the servants of the patriarchs is more beautiful than the laws even of later generations.[3] Another Rabbi remarks that the Torah as a legal code would only have commenced with Exod. 12, where the first (larger) group of laws is set forth, but God's object was to show his people the power of his work,

[1] See *Gen. R.*, 85 2; *Sifre*, 33 *a*; *Sanhedrin*, 99 *b*; *M. T.*, 3 2.
[2] *T. K.*, 89 *b*, and parallels. Cf. Bacher, *Ag. Tan.*, I 720.
[3] *Gen. R.*, 60 8.

"that he may give them the inheritance of the heathen" (Ps. 111 6), and thus, in the end, justify the later history of their conquests.[1]

The Book of Genesis, which contains the history of this manifestation of God's powers, as revealed in the act of creation as well as in the history of the patriarchs, and leads up to the story of the Exodus from Egypt, is, according to some Rabbis, the book of the covenant which Moses read to the people (Exod. 24 7) even before the act of revelation. To come into the possession of this book (the Book of Genesis), which unlocked before them one of the inner chambers of the king (or revealed to them the holy mysteries of God's working in the world), was considered by the Rabbis one of the greatest privileges of Israel, given to them as a reward for their submission to God's will.[2]

Thus *Torah*, even as represented by the Pentateuch, is not mere Law, the Rabbis having discerned and appreciated in it other than merely legal elements. Moreover, the term *Torah* is not always confined to the Pentateuch. It also extends, as already indicated, to the whole of the Scriptures on which the Rabbis "laboured" with the same spirit and devotion as on the Pentateuch. For indeed "the Torah is a *triad*, composed of Pentateuch, Prophets, and Hagiographa." "Have I not written to thee the three things in counsels

[1] See *Tan. B.*, 1 4 *a*. Cf. Rashi to Gen. 1 1.
[2] See *Mechilta*, 63 *b*. Cf. *Cant. R.*, 1 4, on הביאני המלך חדריו.

and in knowledge?"[1] That lessons from the Prophets almost always accompanied those taken from the Pentateuch is a well-known fact,[2] as likewise that the Talmid Chacham, or the student, had to beautify himself with the knowledge of the twenty-four books of which the Bible consists, even as a bride adorns herself with twenty-four different kinds of ornaments.[3] That this injunction was strictly fulfilled by the student is clear from the facility and frequency with which the Rabbis quoted the Prophets and the Hagiographa. A striking instance may be seen in the *Mechilta*, a small work of not more than about seventy octavo pages when stripped from its commentaries; it has about one thousand citations from the Prophets and the Hagiographa.

"The sinners in Israel" (probably referring to the Samaritans), the Rabbis complain, "contend that the Prophets and the Hagiographa are not Torah, but are they not already refuted by Daniel (9 10), who said, 'Neither have we obeyed the voice of the Lord our God, to walk in his Toroth which he set before us by his servants the prophets.'" Hence, the Rabbis proceed to say, Asaph's exclamation in Ps. 78, "Give ear, O my people, to my Toroth."[4] Note, in

[1] See *Tan.*, B. 2 37 *a* (§ 8), and *Midrash Prov.*, 22 19, text and notes, urging the שלישים.

[2] See Zunz, *Gottesdienstliche Vorträge*, p. 3 (2d ed.), and Schürer's *Geschichte*, 2 380 f.

[3] See *Exod. R.*, 41 5.

[4] See *M. T.*, 78 1, and *Tan.*, ראה, 1. Cf. Bacher, *Terminologie*, 2 81.

passing, that this Psalm, which claims to be Torah, is nothing but a *résumé* of Israel's history. With the Rabbinic Jews, the Hagiographa formed an integral part of their holy Scriptures. "The prophets of truth and righteousness" were, as can be seen from the benediction preceding the weekly lesson from the Prophets, God's chosen ones, in the same way as the Torah, as his servant Moses, and his people Israel — the depository of revelation.[1] In olden times they had even a special benediction before they began to read either the Prophets or the Hagiographa, running thus, "Blessed art thou, O Lord our God, who hast commanded us to read the holy writings." [2] This was quite in accordance with their principle regarding prophecy as "the word of God," [3] and the continuation of his voice heard on Mount Sinai,[4] a voice which will cease only with the Messianic times, — perhaps for the reason that the earth will be full of the knowledge of God and all the people of the Lord will be prophets.[5]

[1] See Baer, p. 226. In *Masecheth Soferim*, ch. XIII, the words ובישראל עמו are omitted.

[2] See *Masecheth Soferim*, ch. XIV, and *Notes*,.p. 188.

[3] *Shabbath*, 138 *b*.

[4] See *Sifre*, 92 *a*, and parallels given in the Notes. MHG., ובקולו תשמעו בקול נביאיו. Cf. *ibid.* 114 *a*, סורר על דברי תורה ומורה על דברי הנביאים. See also *Sifre*, 135 *b*, רב״שע כבר כתבת הן ישלח אדם "Lord of the world, thou hast written, If a man put away his wife," etc., which is a verse in Jer. 3 1. Cf. Blau, *Zur Einleitung in die Heilige Schrift*, p. 14. See also Bacher, *Terminologie*, 1 197; 2 229.

[5] See *Jer. Megillah*, 70 *d*, and the commentaries. Cf. also Maimonides' *Mishneh Torah*, הלכות מגילה וחנוכה, 2 18, and the השגת הרא״בד.

Says R. Isaac, "All that the Prophets will reveal in (succeeding) generations had been received by them on Mount Sinai." "And so he says, 'The burden of the word of the Lord to Israel by *the hand* of Malachi.' It is not said '*In the days of Malachi*,' for the prophecy was already in his hands (since the revelation) on Mount Sinai." And so Isaiah, "From the time that it (the Torah) was (revealed) I was there," and received this prophecy, "but it is now that the Lord God and his spirit has sent me."[1]

It is in harmony with this spirit — the Prophets and the Hagiographa being a part of Israel's Torah — that the former are cited in Rabbinic literature with the terms "for it is said" or "it is written" in the same ways as the Pentateuch. Again, in the well-known controversy about the scriptural authority for the belief in resurrection, both the Prophets and the

The special emphasis of the Jerushalmi of the Pentateuch's retaining its importance even after the Messiah has come, is, as is well known, the result of the opposition to sectarian teaching, demanding the abolition of the Law. The answer of the Rabbis was therefore that even the authority of the Messiah himself will not prevail against that of Moses. In this sense also — as opposition to this teaching — must be understood the passage in *Jer. Berachoth*, 3 *b* and parallels, where the prophet, so to say, is required to bring his imprimatur from the Torah, שלי וסמנטרין שלי חותם, the prophet without such a legitimation being very probably an antinomianist. Hence also the effort made by the Rabbis to prove that the Pentateuch already indicated the teachings of the *Kethubim*. See *Taanith*, 9 *a*.

[1] See *Lev. R.*, 28 6 and commentaries. Cf. Oppenheim in Geiger's *Jüdische Zeitschrift*, 11, p. 82 *seq.* See also Frankl in *Ersch und Gruber*, 2 sec., Bd. 33, pp. 15–34.

Hagiographa are quoted under the name of Torah; and the evidence brought forward by them seems to be of as much weight as that derived from the Pentateuch.[1] In the New Testament they also occasionally appear under the title of Nomos or Law. To the Jew, as already pointed out, the term *Torah* implied a teaching or instruction, and was therefore wide enough to embrace the whole of the Scriptures.[2]

In a certain manner it is extended even beyond the limits of the Scriptures. When certain Jewish Bos-

[1] *Sanhedrin*, 91 *b*; see also *Mechilta*, 34 *b*, 40 *b*. Cf. Blau, as above, pp. 16, 17. For more instances, see תורת נביאים by R. Hirsch Chajas, pp. 2 *a* and *b*, 5 *a*, 9 *a*, 10 *b*. This book contains the best exposition of the Rabbinical conception of the importance of the Prophets both from a Halachic and Hagadic point of view, and their relation to the Pentateuch. The student will find that a good deal that was written on the subject by other writers is mere talk due to the ignorance of Rabbinic literature. NB

[2] See Schürer's *Geschichte*, 2 253, note 17, for the references from the New Testament. Following Weber (p. 79), Schürer seizes the opportunity of making the remark that there is perhaps nothing more characteristic of the full appreciation of their importance on the part of the Jews than that they too (the Prophets and the Hagiographa) were not first of all to the Jewish conviction didactic or consolatory works, not books of edification or history, but were considered chiefly as Law, the substance of God's claim upon his people. So far Schürer, which of course only proves again to what misconception the rendering of Torah by Law must lead. Besides, we find that the Rabbis had such specification for the various books in the Bible as ספר יציאת מצרים for the Exodus (see Blau, as above), תוכחות for Deuteronomy (see above). The Psalms again are called the Book of Praises or Hymn Book, whilst the whole of the *Kethubim* are the Books of Wisdom (*P. K.*, 158 *b*), and Isaiah was chiefly characterised as the "work of consolation" (*Baba Bathra*, 14 *a*).

wells apologised for observing the private life of their masters too closely, they said, "It is a Torah, which we are desirous of learning."[1] In this sense it is used by another Rabbi, who maintained that even the everyday talk of the people in the Holy Land is a Torah (that is, it conveys an object lesson). For the poor man in Palestine, when applying to his neighbour for relief, was wont to say, "Acquire for thyself merit, or strengthen and purify thyself" (by helping me);[2] thus implying the adage — that the man in want is just as much performing an act of charity in receiving as his benefactor in giving. In the east of Europe we can, even to-day, hear a member of the congregation addressing his minister, "Pray, tell me some Torah." The Rabbi would never answer him by reciting verses from the Bible, but would feel it incumbent on him to give him some spiritual or allegorical explanation of a verse from the Scriptures, or would treat him to some general remarks bearing upon morals and conduct.

[1] *Berachoth*, 62 *a*. See also Chajas, as above, 2 *b*.

[2] *Lev. R.*, 34 7.

## IX

# THE LAW AS PERSONIFIED IN THE LITERATURE

To return to Torah proper. It is the Torah as the sum total of the contents of revelation, without special regard to any particular element in it, the Torah as a faith, that is so dear to the Rabbi. It is the Torah in this abstract sense, as a revelation and a promise, the expression of the will of God, which is identified with the wisdom of Prov. 8, thus gaining, in the course of history, a pre-mundane existence, which, so to speak, formed the design according to which God mapped out the world. Said Rabbi Hoshayah, "It is written of Wisdom, 'Then (before the world was created) I was with him *amon*, and was daily his delight, rejoicing always before him.' The word *amon* is to be read *uman*, meaning architect. For as a king employs an architect when he proposes to build a palace, and looks into his plans and designs to know where the various recesses and chambers shall be placed, so did God look into the Torah when he was about to create the world." [1]

[1] See *Gen. R.*, 1 and parallels. Cf. Bacher, *Ag. Am.*, 1 107, and his references to Freudenthal and the *Jewish Quarterly Review*, 3 357-360. See also Professor Cheyne, *Job and Solomon*, pp. 160–162. See also above, p. 13, note 4.

How far the idea is originally Jewish is not here the place to discuss. Nor is its meaning quite clear when subject to an analysis. One of the later commentators of the Midrash tries to connect it with the צמצום theory, that is, the limitation-mystery of the later cabalists, according to which the act of creation was an effluence of God's ineffable goodness and mercy — when he withdrew himself into himself, and thus revealed from himself the universe. But it is not quite clear what part the Torah plays in this mystical system.[1] As far as any definite meaning may be attached to such hazy and nebulous ideas, it may perhaps be reduced to this: that the Torah having been long destined to become a main factor in God's government of the world, its creation must have been predesigned by God before he called the world into existence. In this sense the Torah is classed with other creations of God which are endowed with pre-mundane existence, as Israel, the throne of God (kingdom?), the name of the Messiah, hell and paradise (or reward and punishment), and repentance.[2] With regard to repentance, the Chapters of Rabbi Eliezer teach, When God designed the world he found no firm basis for it until he created the quality of repentance.[3] The same thought of the impossibility of a world without a revelation may perhaps also have been present

[1] See פירוש מהרז״ו to *Gen. R.*, I.

[2] See *Gen. R.*, I 4, and all the parallels given there, which are very varying.

[3] See *P. R. E.*, 3. See also below, p. 314.

to the mind of the Jew when he spoke of the premundane existence of the Torah.

Plausible, however, as this explanation may be, it is a little too rationalistic and would hardly account for that exaltation of the Torah which is such a prominent feature in Jewish literature. As soon as the Torah was identified with the Wisdom of Proverbs, the mind did not rest satisfied with looking upon it as a mere condition for the existence of the world. Every connotation of the term *Wisdom* in the famous eighth chapter of Proverbs was invested with life and individuality. The Torah, by this same process, was personified and endowed with a mystical life of its own, which emanates from God, yet is partly detached from him. Thus we find the Torah pleading for or against Israel, as on the occasion of the destruction of the Temple, when the Torah was called to give evidence against Israel, but desisted from it at the instance of Abraham, who said unto her, "My daughter, were not my children the only ones who received thee, when thou wast rejected by other nations?"[1] Nay, even single letters of the alphabet are endowed with a separate life, enabling them to act the same part almost as the Torah.[2] The whole later mystical theory which degenerates into the combinations of letters to which the most important meaning is attached, takes its origin from these personifications.

[1] See *Lament. R.*, Introduction, I. See also *Lev. R.*, 19 and parallels.
[2] See *Gen. R.*, 1. Cf. *P. R.*, 109 *a*.

This notion of the personification of the Torah never hardened into an article of faith. Its influence is less felt in dogma than in literature, particularly in the legends and scriptural interpretations bearing on the subject of the revelation on Mount Sinai. We must, at least, consider them in their main features.

First, the day of revelation is considered as the day on which earth was wedded to heaven. The barrier between them was removed by the fact that the Torah, the heavenly bride, the daughter of the Holy One, was wedded to Israel on that day.[1] The simile is carried further, and even the feature of the capture of the bride is not missing, — the verse in Ps. 68 19, "Thou hast ascended on high, thou hast led captivity captive," being interpreted as referring to Moses, who ascended to heaven and captured the Torah, in spite of the resistance of the angels, who were most reluctant to allow the Torah, the desirable treasure, to be taken away from among them.[2] Our planet is in constant fear lest Israel should imitate the example of their heathen neighbours, which would signify its doom to destruction. Hence the attention of the whole universe is directed to this glorious act. When God gave the Torah we read that the creatures of the firmament paused in their flight, those of the earth ventured not to lift up their voices, the waves of the boisterous

[1] See *P. K.*, 104 *b*, and *Exod. R.*, 30 5, 33 7.

[2] See *Shabbath*, 89 *b*; *P. R.*, 98 *a*, and *b*; and *Exod. R.*, 28 1 and parallels.

seas ceased to roll, and the angels interrupted their eternal song of "Holy, Holy, Holy,"[1] — heaven and earth listening to the good message.

This listening of the universe suggests the universalistic feature of the Sinaitic revelation. Though magnifying Israel for their readiness to receive the Torah, and strongly blaming the gentiles who refused to subject themselves to the word of God, so that a certain animosity comes down from Mount Sinai against the worshipper of idols,[2] these legends still betray a universalistic tendency as to the real and original purpose of the revelation. Thus with reference to Isa. 45 19, God is supposed to have said: "I have not spoken (the word of the revelation) in secret. I did not reveal it in hidden places and in dark corners of the earth." Nor did God postpone the giving of the Torah till Israel should enter into the Holy Land, lest Israel might claim it for themselves and say that the nations of the world have no share in it (in other words, it was not God's intention to make it a national religion). He gave it in open places, in the free desert, so that every man feeling the desire might receive it. Nor did he say *first* to the children of Jacob, "Seek ye me."[3] For, as we read in other places, the Holy

[1] *Exod. R.*, 29 9. [2] *Shabbath*, 89 *a*.

[3] See *Mechilta*, 62 *a*, 66 *b*, the whole passage beginning ויחנו במדבר. The text is not quite correct, but the drift of the thought is as we have it here. See Notes to the passage, and cf. Bacher, *Ag. Tan.*, 2 164, note 1; and *Aruch*, ed. Kohut, s.v. פנגם. See also *Yalkut Machiri on Isa.*, p. 156, read פוגום instead of פנגם. The *MHG.* reads תהו בקשוני לא עשיתיה הפותיקי אלא נתתי מתן שכרה בצדה.

one, blessed be he, came first to the sons of Esau and offered to them the Torah. These asked, "What is written in it?" God answered, "Thou shalt not kill." "We cannot accept it," they rejoined, "killing being our profession." Other nations objected to it on account of the seventh and eighth commandments, immorality and the appropriation of other men's possessions being the purposes of their lives, and the motive-springs of their actions, and so they said, "For the knowledge of thy ways, we have no desire — give thy Torah to thy people." [1]

It is rather characteristic of these legends, which probably reflect the attitude of the Rabbis towards the missionary enterprises of their time, that it is chiefly the moral part of the decalogue to which the nations objected. Esau is broad enough for general principles and will admit the Jewish God into his pantheon, if he submit to the process of accommodation and evolution so that he can share his honours with other gods. Esau objected to the "Do nots." These were too definite to allow of a wide interpretation in which the wisdom of Edom excelled, and might thus interfere with Esau's calling, his gladiators, his legions, and the policy of his procurators.

Thus Mount Sinai becomes the place in which God reveals himself to the world, and Israel undertakes the terrible responsibility of bearing witness to this fact.

[1] See *Mechilta, ibid.; Sifre*, 142 *b*; *Lament R.*, 31; *P. R. E.*, ch. 41; *P. R.*, 99 *b* and parallels.

"If you will not make known my divinity (divine nature) to the nations of the world, even at the cost of your lives, you shall suffer for this iniquity," said God.[1] Though, indeed, the whole of creation has the duty to join in his praise and to bear witness to his divinity (divine power), Israel is especially commanded to invite all mankind to serve God and to believe in him, even as Abraham did, who made God beloved by all the creatures. And so intensely should we love him that we should also make others love him. For those who make God beloved by mankind are much greater than the mere lovers.[2] By this acceptance of the Torah, Israel made peace between God and his world,[3] the ultimate end being that its influence will reach the heathen too, and all the gentiles will one day be converted to the worship of God;[4] for the Torah "is not the Torah of the Priests, nor the Torah of the Levites, nor the Torah of the Israelites, but the Torah of Man (Torath ha-Adam), whose gates are open to receive the righteous nation which keepeth the truth and those who are good and upright in their hearts."[5]

Another important feature in these legends and interpretations is the fact that the revelation was an act of grace and the effluence of God's goodness. When the princes of the world heard the thunders

[1] See *Lev. R.*, 6 5, and commentaries. Cf. also *M. T.*, 19 1.

[2] See Maimonides, ס׳ה׳מ, מ׳ע, א, ב. Cf. *M. T.*, 19 1, and *Midrash Tannaim*, ed. Hoffmann, p. 40. See also *M. T.*, 18 7.

[3] *Gen. R.*, 66 2. [4] See *Berachoth*, 54 *b*. [5] *T. K.*, 86 *b*.

and lightnings which accompanied the revelation, they were frightened, thinking the world was to pass through another judgement as it did in the days of the deluge, whereupon they consulted their prophet Balaam. He calmed their fears, saying: "Fear not, ye kings, he who dwells in heaven has revealed himself to his children in his glory and his mercy. He has appeared, to give to his beloved people Torah, wisdom, and instruction,[1] and to bless them with strength and peace."[2] In another passage it is stated that God appeared on this occasion in the aspect of an instructing Elder, full of mercy.[3] Like rain and light, the Torah was a gift from heaven of which the world is hardly worthy, but which is indispensable to its maintenance.[4]

The gift was a complete one, without any reserve whatever. Nothing of the Torah, God assures Israel, was kept back in heaven.[5] All that follows is only a matter of interpretation. The principle held by the Rabbis was that the words of the Torah "are fruitful and multiply."[6] Thus the conviction could ripen that everything wise and good, be it ethical or ceremonial in its character, the effect of which would be to strengthen the cause of religion, was at least potentially contained in the Torah. Hence the famous adage, that everything which any student will teach at any future time, was already communicated to Moses on Mount Sinai, as also the injunction that any accept-

[1] See *P. R.*, 95 *a*. [2] See *Sifre*, 142 *b*. [3] See *Mechilta*, 66 *b*.
[4] *Gen. R.*, 6 4. [5] *Deut. R.*, 8 6. [6] See *Chagigah*, 3 *b*.

NB

able truth, though discovered by an insignificant man in Israel, should be considered of as high authority as if it had emanated from a great sage or prophet or even from Moses himself.[1] It requires but an earnest religious mind to discover all truth there. For the Torah came down from heaven with all the necessary instruments: humility, righteousness, and uprightness — and even her reward was in her.[2] And man has only to apply these tools to find in the Torah peace, strength, life, light, bliss, happiness, joy, and freedom.[3]

The Torah was, in short, all things to all men. To the Theosophist, who had already come under the sway of Hellenistic influences, it was the very expression of God's wisdom, which he would, as far as it is consistent with Biblical notions, elevate into an emanation of God's essence, and endow with a pre-mundane existence, reaching almost to infinity. To the mystical poet, with his love for the picturesque, it was the heavenly bride adorned with all the virtues which only heaven could bestow on her, at whose presentation to Israel the whole universe rejoiced, for her touch with mankind meant the wedding of heaven to earth. What, then, could the poor mortal do better than to learn to know her and to fall in love with her?

To the great majority of the Rabbis who retained

[1] See *Sifre*, 79 *b*. [2] *Deut. R.*, *ibid.*

[3] See *P. K.*, 105 *b*; *Mechilta*, 36 *b*, 47; *Sifre a*, 82 *b*, 83 *b*; *Exod. R.*, 36 8.

their sober sense, and cared more about what God requires us to be than about knowing what he is, the Torah was simply the manifestation of God's will, revealed to us for our good; the pedagogue, as the Rabbis expressed it,[1] who educates God's creatures. The occupation with the Torah was, according to the Rabbis, less calculated to produce schoolmen and jurists than saints and devout spirits. "Whosoever labours in the Torah for its own sake, merits many things . . . he is called friend, beloved, a lover of God, a lover of mankind; it clothes him in meekness and fear (of God), and fits him to become righteous, pious, and upright; it keeps him far from sin, brings him towards the side of virtue, and gives him sovereignty and dominion and discerning judgement. To him the secrets of the Torah are revealed; he becomes a never failing fountain, he grows modest and long-suffering, forgives insults, and is exalted above all things."[2] On the other hand, his individualism does not make him exclusive, his freedom does not involve the subjection of others, the world rejoices in him, for he enriches it with sound knowledge, understanding, and strength.[3] His life is one even like that of Moses, a continuous mourning for the glory of God and the glory of Israel (at present obscured) and a con-

[1] See *Gen. R.*, I. Cf. אבות עם תלמוד ירושלמי, etc., by R. נח חיים מקברין, *to Kinyan Torah*, 3 *b*, 4 *a*, the passage given there from the *Mechilta* of Ishmael, but not to be found there.

[2] See *Kinyan Torah* and Friedmann, נספחים, p. 15 *seq.*

[3] *Kinyan Torah, ibid.*

stant longing for their salvation,[1] whilst his activity (a continuation of the revelation) is making peace between heaven and earth.[2] In sooth, Israel has recognised the strength (or the secret) of the Torah; therefore, they said, "We forsake not God and his Torah, as it is said: 'I sat down under his shadow with great delight, and his fruit was sweet to my taste'" (Song of Songs 23).[3]

In fine, to the Jew the Torah was anything but a curse. He understood how to find out the sweetness and the light of it and of the Law which formed a part of it.

[1] See *S. E.*, pp. 17 and 63. [2] See *Sanhedrin*, 99 *b*.
[3] See *Exod. R.*, 17 2.

# X

# THE TORAH IN ITS ASPECT OF LAW (MIZWOTH)

R. Simlai, a well-known Agadic teacher and controversialist of the third century, said as follows: "Six hundred and thirteen commandments were delivered unto Moses on Mount Sinai; three hundred and sixty-five of which are prohibitive laws, corresponding to the number of days of the solar year, whilst the remaining two hundred and forty-eight are affirmative injunctions, being as numerous as the limbs constituting the human body."[1] This is one of the earlier comments on the number of the six hundred and thirteen laws, which are brought forward in many of our theological works, with the purpose of proving under what burden the scrupulous Jew must have laboured, who considered himself under the duty of performing all these enactments. The number is, by its very strangeness, bewildering; and the Pharisee, unable to rise to the heights above the Law, lay under

[1] *Makkoth*, 23 *b* and parallels, in the יפה עינים (where פדר״א פמ״ח ought to be corrected into מ״א). Cf. Bacher, *Ag. Am.*, I 558, and notes. The earliest known source for this number is probably *Mechilta* 67 *a*. Cf. also Sifre, 90 *b*. See also Bloch, *Revue des Études Juives*, I 197 *seq.*, and 209 *seq.*

the curse of its mere quantity. A few words as to the real value of these statistics are therefore necessary, before we pass to other questions connected with our subject.

The words with which the saying of R. Simlai is introduced are,[1] "He preached," or "he interpreted," and they somewhat suggest that these numbers were in some way a subject for edification, deriving from them some moral lesson. The lesson these numbers were intended to convey was, first, that each day brings its new temptation only to be resisted by a firm Do not; and, on the other hand, that the whole man stands in the service of God, each limb or member of his body being entrusted with the execution of its respective functions.[2] This was probably the sentiment which the preacher wished to impress upon his congregation, without troubling himself much about the accuracy of his numbers. How little, indeed, we are justified in urging these numbers too seriously is clear from the sequel of R. Simlai's homily. It runs thus: "David came (after Moses) and reduced[3] them (the six hundred and

[1] דרש ר׳ שמלאי in most of the parallels.

[2] Cf. *P. K.*, 101 *a*, and Rashi to *Makkoth*, *ibid.* Cf. also *Tan.*, תצא, 2. There are, however, grave doubts whether the subdivision in 365 and 248 (the words in the Talmud from שס״ה to אדם) is not a later addition. Cf. Bacher, *ibid.*

[3] The word in the Talmud and in *Tan.*, שופטים end is והעמידן, which may mean "compressed" or "reduced." See Bacher, *ibid.* I take here the version of the Talmud, omitting the additional discussions. Cf. also *M. T.*, 15, end.

thirteen commandments) to eleven, as it is said: Lord, who shall abide in thy tabernacle? who shall dwell in thy holy hill? He that walketh uprightly, etc.[1] Then Isaiah came and reduced them to six, as it is said: He that walketh righteously, etc.[2] Then Micah came and reduced them to three: He hath shewed thee, O man, what is good; and what doth the Lord require of thee, but to do justly, etc.[3] Then Isaiah came again, and reduced them to two, as it is said: Thus saith the Lord, Keep my judgements, and do justice.[4] Then Amos came and reduced them to one, as it is said: Seek the Lord and live.[5] Whilst Habakkuk (also) reduced them to one, as it is said: But the just shall live by his faith.[6]" The drift of this whole passage shows that the homily was not so much intended to urge the necessity of carrying out all the commandments with their numerous details, as to emphasise the importance of the moral laws, which themselves, nevertheless, may be compressed into the principle of seeking God, or of faith in God.

Granted, however, that R. Simlai took it seriously with his number of six hundred and thirteen: granted,

[1] Ps. 15 2–5, which verses contain eleven moral injunctions. Cf. Kimchi's commentary to this chapter.

[2] Isa. 33 15, which verse contains six moral injunctions.

[3] Micah 6 8, where three moral injunctions are contained.

[4] Isa. 56 1.

[5] Amos 5 6. This was probably the original version of R. Simlai's words, notwithstanding the objections made there.

[6] Hab. 2 4.

again, that his enumeration rested on some old authority which may be regarded as a guarantee for its exactness,[1] this would prove nothing for the "burden theory." The only possible explanations of our Rabbi's saying are the lists of R. Simon Kiara and of Maimonides.[2] But even a superficial analysis will discover that in the times of the Rabbis many of these commandments were already obsolete, as, for instance, those relating to the arrangements of the tabernacle, and to the conquest of Palestine; whilst others concerned only certain classes, as, for instance, the priests, the judges, the soldiers and their commanders, the Nazirites, the representatives of the community, or even one or two individuals in the whole population, as, for example, the king and the high priest. Others, again, provided for contingencies which could occur only to a few, as, for instance, the laws concerning divorce or levirate-marriages. The laws, again, relating to idolatry, incest, and the sacrifices of children to Moloch, could hardly be considered as coming within the province of the practical life even of the pre-Christian Jew; just as little as we can speak of Englishmen being under the burden of the law when prohibited from burning their widows or marrying their grandmothers, though these acts would certainly be considered as crimes. A careful examination of the six hundred and thirteen laws will prove

[1] This seems to be the opinion of Maimonides.

[2] The former in the הלכות גדולות, the latter in the ספר המצות and the Introduction to the משנה תורה.

that barely a hundred laws are to be found which concerned the everyday life of the bulk of the people.[1] Thus the law in its totality, which by the number of its precepts is so terrifying, is in its greater part nothing else than a collection of statutes relating to different sections of the community and to its multifarious institutions, ecclesiastical as well as civil, which constituted, as I have already said, the kingdom of God.

And here lay the strength of Judaism. The modern man is an eclectic being. He takes his religion from the Bible, his laws from the Romans, his culture from the classics, and his politics from his party. He is certainly broader in his sympathies than the Jew of old; but as a composite being, he must necessarily be lacking in harmony and unity. His sympathies are divided between the different sources of his inspiration, — sources which do not, as we know, always go well together. In order to avoid collision, he has at last to draw the line between the ecclesiastical and the civil, leaving the former, which in fact was forced upon him by a foreign religious conqueror, to a separate body of men whose business it is to look after the welfare of his invisible soul, whilst reserving the charge of the body and the world to himself.

The Rabbinic notion seems to have been that "if religion is anything, it is everything." The Rabbi gloried in the thought of being, as the Agadic expression runs, "a member of a city (or community) which in-

[1] See Schechter, *Studies in Judaism*, p. 301.

cluded the priest as well as the prophet, the king as well as the scribe and the teacher," all appointed and established by God.[1] To consider the administration of justice with all its details as something lying without the sphere of Torah would have been a terrible thought to the ancient Jew. Some Rabbis are anxious to show that the appointment of judges was commanded to Moses, even before Jethro gave him the well-known advice.[2] The Torah, they point out, is a combination of mercy and justice.[3] That the ways of the Torah "are ways of sweetness, and all her paths are peace" (Prov. 3 17. 18), was a generally accepted axiom,[4] and went without saying; what had to be particularly urged was that even such laws and institutions as appear to be a consequence of uncompromising right and of rigid truth, rather than of sweetness and peace, were also part and parcel of the Torah, with her God-like universality of attributes. Hence the assertion of the Rabbis that God threatens Israel with taking back his treasure from them should they be slow in carrying out the principle of justice (*dinim*).[5] "To the nations of the earth he gave some few laws; but his love to Israel was particularly manifested by the fulness and

[1] *Sifre*, 134 *a*. Cf. *Chullin*, 56 *b*. The passage in the text follows more the reading in the *MHG.*, ר"מ אומ׳ כרכא דכולא ביה׳ כהניו מתוכו לוייו מתוכו מלכיו מתוכו נביאיו מתוכו חכמיו מתוכו סופריו מתוכו ומשניו מתוכו, etc.

[2] See *Sifre*, 20 *a*.

[3] *Deut. R.*, 5 7.

[4] See, for instance, *Sukkah*, 32 *a*; *Jebamoth*, 87 *b*, and elsewhere.

[5] *Exod. R.*, 30 28.

completeness of the Torah, which is wholly theirs."[1] And in it they find everything. "If thou wantest advice," the Rabbis say (even in matters secular, or in questions regarding behaviour and good manners), "take it from the Torah, even as David said, From thy precepts I get understanding" (Ps. 119 104).[2]

As a fact, the old Rabbis hardly recognised such a chasm between the material and the spiritual as to justify the domain of religion being confined to the latter. The old Rabbinic literature is even devoid of the words *spiritual* and *material*. The corresponding terms, רוחני and גשמי, were coined by later translators from the Greek and Arabic philosophers, with whom the division between body and soul is so prominent. It is true that the Rabbis occasionally used such expressions as "things of the heaven" and "things of the world," or matters concerning "the eternal life" and matters concerning "the temporal life."[3] But apart from the fact that they were little meant to indicate a theological division between two antagonistic principles, the "things of the heaven" covered a much wider area of human life than is commonly imagined. Thus we hear of a Rabbi who remonstrated with his son for not attending the lecture of his friend R. Chisda. The son

[1] *Exod. R.*, *ibid.*, 9 and parallels. [2] See *P. K.*, 105 *a*.

[3] מילי דשמיא — מילי דעלמא. See *e.g. Berachoth*, 7 *b*, v. *Shabbath*, 33 *b*. Interesting is the arrangement in the complete edition of the ספר יראים in which all the laws concerning conduct and morality are grouped under the heading of the duties towards God and man, whilst the ceremonial come under the heading of duties towards God alone.

apologised, and answered that he had once gone to the school of R. Chisda, but what he heard were "things of the world," the lecture having consisted in the exposition of a set of sanitary rules to be observed on certain occasions. Whereupon the father rejoined indignantly: "He (R. Chisda) is occupied with the life of God's creatures, and dost thou venture to call such matters 'things of the world'?"[1] Elsewhere we find the Rabbis deciding that to teach a child a trade or a handicraft is to be considered as one of the "delights of heaven," for which arrangements may be made even on the Sabbath.[2]

As a rule, the Rabbis spoke of sin and righteousness, a good action or a bad action, מצוה or עבירה, for each of which body and soul are alike held responsible. But no act is in itself the worse or the better for being a function of the body or a manifestation of the soul. When Hillel the Great, who, as it would seem, was the author, or at least the inspirer, of the saying, "Let all thy deeds be for the sake of Heaven," was about to take a bath, he said, "I am going to perform a religious act by beautifying my person, that was created in the image of God."[3]

R. Judah Hallevi, with the instinct of a poet, hit the

[1] *Shabbath*, 82 *a*. [2] חפצי שמים. *Shabbath*, 150 *a*.

[3] See *A. R. N.*, 33 *b*; *Lev. R.*, 34 3; and *P. R.*, 115 *b*. "The fourth degree of love," says St. Bernard somewhere, "is to love self only for God's sake." See also the passage from the *Yelamdenu* reproduced in Jellinek's *Beth Hammidrash*, 6: 85 where it is the נוי (or superior beauty) in which the צלם האל finds expression.

right strain when he said, in his famous Dialogue *Kusari*, "Know that our Torah is constituted of the three psychological states: Fear, love, and joy" (that is to say, all the principal emotions of man are enlisted in the service of God). "By each of these thou mayest be brought into communion with thy God. Thy contriteness in the days of fasting does not bring thee nearer to God than thy joy on the Sabbath days and on festivals, provided thy joy emanates from a devotional and perfect heart. And just as prayer requires devotion and thought, so does joy, namely, that thou wilt rejoice in his commandments for their own sake, (the only reasons for this rejoicing being) the love of him who commanded it, and the desire of recognising God's goodness towards thee. Consider these feasts as if thou wert the guest of God invited to his table and his bounty, and thank him for it inwardly and outwardly. And if thy joy in God excites thee even to the degree of singing and dancing, it is a service to God, keeping thee attached to him. But the Torah did not leave these things to our arbitrary will, but put them all under control. For man lacks the power to make use of the functions of body and soul in their proper proportions." [1]

The law thus conceived as submitting all the faculties and passions of man to the control of the divine, whilst suppressing none, was a source of joy and blessing to the Rabbis. Whatever meaning the words of the Apostle may have, when he speaks of the curse of the Law, it is

[1] *Kuzari* (ed. Sluzki, p. 45).

certain that those who lived and died for it considered it as a blessing. To them it was an effluence of God's mercy and love. In the daily prayer of the Jews the same sentiment is expressed in most glowing words: "With everlasting love thou hast loved the house of Israel, thy people; Torah, commandments, statutes, and judgements hast thou taught us. . . . Yea, we will rejoice in the words of thy Torah and thy commandments forever. . . . And mayest thou never take away thy love from us. Blessed art thou, O Lord, who lovest thy people Israel."[1] Beloved are Israel, whom the Holy One, blessed be he, surrounded with commandments, (bidding them) to have phylacteries on their heads and arms, a mezuzah on their door-posts, fringes on the four corners of their garments. . . . "Be distinguished," said the Holy One, blessed be he, to Israel, "by the commandments in order that ye may be pleasing unto me. Thou (Israel) art beautiful when thou art pleasing."[2] Indeed, there is not a single thing which is not connected with a commandment, be it the farm, or the home, or the garments of the man, or his flocks.[3] And it is on account of this fact that Israel considered themselves blessed in the city and in the field.[4] It is the very light sown for the righteous, God not having loved anything in the world which is not connected with a law.[5]

[1] See Singer, p. 69; Baer, p. 164. Cf. also Berachoth, 33 *b*; Singer, p. 227; and Baer, p. 347.

[2] *Sifre*, 75 *b* and parallels.

[3] *T. K.*, 42 *a*.

[4] *Tan.* תבא, 4.

[5] *Num. R.*, 17 5; cf. *Lev. R.*, 6 3.

## XI

## THE JOY OF THE LAW

LAW and commandments, or as the Rabbinic expression is, *Torah* and *Mizwoth*, have a harsh sound and are suggestive to the outsider of something external, forced upon men by authority from the outside, sinister and burdensome. The citations just given show that Israel did not consider them in that light. They were their very love and their very life. This will become clearer when we consider both the sentiment accompanying the performance of the Law and the motives urging them.

The שמחה של מצוה, the joy experienced by the Rabbinic Jew in being commanded to fulfil the Law, and the enthusiasm which he felt at accomplishing that which he considered to be the will of God, is a point hardly touched upon by most theological writers, and if touched upon at all, is hardly ever understood. Yet this "joy of the Law" is so essential an element in the understanding of the Law, that it "forms that originality of sentiment more or less delicate" which can never be conceived by those who have experienced it neither from life nor from literature.

How anxious a Jew was to carry out a law, and what joy he felt in fulfilling it, may be seen from the following story, which perhaps dates from the very time when the Law was denounced as slavery and as the strength of sin. According to Deut. 24 19, a sheaf forgotten in the harvest field belonged to the poor; the proprietor being forbidden to go again and to fetch it. This prohibitive law was called מצות שכחה, "the commandment with regard to forgetfulness." It was impossible to fulfil it as long as one thought of it. In connection with this we read in the Tosephta: "It happened to a Chasid (saint) that he forgot a sheaf in his field, and was thus enabled to fulfil the commandment with regard to forgetfulness. Whereupon he bade his son go to the temple, and offer for him a burnt-offering and a peace-offering, whilst he also gave a great banquet to his friends in honour of the event. Thereupon his son said to him: Father, why dost thou rejoice in this commandment more than in any other law prescribed in the Torah? He answered, that it was the occurrence of the rare opportunity of accomplishing the will of God, even as the result of some oversight, which caused him so much delight." [1]

This joy of the *Mizwah* constituted the essence of the action. Israel, we are told, receives especial praise for the fact that when they stood on Mount Sinai to receive the Torah, they all combined with one heart to accept

[1] *Tosephta Peah*, 22. Cf. *Midrash Zuta* (ed. Buber, 51 *b*). Of course, we must read there שלא בכונה for בעונה.

the kingdom of heaven in joy. The sons of Aaron, again, were glad and rejoicing when they heard words (of commandment) from the mouth of Moses. Again, "let man fulfil the commandments of the Torah with joy," exclaimed a Rabbi, "and then they will be counted to him as righteousness." [1] The words, "Moses did as the Lord commanded him" (Num. 27 22), are explained to mean that he fulfilled the Law with joy.[2] In a similar manner the words, "I have done according to all that thou hast commanded me" (Deut. 26 14), are interpreted to signify, I have rejoiced and caused others to rejoice.[3] Naturally, it is the religionist of high standard, or as the Rabbis express it, "the man who deserves it," who realises this joy in the discharge of all religious functions, whilst to him "who deserves it not" it may become a trial of purification.[4] But the ideal is to obtain this quality of joy, or "to deserve it." The truly righteous rejoice almost unconsciously, joy being a gift from heaven to them, as it is said, "Thou (God) hast put gladness in my heart." [5]

This principle of joy in connection with the *Mizwah* is maintained both in the Talmud and in the devotional literature of the Middle Ages. The general rule is: Tremble with joy when thou art about to fulfil a

[1] See *Mechilta*, 66 *b*; *T. K.*, 42 *b*. See also *S. E.*, p. 29. Cf. also *ibid.*, p. 95.

[2] *Sifre*, 52 *b*.

[3] *Ibid.*, 129 *a*.

[4] *Yoma*, 72 *b*, זכה משמחתו לא זכה צורפתו.

[5] *S. E.*, p. 97.

commandment.[1] God, his Salvation, and his Law, are the three things in which Israel rejoices.[2] Indeed, as R. Bachye Ibn. Bakudah declares, to mention one of the later moralists, it is this joy experienced by the sweetness of the service of God which forms a part of the reward of the religionist, even as the prophet said, "Thy words were found, and I did eat them; and thy word was unto me the joy and rejoicing of mine heart" (Jer. 15 16).[3] R. Bachye Ibn Chalwah, again, declares that the joy accompanying the carrying out of a religious performance is even more acceptable to God than the *Mizwah* itself. The righteous, he points out, feel this ineffable delight in performing God's will in the same way as the spheres and planets (whose various revolutions are a perpetual song to God) rejoice in their going forth and are glad in their returning;[4] whilst R. Joseph Askari of Safed (sixteenth century) makes joy one of the necessary conditions without which a law cannot be perfectly carried out.[5] And I may perhaps remark that this joy of the *Mizwah* was a living reality even in modern times. I myself had once the good fortune to observe one of those old type Jews, who, as the first morning of the Feast of Tabernacles drew near, used to wake and rise soon after the middle of the night. There he sat, with

[1] *D. E. Z.*, 2. [2] *P. K.*, 147 *a*, 194 *a*.

[3] חובות הלבבות עבודת האלהים פ״ג.

[4] כד הקמח, ch. שמחה.

[5] See חרדים, Warsaw, 1879, p. 9. Cf. also Albo, *Ikkarim*, 3 88; also Luzzato, מסילת ישרים, 28 *a*.

trembling joy, awaiting impatiently the break of dawn, when he would be able to fulfil the law of the palm branches and the willows!

To give one or two further instances how many more things there are in the Synagogue and in the Law than are dreamt of by our divines, I shall allude to the Sabbath and to prayer.

The institution of the Sabbath is one of those laws the strict observance of which was already the object of attack on the part of the compilers of the Synoptic Gospels. Nevertheless, the doctrine proclaimed in one of the Gospels that the Son of man is the Lord of the Sabbath, was also current among the Rabbis. They too teach that the Sabbath is delivered into the hand of man (to break it when necessary), and not man into the power of the Sabbath.[1] And the Rabbis even laid down the axiom that a scholar living in a town, where there could be among the Jewish population the least doubt as to the question whether the Sabbath might be broken for the benefit of a person dangerously sick, was to be despised as a man neglecting his duty; every delay in such a case being fraught with grave consequences to the patient; for, as Maimonides points out, the laws of the Torah are not meant as an infliction upon mankind, "but as mercy, loving-kindness, and peace."[2]

The attacks upon the Sabbath have not abated. "The day is still described by almost every modern

[1] *Mechilta*, 104 *a*.

[2] *Jer. Yoma*, 45 *b*. Cf. Maimonides, הלכות שבת פ״ב ה״ג.

writer in the most gloomy colours, and long lists are given of the minute observances connected with it, easily to be transgressed, which would necessarily make the Sabbath, instead of a day of rest, a day of sorrow and anxiety, almost worse than the Scotch Sunday, as depicted by continental writers." Even Hausrath[1] — who is something more than a theologian, for he also wrote history — is unable to see in the Rabbinic Sabbath more than a day which is to be distinguished by a mere non-performance of the thirty-nine various sorts of work forbidden by the Rabbis on Sabbaths, such as sowing, ploughing, reaping, winnowing, kneading, spinning, weaving, skinning, tanning, writing, etc., etc., — a whole bundle of participles, in the expounding of which the Pharisee took an especial delight.[2] Contrast this view with the prayer of R. Zadok, a younger contemporary of the Apostles, which runs thus: "Through the love with which thou, O Lord our God, lovest thy people Israel, and the mercy which thou hast shown to the children of thy covenant, thou hast given unto us in love this great and holy seventh day."[3] This Rabbi, clearly, regarded the Sabbath as a gift from heaven, an expression of the infinite love and mercy of God, which he manifested toward his beloved children. Thus the Sabbath is celebrated by the very people who observe

[1] See Schechter, *Studies in Judaism*, p. 297 *seq.*

[2] *History of the New Testament Times*, I 101.

[3] *Tosephta Berachoth*, 3 7.

it, in hundreds of hymns, which would fill volumes, as a day of rest and joy, of pleasure and delight, a day in which man enjoys some presentiment of the pure bliss and happiness which are stored up for the righteous in the world to come, and to which such tender names were applied as the "Queen Sabbath," the "Bride Sabbath," and the "holy, dearly beloved Sabbath." Every founder of a religion declares the yoke which he is about to put on his followers to be easy, and the burden to be light; but, after all, the evidence of those who *did* bear the Sabbath yoke for thousands of years ought to pass for something. The assertion of some writers that the Rabbis, the framers of these laws, as students leading a retired life, suffered in no way under them, and therefore were unable to realise their oppressive effect upon the great majority of the people, is hardly worth refuting. The Rabbis belonged to the majority, being mostly recruited, as already pointed out in another place, from the artisan, trading, and labouring classes.[1] This very R. Zadok, whom I have just mentioned, says: "Make not the Torah a crown wherewith to aggrandise thyself, nor a spade wherewith to dig;" whilst Hillel considers it as a mortal sin to derive any material profit from the words of the Torah.[2]

The prayers of the synagogue are another case in point. That Jews could pray, that they had, besides the Temple, a synagogue service, independent of sacri-

[1] See above, p. 110. [2] *Aboth*, 4 7.

fices and priests, does not, as every student must have felt, fit in well with the view generally entertained of the deadly and deadening effects of the Law. The inconvenient Psalms of the later periods were easily neutralised by divesting them of all individualistic tendency, whilst the synagogue was placed under the superintendence of the Rabbis, "whose mechanical tendencies are well known." In their hands, we are told, prayers turn into rubrics, and it is with an especial delight that theologians dwell on the Rabbinical laws relating to prayer, as, for instance, how many times a day a man ought to pray, the fixed hours for prayer, in what parts of the prayer an interruption is allowed, which parts of the prayer require more devotion than others, and similar petty little questions of religious casuistry in which the Rabbi, as an expert, if I may call him so, greatly delighted. But these writers seem to overlook the fact that the very framers of these petty laws were the main composers of the liturgy. And who can say what the Rabbi's feelings were when he wrote, for instance, "Forgive us, our Father, for we have sinned"? The word "Father" alone suggests a world of such ideas as love, veneration, devotion, and childlike dependence upon God. It is easy enough to copy rubrics. They float on the surface of the so-called "Sea of the Talmud," and it requires only a certain indelicacy of mind, or what Renan would have called "the vulgarity of criticism," to skim them off, and pass them on to the world as samples of Jewish synagogue life. If Life and Times writers would only dip a little deeper into this sea, they would notice how easily the Rabbis could disregard all these rubrics. The subject of prayer is too wide to be dealt with here even in a perfunctory manner, but a few passages at least may be cited which will illustrate the sentiment of the Rabbis with regard to this topic. Thus we read, with reference to Jer. 14 8: "God is the *Mikweh* of Israel, which word the Rabbis take to mean "the source of purity" (Israel's purification being established by attachment to God). "God says to Israel, I bade thee read thy prayers unto me in thy synagogues; but if thou canst not, pray in thy house; and if thou art unable to do this, pray when thou art in thy field; and if this be inconvenient to thee, pray on thy bed; and if thou canst not do even this, think of me in thy heart."[1] Prayer is, indeed, as the Rabbis call it, "the service of the heart"; though man should praise the Holy One, blessed be he, with every limb in his body, even as David did who praised him with his head, with his eyes, with his mouth, with his ears, with his throat, with his tongue, with his lips, with his heart, with his reins, with his hands, with his feet, as it is said, "All my bones shall say, Lord who is like unto thee?" (Ps. 35 10); nay, with his soul and his breath.[2]

[1] *P. K.*, 157 *b*, 158 *a*, referring to the meaning "well" or "cistern" rather than "hope."

[2] *Taanith*, 2 *a*. Cf. *Sifre*, 80 *a*; *M. T.*, 5 1, about the prayers of יחיד (individual). See *Mechilta of R. Simon*, p. 151. Cf. also above, p. 50, note 2.

Prayer, and the recitation of the Shema, are among the things which keep the heart of Israel in exile awake,[1] and God requires of Israel that, at least in the time of prayer, they should give him all their hearts;[2] that is to say, that the whole of man should be absorbed in his prayer. "Prayer without devotion is like a body without a soul," is a common Jewish proverb. Indeed, he who prays should direct his heart to heaven, nay, he must consider himself as if the very Divine Presence is facing him.[3] God himself teaches Israel how to pray before him;[4] for nothing is more beautiful than prayer; it is more beautiful even than good works, and of more value than sacrifices.[5] It is the expression of Israel's love to God; God longs for it.[6] Prayer is Israel's chiefest joy.[7] When thou risest to pray, let thy heart rejoice within thee, since thou servest a God, the like unto whom there is none (Ps. 100 3). Hence the benediction in which Israel thank God that they are permitted to pray to him.[8]

And here I must again be allowed an allusion to personal reminiscences. The following passages in the

[1] See *Cant. Rabba*, 5: 2. [2] *Tan.*, תבא 1, end.
[3] See *Berachoth*, 31 *a*, and *Sanhedrin*, 22 *a*.
[4] See *Rosh Hashanah*, 17 *b*. Cf. above, 37.
[5] See *Sifre*, 71 *b*, and *Tan.*, תבא 1.
[6] See *M. T.*, 116 1.
[7] See Yalkut to Ps. 100. Cf. *M. T.* to this chapter.
[8] See *Jer. Berachoth*, 3 *d* (the first lines on the top). Cf. Baer's remarks to the מודים דרבנן, p. 100.

Song of the Unity are recited in some congregations on the Eve of the Day of Atonement: —

We are thy people and thy sheep, who delight to obey thy will.
But how shall we serve, since our hand hath no power, and our sanctuary is burnt with fire?
How shall we serve without sacrifice and meat offering? for we are not yet come unto our rest,
Neither is there water to wash away defilement; lo! we are upon unpurified ground.
But I rejoice at thy word, and I am come according to thy bidding.
For it is written, I will not reprove thee for thy sacrifices, or thy burnt-offerings.
Concerning your sacrifices and your burnt-offerings I commanded not your fathers.
What have I asked, and what have I sought of thee but to fear me?
To serve with joy and a good heart?
Behold, to hearken is better than sacrifice,
And a broken heart than pure offering.
The sacrifices of God are a broken spirit.
In sacrifice and meat-offering thou delightest not; sin-offering and burnt-offering thou hast not asked.
I will build an altar of the broken fragments of my heart, and will break my spirit within me.
The haughty heart I will humble; yea, the haughtiness of mine eyes, and I will rend my heart for the sake of the Lord.

My broken spirit, that is thy sacrifice. Let it be acceptable upon thine altar![1]

But only one who has seen the deep despair reflected on the faces of the worshippers, as they repeat the first stanzas bewailing the loss of sacrifices as a means of atonement, and the sudden transition to the highest degree of joy and cheerfulness at the thought expressed in the last stanzas, that it is neither burnt-offering nor meat-offering which God requires, but that the heart is the real altar and the service of the heart the real sacrifice — only one who has witnessed such a prayer-meeting will be able to conceive how little the capacity of the Rabbi to pray, and to rejoice in prayer, was affected by the rubrics, and how superficial is the common conception of onlookers on this subject.

In the preceding remarks we had a reference to a saying of R. Zadok, prohibiting the making of the Torah a means of aggrandising one's self, and another saying of Hillel to the same effect.[2] The saying in question closes with the words, "Lo, whosoever makes profit from the words of the Torah removes his life from the world."[3] This brings us to the subject of לשמה (*Lishmah*), playing a very prominent part in Rabbinic literature. By *Lishmah* is understood the performance of the Law for its own sake, or rather

[1] שיר היחוד, first day. See *Service of the Synagogue*, Davis and Adler, London, 1906, vol. I, p. 41.

[2] See above, p. 145.

[3] *Aboth*, 4 7.

for the sake of him who wrought (commanded) it, excluding all worldly intentions. Thus, with regard to sacrifices, the words of Lev. 1 9 (ריח ניחוח לה') are explained to mean that the sacrifice must be brought with no other intention but that of pleasing him who created the world.[1] The service of God should be as single-minded as he is single in the world, to whom this service is directed.[2] "It is pleasing unto me that I commanded and my will was done."[3] With reference to other laws, the injunction is, "Do the things (of the Torah) for the sake of him who wrought them, and speak in them for their own sake."[4] Indeed, the Torah is only then pure when man cleanses himself from all sin, and from every thought of profiting by it, so that he must not expect of mankind to serve him or maintain him, because he is a scholar.[5] Nay, it is only the occupation with the Torah for its own sake which is life, "but if thou hast not performed the words of the Torah in this manner, they kill thee."[6] It is just this purity of motive which forms the main difference "between the righteous and the wicked, between him that serveth God and

[1] *T.K.*, 7 *c* and 8 *c*. Cf. *Zebachim*, 37 *b*. See also below, pp. 297 and 298.

[2] *T.K.*, 43 *d*. See below, p. 258. [3] *Sifre*, 39 *a* and 54 *a*.

[4] See *Nedarim*, 62 *a*, reading פועלם. See, however, *Sifre*, 84 *b*. *D. E. Z.* (ed. Tawrogi) has both readings. Cf. Bacher, *Ag. Tan.*, 1 53. Duran in his commentary to אבות, 5 4, has the reading לשם פעלן ודבר בהם לשם שמים.

[5] *Mechilta of R. Simon*, 98.

[6] *Sifre*, 131 *b*; *Taanith*, 7 *a*; cf. Bacher, *Ag. Tan.*, 2 540.

him that serveth him not" (Malachi 3 18).[1] The same thing applies also to other laws. Two men feasted upon their Passover lamb. The one ate it for the sake of the *Mizwah*, the other devoured it in the manner of a glutton. To the former they apply the Scriptural words, "The righteous shall walk in them;" to the latter, "The transgressor shall fall therein" (Hosea 14 10).[2] This is of course the highest ideal of the religionist, though not everybody could attain to this high degree, and some concessions were made in this respect. Hence such statements as "Let a man be occupied in the study of the Torah and the fulfilling of commandments even in the case when they are not performed for their own sake;" but the statement closes with the words, "for this occupation will lead in the end to the desired ideal of the purer intention." This is in harmony with the sentiment expressed by another Rabbi, who was wont to pray, "May it be thy will that you bring peace . . . among those students who are occupied in the study of the Torah, both who do it for its own sake, and those who do not do it for its own sake. And that these latter may come to ultimately occupy themselves with it for its own sake."[3] In any case, this selfish occupation was considered as a Torah wanting in grace.[4]

1 See *M. T.*, 31 9.

2 See *Nazir*, 23 *a*. See also Albo, *Ikkarim*, 3 5 and 28.

3 See *Berachoth*, 17 *a*.

4 (חסר). See *Sukkah*, 49 *b*.

And let it be noticed that the notion of *Lishmah* excluded even the intention of fulfilling a law with the hope of getting such rewards as are promised by the Scriptures. Though the Rabbis never tired of urging the belief in reward and punishment, and strove to make of it a living conviction, they yet displayed a constant tendency to disregard it as a motive for action. The saying of Antigonos of Socho, "Be not like servants that serve their master with the view to receive reward," is well known.[1] All the commentators on the sayings of the Fathers explain this sentence as meaning that love pure and simple is the only worthy motive of the worshipper. But we must not look upon this saying of Antigonos as on one of those theological paradoxes in which divines of all creeds occasionally indulge. It is a sentiment running through the Rabbinic literature of almost every age. Thus the words in Deut. 11 13, "To love the Lord your God," are explained to mean: "Say not, I will study the Torah with the purpose of being called sage or Rabbi, or to acquire fortune, or to be rewarded for it in the world to come; but do it for the sake of thy love to God, though the glory will come in the end."[2] The words in Ps. 112 1, "Blessed is the man who delighteth greatly in his commandments," are interpreted to mean, that he is blessed who delighteth in God's commandments, but not in the reward promised for his commandments.[3] This proves, by

[1] *Aboth*, 1 : 3. [2] *Sifre*, 84 *a*. Cf. above, p. 68. [3] *Abodah Zarah*, 19 *a*.

the way, that the Rabbis could depart from the letter of the Scripture for the sake of the spirit, the succeeding verses in this very Psalm being nothing else than a description of the reward awaiting the pious man who fulfils God's commandments. In another place, those who, in view of Prov. 3 16, look out for the good things which are on the left side of wisdom, namely, riches and honours, are branded as wicked and base.[1] And when David said, "I hate them that are of a double mind, but thy law do I love," he indicated by it, according to the Rabbis, his contempt for mixed motives in the service of God, as the Law should not be fulfilled either under compulsion or through fear, but only from the motive of love. Indeed, God bears evidence to the unselfishness of Israel and their full confidence in him, saying, "I gave them affirmative commands and they received them; I gave them negative commands and they received them, and though I did not explain their reward, they said nothing" (making no objection).[2] In the devotional literature of the Middle Ages there is hardly a single work in which man is not warned against serving God with any intention of receiving reward, though, of course, the religionist is strongly urged to believe that God does reward goodness and does punish wickedness.[3]

[1] See *Num. R.*, 22 9. [2] *M. T.*, 119 46, and *ibid.*, 119 1.

[3] See ספר חסידים, Parma, p. 254. Cf. also Azulai, מדבר קדמות, s.v., לשמה. See also above, pp. 67 *seq.* and 68 *seq.* Cf. also Schechter, *Studies in Judaism*, 2d series, the essay on *Saints and Saintliness.*

Nor does salvation exactly depend on the number of the commandments man accomplishes. It is true that every law gives Israel an opportunity of acquiring merit (*Zachuth*), and inheriting thereby the world to come; for which reason the Holy One, blessed be he, multiplied to them Torah and commandments.[1] But this multiplication only aims at an increase of opportunities enabling man to accomplish at least *one* law in a perfect manner, which alone possesses the virtue of saving. "Even he who has done *one* of those things (enumerated in the 15th Ps.) is valued as much as if he had done all those things and shall never be moved,[2] and only he shall not escape the mouth of Sheol who has not accomplished a single law."[3] But the accomplishment of this single law must be, as already indicated, in the most perfect way. As R. Saadya Gaon states on Talmudic authority, the worshipper (*Obed*) is to be considered the man who at least set one law apart for himself which he should never transgress, or fall short of in any way.[4]

[1] See *Makkoth*, 23 *b*, Mishnah. Cf. *Tan. B.*, 4 87 *a*, and *Num. R.*, 17 2, and Friedmann, נספחים, p. 23.

[2] See *Makkoth*, 24 *a*; *M. T.*, 16 7. Cf. also *Sanhedrin*, 81 *a*. It should be remarked that the paraphrase of the Rabbis of this Ps. and of Ez., 18 6 *seq.*, implies even a higher standard than suggested by the literal sense of the Biblical text.

[3] See the statement of R. Jochanan in *Makkoth*, *ibid.* Cf. Rabbinowicz in *Variae Lectiones*, *a. l.*

[4] אמונות ודעות, 5 : 8. His authority is *Jer. Kiddushin*, 61 *d*. As an instance of such a law, the commandment of honouring father and mother is given there.

In conformity with this is the view of Maimonides, who declares that it is an essential belief of the Torah that if a man fulfils even (only) one of the six hundred and thirteen laws in a perfect manner, so that it is not accompanied by any worldly consideration but done for the sake of the love of God, he becomes thereby worthy of the life of the world to come.[1] Maimonides illustrates his point by the story of a Rabbi (of the Tannaitic age), who was about to die the death of a martyr, but shortly before he suffered, he discussed with his friend his prospects of sharing in the life of the world to come. The answer he received was to the effect that if ever there came "an action into his hands," he may hope for it; that is, if he ever met with a case requiring a special effort to carry the law into effect. The Rabbi then remembered that in his capacity as treasurer of the charities in his city such a case did occur, and that he performed his duty to the full. It is thus neither the martyrdom which he was to undergo nor the routine life in accordance with the law which may readily be expected of any Rabbi, but the accomplishment of one commandment in a perfect way that secures salvation.[2] Somewhat similar is the

[1] See Maimonides, Commentary to *Mishnah Makkoth*, 3 16. It is not impossible that both R. Saadya and Maimonides were also thinking of *Mechilta* 33 *b*, where we read in the name of R. Nehemiah, "He who receives upon himself (even) a single law, in faith, is worthy that the Holy Spirit should rest upon him."

[2] See Maimonides, *ibid.* See also *Abodah Zarah*, 18 *a*. Cf. Albo, *Ikkarim*, 5 29.

following story: A certain Rabbi who held communion with Elijah asked the prophet one day when standing in the market whether he could discover among the crowd there any person destined for the life of the world to come. "No," answered the prophet. Subsequently Elijah perceived a certain person, then he said to the Rabbi, "This is the man of the world to come." Upon inquiry by the Rabbi, it was found that he was a jailer, and that he possessed the merit of watching over the chastity of the daughters of Israel, whom misfortune brought under his authority. A little later, the prophet again pointed out two more individuals as men of the world to come. When the Rabbi asked after their profession they answered, "We are cheerful persons and cheer up the depressed ones. Again, when we see two persons quarrelling, we endeavour to make peace between them."[1]

It must further be noted that even mere negative virtues are not without a certain saving power. "He who refrains from committing a sin, they reward him as if he accomplished a commandment."[2] It should however be stated that this view is greatly modified by some other opinions that only admit the merit of this negative disposition when the temptation to sin was very great, or when the man out of conscientious scruples abstained from an action, the sinful feature of which

[1] See *Taanith*, 22 *a* and *Jer. Taanith*, 64 *b*. Cf. also Albo, *ibid.*

[2] See *Mishnah Makkoth*, 3 15. Cf. *Sifre*, 125 *a*, *Kiddushin*, 39 *b*, and *Jer. Kiddushin*, 61 *d*.

was not fully established.[1] It is further modified by the following statement: "A man might think," the Rabbis teach, "considering that he avoids every opportunity of sin and is on his guard against evil (with his tongue) and falsehood, he can now indulge in sleep (idleness), neither committing sin nor doing good; therefore it is said 'Depart from evil and do good,'" (Ps. 34 14). And by "good" is meant the occupation with the Torah.[2]

The real motive of this enthusiasm for the Law must be sought in other sources than the hope of reward. Those who keep the commandments of God are his lovers. And when the lover is asked, Why art thou carried away to be burned, stoned, or crucified? he answers, Because I have studied the Torah, or, Because I have circumcised my son, or, Because I have kept the Sabbath; but he considers the suffering as wounds inflicted upon him for the sake of his beloved one, and his love is returned by the love of God.[3] The Law is thus a means of strengthening the mutual relations of love between God and his people.[4] The fulfilment of the Law was, in the eyes of the Rabbis, a witnessing on the part of the Jews to God's relationship to the world. "Why does this man," they say, "refrain from work on the Sabbath? why does he close his business on the seventh day? He does so in order to bear

[1] See *Kiddushin*, 31 *b*, and *Jer. Kiddushin*, 61 *d*. Cf. also *M.T.*, 1 7.
[2] See *Abodah Zarah*, 18 *b* and 19 *a*, and *M. T.*, 1 6.
[3] *Mechilta*, 68 *b*.
[4] See *Mechilta*, 98 *a*.

witness to the fact of God's creation of the world, and to his providence over it." [1] The Law, according to the Rabbis, was a source of holiness. Each new commandment with which God blesses Israel adds holiness to his people; but it is holiness which makes Israel to be God's own.[2] They deduce this doctrine from Exod. 20 30, which verse they explain to mean that it is the fact of Israel being holy men אנשי קדש which gives them the privilege of belonging to God. Hence the formula in many benedictions: "Blessed art thou, O Lord our God, . . . who hast sanctified us by thy commandments, and found delight in us." [3] Another version of the same sort is, "Beloved are the commandments by which the Holy One, blessed be he, exalted the seed of his friend Abraham and gave them unto Israel with the purpose of beautifying and glorifying them; whilst Israel, his holy people, and his inheritance, glorify his name for the commandments and statutes he gave them. And it is because of these commandments that Israel are called holy.[4] These reasons, namely, the motive of love, the privilege of bearing witness to God's relationship to the world, the attainment of holiness in which the Law educated Israel, as well as the other spiritual motives which I have already pointed out, such as the joy felt

[1] See *Mechilta*, 104 *a*. [2] *Ibid.*, 98 *a*. [3] Baer, p. 198.

[4] See ספר המוסר, ed. Mantua, 126 *b*. The diction of the passage shows that it has been taken from some ancient Midrash. See also above, p. 147. and below, p. 209.

by the Rabbis in the performance of the Law and the harmony which the Rabbis perceived in the life lived according to the Torah, were the true sources of Israel's enthusiasm for the Law. At least they were powerful enough with the more refined and nobler minds in Israel to enable them to dispense utterly with the motives of reward and punishment; though, as in every other religion, these lower motives may have served as concurrent incentives to a majority of believers.

# XII

## THE *ZACHUTH* OF THE FATHERS

### IMPUTED RIGHTEOUSNESS AND IMPUTED SIN

THE last chapter having treated of the righteousness achieved through the means of the Law and the sin involved by breaking it, it will be convenient to deal here with the doctrine of the זכות אבות (the Merits of the Fathers), the merits of whose righteousness are charged to the account of Israel. This doctrine plays an important part in Jewish theology, and has its counterpart in the belief that under certain conditions one person has also to suffer for the sins of another person. We have thus in Judaism both the notion of imputed righteousness and imputed sin. They have, however, never attained such significance either in Jewish theology or in Jewish conscience as it is generally assumed. By a happy inconsistency, in the theory of salvation, so characteristic of Rabbinic theology, the importance of these doctrines is reduced to very small proportions, so that their effect was in the end beneficial and formed a healthy stimulus to conscience.

The term זכות (*Zachuth*) is not to be found in the

Bible, though the verb occurs in the sense of being pure or of being cleansed.[1] In the Rabbinic literature, the verb זכה is sometimes used as a legal term meaning to be acquitted, to be in the right, to have a valid claim; whilst the noun *Zachuth* means acquittal.[2] Occasionally it also means to be worthy of a thing, or to be privileged.[3] In the *pi'el* it means to argue, to plead for acquittal.[4] Further, in a theological sense, to lead to righteousness,[5] to cause one or to give one the opportunity to acquire a merit, while the noun *Zachuth* is used in the sense of merit, virtue, which under certain conditions have a protective or an atoning influence.[6]

For the sake of obtaining a clearer view of the subject, which is rather complicated, we shall treat it under the following headings: (1) The *Zachuth* of a Pious Ancestry; (2) The *Zachuth* of a Pious Contemporary; (3) The *Zachuth* of the Pious Posterity.

(1) The *Zachuth* of the pious ancestry may generally be described as the זכות אבות (the *Zachuth* of the Fathers), but the term *Fathers* is largely limited in Rabbinic literature to the three patriarchs, Abraham, Isaac, and Jacob, God's covenant with whom is so often ap-

[1] See Micah 6 11; Ps. 119 9; Job 25 4.

[2] See *Baba Meziah*, 107 *b*; *Mishnah*, *ibid.*, 1 4; *Mishnah Sanhedrin*, 4 1. See Jastrow's *Dictionary*, s.v. See also Bacher, *Terminologie*, I 50.

[3] See *Sota*, 17 *a*; *Chagigah*, 5 *b*.

[4] See, for instance, *Mishnah Sanhedrin*, 3 5.

[5] See *Aboth*, 5 18. [6] See *Jer. Kiddushin*, 61 *d*, and *P. R.*, 38 *b*.

pealed to already in the Bible. The Rabbinic rule is, "They call not Fathers but the three (patriarchs), and they call not Mothers but four" (Sarah, Rebeccah, Rachel, and Leah).[1] The last statement with regard to the Mothers suggests also that there is such a thing as the זכות אמהות (the *Zachuth* of the Mothers). This is in conformity with the Rabbinic statement in reference to Lev. 26 42 regarding God's remembering his covenant with the patriarchs, that there is also such a thing as the covenant with the Mothers.[2] In another place they speak even distinctly of the *Zachuth of the Mothers*, "If thou seest the *Zachuth* of the Fathers and the *Zachuth* of the Mothers, that they are on the decline, then hope for the grace of God."[3] And it would even seem that they would invoke the *Zachuth* of the Mothers together with the *Zachuth* of the Fathers in their prayers on public fasts prescribed on the occasion of general distress.[4] In connection with the same verse (Lev. 26 42), the Rabbis speak also of the covenant with the Tribes ("the servants of the Lord"), to whom God has also sworn as he did to the patriarchs,

[1] *Berachoth*, 16 *b*. See, however, *D. E. Z.*, ch. 1, where they speak of seven Fathers who entered into a covenant with God. In *Sirach* (heading to c. 44), the expression *Fathers* is even more extensive.

[2] *T. K.*, 112 *c*.

[3] See *Jer. Sanhedrin*, 27 *d*, and *Lev. R.*, 36 6. Cf. commentaries, and see also *Cant. R.*, 2 9.

[4] See Pseudo-Jonathan to Exod. 18 9 and *Mechilta*, 54 *a*. In our liturgy, the invocation to the *Zachuth* of the Mothers is very rare. A *Piyut* (hymn) by R. Gershom b. Judah, recited on the eve of the New Year, has a reference to the covenant of the Mothers.

and whose *Zachuth* Moses is also supposed to have invoked, as he did that of the Fathers.[1]

It is, however, the *Zachuth* of the Fathers which figures most prominently in Rabbinic literature. The thought of the creation of the Fathers preceded the creation of the world.[2] They are the rocks and the hills,[3] but also the foundations of the world, for it is on their *Zachuth* that the world is based.[4] Abraham is the very *petra* on which the Holy One, blessed be he, established the world,[5] as it is said, "For the foundations of the earth are the Lord's" (1 Sam. 2 8), whilst the *Zachuth* of the Fathers is also occasionally called "rock."[6]

It is true that the Fathers are not considered absolutely perfect. They could not, according to some authorities, stand the rebuke (or judgement) of God.[7] And though their position is so exalted that their abode would have been translated into the regions above had they wished it, nevertheless, they did not receive the epithet "Holy" until they died.[8] Yet, in general, they are considered as the greatest and

[1] *T. K.*, 112 *c*; *Exod. R.*, 44 9 and 10. Cf. Isa. 63 17. See also *P. R.*, 191 *a*.

[2] *P. R. E.*, 3. Cf. *Gen. R.*, 1 4.

[3] See *Mechilta*, 54 *a*, and *Sifre*, 140 *a*. Cf. also *Exod. R.*, 28 1.

[4] *Exod. R.*, 15 6.

[5] See *Yalkut* to *Pent.*, § 766, reproduced from the *Yelamdenu*. Cf. above, p. 59.

[6] See *Yalkut* to *Pent.*, § 763, reproduced from the *Yelamdenu*.

[7] See *Arachin*, 16 *a*. [8] *M. T.*, 16 2. See also commentary.

the most weighty among Israel,[1] except the King Messiah, according to certain Rabbis also except Moses.[2] It is because of the *Zachuth* of the Fathers, or the Covenant with the Fathers, that Israel was redeemed from Egypt.[3] That Moses was permitted to ascend Mount Sinai and to mingle there with the celestials and receive the Torah, was also for the sake of the *Zachuth* of the Fathers.[4] When Israel sinned in the desert (by the worshipping of the golden calf), Moses uttered ever so many prayers and supplications and he was not answered. Indeed, his pleading for Israel lasted not less than forty days and forty nights, but all in vain. Yet when he said, "Remember Abraham, Isaac, and Jacob thy servants" (Exod. 32 13), his prayer was heard at once.[5] One Rabbi gets so exalted at the thought of the *Zachuth* of the Fathers that he exclaims to the effect: Blessed are the children whose fathers have a *Zachuth*, because they profit by their *Zachuth;* blessed are Israel who can rely upon the *Zachuth* of Abraham and Isaac and Jacob, it is their *Zachuth* which saved them. It saved them on the occasion of the exodus from Egypt, when they worshipped the golden calf, and in the times of Elijah,

[1] See *Sifre*, 94 *a*.

[2] See *Tan. B.*, 1 70, text and commentary, and *Sifre*, 27 *b*.

[3] See *Exod. R.*, 1 36. See also *Mechilta*, 48 *a*, where the patriarchs are described as sinless. The opinions seem to have been divided. Cf. ספרי דאגדתא, ed. Buber, 25 *a*. See also Nachmanides' commentary to Exod. 12 10.

[4] *Gen. R.*, 28 1 and 2.

[5] *Shabbath*, 42 *a*. Cf. *Exod. R.*, 44 1.

and so in every generation.[1] Indeed, Israel is compared to a vine, because as the vine is itself alive, but is supported by dead wood, so Israel is living and lasting, but is leaning upon the deceased Fathers.[2] It is by reason of this support, that the righteous deeds of the Fathers are remembered before God. "Who was so active before thee (God) as Abraham, the lover of God? Who was so active before thee as Isaac, who allowed himself to be bound upon the altar? Who was so active before thee as Jacob, who was so thankful to God?"[3] Therefore, whenever Israel comes into distress they call into remembrance the deeds of the Fathers.[4]

Besides the *Zachuth* of the Fathers, *κατ' ἐξοχήν* limited to the patriarchs, there is also apparently the *Zachuth* of every man's ancestry. The father, we are taught, transfers (זוכה) to his son the benefits of beauty, strength, wealth and wisdom and (old) age.[5]

[1] *Ag. Ber.*, ch. 10. [2] *Exod. R.*, 44 1. Cf. *Lev. R.*, 36 2.

[3] See *Cant. R.*, 1 4. The special activities here are supplied from *Sifre*, p. 73 *b*.

[4] *Aggadath Shir Hashirim*, p. 14. With regard to the sacrifice of Isaac, playing such an important part in the liturgy, see *Midrashim* to Gen., ch. 22; *P. K.*, 154 *a* and *b*, text and notes, and *P. R.*, 171 *b*, and reference given there. Cf. also *MHG.*, 314 *seq.*, and Beer, *Leben Abrahams*, pp. 57 *seq.*, 175 *seq.*

[5] *Mishnah Eduyoth*, 2 9. Cf. *Tosephta*, *ibid.*, p. 456, and *Tosephta Sanhedrin*, 4 32, and *Jer. Kiddushin*, 61 *a*. See also 63 *c*, and references, and *Tan. B.*, 1 64 *b*. Cf. also *Kinyan Torah; A. R. N.*, 55 *b*, note 11, and 60 *b*, note 24, and Friedmann, נספחים, pp. 19 and 20, text and notes.

Though these benefits are all personal and merely hereditary, it would seem that they were not quite dissociated in the mind of the Rabbis from the notion connected generally with *Zachuth* and its theological possibilities. This is the impression, at least, we receive from the remark of one of the ancient Rabbis, who declares that these benefits cease with the moment man has attained his majority, when he becomes responsible for his conduct, and that it depends upon his own actions whether these benefits should continue or not.[1] In the well-known controversy between the patriarch Rabban Gamaliel the Second and his opponents, the general opinion was that preference should be given to R. Eliezer b. Azariah, above other nominees, because he was a man who enjoyed the *Zachuth* of his fathers, having been a descendant of Ezra.[2] "The son of fathers" (that is, a man of noble descent) was generally respected, though some would place him below the scholar or "the son of the Torah." [3] Indeed, he who had *Zachuth* of his fathers was thought that he could with less risk expose himself to danger than any other man.[4] They were also considered fit to act as the representatives of communities. "Let all men," said a Rabbi, "who are

[1] See *Tosephta Eduyoth*, *ibid.*, and compare Maimonides' commentary to the *Mishnah*, *ibid.* From the references given in *A. R. N.*, *ibid.*, and Friedmann, נספחים, *ibid.*, it is also evident that the transferring of benefits are a special privilege of the righteous. Cf. also the *Responsa of the Geonim*, ed. Harkavy, p. 176.

[2] *Berachoth*, 27 *a*. [3] See *Menachoth*, 53 *a*. [4] See *Shabbath*, 129 *b*.

labouring with a Congregation (that is, leaders of communities occupied in social duties), act with them in the name of heaven, for the *Zachuth* of the fathers sustains them." And the larger the number of these righteous fathers, the more effective is the *Zachuth* by which their children profit.[1]

All these statements, however, with their exaggerating importance of the *Zachuth* of a righteous ancestry, are greatly qualified by another series of Rabbinic statements, reducing the *Zachuth* to small proportions. With regard to the *Zachuth* of the Fathers (or patriarchs), we have the astonishing assertion by the Rabbis that this *Zachuth* was discontinued long ago. The passage in question begins with the words, "When did the *Zachuth* of the Fathers cease?" In a parallel passage, it runs, "How long did the *Zachuth* of the Fathers last?" Various dates are fixed by various Rabbis, but none of them is later than the age of the King Hezekiah. The Scriptural proofs adduced by these Rabbis are not very cogent. The way, however, in which the question is put impresses one with the conviction that this cessation of the *Zachuth* of the Fathers was a generally accepted fact and that the only point in doubt was the exact date when this cessation took place.[2] But when this date was reached, the Holy One, blessed be he, exclaimed, "Until now you possessed the *Zachuth* of the Fathers, but for the

[1] *Aboth*, 2 12. See also *M. T.*, 59 1.

[2] See *Shabbath*, 55 *a*; *Jer. Sanhedrin*, 27 *d*; and *Lev. R.*, 39 6.

future, every one will depend on his own actions. I shall not deal with you as I dealt with Noah (who, according to certain Rabbis, protected with his *Zachuth* his unworthy sons). Fathers will no longer save their children."[1] Of course, Israel need not despair, for when every *Zachuth* of the ancestral piety disappears, Israel can always fall back on the grace of God, never to be removed.[2] Thus on the day when the Holy One, blessed be he, will judge Israel, the latter will look at the Fathers that they should plead for them, but there is no father who can save his son, and no man can save his brother in this distress. Then they will lift up their eyes to their Father in Heaven. In another place, the same thought is expressed to the following effect: Those generations (who passed through distress) will say unto him, "Master of the World, those of yore had the Fathers, whose *Zachuth* stood by them, but we are orphans, having no father, but thou hast written, 'For in thee the fatherless findeth mercy'" (Hosea 14 4).[3] There is however one Rabbi who objects to all the dates given, maintaining that the *Zachuth*

[1] *Ag. Ber.*, ch. 10. The authority of *Ag. Ber.* seems to be an old *Baraitha*. Cf. *Midrash Tannaim*, p. 62, § 9, where it even seems that the *Zachuth* of Noah continued much longer than the *Zachuth* of the Fathers, Israel only living on the *Zachuth* of the commandments. See also *Tan.* ויצא, § 13, with reference to Gen. 31 42, where the remark is made that the *Zachuth* of (honest) handicraft is greater than the *Zachuth* of the Fathers. Cf. *Berachoth*, 8 *a*.

[2] *Lev. R.*, *ibid.* See above, p. 172, note 3, with regard to the *Zachuth* of the Mothers.

[3] See *M. T.*, 121 1; *Ag. Ber.*, ch. 83.

of the Fathers lasts forever, and that Israel can always appeal to it, as it is said, "For the Lord, thy God, is a merciful God; he will not forsake thee, neither destroy thee, nor forget the covenant of thy fathers which he sware unto them" (Deut. 4 31).[1] This, however, is more of an appeal to the covenant with the Fathers than to the *Zachuth*, the covenant being unconditional and everlasting, independent of Israel's actions.[2] "And the truth of God endureth forever" (Ps. 117 2), is the covenant which God has established with the Fathers.[3] This is in accordance with the remark of one of the mediæval commentators of the Talmud, who says, "Though the *Zachuth* of the Fathers has ceased, the covenant of the Fathers never ended." He points to the liturgy where we bring into remembrance the covenant, *not* the *Zachuth*, of the Fathers.[4] Another commentator, again, explains that it is only the very wicked who may not rely any longer

[1] *Jer. Sanhedrin*, 27 *d*. Cf. *Lev. R.*, 39 6.

[2] Remarkable is the expression in the *Mechilta of R. Simon*, p. 94, ברית אבות וזכות בנים.

[3] *M. T.*, 117 2.

[4] See *Tosafoth Shabbath*, 55 *a*. The appeal to the *Zachuth* of the Fathers is hardly represented in the original prayers, except if we take as such the words, "who rememberest the pious deeds of the patriarchs," in the first benediction of the Eighteen Benedictions. These words, however, are omitted in the most ancient versions of the Eighteen Benedictions. To the *covenant* with the Fathers, however, we have a very emphatic appeal in the *Musaf* (Additional) Prayer of the New Year. It is in the later liturgy where the *Zachuth* of the Fathers plays such an important part. See Zunz, *Synagogale Poesie*, p. 455. Cf. Rev. S. Levy's *Original Virtue*, p. 7.

on the *Zachuth* of the Fathers, whilst the righteous still profit by it. He further suggests that together with prayer the *Zachuth* of the Fathers may prove efficacious even now. This opinion receives some support from a statement of an ancient Rabbi, who declares that the *Zachuth* of the Fathers, which was so potent a factor on the occasion of the exodus from Egypt, would have been of little use but for the fact that Israel did repentance in time, since there was against their account also the consideration that they were soon to commit the sin of the golden calf.[1] Generally, it may be stated that the *Zachuth* of the Fathers still retained its hold on Jewish consciousness, at least in its aspect of the covenant, if not directly, as a fountain of grace on which the nation can rely at all times. In fact, the two aspects are sometimes closely combined. Thus we are told that God removes the sin of Israel on account of the *Zachuth* of the conditions (or covenant) which he made with Abraham, their father (between the Pieces).[2] Again, "When Moses the Prophet began to say those words (the Curses of Deut. 28 15-68) . . . the Fathers of the World

[1] See the commentaries to *Lev. R.*, 36 6, and *Exod. R.*, 1 36. Cf. Beer, *Leben Abrahams*, p. 202 *seq.*

[2] See *Cant. R.*, 1 14. Cf. Gen. 15 10. Cf. also *Deut. R.*, 2 23, where the verse to prove the effect of the *Zachuth* of the Fathers upon the redemption is Deut. 4 31, "For the Lord . . . will not . . . forget the covenant of thy fathers which he sware unto them." See also *Deut. R.*, 6 4, where they speak of the *Zachuth* of the Fathers, the covenant and the oaths, which are afterwards reduced to the *Zachuth* of the Fathers alone.

(the patriarchs) lifted their voices from their graves . . . and said, 'Woe to our children when they are guilty, and all these curses come upon them. How will they bear them? Will he make an end of them, as our *Zachuth* will not protect them, and there will be no man who will pray for them?' Then there came a daughter voice from the high heavens, and thus she said, 'Fear not, ye Fathers of the World. Even if the *Zachuth* of the generations should cease, your *Zachuth* will never end, nor will the covenant I made with you be dissolved and (these) will protect them.'"[1]

It was different with the *Zachuth* of the fathers, or ancestral piety in general, where no such covenant exists. Various passages have also been reproduced in proof of the Rabbinic belief in this *Zachuth*.[2] It is hardly necessary to remind one of the Biblical authority for this belief, the very Decalogue containing the words, "For I the Lord thy God am a jealous God, visiting the iniquity of the fathers upon the children unto the third and fourth generations of them that hate me; and showing mercy unto thousands of them that love me, and keep my commandments" (Exod. 20. 5 and 6). Some Rabbis, urging the plural "unto thousands," (meaning at least two thousand), infer from this that the period of grace is to last five hundred times as long as that of punishment,[3] the visiting of iniquity extending only to the third and fourth generations.

[1] *Pseudo-Jonathan*, Deut. 28 15. [2] See above, p. 175 *seq.*
[3] See *Tosefta Sotah*, 298; *Sotah*, 11 *a*. Cf. *Yoma*, 76 *a*.

Other Rabbis explain these words to stand for generations of indefinite number and without end,[1] or, as it is expressed in another place, by the accomplishment of a religious act man acquires merit for himself and for his posterity, "until the end of all generations."[2] But this *Zachuth* experiences many limitations. Thus, with reference to Deut. 7 9, in which the extension of this *Zachuth* is confined to a *thousand* generations, and which the Rabbis took as contradicting the verse just quoted from Exodus (extending it to two thousand generations), the explanation is given that this former verse refers to cases in which those who transfer the merit serve God only through motives of fear; hence, their merit is not so enduring and is subject to limitations in time.[3] The *Zachuth*, thus to have a more lasting effect, has to be acquired by the highest degree of perfection in the service of God, which is that accomplished through the motive of love. But even of more importance are the limitations made on the part of those who are to profit by these merits. We are referring to the emphatic statement of Hillel, who said, "If I am not for myself, who is for me, and being for myself, what am I?" which is explained to mean, "I must work out my own sal-

[1] *Mechilta*, 68 *b*. Cf. also לקח טוב to Deut. 7 9.

[2] *T. K.*, 27 *a*. Cf. also *Yoma*, 87 *a*, where it is stated that both *Zachuth* and guilt have their effect until the end of all generations.

[3] See *Sotah*, 31 *a*. See Rashi's commentary as to the meaning of fear and love.

vation, yet how weak are my unaided efforts!"[1] This interpretation is supported by a paraphrase given of it in an older source, "If I have not acquired merit for myself, who will acquire merit for me, making me worthy of the life of the world to come? I have no father, I have no mother, I have no brother" (upon whose merits I can rely).[2] A similar opinion of the Rabbis is expressed with reference to Deut. 32 39, "Fathers save not their children: Abraham saved not Ishmael, Jacob saved not Esau; brothers save not brothers, . . . Isaac saved not Ishmael, Jacob saved not Esau. All the money in the world established no ransom, as it is said, 'Surely a brother redeemeth not a man, nor giveth to God a ransom for him" (Ps. 49 8).[3] Again, "Let not a man say, my father was a pious man, I shall be saved for his sake. Abraham could not save Ishmael, nor could Jacob save Esau."[4] Indeed, it would seem as if this were a generally accepted axiom, expressed in the words, "A father cannot save the son."[5] In the face of such statements, some of which became almost proverbial, there can be no doubt that the *Zachuth* of the fathers in no way served to silence the conscience of the individual, relieving him from responsibility for his actions. What this *Zachuth*

[1] *Aboth*, I 15. Cf. Taylor on this saying. See also *A. R. N.*, 27 *b*, note 58.

[2] *A. R. N.*, 27 *b*.

[3] See *Sifre*, 139 *b*. Cf. *Targum* to Ps. 49 8 and 10, authorised version. See also *A. R. N.*, *ibid.*, and *Sanhedrin*, 104 *a*.

[4] *M. T.*, 46 2.

[5] *Sanhedrin*, *ibid.*

served mostly to establish was the consciousness of the historic continuity, and to increase the reverence for the past which has thus become both foundation and inspiration. But this very idea brought Israel new duties. "We are thy people," runs an old prayer, "the children of thy covenant, the children of Abraham, thy friend . . . the seed of Isaac . . . the congregation of Jacob, thy first-born son. . . . Therefore it is our duty to thank, praise, and glorify thee, to bless, to sanctify, and to offer praise and thanksgiving unto thy name."[1] And it is in the end the grace of God himself to which the congregation of Israel appeals. The congregation of Israel says to the holy one, blessed be he: We have no salvation but in thee, we hope only in thee.[2] Again, when Israel comes into distress, they say unto the Holy One, blessed be he: Redeem us! but God says unto them: Are there among you righteous and God-fearing men (by whose *Zachuth* they could profit)? They answer: In the former times of our ancestors, the days of Moses, Joshua, David, Samuel, and Solomon, we had (such righteous men), but now, the longer the exile lasts, the darker it becomes. Then God says, "Trust in my Name, and my Name will save you."[3] Again, the congregation of Israel said before the Holy One, blessed be he, "It is not for the sake of our righteousness and the good deeds we possess, that thou wilt

[1] See Singer, p. 8; Baer, p. 45. [2] See *M. T.*, 88 1.
[3] See *M. T.*, 31 1 and references.

save us, but whether to-day or to-morrow, deliver us for the sake of thy righteousness." [1] And indeed, it was for his Name's sake that he redeemed them from Egypt; that he brought them to the Holy Land was also for his Name's sake, not for the sake of Abraham, Isaac, and Jacob; and so will the future redemption from Edom be effected for his Name's sake. [2]

Corresponding to the ancestral piety is the ancestral sin, which is charged, as indicated above, to the account of posterity that it may be made to suffer for it. As in the case of imputed righteousness, so they had also for the belief in imputed sin Biblical authority in the words of the Decalogue, "Visiting the iniquity of the fathers upon the children unto the third and fourth generation of them that hate me" (Exod. 20 5). But it did not escape the Rabbis that this is in contradiction with the verse, "The fathers shall not be put to death for the children, neither shall the children be put to death for the fathers: every man shall be put to death for his own sin" (Deut. 24 16).

[1] *M. T.*, 71 2.

[2] See *M. T.*, 107 1. This is in contradiction to the statement made above, p. 174, that it was the *Zachuth* of the Fathers which was effective at the redemption from Egypt. According to other Rabbis at every redemption both in the past and in the future, various factors come into consideration, among them the *Zachuth* of the Fathers and repentance. See also *M. T.*, 114 5, and references given there, with regard to the *Zachuth* which was effective on the occasion of that redemption. Cf. *Jer. Taanith*, 63 *d*; *M. T.*, 106 9; *Deut. R.*, 2 23; *P. R.*, 184 *b*. The last adds, "It is repentance which causes the mercy of God and the *Zachuth* of the Fathers (to be effective)."

They tried to meet this difficulty by explaining that children are made to suffer for the sins of their fathers only when they perpetuate the wicked deeds of their parents, in which case they are considered as identical with their parents, for whose sins they are thus punished in addition to their own.[1] Rather interesting is the way in which one of the Rabbis puts this contradiction: "When the Holy One, blessed be he, said unto Moses, that he was visiting the sins of the fathers upon the children, Moses answered, 'Master of the world, how many wicked people have begot righteous children? Shall they share in the sins of their parents? Terah worshipped images, and Abraham his son was righteous; Hezekiah was righteous, whilst his father Ahaz was wicked. . . . Is it proper that these righteous sons should be punished for the sins of their fathers?' Thereupon, the Holy One, blessed be he, said unto him, 'Thou hast instructed me well. By thy life, I shall remove my words and will establish thy words,' as it is said, 'Fathers shall not be put to death for their children,' etc. (Deut. 24 16). 'By thy life, I will ascribe (these words) to

[1] See *Onkelos* and *Pseudo-Jonathan* to the verse in Exodus. *Sanhedrin*, 27 *b*. Cf. also *Mechilta*, 78 *b* and 114 *a*, and *P. K.*, 167 *b*, as well as *T. K.*, 112 *b*, with reference to Lev. 26 39. Nachmanides in his commentary to this passage in Exodus explains this contradiction that the visiting of the sins of the fathers takes place only in the case of idolatry, whilst in other sins the suffering or the punishment is confined to the individual who committed the crime. However, he gives no Rabbinical authority for this opinion. Perhaps he was thinking of *Mechilta* 68 *a*, which explains that it is only in the case of idolatry that he is an אל קנא, whilst in the case of other sins he is רחום וחנון.

thy name,' as it is said, 'But the children of the murderers he slew not: according unto that which is written in the book of the law of Moses, wherein the Lord commanded, saying, "The fathers shall not be put to death for the children,"'" etc. (2 Kings 14 6).[1] The same contradiction the Rabbis also saw between Exodus 20 5 and Ezekiel 18 20, "The soul that sinneth, it shall die. The son shall not bear the iniquity of the father, neither shall the father bear the iniquity of the son: the righteousness of the righteous shall be upon him, and the wickedness of the wicked shall be upon him," and tried to reconcile it in the following way: That in the case of a man who is righteous, his wicked posterity is not liable to suffer for their *own* sins so quickly, the punishment being suspended for a time by the merits of their fathers; but in the case that a man is wicked, the visiting of his sins upon his wicked posterity will hasten the judgement of God, so that his children will at once be punished for their *own* evil deeds. In no case, however, will they suffer for the sins of their fathers.[2] Other Rabbis, however, saw in this contradiction a direct prophetic improvement upon the words of the Torah. "Moses said, 'God visits the sins of the fathers upon the children,' but there came Ezekiel and removed it and said, 'The soul that sinneth, it shall die.'"[3]

[1] See *Num. R.*, 19 33. [2] See *Mechilta of R. Simon*, p. 106.

[3] *Makkoth*, 24 *a*. Cf. also *Ag. Ber.*, ch. 10, where it would seem that there was a certain point in history when neither ancestral righteousness nor ancestral wickedness were of any consequence to the children.

The prophetic view is the one generally accepted by the Rabbis.[1] As an exception we may perhaps consider the sin of Adam, causing death and decay to mankind of all generations.[2] When the Holy One, blessed be he, created Adam, the first, he took him around all the trees of the Paradise and he said to him: "See my works, how beautiful and excellent they are. All that I have created I have created for thy sake. Take heed that thou sinnest not and destroy my world. For if thou hast sinned, there is none who can repair it. And not only this, but thou wilt also cause death to that righteous man (Moses). . . ." It is to be compared to a woman with child who was in prison. There she gave birth to a son, whom she brought up within the prison walls before she died. Once the King passed before the door, and the son began crying: "My master, the King! Here was I born, here was

[1] See ספר חסידים, Parma, pp. 32 and 39, for some interesting remarks and fine distinctions on this point. See also Schechter, *Studies in Judaism*, p. 266 *seq.*

[2] See *Eccles. R.*, 7 13, but see also *Gen. R.*, 14 6. Cf. *T. K.*, 27 *a.* Cf. *Num. R.*, 9 49. Cf. *Pugio Fidei*, p. 675 (865), who seems, however, to have tampered with the text. There can be little doubt that the belief in the disastrous effects of the sin of Adam on posterity was not entirely absent in Judaism, though this belief did not hold such a prominent place in the Synagogue as in the Christian Church. It is also thought that in the overwhelming majority of mankind there is enough sin in each individual case to bring about death without the sin of Adam. *See Tan. B.*, 1 11 *a*, and Shabbath 52 *a* and *b*. The doctrine was resumed and developed with great consistency by the Cabalists of the sixteenth century. Cf. also Ginzberg, *Die Haggada bei den Kirchenvätern*, p. 46.

I brought up; for which crime am I placed here?" The King answered, "For the crime of your mother." Likewise there are certain national sins, as, for instance, the sin of the golden calf, in the expiation of which each generation contributes its small share, at least in the coin of suffering.[1]

(2) The *Zachuth* of a Pious Contemporary (and Contemporary Sin). The most important passage to be considered in this connection is that relating to the scale of merit and the scale of guilt. Believing fully in the justice of God, the Rabbis could not but assume that the actions of man form an important factor in the scheme of his salvation, whether for good or for evil. Hence the statement that man is judged in accordance with the majority of his deeds, and the world in general, in accordance with the number of the righteous or wicked men it contains.[2] In accordance with this is the notion of the scale of merit (or *Zachuth*) and the scale of guilt. Assuming a man to be neither particularly righteous nor particularly wicked, and the world in general to consist of an equal number of rightous and wicked men, the fate of the world may be determined by a single action added to the scale which outbalances the other, and so may the fate of the whole world depend on it. "He performed one commandment, and bliss is unto him, for he may by this have inclined the scales (הכריע) both with regard to himself

[1] See *Jer. Taanith*, 68 *c*, and *Sanhedrin*, 102 *a*.

[2] See *Tosephta Kiddushin*, 336. *Kiddushin*, 40 *b*, and *Eccles. R.*, 10 1.

and with regard to the whole world to the side of *Zachuth*. He committed one sin, woe is unto him, for he may by this have inclined the scales both with regard to himself and with regard to the whole world to the side of guilt." [1]

The protective power of the *Zachuth* of the pious contemporary not only turns the scales to the side of *Zachuth* but "even maintains the world that was created by Ten Sayings." [2] The authority for such a belief is given in the well-known dialogue between God and Abraham regarding the absence of the righteous men in Sodom and Gomorrah (Gen. 18 24 *seq.*). And it is with reference to this dialogue that we are told that Abraham received the good message that the world will never be lacking in a certain number of righteous men even like himself, for whose sake the world will endure.[3] This number is differently given in the various sources, ranking between fifty and one. "Even for the sake of one righteous man the world is maintained, as it is said, 'the righteous is the foundation of the world'" (Prov. 10 25). Indeed, every day a daughter-voice comes from Mount Horeb, that says, "The whole world is fed for the sake of my son Chaninah, but he himself lives the whole week on a *Kab* of carobs." [4]

[1] See *Kiddushin*, 40 *b*, and references. [2] See *Aboth*, 5 1.

[3] See *Gen. R.*, 49 3. The number given there is thirty. *Chullin*, 92 *a*, speaks of forty-five. *P. R. E.*, ch. 25, has fifty. Cf. *P. K.*, 88 *a*, and *MHG.*, 278. The statement given in the text is from *Yoma*, 38 *b*.

[4] *Berachoth*, 17 *b*. See also *Tan. B.*, 5 25 *a*. For the contemporary *Zachuth* on a more limited scale, see among others, *Taanith*, 20 *b* and 21 *b*; *Baba Mezia*, 85 *a*; *Sanhedrin*, 114 *a*; and *Chullin*, 86 *a*.

As to the effect of contemporary sin it is hardly necessary to point out that a difference is to be made between the punishment to be decreed by the worldly court and that inflicted by heaven. The court in Rabbinic notion is strictly confined in its dealings to the sinner himself. In the case of Achan, it is even declared against the literal sense of the Scriptures, that his children did not really suffer. According to the Rabbis, they were only made to be present at the execution of their father, in order to come under the deterring effect of the whole procedure.[1] The judgement of heaven, however, makes the community responsible for the sins of the individual. They indeed fall heavily into the scale, but not on the ground of imputation, but by reason of solidarity, which was very strongly felt in the ancient Jewish community. "Israel," an ancient Rabbi expressed himself, "is like one body and one soul. . . . If one of them sinned, they are all of them punished."[2] The great principle was, all Israel are surety one for another.[3] "You are all surety for each other. If there is one righteous man among you, you will all be sustained by his merit, and not only you alone, but also the whole world; and when one sins, the whole generation will be punished."[4] This responsibility affects

[1] See Joshua 7 24 and 25. Cf. *Targum* and commentaries to these verses, and *Sanhedrin*, 44 *a*. Against this is to be noticed *P. R. E.*, 38, text and commentaries.

[2] See *Mechilta of R. Simon*, p. 95. Cf. *Lev. R.*, 4 6. See also Lewy, *Ein Wort über die Mechilta des R. Simon*, p. 25.

[3] See *Sanhedrin*, 27 *b* and references.

[4] *Tan. B.*, 5 25 *a* and references.

the community differently with different sins. In the case of a false oath, not only the transgressor suffers, but also his family as well as the rest of the world are visited by the divine judgement. In lighter sins, the community is only made responsible in the case when they could have protested against the crime to be committed, but failed to do so.[1] The family of the criminal suffers, of course, in a higher degree than strangers.[2] It would seem, further, that, as far at least as the judgement of heaven was concerned, there was a tendency to consider the relatives of a criminal as a sort of accessories to the crime. Thus the question is put with reference to Lev. 20 5, "If he sinned, what crime did his family commit?" The answer given is, "There is no family counting among its members a publican in which they are not all publicans. There is no family counting among its members a highwayman in which they are not all highwaymen."[3] Little children seem to form almost a part of their fathers' selves and suffer on that account for the sins of their parents. They are not included in the classes of children exempt by the law of Lev. 24 16.[4] The elders

[1] See *Shebuoth*, 39 *a*. [2] See *Shebuoth*, 39 *b*. See, however, next note.

[3] See *T. K.*, 91 *c*, *Pseudo-Jonathan* to the verse in Leviticus, and *Shebuoth*, *ibid*. The comment of the *Gemara* seems to labour under the difficulty of reconciling various Rabbinic sayings. More probable it is that this heavy responsibility of the family refers on the whole to the sins of a very serious nature, such as a false oath, the worshipping of Moloch, etc.

[4] See *Sifre*, 124 *a*, and cf. below, p. 175, where the reason is given that they stand surety for their parents. From a Midrash quoted in

and leaders, again, of the community are burdened with a special responsibility, as it is assumed that their protest may, by reason of their authority, prevent crime.[1]

The Scriptural words, "Cursed be he that confirmeth not all the words of this law to do them" (Deut. 27 26), are interpreted to refer to the worldly tribunal which fails in its duty to enforce the law and to protest against crime.[2] Again, with reference to Prov. 6 1, the Rabbis remarked: This verse refers to the student. As long as one is a mere student, he is not concerned in the community and will not be punished for the sin of the latter. But when he is appointed at its head and has put on the gown (a special dress which the Rabbi used to wear in his judicial capacity) . . . the whole burden of the public is upon him. If he sees a man using violence against his neighbour or committing an immoral action and does not protest, he will surely be punished.[3] Indeed, he who has the power of protesting and does not protest, he who has the power to bring Israel back to the good and does not bring them back, is responsible for all the bloodshed in Israel, as though he would have com-

*MHG.*, 4 6, MS., it would still seem that the loss of children is only another kind of punishment of the father. אבל הצלת הקטנים אינה מצלת אלא לאביהן הקרוב בלבד מפני שנתיסר בהן. See also *Midrash Zuta*, 47, that this death or suffering of children for the sin of their fathers is only up to the age of 13. After this age it is for the child's own sin. Cf. also Löw's *Lebensalter*, p. 411.

[1] See *Shabbath*, 55 *a*. Cf. *Tan. B.*, 3 21 *a* and references there.

[2] See *Jer. Sotah*, 21 *d*.

[3] *Exod. R.*, 27 9.

mitted the murder himself. For, as already stated, all Israel are surety one for another. They are to be compared to a company sailing in a ship, of whom one took a drill and began to bore a hole under his seat. When his friends protested, he said, "What does this concern you? Is not this the place assigned to me?" They answered him, "But will not the water come up through this hole and flood the whole vessel?" Likewise the sin of one endangers the whole community.[1]

The community, however, according to the majority of the Rabbis, is not responsible for the sins committed in secret. "When Israel stood on Mount Sinai they all made up one heart to receive the kingdom of heaven in joy, and not only this, they pledged themselves one for the other. When the Holy One, blessed be he, revealed himself to make a covenant with them which should also include the secret things, they said, 'We will make a covenant with thee for the things seen, but not for the things secret, lest one among us commit a sin in secret and the whole community be made responsible.'"[2] This condition of Israel was accepted by God. "Things hidden are revealed to the Lord, our God, and he will punish for them, but things seen are given over to us and to our children forever, to do

[1] See *S. E.*, p. 56. Cf. also *Lev. R.*, 4 6.

[2] *Mechilta*, 66 *b*. The reading there is not quite certain. Cf. commentary. In the text the reading of the *Yalkut* was partly followed. For opposite views, see Friedmann, Introduction to *S. E.*, p. 73, and references given there to *Sanhedrin*, 43 *b*.

judgement concerning them."[1] Quite isolated seems to be the opinion according to which this exemption from mutual responsibility extended after the Revelation on Mount Sinai also to things seen. It is expressed in the following way: From the moment that God gave the Torah, it is only he who sins that will be punished, though before that the whole generation was responsible for the sin of the individual. Thus there were many righteous men swept away with the deluge in the times of Noah.[2] On the other hand, we have also the view that this responsibility extended also to things secret with the moment all Israel passed the Jordan (and established there a proper commonwealth).[3] It was only after the destruction of the Second Temple, when the Sanhedrin gathered in Jabneh, that they were relieved from this responsibility, a voice from heaven proclaiming, "You need not busy yourselves with things hidden;"[4] that is to say, that with the loss of Israel's political independence, and proper jurisdiction of the community over all its members connected with it, the solidarity was also, partially at least, relaxed.

(3) The *Zachuth* of a Pious Posterity, or the sin of a wicked posterity which has a retroactive influence upon their progenitors. With regard to sin there is

[1] See *Pseudo-Jonathan* to Deut. 29 6. [2] *Tan.*, ראה, 3.

[3] See *Sanhedrin*, 43 *b*. The reading is uncertain. See commentaries. Cf. also *Sifre*, 18 *a*; *A. R. N.*, 50 *a* and *b*, and references.

[4] *Jer. Sotah*, 22 *a*.

only a faint trace of such a belief left in the earlier Rabbinic literature. It is with reference to Deut. 21 8, where the statement is made that even the dead are in need of an atonement, but the context shows that such an atonement is only needed in case of murder, which is supposed to have a damaging effect upon the ancestors of the murderer. It is not impossible that this notion was suggested by Ezekiel 18 10, "And if he begat a son that is a robber or a shedder of blood." The murderer is thus born already with the taint of his subsequent sin. But, if the ancestor can be affected by a sin not committed by himself, it is only reasonable that he should secure pardon by an atoning action accomplished by posterity.[1] More ample are the references to the *Zachuth* of a pious posterity. Thus the Holy One, blessed be he, acts kindly with the first (fathers) for the sake of the *Zachuth* of the latter ones (descendants), as was the case with Noah, who was saved for the sake of his children.[2] Abraham, again, became worthy of taking possession of the land for the sake of the *Zachuth* attaching to the commandment of bringing the first sheaf of their harvest, which Israel will accomplish.[3] There was even a saying that a son can make his father acquire a merit,[4] "for so they said,

[1] See *Sifre*, 112 *b* (§ 110), text and commentary, especially note 6. The text is not quite certain. The Halachic point of view of this question is fully treated by Azulai, שער יוסף, p. 54 *seq.*

[2] *Gen. R.*, 29 5.

[3] See *P. K.*, 71 *a*; *Lev. R.*, 28 6.

[4] See *Sanhedrin*, 104 *a*.

Children save their parents from the judgement of Gehenna." And so Solomon said, "Correct thy son and he shall give thee rest; yea, he shall give delight unto thy soul" (Prov. 29 17); that is, he will deliver thee from the judgement in the Gehenna, and will delight thy soul in Paradise with the righteous.[1]

This relief coming from the children is, according to the source of the statement just given, only for four generations, God suspending the judgement of the ancestors till their great-grandchildren are grown up, by whose righteousness they might be relieved. "And so Samuel said to Israel, 'But if ye will not obey the voice of the Lord, but rebel against the commandment of the Lord, then shall the hand of the Lord be against you and against your fathers' (1 Samuel 12 15). Be therefore careful that you do not provoke the wrath of God and receive punishment, so that even your fathers, whose sins were in suspense, who were hoping for your redeeming merits will now be judged according to their deeds."[2] The relief by

[1] *MHG.*, Num. Ms., 81 *a*.

[2] *MHG.*, *ibid.* He derives this doctrine from Exod. 20 5, taking the word פקד in the sense of depositing or entrusting. See *Mechilta of R. Simon*, p. 106, text and notes, and cf. *P.K.*, 167 *a*. This interpretation is preceded by a long argument ascribed to Tannaitic authorities in favour of this doctrine. Cf. *Reshith Chochmah*, Section גדול בנים, ed. Cracow, pp. 332 *b*, 334 *b*, and 375 *a* and *b*, where the contents of these extracts from *MHG.* are to be found, but in a rather corrupt text. Some reminiscence of it is to be found in *Eccles. R.*, 4 1. See also רב פעלים, by R. Abraham of Wilna, p. 34 *b*, and ספר הלקוטים by Grünhut, 3 *a*, seg. Cf. also ספר חסידים, Parma, pp. 76 and 261. See also Rashi and Kimchi to Samuel 12 15.

the posterity is extended from children to the general public, and a principle is laid down that the living redeem the dead,[1] and indeed we find cases in Rabbinical literature where prayers were offered for the benefit of the dead.[2] It does not seem, however, that the doctrine took root in Jewish conscience. The whole of the original liturgy has not a single reference to the dead, nor is there during the first ten centuries of our era to be found a single fixed prayer for the benefit of those departed. The first time we meet with the practical question of the use of offering alms or prayers for the dead is in the *Responsa* of a certain Gaon in the eleventh century, who was asked whether the offerings made for the dead can be of any advantage to them. He seems to have been quite astonished by this question, and confesses his ignorance of such a custom.[3]

[1] See *Tanchuma*, האזינו, I; *Tan. B.*, Introduction, 90 *a*.

[2] See *Gen. R.*, 98 2, and reference given there; *Chagigah*, 15 *b*; *Sotah*, 10 *b*; *Makkoth*, 11 *b*. Cf. also Friedmann's נספחים, p. 23 *seq.*; 2 Maccabees, 13 43 *seq.*

[3] See קבץ על יד of the Mekize Nirdamim, Berlin, 1886, pp. 16 and 17, and cf. *Hechaluz*, 13 93. Cf. also הגיון הנפש by R. Abraham b. Chiya, p. 58 *seq.*, and 32 *a*.

## XIII

# THE LAW OF HOLINESS AND THE LAW OF GOODNESS

HOLINESS is the highest achievement of the Law and the deepest experience as well as realisation of righteousness. It is a composite of various aspects not easily definable, and at times even seemingly contradictory. But diverging as the ideals of holiness may be in their application to practical life, they all originate in the conception of the kingdom, the central idea of Rabbinic theology, and in Israel's consciousness of its close relation to his God, the King.[1] In its broad features holiness is but another word for *Imitatio Dei*, a duty intimately associated with Israel's close contact with God. The most frequent name for God in the Rabbinic literature is "the Holy One," occasionally also "Holiness,"[2] and so Israel is called holy.[3] But the holiness of Israel is dependent on their acting in such a way as to become God-like.[4] "Ye shall be

[1] See above, p. 65 *seq.*

[2] See Blau, *Zur Einleitung*, p. 13; Bacher, *Terminologie*, I 169. See also Friedmann. Introduction to נספחים, p. 20.

[3] See *Tan. B.*, 3 37 *b*; *P.K.* 111 *a*; *S.E.* 133. Cf. also *Shabbath*, 86 *a*, and references given there.

[4] See *Num. R.*, 9 4 and 17 6.

holy, for I the Lord am holy" (Lev. 19 2). These words are explained by the ancient Rabbinic sage Abba Saul to mean "Israel is the *familia* (suite or bodyguard) of the King (God), whence it is incumbent upon them to imitate the King." [1] The same thought is expressed in different words by another Rabbi, who thus paraphrases the verse from Leviticus which has just been cited. "Ye shall be holy, and why? because I am holy, for I have attached you unto me, as it is said, 'For as the girdle cleaves to the loins of a man, so I have caused to cleave unto me the whole house of Israel'" (Jer. 13 11).[2] Another Rabbi remarked, "God said to Israel, Even before I created the world you were sanctified unto me; be ye therefore holy as I am holy;" and he proceeds to say, "The matter is to be compared to a king who sanctified (by wedlock) a woman unto him, and said to her: Since thou art my wife, what is my glory is thy glory, be therefore holy even as I am holy." [3] In other words, Israel having the same relation to God as the *familia* to the king, or as the wife to the husband, or as children to the father,[4] it follows that they should take him as their model, imitating him in holiness.

Before proceeding to some analysis of this *Imitatio Dei*, or holiness, as suggested by the Rabbinic literature,

[1] *T.K.*, 86 *c*. Cf. Bacher, *Ag. Tan.*, 2 367, and Lewy, *Ueber einige Fragmente aus der Mischna des Abba Saul*, p. 23.

[2] *Tan. B.*, 3 37 *b*. Cf. also *P.K.*, 16 *a*.

[3] *Tan. B.*, 3 37 *a*.

[4] See *Lev. R.*, 24 4.

it must be remarked that the Hebrew term *Kedushah* does not quite cover our term *holiness*, the mystical and higher aspect of it being better represented by the Hebrew term *Chasiduth* (saintliness), for which Kedushah is only one of the preparatory virtues;[1] though the two ideas are so naturally allied that they are not always separated in Rabbinical texts. I shall, nevertheless, in the following pages classify my remarks under the two headings of *Kedushah* and *Chasiduth*. The former moves more within the limits of the Law, though occasionally exceeding it, whilst the latter, aspiring to a superior kind of holiness, not only supplements the Law, but also proves a certain corrective to it.

As we have seen, holiness, according to Abba Saul, is identical with Imitation of God. The nature of this imitation is defined by him thus: "*I and he*, that is like unto him (God). As he is merciful and gracious, so be thou (man) merciful and gracious."[2] The Scriptural phrases "walking in the ways of God" (Deut. 11 22), and "being called by the name of God" (Joel 3 5), are again explained to mean, "As God is called merciful and gracious, so be thou merciful and

[1] See *T. B. Abodah Zarah*, 20 *b*, and Rabbinowicz, *Variae Lectiones* to the passages. All the parables, however (given by Bacher in his *Ag. Tan.* 2, p. 496, note 5, to which *Midrash Prov.*, 15, is also to be added), have חסידות close to רוה"ק

[2] *Mechilta*, 37 *a*, and *Shabbath* 133 *b* and parallels. The interpretation of Abba Saul is based on the word ואנוהו in Exod. 15 2, which he divides into אני והו, meaning, "I (man) and he (God)." See also above, pp. 90 and 119.

gracious; as God is called righteous, so be thou righteous; as God is called holy, so be thou holy."[1] Again, as the way of heaven is that he is ever merciful against the wicked and accept their repentance, so be ye merciful against each other. As he bestows gifts on those who know him and those who know him not and deserve not his gifts, so bestow ye gifts upon each other.[2] "The profession of the Holy One, blessed be he, is charity and loving-kindness, and Abraham, who will command his children and his household after him 'that they shall keep the way of the Lord' (Gen. 18 19), is told by God: 'Thou hast chosen my profession; wherefore thou shalt also become like unto me, an ancient of days.'"[3] The imitation receives practical shape in the following passage: "The members of the house of Israel are in duty bound to deal with one another mercifully, to do charity (*Mizwah*), and to practise kindness. For the Holy One, blessed be He, has only created this world with loving-kindness and mercy, and it rests with us to learn from the ways of God." Thus said Rabbi Chama b. Chaninah, ". . . Walk in the attributes of God (or rather make his attributes the rule for thy conduct). As he clothes the naked (Gen. 3 21), so do thou clothe the naked; as he nurses the sick (Gen. 18 1), so do thou nurse the sick; as he comforts the mourners (Gen. 25 11), so do thou comfort the mourners; as he buries the dead

[1] *Sifre*, 85 *a*. It seems that the Rabbis read in Joel יִקָּרֵא.

[2] *S.E.*, p. 135. Cf. *Mechilta*, 59 *a*.

[3] See *Gen. R.*, 58, 9.

(Deut. 34 5), so do thou bury the dead."[1] Again, when R. Judah b. Ilai interrupted his lectures in order to join the bridal procession, he would address his disciples with the words, "My children! rise and show your respect to the bride (by joining the procession), for so we find that the Holy One, blessed be he, acted as best man to Eve."[2] Indeed, it is maintained that God himself observes the commandments, acting in this respect as an example to his children.[3] The imitation is further extended to mere good manners, in which God is also taken as a model. Thus, for instance, we are told by the Rabbis: Let man learn proper behaviour from the Omnipresent, who, though knowing the absence of righteous men from Sodom and Gomorrah, did not interrupt Abraham in his intercession for these cities, but waited until he finished his pleading and even took leave before parting with him.[4]

It is to be remarked that this God-likeness is con-

[1] *Sotah*, 14 *a*. The beginning of the passage is taken from the שאילתות פ׳ בראשית. According to the Agadic explanations Abraham was in an invalid state when God appeared to him in the plains of Mamre. The blessing, again, spoken of in Gen. 25 11, which took place after the death of Abraham, was meant as a message of condolence.

[2] See *A. R. N.*, 10 *a*. The words, "And he brought unto the man" (Gen. 2 23), are understood by the Rabbis that God took particular care to present Eve to Adam in the adorned state of a bride. See *Gen. R.*, [illegible]1.

[3] See *Jer. Bikkurim*, 66 *c*, and *Lev. R.*, 35 8.

[4] See *D. E.*, ch. 5. I supplemented the passage with the parallel in *A. R. N.*, 56 *a*. Cf. also *Gen. R.*, 8 8; *Tan. B.*, I 28 *b*; and *Sukkah*, 30 *a*.

fined to his manifestations of mercy and righteousness, the Rabbis rarely desiring the Jew to take God as a model in his attributes of severity and rigid justice, though the Bible could have furnished them with many instances of this latter kind. Interesting in this connection is the way in which the commandment of the Imitation was codified by some of the later authorities: "The Holy One, blessed be He, ordained that man should cleave to his ways, as it is written, 'Thou shalt fear the Lord thy God, him shalt thou serve, and to him shalt thou cleave' (Deut. 10 19). But how can man cleave to the *Shechinah?* Is it not written, 'For the Lord thy God is a consuming fire, a jealous God'? (Deut. 4 24). But cleave to his ways: as God nurses the sick, so do thou nurse the sick, and so forth."[1] The feature of jealousy is thus quite ignored, whilst the attributes of mercy and graciousness become man's law. Indeed, it is distinctly taught that man should not imitate God in the following four things, which He alone can use as instruments. They are, jealousy (Deut. 6 5), revenge (Ps. 94 1), exaltation (Exod. 15 21, Ps. 93 1), and acting in devious ways.[2] The prophet Elijah, who said, "I have been very jealous for the Lord God of Hosts" (1 Kings 19 10), and even repeated the denunciation of Israel (*ibid.*

[1] R. Eliezer of Metz, ספר יראים, § 3. See also Maimonides, ס'ה'מ, מ'ע ח'.

[2] *MHG.*, p. 549; cf. פרקא דרבינו הקדוש, ed. Schönblum, § 34 in the Five Groups.

v. 14), was, according to the Rabbis, rebuked by God, who answered him, "Thou art always jealous," and was removed from his prophetic office, Elisha being appointed prophet in his stead.[1]

The second or negative aspect of holiness is implied in the Hebrew word *Kedushah*, the original meaning of which seems to be "separation" and "withdrawal." [2] So the Rabbis paraphrase the verse, "Sanctify yourselves, therefore, and be holy, for I am holy" (Lev. 11 44), with the words, "As I am separated, so be ye separated." [3] By the separateness of God is not meant any metaphysical remoteness, but merely aloofness and withdrawal from things impure and defiling, as incompatible with God's holiness, whence Israel should also be removed from everything impure and defiling.

Foremost among the things impure, which range very widely, are: idolatry, adultery, and shedding of blood. To these three cardinal sins the term *Tumah* (defilement) is especially applied.[4] The defiling nature of the second (including all sexual immorality) is particularly dwelt upon in Rabbinic literature. Thus

[1] See *S. E. Z.*, p. 187; and *Yalkut* to *Kings*, § 217. Cf. also *Cant. R.*, 1 6; *Agadath Shir Hashirim*, p. 45. See also above, p. 52.

[2] See Robertson Smith's *Religion of the Semites*, p. 140, about the uncertainty of the original meaning of the word.

[3] *T. K.*, 57 *b*. Cf. *ibid.*, 86 *c*.

[4] See *Moreh Nebuchim*, 3 47. Maimonides' explanation was undoubtedly suggested to him by *T. K.*, 81 *a* (to Lev. 16 16). Cf. below, p. 122 *seq*. See also *Sifre*, 113 *a*, where it is said of the daughters of Israel that they are קדושות וטהורות.

the Rabbis interpret the verse, "And ye shall be unto me a kingdom of priests and a holy nation" (Exod. 19 1), with the words, "Be unto me a kingdom of priests, separated from the nations of the world and their abominations."[1] This passage must be taken in connection with another, in which, with allusion to the scriptural words, "And ye shall be holy unto me . . . and I have severed you from other people that you should be mine" (Lev. 20 26), the Rabbis point to the sexual immorality which divides the heathen from Israel.[2] In fact, all incontinence was called *Tumah* (impurity), indulgence in which disqualifies (or cuts man off from God); God says, "What joy can I have in him?"[3] but he who surrounds himself with a fence against anything unchaste is called holy,[4] and he "who shutteth his eyes from seeing evil (in the sense of immorality) is worthy of receiving the very presence of the *Shechinah*."[5]

The notion of impurity is further extended to all things stigmatised in the Levitical legislation as unclean, particularly to the forbidden foods "which

[1] *Mechilta*, 63 *a*. A few lines before these is given another explanation to the words וגוי קדוש, which was taken by the great master of the Agada, Lector Friedmann, to contain a protest against proselytising. The text, however, seems to be corrupt, and reads in the *MHG.*, יכול מלכים בעלי מלחמה ת״ל כהנים אי כהנים יכול בטלנים כענין שכ׳ ובני דוד כהנים היו ת״ל וגוי קדוש. Cf. *Mechilta of R. Simon*, p. 95.

[2] *T. K.*, 93 *b*. Cf. *Num. R.*, 9 7.

[3] *T. K.*, 86 *d*.

[4] *Lev. R.*, 26 6.

[5] See *Lev. R.*, 23, end.

make the soul abominable," the command being, "Be holy in your body." The observance of these laws the Rabbis seem to consider as a special privilege of Israel, marking the great distinction between them and the "descendants of Noah,"[1] whilst in the transgression of them they saw the open door leading to idolatry; in a word, to a deeper degree of impurity.[2]

The soul is also made abominable — and hence impure — according to the Rabbis, by doing anything which is calculated to provoke disgust, as, for instance, by eating from unclean plates or taking one's food with filthy hands.[3] In fact, to do anything which might have a sickening effect upon others is ranked among the hidden sins which "God shall bring into judgement";[4] but he who is careful to refrain from things filthy and repulsive brings upon himself a particular holiness purifying his soul for the sake of the holy one; as it is said, "Ye shall sanctify yourselves."[5]

[1] See *Exod. R.*, 30 9, and *ibid.*, 31 9. Cf. *Tan. B.*, 3 14 b, and see also *Pseudo-Jonathan* to Lev. 20 7.

[2] This seems to me to be the meaning of the words in *D. E. Z.*, ch. 3, תחלת טומאות פתח לע״ז. See *T. K.*, 57 *b*, ואם טמאים אתם בהם סופכם ליטמא בם and cf. the ראב״ד. The other explanation given there suggests our passage to be a parallel to that quoted in the preceding note from the *D. E. Z.* Perhaps we should read in *T. K.*, סופכם ליטמא בע״ז.

[3] See *T. B. Makkoth*, 16 *b*, and Maimonides, הלכות מאכלות אסורות, § 17, the last five הלכות.

[4] See *T. B. Chagigah*, 5 *a*, the explanation of Rab. to Eccles., 12 14.

[5] Maimonides, *ibid.* Cf. *T. B. Berachoth*, 53 *b*, the last line of the page.

Lastly, we have to record here that view which extends the notion of impurity to every transgression of Biblical law. Every transgression has the effect of stupefying the heart,[1] whilst the observance of the laws in the Torah is productive of an additional holiness.[2] According to this view, all the commandments, negative and affirmative, have to be considered as so many lessons in discipline, which if only as an education in obedience, result in establishing that communion between man and God which is the crowning reward of holiness. Thus the Rabbis say, with allusion to the verse, "That ye may remember and do all my commandments and be holy unto your God" (Num. 15 40), "Heart and eyes are the two middlemen of sin in the body, leading him astray. The matter is to be compared to a man drowning in water, to whom the shipmaster threw out a cord, saying unto him, Hold fast to this cord, for if thou permit it to escape thee, there is no life for thee. Likewise, the Holy One, blessed be he, said to Israel, 'As long as you cling to my laws, you cleave unto the Lord your God (which means life). . . . Be holy, for as long as you fulfil my commandments you

[1] See *T. B. Yoma*, 39 *a*, תני דבי ר שמעאל עבירה, etc. By עבירה in this passage is meant the transgression of any law.

[2] See *Mechilta*, 98 *a*, and *T. K.*, 35 *a*, and 91 *d*, קדושת כל המצות. The *MHG.* also seems to read in *T. K.* (to Lev. 11 44), והתקדשתם זו קדושת מצות; a reading which is confirmed by Maimonides when he says (*Moreh Nebuchim*, 3 33. 47), אמנם אמרו יתעלה והתקדשתם ··· לשון ספרא זו קדושת מצות. Cf. also his ס׳ה׳מ, § 4.

are sanctified, but if you neglect them, you will become profaned.'"[1]

Thus far holiness still moves within the limits of the law, the obedience to which sanctifies man, and the rebellion against which defiles. There is, however, another superior kind of holiness which rises above the Law, and which, as already indicated in the opening remarks of this chapter, should be more correctly termed *Chasiduth* (saintliness). The characteristic of the Chasid, as it is somewhere pointed out, is that he does not wait for a distinct commandment. He endeavours to be pleasant to his Maker, and like a good son studies his father's will, inferring from the explicit wishes of the father the direction in which he is likely to give him joy.[2] Hence the tendency of the Chasid to devote himself with more zeal and self-sacrifice to one law or group of laws than to others; just according to the particular bent of his mind, and the individual conception of the will of his father. Thus Rab Judah perceives the "things of *Chasiduth*" in paying particular attention to the tractate *Nezikin* (Damages), including the laws regarding the returning of lost goods, prohibition of usury, etc., and in avoiding anything which might result in injury to a fellow-man. Rabba again defines *Chasiduth* as carrying out the prescriptions in the tractate of *Aboth;* a tractate, be it observed, in which the ritual element is quite absent, as it is limited

[1] *Num. R.*, 17 *6*. See also above, p. 168.

[2] See Luzzatto, מסילת ישרים, ed. Warsaw, p. 24 *b*.

to the moral sayings and spiritual counsels given by the ancient Jewish authorities. Another (anonymous) author thinks that *Chasiduth* consists in closely observing the laws prescribed in the (liturgical) tractate *Berachoth* (Benedictions), prayer and thanksgiving having been probably the particular passion of this Rabbi.[1]

The principle of *Chasiduth* is perhaps best summarised by the Talmudic formula, "Sanctify thyself even in that which is permitted to thee." [2] R. Eliezer, of Worms, who takes this saying as the motto to one of his chapters on the *Regulations of Chasiduth*, comments upon it to the effect: "Sanctify thyself and thy thoughts, reflect upon the unity (of God, and think of) whom thou art serving, who (it is that) observes thee, who (it is that) knows thy deeds, and who (it is) to whom thou wilt return. . . . Hence be (in ritual questions) stringent with thyself and lenient towards others. . . . The Torah in certain cases made concessions to the weakness of the flesh (hence the law cannot always be taken as the supreme standard of conduct). Take no oath even for the truth. . . . Keep thee from every wicked thing (Deut. 23 11), which means, among others, not to think even of the things impure," etc.[3] Impure thinking was, in the Rabbinic

[1] See *Baba Kama*, 30 *a*, text and commentaries, especially the ר"ן to their corresponding place in the רב אלפס. For the ten things of the *Chasiduth* which Rab is said to have observed (mixture of the ceremonial and moral) see *Sefer Ha-Orah*, ed. Buber, pp. 3 and 4.

[2] See *Sifre*, 95 *a*; *T. B. Jebamoth*, 20 *a*.

[3] See R. Eliezer of Worms, Introduction to the רוקח.

view, the antecedent to impure doing, and the ideal saint was as pure of heart as of hand, acting no impurity and thinking none.

Very expressive is Nachmanides, whose comments on the Rabbinic paraphrase of Lev. 11 44, "As I am separated so be ye separated," are to the following effect: —

According to my opinion, by the Talmudic term פרישות *separateness*, is not meant the abstaining from *Arayoth* (sexual intercourse forbidden in the Bible), but something which gives to those who practise it the name of Perushim. The matter (is thus): The Torah has forbidden *Arayoth* as well as certain kinds of food, but allowed intercourse between man and his wife as well as the eating of meat and the drinking of wine. But even within these limits can the man of (degenerate) appetites be drenched in lusts, become a drunkard and a glutton, as well as use impure language, since there is no (distinct) prohibition against these things in the Torah. A man could thus be the worst libertine with the very license of the Torah. Therefore the Scriptures, after giving the things forbidden absolutely (in detail), concluded with a general law (of holiness), to show that we must also abstain from things superfluous. As for instance, that even permitted sexual intercourse should be submitted to restrictions (of holiness), preserving it against degenerating into mere animal lust; that the drinking of wine should be reduced to a minimum, the Nazir being called holy because he abstains from drink; and that one should guard one's mouth and tongue against being defiled by gluttony and vile language. Man should indeed endeavour to reach a similar degree of holiness to R. Chiya, who never uttered an idle word in his life. The Scriptures warn us to be clean, pure, and separated from the crowd of men who taint themselves with luxuries and ugliness.[1]

It will be observed that this corrective of the Law is not considered by Nachmanides as a new revelation; according to him it is implied in the general scriptural rule of holiness, which, of course, considering the indefinable nature of holiness, can be extended to any length. Nor were the Rabbis conscious of any innovation in or addition to the Torah when they promulgated the principle of sanctifying oneself by refraining from things permitted; a principle which can be and was applied both to matters ritual as well as to morals and conduct.[2] As it would seem, they simply looked upon it as a mere "Fence" (*Geder*) preventing man from breaking through the limits drawn by the Torah itself. Very instructive in this respect is the conversation which the Talmud puts in the mouth of King David and his friend Hushai, the Archite. When David was fleeing before his rebellious son Absalom, he is reported to have been asked by Hushai, "Why hast thou married a cap-

[1] Commentary to the Pentateuch, Lev. 19 2.

[2] See רוקח, *ibid.*, where he deducts from it certain stringent rules, regarding the dietary laws as well as others bearing on conduct.

tured woman?" For, according to Rabbinic legend, Absalom's mother Maacah (2 Sam. 3 3) was a woman taken captive in war. Hushai thus accounted for the misfortune which had befallen David by this unhappy marriage. But David answered him, "Has not the Merciful allowed such a marriage?" (Deut. 21 10-13), whereupon Hushai rejoins, "Why didst thou not study the order of the Scriptures in that place?" In other words, the fact that the regulations regarding the woman taken captive in war are closely followed by the law concerning the stubborn and rebellious son (Deut. 21 18-21), indicates that the Torah, though not absolutely forbidding it, did not wholly approve of such a marriage, but foretold that its offspring was likely to prove a source of misery to his parents.[1] The corrective of the Law, for the neglect of which corrective David is so terribly punished, is thus effected, not by something antagonistic to or outside of it, but by its own proper interpretation and expansion. As another instance of this kind I quote the following, which, rendered in the old Rabbinic style, would run thus: "We have heard that it is written, 'Thou shalt not kill' (Exod. 20 13). We should then think that the prohibition is confined to actual murder. But there are also other kinds of shedding blood, as, for instance, to put a man to shame in public, which causes his blood to leave his face. Hence to cause this feeling is as bad as murder, whence he who is guilty of it loses his share in the world to come.[2] Again,

[1] See *T. B. Sanhedrin*, 107 *a*. [2] See *T. Z. Baba Mezia*, 59 *a*.

we have heard that it is written, 'Thou shalt not commit adultery' (Exod. 20 14). But the phrase in Job (24 15), 'The *eye* also of the adulterer waiteth for twilight,' teaches us that an unchaste look is also to be considered as adultery; and the verse, 'And that ye seek not after your own heart and your own eyes, after which ye used to go a whoring' (Num. 15 39), teaches us that an unchaste look or even an unchaste thought are also to be regarded as adultery." [1]

The law of goodness, closely connected with the law of holiness, is another corrective of the Law. It developed from such general commandments as the one in Deuteronomy, "And thou shalt do that which is right and good in the sight of the Lord" (6 18), which, as Nachmanides aptly remarked, means that the Torah bids man to direct his mind to do what is good and upright in the sight of God, seeing that God loves goodness and uprightness. He proceeds to say, "This is an important point, for it is impossible to refer in the Torah to all the relations between man and his neighbours, and his friends, his business affairs, and to all the improvements bearing upon one's community and one's

[1] See *Lev. R.*, 23 11. Cf. *P. R.*, 124 *b*, text and notes. See also *Mechilta* of R. Simon, 111, ד״א לא תנאף שלא ינאף ··· ולא בעין ולא בלב ומנין שהעין והלב מזנין דכתיב ולא תתורו אחרי לבבכם ואחרי עיניכם. Cf. also New Testament, Matt. 5 21 and 27. I suspect that the expression in the N. T., "Ye have heard," had originally something to do with the Talmudic formula שומע אני ··· ת״ל, or לא שמענו ··· אלא ··· ת״ל, or במשמע ··· ת״ל (see *Mechilta*, 81 *b*, 82 *b*, and 84 *a*). Cf. also below, 224 *seq.*

country." But after the Torah had mentioned many such laws in another place (Lev. 19), it repeats in a general way that man has to do what is good and upright, which includes such things as arbitration (in the case of money litigations) and the not insisting upon the strict law. It further includes certain laws relating to neighbourly considerations as well as to kindly behaviour towards one's fellow-men.[1] Jerusalem indeed was destroyed only because of the sin that they insisted upon the law of the Torah,[2] thereby transgressing the law of goodness. According to others, this precept of not insisting upon the law of the Torah, and acting in a merciful way, is to be derived from Exod. 18 20, where Moses is asked to make Israel acquainted both with the Law and with the (merciful) actions going beyond the Law.[3] As a practical illustration of this law of goodness, we quote here the following case: Rabba Bar bar Chana had a litigation with carriers who broke (during their work) a cask of wine. He then took away their clothes; whereupon they brought to Rab a complaint against him. Rab

[1] See Nachmanides' commentary to Deut. 6 18. Cf. Deut. 12 28 and 14 19. See also *Sifre*, 91 *a* and 94 *a*, on these verses. Cf. also Maimonides, שכנים, 14 8, text and commentaries.

[2] *Baba Meziah*, 13 *b*.

[3] See *Mechilta*, 59 *b*; *Baba Meziah*, 30 *b*; cf. also *Pseudo-Jonathan* to this verse in Exod., where it is emphasised that this merciful treatment beyond the law should extend also to the wicked. דין and לפנים משורת הדין correspond often with מדת הדין and מדת הרחמים, the quality of law or justice and the quality of mercy. See *Jer. Baba Kama*, 6 *c*. Note the use of these terms of men.

said to him, "Give them back their clothes." Rabba then asked, "Is this the law?" He said, "Yes (as it is said, 'Thou mayest walk in the way of the good' [Prov. 2 20])." He gave them back their clothes. The carriers then said, "We are poor men and laboured the whole day, and now we are hungry and have nothing to eat." Rab then said, "Pay them their wages." Whereupon Rabba again asked, "Is this the law?" He said, "Yes (as it is said), 'And keep the path of the righteous' [Prov. *ibid.*]."[1] A not less striking case is the following: The Roman army once besieged the town of Lydda, and insisted upon the delivering up of a certain Ula bar Koseheb, threatening the defenders with the destruction of the place and the massacre of its inhabitants in case of further refusal. R. Joshua ben Levi then exerted his influence with Ula, that he would voluntarily deliver himself to the Romans so that the place might be saved. Thereupon, the prophet Elijah, who often had communion with R. Joshua ben Levi, stopped his visits. After a great deal of penance, which the Rabbi imposed upon himself, Elijah came back and said, "Am I expected to reveal myself to informers?" Whereupon the Rabbi asked, "Have I not acted in accordance with the strict letter of the law?" "But," retorted Elijah, "this is not the law of the saints."[2]

[1] *Baba Meziah*, 83 *a*. See also Rabbinowicz, *Variae Lectiones*, *a.l.*

[2] See *Jer. Terumoth*, 46 *b*. Cf. Schechter, *Studies in Judaism*, Second Series, pp. 116 *seq.* and 166 *seq.*

The crowning reward of *Kedushah*, or rather *Chasiduth*, is, as already indicated, communion with the Holy Spirit, "Chasiduth leading to the Holy Spirit," or, as it is expressed in another place, "Holiness means nothing else than prophecy." [1] This superior holiness, which implies absolute purity both in action and thought, and utter withdrawal from things earthly, begins, as a later mystic rightly points out, with a human effort on the part of man to reach it, and finishes with a gift from heaven bestowed upon man by an act of grace.[2] The Talmud expresses the same thought when we read, "If man sanctifies himself a little, they (in heaven) sanctify him much; if man sanctifies himself below (on earth), they bestow upon him (more) holiness from above." [3] "Everything is in need of help (from heaven)." [4] Even the Torah, which is called pure and holy, has only this sanctifying effect, when man has divested himself from every thought of pride, when he has purified himself from any consideration of gold and silver, when he is indeed quite pure from sin." [5] Only Torah with holiness can bring about communion with God. Thus runs a prayer, or rather prophecy, by an ancient Rabbi: "Learn with

[1] ואת הקדוש והקריב אין קדושה אלא נבואה שנאמר אין קדוש כה׳, *Midrash* in Ms. Cf. also *Monatsschrift*, vol. 50, beginning of p. 410, given from the *Sifre Zuta*.

[2] ענין הקדושה · · · תחלתו השתדלות וסופו מתנה, 36 *a*, מסילת ישרים.

[3] *T. B. Yoma*, 39 *a*.

[4] *Midrash* to Ps. 20. Cf. *Tan.* קדושים, 9.

[5] See *Mechilta of R. Simon*, 98. Cf. above, p. 160.

all thy heart and all thy soul to know my ways, and to watch the gates of my Torah. Preserve my Torah in thy heart, and may my fear be present before thy eyes. Guard thy mouth against all sin, and make thyself holy against all sin and injustice, and I will be with thee."[1] Hence the prayer which so often occurs in the Jewish liturgy, "Sanctify us by thy commandments," for any thought of pride or any worldly consideration is liable to undo the sanctifying effect of the performance of any divine law.

[1] *T. B. Berachoth*, 17 *a*. See also Rabbinowicz, *Variae Lectiones*, to the passage.

## XIV

## SIN AS REBELLION

The teaching of the Rabbis with regard to the doctrines of sin, repentance, and forgiveness is in harmony with their conception of man's duty towards the Law. This duty, as we have seen, is a result of the doctrine of God's Kingship.[1] As a consequence, sin and disobedience are conceived as defiance and rebellion. The root פשע, used in the confession of the High Priest on the Day of Atonement, denoting, according to the Rabbis, the highest degree of sin, is explained by them to mean rebellion, illustrating it by parallel passages in 2 Kings 1 1, 3 4 and 7.[2] The generation of Enosh, the generation of the deluge, and the generation which built the Tower of Babylon are described as *rebels* who transferred the worship of God to idols or to man and thus profaned the Holy Name.[3] The same remark is also made of Nimrod, who made man rebel against God, and of the people of Sodom and Gomorrah. These latter, and the generation of Enosh and the generation of the deluge, as well as the people of Egypt, are further described as those

[1] See above, p. 116. Cf. also *Pseudo-Jonathan*, Exod. 34 7, Lev. 16 21, and Num. 14 18.

[2] *T. K.*, 80 *d*. Cf. Lev. 16 16 and 21.

[3] See *T. K.*, 111 *b*, *Gen. R.*, 23 7 and 26 4.

who caused pains to the Holy One, blessed be he, and spited him by their wicked deeds.[1] As men spiting God, reference is also made to certain kings of Judah, as Ahaz, Amon, and Jehoiakim.[2] In the Halachic literature we meet also with the *spite apostate*, or the apostate out of spite, מומר להכעים, who commits sin, not for the sake of satisfying his appetite, but with the purpose of showing his rebellious spirit.[3]

Closely connected with rebellion is the *porek ol* (פורק עול), that is, he who throws off the yoke of the Omnipresent, or of heaven.[4] The term *porek ol* is differently explained by various Rabbis, meaning according to some, the worshipper of idols,[5] according to others, the man who treats the Torah as antiquated matter and declares its laws as abrogated.[6] The throwing off of the yoke is classed together with the removing of the Covenant made by God with Israel on Mount Sinai,[7] and the uncovering of faces,[8] that is,

[1] *Gen. R.*, 27 2. Cf. also *Sifre*, 136 *a*; *Mechilta*, 35 *b* and 36 *a*; and *Num. R.*, 9 24.

[2] *Sanhedrin*, 103 *b*.

[3] See *Horayoth*, 11 *a*. See also Rabb. Dictionaries.

[4] See *Sifre*, 93 *a*, and *Sanhedrin*, 111 *b*.

[5] See *Sifre*, 31 *b*, with references to Num. 15 22.

[6] See *Jer. Peah*, 16 *b*, and *Jer. Sanhedrin*, 27 *c*. Cf. Friedmann's essay in the *Beth Talmud*, I 331–334.

[7] See *Jer. Peah* and *Sanhedrin* as above; *Sifre*, 31 *b* and 33 *a*. According to others, by this Covenant is meant the Covenant of Abraham; see *Sifre*, 31 *b*, § 111 (to Num. 15 22), and the commentary of R. Hillel, quoted by Friedmann in his Notes (Note 3). Cf. also in Friedmann, *Beth Talmud*, I, p. 334.

[8] See *Sifre*, *ibid.* (to Num. 15 31). Cf. *Mishnah Aboth*, 3 13, and *A. R. N.*, I 41 *b*, text and Note 16 for other parallels. The best Mss.

the treatment of the words of the Torah irreverently or ridiculing them, as Manasseh, the son of Hezekiah, did, when he preached "scandalous homilies, asking 'Could not Moses have written other things than, "And Reuben went in the days of the wheat-harvest," etc. (Gen. 30 14), or "And Lotan's sister was Timna" (Gen. 36 22)'?".[1] To both these classes, according to some Rabbis, the words of the Scriptures refer: "But the soul that does aught presumptuously . . ." or "who hath despised the word of the Lord and has broken His Commandments" (Num. 15 30 and 31).[2]

have not the words שלא כהלכה. Cf. Bacher, *Ag. Tan.*, I 197; *Terminologie*, I 149. See also his *Die Bibelexegese Moses Maimonides*, p. 16, note 4. Cf. also *P. R. E.*, ch. 44, where this explanation of uncovering the faces is used of men in the sense of putting them to shame.

[1] This is the explanation of the *Sifre*, 33 *a* (to Num. 15 30); cf. *Jer. Peah* and *Sanhedrin*, *ibid.* Certain Rabbis of a later date think that the uncoverer of faces is he who denies revelation (cf. *Sanhedrin*, 99 *a*) or "he who transgresses the word of the Torah in public, as the king Jehoiakim the king of Judah and his associates," while in the *Bab. Sanhedrin*, 99 *b*, the phrase is explained to mean he who despises the scholars. Cf. Friedmann, *ibid.*, pp. 334 and 335.

[2] *Sifre*, *ibid.* Cf. *Sanhedrin*, 99 *b*. See also Guttmann, *Monatsschrift*, 42, p. 337 *seq.* He tries to justify the reading שלא כהלכה, explaining it to mean the allegoric interpretation of Scriptures, in opposition to its literal meaning (especially the legal portions), with the intention of abolishing the law. Dr. Guttmann's explanation receives support from the fact that the interpretations of the Rabbis in the *Sifre* in the quoted places are undoubtedly strongly polemical, as may be seen from the following passage, forming a comment on Num. 15 22 and 23: "Where is it to be inferred from that he who believes in the worship of idols is as much as if he denied the Ten Words (the Decalogue)? . . . Where is it further to be inferred from that it is as much as if he would deny all that was commanded to Moses, . . . that

Another expression suggesting rebellion is "stretching the hand into the root." By this is chiefly meant blasphemy and other sins punishable by stoning.[1] Blasphemers are sometimes classified together with those who commit sins in secrecy, and act insolently in public, and those who are men of strife. They will end as Korah and his congregation.[2]

The transgressions of which the most prominent of the rebels (especially the generations of the deluge, and the people of Sodom and Gomorrah) were guilty are the three cardinal sins[3] causing contamination and defilement[4] which the Jew is bound to undergo martyrdom for rather than commit.[5] These three things are:—

*Idolatry.* — "He who worships idols is called 'desolation, abomination, hateful, unclean, and iniqui-

was commanded to the Prophets, . . . that was commanded to the Patriarchs? . . . Thus, the Scripture teaches that he who believes in the worship of idols is as much as if he would deny the Ten Words, the commandments that Moses was commanded, the commandments that the Prophets were commanded, the commandments that the Patriarchs were commanded; and he who denies the worship of idols is as much as if he would confess the whole of the Torah."

[1] See *Jer. Sanhedrin*, 23 *c*.

[2] See *A. R. N.*, 2 85; *D. E.*, ch. 2, and *S. E.*, p. 77. It will be seen from these parallel passages that the reading is doubtful. Interesting is it that in the *S. E.* and *D. E. R.*, the various groups of heavy sinners include both the heretic, the sectarian, and the apostate, as well as those who corner wheat, who lend on usury, and who gamble. Cf. above, p. 113.

[3] See *Gen. R.*, 28 8 and 9; 31 6; 32 41; 41 27. Cf. *A. R. N.* 36 *b seq.*, and *Sanhedrin*, 107 *b* and 109 *a*.

[4] See *T. K.*, 81 *c*, and *Num. R.*, 7, § 10.

[5] See *Sanhedrin*, 74 *a*. Cf. Graetz's *Geschichte d. Juden*, 3, pp. 156 and 431.

tous, and causes five things: the contamination of the land, the profanation of the name of God, the removal of the Shechinah, the delivering of Israel to the sword, and the banishment of them from their land.'"[1] But the three cardinal sins have their appurtenances, of which a few will be given here. Thus, pride is another form of idolatry, and has the same grave results. "Moses was considered worthy to draw near the thick darkness (Exod. 20 21), because of his humility, as it is said, 'The man Moses was very humble' (Num. 12 3). The Scriptures teach that he who is humble will as a result make the Shechinah dwell with man on earth, as it is said, 'For thus said the high and lofty One that inhabiteth eternity, whose name is Holy, "I dwell in the high and holy place with him also that is of a contrite heart and humble spirit"'"[2] (Isa. 57 15). "But he who has a proud heart will bring defilement to the land and cause to remove the Shechinah, to remove as it is said, 'He who has a proud heart and high looks, with him I cannot be together' (Ps. 101 5).[3] Again, he who is proud of heart is called abomination (Prov. 16 5) as the idol is called abomination (Deut. 7 26), but as idolatry causes the defilement of the land and the removal of the Shechinah, so does he who is proud of heart" cause the same things.[4] It is only by forget-

[1] See *Sifre*, 104 *a*, text and Note 7. הסתר פנים=סילוק שכינה. Cf. *Onkelos*, *Deut.* 31 : 18.

[2] In the text are given also citations from Isa. 61 1; 66 2; Ps. 51 19.

[3] The Rabbis interpreted it as if they read אִתּוֹ, "with him," instead of אותו. See *Arachin*, 15 *b*.

[4] *Mechilta*, 72 *a*.

ting God that man's heart can be lifted up by conceit (Deut. 8 14).[1] There is no room for the Divine beside him, the Holy One saying, "He and I cannot dwell in the same place." [2] Something similar is said of the man who is wroth. The very Shechinah is not respected by a man in a violent temper.[3] Indeed, he sets up the strange god which is in himself which he worships.[4]

*Adultery.*—"All forbidden sexual relations are called contamination . . . (*Tumah*). If you pollute yourself by them (God says) you are hewn off (or cut off) from me; what joy have I in you? you have incurred the penalty of extermination.[5] As the idolater, the adulterer (or even the one who does any action which may lead to adultery) is also called desolation, abomination, hateful, unclean, and iniquitous.[6] Again, before they sinned, the Shechinah was dwelling with every one of Israel, as it is said, "The Lord, thy God walketh in the midst of thy camp" (Deut. 23 15), but after they sinned (abandoning themselves to immorality), the Shechinah was removed, as it is said, "that he see no unclean thing in thee, and turn away from this" (Deut. *ibid.*).[7] The sin of adultery further involves the sin of heresy, or that of denying God's knowledge of the secret actions of man. Thus, with reference to Job 24 15,

[1] See *Sotah*, 4 *b*.
[2] *Sotah*, 5 *a*. Cf. also *Berachoth*, 43 *a*.
[3] *Nedarim*, 22 *b*.
[4] *Shabbath*, 105 *b*.
[5] *T. K.*, 86 *d*.
[6] *Sifre*, 115 *b*.
[7] See *Sotah*, 3 *b*; cf. *Sifre*, 120 *b* and 121 *a*; *A. R. N.*, 1, 58 *a*.

the Rabbis paraphrase it in the following way: "The eye also of the adulterer waiteth for the twilight, saying, No Eye (that is, the Eye of the Above) shall see me."[1] For so the adulterer says, no creature knows it. But the eyes of the Holy One, blessed be he, run to and fro through the world. . . . Grave is (the case of) the adulterer, and that of the thief, both causing the removal of the Shechinah. . . . Is not the Holy One, blessed be he, everywhere? Can any one hide himself in secret places that I shall not see him? saith the Lord. Do I not fill heaven and earth? saith the Lord (Jer. 23 24). But the adulterer acts in such a way (as if) he said to God, "Remove thyself for a short while, and make room for me."[2] But adultery includes every unchaste action or unchaste thought, the Biblical prohibitions extending to all kinds of unchastity, whether in action or in thought.[3] Heresy is also considered an unclean thought and comes also under the heading of the commandment, "Then keep thee from every wicked thing" (Deut. 23 10).[4] The *Olah* (burnt-offering), though belonging to the voluntary offerings, is declared to have

[1] See *Num. R.*, 9, 1.

[2] *Tan. B.*, 4 14 *b*, 15 *a*. Cf. Zach. 4 10. Cf. also *Tan. B.*, *ibid.*, 13 *b* and 14 *a*, and *Num. R.*, 9 12; where it is maintained that adultery means a breach of all the Ten Commandments. The breach with the first commandment is proved from *Jeremiah* 5 12.

[3] For references, see above, p. 214, note 1, to which are to be added *Sifre*, 35 *a*; *Berachoth*, 12 *b*. Cf. Maimonides, סה״מ, מל״ת מ״ז.

[4] See *Sifre*, 120 *b*, and *Abodah Zarah*, 20 *b*.

the function of atoning for the (sinful) meditations of the heart, as it is even said of Job: "And (Job) offered burnt-offerings, according to the number of them all: for Job said, It may be that my sons have sinned, and cursed God in their hearts. Thus did Job continually" (Job 1 5).[1] The uttering of obscene words brings distress and death into the world.[2] In fact, he who uses foul language is included among these wicked, of whom it is said, "Behold the day cometh, that shall burn as an oven, and . . . shall burn them up" (Mal. 3 19), whilst he who indulges in impure thought is not admitted into the presence of God.[3]

*Shedding of Blood* also has the effect of contaminating the land and removing the Shechinah, besides that of leading to the destruction of Israel's sanctuary.[4] He who commits murder acts like one who overturns the statue of the king, destroys his image, and mutilates his impress (on the coins). "For in the image of God made he man" (Gen. 9 6).[5] "But he who transgresses a light commandment will end in violating the more heavy one. If he neglected (the injunction of) 'Thou shalt love thy neighbour as thyself' (Lev. 19 18), he will soon transgress the commandment of 'Thou

[1] See *Tan. B.*, 3 9 *a*. See below, p. 300, note 2.

[2] See *Shabbath*, 33 *a*.

[3] See *Niddah*, 13 *b*. Cf. English version, Mal. 4 1. Cf. above, pp. 207 and 214.

[4] *T. K.*, 62 *a*; cf. *Shabbath*, 33 *a*.

[5] See *Mechilta*, 70 *b*. Cf. *Mishnah Sanhedrin*, 4 5, and *Exod. R.*, 30 16.

shalt not hate thy brother in thine heart' (*ibid.*, v. 17), and that of 'Thou shalt not avenge or bear grudge against the children of thy people' (*ibid.*, v. 18), which, terminating in acting against 'And thy brother shall live with thee' (*ibid.*, 25 36), will lead to the shedding of blood."[1] In fact, "wanton hatred" is as great a sin as idolatry, adultery, and shedding of blood, all combined.[2] Likewise the sin of slander and back-biting is even worse than the three cardinal sins,[3] for man would never make these utterances unless he "denied the root"[4] (the existence of God), and they have the effect of removing the Shechinah from the world.[5]

Again, he who robs his neighbour, even if the goods robbed do not amount to more than the value of a Perutah, is as much as if he murdered him.[6] Some Rabbis maintain the sin of the generation of the deluge to have consisted in robbery (גזל), that is, the appropriation of wealth by violence and other unlawful means. "Behold," says Rabbi Jochanan, "how terrible are the effects of robbery, for, though the generation of the deluge transgressed everything, their verdict (of extermination) was not sealed till they stretched forth their hands to acquire wealth by un-

[1] See *T. K.*, 108 *b*; cf. *D. E.*, ch. 11. [2] *Yoma*, 9 *b*.
[3] *M. T.*, 52 2. Cf. also *ibid.*, 39 1, and *Arachin*, 15 *b*.
[4] *Jer. Peah*, 16 *a*. Cf. *M. T.*, 52 2.
[5] *Jer. Peah*, *ibid.*, and *P. K.*, 31 *b*, and *M. T.*, 7 7.
[6] *Baba Kama*, 119 *a*. Cf. *Lev. R.*, 22 16.

lawful means."[1] Again, the prophet Ezekiel in his exhortation (c. 22 3-12) enumerated twenty-four sins, but wound up with the words, "And thou hast greedily gained of thy neighbours by extortion, and hast forgotten me, said the Lord God."[2] Nay, God calls him "wicked" even after he made restitution.[3]

Sacrifices brought by the man who is not quite free from the sin of robbery are rejected. "If thou dost wish to bring an offering, rob no man first, for I, the Lord, love judgement, 'I hate robbery for burnt-offering' (Isa. 61 8). I shall only accept it when thou wilt have cleansed thy hands from plunder."[4] Something similar is said of charity: Here is a man who committed an immoral action, on which he spent his money, but he hardly left the place when a poor man met him and addressed him for alms. This man thinks that God put this poor man in his way with the purpose of making him find pardon through the alms he gave, but the Holy One, blessed be he, says: Wicked man, think not so. The hand which gives alms will not cleanse the other from the evil which it did by paying the wages of sin.[5] Indeed, the prayers of the man whose hands are tainted by robbery are not answered, for his supplication is turbid, being under transgression. Therefore man is bound to

[1] *Sanhedrin*, 108 *a*. Cf. *Tanhuma Noah*, 4.
[2] See *Lev. R.*, 33 3; *MHG.*, p. 143.
[3] *Yalkut* to *Ezekiel*, § 782, reproduced from *Yelamdenu.*
[4] *Tan. B.*, 3 7 *a*.
[5] See *Midrash Prov.*, ch. 11.

cleanse his heart (from every covetousness) before he prays, as it is said, "No robbery in mine hands, and my prayer is clean" (pure) (Job 16 17).[1]

The wrong administration of justice may also be classified under this heading: The Holy One, blessed be he, does not cause his divine presence to rest upon Israel, until the false judges and bad officers shall have disappeared from their midst.[2] "When three establish a court, the Shechinah is with them,"[3] and God says to the judges, "Think not that you are alone, I am sitting with you,"[4] but when they are about to corrupt judgement, that is, to give a false verdict, God removes his Shechinah from among them, as it is said, "For the oppression of the poor, for the sighing of the needy (caused by injustice), now I will rise (to leave the Court), saith the Lord."[5] The same thought is expressed elsewhere as follows: "When the judge sitteth and delivereth just judgement, the Holy One, blessed be he, leaves — if it were possible to say so — the heaven of heavens and makes his Shechinah dwell on his side, as it is said, 'And when the Lord was with the judge' (Judg. 2 18), but when he sees that the judge is a respecter of persons, he removes his Shechinah, and returns to heaven. And the angels say unto him, 'Master of the world, what hast thou done?' (what is the reason for this removal), and he answers, 'I have found that the judge is a respecter of persons,

[1] See *Gen. R.*, 22 8. [2] See *Shabbath*, 139 *a*.
[3] See *Berachoth*, 6 *a*. [4] *M. T.*, 82 1. [5] *M. T.*, 12 2.

and I rose from there.'"[1] For, the respecters of persons are men "who have thrown off the yoke of heaven and loaded themselves with the yoke of men."[2] But it is written, "Ye shall do no unrighteousness in judgement, in meteyard," etc. (Lev. 19 35), which teaches "that he who is occupied in measuring, weighing, performs the function of judge, but if he gave false measure, he is called iniquitous, etc., . . . and causes the Shechinah to be removed from the earth."[3] Israel, indeed, was brought out of the land of Egypt, on the condition that they accept the fulfilment of the commandment relating to just measure, and he who denies this commandment "denies also the exodus from Egypt" (that is, God's special relation to Israel in history).[4]

Something similar is remarked of usury. The Rabbinic interpretation is in reference to the commandment: "Thou shalt not give him thy money upon usury, nor lend him thy victuals for increase. I am the Lord your God which brought you out of the land of Egypt" (Lev. 25 37–38). Whereupon, the Rabbis from the proximity of the two verses infer, "That he who receives upon himself the yoke of the commandment of usury receives upon himself the yoke of heaven, and he who removes the yoke of the commandment of usury removes from himself the yoke of heaven." And they then proceed to comment on the latter verse:

[1] See *Exod. R.*, 30 24.
[2] *Sotah*, 47 *b*.
[3] *T. K.*, 91 *a*.
[4] *T. K.*, *ibid.*

"Upon that condition I brought you forth out of the land of Egypt 'that you will receive upon yourselves the commandment regarding usury.' Because he who confesses this commandment acknowledges the fact of the exodus from Egypt, and he who denies it denies also the fact of the exodus from Egypt."[1] It is evident from this interpretation of the Scriptures that the Rabbis thought that each *Mizwah*, that is, the fulfilment of a commandment, had also a certain doctrinal value, bearing evidence to God's relation to man in general and his historic relation to Israel in particular.

The act of lending upon usury, which is also said to weigh as heavily as murder,[2] was, as it seems, considered as containing also an ironic implication directed by the man of affairs against the man of religion. He thereby declares Moses untrue and his Law false, saying, "If Moses would have known that there was so much profit in it, he would never have written it."[3] Hence to witness a bill in which interest of money is promised, is as much as to give evidence that the lender has denied the God of Israel.[4] It is probably for the same reason that the Rabbis say in another place, "Be careful not to be unmerciful, because he who keeps back his compassion from his neighbour is to be compared to the idolater and to the one who throws off the

[1] *T. K.*, 109 *c*. Cf. *Exod.*, 20 2.

[2] See *Baba Mezia*, 60 *b*. [3] See *Baba Mezia*, 75 *b*.

[4] *Baba Mezia*, 71 *a*. See also *Rashi* to that passage.

yoke of heaven from himself,"[1] since he could not act cruelly without considering the laws commending charity and charitableness impracticable, and devoid of all divine authority. Indeed, the notion is that no man betrays the confidence put in him by his neighbour until he has first denied the root (God); that no man engages in sin until he has first denied him who forbade it.[2]

The three cardinal sins, as well as blasphemy and slander, are called the evil things.[3] An impure thought is also described as evil.[4] All of these cause separation between man and God (as it is said), "Neither shall the evil dwell with thee" (Ps. 5 5). The scoffers, the liars, the hypocrites, are also excluded from the Divine Presence.[5] Every deed, again, implying a certain disrespect for those who deserve to be honoured on the ground of their being the teachers of Israel, as well as the showing impatience with the performance of religious actions, have the effect of the divine presence being removed from Israel.[6] This punishment of separation, as it would seem, is extended to sin in general. "Blessed be the man," says a Jewish teacher, "who is free from transgression, and possesses no sin or fault, but is devoted to good actions, to the study of the Torah, is low of knee (meek) and humble.

[1] *Sifre*, 98 *b*. [2] See *Tosephta Shebuoth*, 4 50. Cf. *T. K.*, 27 *d*.
[3] *Sifre*, 120 *b*. [4] See *Niddah*, 13 *b*.
[5] *Sanhedrin*, 103 *a*. See also above, p. 33 *seq*.
[6] *Berachoth*, 17 *b* and 5 *b*.

The Holy One, blessed be he, says this is the man who dwells in heaven with him" (Isa. 57 15). The wise man said, "Thy deeds will bring thee near, and thy deeds will remove thee." How is this? If a man performed ugly deeds and unworthy actions, his deeds removed him from the Shechinah, as it is said, "But your iniquities have separated between you and your God, and your sins have hid his face from you, that he will not hear" (Isa. 59 2).[1]

From the preceding remarks it is clear that sin is conceived as an act of rebellion, denying the root, that is the existence of God, or his providence, or his authority, indeed, excluding him from the world. This extends also, as we have seen, to a sinful thought, in fact from the moment that a man thinks of sin it is as much as if he would commit treason against God.[2] It is also described as contamination and contaminating. The favourite expression for sin of the *Seder Elijah* is "ugly things and ugly ways." [3] This term is occasionally used also by older Rabbis. "Remove thyself," said "the wise men," in speaking of sin, "from ugliness and from that which is like ugliness." [4] Another similar expression is "dirt." Thus, Abraham is commanded to leave the land of his birth which is "dirtied" by idolatry.[5] The man, again, whose hands are "dirtied"

[1] *S. E.*, p. 104. See above, p. 33.

[2] *Sifre Zuta*, as communicated by *Num. R.* 8 5. Cf. also *Yalkut* to *Pent.* § 701. [3] See Friedmann's Introduction, ch. 10 (p. 105).

[4] *Chullin*, 44 *b*; *A. R. N.*, 5 *a* I, text and note 22.

[5] *MHG.*, p. 201. See also *Aruch Completum*, s.v. מנף.

by robbery is bidden not to pray, or is warned that his prayers will be of no avail.[1] In another passage, the Rabbis speak of the effect of the Day of Atonement, which is to purify Israel who are "dirty" by sin, throughout the whole year.[2] The verse in Proverbs, "As a jewel of gold in a swine's snout, so is a fair woman which is without discretion" (11 22) is illustrated by the Rabbis, "If thou puttest a vessel of gold into the nose of a swine, he will 'dirty' it with mire and refuse;" so is the student of the Torah if he abandon himself to immorality, he makes his Torah "dirty."[3] More frequent, we have the term of putrefaction and offensive smell, in connection with sin. The sin of the golden calf is described as a putrefaction. Song of Songs 1 12, is paraphrased in the Targum as follows: "And whilst their master Moses was still in heaven to receive the two tablets of stone, and the Torah, and the Commandments, there arose the wicked men of that generation and made a calf of gold. . . . And their deeds became putrefied, and their evil fame spread in the world."[4] The expression seems especially connected with rebellion and disobedience. Thus, the parable of a later Rabbi who began a sermon with the words, "And it came to pass, when the flock gave an offensive smell and obeyed not the words of its master, they hated the shep-

[1] *Exod. R.*, 22 3.

[2] See *M. T.*, 15 5. The right reading is from *Yalkut Machiri*, 42 *b*. See also *Tan.* בשלח, 28.

[3] *Yalkut* to *Prov.*, § 14.

[4] *Targum*, Song of Songs, 1 12.

herds and the good leaders, and went away far from them."[1]

Sin is thus a symptom of corruption and decay in the spiritual condition of man. He who committed a transgression is as one who was defiled by touching the corpse of a dead man.[2] The thoroughly wicked man is therefore even in life considered as dead.[3] Nay, the sin becomes also a part of himself and clings to him and appears with him together on the Day of Judgement.[4] The presence of the man of sin has, so to speak, a sickening and offensive effect upon everything pure and holy, so that he has to be removed from its neighbourhood. With reference to the scriptural words, "Ye shall therefore keep all my statutes, and all my judgements, and do them: that the land, whither I bring you to dwell therein, spew you not out" (Lev. 20 22), the Rabbis remark, "The land of Israel (by reason of its holiness) is not as the rest of the world. It cannot tolerate men of transgression. It is to be compared to the son of a King, whom they made to eat food that was coarse (that is, indigestible), which he is compelled (by reason of his delicate constitution) to vomit out."[5] The voice of God, which gave Adam delight and enjoyment, became a terror to him,[6] whilst he lost also his power over the lower creation which before his

[1] *P. R.*, 128 *b*. Cf. also *Aruch Completum*, s.v. סרח.

[2] *M. T.*, 51 2.

[3] *Berachoth*, 18 *a* and *b*.

[4] *Sotah*, 3 *b*.

[5] *T. K.*, 93 *a*.

[6] *P. K.*, 44 *b*, and *P. R.*, 68 *b*; see notes for parallels.

sin stood in awe and fear of him. His very stature was diminished, and instead of longing after, he feared the nearness of the Divine Presence.[1] His face, originally bearing the image of God, became disfigured and hateful.[2] Before Israel sinned (by worshipping the golden calf) their eyes saw the glory of God which was surrounded by (seven) walls of fire, and they feared not, as it is said, "And the sight of the glory of the Lord was like devouring fire on the top of the Mount in the eyes of the children of Israel" (Exod. 24 17); but after they sinned they could not even bear to look at the face of the middleman (Moses), as it is said, "And when Aaron and all the children of Israel saw Moses, behold, the skin of his face shone; and they were afraid to come nigh him" (Exod. 34 30).[3]

As in the Bible, sin is described in Rabbinic literature also as folly. The Rabbinic expression טפש, fool, like the Biblical term כסיל, has the original meaning of being fleshy and fat. They who know not God are טפשים, "fools."[4] By the act of sinning, man becomes a fool,[5] whilst the neglect of the Torah was the cause of Israel's becoming stupid and fools.[6] But more frequent is the expression of שוטים, fools, or שטות, folly. Thus, we read, "he whose heart is arrogant in decision is a fool (שוטה), a wicked man and puffed up in spirit."[7]

[1] *P. K.* and *P. R.*, *ibid.* See also *Eccles. R.*, 8 1.

[2] *P. K.*, 37 *d*; *P. R.*, 62 *a*; and *Gen. R.*, 11 2.

[3] *P. K.* and *P. R.*, *ibid.*

[4] See *Agadath Shir Hashirim*, p. 90.

[5] See *Targum* to 1 Kings 8 47.

[6] *Sifre*, 132 *b*.

[7] *Aboth*, 4 11.

Again, a discussion as to God's suffering the sin of idolatry, considering that he could easily destroy the objects of the heathen's worship, the Rabbis answered, "Shall God cause his world to perish because of the fools (שוטים), who worship also the sun and the moon?"[1] The sin of idolatry is also described as folly. The word שטים in Num. 25 1 is held to indicate that Israel abandoned themselves there to folly (שטות).[2] But it must be remarked that the word שוטה, or שטות, implies also madness. "No man," the Rabbis say, "would ever commit a sin but for the fact that there came unto him a spirit of שטות,"[3] whilst in another place we read that no man abandons himself to immorality if he were in his right sense.[4] Similarly, it is said of the suspected woman, that her fall could only be explained as the effect of madness.[5]

The effects of sin extend even further. It has, apparently, a blighting influence upon the world, under which even the righteous suffer. The light which the Holy One, blessed be he, created on the first day was such that a man could see from one end of the world to the other, but it was concealed because of the sin of Adam; according to others, because of the future corrupt actions of the men of the deluge and of the men of the Tower of Babel.[6] Moses, who before Israel

[1] *Aboaah Zarah,* 54 *b.*
[2] *Bechoroth,* 5 *b*; *Num. R.,* 20 22.
[3] *Sotah,* 3 *a.*
[4] *Num. R.,* 9 6.
[5] *Num. R., ibid.,* reading in Num. 5 12 תשטה instead of תשטה, "she went mad."
[6] *Gen. R.,* 11 2, and *P. R.,* 107 *a.*

sinned could not be approached even by the archangels Michael and Gabriel, is after that in fear of the angels of destruction, Anger and Wrath.[1] Hillel and Samuel Hakaton were both worthy that the divine presence should rest upon them, but they were deprived of this gift because of the unworthiness of the generations in which they lived.[2] In another passage we read that it is sin which made Israel deaf so that they could not hear the words of the Torah, and blind so that they could not see the glory of the Shechinah.[3] The exodus from Babel (in the time of Ezra) was of such importance that such miracles could have been performed for it as at the exodus from Egypt, but sin made such a manifestation of the divine power impossible.[4]

More emphatically this doctrine is taught in the following words: "He who committed one sin, woe is unto him, for he inclined the balance both with regard to himself and with regard to the whole world toward the side of guilt," as it is said, "But one sinner destroys much good" (Eccles. 9 18). Thus by a single sin which man committed he deprived himself and the world from much good.[5] But the most bitter result of sin is that they (the sinners) are, as the Rabbis express it, "weakening the Power of the Above"; that is, that they prevent the channels of

[1] *P. K.*, 45 *a* and 45 *b*; *P. R.*, 69 *a*.
[2] *Sotah*, 48 *b*.
[3] *Ag. Ber.*, ch. 69.
[4] *Berachoth*, 4 *a*.
[5] *Tosephta Kiddushin*, I; Cf. also *Eccles. R.*, 10 1. See also above, p. 191.

grace to flow so freely and fully as intended by the Merciful Father. "As often," says God, "I desired to do good unto you, you weaken the power from above by your sins. . . . You stood at Mount Sinai and said, 'all that the Lord hath said we will do and be obedient' (Exod. 24 7), and I desired to do you good, but you altered your conduct and said to the golden calf, 'These be thy gods, O Israel, which have brought thee out of the land of Egypt' (Exod. 32 8), and thus weakened the Power."[1] In another place, the same thought is expressed in somewhat different language. When Israel accomplishes the will of God, they add Power to Might (גבורה), as it is said, "And now let the power of the Lord increase" (Num. 14 17). According to another Rabbi, this is to be inferred from Ps. 60 14, which he translates, "*In* God we shall make our power."[2] If they act against the will of God (one might almost apply to them), "And they are gone without Power" (Lam. 1 6).

It is in harmony with this conception that the Rabbis exclaim, Woe unto the wicked who turn the attribute of mercy into that of strict judgement! for everywhere the Tetragrammaton is used it implies the attribute of mercy (as we can learn from Exod. 34 6, "The Lord, the Lord God, merciful and gracious"); but the same name of God is used in connection with the destruction of the men of the generation of the deluge, where we

[1] *Sifre*, 136 *b* and 137 *a*.

[2] *P. K.*, 166 *b*. See also above, p. 34.

read, "And God saw the wickedness of man was great in the earth" (Gen. 6 5).[1] In another place we read, "This is what Isaiah said, 'A sinful nation . . . they have forsaken the Lord' (Isa. 1 4), they have made me forsake myself; I am called the 'merciful and gracious,' but through your sins I have been made cruel and I have converted my attribute (of mercy) into that of strict judgement; as it is said, 'The Lord was an enemy' (Lam. 2 5); and so he says also in another place, 'But they rebelled and vexed his Holy Spirit; therefore he was turned to be their enemy'" (Is. 63 10).[2]

It is further to be remarked that this abhorrence of sin is not entirely confined to sins committed wilfully. It extends also to sins committed unintentionally, as it is said, "Also that the soul be without knowledge is not good, and he who is hasty with his feet sinneth" (Prov. 19 2). Again, with reference to Eccles. 12 14, "For God shall bring every work into judgement, with every secret thing, whether it be good or it be evil," a Rabbi exclaimed in tears, "What hope is there for a slave whose master reckons unto him the unintentional sins as the intentional?"[3]

They took it as a sign of carelessness, which might have more serious consequences. "Men," they say, "need not feel distressed on account of an unintentional sin,

[1] *Gen. R.*, 33 8.

[2] *Tan. B.*, 3 55 *a*. Cf. *Yalkut Machiri* to Isaiah, p. 7.

[3] *Tan. B.*, 3 8 *b*. Cf. *Chagigah* 5 *a*. The Rabbis interpret the word נעלם in Eccles. 12 14, that the sin was concealed even from the man who committed it.

except for the reason that a door to sin is thus opened to them, leading both to more unintentional and even intentional sins." [1] They even expressed their wonder that a soul coming from a place of righteousness, free from sin and transgression, shall sin through ignorance. "The soul," they say, "is the child coming from the palace above," knowing all the etiquette of the court, therefore sin should be impossible to it, and if it does sin even through ignorance, it is also considered a transgression.[2] The same thought takes a deeper aspect with the mystics. Thus Nachmanides, in alluding to Lev. 4 2, "If a *soul* shall sin through ignorance," remarks, "Since thought concerns only the soul, and it is the soul which is ignorant, the Scripture mentioned Soul here (in contradistinction to Lev. 1 2, where it speaks of *Man*), and the reason for bringing a sacrifice for the ignorant soul is because all sin leaves a taint in her, causing her to have a blemish, and she will not be worthy to face the Presence of the Maker, but when she is free from all sin." [3] The later mystics dwell on this thought at great length: the soul, they say, is an actual part of the divine, as it is said, "For the Lord's portion, is his people" (which they interpret to mean that his people are a portion of the Lord). Every sin, therefore, taints the divine in man, breaking all communion with heaven.[4]

[1] *Tan. B., ibid.* [2] *Tan. B.*, 3 4 *a* and *b*.
[3] Nachmanides, *Commentary to the Pentateuch.*
[4] See *Reshith Chochmah*, Section יראה, 9 and 10.

## XV

# THE *EVIL YEZER:* THE SOURCE OF REBELLION

SIN being generally conceived as rebellion against the majesty of God, we have now to inquire after the source or instigator of this rebellion. In Rabbinic literature this influence is termed the יצר הרע (*Yezer Hara*). This is usually translated "evil imagination," but the term is so obscure and so variously used as almost to defy any real definition.[1]

The term יצר הרע was probably suggested by Gen. 6 5 and *ibid.* 8 21, where the noun יצר is followed by the predicate רע, *evil.* Deut. 31 21 is also another case in point. After predicting that Israel will turn to strange gods and worship them, and provoke God to break his covenant, the Scriptures proceed to say: "For I know his *Yezer* (יצרו)," etc. It is thus the *Yezer* generally which is represented as something unreliable, and made responsible for Israel's apostasy. And it is in accordance with this notion that Pseudo-Jonathan renders it "their *Evil Yezer,*" though the Hebrew original has not the word רע in this place. A parallel to this we have in Ps. 103 14, "For he knows our

[1] See on this subject Dr. F. C. Porter's article, *The Yeçer Hara*, in *Yale Biblical and Semitic Studies*, 1901, pp. 91–156.

*Yezer*," which the Targum renders, "the *Evil Yezer* that causes to sin."[1] 1 Chron. 28 9 and 29 18, in which the expression יצר מחשבות occurs, are generally understood to mean simply imagination, or desire, whatever the nature of this desire may be, good or evil. But it is to be remarked that the word לבבות in 28 9 is explained by some Rabbis to mean two hearts and two *Yezers:* the bad heart with the *Evil Yezer*, the good heart with the *Good Yezer*.[2]

The more conspicuous figure of the two *Yezers* is that of the *Evil Yezer*, the יצר הרע. Indeed, it is not impossible that the expression *Good Yezer*, as the antithesis of the *Evil Yezer*, is a creation of a later date.[3]

The names applied to the *Evil Yezer* are various and indicative both of his nature and his function. R. Avira, according to others R. Joshua b. Levi, said: "The *Evil Yezer* has seven names. The Holy One, blessed be he, called him *Evil* (Gen. 8 21); Moses called him *uncircumcised* (Deut. 10 16); David called him *unclean* (Ps. 51 12); Solomon called him *fiend* (or *enemy*) (Prov. 15 31); Isaiah called him *stumbling-block* (Isa. 57 14); Ezekiel called him *stone*

[1] See, however, English versions to this verse and Baethgen in his commentary to the Ps., *ibid.*

[2] See *M. T.*, 14 1. Cf. notes for another reading: "These are two hearts: the *Good Yezer* and the *Evil Yezer*." See also below, 255, note 2, and 257, note 2.

[3] See, however, *Mishnah Berachoth*, 9 5; *Sifre*, 73 *a*; *A. R. N.*, 47 *a*; *Berachoth*, 61 *b*; where it is clear that the Tannaim were already acquainted with this expression.

(Ezek. 36 26); Joel called him the *hidden-one* (צפוני) in the heart of man (Joel 2 20).[1]

Other names applied to this *Yezer* are: the *foolish old king* who accompanies man from his earliest youth to his old age, and to whom all the organs of man show obedience;[2] the *spoiler* who spares none, bringing man to fall even at the advanced age of seventy or eighty;[3] and the *malady*.[4] He is also called the *strange god*, to obey whom is as much as to worship idols, and against whom Scripture warns, "There shall be no strange god in thee" (Ps. 81 10), whilst the words, "Neither shalt thou prostrate thyself before a strange god" (Ps., *ibid.*), are taken to mean "appoint not the strange god to rule over thee."[5]

The activity of the *Evil Yezer* is summed up by R. Simon b. Lakish, who said, "Satan and *Yezer* and the Angel of Death are one,"[6] which view is confirmed

[1] *Sukkah*, 52 *a*. Cf. also the כבוד חופה by Horwitz, p. 55, where Ezekiel is cited before Isaiah, thus agreeing with the ancient order of the Prophets given in *Baba Bathra*, 14 *b*. It has also the additional words to "Zephoni": זה יצר הרע שהוא צפון בלבושו את פניו ("The *Evil Yezer* who is hidden when disguising his face"). With reference to the name *stone*, see *Gen. R.*, 89 1, where it would seem the *Evil Yezer* is (with allusion to Job 28 3) identified with "the stone of darkness and the shadow of death."

[2] See *Eccles. R.*, 4 13, and *M. T.*, 9 5 and ref.

[3] See *P. K.*, 80 *b*; *Gen. R.*, 54 1; *M. T.*, 34 2.

[4] See *Lev. R.*, 16 7.

[5] See *Jer. Nedarim*, 41 *b*, and *Shabbath*, 105 *a*.

[6] *Baba Bathra*, 16 *a*. See *Targum* to *Zechariah*, ch. 3, where *Satan* is rendered with חמאה.

by the statement of an earlier anonymous Tannaitic authority: "He cometh down and leadeth astray; he goeth up and worketh up wrath (accuses); he cometh down and taketh away the soul."[1] His rôle as accuser is described in another place with the words, "The *Evil Yezer* persuades man (to sin) in this world, and bears witness against him in the future world;"[2] whilst his function as Angel of Death is expressed in the words, "He accustoms (or entices) man to sin and kills him."[3] Some modification of this thought we may perceive in another statement of R. Simon b. Lakish, who says, "The *Yezer* of man assaults him every day, endeavouring to kill him, and if God would not support him, man could not resist him; as it is said, 'The wicked watcheth the righteous and seeketh to slay him' (Ps. 37 32)."[4]

The identification of the *Evil Yezer* with the Angel of Death is sometimes modified in the sense of the former being the cause of death consequent upon sin rather than of his performing the office of the executioner. This is the impression, at least, one receives from such a passage in the *Mishnah* as the following: "The evil eye (envy), the *Evil Yezer*, and the hatred of one's fellow-creatures put man out of the world."[5] According to an ancient paraphrase of this passage, the rôle of the *Evil Yezer* who accosts man from the very moment of his birth, is of a passive nature, neglecting

[1] *Baba Bathra, ibid.* [2] *Sukkah*, 52 *b.* [3] *Exod. R.*, 30 18.
[4] *Sukkah*, 52 *b.* Cf. also *Kiddushin*, 30 *b.* [5] *Aboth*, 2 16.

to warn him against the dangers following upon the committing of such sins as profaning the Sabbath, the shedding of blood, and the abandoning of oneself to immorality.[1] A close parallel to the passage quoted above, likewise found in the *Mishnah*, is the following saying, in which the same expression is used with regard to the consequence of sin. It reads: "Envy, lust, and conceit put man out of this world."[2] "Lust" here apparently corresponds to *Evil Yezer*, and as the context shows, can only mean that it is the cause of death. In another place, these three evil impulses are said to have incited the serpent to his invidious conversation with Eve, resulting in her transgressing the first commandment given to man and finally in death.[3] The identification in the *Zohar* of Samael with the *Evil Yezer* is probably in some way connected with the given Rabbinic passages,[4] since in another place the tempting serpent is said to have been Samael in disguise, originally a holy angel, but who through his jealousy of man, determined to bring about the latter's fall.[5]

The *Evil Yezer* is also credited with inflicting other kinds of punishment upon man besides death, as, for instance, in the story of the Men of the Great Assembly in their effort to destroy the *Yezer*. When, perceiving

[1] *A. R. N.*, 31 *b*. [2] *Aboth*, 4 28. Cf. *Aboth*, 3 14.

[3] See *P. R. E.*, ch. 13.

[4] See *Zohar*, Gen. 41 *a*. On page 248, *ibid.*, the *Evil Yezer* is identified with the Angel of Destruction אגירימון.

[5] See *P. R. E.*, *ibid.*, and *Pseudo-Jon.*, Gen. 3 6.

the *Evil Yezer*, they exclaimed: "Here is the one who has destroyed the sanctuary, burned the Temple, murdered our saints, and driven Israel from their country." [1]

But it must be noted that in other places it is sin itself that causes death. "See, my children," said the saint R. Chaninah b. Dosa to his disciples, "it is not the ferocious ass that kills, it is sin that kills." [2] Again, with allusion to Prov. 5 22, the Rabbis teach, "As man throws out a net whereby he catches the fish of the sea, so the sins of man become the means of entangling and catching the sinner." [3] It must be further noticed that both the function of the accuser and witness are sometimes ascribed to God himself: "He is God, he is the Maker, he is the Discerner, he is the Judge, he is the Witness, he is the Complainant." [4] Again, with allusion to Mal. 3 5, an ancient Rabbi remarked, "What chances are there for a slave whose master brings him to judgement and is eager to bear witness against him?" [5] In another passage, the function of bearing witness is ascribed to the two angels accompanying man through life, whilst others think that it is the soul of man or his limbs that give evidence. Nay, the very stones of man's abode and the beams in it cry out against man and accuse him, as it is said, "For the stones shall cry out of the wall and the beam out of the timber shall answer it" (Hab. 2 11).[6]

1 *Yoma*, 69 *b*.
2 *Berachoth*, 33 *a*.
3 *Midrash, Prov.*, ch. 5.
4 *Aboth*, 4 29.
5 *Chagigah*, 5 *a*. Cf. *P. K.*, 164 *b*.
6 *Chagigah*, 16 *a*.

Neither the function of bearing witness against man and accusing him, nor that of executing the judgement, can thus be exclusively ascribed to the *Evil Yezer*. His main activity consists in seducing and tempting. His ways are of the insinuating kind, appearing first to the man as a modest traveller (הלך), then as a welcome guest (אורח), and ending in exacting obedience as the master of the house (איש).[1] He shows himself also more as an effeminate being with no capacity for doing harm, but afterwards overwhelms with masculine strength.[2] The snares in which the *Evil Yezer* entangles man are at first sight as insignificant and vain as the thin thread of the cobweb, but take soon the dimensions of the rope, making it impossible for man to free himself from it.[3] In another place this treachery of the *Evil Yezer* is compared with that of the dogs in the city of Rome: they lie down before a baker's shop and simulate sleep; but when the baker in his security allows himself to take a nap, they quickly jump up, snatch away a loaf, and carry it away. The *Evil Yezer* deals with man in the same way, feigning weakness and helplessness, but as soon as man is off his guard, he jumps on him and makes him sin.[4]

The man who is most exposed to the allurements of

[1] *Sukkah*, 52 *a*. Cf. *Gen. R.*, 22 6. [2] *Gen. R.*, *ibid.*

[3] See *Sukkah*, *ibid.*; *Sanhedrin*, 99 *b*. Cf. *Gen. R.*, *ibid.* and Rabb. Dictionaries, s.v. כוביא. *Sifre*, 33 *a*, this simile is made of sin itself.

[4] See *Gen. R.*, 22 6.

the *Evil Yezer* is the vain one. "*Yezer*," the Rabbis say, "does not walk in retired places. He resorts to the middle of the highroads. When he sees a man dyeing his eyebrows, dressing his hair, lifting his heels, he says, 'That is my man!'"[1] Again, when Simon the Just asked a Nazarite of stately appearance, beautiful eyes, and curly hair, "My son, why didst thou choose to have thy beautiful hair destroyed?" (the Nazarite having, according to Num. 6 18, to have his hair shaved when the days of his separation are fulfilled), he answered, "I acted as father's shepherd in my town. Once, I went to fill the casket from the well; but when I saw the image reflected in the water, my *Yezer* grew upon me and sought to turn me out from the world. Then I said to him, 'Thou wicked one! why dost thou pride thyself with a world which is not thine; thou, whose destiny is to become worm and maggots? I take an oath that I will have thee shaved in the service of heaven!'"[2] It is interesting to notice in passing that this instantaneous resistance to the *Evil Yezer* is also recommended in another place. "He that spoils his *Yezer* by tender and considerate treatment (that is, allows him slowly to gain dominion over himself without rebuking him) will end in becoming his slave."[3]

[1] *Gen. R.*, 22 6. Cf. *MHG.*, p. 119, reading מסמסם for ממשמש. Cf. also *Zohar*, I 190 (Gen. 39 12), where the vanity of fine clothes is added.

[2] *Sifre*, 9 *b*; *Nedarim*, 9 *b*; *Num. R.*, 10 7 and references. Cf. also *Yoma*, 35 *b*.

[3] *Gen. R.*, *ibid.* Cf. *Rashi* to Prov. 29 21.

The two great passions which the *Yezer* plays most upon are the passions of idolatry and adultery. The latter is called the יצרא דעבירה, the passion of sin; just as מצוה in many places means charity, so does עבירה in a large number of passages refer to immorality.[1] The passion of idolatry, though once more general and more deeply rooted in the nature of man than any other passion, is stated, however, to have already disappeared from the world through the work of the Men of the Great Assembly who prayed for its extinction.[2]

Of the two passions, it is pointed out that the passion of idolatry was (once) even stronger than that of adultery; the former having such a power over man as to induce him to have his sons and daughters sacrificed to idols. It knows no shame, performing its office both in public and in private, and sparing no class of society, enlisting in its service both small and great, old and young, men and women.[3] It is worth noting that the desire for acquiring wealth is not counted by the Rabbis among the grand passions, though it is stated in another place that it is the sin of dishonesty in money transactions under which the great majority of mankind is labouring. It is there further remarked that the sin of immorality involves only the minority, whilst none escape the sin of slander-

[1] See Levy's Rabb. Dictionary, *s.v.*

[2] See *Yoma*, 69 *b*. See also *Midrash Cant.*, 7 8. Cf. also *Jer. Abodah Zarah*, 40 *c*.

[3] *MHG.*, p. 120.

ing, or at least of invidious talk against their neighbours.[1] Scepticism is another means by which the *Evil Yezer* reaches man. Sometimes he questions the nature of the Deity, ascribing to God corporeal qualities, such as to be in need of food;[2] at others, his attacks are directed against the Biblical precepts relating to the dietary laws, and certain ritual observances known under the name of חוקים (statutes), the reason for which is unknown.[3] The *Yezer* is especially anxious to show him that the ceremonies and the cult of other religions are more beautiful than those of the Jew.[4] Sometimes he even deigns to bring evidence from Scripture, as in the case of Abraham. When Abraham was on his way to Mount Moriah to sacrifice his son Isaac, Satan met him and said, "Old man, where art thou going?" He answered, "I am going to fulfil the will of my Father in Heaven." Then Satan said unto him, "What did he tell thee?" Abraham answered, "To bring my son to him as a burnt-offering." Thereupon Satan said, "That an old man like thee should make such a mistake! His attention was only to lead thee astray and to tire thee! Behold, it is written, 'Whoso sheds man's blood, by man his blood shall be shed' (Gen. 9 6). Thou art the man who bringest mankind under the wings of the Shechinah.

1 *Baba Bathra*, 165 *a*.

2 See *Tan. B.*, 4 48 *b*. See also below, p. 298.

3 See *T. K.*, 86 *a*. See also *P. R.*, 64 *a*, text and notes.

4 *T. K.*, *ibid.*, שלהם נאים משלנו, apparently relating to matters of cult.

If thou wilt sacrifice thy son, they will all leave thee and call thee murderer."[1] The name Satan here is identical with the *Evil Yezer*, who, as in the case of Job, performs the office of the informer against Abraham. *Yezer*, indeed, shows special anxiety for man's duty to his family. Thus when man "loves in his heart" to do a מצוה (give charity), the *Evil Yezer* in him says, "Why should you do a מצוה and diminish thy property? Rather than to give to strangers, give to thy children."[2] Sometimes he appeals to his vanity, telling man, for instance, not to pay a visit of condolence, because he is too great a man.[3] When all fails, he will appeal to the mercy of God, saying to man, "Sin and the Holy One, blessed be he, will forgive thee."[4]

The beginning of the association of the *Evil Yezer* with man is a controverted point among the Rabbis. According to some, the *Evil Yezer* arises with the act of cohabitation. Thus R. Reuben b. Astrobolis expresses himself to the effect: How can man keep aloof from the *Evil Yezer* considering that the very act of generation came through the strength of the *Evil Yezer*, constantly gaining in strength till the time of his birth arrives? The *Evil Yezer* dwells at the opening of his heart.[5] This is in accordance with the view of R.

[1] *MHG.*, pp. 304 and 305. Cf. notes 3 and 4.

[2] *Exod. R.*, 36 3.

[3] *P. R.*, 150 *a*.

[4] *Chagigah*, 16 *a*.

[5] *A. R. N.*, 32 *b*, according to the text given in the Note 22. Cf. *MHG.*, p. 106.

Acha, who, with reference to Ps. 51 7, expressed himself to the effect that in sexual intercourse even the saint of saints cannot well escape a certain taint of sin, the act of cohabitation being performed more with the purpose of satisfying one's animal appetite than with the intention of perpetuating the human species.[1] Very near to this notion, though not quite identical, is that which teaches that the *Evil Yezer* enters into man when he is still in the embryonic state; but this seems to have been an isolated opinion, having been abandoned by the very authorities who taught it first. This can be seen from the following passage, which is to the effect that Antoninus put the question to R. Judah the Saint, "When does the *Evil Yezer* begin his rule over man: from the moment of his formation into bones, muscles, and flesh, or from that of his birth?" R. Judah was inclined to the former view, to which Antoninus objected on the ground that we have no proof of any malign tendency on the part of the embryo. Thereupon R. Judah declared himself in favour of the latter view, and in a public lecture made the statement, "This fact Antoninus taught me, and Scripture is in his support; as it is said, 'At the door (of man's entering the world) the sin lieth.'"[2] Likewise isolated is another opinion, which is to the effect: that the child

[1] *Lev. R.*, 14 5. The sense of the passage is not very clear. See also *Yalkut Machiri. Ps.* to this verse and cf. Bacher, *Ag. Am.*, 3 144.

[2] See *Sanhedrin*, 91 *b*. Cf. *Gen. R.*, 34 6, and *Jer. Berachoth*, 6 *d*. Cf. Löw's *Lebensalter*, p. 64 *seq*.

of six, seven, eight, and nine years sins not; only from the age of ten he begins to grow (or perhaps to magnify, or to cultivate) the *Evil Yezer*.[1] The general notion seems to be the one accepted by R. Judah, which is that the *Evil Yezer* accompanies man from his earliest childhood to his old age, by reason of which he enjoys a priority of not less than thirteen years over the *Good Yezer*, who only makes his appearance at the age of puberty.

It is on account of this seniority that he establishes a certain government over man and is thus called "the old foolish king."[2] It is true that children enjoy a certain immunity from sin, on account of their undeveloped physical condition, so that the Rabbis speak of the breath of the school children, in which there is no (taint of) sin. Indeed, the death of children is mostly explained as an atonement for the sins of their parents or their grown-up contemporaries.[3] Yet, they are, as already indicated, not quite free from the *Evil Yezer*, who, as we have seen, accosts man from his earliest childhood. "Even in his state as minor, man's thoughts are evil."[4] As it would seem,

[1] See *Tan.* בראשית, 7.

[2] See *A. R. N.*, 32 *b*; *Eccles. R.*, 4 13 and 9 15; *Nedarim*, 32 *b*; M., T. 9 5, and *Tan. B.*, I, 102 *a* and *b*. From *Tan. B.*, I 63 *a*, it would seem that it is at the age of fifteen that the effects of the *Evil Yezer* become visible. The reading is, however, not certain. See Note 5, *ibid.*, on the various parallel passages and the different readings.

[3] See *Shabbath*, 119 *b* and 33 *b*. Cf. *Gen. R.*, 58 2 and commentaries. See also above, p. 193, below, p. 311.

[4] *Jer. Berachoth*, 6 *b*.

it is in the aspect of "fool" (stupid and wanting in caution and foresight) that the influence of the *Evil Yezer* makes itself felt in the child. "From the moment man is born, the *Evil Yezer* cleaves to him." And this is illustrated by the following fact: If a man should attempt to bring up an animal to the top of the roof, it will shrink back; but the child has no hesitation in running up, with the result of tumbling down and injuring himself. If he sees a conflagration, he will run to it; if he is near burning coals, he will stretch out his hands to gather them (and be burnt). Why (this audacity and want of caution), if not because of the *Evil Yezer* that was put in him?[1]

The seat both of the *Evil* and the *Good Yezer* is in the heart, the organ to which all the manifestations of reason and emotion are ascribed in Jewish literature.[2]

[1] See *A. R. N.*, 32 *a*, 32 *b*, text and notes.

[2] The importance of this organ in Rabbinic literature will be more clearly seen by the reader through reproducing here the following passage in *Eccles. R.*, I 16, omitting such clauses as seem to be mere repetition, as well as the Scriptural verses cited there in corroboration of each clause. Cf. *P. K.*, 124 *a* and *b*, text and notes: "The heart sees, the heart hears, the heart speaks, the heart walks, the heart falls, the heart stops, the heart rejoices, the heart weeps, the heart is comforted, the heart grieves, the heart is hardened, the heart faints, the heart mourns, the heart is frightened, the heart breaks, the heart is tried, the heart rebels, the heart invents, the heart suspects (or criticises), the heart whispers, the heart thinks, the heart desires, the heart commits adultery, the heart is refreshed, the heart is stolen, the heart is humbled, the heart is persuaded, the heart goes astray, the heart is troubled, the heart is awake, the heart loves, the heart hates, the heart is jealous, the heart is searched, the heart is torn,

It is in this heart, with its manifold functions, that the *Evil Yezer* sets up his throne. The *Evil Yezer* resembles a "fly" (according to others, a "wheat" grain), established between the two openings (valves) of the heart.[1] More minute are the mystics, who describe the heart as having two cavities, the one full of blood, which is the seat of the *Evil Yezer;* the other empty, where the *Good Yezer* dwells.[2] Somewhat different is the statement, "Two reins are in man: the one counsels him for good, the other for evil," and they proceed to say it is evident the former is on the right side, the latter on the left side; as it is said, "The heart of the wise man is on his right, the heart of the fool is on his left" (Eccles. 10 2).[3] The reins in this case seem to have an auxiliary function. "The reins counsel and the heart understands (to decide for action)." It should, however, be noted that in another place, this very verse is

the heart meditates, the heart is like fire, the heart is like stone, the heart repents, the heart is warned, the heart dies, the heart melts, the heart accepts words (of comfort), the heart accepts the fear (of God), the heart gives thanks, the heart covets, the heart is obstinate, the heart is deceitful, the heart is bribed, the heart writes, the heart schemes, the heart receives commandments, the heart does wilfully, the heart makes reparation, the heart is arrogant."

[1] *Berachoth*, 61 *a*. The first view, which is that of Rab, is derived from Eccles. 10 1, "Dead flies cause the precious oil of the apothecary to become stinking and foaming; so doth a little folly, him that is valued for wisdom and honour." The second, ascribed to Samuel, is a play on the word חטאת (Gen. 4 7) = חטה. This latter interpretation is probably connected with the legend maintaining that the Tree of Knowledge grew wheat (*Berachoth*, 40 *a*).

[2] *Zohar*, *Exod.*, 107 *a*.

[3] See *Berachoth*, *ibid.*

interpreted to mean that the wise man's heart on the right is the *Good Yezer*, which is placed on the right of man; and the fool's heart to his left is the *Evil Yezer*, which is placed to his left.[1] We are thus brought to the notion identifying the two *Yezers* with the two hearts, of which the Rabbis speak occasionally. What is the meaning, they say, of the verse, "For the Lord searcheth all the hearts"? (1 Chron. 28 9). These are the two hearts and the two *Yezers:* the bad heart with the *Evil Yezer*, and the good heart with the *Good Yezer.*[2] Indeed, the angels, who have only one heart, are free from the *Evil Yezer*, a blessing to which Israel will attain only in the Messianic times.[3] Therefore, man is bidden not to have two hearts when he prays, one directed to the Holy One, blessed be he, and the other occupied with worldly thoughts; just as the priests are bidden not to have two hearts, one directed to the Holy One, blessed be he, and the other directed to something else, when they are performing their sacrificial rites.[4] Indeed, the pious generation of the prophetess Deborah had only one heart, directed towards their Father in Heaven.[5] The same thought is expressed in different words in another place: Moses

[1] *Num. R.*, 22 9.

[2] See above, p. 243, note 2 and reference there to a differing reading. To this should be added *Midrash Prov.*, 12, where, with reference to Ps. 7 10, it is distinctly remarked, "Has a man two hearts? But by these are meant, the *Good Yezer* and the *Evil Yezer.*"

[3] *Gen. R.*, 48 11.

[4] *Tan.*, חבא, 1 and 2. Cf. *Tan. B.*, 5 23,*b.* [5] *Megillah*, 14 *a.*

said to Israel, "Remove the *Evil Yezer* from your hearts, so that ye may be all in one fear of God and in one counsel to serve before the Omnipresent. As he is alone in this world, so shall your worship of him be only to him (single-hearted)," as it is said, "Circumcise therefore the foreskin of thy heart." [1]

The loose manner in which heart and *Evil Yezer* are interchangeably used in the foregoing passage, suggest the close affinity between the two, as indeed, heart sometimes stands for *Yezer*.[2] "The eyes and the heart are the agents of sin," but as it is pointed out by an ancient Rabbi, the first impulse comes from the heart, the eyes following the heart.[3] There is a clean heart for which the Psalmist prays (51 12), and there is the contaminated heart to which the *Evil Yezer* owes the name of "unclean." [4] Again, it is the heart that brings the righteous to Paradise, it is the heart that hurls down the wicked to Hell, as it is said, "Behold, my servants shall sing for joy of *heart*, but ye shall cry for sorrow of *heart*" (Is. 65 14).[5] We must, however, not press this point too much so as to identify the heart with the *Evil Yezer*, for not only have the Rabbis, as we have

[1] *T. K.*, 33 *d*. See above, 160.

[2] See *Sukkah*, 52 *a* (heart of stone), and cf. above, 243. In *Pseudo-Jonathan* the לב is in most cases rendered with יצרא. Cf. Exod. 4 21; 7 3; 13 and 14; 8 15. 28; 9 7. 34; 10 1. 20. 27; 11 10. Deut. 5 26; 11 16; 29 25; 30 6.

[3] See *Jer. Berachoth*, 3 *c*; *Sifre*, 35 *a*, and *Num. R.*, 17 6.

[4] See above, p. 243, and reference given there to *Sukkah*, 52 *a*.

[5] *M. T.*, 119 6 (146 *b*).

seen, assigned to it the seat of the *Good Yezer*, but they have even declared it as the abode of wisdom.[1] The good heart, again, is the most desired possession.[2] In the later literature, the heart is described as outweighing all the other organs of man, hatred and love having their seat in the heart; as it is said, "Thou shalt not hate thy brother in thine heart" (Lev. 19 17), whilst it is also said, "And thou shalt love the Lord, thy God, with all thy heart" (Deut. 6 5).[3] It is also maintained that the heart is purer than anything else, and that everything good proceeds from it.[4] All that the heart is accused of is inconsistency. God says, "Two hundred and forty-eight organs have I created in man; all of these keep in the same manner as I have created them, except the heart;" (and) so said Jeremiah, "The heart changeth from moment to moment. It alters itself and perverts itself."[5] These changes apparently depend upon the nature of the tenant who gets possession of the heart. "As often as the words of the Torah appear and find the chambers of the heart free, they enter and dwell therein. The *Evil Yezer* has no dominion over these, and no man can remove them."[6]

The heart is thus not in itself corrupt; at least, not more corrupt than any other organ. Indeed, when

[1] *Midrash Prov.*, ch. 1.
[2] See *Aboth*, II 9.
[3] אותיות דר״ע אות ל״.
[4] *Zohar, Num.*, 225 *a*.
[5] See *Ag. Ber.*, ch. 2. Cf. Jeremiah, 17 19.
[6] *A. R. N.*, 15 *b*; *Midrash Prov.*, ch. 24.

man is under the incitement of sin, all his members are obedient to the *Evil Yezer*, who is king over man's two hundred and forty-eight members; whilst when he makes an effort to perform good work, they all show laziness and reluctance.[1] Again, when the *Evil Yezer* lays siege to man, it is all the members, not the heart in particular, that act as auxiliaries.[2] It is only because of the heart's various functions, as pointed out above, that it is more often liable to be enlisted in the service of the *Evil Yezer* than any other organ, and therefore more blamed than any other part of the human body, but not on account of a special depravity attaching to it. As a matter of fact, the heart in this respect is only synonymous with soul in the Bible, where it is the נפש which commits sin, and even the Rabbis occasionally speak of the "soul of man," with its greed after wealth (even when acquired by dishonest means) and its tendency towards lust.[3] Indeed, according to the Rabbis, Scripture is astonished that the soul coming from a place where there is no sin should sin, but nevertheless, the fact is accepted that it shares in sin as much as the body, though the body comes from a village and the soul comes from the court and is well acquainted with the etiquette of the court. But it is this very fact which makes this sin of the soul less excusable; and the Holy One, blessed be he, says

[1] *A. R. N.*, 32 *a*; *MHG.*, p. 109.
[2] *Nedarim*, 32 *b*.
[3] *Mishnah Makkoth*, end. See also *Sifre*, 125 *a*.

to the soul, "All that I have produced in the first six days of creation I have produced for thy sake, but thou didst rob, sin and commit violence. . . ." "But it is impossible for the body to be without the soul, and if there is no soul there is no body, and if there is no body there is no soul; they sin together; (hence) 'the soul that sinneth, it shall die' (Ezekiel 18 20)."[1]

The passages indicating a tendency to identify the heart (or the soul) with the *Evil Yezer* have further to be qualified by other Rabbinic statements looking for the source of sin to some force outside of man. For

[1] See *Tan. B.*, 3 4 a and b, and *Eccles. R.*, 6 6. The simile of the villager and the courtier will be better understood by the following Rabbinic passages, on which it was probably based: *Mechilta* 36 *b* and *Mechilta of R. Simon*, p. 59, where Antoninus asks Rabbi, "Considering that the man is dead and the body in a state of decay, whom does God bring to judgement?" Whereupon Rabbi answered him, "*Before thou asketh me about the body which is impure, ask me about the soul which is pure.*" This is followed by the well-known parable of the blind and the lame, who robbed the garden of the king, etc. "Pure" and "impure" apparently stand here for lasting and decaying. It should be remarked that the words in italics are missing in the parables of *Sanhedrin*, 91 *a*; *Lev. R.*, 4 5; *Tan. B.*, 3 4 b, and *Tan.* ויקרא 6. In *Sifre*, 132 *a*, man is defined as the only creature whose soul is from heaven and his body from the earth. If he obeyed the Torah and performed the will of his father in heaven, he is like one of the creatures above; if he did not obey the Torah and the will of his father in heaven, he is like one of the creatures below. Closely corresponding with it is the passage in *Gen. R.*, 8 11, where also man is described as a combination of those above (angels) and those below (animals). See also *Gen. R.*, 14 2 and 27 4; *Chagigah*, 16 *a*; and *A. R. N.*, 55 *a*, text and notes. See also *Tan. B.*, 1 15 *b*. Cf. also above, 81 and 241, and below, 285.

apart from what we may call the mythological view, identifying the *Evil Yezer* with the serpent, or Samael, and of which some other names of the *Evil Yezer* in Rabbinic literature are to be considered as reminiscent at least,[1] the comparison of the *Yezer's* visitations to man with the passing traveller and other similar passages[2] point also to the fact that the Rabbis did not entirely view man in the light of a corrupt being. We have further to note that the *Evil Yezer* is, as indicated above, more conspicuous in the Jewish literature than the *Good Yezer*, whilst by *Yezer*, without any further specification, is often meant the *Evil Yezer*.[3] This would suggest that there is in fact only one *Yezer*, the *Evil Yezer*, and we may further conclude that it is man himself, by his natural tendency, that represents the *Good Yezer*. Accordingly, when he commits evil, he acts under certain impulses not exactly identical with his own natural self. The Rabbis further speak of the *leaven in the dough*, preventing man from doing his (God's) will.[4] This metaphor is taken by some as indicating some inner physical defect in human nature, but in another place forming a parallel passage to the one just quoted, the leaven in the dough appears together with the subjection to foreign governments that make compliance with God's

[1] See above, p. 243.

[2] See above, p. 248.

[3] See *e.g.* *Sukkah*, 52 *b*; *Gen. R.*, 59 6; *Aboth*, I 4; *Sifre*, 74 *a*; *Targum* to Ps. 4 6.

[4] *Jer. Berachoth*, 7 *d*. See below, p. 265, where the passage is given.

will hard, if not impossible.[1] It is thus a certain quasi-external agency which is made responsible for sin, whilst man himself, by his spontaneous nature, is only too anxious to live in accordance with God's commandments.

[1] *Berachoth*, 17 *a*.

# XVI

## MAN'S VICTORY BY THE GRACE OF GOD, OVER THE *EVIL YEZER* CREATED BY GOD

THE opinions recorded in the preceding chapter, some of which suggest the placing of the *Evil Yezer* outside of man, and the further fact that he is described as the source of rebellion, must, however, not be pressed to such an extent as to give the *Evil Yezer* an independent existence, representing a power at warfare with God. As is so often the case in Jewish theology, the Rabbis, consciously or unconsciously, managed to steer between the dangerous courses, never allowing the one aspect of a doctrine to assume such proportions as to obscure all other aspects. First, it must be noted that the *Evil Yezer*, whatever its nature, is, as is everything else in the universe, a creature of God. Thus with reference to Gen. 2 7, a Rabbi interprets the fact of the word וייצר being written with two *Yods* to indicate that God created man with two *Yezers:* the *Good Yezer* and the *Evil Yezer*.[1] For "God hath also set the one against the other" (Eccles.

[1] *Gen. R.*, 14 7; *Berachoth*, 61 *a* and references. Cf. also *Pseudo-Jonathan*, Gen. 2 14. Cf. also below, p. 313, the quotation given there from *M. T.*, 32 4.

7:14), which verse Rabbi Akiba explains to mean that God created the righteous and God created the wicked.[1] In a later semi-mystical Midrash, the same thought is repeated, "God created the world in pairs, the one in contrast to the other," as life and death, peace and strife, riches and poverty, wisdom and folly, the righteous and the wicked.[2] This thought was so familiar to the people that the Rabbis tell a story of one of their colleagues who overheard a young girl praying thus: "Lord of the universe! Thou hast created paradise, thou hast created hell, thou hast created the righteous, thou hast created the wicked. May it be thy will that the sons of men should not be ensnared by me!" that is, that she might not prove the opportunity for the wicked.[3]

We have already referred to the metaphor of the *leaven in the dough* as applied to the *Evil Yezer*. The metaphor occurs in a Rabbinic prayer running thus: "May it be thy will, O my God, and the God of my fathers, that thou breakest the yoke of the *Evil Yezer* and removest him from our hearts; for, thou hast created us to do thy will, and we are in duty bound to do thy will. Thou art desirous and we are desirous. But who prevents it? The leaven in the dough. It is revealed and it is known before thee that we have not the strength to resist him; but may it be thy will,

[1] *Chagigah*, 15 *a*. [2] See *Midrash Temurah*.

[3] See *Sotah*, 22 *a*. Cf. Edeles. The parallel, however, in *Baba Bathra*, 16 *a* (cf. below, p. 273), shows that by creation of the wicked is meant creation of *Evil Yezer*.

O Lord my God, and the God of my fathers, that thou wilt remove him from us, subject him, so that we may do thy will as our will, with a perfect heart." But this leaven is a creation of God, which fact called forth the remark (with reference to Gen. 8 21), "How wretched must the leaven be, that he who has created it bears witness" (that it is bad)! [1] More emphatically the same thought is expressed in another place with reference to Gen. 6 6. The Holy One, blessed be he, said, "It is I who put the leaven in the dough; but for the *Evil Yezer* which I have created in him, he (man) would have committed no wrong." [2]

But the leaven, evil as it is, has, according to the Rabbis, its good purpose and its proper place in the universe, as anything created by God, indeed, cannot be entirely evil. Thus, the Scriptural words, "And God saw everything that he had made and behold, it was very good" (Gen. 1 31), are explained among other things to refer to the *Evil Yezer;* whereupon the question is put, "Indeed, can the *Evil Yezer* be considered as very good?" The answer given is that but for the *Evil Yezer* a man would neither build a house, nor marry

[1] See *Jer. Berachoth*, 7 *d*; *Gen. R.*, 34 10. Cf. ר׳ד׳ל, note 12. Cf. above, p. 145, note 6. It should be noticed that *Gen. R.*, 34 10, has also one opinion to the effect: "How poor must the dough be, that the baker bears witness against it." This would, acccording to some commentators, include the whole of man and the condemnation of his all being bad, but this opinion seems to be isolated, and is not reproduced in the parallel passages, such as the *MHG.*, p. 132, and *Tan. B.*, 1 15 *b*, which has also שאור רע.

[2] See *MHG.*, p. 132. Cf. *Gen. R.*, 27 4, and *T. B.*, 1 15 *b*.

a wife, nor beget children, nor engage in commerce. As further proof of this is given the verse, "Again I considered all travail, and every right work, that for this a man is envied of his neighbour" (Eccles. 4 4).[1] Envy itself, which is one of the ugliest qualities, can thus be made serviceable for a good purpose. This corresponds with another statement, according to which the three things upon which the world is based are: envy, lust, and mercy. In another version the same statement is paraphrased in the following way: "Three good qualities, the Holy One, blessed be he, created in this world, namely, the *Evil Yezer*, *Envy*, and *Mercy*."[2] The *Evil Yezer* has thus little in common with the evil principle of theology, but is reduced to certain passions without which neither the propagation of species nor the building up of the proper civilisation would be thinkable. They only become evil by the improper use man makes of them. It is probably in this sense that the *Evil Yezer* is called once the servant of man. "The Holy One, blessed be he, said: 'See what this wicked people do. When I created them I gave to each of them two servants, the one good and the other evil. But they forsook the good servant and associated with the evil one.'"[3] But even the *Evil Yezer* in his aspect of

[1] *Gen. R.*, 9 7. Cf. also *Eccles. R.*, 3 11.

[2] *A. R. N.*, 9 *a*, text and note 9.

[3] *Ag. Ber.*, 1 4. Cf. *Tan. B.*, 1 13 *a*. The latter reads, "Two creations I made in man: the *Good Yezer* and the *Evil Yezer*." But a comparison of the two texts shows that in this case the *Ag. Ber.* pre-

adversary and enemy of man, as his identification with Satan suggests, is not supposed to be entirely evil. Thus Satan is said to have had godly intentions in his denunciation of Job. His purpose was that the merit of Abraham should not be entirely obscured by that of Job. Satan proved himself so grateful for this appreciation of his nature, that he is reported to have kissed the Rabbi on his knees, who thus interpreted his intentions in this generous way.[1] One Rabbi went even so far as to make man responsible for the wickedness of *Yezer*. This opinion is expressed in connection with the verse, "Lo, this only have I found, that God hath made man upright" (Eccles. 7 29), on which the Rabbi remarked: The Holy One, blessed be he, who is called righteous and upright and created man in his image, did this only with the intention that man should be as righteous and upright as he himself. If man will argue, why did he then create the *Evil Yezer* of whom it is written that he is evil from the very youth of man? If God described him as evil, who then could make him good? God's answer is, "Thou (man) hast made him bad." As a proof is given that

served the better reading. Cf. also *S. E. Z.*, p. 176, about the two angels or three, and יפה תואר to *Gen. R.*, 34 10. Cf. also R. Simon Duran's commentary (אוהב משפט) to Job (ed. Venice), 29 *b* and 47 *b*. It is interesting to see there how the rationalistic school, taking its clew from non-Jewish philosophy, insists upon making the body (or the flesh) responsible for the *Evil Yezer*, maintaining the dualism of flesh and spirit in the most positive manner; whilst the mystical school objects to it and endeavours to ascribe all evil to powers outside of man.

[1] *Baba Bathra*, 16 *a*.

little children commit no sin, and as it is man who breeds the *Evil Yezer* it is thus with the growth of man that sin comes. God further reproaches man, saying, that there are many things harder and bitterer than the *Evil Yezer*, but man finds the means to sweeten them. If man succeeds in making things palatable that are created bitter, how much more could he succeed in tempering the *Evil Yezer* who is delivered into the hands of man? [1]

By making him "bad" is meant, the abuse of those passions which are in themselves a necessity. The same question as to why God has created the *Evil Yezer* is answered in another place to the following effect: The matter is to be compared to a king who had slaves separated from him by an iron wall. The king proclaimed, "He who loves me shall climb this wall and come up to me. He will prove by this effort that he fears the king, and loves the king." [2] The text is not quite clear, but the general drift is that the *Yezer* who forms such an obstacle on the path of righteousness was created with the purpose that man should make a strong effort to overcome him, thereby testifying his loyalty and devotion to the King God, and increasing his reward when all the obstacles have been overcome.

Though these two opinions differ as to the nature and purpose of the *Evil Yezer*, they both agree that he

[1] *Tan.*, בראשית, 7.
[2] *S. E. Z.*, p. 193.

is in the hands of man, who is able to overcome him with a strong effort. Man is warned not to be intimidated by the fact that the *Evil Yezer* is a creation of God, and say that he has no authority over him, for it is written in the Torah, "And unto thee shall be his desire, but thou shalt rule over him" (Gen. 4 7).[1] This verse is paraphrased, "If thou wilt mend thy actions in this world, everything shall be forgiven and pardoned in the world to come. But if thou wilt not mend thy deeds in this world, thy sin will be preserved for the great Day of Judgement. And at the door of thy heart he lies, but in thy hand I have given the *Evil Yezer*, and thou shalt rule over him both for good and for evil." [2] Man has the power in his own hands,[3] and it is only by man's own neglect and weakness that the *Evil Yezer*, who appears first quite effeminate and powerless, gains masculine strength, enabling him to dictate to man. If man does well, he finds forgiveness; but if he does not well, he is delivered into the hands of the *Evil Yezer* who lies at the door.[4]

The difference between the wicked and the righteous is that the wicked are in the power of their hearts, while the righteous have the heart in their power.[5] Indeed, it would seem as if everything depended upon man. Either Satan enters into his body and gains dominion

[1] *Gen. R.*, 22 6. Cf. the commentary of מהרז״ו.

[2] *Pseudo-Jonathan*, Gen. 4 7.

[3] See *MHG.*, p. 109.

[4] See *MHG.*, p. 107. See above, p. 249.

[5] See *Gen. R.*, 34 10. By "heart" is of course meant here the *Yezer*.

over man and sin becomes his master, or man gains mastery over Satan and he suppresses him.[1] Nay, man has in his power not only to resist the *Evil Yezer*, but to turn his services to good purpose. At least the wicked are reproached for their failing to make the *Evil Yezer* good.[2] It is simply a question of choice, the wicked preferring the *Evil Yezer*, while the righteous decide for the *Good Yezer*.[3] Again, the men of the deluge are described as those who themselves made the *Evil Yezer* rule over them, by following his devices.[4] On the other hand, Abraham is said to have had dominion over the *Evil Yezer*,[5] whilst all the patriarchs are recorded to have enjoyed the blessing that the *Evil Yezer* had no dominion over them.[6] Joseph, again, is called the ruler over his *Evil Yezer*.[7] When the *Evil Yezer* is about to overpower man, the righteous will resist him with an oath, as we find in the case of Abraham, Boaz, David, and Elijah, who all conjured their *Yezer* to desist from his evil intentions, while the wicked will conjure their *Yezer*, urging him to commit the evil deed, as in the case of Gehazi.[8] Counsel is given to man that he should prove himself higher and above his sin, not allowing himself to become its slave and be buried under

[1] See Wertheimer, לקט מדרשים, p. 4 *b*.

[2] See *Ag. Ber.*, ch. 1.

[3] *Eccles. R.*, 9 1.

[4] *MHG.*, p. 131.

[5] *MHG.*, p. 354.

[6] See *Baba Bathra*, 17 *a*.

[7] *Num. R.*, 14 6. Cf. *Deut. R.*, 2: 33.

[8] See *Sifre*, 74 *a*; *Gen. R.*, 87 5; *Lev. R.*, 23 11; and references given there. Cf. also *MHG.*, p. 585, text and note 31.

its heavy burden.[1] If man has to make a goad to direct the animal, which he uses for the purpose of ploughing, etc., how much more should he be careful to use the goad for the purposes of directing his *Yezer*, who can by his seduction remove him from this world and the world to come? [2]

Man is further advised to stir up (to war) the *Good Yezer* against the *Evil Yezer*.[3] In this war, man is not supposed to be neutral. It is his duty not only to assist the *Good Yezer* and save him from his enemy, the *Evil Yezer*, but he should also make an effort to establish the kingdom of the *Good Yezer* over the *Evil Yezer*.[4] As an instance of such a victory of the *Good Yezer* over the *Evil Yezer* the following story may be given: The Saint, Abba Tachna, returned to his village on the eve of the Sabbath, when darkness was about to set in. He had his pack on his shoulders, but there he found at the crossroad a leper, lying, who said unto him, "Rabbi, do with me a righteousness (or act of mercy), and carry me to the town." Abba Tachna said, "If I leave here my pack (which contained all his earnings) how shall I and my family maintain ourselves? But if I leave here this leper, I forfeit my soul." But he declared the *Good Yezer* king over the *Evil Yezer*, and carried the leper to the town, and then came back and took

[1] See *Gen. R.*, 22 6. It is with allusion to Ps. 32 1.

[2] See *Lev. R.*, 29 17; *Eccles. R.*, 2 11.

[3] *Ber.*, 5 *a*. Cf. *P. K.*, 158 *a*.

[4] *Lev. R.*, 34 1; See also *M. T.*, 41 2, text and notes.

his pack and arrived at the town again just about sunset. They all wondered and said, "Is this the Saint Abba Tachna?" He himself had some regrets in his heart about it, fearing that he had profaned the Sabbath, but just at this time the Holy One, blessed be he, caused the sun to shine.[1]

The weapons used in this war against the *Evil Yezer* are mainly: occupation with the study of the Torah and works of loving-kindness. "Blessed are Israel," the Rabbis say; "as long as they are devoted to the study of the Torah, and works of loving-kindness, the *Evil Yezer* is delivered into their hands."[2]

It is especially the Torah which is considered the best remedy against the *Evil Yezer*. When Job remonstrated with God, "Thou hast created Paradise, thou hast created Hell, thou hast created the righteous, and thou hast created the wicked. Who prevented thee (from making me righteous?)," he sought by this argument to release the whole world from judgement, seeing that they sin under compulsion.—But his friend answered him, "If God has created the *Evil Yezer*, he also created the Torah as a spice (remedy) against him."[3] To the same effect is another passage, "My son, if this ugly one (the *Evil Yezer*) meets you, drag him into the schoolhouse (Beth-Hammidrash). If he is a stone, he will be ground (into powder); if he is iron, he will be broken into pieces; as it is said, 'Is not my word like

[1] See *Eccles. R.*, 9 7.
[2] *Abodah Zarah*, 5 *b*.
[3] *Baba Bathra*, 16 *a*.

unto a fire? saith the Lord, and like a hammer that breaketh the rocks in pieces?'" (Jer. 23 29).[1]

The words in the Psalms, "Order my steps in thy word, and let not any iniquity have dominion over me" (Ps. 119 133), are paraphrased in the following way: "David said, 'Allow not my feet to go where they wish, but let them go all the time to thy Torah in the Beth-Hammidrash, for the *Evil Yezer* does not enter the Beth-Hammidrash. He may pursue man all the way, but as soon as they reach the Beth-Hammidrash, Satan must abandon the race.'"[2] Again, he whose heart is absorbed in the words of the Torah removes thereby from himself all idle thoughts as well as the thoughts insinuated by the *Evil Yezer*.[3] The name *stone* given to the *Evil Yezer* suggested also the following allegorical explanation of Gen. 29 2: "*And Jacob looked, and behold there were three flocks of sheep.* By these are meant the three masters of the Synagogue; *For out of this well they watered the flocks;* by this is meant the Torah; *but the stone is great;* this is the *Evil Yezer*, who can only be removed by the efforts of the whole congregation; *who rolled the stone from the well's mouth*, by means of their listening to the Torah. But as soon as they left the Synagogue, the *Evil Yezer* reasserted himself."[4] The fact, however, that a part of the Torah, or rather the Decalogue, was written on stone or

[1] *Kiddushin*, 30 *b*. [2] *M. T.*, 119 62. [3] *A. R. N.*, 35 *b*.

[4] *Gen. R.*, 70 8. The word קרואים is doubtful, and still requires a proper explanation. See above, p. 244, note 1.

on "tablets of stone" (Exod. 24 22), suggested the following explanation: "Since the *Evil Yezer* is also called *stone*, as it is said, 'And I will take away the stony heart'" (Ezek. 36 26), "it is only proper that stone should watch over stone." [1] The effects of the Torah in this battle with the *Yezer* seem to be differently understood by the different authorities, for while one Rabbi gives as advice, "If the *Yezer* come to make you merry (or frivolous), then kill him (or throw him down) by the word of the Torah," the other Rabbi counsels us "to rejoice the *Yezer* with the words of the Torah"; that is, to use the inclination of man towards joy and cheerfulness for the joy and the happiness which man should find in accomplishing the will of God.[2] The killing of the *Evil Yezer* is further recommended in the following words, "To him who kills his *Yezer* and confesses upon it, it is reckoned as if he would have honoured the Holy One, blessed be he, in two worlds, this world and the world to come." [3] But it would seem that this is not considered as the highest attainment of man; for it is said of Abraham, that he made the *Evil Yezer* good. Indeed, the *Evil Yezer* compromised with him, entering into a covenant that he would not make Abraham sin, whilst David, who could not resist the *Evil Yezer*, had to slay him in his heart.[4]

[1] *Lev. R.*, 35 5; cf. also *Num. R.*, 14 4, and *Cant. R.*, 6 11.

[2] See *Gen. R.*, 22 6, text and commentaries. Cf. *MHG.*, p. 110, for varying readings. Cf. Theodor's ed. of *Gen. R.*, p. 212.

[3] *Sanhedrin*, 43 *b*. Cf. *Lev. R.*, 9 1. See also below, p. 335 *seq.*

[4] *Jer. Berachoth*, 14 *b*. See also above, p. 67.

Another means of defeating the machinations of *Yezer* is the contemplation of death.[1] This can be best illustrated by the following passage of Akabiah b. Mahalaleel, "Consider three things, and thou wilt not come into the hands of sin. Know whence thou comest, and whither thou art going, and before whom thou art to give account and reckoning."[2] Another version of the same saying is, "He who thinks of the following four things will never sin again: that is, from whence he comes, where he is destined to go, what will become of him, and who is his Judge."[3] Sin or the *Evil Yezer* in this case is chiefly representative of the passion of vanity. These passages could be multiplied to any extent, but they are all to the effect that man, meditating upon his lowly origin and his sad end, will not be slow to give up all pretensions that come from pride and conceit. Sometimes, the remembrance of death serves also as a damper to man's tendency towards excess. An instance of this we have in the following: "At the wedding of the son of Rabina, the students there present said unto Rab Hamnuna Zuta, 'Let the master sing a song unto us,' whereupon he began to sing, 'Woe unto us that we shall die! Woe unto us that we shall die!' When they asked for the refrain, he gave the words, 'Where is the Torah, and where are the good works that will protect us?'"[4]

[1] *Berachoth*, 5 *a*.
[2] *Aboth*, 3 1.
[3] *D. E.*, p. 3. Cf. *A. R. N.*, 35 *a*, text and notes.
[4] *Berachoth*, 31 *a*.

There may further be brought together under this category other remedies against the *Evil Yezer* which are of an ascetic nature. The story of the Nazarite who had his hair cut off with the purpose of subduing his *Yezer* has already been referred to.[1] A certain Rabbi, again, is recorded to have prayed for the death of his nearest kin, when he was under the impression that she would become the cause of sin.[2] The later Jewish moralists prescribed a whole set of regulations, which are more or less of an ascetic nature, and calculated to make a fence against transgression. But the underlying idea of all of them is that all opulence, wealth, gluttony, and other opportunities of satisfying one's appetite are so many auxiliaries to the *Evil Yezer*. Thus the Scriptural verses in Deut. 11 15–16 are paraphrased, "Moses said unto Israel, 'Be careful that you rebel not against the Holy One, blessed be he, because man does not enter upon this rebellion, but when he is full,'" that is, revelling in food and other luxuries.[3] The proverb was, "A lion does not roar from the midst of a heap of straw, but from the midst of a heap of meat." Another proverb was, "Filled stomachs are a bad sort (or plenty is tempting)."[4] Hence the homily of the Rabbi with reference to the verse, "Behold, I have refined thee, but not with silver; I have chosen thee in the furnace of poverty" (Isa. 48 10), that it teaches that the Holy One, blessed be he, searched all good

[1] See above, p. 249.
[2] *Taanith*, 24 *a*.
[3] *Sifre*, 80 *b*. Cf. *ibid.*, 136 *a*.
[4] *Berachoth*, 31 *a*.

things but found nothing better for Israel than poverty.[1]

It should, however, be remarked that even the Torah is not an all-powerful remedy in itself without the aid of heaven, which gives the Torah its real efficiency. Thus with reference to the verse, "Let my heart be sound (תמים) in thy statutes, that I be not ashamed" (Ps. 119, 80), the Rabbis remark, "David said, 'Master of the world, when I am occupied in Thy Law, allow not the *Evil Yezer* to divide me . . . that the *Evil Yezer* may not lead me astray . . . but make my heart one, so that I be occupied in the Torah with soundness (perfection or fulness).'" [2] Again, with reference to another verse, "Make me understand the way of thy precepts" (Ps. 119 27), it is remarked that David said, "My Master, say not unto me, behold they (the words of the Torah) are before thee, meditate upon them by thyself. For if thou wilt not make me understand them, I shall know nothing." [3] The Torah by itself is thus not sufficient to defeat the *Evil Yezer*. The conquest comes in the end from God. We are thus brought to the necessity of grace forming a prominent factor in the defeat of the *Yezer*. Hence, the various prayers for the removal or the subjugation of the *Evil Yezer*. Specimens of such prayers have already been given.[4] Here we might further refer to the

[1] See *Chagigah*, 9 *b*.

[2] *Exod. R.*, 19 2. The reading is not quite clear. I have adopted the reading suggested by רד"ל, note 8.

[3] *M. T.*, 119 16. See also *ibid.* to verse 33. [4] See above, p. 265,

individual prayer of R. Judah the Saint, in which he supplicates that God may save him from the *Evil Yezer*.[1] A similar prayer we have from another Rabbi of a later date.[2] Other Rabbis, again, put their prayers in a more positive form, as, for instance, those who prayed that God would endow them with a *Good Yezer*.[3] Sometimes neither the *Evil Yezer* nor the *Good Yezer* is mentioned, the prayer being more directed against sin, as for instance, the one running, "May it be thy will that we shall not sin, and then we shall not be put to shame." [4] The heart plays a special part in these prayers, as for instance the one which is to the effect, "May our heart become single in the fear of thy name. Remove us from all thou hatest. Bring us near to all thou lovest, and do with us a righteousness for thy Name's sake." Another similar prayer is, "May it be thy will, Lord God, and the God of our fathers, that thou put into our hearts to do perfect repentance." [5] As typical in this respect we may perhaps mention the lines in the daily prayer-book, "Make us cleave to the *Good Yezer* and to good deeds; subjugate our *Evil Yezer* so that it may submit itself unto thee." [6] A prayer fairly combining all these features is the one repeated several times on the Day of Atonement, running thus: "Our God and God of our

[1] *Berachoth*, 16 *b*. [2] *Berachoth*, 17 *a*.

[3] See *Berachoth*, 17 *b*, and *Jer. Berachoth*, 4 *c*.

[4] *Berachoth*, 17 *b*. [5] *Jer. Berachoth*, 7 *d*.

[6] See *Berachoth*, 60 *b*, the text of which differs in some minor points from that in our prayer-books. Cf. *Singer*, p. 7, Baer, p. 43.

fathers, forgive and pardon our iniquities on this Day of Atonement. . . . Subdue our heart to serve thee, and bend our *Yezer* to turn unto thee; renew our reins to observe thy precepts, and circumcise our hearts to love and revere thy Name, as it is written in thy Law: And the Lord thy God will circumcise thy heart and the heart of thy seed, to love the Lord thy God with all thine heart and with all thy soul, that thou mayest live."[1] The underlying idea of these passages, which can be multiplied by any number of parallel passages, is man's consciousness of his helplessness against the powers of temptation, which can only be overcome by the grace of God. The oldest prayer of this kind, of course, is the one in the Eighteen Benedictions, praying for God's help to bring man back unto him or his Torah and to his service, as well as the one for repentance.[2]

A special feature about the Rabbinic passages emphasising the necessity of grace in the struggle with the *Evil Yezer*, is the implication of God's responsibility for the existence of the *Evil Yezer*. The pleading of Job and his insistence upon God's power to prevent sin has already been quoted, but there Job is censured for it.[3] Indeed, he was considered as an heretic for making this plea. A similar case we have with Cain. When reproached for murdering his brother, he is described as saying, "Master of the world, if I have

[1] See Festival Prayers, Day of Atonement, Part II, pp. 14, 185, 234.
[2] See below, p. 341. [3] See above, p. 273, note 3.

killed him, it is thou who hast created in me the *Evil Yezer*. Thou watchest me and the whole world. Why didst thou permit me to kill him? It is thou who hast killed him . . . for if thou hadst received my sacrifice, as thou didst receive his (Abel's) sacrifice, I would not have become jealous of him." [1] But of course Cain represents the bad type of humanity. Yet it is not to be denied that the Rabbis themselves sometimes employed similar arguments. Thus, with reference to the verse, "O Lord, why hast thou made us to err from thy ways, and hardened our heart from thy fear?" (Isa. 63 17), the Rabbis plead in favour of the brothers of Joseph, "When thou (God) didst choose, thou didst make them love; when thou didst choose, thou didst make them hate." [2] Something similar is hinted about the affair of Cain and Abel. R. Simon b. Jochai said, "It is a thing hard to say, and it is impossible for the mouth to utter it. It is to be compared to two athletes who were wrestling in the presence of the king. If the king wills, he can have them separated; but the king wills not; (in the end) one overwhelmed the other and killed him. And (the dying) man shouted: 'Who can now demand justice for me (seeing that the king was present and could have prevented it)?'" [3] In another place we read with reference to the verses in Micah 4 6, Jer. 18 6, and Ezek. 36 26, that but for such statements as these, implying the pos-

[1] See *MHG.*, p. 112, and note 36.

[2] *Gen. R.*, 18 20.

[3] *Gen. R.*, 22 9.

sibility of God's power to exterminate the *Evil Yezer*, there would be no hope for Israel, such a possibility serving in extenuation of their guilt.[1] Again, with reference to the verse, "For he knoweth our frame (יצרנו); he remembereth that we are dust," we are told that this fact will save Israel from seeing Hell. So Israel will plead before the Holy One, blessed be he, "Master of the world, thou knowest the *Evil Yezer* who seduces us." [2] It is with reference to the same verse, that we read as stated in another place, "Wretched, indeed, must be the leaven, if he who has created it declares it as evil." [3] The "whisper from above" (heaven) makes the serpent (or the *Evil Yezer* whose creation God regrets) bite or commit violence on earth; because of which fact "a door of mercy is opened to the sinners in Israel that they may be received as penitents; as they will plead before him, Master of the world: it is revealed and known unto thee that it is the *Evil Yezer* that incites us. In thy great mercy receive us in perfect repentance." [4]

More emphatic, even, is another remark on the verse of Jer. 18 6, "Israel said, 'Master of the world . . . even when we sin and make thee angry, be not removed from us, for we are the clay, and thou art the potter! . . .' Israel said, 'Thou hast created in us the

[1] *Berachoth*, 32 *a*, and *Sukkah*, 52 *b*.

[2] *A. R. N.*, 32 *a* and *b*. Cf. *Sanhedrin*, 105 *a*, homily on Isa. 28:26.

[3] *Gen. R.*, 34 10. Cf. *M. T.*, 103 14, text and Note 55. See above, 266.

[4] See *S. E.*, p. 63 *a*, text and notes. Cf. *Eccles. R.*, 10 1.

*Evil Yezer* from our very youth. It is he who causes us to sin before thee, but thou dost not remove from us the sin. We pray thee, cause him to disappear from us, so that we may do thy will.' Whereupon God says, 'So I will do in the world to come.'"[1] Nay, there are recorded cases of men belonging to the best type of humanity, who make the same plea as Job and Cain, though in somewhat more modest terms. Thus, Moses is said to have "knocked words against the height" (reproached God), arguing it was the gold and silver which he gave to Israel that was the cause of their making the golden calf.[2] Again, Elijah "knocked words against the height," saying to God, "Thou hast turned their heart back again" (1 Kings 18 37). And the Rabbis proceed to say that God confessed that Elijah's contention was right.[3]

For, indeed, God sometimes does make sin impossible, as in the case of Abimelech, to whom God said, "For I also withheld thee from sinning against me: therefore suffered I thee not to touch her" (Gen. 20 6). The Rabbis illustrate this in the following way: "It is to be compared to a strong man riding on a horse. But there was a child lying on the road which was thus in danger of being run over. But the man drove the horse so that it avoided the child. The praise in this case is certainly due to the rider, not to the horse. In a similar way Abimelech claimed a special merit for not having sinned. But God said unto him, 'The

[1] *Exod. R.*, 46 4. [2] *Berachoth*, 32 *a*. [3] *Berachoth*, *ibid.*

*Yezer* who causes you to sin is in my power, and it was I who drew thee away from sin.'"[1]

This direct interference, however, with the *Evil Yezer* seems exceptional. What was prominent in the mind of the Jew was first, that God, "who is a law unto himself," does not choose to make use of this prerogative of his, though the *Evil Yezer* evidently belongs to this class of creation which the Holy One, blessed be he, regrets to have called into existence, if one can say so.[2] "There is astonishment before me" (God says), "that I have created in man the *Evil Yezer*, for if I would not have created in man the *Evil Yezer*, he would not have rebelled against me."[3] This regret of God is expressed by another Rabbi in the following way: "After the Holy One, blessed be he, created this world he regretted the creation of the *Evil Yezer*, as it is said, 'O that there were such an heart in them that they would fear me and keep my commandments always' (Deut. 5 29). This teaches that God longs that Israel should labour in the Torah. From this thou inferrest that the authority (choice) of man is given unto him; therefore if he does what he is commanded, he merits to receive reward, as it is said, 'That it might be well with them and their children for ever' (Deut. 5 26)."[4] Apparently, the world is so constituted that man should be a hybrid of angel and beast with the

[1] *Gen. R.*, 52 7. Cf. *Exod. R.*, 21, and *P. K.*, p. 176 *b*.

[2] *Sukkah*, 52 *b*. Cf. *S. E.*, p. 63.

[3] *Gen. R.*, 27 4.

[4] *MHG.*, Deut., p. 46 *b*, Ms.

possibility of sin, which spells death, and that of conquering sin, which means life.[1] Angels have no *Evil Yezer* and are thus spared from jealousy, covetousness, lust, and other passions, but those who dwell below are under the temptation of the *Evil Yezer*, and therefore require a double guard of holiness to resist him.[2] This double guard they have in the Torah, as indicated above; otherwise man is a free agent. To secure this freedom, it would seem that God has even foregone his prerogative in respect of preventing sin, so that the bold statement of the Rabbi that everything is in the power of God except (the forcing upon man of) the fear of God, has become a general maxim, though, as is well known, this maxim is not without its difficulties.[3] All that God does is only in the way of warning, and reminding man that there is an Eye watching him, and that he will be responsible for his choice. "Everything is seen, and freedom of choice is given . . . the shop is open; and the dealer gives credit; and the ledger lies open; and the hand writes; and whosoever wishes to borrow may come and borrow."[4] In another place,

[1] See *Gen. R.*, 14 8. See above, p. 261, note 1, and below, 292.

[2] See *Shabbath*, 89 *a*; *Gen. R.*, 48 11; *Lev. R.*, 24 8 and 26 5.

[3] See *Berachoth*, 33 *b*; *Megillah*, 25 *a*; *Niddah*, 16 *b*; *Tan.* פקודי, 3. Cf. *Tosafoth* to the passages in the Talmud.

[4] See *Aboth*, 3 15. Cf. Taylor, 3 24, and Bacher, *Ag. Tan.*, I 282. See also *A.R.N.*, 58 *b*. According to the version given there of this saying of R. Akiba, it is altogether very doubtful whether the Rabbi really meant to emphasise the antithesis of predestination and free will. Cf. Commentaries to *Aboth*. See also *A.R.N.*, 75 *a* and 81 *b*, suggesting that the צפוי refers to man.

the responsibility for his choice is expressed in the following words: "As it was said, 'I have set before you life and death, blessing and cursing' (Deut. 30 19), Israel might perhaps say, 'Considering that the Holy One, blessed be he, placed before us two ways, the way of life and the way of death, we might go in any of these which we like,' therefore it is further said, 'Choose life, that both thou and thy seed may live' (Deut., *ibid.*)."[1] Life is identical with the good way. Deut. 30 15 is paraphrased, "Behold, I have set before you this day the way of life, which is the good way, and the way of death, which is the bad way."[2] The sin of Adam, indeed, consisted in the fact that he made choice of the evil. The Omnipresent placed before him two ways, the one of death and the one of life, and he (Adam) chose the way of death.[3] The same complaint is made of other transgressors in history, of whom it is said, "He setteth himself in a way that is not good" (Ps. 36 5). They walk in iniquity and meditate iniquity: they have two ways, the one for good and the one for evil. And so Solomon said, "Who leave the paths of uprightness to walk in the ways of darkness." For indeed the heart was created to speak truth, but your heart works wickedness; the hands were created to accomplish goodness and righteousness, and you do violence and robbery, and so the

[1] See *Sifre*, 86 *a*. Cf. *Tan.*, ראה, § 3.
[2] See *Pseudo-Jonathan* to this verse.
[3] *Mechilta*, 33 *a*. Cf. *Gen. R.*, 20 5 and references.

blind walk in the evil way and the open-eyed ones walk in the way of good.[1]

The verse, again, "Surely he scorneth the scorners; but he giveth grace unto the lowly" (Prov. 3 34), is interpreted, he who desires to contaminate himself they open unto him, he who desires to purify himself they aid him (from heaven). "For indeed things defiling do not come upon man unless he turned his mind to them and became defiled by them," whilst God increases the strength of the righteous that they may do his will, but he that guards himself against sin for three times, has the promise that henceforth God will guard him[2] In different words, the same thought is expressed in another place, "In the way in which a man chooses to walk, they guide him (or allow him to walk). This is to be derived from the Torah, where it is written (with regard to Balaam), first, 'Thou shalt not go with them' (Num. 25 12), and then, 'Rise up and go with them' (*ibid.* 20); from the Prophets, where it is said, 'I am the Lord, thy God, which teacheth thee to profit, which leadeth thee by the way that thou shouldst go' (Isa. 48 17); and from the Hagiographa, where it is said, 'Surely, he scorneth the scorners; but he giveth grace unto the lowly' (Prov. 3 35)."[3]

A peculiar paraphrase of the verses quoted above from

[1] *M. T.*, 36 8 and 58 2; *Exod. R.*, 30 20.

[2] *Shabbath*, 104 *a*. See also *T. K.*, 91 *a*; *P. K.*, 161 *a*; and *Jer. Kiddushin*, 61 *d*.

[3] *Makkoth*, 10 *b*.

Deuteronomy (30 15), we have in the following passage taken from a later Midrash: "Rabbi Eliezer said, 'I heard with my ears the Lord of Hosts speaking. And what did he say? "Behold, I have set before you this day the life and the good, death and the evil." The Holy One, blessed be he, said, "Behold, these two ways I have given to Israel, the one for good and the one for evil: that of good is of life, that of evil is of death." That of good branches off in two ways: of righteousness and of loving-kindness: Elijah is placed in the middle. And when a man is about to enter upon them, he exclaims and says, "Open ye the gates, that the righteous nation . . . may enter in" (Isa. 26 2). . . . But that of the evil has four doors: upon each door seven guardians are seated: four within and three without. Those outside are merciful angels. . . . And when he is about to enter in the first door, the merciful angels meet him first and say unto him, "Why dost thou want to enter into this fire, among the wicked and the coals? Listen unto us and do repentance. . . ." When he comes to the second door, they say unto him, "Behold, thou hast already passed in through the first door, do not enter into the second! Why dost thou want to be removed from the Torah of God, that they call thee 'unclean,' and flee from thee?" . . . When he comes to the third door, they tell him, "Thou hast already passed the second door! Why come into the third? Why wilt thou be wiped out from the book of life? . . .

Listen unto us and return!" When he reaches the fourth door, they say unto him, "Thou hast passed already the third door! do not come into the fourth door! . . . Thou hast not listened and stayed thy steps hitherto . . . the Holy One, blessed be he, forgives the sins and pardons, and says every day, 'Return, ye backsliding children!'" If he listens unto them, well; if not, woe unto him and to his star.'"[1]

The quoted passage, with the constant reminder coming from the angels of mercy, brings us back to the idea of grace, or the thought of man standing in need of the aid of heaven in his struggle with *Yezer.* Besides the passages given above, we may add here the following statement, "Every day the *Yezer* of man assaults him and endeavours to kill him, and but for the Holy One, blessed be he, who helps man, he could not resist him."[2] It may be that it was this feeling of man's comparative helplessness in such a condition which wrung the cry from the Rabbi, "Woe unto me of my (*Evil*) *Yezer* and woe unto me of my *Yozer* (Creator)."[3] But man has to show himself worthy of this grace, inasmuch as it is expected that the first effort against the *Evil Yezer* should be made on his part, whereupon the promise comes that *Yezer* will be finally removed by God. Thus with reference to the

[1] *P. R. E.*, ch. 15. Cf. the commentary of רד"ל. Cf. Mr. C. G. Montefiore, *Rabbinic Conception of Repentance*, *Jewish Quarterly Review*, *v.* 16, pp. 209–257.

[2] *Sukkah*, 52 *b*.

[3] See *Berachoth*, 61 *a*.

Scriptural verse, "O Israel, return unto the Lord thy God; for thou hast stumbled by thine iniquity" (Hos. 14 1), the Rabbis remark that it is to be compared to a huge rock that was placed on the crossways, on which men used to stumble; whereupon the king said unto them, "Chip it off little by little until the hour comes when I will remove it altogether."[1] Another version of the same saying is, "Israel said before the Holy One, blessed be he, 'Master of the world, thou knowest the power of the *Evil Yezer*, which is very hard.' Whereupon the Holy One, blessed be he, said unto them, 'Move the stone a little in this world, and I will remove it from you in the next world, as it is said, "Cast up, cast up the highway; gather out the stones" (Isa. 62 10), whilst in another place it is said, "Cast ye up, cast ye up, prepare the way, take up the stumbling-block of my people"' (Is. 57 14)."[2]

The struggle with the *Evil Yezer* will cease with the advent of the Messiah, "when the Holy One, blessed be he, will bring the *Evil Yezer* and kill him in the presence both of the righteous and of the wicked." To the righteous he will appear in the shape of a big mountain, and they will cry and will say, "How were we able to subdue such an obstacle?" In the eyes of the wicked, he will resemble a thin hair, and they will cry and say, "O that we were not strong enough to defeat such an insignificant impediment!"[3] In another

[1] *P. K.*, 165 *a*. [2] *Num. R.*, 15 16. Cf. *Tan. B.*, 4 28 *a*.

[3] *Sukkah*, 52 *a*. Cf. also *Gen. R.*, 48 11 and 89 1; *Exod. R.*, 41 7 and 46 4, and *Num. R.*, 17 6; *Deut. R.*, 2 30 and 6 14; *P. R.*, 29 *a*.

place, the removal of the *Yezer* from the world is described as follows: "If your scattered ones will be in the end of the heaven, from there the word of the Lord your God will gather you through Elijah the High Priest, and from there he will bring you near through the hands of the King Messiah. And the word of the Lord your God will bring you to the land which your fathers inherited, and you shall inherit it; and he will do you good, and multiply you above your fathers. And the Lord your God will remove the folly of the hearts of your children, for he will make the *Evil Yezer* cease from the world, and will create the *Good Yezer*, who will counsel you to love the Lord your God with all your hearts, and all your souls, that your lives may last forever." [1]

Only once in history Israel had a presentiment of these Messianic times. When Israel (on the occasion of the Revelation on Mount Sinai) heard the commandment "Thou shalt have no other gods before me" (Exod. 20 3), the *Evil Yezer* was uprooted from their hearts; but when they came to Moses and said unto him, "Our master Moses, become thou the messenger between us (Israel and God), as it is said, 'Speak thou with us . . . but let not God speak with us lest we die' (Exod. 20 19), the *Evil Yezer* came back at once in his place." They came again to Moses and said, "Our master Moses, we wish that he (God) should reveal himself again unto us." He answered them,

[1] *Pseudo-Jonathan*, Deut., 30 4.

"This is impossible now (but it will take place in the future to come)." [1] Every separation from God, though not with the intention of sin, but with the purpose of establishing an intermediary, is, as we see, considered as the setting up of another God, who is the cause of sin; whilst on the other hand, it is suggested that it is by the conquering of the *Evil Yezer* that man enters into close communion with God. Thus Lev. 9 6 is paraphrased, "Remove the *Evil Yezer* from your heart and the Divine Presence will at once be revealed to you." [2] But it is this struggle on the part of man which places him above the angels. "The angels said in the presence of the Holy One, blessed be he, 'Master of the world, why are we not allowed to intone our song here in heaven (in the praise of God) before Israel sing their song below on earth?' And the Holy One, blessed be he, answered to them, 'How shall you say it (the song) before Israel? Israel have their habitation on earth; they are born of women, and the *Evil Yezer* has dominion among them, and nevertheless they oppose the *Yezer* and declare my unity every day, and proclaim me as King every day, and long for my Kingdom and for the rebuilding of my Temple.'" [3]

[1] *Cant. R.*, I 2. [2] *Pseudo-Jonathan*, Lev. 9 6.
[3] See Friedmann, נספחים, p. 56. See above, p. 91, note 2.

# XVII

# FORGIVENESS AND RECONCILIATION WITH GOD

THE various aspects of the doctrine of atonement and forgiveness as conceived by the Rabbis may be best grouped round the following Rabbinic passage: "They asked Wisdom (Hagiographa), 'What is the punishment of the sinner?' Wisdom answered, 'Evil pursues sinners' (Prov. 13 21). They asked Prophecy, 'What is the punishment of the sinner?' Prophecy answered, 'The soul that sinneth, it shall die' (Ezek. 18 4). They asked the Torah, 'What is the punishment of the sinner?' Torah answered, 'Let him bring a guilt-offering and it shall be forgiven unto him, as it is said, "And it shall be accepted for him to make atonement for him"' (Lev. 1 4). They asked the Holy One, blessed be he, 'What is the punishment of the sinner?' The Holy One, blessed be he, answered, 'Let him do repentance and it shall be forgiven unto him, as it is said, "Good and upright is the Lord: therefore will he teach sinners in the way"' (Ps. 25 8)—that is, that he points the sinners the way that they should do repentance."[1] It need hardly be remarked that to the Rabbi the whole of the Bible was the word of God, and he could not thus fairly have seen a contradiction between the dictum of the Holy One, blessed be he, and the dicta of the Torah and those of the "Prophets of truth and righteousness." Besides, it could not have escaped the Rabbi that both the Torah and the Prophets have passages enough insisting upon the importance of repentance. Again, sacrifices, as we shall see presently, according to the Rabbis are always accompanied by repentance, whilst the chief function of repentance is limited to such cases as those in which sacrifices are of no avail. What the Rabbi really meant is, that forgiveness is achieved in various ways, through suffering and death, through atonement of sacrifices, but more prominently through repentance, which latter is the most divine aspect of the three. It should be premised that the prerogative of granting pardon is entirely in the hands of God, every mediator being excluded from this prerogative; "for he will not pardon your transgressions," being a mere messenger to accomplish what he is bidden to do. And so David said, "Master of the world, wilt thou deliver me into the hand of an angel who wilt not lift up his countenance? Forgiveness is with

[1] See *Jer. Makkoth*, 31 *d*, and *P. K.*, 158 *b*. The texts are in both places defective, but they supplement each other. Cf. *Yalkut Machiri* to Ps. 25 8, reproducing the passage from *Jer. Makkoth* in the order of Torah, Prophecy, Hagiographa, and God, adding also between Prophets and Hagiographa David, with a reference to Ps. 104 35.

thee (God), as it is said, 'But there is forgiveness with thee' (Ps. 130 4)."[1] David also prayed, "Let my sentence come from thy Presence (Ps. 17 1); do thou judge me, and deliver me not into the hands of an angel, or a seraph, or a cherub, or an *ofan*, for they are all cruel," as indeed they do object to the acceptance of the penitents altogether.[2] Indeed, God is desirous of acquitting his creatures and not of declaring them guilty. When the Holy One, blessed be he, said unto Moses, "What is my profession (אומנות)?" he answered, "Thou art merciful and gracious and long-suffering and abundant of goodness." [3] When they sin and provoke his anger, the Holy One, blessed be he, seeks for one to plead on their behalf and paves the way for him.[4]

As sacrifice as a means of atonement is a prominent feature both in the Torah and in Rabbinic literature, it will perhaps be best here to treat first of this aspect. It should be remarked that sacrifices are, as just hinted at, very limited in their efficacy as a means of atonement and reconciliation. Thus with reference to Lev. 4 1, "If a soul shall sin through igno-

[1] See *Tan. B.*, 2 44 *b*, text and notes. Cf. *Sanhedrin*, 38 *b*, the references there to Exod. 23 21. Cf. above, p. 41, text and notes.

[2] See *Ag. Ber.*, ch. 9. See also below, pp. 319 and 321. Cf. *S. E.*, p. 109. See also Hoffmann's remark, *Das Buch Leviticus*, 1186, that whilst it is the priest who atones, וכפר הכהן, the pardon comes from God, ונסלח.

[3] See *Yalkut* to Num. 14 8 and Job, § 907, reproduced from the *Yelamdenu*.

[4] *Tan.*, וירא, 8. Cf. *P. R.*, *ibid.*

rance," the general rule is laid down, "One brings a sin-offering for sins committed in ignorance, but brings no sin-offering for sins committed wilfully," which rule is also applied to sin-offerings.[1] In another place, with reference to Prov. 21 2, it is pointed out that the superiority of practising the works of charity and justice over sacrifices consists in this, that whilst the atoning effect of the former extends also to the sins committed wilfully, that of the latter is confined only to sins committed unintentionally.[2] It is further to be noticed that the great majority of sacrifices are largely confined to matters ritual and ceremonial, and certain other transgressions relating to Levitical impurity; whilst all those sins which concern a person and which fall mostly under the heading of moral laws could not be atoned without proper restitution.[3] Lastly, it is to be remarked, that sin- and guilt-offerings, according to the opinion of the majority of the Rabbis, are accompanied by repentance and by a confession of sins on the part of the man who brings the sacrifices.[4] The injunction is, "Be not like the fools who bring a sacrifice for their offences, but turn not from

[1] See *Kerithoth*, 9 *a*; *T. K.*, 15 *b*; *Sifre*, 32 *b*.

[2] *Deut. R.*, 5 3. See commentaries.

[3] See Maimonides, הלכות שגגות, ch. 1 and 9, regarding the cases in which a sin- or guilt-offering is brought.

[4] See *Shebuoth*, 13 *a*; *Kerithoth*, 7 *a*; *Tosephta Yoma*, p. 190 (§ 9). Cf. also *Sifre*, 2 *a*, with regard to Confession. See also Maimonides, תשובה, I., and Hoffmann, *Das Buch Leviticus*, I., p. 202. Cf. also below, p. 337, note 1.

the evil deeds which they have in their hands, and are not accepted in grace." [1]

A main condition in the sacrificial service aptly described sometimes in contradistinction to prayer as the "service of deeds" is the purity of intention and the singleness of purpose with which the sacrifice is brought. It has to be brought with the intention "of giving calmness of spirit for the sake of him who created the world." Quantity is of no consideration, considering that both the burnt-offering of an animal and the burnt-offering of a mere bird form a sweet savour unto the Lord (Lev. I 9 and 17). "This is to teach," as the Rabbis proceed to say, "that both he who increases (his offering) and he who diminishes his offering are alike pleasing unto the Lord, provided each directs his mind toward heaven." [2] From another place, it would almost seem as if it were the less costly sacrifice that is the more acceptable. It is with reference to the circumstance that the term והקריב used of the sacrifice consisting in a ram (Lev. I 13) is omitted at the sacrifice consisting of a bullock (Lev. *ibid.*, 9). On this the Rabbis remark, "Let no man think, 'I will do things ugly and things unworthy, but will afterwards bring a bullock which has much flesh and cause it to be brought upon the altar.' How! will God respect per-

[1] *Targum*, Eccles. 4 17; cf. *Berachoth*, 23 *a*.

[2] See *T. K.*, 8 *b* and 9 *b*. See also *Zebachim*, 46 *b*. Cf. Hoffmann as above, p. 92. The words "calmness of spirit" are a sort of paraphrase of the Hebrew equivalent, ריח ניחח, usually rendered into English by "sweet savour." Cf. above, p. 160.

sons? 'But let man do good deeds and devote himself to the study of the Torah and bring the lean ram . . . and I shall have mercy with him and accept his repentance.'"[1] If the sacrifice is not brought with the intention of pleasing God, it is reckoned unto them as if they have brought it only for their own purposes.[2] Indeed, it would seem that according to the Rabbis the only *raison d'être* for sacrifices is man's compliance with God's will, who prescribed this order of service. Thus, with reference to Num. 28 2, it is remarked, "It is a calmness of spirit for me, I, who commanded it and my will was done." The Rabbi proceeds then to prove that the sacrifices have not the purpose of providing the Holy One, blessed be he, with food, and quotes the well-known verses of the 50th Psalm, and concludes to the effect: "But why did God say sacrifice unto him, in order to accomplish his will?"[3]

[1] See *S. E.*, pp. 36 and 38, and *Lev. R.*, 2 12. The term והקריב (to bring near) is interpreted to mean the closer communion with God which is to be established by the sacrifice in question. See the commentary, יפה תואר, to this passage in *Lev. R.*

[2] See *T. K.*, 12 *c*. Cf., however, the commentary of R. Abraham b. David to this passage.

[3] See *Sifre*, 54 *a*. Cf. *P. K.*, 56 *seq.*, and *P. R.*, pp. 80, 194 *a seq.*, and references, given there in the commentaries. See also *Yalkut Machiri* to Ps. 50 4–14. It ought to be remarked that the reading in the concluding sentence of our passage in the *Sifre* is not certain. According to the *Machiri*, this sentence reads to the effect that, "Indeed, God is in no need of sacrifices, but only told man to sacrifice unto him in order to do his (man's) will," which reading received some support from *P. R.*, 195 *a*, where it reads that "the sacrifices were only instituted for thy (man's) atonement and honour." Neverthe-

The atoning effect of sacrifices differs with the various sacrifices. The sin-offering brings complete reconciliation, whilst others have only the power of partial atonement or of suspending the judgement of God.[1] Interesting is the following controversy between the School of Shammai and the School of Hillel with reference to the "continual burnt-offering" consisting of two lambs (Num. 28 3, *seq.*). According to the School of Shammai, "they only subdue the sins of Israel," as it is said, "He will subdue our iniquities; and thou wilt cast all their sins into the depths of the sea" (Micah 7 19), but the School of Hillel teaches that, "Everything which is subdued (or sunk) may, in the end, come to the surface," but the name of this sacrifice means that the two lambs have the effect to wash away the sins of Israel.[2] It is in this way, it is

less I am not inclined to think that the Rabbis entertained any such rationalistic views as those with regard to sacrifices. Excepting the well-known passage in *Lev. R.*, 22 8, the meaning of which is, however, very doubtful, there is nothing to prove that they in any way deprecated it. Cf. Hoffmann, *Das Buch Leviticus*, pp. 79–92. On the other hand, the facility with which the Rabbis adapted themselves after the destruction of the Holy Temple to the new conditions must impress one with the conviction that the sacrificial service was not considered absolutely indispensable.

[1] Cf. Hoffmann, *ibid.*, pp. 79–92. About sacrifices atoning only partially or having only suspending power, תולה, see *Yoma*, 85 *b*, text and commentaries.

[2] *P. K.*, 61 *b*; *P. R.*, 84 *a* and commentaries. The *Beth Shammai* take the word כבשים as if it were written with a ש, thus meaning "suppressing" or "subduing," and corresponding to יכבש of Micah. The *Beth Hillel* take the word כבשים as if it would have a ס instead of a ש, which would thus mean "washing" and refer to Jeremiah, 4 14.

pointed out, that the man living in Jerusalem could be considered as righteous, considering that the continual offering of the morning atoned for the transgressions of the night, and the continual offering of the afternoon atoned for the transgressions of the day.[1]

The continual offering was a communal offering, nor is there in the Bible ascribed to it any atoning power; but there is a marked tendency in Rabbinic literature to bestow on all sacrifices, even such as the burnt-offering and the peace-offering, some sort of atoning power for certain classes of sins, both of commission and omission, for which the Bible ascribes no sacrifice at all.[2] We find, further, that they ascribed an atoning power to the vestments of the high priests. All such passages have to be taken *cum grano salis;* they are in no way meant to relieve the individual from his duty to perform or to refrain from certain actions, nor from any punishment or fine connected with the transgression in question, be it of a prohibitive or affirmative nature. Such atonements, especially those connected with the vestments of the high priests or with communal offerings, extend chiefly to the community, which, in accordance with the Rabbinic high conception of the close solidarity

[1] See *Pseudo-Jonathan* to Num. 28 4; *P. K.*, 55 *b*; and *P. R.* 78 *b*.

[2] See above, p. 226, with regard to the function of the burnt-offering, which atones for the evil meditations of the heart. According to others, it atones for failing to accomplish the affirmative laws of the Bible. See *Arachin*, 16 *a*, with regard to incense. See also *Tan.* תצוה, 15.

of Israel, was greatly responsible for the sins of the individual, but practically helpless to prevent them. Following, as it seems, the precedent of the expiatory ceremony of the heifer beheaded in the valley in the case of unknown murder (Deut. 21 1–9), they also came to perceive in almost every object connected with the sanctuary or the high priest as many symbolic atonements protecting the community against the consequences of sins beyond its ken and its power to interfere.[1]

The Day of Atonement, with its various atoning functions, is also, as is well known, largely the means of protection for the community, and is chiefly concerned with sins connected with Levitical impurity. According to the Rabbis, the atoning effect of the scapegoat (Lev. 16 21) extends also to the individual, and expiates also for other "transgressions of the Law, the light and the heavy ones, committed intentionally or unintentionally, knowingly or unknowingly, of an affirmative or prohibitive nature, punished by excision from the community or even by capital punishment." [2] It is

[1] See *J. T. Yoma*, 44 *b*; *Arachin*, 15 *a*; *Zebachim*, 88 *b*, text and commentaries; *Lev. R.*, 10 6, and *Cant. R.*, 4 4. Some sort of a precedent is given in the diadem on the forehead of the high priest, to which an atoning efficacy is ascribed in the Scriptures. See Exod. 28 38. Cf. also Epstein's commentary, תורה תמימה, to Exod. 29 1. The explanation given in the text here is that suggested by certain commentators of the Talmud, which is undoubtedly the only true one, though the Agadic expressions are very vague and not always consistent.

[2] See *Shebuoth*, 2 *b*, *Mishnah* and *Gemara*, 2 *b* and 6 *b* to 14 *a*. Cf. *Yoma*, 85 *b*, *Mishnah*; *T. K.*, 82 *b*. The distribution of the vari-

further to be noticed that, according to the Rabbis, it is the *Day* of Atonement that atones "even when there is no sacrifice and no goat," it being the day itself which has this efficacy, independent of the sacrificial worship.[1] But, on the other hand, this efficacy is subject to the following two important conditions: first, that it has to be accompanied by repentance on the part of those who are meant to profit by it;[2] and, further, that in matters between man and man the

ous atonements over the various sacrifices brought on the Day of Atonement and other festivals and the particular function of each sacrifice is one of the most complicated subjects in Rabbinic literature, and is discussed at great length by different schools both in the Talmud of Babylon, and the Talmud of Jerusalem of the Tractates just named. Briefly stated, it comes to this, that all the sacrifices brought by the congregation (צבור) on new moons and the various festivals which the Scriptures describe as a sin-offering or as intended to make atonement (cf. Lev. 23 19; and Num. 28 15. 22. 29; 29 4. 9. 16. 19. 22. 25. 28. 31. 34. 38) are limited in their efficacy to Levitical impurity. This is also the case with the various sin-offerings brought on the Day of Atonement, as detailed in Lev., ch. 16. An exception is made with reference to the scapegoat, whose atonement extends to all possible cases. See especially *Tosephta Shebuoth*, p. 445, where the importance of Levitical purity is proved by the fact that any breach against it was atoned for by not less than thirty-two sacrifices every year. Cf. also Maimonides, שגגות, 3 9 and 11 9. See also Maimonides, תשובה, 1 2. For the statement of Maimonides, that the scapegoat atones in lighter transgressions even without repentance, see טורי אבן by R. Eleazar Rokeach (in *Mishneh Torah*, ed. Warsaw, 1900), that it refers only to cases when the person remained ignorant of his sin, לא הודע.

[1] See *T. K.*, 83 *a*. Cf. also *Jer. Yoma*, 45 *c*.

[2] This is the general opinion of the Rabbis. See *T. K.*, 102 *a*; *Jer. Yoma*, 45 *b*; and *B. T.*, *ibid.*, 85 *b*. Cf. Maimonides, תשובה, ch. 3. The contrary opinion of R. Judah, the Patriarch, forms the only exception and stands entirely isolated.

Day of Atonement loses its atoning power until proper restitution is made to the wronged person. "Matters between thee and the Omnipresent they forgive thee; matters between thee and thy fellow-man they forgive not until thou hast appeased thy neighbour." [1] In such matters touching one's fellow-man God neither respects persons nor will he by any means clear the guilty.[2] But apparently, in wronging one's fellow-man, there is also an offence against the majesty of God. Whence the formula in the case of asking forgiveness for the injury done to a man who died before satisfaction could be given him is, "I have sinned against the Lord, the God of Israel, and against the man I have injured." [3] Man is thus also in need of the pardon of heaven, besides the achieved reconciliation from his fellow-man or through the worldly tribunal. Through these conditions, the Day of Atonement becomes practically the great Day of Repentance, the culmination of the Ten Days of Repentance. It brings with itself purification, the Father in Heaven making white the sin committed by the son, by his forgiveness and pardon.[4] "It is the Day of the Lord, great and very terrible," inasmuch as it becomes a day of judgement,[5] but also the Day of Salvation.[6]

[1] *T. K.*, 83 *a*; *Yoma*, 85 *a*.

[2] See *Sifre Zuta* as reproduced by *Yalkut* to *Pent.*, § 711, and *Num. R.*, 11 6. Cf. *Rosh Hashanah*, 17 *b*. The Rabbinic interpretation deals there with the seeming contradiction between Num. 6 26 and Deut. 10 17.

[3] See *Yoma*, 87 *a*. See also *Mishnah*, *Baba Kama*, 8 7.

[4] *M. T.*, 9 4. [5] See *Tan.*, וישלח, 2. [6] *P. R.*, 175 *b*.

"Israel is steeped in sin through the *Evil Yezer* in their body, but they do repentance and the Lord forgives their sins every year, and renews their heart to fear him."[1] "On the Day of Atonement I will create you a new creation."[2] It is thus a penitential day in the full and in the best sense of the word.

Death and suffering may be viewed either as a punishment satisfying the claims of justice or as an atonement, bringing pardon and forgiveness and reconciling man with God. The first aspect finds its most emphatic and most solemn expression in the following Tannaitic statement: The born are to die; and the dead to revive; and the living to be judged; for to know, and to notify, and that it may be known, that he is the framer, and he the creator, and he the discerner, and he the judge, and he the witness, and he the complainant, and he is about to judge, with whom there is no iniquity, nor forgetfulness, nor respect of persons, nor taking of bribe, for all is his, and know that all is according to reckoning. Let not thine *Yezer* assure thee that the grave is a place of refuge for thee; for perforce thou wast framed, and perforce thou wast born, and perforce thou livest, and perforce thou diest, and perforce thou art about to give account and reckoning before the King of the king of kings, the Holy One, blessed be he.[3] But "the judgement (to proceed with another Tannaitic statement of R. Akiba) is a

[1] *Exod. R.*, 1 6. [2] *P. R.*, 169 *a*.
[3] *Aboth*, 4 22. Cf. *Taylor*, 4 31-32; Bacher, *Ag. Tan.*, 2 502.

judgement of truth."[1] And when Pappos, on the authority of Job 23 13, expressed views implying a certain arbitrariness on the part of God because of his being One (alone), he was severely rebuked by R. Akiba, the latter Rabbi interpreting the meaning of the verse mentioned, "There is nothing to answer to the words of him by whose word the world was called into existence, for he judges all in truth and everything in judgement (justice)."[2] The same thought is somewhat differently expressed by another Rabbi, in allusion to Deut. 32 4: "'He is the Rock, his work is perfect: for all his ways are judgement: a God of truth and without iniquity, just and right is he.' His work is perfect towards all who come into the world (mankind), and none must allege that there is the slightest injustice. Nobody must brood upon and ask, why was the generation of the deluge swept away by water; why was the generation of the Tower of Babel scattered over all the world; why were the generations of Sodom and Gomorrah consumed by fire and brimstone; why was Aaron found worthy to be endowed with the priesthood; why was David worthy to be presented with the kingdom; and why were Korah and his congregation swallowed up by the earth? . . . He sits in judgement against every

[1] *Aboth*, 3 15.

[2] See *Mechilta*, 33 *a*; *Cant. R.*, 1 9. The parallel in *Tan. B.*, 2 4 *b*, to the effect that God occupies only the position of the president of the heavenly court composed of angels, seems to be a younger paraphrase of the statement of R. Akiba. See *Exod. R.*, 6 1. Cf. Bacher, *Ag. Tan.*, 3 26.

one and gives every one what is due to him."[1] It is with reference to the same verse (Deut. 32 4) that a later Rabbi makes the remark to the effect: He who says the Holy One, blessed be he (or the Merciful One), is loose (or lax) in his dealing out justice, let his life become loose. He is long-suffering but collects his (debt) in the end.[2] In another place the same thought is expressed in the words: God says, "I am the merciful one, but also a judge to punish."[3]

It should, however, be remarked that the same R. Akiba, who insists on the strict (true) judgement of God, teaches also that the world is judged by grace.[4]

[1] See *Sifre*, 133 *a*. Cf. also לקט מדרשים, ed. Werthheimer, p. 6 *b*, with reference to Job 11 7.

[2] See *Baba Kama*, 50 *a*; *Jer. Shekalim*, 48 *d*; *M. T.*, 10 8, text and notes.

[3] *Gen. R.*, 16 6.

[4] *Aboth*, 3 15. Cf. Taylor, 3 24. It should be remarked that this sentence is followed in the editions by the words והכל לפי רוב המעשה ("everything is according to the majority of the actions"). This reading receives some support from *Kiddushin*, 40 *a*, and *Eccles. R.*, 10 1, that both the world and the individual are judged according to the majority of good actions. Cf. Bacher, *Ag. Tan.*, I 282. But there are also other readings, as "But not everything is according to the majority of deeds;" or merely, "But not according to the deed." Cf. Taylor, *ibid.*, and his Appendix, p. 153. From *Jer. Kiddushin*, 61 *d*, it would seem that this insistence upon a majority of good actions applies only to the judgement in the next world, but in this world even one good action can save a man. If we should assume that this represents also the opinion of R. Akiba, there would be no real contradiction. Cf. *A. R. N.*, 81 *b*, and the commentary to *Aboth* in *Machsor Vitri*, p. 514, where *Aboth* 3 15 is explained in the way just indicated. Cf. above, p. 15, note 1.

But it would seem that this grace is only confined to this world. In the next world there is only strict justice prevailing. Even Israel, apparently, enjoying otherwise so many privileges, is not exempt from the punishment awaiting the sinners in the next world. When Moses ascended from hell, he prayed, "May it be thy will . . . that thou savest thy people Israel from this place." But the Holy One, blessed be he, said unto him, "Moses, there is not with me respect of persons, nor taking of bribe. He who will do good will be in the Paradise, he who will do evil will be in hell, as it is said, 'I the Lord search the heart, I try the reins, even to give every man according to his ways, and according to the fruit of his doings' (Jer. 17 10)."[1] But even in this world, "when man sees that suffering comes upon him, he has to examine his actions," to see whether it has not come as a punishment for his sins. Likewise is death considered, in the majority of cases at least, as a punishment for the sin of the individual. For God is not suspected to execute judgement without justice.[2]

But besides satisfying the claims of a just God or of justice, death and suffering also atone and reconcile

[1] See בתי מדרשות, ed. Werthheimer, 4 29 *a*. Against this view are *Cant. R.*, 8 8; *Exod. R.*, 30 16. Cf. also *M. T.*, 15 24, text and notes, but the view given in the text appears to be the older one. Cf. *Sifre*, 12 *b*, text and notes 5 and 6, and *Num. R.*, 11 7.

[2] See *Berachoth*, 5 *a* and *b*. For the difficulties in the way of this theory and the manner in which the Rabbis tried to solve it, see Schechter, *Studies in Judaism*, Essay on Retribution, p. 259 *seq.*

man with God. They form, according to the Rabbis, two of the four (or the three) kinds of atonement taught by the Scriptures.[1] Self-inflicted suffering, such as fasting, assumes naturally the aspect of sacrifices. Hence the prayer of a Rabbi after a fast that the fat and blood which he lost through the fast should be accounted to him as a sacrifice on the altar, and have the same effect as the sacrifice in the days of yore when the Holy Temple was in existence.[2] This was considered as a kind of self-sacrifice, or rather sacrifice of his soul,[3] but this notion was not entirely limited to voluntary suffering. Every loss of property sustained by man, as well as every kind of physical suffering which he happens to undergo, are considered an atonement. "A man stumbled in a transgression, and became guilty of death by heaven (in contradistinction of the worldly tribunal). By what means shall he atone? His ox died, his chickens went astray, or he stumbled on his finger so that blood came out — by these losses and suffering, his debts (to the account of heaven against him) are considered paid."[4] Indeed, the loss of blood

[1] See *Mechilta*, 68 *b* and 69 *a*. *A. R. N.*, 44 *b*, text and notes for other references. The other kinds of atonement are the Day of Atonement and Repentance, but since they are all accompanied by repentance, there are practically only three kinds. The Scriptural references are Lev. 16 30, for the Day of Atonement, Isa. 22 14, for death, Jer. 3 22, for repentance, and Ps. 89 33, for suffering.

[2] See *Berachoth*, 17 *a*. Cf. *M. T.*, 25 8.

[3] See *Lev. R.*, 3 4 and commentaries.

[4] See *Jer. Sotah*, 17 *a*; *Eccles. R.*, 7 27; *Pesachim*, 118 *a*.

through any accident atones as the blood of a sacrifice.[1]

It is further maintained that the appearance of leprosy on the body of a man is the very altar of atonement.[2] Hence the dictum, "Beloved is suffering, for as sacrifices are atoning, so is suffering atoning." Nay, suffering has even a greater atoning effect than sacrifice, inasmuch as sacrifice affects only man's property, whilst suffering touches his very self.[3] "Who caused the son to be reconciled to his father (in heaven), if not suffering?"[4] "Therefore, let man rejoice in suffering more than in prosperity," for it is suffering through which he receives pardon and forgiveness.[5] "If thou seekest for life, hope for suffering," as it is said, "And reproof of chastisement (is) the way of life" (Prov. 6 3).[6] Indeed, the good son does not even pray that the suffering should cease, but says, "Father, continue thy chastisement."[7] This suffering has to be a sacrifice accompanied by repentance. The sufferer has to accept the suffering prayerfully and in a spirit of submission, and has to recognise that the visitation of God was merited by him. Man knows well in his heart when weighing his deeds with the suffering which came upon him that he was dealt with mercifully.[8] Indeed, the great difference between Israel and

[1] See *Chullin*, 7 *b*.
[2] See *Berachoth*, 5 *b*.
[3] See *Sifre*, 73 *b* and reference given there.
[4] *Sifre*, *ibid.*
[5] *Sifre*, 73 *b*.
[6] *M. T.*, 16.
[7] See Minor Tractate, *Semachoth*, 8.
[8] *Sifre*, *ibid.*

the gentiles, is that the gentiles rebel when suffering comes upon them, and curse their gods; but Israel becomes humble and prays, as it is said, "I found trouble and sorrow. Then called I upon the name of the Lord," etc. (Ps. 116 34).[1]

The atonement of suffering and death is not limited to the suffering person. The atoning effect extends to all the generation. This is especially the case with such sufferers as cannot either by reason of their righteous life or by their youth possibly have merited the afflictions which have come upon them. The death of the righteous atones just as well as certain sacrifices.[2] "They are caught (suffer) for the sins of their generation. If there are no righteous, the children of the schools (that is, the innocent young children) are caught for the sins of their generation."[3] There are also applied to Moses the Scriptural words, "And he bore the sins of many" (Isa. 53 12), because of his offering himself as an atonement for Israel's sin with the golden calf, being ready to sacrifice his very soul for Israel, when he said, "And if not, blot me, I pray thee, out of thy book (that is, from the Book of the Living), which thou hast written" (Exod. 32 32).[4] This readiness to sacrifice oneself for Israel is characteristic of all the great men of Israel, the patriarchs and the Prophets

[1] See *Mechilta*, 72 *b* and reference given there. Cf. *T. B.*, 5 24 *b*.

[2] See *Moed Katon*, 28 *a*.

[3] See *Shabbath*, 32 *b*.

[4] *Sotah*, 14 *a*, and *Berachoth*, 32 *a*.

acting in the same way, whilst also some Rabbis would, on certain occasions, exclaim, "Behold, I am the atonement of Israel."[1] This sacrifice is, of course, voluntary. But this is also the case with the sacrifice on the part of the children who in some mystical way are made to take upon themselves this surety. When God was about to give the Torah to Israel, Rabbinic legend relates that he asked for some guarantee that Israel will on its part fulfil the obligations which the Revelation will devolve upon them. Then Israel offered as such the patriarchs and the Prophets, but they were not found sufficiently free from debt (faultless) to be worthy of this confidence. At last they offered their children, and the Holy One, blessed be he, accepted them willingly. But he first asked them, "Will you serve as surety for your parents, that they fulfil the Torah which I am about to give them, and that you will suffer in case they do not fulfil it?" They said, "Yes." Then the Act of Revelation began, which also the children witnessed, even those who were still in the embryonic state, when they gave their consent to each commandment revealed. This is what is said, "Out of the mouths of babes and sucklings hast thou ordained strength" (Ps. 8 2).[2]

[1] See *Mechilta*, 2 *a*; *Mishnah Negaim*, 2 1. Cf. Introduction to *S. E.*, 127. By patriarchs is understood in that place, David. Cf. 2 Samuel 24 17. Cf. above, p. 52 *seq.*

[2] See *M. T.*, 8; *Midrash Cant.*, 1 8 and references given there. Cf. also above, pp. 193 and 254.

Atoning power is also ascribed to Torah and charity. The descendants of Eli could find no atonement by sacrifice and meat-offering, but they might receive pardon through the occupation with the study of the Torah and acts of loving-kindness.[1] Indeed, the Holy One, blessed be he, foresaw that the Holy Temple would be destroyed and promised Israel that the words of the Torah, which is likened unto sacrifices, will, after the destruction of the Temple, be accepted as a substitute for sacrifices.[2] Something similar is maintained with regard to acts of loving-kindness, which take the place of sacrifice, atoning for the sins of Israel after the destruction of the Temple; nay, it is even maintained that acts of loving-kindness or charity are more important than sacrifices.[3] Reference may be made here also to the atoning effect ascribed to the dining-table in the household of a man, which is considered, by reason of the hospitality offered on it to the poor, as the altar in the Temple, on which the sacrifices were brought.[4] The chaste woman is also likened to the altar; as the altar atones (for the sins of Israel), so she atones for her house.[5]

1 *Rosh Hashanah*, 18 *a*.

2 *Tan.*, אחרי, 10. Cf. *Tan. B.*, 3 85 *a*.

3 See *A. R. N.*, 11 *a* and *b*, text and notes, and *Sukkah*, 49 *b*. See above, p. 308.

4 *Berachoth*, 55 *a*. See, however, A. Epstein, אלדד הדני, p. 117, note 126.

5 *Tan.*, וישלח, 6.

## XVIII

## REPENTANCE: MEANS OF RECONCILIATION

THE prayer of the Psalmist, "Be merciful unto me, O God" (Ps. 56 2), is paraphrased by the Rabbis in the following way, "Be merciful unto me that I shall not be brought to fall by sin, but when I have sinned (God forefend) be merciful unto me that I may return in repentance." In another place the same thought is expressed in the following way: The Holy One, blessed be he, says (unto man), "I made the *Evil Yezer.* Be careful that he should not make thee sin; but if he did make thee sin, be eager to do repentance, then I will forgive thy sins." And as we have seen, repentance is the remedy offered by the Holy One, blessed be he, himself.[1] As it must further be clear from the preceding remarks, it is practically considered a necessary accompaniment of all other modes of atonement. Indeed, it would seem as if repentance is the only means of cleaning the guilty, though God is long-suffering, and forgiving iniquity and transgressions.[2] Its im-

[1] *M. T.*, 57 1. See also *ibid.*, 32:4. See Montefiore (as above, p. 289, note 1) on the subject.

[2] See *Sifre Zuta* as communicated in the name of Ben Azai in *Num. R.*, 11 7. Cf. *Yoma*, 86 *a*, and *Midrash Prov.*, 10. The interpretation is based on Exod. 34 7, where the Rabbis, in a homiletical way, separated the infinitive of ונקה from the verb לא ינקה.

portance is so great that it forms one of the things which preceded creation,[1] as a preliminary condition to the existence of the world. "When he drew the plan of the world he found that it could not stand (endure) until he had created repentance," since, as the early commentators explained it, the nature of man is so constituted that he cannot well escape sin. His existence would therefore have proved impossible without the remedy of repentance.[2] In agreement with this explanation is another passage from a semi-mystical book, running thus: "Rabbi Ishmael said, 'The world could never have existed but for the fact that repentance was created (first), and the Holy One, blessed be he, stretches out his right hand to receive penitence every day.' The sages said, 'After God thought to create the *Evil Yezer* he began to regret it, but prepared the cure before the affliction, and created repentance.'"[3]

God not only created repentance, but he continues to instruct mankind in repentance. "Good and upright is the Lord, therefore will he teach sinners in the way" (Ps. 25 8). This way is, as the Rabbis explained, the way of repentance which God points out to the

[1] See *Gen. R.*, 1 4, and *Pesachim*, 54 *a*, and references, especially *M. T.*, 9 11, text and note 69.

[2] See *P. R. E.*, 11; cf. *MHG.*, p. 8, and the commentary on the *Sefer Yezirah*, of R. Jehudah Barzillai of Barcelona, pp. 88 and 96. Cf. also above, p. 128.

[3] Quoted by a commentary to *Aboth* in Ms. (in the Library of the Jewish Theological Seminary) forming a kind of *Yalkut* to this Tractate (22 *a*). The use of the word אלהים in the text would point to the *Yelamdenu* as the original source.

sinner.[1] In other places, the Rabbis speak of the "doors of repentance," or "the gates of repentance," which are likewise opened by God himself.[2] Such a "door" God opened to Adam after his fall, saying unto him, "Do repentance," but of this offer he did not avail himself; whereupon he was expelled from Paradise.[3] Adam only learned the force of repentance from his son Cain, whom God established as a "mark" (or standard, example) for penitence.[4] He then submitted to a course of repentance and prayed, "Lord of the world, remove my sin from me and accept my repentance, so that all generations should learn that there is repentance and that thou hast accepted the repentance of those who return unto thee."[5] It is further recorded that God gave warning (by certain phenomena in nature) and opportunity for repentance to the generation of the deluge,[6] the generation of the Tower of Babel,[7] as well as to the men of Sodom[8] in

[1] See *Jer. Makkoth*, 31 *d*; *P. K.*, 158 *b*; *M. T.*, 25 10; and *Yalkut Machiri* to this verse. Cf. *Sanhedrin*, 105 *a*, on Isa. 28: 26, יורנו.

[2] See *P. K.*, 157 *a*; *Deut. R.*, 2 12 and references. See also M. Grünbaum, *Gesammelte Aufsätze*, etc., pp. 505 *seq.* and 510 *seq.*

[3] See *Gen. R.*, 21 6; *P. R.*, 26 *b*, text and notes.

[4] See *Gen. R.*, 22 12 and 13.

[5] See *P. R. E.*, ch. 20; cf. *Erubin*, 18 *b* and *Tan.*, תזריע, § 9. This is in contradiction with another Agadic statement which describes Reuben, the first-born of Jacob, as the first man to do repentance. Cf. *Gen. R.*, 82 11 and 84 19.

[6] See *A. R. N.*, 1 32 and reference given there.

[7] See *Gen. R.*, 38 9.

[8] See *Gen. R.*, 49 6; cf. also *Tan.* נח, 18, and בשלח, 15.

spite of their open rebellion against God. A similar opportunity was given to Korah, Moses deferring the action of offering the incense which brought about the catastrophe until "to-morrow," for the purpose of giving him and his adherents time to reconsider their evil behaviour and to repent.[1] With regard to Israel, it is stated that the Divine Presence tarried, before the destruction of the Temple, on the Mount of Olives for not less than thirteen and a half years (after it removed from the Temple), proclaiming three times a day, "Return, ye backsliding children, and I will heal your backslidings" (Jer. 3 22).[2] When the Temple was destroyed, God prays, "May it be my will that I exterminate the *Evil Yezer* that brings my children to sin, so that they do repentance and I hasten the rebuilding of my house and my sanctuary."[3] But this mercy of God is not confined to Israel, the Holy One, blessed be he, hoping for the nations of the world that they might do repentance that he should bring them near under his wings (by becoming proselytes).[4] The example set by God (in praying for the regeneration of the sinner) is imitated both by Moses and by Aaron, who prayed for the sinners in Israel that they might become penitents.[5] It is also narrated that

[1] See *Num. R.*, 18 7; cf. Deut. 16 5 *seq.*

[2] See *P. K.*, 115 *a*, text and notes; and *Lament. R.*, ed. Buber, 15 *b*, text and notes.

[3] *M. T.*, 76 8. See text and notes.

[4] See *Num. R.*, 10 1; *Cant. R.*, 61 1 (§ 5).

[5] See *Sotah*, 14 *a*, and *T. K.*, 46 *a*.

the Saint Abba Hilkia had certain outlaws in his neighbourhood for whose death he prayed, but his wife prayed that they might return to repentance, and that her actions were approved by signs from heaven.[1]

It is further assumed that great moral catastrophes were almost providentially brought about with the purpose of setting the good example to sinners that no sin is so great as to make repentance impossible. As such examples, are cited: David, who committed the sin of adultery; and the whole congregation of Israel, the contemporaries of Moses, who worshipped the golden calf. Neither David nor Israel, considering their high moral standing, were, the Rabbis declare, capable of such crimes, but it was brought about against their own will, as just stated, to give a claim for repentance in the future both in the case of the individual, as David, and in the case of the whole community, as that of the golden calf, in which the whole of Israel was involved, and thus showing that there is no room for despair of reconciliation with God, be the sin never so great and all-embracing.[2] Indeed, David became a "witness to the people," bearing evidence to the power of repentance, for "he who is desirous to do repentance has only to look at David." Hence, he

[1] See *Taanith*, 23 *b*. Cf. *Berachoth*, 10 *a*, the story of R. Meir and Berurya.

[2] See *Abodah Zarah*, 4 *b* and 5 *a*, text and commentaries; cf. *Shabbath*, 65 *a*.

is called the man that established the sublimity of repentance.[1]

The encouragement of mankind to repentance is carried so far on the part of heaven that the "door" is opened even when this repentance is not entirely the expression of real remorse and regret, having been brought about only by pressure, and furthermore meant to atone for crimes of a most revolting kind. Such a case is particularly that of Manasseh, the son of Hezekiah, the wicked King of Judah, whose reign was, according to the testimony of the Scriptures, one long series of the most atrocious crimes" (2 Kings 21 2 *seq.* and 2 Chron. 33 2 *seq.*). "When he found himself during his captivity in Babel, in real distress, there was no idol he failed to invoke. . . . But when he saw that they were of no help to him, he said, 'I remember that my father made me read, "When thou art in tribulation, and all these things are come upon thee, even in the latter days, if thou turn to the Lord, thy God, and shalt be obedient unto his voice: For the Lord thy God is a merciful God; he will not forsake thee, neither destroy thee" (Deut. 4 30. 31). I will now invoke him. If he will answer me, well; if not, I will declare that all Powers are alike.' The angels thereupon shut the openings of heaven and said before the Holy One, blessed be he, 'Shall repentance avail

[1] See *M. T.*, 40 2 and 51 8. Cf. Isa. 55 4. See also *Moed Katon*, 16 *b*, and Rashi's commentary as given in the עין יעקב to this passage. Cf. also *Num. R.* 18 21, text and reference given there.

for a man who placed an image in the very *Hechal* (sanctuary)?' (2 Kings 21 7 and 2 Chron. 33 7). Then the Holy One, blessed be he, said, 'If I accept not his repentance, I thereby shut the door against all other penitents.' He then dug for Manasseh's repentance a special passage from below the Throne of Glory (over which the angels have no control) and through this was heard Manasseh's supplication." [1] "Thus, if a man would tell thee that God receives not the penitents, behold Manasseh, the son of Hezekiah, he will bear evidence that no creature in the world ever committed before me so many wicked deeds as he did, yet in the moment of repentance I received him." [2] Some Rabbis even resented the apparently ancient tradition excluding Manasseh from the bliss of the world to come, inasmuch as it may have the effect to "weaken the hand of penitence," that is, to make sinners despair of the efficacy of repentance.[3]

Of Jeroboam it is said that the Holy One, blessed be he, laid hold of him and said, "Return (in repentance), and I and the son of Jesse and thou shall walk together in Paradise." The conceit of Jeroboam, however,

[1] See *P. K.*, 162 *a* and *b*; cf. *Jer. Sanhedrin*, 78 *c*, and *B. T. Sanhedrin*, 103 *a*; *Lev. R.*, 30 3; *Deut. R.*, 2 20; *Ruth R.*, 5 14; *P. R. E.*, ch. 43; and *Targum* to *Chron.*, *a. l.* See also *Ag. Ber.*, ch. 9, and *Sifre*, 144 *b*. Cf. also *M. T.*, 4 : 5, where the statement is more general, but is based on the Manasseh legend.

[2] See *Num. R.*, 14 1 and references. Cf. also *Gen. R.*, ed. Wilna, Appendix on the Blessing of Jacob, p. 376, col. 2, the story there about Cain.

[3] *Sanhedrin*, 103 *a*.

made him refuse God's offer, as he was not willing to be second to the son of Jesse.[1] Naturally such a *Teshubah* as that of Manasseh, undertaken amidst suffering and through fear of punishment, is not considered the highest degree of repentance, leaving man in a state of slavery, whilst the repentance undertaken through the motive of love reëstablishes man's child-like relations to his Father in Heaven.[2]

This consideration, that nothing should be said or done which might lead to the discouragement of the penitent, had also an influence on certain ordinances of the Rabbis which were introduced for the special benefit of those who "returned." Thus, in certain cases, the restitution of the article appropriated in a dishonest way was not insisted upon, the robber being allowed to repay its value in money. It seems that even for the cattle-drivers and the tax-gatherers and the publicans, whose repentance meets with difficulties (because of their plundering the community at large, so that they are not in a condition to make restitution to the wronged person), certain provisions were made to make their repentance possible.[3] The rule was also that they would accept sacrifice from sinners in Israel in order that they might return as penitents.[4]

[1] See *Sanhedrin*, 102 *b*.

[2] See *Yoma*, 86 *a*. See also Rabbinowicz, *Variae Lectiones*, *a.l.*

[3] תקנת השבים. See *Eduyoth*, 7 9. See *Baba Kama*, 94 *b* and 95 *a*. Cf. also Maimonides, ה׳ גזלה ואבדה, 1 13.

[4] See *Chullin*, 5 *a*, and Maimonides, מעשה הקרבנות, 3 4, about the various modifications of this law. Cf. also *P. R.*, 192 *a*.

We find even that friendly relations were entertained with sinners in the hope that intercourse with saintly men would engender in them a thought of shame and repentance. Thus it is said of Aaron the High Priest, who "did turn many away from iniquity" (Mal. 2 6), when he met a wicked man he would offer him his greetings. When the wicked man was about to commit a sin, he would say to himself, "Woe unto me, how can I lift my eyes and see Aaron? I ought to be ashamed before him who gave me greetings." And he would then desist from sin.[1] It was also forbidden to say to the penitent, "Remember thy actions of former days," such a reference to the former depraved life of the penitent being considered an oppression and coming under the Scriptural prohibition of, "Ye shall therefore not oppress one another: but thou shalt fear thy God: for I am the Lord, your God" (Lev. 25 17).[2]

The objection of the angels to the admittance of repentance is not confined to such extraordinary cases as the one of Manasseh. As it would seem, they oppose repentance in general. "When a man commits a transgression, the angels come and denounce him, and say, 'Master of the Universe, bow down thy heavens, O Lord, and come down: touch the mountains and they shall smoke,' etc. (that is, they demand immediate

[1] *A. R. N.*, 24 *b.* Cf. *Sanhedrin*, 37 *a*, the story of R. Zera, who entertained certain relations with the outlaws in his neighbourhood for the same purpose.

[2] See *Baba Mezia*, 58 *b.*

satisfaction). But the Holy One, blessed be he, says, 'Man may be hard for the time, but if he will do repentance, I will receive him.'"[1] But it should be remarked that in other places this opposition to the admittance of repentance is ascribed to the Divine attribute of strict justice, which is overruled by the Divine attribute of mercy.[2] Nay, repentance is so beloved by the Holy One, blessed be he, that he is ready to overrule his own Law for its sake. It is written in the Torah, "When a man hath taken a wife and married her, and he has found some uncleanness in her, then let him write a bill of divorcement. . . . And if the later husband hate her, and write her a bill of divorcement, . . . her former husband which sent her away cannot take her again to be his wife, after she is defiled" (Deut. 24 1, 3, and 4). But this is not so with the Holy One, blessed be he, for though they have forsaken him and worshipped another, he said unto them, "Do repentance and come back unto me and I will receive you."[3] It is the right hand of God which is stretched out to receive penitence, against the pleading of angels, and as we may add also against

[1] See *M. T.*, 94 4; see also *Yalkut Machiri Ps.*, *a. l.*, who gives a better reading, which is reproduced here.

[2] See *Sanhedrin*, 103 *a*, and *Pesachim*, 119 *a*. See also *Pseudo-Jonathan S. E. Z.*, p. 37. This is an interesting case of hypostatised attributes, to which others might be added. The subject is still in need of a good monograph.

[3] *P. R.*, 184 *a*. Cf. *Yoma*, 86 *b*. This homily forms a paraphrase of Jer. 3 1.

the view of the Prophets demanding punishment by death, and the decision of the Torah, demanding at least a sacrifice. The "right hand" represents the attribute of mercy, which is also called "the strong hand," inasmuch as it has to repress the attribute of strict justice.[1] This suggests that the admittance of repentance is an act of grace on the part of God, as forgiveness in general is. "There is no creature which is not in debt (or rather guilty) to God, but he is merciful and gracious and forgives the sins of the past," when succeeded by repentance.[2] When the Holy One, blessed be he, said to the Torah, "Let us make man in our image after our likeness," the Torah answered, "Master of all worlds, the world is thine, but the men thou desirest to create are 'of few days and full of trouble' and will fall into the power of sin, and if thou wilt not defer thy anger, it is better for him (man) that he should not come to the world." Then the Holy One, blessed be he, said to her, "Is it for naught that I am called long-suffering and abundant in goodness?" [3] "I am," says God, "the same (in my attribute of mercy) before man sins and (the same in my attribute of mercy) after man has sinned, if he will do repentance." [4] Indeed,

[1] See *Sifre*, 50 *b*.

[2] See *Exod. R.*, 31 1.

[3] See *P. R. E.*, ch. 12, text and notes of Loria, especially his reference to ch. 3, *ibid.* The connection of the attribute of long-suffering with repentance is also given in *P.K.*, 161 *b*, with allusion to Joel 2 13. Cf. Gen. 1 26; Exod. 34 7; Job 8 1.

[4] See *Rosh Hashanah*, 17 *b*; cf. *P.R.*, 145. The text forms an interpretation to Exod. 34 6, referring to the two mentions of the Tetra-

repentance is described as the good portion which God assigned to his world, which proved effective even in the case of an Ahab,[1] and the call to repentance embodied in the words of Amos, "Seek ye me and ye shall live" (5 4), is considered as the sweet message.[2] The sinner even receives the promise that after a sincere repentance entered upon through the motive of love (of God) his very intentional sins during his unregenerated life will be charged unto him as so many merits.[3]

The verse from Amos just quoted is paraphrased, "My children, what do I ask of you but seek me and you shall live." [4] It is, as we have just seen, the sweet message; but it assumes an endeavour on the part of man to break with his sinful past.[5] For, though repentance is, as just pointed out, an act of grace, there is, as in other such cases, a certain initiative and co-operation expected on the part of man.[6] Every encouragement is given to the penitent. No false shame should stand in the way of the repentant in seeking reconciliation with God. "Said the Holy One, blessed be he,

grammaton in that verse, which Divine Name represents, in Rabbinic literature, the attribute of mercy.

[1] See *Jer. Sanhedrin*, 78 *b*. I am inclined to think that the word מנה should be amended to מתנה. The sense then would be that repentance is one of God's good gifts to the world.

[2] See *Cant. R.*, 6 1.

[3] See *Yoma*, 86 *b*. Cf. *Cant. R.*, 6, *ibid.*

[4] See *P. R.*, 158 *b*; cf. also *ibid.*, 157 *a*.

[5] See *Cant. R.*, *ibid.*

[6] See above, 289.

to Jeremiah, 'Go and bid Israel to do repentance.' He went and delivered his message. Thereupon they said to him, 'With what face can we enter before his presence? Have we not made him angry; have we not provoked his wrath? Are not those mountains and hills on which we worshipped the idols, still existing? We lie down in our shame and our confusion covers us.' He came back to the Holy One, blessed be he, and said so (repeating their answer). Then God said to him, 'Go back and tell them, "If you return to me, is it not to your Father in Heaven to whom you come? For I am a Father to Israel, and Ephraim is my first-born."'"[1] Nor must man despair because of the quantity of his sins. When David, and after him Ezra, said, "Our iniquities are increased over our heads and our trespass is grown up to the heavens," the Holy One, blessed be he, answered, "Fear not because of this thing, even if they (the sins) reached the very heaven, and if you do repentance, I will forgive; and not only the first heaven . . . but even if they reached the very Throne of Glory, and if you will do repentance, I will receive you at once (as it is said): 'O Israel, return unto the Lord thy God' (Hos. 14 1)."[2] In another place, the words "unto thy God" are interpreted to refer to the *quality* of sins, be they even of such a nature that they touched the very Deity itself, as, for instance, when man

[1] See *P. K.*, 165 *a*; cf. also Jer. 3 25, 31 9, and Hosea 4 18. See also *Tan. B.*, Introduction, 68 *b* and 69 *a*.

[2] See *P. R.*, 155 *a*; cf. Ps. 38 5; Ezra 9 6.

denied the very root (the existence of God) or committed blasphemy. It is customary, the Rabbis say, when a man insults his neighbour in public and after a time he seeks for reconciliation with him that the latter insist that he should ask for his pardon in public. "But with the Holy One, blessed be he, it is not so. Man rises and blasphemes in the market-place. But the Holy One, blessed be he, says unto him, 'Do repentance between thee and me and I will receive thee.'"[1] And when Israel, under the heavy burden of sin, says, "Master of the world, wilt thou receive us if we shall do repentance?" God answers them, "I have received the repentance of Cain . . . the repentance of Ahab . . . the repentance of the men of Anathoth . . . the repentance of the men of Nineveh . . . the repentance of Manasseh . . . the repentance of Jehoiachin, against all of whom there were ordained heavy decrees, shall I not receive your repentance?"[2] indeed, even as David said, "Master of the world, thou art a great God and my sins are also great. It is only becoming for the great God that he should forgive the great sins."[3]

Thus neither the quantity of sins, nor the quality of sins, need make man hesitate to follow the Divine call to repentance. He has only to approach, so to speak, the "door" with the determination of repentance, and

[1] See *P. K.*, 163 *b*; see also *S. E.*, p. 189.

[2] See *P. K.*, 160 *a* to 163 *b*.

[3] See *Lev. R.*, 5 8, text and commentaries.

it will be widely opened for his admittance. Thus said the Holy One, blessed be he, to Israel, "Open unto me the door of repentance, be it even as narrow as the sharp point of a needle, and I will open it so wide that whole wagons and chariots can pass through it."[1] Indeed, it would seem that this Divine call of repentance implies also a certain mutual repentance, so to speak, or returning on the part of God, who meets Israel half-way. "It is to be compared to the son of a king who was removed from his father for the distance of a hundred days' journey. His friends said to him, 'Return unto your father,' whereupon he rejoined, 'I cannot.' Then his father sent a message to him, 'Travel as much as it is in thy power, and I will come unto you for the rest of the way.' And so the Holy One, blessed be he, said, 'Return unto me and I will return unto you' (Mal. 3 7)."[2] In another place, with reference to a Korahite's Psalm (55 7), we read, "The sons of Korah said, 'How long will you say, "Turn, O backsliding children"?' (Jer. 3 14) whilst Israel said, 'Return, O Lord, how long?' (Ps. 90 15). . . . But neither thou (God) wilt return by thyself, nor will we return by ourselves, but we will return both together as it is said, 'Turn us, O God of our salvation.

[1] See *Cant. R.*, 5 2 and 6, and *P. K.*, 163 *b*, text and notes. See also *Targum a. l.*

[2] See *P. R.*, 184 *b* and 185 *a*; see also *ibid.*, 144 *a*, the comparison with the sick prince, where it would seem that God takes the initiative of returning to Israel on his part.

. . . Wilt thou not come back and revive us?' (Ps. 85 4.5 and 6). As Ezekiel said, 'Behold, O my people, I will open your grave . . . and shall put my spirit in you, and ye shall live' (Ezek. 37 12-14)."[1]

The statement that neither the quantity nor the quality of sins can prevent repentance is subject to certain modifications in Rabbinic literature. The most important, though somewhat obscure, passage is the following: "Five are exempt from forgiveness: He who repeatedly does repentance and repeatedly sins; he who sins in a righteous generation; he who sins with the intention to repeat; and he who has in his hands (on his conscience) the sin of the profanation of the Name of God."[2] The passage is, as just stated, obscure and undoubtedly corrupt, but as with all these groups of numbers, it probably forms only a résumé of Tannaitic statements, scattered over the Rabbinic literature, bearing on the subject of the efficacy of repentance. As such, the following may be cited, in illustration and elucidation of the text just given: He who says, "I will sin and repent, I will sin and repent," they do not make it possible for him to repent.[3] As a reason is given in the Talmud the psychological fact that when a man has committed the same sin twice it becomes to him a thing permitted (that is, he ceases to consider it a sin), and he is therefore unable any more to repent and

[1] See *M. T.*, 85 3; cf. *Lament. R.*, 5 21.
[2] See *A. R. N.*, 58 *b*.
[3] See *Mishnah Yoma*, 85 *b*.

to leave off doing it.[1] The same sentiment is expressed elsewhere in the following words, "Let not a man say, 'I shall commit ugly deeds and things unworthy and will then bring a bull that has much flesh which I will sacrifice upon the altar and then God will have mercy upon me and accept me as a penitent.'"[2] In another place, we read, "He who causes the multitudes to sin, they do not make it possible for him to do repentance."[3] As to the profanation of the Name of God, we have the statement that "for him who has committed this sin, there is no power in repentance to suspend (the punishment), nor in the Day of Atonement to atone, nor in suffering to purify," full forgiveness only being obtained when the sinner dies.[4] For the whole of the Torah was only given with the purpose to sanctify his Great Name.[5] From these illustrating passages it will be readily seen that the statement that certain transgressions are excluded from forgiveness means in most cases that these transgressions are of such a nature that man is not likely to enter upon a course of real repentance such as would be followed by forgiveness. Some-

[1] See *Yoma*, 87 *a*.

[2] See *Lev. R.*, 2 12. See also commentaries. See also *S.E.*, p. 36.

[3] See *Aboth*, 5 18. See also *A. R. N.*, 60 *b*; *Yoma*, 87 *a*; and *Tosephta Yoma*, 4. See also *Sotah*, 47 *a*. This may perhaps be the meaning of the clause in *A. R. N.*, "He who sins in a righteous generation," that is, the generation by itself is righteous, but is caused to sin by his criminal example.

[4] See *Mechilta*, 69 *a*; *Yoma*, 86 *a*.

[5] See *S. E.*, p. 74.

times the two expressions occur together. Thus we read, "He who is confirmed (מוחלט) in transgressions (that is, a confirmed or inveterate sinner) cannot repent, and there is never forgiveness for him." [1] Indeed, there is a class of sinners who, at the very door of Gehenna, continue their rebellion and never repent.[2]

This is even more distinctly seen from another group of numbers commencing with the words, "Twenty-four things prevent repentance," which include also some of those just mentioned. They are: "He who is accustomed to slander; he who indulges in anger; he who entertains evil thoughts; he who associates with the wicked; he who looks at women; he who shares with thieves; he who says I will sin and repent, I will sin and repent; he who exalts himself at the disgrace (expense) of his neighbour; he who separates himself from the community; he who slights his masters;[3] he who curses the many;[4] he who prevents the many from doing charity; he who causes his neighbour to leave the good way for the evil way; he who makes use of the pledge of the poor;[5] he who receives bribery with the purpose of making others act unjustly; he who finds lost goods and does not return it to its owner;

[1] See *M. T.*, I 22; cf. *Yoma*, 86 *b*. See also *A. R. N.*, 62 *a*.

[2] See *Erubin*, 19 *a*, and *M. T.*, *ibid.*

[3] Reading רבותיו instead of אבותיו.

[4] Perhaps we should read המכשיל instead of המקלל, meaning, "he who puts a stumbling-block in the way of the many." Cf. the expression: המביא תקלה לרבים.

[5] See *Deut.* 24 12.

he who sees his children embracing a depraved life and does not protest; he who eats the plunder of the poor and the widows;[1] he who criticises the words of the wise man; he who suspects upright men; he who hates admonition; and he who scoffs at the commandments. Of these the Scripture says, 'Make the heart of the people fat, and make their eyes heavy, and shut their eyes; lest they see with their eyes, and hear with their ears, and understand with their heart, and convert, and be healed'" (Is. 6 10).[2] But as it is rightly pointed out by the authorities, it is not because real repentance is unacceptable, but because the nature of these sins is such that they are so habitual, or so little conspicuous, that man hardly looks upon them as sins; or because of the difficulties in the way of making proper restitution. Maimonides, who in his Law of Repentance gives the above passage with some comments, distinctly adds that though these things delay repentance, they do not make it impossible. "If a man does return, he is considered a penitent, and has a share in the world to come." [3]

[1] Reading שוד instead of שור (ox). There is, however, some justification for this latter reading. See Job 24 3. 4.

[2] See Maimonides, תשובה, ch. 4. This group is also known to many of the earlier post-Talmudic authorities, such as *Alfasi*, the *Machsor Vitri*, and others. The original source is unknown, but there can be but little doubt that it formed once a part of the Minor Tractate. See Friedmann, נספחים pp. 7 and 8, and his remarks there, on which the reader will find the authority for the corrections given in the text. See also Friedmann, *ibid.*, p. 8, for the expression cited on p. 330, Note 4. [3] See Maimonides, *ibid.*, at the end of the chapter.

The "fattening" of the heart referred to above, which makes man impervious to the thought of repentance, has a close parallel in the "hardening" of the heart used in connection with Pharaoh.[1] But there it is God himself who hardens the heart of Pharaoh (Exod. 10 1). And the Rabbis felt the difficulty, since under these conditions Pharaoh had it no longer in his power to do repentance. The answer given is that "after the Holy One, blessed be he, has given man warning three times (to do repentance) and he did not return, God shuts his heart against repentance in order to punish him for his sins."[2] "After the Holy One, blessed be he, hoped (waited) for the wicked that they will do repentance, if they do not, then he takes away their heart so that they cannot return even if they want to. Nay, he makes it impossible for them to pray."[3] This is in agreement with another statement of the Rabbis, according to which pardon is only granted for three times, but there is no forgiveness for the fourth time,[4] and cases are recorded where men hear voices from heaven giving them the sad message that there is no hope for them. Others, again, feel themselves such outcasts that they appeal to heaven and

[1] See Exod. 7 3, 10 1, and 11 10. [2] See *Exod. R.*, 13 3 and 11 6.

[3] See *Exod. R.*, 11 1. This homily seems to be based on Job 36 9-18. It is to be noted that according to other interpretations God gave to Pharoah the opportunity of repentance to the very last. See *Exod. R.*, 12 1 and especially 13 4.

[4] See *Yoma*, 86 *b*, in the name of R. Jose b. Judah. Cf. Job 33 29; *Amos* 2 4. 6. The sense of the passage is not clear. Cf. Edeles, *a. l.*

earth, to mountains and hills, to sun, moon, and planets, to pray for them, which, however, decline.[1] Legend also records that the Prophet Elisha made a special journey to Damascus to cause Gehazi (who is supposed to have stirred up people to worship idols) to do repentance, but that Gehazi referred him to a tradition which he had from the Prophet himself, that they do not make it possible for him to do repentance who causes others to sin.[2] It seems also that where reparation was impossible, repentance was also regarded as unacceptable. Such cases are: the robbery of the public, as for instance, the man who gives a false measure, since he cannot well reach those whom he cheated,[3] and murder[4] and adultery,[5] since the wrongs resulting from these sins can never be rectified.

All these qualifications, however, have to be taken as mere hyperboles, emphasising and intensifying the evil consequences of sin, and the difficulty of doing real repentance. The general rule is that accepted by all authorities, that there is nothing which can stand in the way of the penitent, be the sin ever so great,[6] or as

[1] See *Chagigah*, 25 *a*, and *Abodah Zarah*, 17 *a*.

[2] *Sotah*, 47 *a*.

[3] *Baba Bathra*, 88 *b*, and *Jebamoth*, 21 *a*.

[4] *Sanhedrin*, 7 *a*.

[5] See *Chagigah*, 9 *a* and *b*, and *Jebamoth*, 22 *b*.

[6] *T. J. Peah*, 17 *b*; R. Saadya Gaon, אמונות ודעות, 5 6. See also Maimonides, *Teshubah*, 33 14. Cf. *Sefer Chasidim*, Parma, p. 38. See also the *Responsa* of R. David b. Zimra, 2 45, in the section on Maimonides. A peculiar case is that given in the *Responsa* of R. Joseph

the outcasts above mentioned said after all intercession was declined, "The matter is only depending on me." Man has only to determine and he may be sure of acceptance. Let not man say, "I have sinned and there is no hope (of restoration or mending) for me," but let him put his confidence in the Holy One, blessed be he, and he will be received.[1] Rather bold but true is the assertion of the mystic that even a voice from heaven telling man that he is excluded from repentance should not be obeyed, it being the will of God himself that man should become importunate with his prayers and supplications, and persist in his entreaties until he finds admittance through the door of repentance.[2]

As to the nature of repentance, it is as the word תשובה suggests, first of all the returning from the evil ways, that is, a strong determination on the part of the sinner to break with sin. To enter upon a course of repentance and not to leave off sinning is compared to the man who enters a bath with the purpose of cleansing himself of a Levitical impurity, but still keeps in his hands the dead reptile which is the cause of all this

Trani (2:8), where the sinner confesses to have been especially guilty of the three cardinal sins, — idolatry, adultery, and the shedding of blood, and the Rabbi nevertheless prescribes for him a course of repentance.

[1] See *M. T.*, 40 8. See also *Abodah Zarah*, 17 *a*, with reference to the outcasts.

[2] See *Reshith Chochmah*, Section קדושה 17. See also *Responsa* of R. Joseph Trani, 2 8.

impurity. "What shall he do? Let him throw away the thing impure and then take the bath and he shall be purified." [1] In the addresses to the people on fast days, the elder would say, among other things, "My brethren, it is not sackcloth and fasts which cause forgiveness, but repentance and good deeds: for so we find of the men of Nineveh, that it is not said of them that God saw their sackcloth and fasts, but that 'God saw their works that they turned from their evil way' (Jonah 3 10)." [2]

Repentance begins in thought, and its effect is instantaneous.[3] But it is further followed up by words of confession. As Maimonides puts it, "Repentance means that the sinner gives up the sin, removing it from his mind, and determining in his heart not to repeat the evil action again; and so also he must regret his past . . . he must also confess with his lips and give expression to the thoughts which he determined in his heart." [4] The regret includes the feeling of shame, for "to him who commits a transgression and

[1] See *P. R.*, 182 *b*. The simile with the reptile occurs first in *Tosephta Taanith*, 1. Cf. *Jer. Taanith*, 65 *b*; *Lament. R.*, 3 8; and *B. T. Taanith*, 16 *a*.

[2] *Taanith*, 16 *a*.

[3] See *P. R.*, 185 *a*; *P. K.*, 163 *b*; cf. *Kiddushin*, 49 *b*, and *Gittin*, 57 *b*. Cf. *M.T.*, 45: 4. The Rabbinic expression is, "He thought (or conceived) the thought of repentance in his heart (or in his mind)." See above, p. 31.

[4] See Maimonides, תשובה, 2 2, and *ibid.*, 1 1. Cf. also *Chagigah*, 5 *a*, that forgiveness depends on regret on the part of the sinner. Cf. Dan. 7 7 and 8; Ezra 9 6.

afterwards is ashamed of it, they forgive all his sins."[1] Indeed, God asks nothing more of man but that he shall say before him, "I have sinned."[2] And the judgement which he brought on Jerusalem was because she said, "I have not sinned."[3] But when man says, "I have sinned," no angel (of destruction) can touch him.[4] That David (after his sin) became worthy of eternal life was because he said, "I have sinned."[5] For he who knows that he sins and prays against the sin and fears the sin and argues (pleads or confesses) it between him and the Holy One, blessed be he, shall receive forgiveness.[6] And so it is with Israel in general, upon whom God will have mercy as soon as they will have confessed their sins (as repentants).[7] At the waters of Marah, Israel was supplicating and praying to their Father in Heaven, as a son who implores his father, and a disciple who beseeches his master, saying unto him, "Master of the world, we have sinned against thee when we murmured on the sea."[8] Confession thus becomes an essential feature of repentance, preceding

[1] See *Berachoth*, 12 *b*.

[2] See *Jer. Tanith*, 65 *d*. Cf. *Midrash Shemuel*, ch. 13.

[3] See *Tan. B.*, 2 91 *b*; cf. Jer. 2 35.

[4] See *Tan. B.*, 4 70 *a*.

[5] See *M. T.*, 51 1.

[6] See *M. T.*, 51 2.

[7] See *T. K.*, 112 *b*; cf. Lev. 26 40.

[8] See *Mechilta*, 45 *b*. Cf. Exod. 14 11. Cf. Jastrow's Dictionary, p. 273, col. 1, about the correct reading of this passage. See also above, 34.

the various kinds of atonements,[1] at the same time expressive of the determination of man to leave off sin-

[1] The most important Halachic aspect of this institution is given in Maimonides, *Teshubah*, 1 1. "If a person has transgressed any law in the Torah, be it affirmative or prohibitive, whether intentionally or unintentionally, he is under the obligation of confession before the Lord, blessed be he; as it is said, When a man or a woman commit any sin, etc., 'then they should confess their sin' (Num. 5 6 and 7), by which is meant the confession in words. This confession is an affirmative command. How do they confess? One says, 'O God, I have sinned, I have perverted, I have rebelled against thee. I have committed such and such an action, and behold, I regret it and am ashamed of my deeds and never will I return to that thing.' These are the contents of confession. . . . Likewise, those who bring a sin-offering or a guilt-offering (for sins) committed, intentionally or unintentionally, are not atoned for by their sacrifices until they have done repentance and uttered confession; as it is said, 'And he shall confess that he has sinned' (Lev. 55 5). Likewise, those who are under the sentence of death or of receiving thirty-nine lashes are not atoned for by their execution or by the fact of their having received the lashes, unless they have first done repentance and confessed. Likewise, he who injured his neighbour (bodily) or damaged him in money matters, though he made restitution for what he owed him, is not atoned for until he confessed and determined never to repeat the offence." The statement in Maimonides is based on *Sifre Zuta*, reproduced in the *Yalkut*, I. § 701, and partially also in *Numb. R.*, 8 5. Cf. also Friedmann, *Mechilta*, 121 *b*, the quotation given there from Maimonides, ספר המצות, and Horowitz, *Monatsschrift* (1906), pp. 76 and 77. See also *T. K.*, 24 *b*; *Sanhedrin*, 43 *b*; and *Sifre*, 2 *a*. Whether those who are about to die a natural death are also included in the duty of confession as derived by the Rabbis from Num. 5 6, depends largely on the reading מומתים (killed) (executed) or מתים (dying) in the *Sifre* and *Sifre Zuta*, referred to, which is difficult to determine, though there is good authority for the latter reading. Cf. R. Isaac Ibn Guiath, מאה שערים, 2 28 *b*. In any event, the institution of confession before death (even natural) is very ancient. See *Shabbath*, 32 *b*; Tractate *Semachoth Zutarti*, ed. C. M. Horowitz, pp. 30–31, text and the reference

ning.[1] "He that covers his sins shall not prosper, but whoso confesses (on the condition) with the determination to forsake his sin, shall receive mercy."[2] It is in this sense that confession is regarded as a means of killing the *Yezer*,[3] and effects a reconciliation with God. "Take with you words and turn to the Lord" (Hos. 14 2). This verse is paraphrased, "The Holy One, blessed be he, said unto Israel, 'My children, I will accept from you neither burnt-offerings nor sin-offerings nor guilt-offerings nor meat-offerings, but (I expect from you) that you will be reconciled unto me by prayer and supplication and by the direction of your heart . . . with confession and prayers and tears.'"[4] It is probably prayer of this kind, asking for forgiveness and acknowledging the sin, which is occasionally quoted together with repentance;[5] this being one of the features of repentance,

given there in the notes. See also *N. T.*, James 5 16, which, as may be seen from the contents, relates to the sick on the death-bed, and apparently is an echo of Ecclus. 38 9-10. Ancient is also the confession on the Day of Atonement (see *Yoma*, 87 *b*), taken over probably from the Temple. (See Lev. 16 21; and cf. *T. K.*, 82 *a*; *Yoma*, 66 *a*; and *Jer. Shebuoth*, 1 5.) It is then extended to other fasts. See *M. T.*, 141 : 2. Cf. also *Yoma*, 87 *b*, about the confession of Raba throughout the whole year.

1 About the various formulas of confession, see *Jer. Yoma*, 87 *b*, and *Lev. R.*, 3 8; *P. R.*, 160 *b*, text and notes. Cf. also Landshut and Baer in their edition of the Prayer Book.

2 See *P. K.*, 159 *a*, paraphrasing Prov. 28 13.

3 See *Lev. R.*, 9 : 1.

4 See *P. R.*, 198 *b*.

5 See *Rosh Hashanah*, 16 *b*; cf. *P. K.*, 191 *a*; *P. R.*, 200 *b* and references given there.

as Maimonides explains it, that the penitent should constantly cry before God with tears and supplication.[1]

Neither, however, the determination to leave off sin nor the regret of the past and the shame and confusion of sin expressed in confession and prayer seem to have been deemed a sufficient guarantee against a relapse into the former habits of sin. As R. Saadya Gaon remarks, we may fairly rely on the great majority of our people that during their prayer and fast they do really mean to forsake sin and regret it, and seek atonement; but what the Gaon is afraid of is, repetition, that is, relapse into sin. The Rabbis, therefore, think that this claim to real exemption from any particular sin can only be maintained after the penitent had twice at least the full opportunity to commit the sin under which he was labouring during his unregenerate life, and escaped from it.[2] Fasting is also mentioned together with repentance, indeed, following closely upon repentance; as it is said, "Therefore also now, saith the Lord, turn ye even to me with all your heart, and with fasting, and with weeping, and with mourning"[3] (Joel 2 12), but they deal treacherously who fast without doing repentance, and shall be put to shame.[4] It is in conformity with

[1] See Maimonides, תשובה, 2 4.

[2] See *Yoma*, 86 *b*. Some of the best authorities omit the word "twice." See above, p. 333, note 6, the reference to R. Saadya.

[3] *M. T.*, 25 5, with allusion to Ps. 25 8.

[4] *Midrash Prov.*, 6: 4. There can be little doubt that the copyist shortened the quotation from the Bible, omitting verse 12, on which the interpretation of the *Midrash* is based. See also above, p. 308, for

this sentiment, for which there is abundant authority both in the Scriptures and in the Talmud, that ascetic practices tending both as a sacrifice and as a castigation of the flesh, making relapse impossible, become a regular feature of the penitential course in the mediæval Rabbinic literature.[1]

But repentance is not confined to the habitual sinner nor to a particular time. True, the Rabbis admit repentance on the death-bed. If a man was absolutely wicked all his days and did repentance in the end, God will receive him.[2] "For as long as man lives, the Holy One, blessed be he, hopes for his repentance; when he dies his hope perishes: as it is said, 'When a wicked man dies his hope shall perish' (Prov. 11 7),"[3] denying the possibility of repentance to the wicked after their death even if they desire to do it.[4] For indeed this world is like the vestibule before the hall, and he who has not prepared himself in the vestibule, how shall he come into the hall? And when the wicked say, "Leave us, and we shall do repentance," the Holy

the quotation given there with reference to fasting, to which any number of references might easily be added.

[1] See *Sanhedrin*, 25 *a*; cf. Saadya, *ibid.*; *Bachye*, חובות הלבבות, section תשובה. See especially Introduction to רוקח, by Rabbi Eleazar of Worms, with his four kinds of repentance, which is reproduced by any number of moralists writing on this subject.

[2] See *Kiddushin*, 40 *b*; cf. *Gen. R.*, 65 22, the case of *Joseph*, משיתא, and of *Yakum*, איש צרורות; *Ruth R.*, 6 4, the case of Elisha b. Abuyah; and *Abodah Zarah*, 17 *a*, the case of Eleazar b. Durdaya.

[3] See *Eccles. R.*, 7 15.

[4] See *Eccles. Targum*, 1 15 and 3 20. Cf. *P. R.*, 184 *a* and *b*.

One, blessed be he, says unto them, "Repentance is possible only before death."[1]

But this death-bed repentance is not regarded as repentance of the highest order, though it may secure final salvation. "Blessed be he who does repentance when he is still a man" (possessing still his manly vigour).[2] The saying of the sage was, "Repent one day before thy death," but when his disciples asked him, "How does man know which day he will die?" he answered, "The more reason that he should repent every day lest he shall die on the following day, so that all his life is spent in repentance."[3] Hence, the benedic-

[1] See *Midrash Prov.*, ch. 6; *Eccles. R.*, 1:15 and 7:15, and *P. R. E.*, ch. 43, text and commentaries. This is the generally accepted view by almost all Jewish moralists. Cf. commentaries to *Aboth* 4:16 and 17, and the *Books of Discipline* (*Sifre Mussar*) generally. There is, however, a statement in the name of R. Joshua b. Levi, according to which the wicked will do repentance in the Gehenna and justify upon themselves the judgement of God, which repentance will contribute to their salvation in the end. As it is clear, however, from other Talmudic passages, this promise does not extend to all classes of sinners. See *Tosafoth and Edeles, a. l.* The saying of R. Joshua b. Levi may also have some connection with the Purgatory state after the wicked have already suffered for a time. There is also a whole circle of later Agadoth in which the wicked in the Gehenna secure a release by their answering "Amen" after the *Kaddish*, to be recited by Zerubbabel on the Day of Judgement succeeding the Resurrection. (?) See Friedmann, נספחים, pp. 32, 33, text and notes and reference given there to *Yalkut* and *Beth Hammidrash*, ed. Jellinek. Cf. the controversy between the Schools of Hillel and Shammai, *Rosh Hashanah*, 17 *a*. See also Nachmanides' *Shaar Haggemul.*

[2] See *Abodah Zarah*, 19 *a*.

[3] See *Aboth*, 2 10. Cf. *Shabbath*, 153 *a*, and *Eccles. R.*, 1 7.

tion in the daily prayer for repentance, running originally, "Turn thou us unto thee, O Lord, and we shall be turned; renew our days as of old. Blessed art thou, O Lord, who delightest in repentance."[1] This is an answer to the call coming daily from heaven, exclaiming, "Return, ye backsliding children."[2] The call, however, seems to have been especially heard on the nine days forming a preparation to the Day of Atonement, which, including this latter day, constitute the Ten Penitential Days. It is on the first of these (New Year's Day — the first of *Tishri*), on which the "Lord shall utter his voice" through the sound of the *Shofar*, which is an invitation to repentance;[3] whilst all the Ten Penitential Days are considered as an especial time of grace "to seek the Lord while he may be found."[4] The Day of Atonement forms the climax, but it would have no atoning efficacy without repentance. These Ten Penitential Days are distinguished by special liturgies and by special ascetic practices.[5]

[1] See Schechter, *J. Q. R.*, 10 654 *seq.*; cf. Dalman, *Die Worte Jesu*, p. 299. Cf. Lam. 5 21. The text in our prayer-books omits the verse, and substitutes for it, "Cause us to return, O our Father, unto thy Law; draw us near, O our King, unto thy service, and bring us back in perfect repentance unto thy presence. Blessed, etc. . . ." See Singer, p. 46; Baer, p. 90.

[2] See *P. R. E.*, ch. 15 and 43 and commentaries.

[3] See *Tan.*, וישלח, 2; cf. *P. K.*, 187 *b*. Cf. Joel 2 11.

[4] See *Rosh Hashanah*, 18 *a*, and *P. R.*, 155 *b*. Cf. Isa. 55 6. Cf. also *Jer. Bikkurim*, 64 *d*.

[5] See *Tur Orach Chayim*, par. 602 and 603, and the commentaries given there. See above, p. 303 *seq.*

But they are only set apart, as already indicated, as a special time of grace, but not as the only days of repentance. For repentance is as wide as the sea, and as the sea has never closed and man can always be cleansed by it, so is repentance, so that whenever man desires to repent, the Holy One, blessed be he, receives him.[1]

[1] See *P. K.*, 157 *a*, and *M. T.*, 65 4 and references.

## ADDITIONS

Page 26. Cancel "stay of the world," and corresponding note.

Page 55, Note 1. See *Sifre*, 113 *a*, and *Jebamoth*, 48 *b*, with reference to Deut. 21 : 13, where the words את אביה ואת אמה are explained to mean ע״ז (her former idols). As a proof is given Jer. 2 : 27, "Saying to a stock, thou art my father; and to a stone, thou hast brought me forth." If this explanation reflected the pagan usage of the Tannaitic time, which is not impossible, we might easily explain the fact that some Rabbis, at least, were sparing with the epithet Father in reference to the Deity.

Page 57, Note 1. See also R. Joseph Ibn Yachya in *Torah Or*, ch. 77, where he speaks of two fundamental doctrines, האמונה בה׳ שהוא אלהינו ואין זולתו מהאלוהות ושאנחנו ישר׳ עמו ולא זולתנו מהאומות.

Page 100, Note 1. Attention should be called to the statement of R. Simon b. Lakish, in which the מלכות שמים is contrasted with the מלכות הארץ, and the compliment is even paid to the latter that it establishes order and law. See *Gen. R.* 9 : 13, and *Gen. R.*, ed. Theodore, p. 73. The context makes it clear that by the Kingdom of the Earth is meant Rome, but this favourable estimation of the Roman Government does not represent the general opinion of the Jews. I found also these terms in a Genizah fragment from an unknown *Mechilta* to Deuteronomy. In connection with this, the following extract from another Genizah fragment is instructing. It forms the conclusion of the third benediction in the *Grace After Meals* in the House of Mourning, and read thus: ברוך אתה ה׳ הבונה ברחמיו את ירושלים. אמן בחיינו אמן במהרה בימינו תבנה ציון ברנה ותכון עבודה בירושלים וארמון על משפטו ורומי הרשעה תפול.

Page 101, Note 2, and 102, Note 2. It is suggested by various writers that the saying of R. Hillel was directed against Christianity, which gave undue emphasis to the belief in the Messiah at the expense of the Law. R. Hillel in a certain measure found a follower a thousand years later in R. Joseph Albo, who was prompted probably by the same tendency. (See *Ikkarim* 4 : 42.) And something similar may be observed of R. Moses Sofer of the nineteenth century (Responsa II, par. 356), who likewise protested against Maimonides, who includes the belief in the Messiah among the *fundamental* doctrines of Judaism, though his protest was, as it seems, less directed against Christianity than against the antinomian tendencies of his time. It is hardly necessary to say that both Albo and Sofer considered the belief in the advent of Messiah an essential Jewish doctrine, though not a fundamental doctrine. Rashi explains the saying of Hillel to the effect that the future redemption of Israel will not be by the Messiah, but by God himself. This explanation, though seeming a little far-fetched, becomes plausible by similar statements of other Rabbis. Thus, with reference to Isa. 35 : 10, "And the redeemed of the Lord shall return," a Rabbi remarks, "They are the redeemed of the Lord, and not the redeemed of Elijah, nor the redeemed of the King Messiah." (See *M. T.* 106 : 1.) Again, with reference to Deut. 17 : 14, we are told that after the sad experience Israel had with their various kings, they began to exclaim: "We have no desire for a King any longer. We want back our first King, God; as it is said, 'The Lord is our King, he will save us'" (Isa. 33 : 22). Thereupon, the Lord said, "By your life I will do so, as it is said, 'And the Lord shall be King over the earth, etc.'" (Zech. 14 : 9). (*Deut. R.* 5 : 11.) The Wilna edition is mutilated by the censorship. (Cf. also *S. E.*, Introduction, p. 26.) It is, however, not impossible that these passages and similar ones were provoked by polemics with Christians.

Page 192–193, Note 1. The statement of the *Midrash Zuta* is probably based on an older Tannaitic interpretation of Deut. 24 : 16. Cf. Hoffmann, לקוטי בתר לקוטי of the *Mechilta to Deut.*, p. 31, text and notes.

Page 305, Note 2. This later version of the statement of R. Akiba has a parallel in the saying of R. Jochanan. (See *Jer. Sanhedrin*, 18 *a*.) Cf. *Exod. R.* 6 : 1. See Bacher, *Ag. Tan.* 3 : 26. These bold statements (all in contradiction to *Aboth*, 4 : 8) have the purpose of refuting the tendency of making God's judgement arbitrary and despotic.

Page 324, Note 3. Cf. also *Berachoth*, 34 *b*, the well-known statement of R. Abahu with reference to the high position to be occupied by the penitents, even higher than that of the perfect righteous. See also Dr. Ginzberg's *Genizah Studies*, p. 377, reproducing the following extract from an unknown Sheelta: —

ופליגא דר׳ אבהו מקום שבעלי תשובה עומדין אין צדיקים
גמורים עומדים והאיך דומים בעלי תשובה למלך שהיו לו שני

בנים אחד הלך בטוב ל·· ואחד יצא לתרבות רעה שנ׳ שלום
שלום לרחוק ולקרוב מאי רחוק.

The text is defective, but it can hardly be doubted, as Dr. Ginzberg points out, *ibid.*, p. 351, that in its completeness the comparison represented the well-known parable of the prodigal son in the *N. T.* Cf. *Num. R.*, 8 : 2.

Page 333, Note 6. See *Meor Enayim*, by R. Azariah de' Rossi, p. 235, ed. Cassel. (Wilna, 1866.)

# LIST OF ABBREVIATIONS AND BOOKS NOT QUOTED WITH FULL TITLE

Abarbanel, Isaac, משמיע ישועה, Königsberg, 1860.

*Ag. Ber.* = *Agadath Bereschith*, ed. Buber, Cracow, 1902, quoted by chapters.

*Agadath Shir. Hashirim*, ed. Schechter, Cambridge, 1896.

Albo, *Ikkarim*, Pressburg, 1853, quoted by book and chapter.

*A. R. N.* = *Aboth de Rabbi Nathan recensiones duas*, ed. S. Schechter, Vienna, 1887, quoted by chapter or folio.

Azulai, מדבר קדמות, Leghorn, 1793, printed together with the same author's יעיר אזן.

Azulai, שער יוסף, Leghorn, 1757.

Bacher, *Ag. P. Am.* = *Die Agada der Palaestinensischen Amoräer*, I, Strassburg, 1892; II, *ib.*, 1896; III, *ib.*, 1899.

Bacher, *Ag. Tan.* = *Die Agada der Tannaiten*, I, Strassburg, 1884; II, *ib.*, 1890.

Bacher, *Terminologie* = *Die exegetische Terminologie der jüd. Traditionsliteratur*, I–II, Leipzig, 1899–1905.

Bachye ibn Bakudah, חובות הלבבות ed. Sluzki, Warsaw, 1870.

Bachye ibn Chalwah, כד הקמח, ed. Breit, Lemberg, 1880–92.

Baer, עבודת ישראל, Roedelheim, 1868.

Berliner, *Targum* = *Targum Onkelos*, I–II, Berlin, 1884.

*Beth Talmud*, Periodical ed. Friedmann and Weiss, I–V, Vienna, 1880–89.

Blau, *Zur Einleitung in die Heilige Schrift*, Budapest, 1894.

*DE* = *Derek Erez Rabba* in the Talmud, at the end of the fourth order.

*DEZ* = *Derek Erez Zutta*, ed. A. J. Tawrogi, Königsberg i. Pr., 1885.

Duran, Simon, *Magen Abot*, commentary to Aboth, Leipzig, 1855.

Edeles, חידושי מהרש"א, commentary to the Talmud, ed. Wilna.

Epstein, אלדד הדני, Pressburg, 1891.

Friedmann, הציון, commentary to Ezekiel, ch. 20, Vienna, 1888.

Friedmann, נספחים לסדר = נספחים אליה זוטא. *Pseudo-Seder Eliahu Zuta*, Vienna, 1904.

Ginsburger, *Das Fragmententargum* (*Thargum Jeruschalmi zum Pentateuch*), Berlin, 1899.

Grünhut, ספר הלקוטים, I–VI, Jerusalem, 1898 *seq.*

Güdemann, *Culturgeschichte* = *Geschichte des Erziehungswesens und der Cultur der abendlaendischen Juden*, I, Vienna, 1880.

*Hechaluz* XIII by Osias H. Schorr, Vienna, 1889.

Jellinek, *Bet ha-Midrasch*, I–IV, Leipzig, 1853–57; V–VI, Vienna, 1873–77.

*Jer* = Talmud of Jerusalem quoted by treatise, folio, and column of ed. Krotoschin, 1866, corresponding to ed. Venice, *ca.* 1523.

Joel, *Blicke* = *Blicke in die Religionsgeschichte zu Anfang des zweiten christlichen Jahrhunderts*, I–II, Breslau and Leipzig, 1880–83.

Judah Hallevi, *Kuzari*, ed. Sluzki, Leipzig, 1864.

*Kinyan Tora*, Sixth chapter of *Aboth*, being an appendix.

Landshut, מקור ברכה in Edelmann, סדור הגיון לב, Königsberg, 1845.

Luzzatto, מסילת ישרים, Warsaw, 1889. An excellent edition with German translation by I. Wohlgemuth appeared lately, Berlin, 1906.

*Machzor Vitry*, ed. S. Hurwitz, Berlin, 1889–93.

Maimonides, *Mishneh Torah*, Wilna, 1900, quoted by book, chapter, and paragraph.

Maimonides, *Moreh Nebuchim*, Warsaw, 1872; quoted by book and chapter.

Maimonides, ספר המצות = סה"מ with many commentaries, Warsaw, 1891, quoted by the number of the precepts (מצות עשה = מ"ע) or prohibitions (מצות לא תעשה = מל"ת).

*Mechilta* = *Mechilta de-Rabbi Ismael*, ed. Friedmann, Vienna, 1870, quoted by folio.

*Mechilta* of R. Simon = *Mechilta de-Rabbi Simon b. Jochai*, ed. Hoffmann, Frankfurt a. M., 1905, quoted by folio; often also the number of the verse is given.

Meïr ibn Gabbai, עבודת הקדש, Warsaw, 1883.

*M.H.G* = *Midrash Hag-gadol*, ed. S. Schechter, I, *Genesis*, Cambridge, 1902. The other volumes are quoted from Mss. in the possession of the author.

*Midrash Agadah ed. B.* = *Agadischer Commentar zum Pentateuch*, ed. Buber, Vienna, 1894.

*Midrash Prov.* = *Midrasch Mischle*, ed. Buber, Wilna, 1893, quoted by chapter.

*Midrash Shemuel B.* = *Midrasch Samuel*, ed. Buber, Cracow, 1893, quoted by chapter and paragraph.

*Midrasch Suta*, ed. Buber, Berlin, 1894, quoted by folio.

*Midrasch Tannaim zum Deuteronomium*, excerpted from the *M.H.G.* by D. Hoffmann, I, Berlin, 1908.

*Mishna*, quoted by treatise, chapter, and paragraph. Occasionally *ed. Lowe* = The Mishnah on which the Palestinian Talmud rests, ed. by W. H. Lowe, Cambridge, 1883, is referred to.

*M. T.* = *Midrasch Tehillim (Schocher Tob)*, ed. Buber, Wilna, 1891, quoted by chapter and paragraph.

Nachmanides, *Shaar Haggemul*, Ferrara, 1556.

Pentateuch with *Targum Onkelos*, *Pseudo-Jonathan and Jerushalmi* and the commentaries of Rashi, Ibn Ezra, Nachmanides, etc., ed. Netter, Vienna, 1860.

*P. K.* = *Pesikta von Rab Kahana*, ed. Buber, Lyck, 1868, quoted by folio.

*P. R. Pesikta Rabbati*, ed. Friedmann, Vienna, 1880, quoted by folio.

*PRE* = *Pirke Rabbi Eliezer* with commentary of R. David Loria (רד"ל), Warsaw, 1852, quoted by chapter.

*Pseudo-Jonathan (Targum Jonathan ben Usiël zum Pentateuch)*, ed. Ginsburger, Berlin, 1903.

*Pugio Fidei* by Raymundus Martini, ed. Carpzov, Leipzig, 1687.

*R* after the books of the Pentateuch or the Five Scrolls means *Midrash Rabba* with many commentaries, Wilna, 1878, quoted by chapter and paragraph of this edition, except for *Cant. R.*, where the numbers refer to chapter and verse of the Biblical book. The introductions in the beginning of *Lament. R.* are quoted with their respective numbers.

R. Rabbinovicz, *Variae lectiones in Mischnam et in Talmud Babylonicum*, I–XV, Munich, 1877–86, XVI, Przemysl, 1897.

*Reshith Chochmah* by R. Elijah de Vidas, Cracow, 1593.

Responsa of R. David b. Zimra = שו״ת הרדב״ז, II, Venice, 1749.

Responsa of the Geonim, ed. Harkavy, Berlin, 1887 (*Studien und Mittheilungen aus der Kaiserlichen Oeffentlichen Bibliothek zu*, St. Petersburg, IV).

Responsa of R. Isaac b. Sheshet = שו״ת הריב״ש, Constantinople, 1547.

Responsa of R. Josef Trani = שו״ת מהרי״ט, Fürth, 1768.

Saadya, אמונות ודעות, Josefow, 1885.

*S.E.* = *Seder Eliahu rabba und Seder Eliahu zuta* (*Tanna d'be Eliahu*), ed. Friedmann, Vienna, 1900. Introduction, *ib.*, 1902.

*Seder Rab Amram*, Warsaw, 1865.

*Semachoth Zutarti* in C. M. Horowitz, Uralte Tosefta's, II–III, Frankfurt a. M., 1890, pp. 28–40.

*Semachoth* in the Talmud at the end of the fourth order.

*S.E.Z.* = *Seder Eliahu zuta; see* S.E.

*Sifre* = *Sifre debê Rab*, ed. Friedmann, Vienna, 1864, quoted by folio.

*Sifre Zuta*, a Tannaitic commentary on Numbers known through quotations in Yalkut and *M.H.G.* and a fragment ed. Schechter (*Jewish Quarterly Review*, VI, 656–63). A collection of these quotations was begun by Königsberger, Frankfurt a. M., 1894 and 1907, and by S. Horovitz in *Monatsschrift f. Geschichte und Wissenschaft des Judentums*, 1905 *seq.*

Simon Kiara, הלכות גדולות, ed. Traub, Warsaw, 1874. A different version, ed. Hildesheimer, Berlin, 1888–92.

Singer, *The Authorised Daily Prayer Book with a New Translation*, London, 1890.

Talmud, ed. Wilna, 1880–86, contains the commentaries of R. Chananel, R. Gershom, etc.; quoted by treatise and folio, all editions having the same pagination.

*Tan.* = *Tanchuma;* quoted by section of the Pentateuch and paragraph of ed. Lublin, 1879, with commentary עץ יוסף.

*Tan. B.* = *Midrasch Tanchuma*, ed. by S. Buber, Wilna, 1885, 5 vols., quoted by volume (book of the Pentateuch) and folio.

*T. K.* = *Torat Kohanim*, called also Sifra, ed. with the commentary of R. Abraham b. David (ראב״ד), by I. H. Weiss, Vienna, 1862, quoted by folio and column.

T. Müller, *Masechet Soferim*, Leipzig, 1878.

*Tosephta*, quoted by folios of ed. M. S. Zukermandel, Pasewalk, 1881. Occasionally A. *Schwarz*, Tosifta juxta Mischnarum ordinem recomposita, I, Ordo Seraim, Wilna, 1890, is referred to.

*Tur Orach Chayim* by R. Jacob b. Asher, Königsberg, 1861.

Weiss, דור דור ודורשיו = דו״ד *Zur Geschichte der jüdischen Tradition,* I–V, Vienna, 1871–91.

Wertheimer, בתי מדרשות, I–IV, לקט מדרשים Jerusalem, 1903.

Wertheimer, Jerusalem, 1893–97.

*Yalkut* = *Yalkut Shimeoni,* Frankfurt a. M., 1687; Part I to Pentateuch; Part II to Prophets and Hagiographa, quoted by paragraphs.

*Yalkut Machiri* on Isa. = The Yalkut on Isaiah of Machir b. Abba Mari, ed. Spira, Berlin, 1894.

*Yalkut Machiri* = *Jalkut Machiri zu den Psalmen,* ed. Buber, Berdyczew, 1899.

*Yelamdenu,* lost Midrash to the Pentateuch, frequently excerpted by the Yalkut and others. Quotations are collected by L. Grünhut, ספר הליקוטים, IV *seq.,* Jerusalem, 1900 *seq.*

*Zohar,* Krotoschin, 1844–45, 3 vols.

אותיות דרבי עקיבא = אותיות דר״ע, in Jellinek, Bet ha-Midrasch, III, pp. 12–64.

בחיי, commentary to the Pentateuch by Bechaye Ibn Chalwa, Amsterdam, 1726.

ס׳ חסידים, Parma = *Das Buch der Frommen nach Cod. De Rossi,* No. 1133, ed. Wistinetzki, Berlin, 1891.

יפה עינים, R. Arje Loeb Jellin's glosses to the Talmud, Wilna, 1880–86.

ל״ב מדות of R. Eleazar b. Jose of Galilee. Rules of interpretation printed in the first volume of the Talmud and in the introduction to *M.H.G.* Separate edition under the title נתיבות עולם, with commentary by Katzenellenbogen, Wilna, 1858.

לקח טוב, *Lekack-Tob,* commentary by R. Tobia b. Eliezer. Genesis and Exodus, ed. Buber; Leviticus, Numbers, and Deuteronomy, ed. Padua, Wilna, 1880.

מורינו הרב רבי זאב וואלף = מה״רזוו איינהאדן, author of a commentary to Midrash Rabba, ed. Wilna, 1878.

מסכת אבות עם תלמוד בבלי וירושלמי, by Noah Chajjim of Kabrin, Warsaw, 1878.

ספר מצות קטן = סמ״ק, by R. Isaac of Corbeil, also called עמודי גולה, Cremona, 1556.

ספר המוסר, by R. Jehuda Kalaz, Mantua, 1560.

ספר יראים, by R. Eliezer of Metz, Warsaw, 1881.

ספרי דאגדתא, *Sammlung agadischer Commentare zum Buche Esther,* ed. Buber, Wilna, 1886.

עין יעקב, by R. Jacob ibn Chabib, Wilna, 1883, 3 vols.

פרקי דרבי אליעזר = פדר״א.

פרקא דרבינו הקדוש in Schoenblum, שלשה ספרים נפתחים, Lemberg, 1877.

פרקי היכלות, Jellinek, Bet ha-Midrasch, III, pp. 83–108; from a different Ms. ed., Wertheimer, Jerusalem, 1890.

רבי דוד לוריא = רד״ל, author of notes to Midrash Rabba, ed. Wilna, 1878, and a commentary to *PRE.*

רוקח, by R. Eleazar of Worms, Warsaw, 1880.

שאלתות, by R. Achai Gaon, with commentary by R. Isaia, Berlin, Dyhernfurt, 1786.

שארית ישראל, Amsterdam, s. a.

תנא דבי אליהו = תדב״א, title of the old editions of S.E.

# INDEX

Aaron, prays for the regeneration of the sinner, 316; encourages sinners to repent, 321.
Abba Hilkia, wife of, prays that outlaws may repent, 317.
Abba Saul, Rabbi, on *Imitatio Dei*, 200, 201–2.
Abba Tachna, illustrates the victory of the *Good Yezer* over the *Evil Yezer*, 272–3.
Abimelech, protected by the grace of God against the *Evil Yezer*, 283–4.
*Aboth*, Mishnic tractate, and *Chasiduth*, 209–10.
Abraham, God pays a sick visit to, 37; God argues with, 37; the rock, 59; as proselytiser, 77, 84, 93; the friend of God, 84; and the kingship of God, 83–4; testifies for Israel against the Torah, 129; the world established on, 173; and the *Zachuth* of posterity, 196; attacked by the *Evil Yezer*, 251–2; the merits of, guarded by Satan, 268: has dominion over the *Evil Yezer*, 271, 275.
*See also* Fathers, the; Patriarchs, the.
Absalom, alluded to, 213.
Abuhah, Rabbi, as a geologist, 19.
Accuser, the. *See* Satan.
Acha, Rabbi, on the taint of sin in sexual intercourse, 253.
Achan, and the doctrine of imputed sin, 191.
Adam, God at the wedding of, 37, 203; acknowledges God as king, 82, 93; and the doctrine of imputed sin, 188; corrupting effect of sin on, 235–6; the sin of, conceals the light of the first day, 237; urged by God to repent, 315.
Admonition, hating, prevents repentance, 331.
Adulterer, the, names for, 224.
Adultery, a cardinal sin, 205; extended meaning of, 214; penalty for, 224–5; removes the Shechinah, 224–5; what is included under, 225; heresy a form of, 225–6; and the *Evil Yezer*, 250; forced upon David, to make him an example of repentance, 317–18; not subject to repentance, 333.
Affirmative injunctions, the number of, 138.
Agadah, the, character of, 3; retells the Bible stories with application to later conditions, 24–5; and corporeal terms applied to God, 35.
*See also under* Rabbis, the.
Agadic saying, on the Mizwoth, 138–40.
Ahab, the repentance of, 324, 326.
Ahaz, spites God, 220.
Akabiah ben Mahalaleel, on the contemplation of death as a remedy against the *Evil Yezer*, 276.
Akiba, Rabbi, on justification by grace or works, 15–16; considers the paternal relation between God and Israel unconditional, 54; rejoices in the yoke of the kingdom of heaven, 71–2; on the justice of God, 304–5; on the grace of God, 306.

Alcimus, high priest, alluded to, 92.
Allegoric interpretation of Scripture, prejudice against, 4.
Allegorising method, the, and the Rabbis, 39–44.
*See also* Corporeal terms.
Alphabet, the, endowed with life, 129.
Amalekites, the, impair the perfection of the kingdom of God, 99–101; identified with Esau and Rome, 99.
Amon, spites God, 220.
Amos, the Book of, cited, in connection with the Mizwoth, 140; with repentance as a sweet message, 324.
Anathoth, the repentance of the men of, 326.
Ancient One of the world, epithet for God, 26.
Angel of Death, the, identified with the *Evil Yezer*, 244–5.
Angels, the, surrounding God, 28, 32; lower than Israel, 49; incapable of sin, 81; object to the removal of the Torah from heaven, 136; free from the *Evil Yezer*, 257, 285; object to the repentance of Manasseh, 318–19; oppose repentance in general, 321–2.
Anger, akin to idolatry, 224; habitual, prevents repentance, 330.
Antigonos of Socho, on purity of motive in performance of the Law, 162.
Antinomian influence of the Apostle Paul, 4.
Antinomianism, and the mystic, 78.
Antoninus, on the time the *Evil Yezer* takes possession of man, 253.
Apocalyptic works, not useful as a source of Rabbinic theology, 5.
Apocryphal works, not useful as a source of Rabbinic theology, 5.
Apologetics, and Rabbinic theology, 18–19.
Apostasy, changes the relation of Israel to God, 55 n.
Apostate, spite, 220.
Apostles, the, meagreness of Rabbinic literature contemporary with, 8.
Araboth, the seventh heaven, the abode of God, 28–9, 30–1, 32.
*Arayoth*, forbidden sexual intercourse, 211.
Arbitration of disputes, a law of goodness, 215.
Archelaus, king, alluded to, 93.
Ascetic practices, to guard against relapsing into sin, 340; connected with the Ten Penitential Days, 342.
Ascetic remedies, against the *Evil Yezer*, 277–8.
Askari. *See* Joseph Askari.
Astruc, alluded to, 19.
Atonement, needed by the dead, 196; through sacrifices limited in efficacy, 295–7; resides in sacrifices, 300–1; by sacrifices intended for the community, 300–1; through death and suffering, 304, 307–8; Scriptural kinds of, 308; through children and the righteous, 310–11; through the Torah and charity, 312; repentance must accompany all kinds of, 313.
*See also* Forgiveness; Reconciliation.
Atonement, the Day of, Scriptural and Prophetical portions for, 119; purifies Israel, 234; prayer on, for grace to conquer the *Evil Yezer*, 279–80; atones for the community and the individual, 301 n.; repentance on, 302–4; inefficacious without repentance, 34[illegible].
Attributes, of God, 38.
*See also* Mercy; Justic

Avira, Rabbi, enumerates seven names for the *Evil Yezer*, 243–4.
Azariah, justified in rebelling against Nebuchadnezzar, 107.

Bachye Ibn Bakudah, on love of God, 68–9, 72–3; on the joy of the Law, 151.
Bachye Ibn Chalwah, on the unity and the kingdom of God, 96; on the joy of performing the Mizwoth, 151.
Backbiting, a form of bloodshed, 227.
Balaam, and the grace of the revelation, 134.
Benaha, Rabbi, as the forerunner of Astruc, 19.
Ben Azai, on "The Book of Generations of Adam," 120.
Benedictions, the, preceding the Prophets and Hagiographa, 123; convey the idea of holiness through commandments, 168.
*Berachoth*, Talmud tractate, and *Chasiduth*, 210.
Beth-Hammidrash (schoolhouse), the, a refuge from the *Evil Yezer*, 273, 274.
Blasphemy, a sin of rebellion, 222; called an evil thing, 232; repentance possible for, 326.
Bloodshed, a cardinal sin, 205; different kinds of, 213; the consequences of, 326–7; slander, a form of, 227; robbery, a form of, 227–9; bad administration of justice, a form of, 229–30; due to the *Evil Yezer*, 246.
*See also* Murder.
Boaz, banishes the *Evil Yezer*, 271.
Body, the, liable to sin, 260–1.
"Book of Generations of Adam, The," on the dignity of man, 120.
Bribery, prevents repentance, 330.
Bride, term for the relation between God and Israel, 47; term applied to the Sabbath, 154.
Brother, term for the relation between God and Israel, 47, 56.
Burnt offering, the, instituted for heresy, 225–6; the continual, controversy on the atoning power of, 299–300.

Cabalists, the, and the creation of the world, 128.
*See also under* Mystic.
Cain, makes the *Evil Yezer* responsible for his crime, 280–1; an example of penitence, 315; repentance of, acceptable, 326.
Captives, objections to marriage with, 213.
Cardinal sins, the, enumerated, 205–6.
*See* Sins, the cardinal.
Catastrophes, to teach that repentance is possible for the greatest sins, 317.
Chama ben Chaninah, Rabbi, quoted, on the imitation of God, 202–3.
Chambers, Chapters of the, mystical description of the heavens, 29.
Chaninah ben Dosa, Rabbi, miracle-worker, lacks influence on Jewish thought, 7; on sin as the cause of death, 247.
Chanukah Candles, the Lighting of the, as a command, 13.
Chapters of the Chambers, mystical description of the heavens, 29.
Charity, invalidated by robbery, 228; disparaged by the *Evil Yezer*, 252; superior to sacrifices as a means of atonement, 296, 312; the atoning power of, 312; preventing, makes repentance impossible, 330.

Charity system, the, of the Rabbis, 112.

*Chasiduth*, saintliness supplementing the Law, 201, 209; discriminates between one and another group of laws, 209; various definitions of, 209–10; summarised in a Talmudic formula, 210; Eliezer of Worms on, 210; abstention from superfluous things, according to Nachmanides, 211–12; a corrective of the Law, 212–14; the reward of, 217–18.
*See also* Holiness.

*Chasiduth, Regulations of*, by Eliezer of Worms, quoted, 210.

Chaste women, the, the atoning power of, 312.

Chayoth, the, surrounding God, 28.

Cheating, not subject to repentance, 333.

Cherubim, the, surrounding God, 32.

Children, term for the relation of Israel to God, 46, 49 (*bis*); not saved by their fathers, 178; and the doctrine of imputed sin, 191, 192–3; the *Evil Yezer* in, 253–5; the death of, an atonement for the sins of adults, 254; are without sin, 269; the atoning power of, 310–11.
*See also Zachuth*, the, of a pious posterity.

Chisda, Rabbi, criticised by a pupil, 144–5.

Chiya, Rabbi, the holiness of, 212.

Choni Hammaagel, miracle-worker, lacks influence on Jewish thought, 7.

Chosen ones, a term applied to Israel by God, 47.

Christianity, the essential principle of, in the Book of Leviticus, 120.

Chronicles (I), the Book of, cited, in connection with the uniqueness of Israel, 48; with the *Evil Yezer*, 243 (*bis*); with the heart as the seat of the *Yezers*, 257.

Chronicles (II), the Book of, cited, in connection with the repentance of Manasseh, 318, 319.

Civil law, in the Mishnah, 2.

Commandment, the performance of one, and the salvation of the world, 189–90.

Commandments, the, kept by God, 203.
*See Mizwoth*, the.

Communion, with the Holy Spirit, brought about by *Chasiduth*, 217; with God, follows the banishment of the *Evil Yezer*, 292.

Community, the, responsibility of, and the doctrine of imputed sin, 191–5; and the atoning power of sacrifices, 300–1; and the Day of Atonement, 301; separation from, prevents repentance, 330.
*See also* Solidarity.

Compilation, a, inadequate as a theologic source, 3–5.

Conceit, causes death, 246.
*See also* Pride.

Conduct, determines man's nearness to God, 33.

Confession of sins, the, accompanies certain sacrifices, 296; a part of repentance, 335–8.

Contamination, description of sin, 233–4.

Corporeal terms applied to God, mitigated, 35–6; exaggerated, 40.
*See also* Allegorising method, the.

Corrective of the Law, *Chasiduth*, 212–14; the law of goodness, 214–16.

Corruption, sin a symptom of, 235.

Court of justice, the, duties of, and the doctrine of imputed sin, 191, 192, 193–5.

Covenant, the, of God with Israel and the *Porek ol*, 220 and n.

Covenant with the Fathers, the, unlimited, 179.
*See also Zachuth*, the, of the Fathers.
Creation, Master of all, epithet for God, 22.
Creation of man, the, subject of controversy, 8.
Creation of the world, the, a glorification of God, 80–1; man the centre of, 82; and wisdom, 127–8; according to the Cabalists, 128; repentance indispensable to, 128, 314.
Creator, epithet for God, 26.
Creed, The Thirteen Articles of the, by Maimonides, contain no mention of Israel's election, 57.
Criminal procedure, in the Mishnah, 2.
Criticism of the wise, prevents repentance, 331.
Cursing the many, prevents repentance, 330.

Daniel, Rome in the vision of, 100.
Daniel, the Book of, cited, in connection with God as a teacher of the Torah, 43; with the extent of the Torah, 122.
David, the consequences of the marriage of, with a captive, 212–13; name given to the *Evil Yezer* by, 243; banishes the *Evil Yezer*, 271; slays the *Evil Yezer*, 275; made to sin as an example of repentance, 317–18; and Jeroboam, 319; confident of God's forgiveness, 326; confesses his sin, 336.
Dead, the, and the doctrine of imputed sin, 196; and the *Zachuth* of posterity, 198; prayers for, 198.
Death, caused by the *Evil Yezer*, 244–7; caused by sin, 245, 247; of children, 254; the contemplation of, conquers the *Evil Yezer*, 276; the punishment of the sinner, 293, 294, 304; an atonement, 304, 307–8, 310.
Death, the Angel of. *See* Angel of Death, the.
Death-bed repentance, 340–1.
Deborah, the generation of, has a single heart, 257.
Decalogue, the, the tablets of, suggest an explanation concerning the *Evil Yezer*, 274–5.
*See also* Law, the; Torah, the.
Defilement, term applied to the cardinal sins, 205, 206.
*See also* Impurity.
Defilement of the land, caused by idolatry, 223; caused by pride, 223; caused by murder, 226.
Deification of man, objected to by the Rabbis, 38–9.
Deluge, the, and the doctrine of imputed sin, 195; generation of, rebels, 219, 222; causes pain to God, 219–20; robbery the capital sin of, 227; and the Tetragrammaton, 239; give the *Evil Yezer* sway, 271; warned to repent, 315.
Depravity in children, left unprotested, prevents repentance, 331.
Desert, the, reason for giving the Torah in, 131.
Deuteronomy, the Book of, cited, in connection with Moses' acknowledgement of God, 26; with the might of God, 38; with the justice of God, 38; with the faithfulness of God, 38; with the unity of God, 48; with Israel's exalted place, 48; with the election of Israel, 58 (*bis*), 63–4; with the kingdom of God, 67 (*bis*); with love of God, 67, 68, 69, 79 (*bis*); with man's righteousness and the kingdom of God, 90 (*bis*), 91; with the kingship benediction, 96; with the superiority of the Torah, 118; an *Imitatio Dei*, 119; cited in

connection with the commandment of forgetfulness, 149; with the joy of the Law, 150; with performing the Law with a view to reward, 162; with *Zachuth*, 179; with the *Zachuth* of a pious ancestry, 182, 183; against imputed sin, 185, 186; cited in connection with the duties of a court of justice, 193; with imputed sin through posterity, 196; with walking in the ways of God, 201; with the imitation of God, 203; with cleaving to God, 204 (*bis*); with jealousy, 204; with marriage with a captive, 213; with a rebellious son, 213; with the law of goodness, 214; with pride, 223, 224; with the Shechinah, 224 (*bis*); with heresy, 225; with the *Evil Yezer*, 242, 243; with the good heart, 259; with remedies against the *Evil Yezer*, 277; with God's regret at having created the *Evil Yezer*, 284 (*bis*); with free will and the *Evil Yezer*, 286 (*bis*), 288; with the communal sacrifices, 301; with the justice of God, 305, 306; with the repentance of Manasseh, 318; with God's attribute of mercy in relation to repentance, 322.

Devious ways, and the imitation of God, 204.

Devotion, a necessary element in prayer, 156–9.

De Wette, definition of mysticism by, 77.

*Dibbur*, as used by the Rabbis, 43 n.

Dietary laws. *See* Forbidden food.

Dining-table, the, the atoning power of, 312.

Dishonesty, a widespread sin, 250, 260.

Disobedience. *See* Sin.

Disrespect, removes the Divine Presence, 232.

Divine Presence, the. *See* Shechinah, the.

Divorce laws, in the Mishnah, 2.

"Duties of the Heart," by Bachye Ibn Bakudah, quoted, 68–9, 72–3.

*Ecce Homo*, quoted, on the ideal of Jesus, 112.

Ecclesiastes, the Book of, cited in connection with corrupt government, 107; with the weakening influence of sin, 238; with unintentional sins, 240; with the heart as the seat of the *Yezers*, 256; with the two *Yezers*, 265; with the good uses of the *Evil Yezer*, 267; with man's responsibility for the *Evil Yezer*, 268.

Edom, the prototype of Rome, 99, 108.

Egypt, the people of, cause pain to God, 219–20.

Eighteen Benedictions, the, prayer for grace to conquer the *Evil Yezer* in, 280.

Eleazar ben Jose of Galilee, on allegoric interpretation of Scriptures, 41 n.

Election of Israel, the, treated by the Agadah, 3; indicates the close relation to God, 57; an unformulated dogma, 57; in the liturgy, 57; in the Scriptures, 58; the Rabbis on, 58–64; reasons for, 58–62; predestined, 59; not exclusive, 62–4.

Eli, the sons of, deny the kingdom of God, 87.

Eliezer, Rabbi, Chapters of, on God before the creation of the world, 80; on repentance, 128; on free will and the *Evil Yezer*, 288–9.

Eliezer ben Azariah, and the *Zachuth* of his ancestors, 176.

Eliezer of Worms, quoted, on love of God, 74–5; on *Chasiduth*, 210.

Elijah, held up as a model to Hiram, 39; rebuked for excessive zeal, 52–3; and the inheritors of the future world, 166; rebuked for excessive severity, 204–5; and the law of saints, 216; banishes the *Evil Yezer*, 271; reproaches God for the *Evil Yezer*, 283.
Elisha, why made to supersede Elijah, 53, 205; urges Gehazi to repent, 333.
*Elohim*, God as judge, 35.
*El Shadai*, the God of pardon, 35–6.
*Enemy*, name for the *Evil Yezer*, 243.
Enosh, generation of, rebels, 219; cause pain to God, 219–20.
Envy, causes death, 245, 246; serviceable for a good purpose, 267.
Epithets for God, 21–2, 26–8, 34, 35–6; as used by the Rabbis, 39; in the liturgy, 44.
Esau, identified with Amalek and Rome, 99–100, 108; supreme in this world, 100; the Torah offered to, 132.
Eve, God at the wedding of, 37, 203.
*Evil*, name for the *Evil Yezer*, 243.
Evil, the punishment of the sinner, 293, 294.
Evil eye, the, causes death, 245.
Evil inclination, the. *See Evil Yezer*, the.
Evil thoughts, indulgence in, prevents repentance, 330.
*Evil Yezer*, the, and the love of God, 67–8; suppressed by Israel to acknowledge the kingdom of God, 97–8; Scriptural passages on, 242–3; names for, 243–4; activities of, 244–7, 248; corresponds to lust, 246; punishment meted out by, 246–7; and vanity, 248–9, 276; instantaneous resistance to, recommended, 249; connected closely with idolatry and adultery, 250; and scepticism, 251–2; disparages charity, 252; when it takes possession of man, 252–5; the heart the seat of, 255–61; not equivalent with the heart, 258–9; has no dominion over the heart filled with Torah 259; prominent in Jewish literature, 262; the leaven in the dough, 262–3; a creature of God, 264–6; God acknowledges the creation of, 266, 280–3; uses of, 266–7; called a good quality, 267; the servant of man, 267; man responsible for, 268–9; created for man to overcome, 269; can be overcome by man, 269–70; can be turned to good purposes, 271; how to banish, 271–2; the *Good Yezer* to be stirred up against, 272–3; two weapons against, 273; conquered by the study of the Torah, 273–5; conquest of, an honouring of God, 275; conquered by the contemplation of death, 276; various remedies against, 277–8; grace needed to conquer, 278–84, 289–90; God regrets the creation of, 284; and free will, 284–9; to cease with the advent of the Messiah, 290–2; the appearance of, to the righteous and the wicked, 290; Israel's reward for banishing, 292; repentance for, 304, 313, 314; God prays for the destruction of, 316; killed by a confession of sin, 338.
Exaltation, and the imitation of God, 204.
Exodus, the, due to the *Zachuth* of the Fathers, 174, 180, 185 n.; denied by the perverter of justice, 230; fulfilment of the commandment on usury, a condition of, 230–1.
Exodus, the Book of, cited in connection with the might of God, 38; with the mercy of God, 38;

with the pride of a mortal, 38; with Jethro's acknowledgement of God, 25; with the name of God, 35, 36; with God's presence at Mount Sinai, 36; with God's speech with man, 41; with God as a man of war, 43; with the affliction of Israel, 44; with God's dwelling on earth, 48; with God's paternal interest in Israel, 50, 51; with Moses as a sacrifice for Israel, 53; with the election of Israel, 58, 63; with the glorification of God through creation, 80; with the kingdom of God as established by Israel, 85–6; with the sanction of the Law, 116; the legal part of the Torah begins in, 120; the book of the covenant mentioned in, 121; cited in connection with Israel's holiness, 168; with the *Zachuth* of the Fathers, 174; with the *Zachuth* of a pious ancestry, 181; with imputed sin, 185, 187; with exaltation, 204; with sexual immorality, 206; with murder, 213; with adultery, 214; with mercy, 215; with humility, 223; with the sight of the glory of God, 236 (*bis*); with the weakening influence of sin, 239 (*bis*); with the Tetragrammaton, 239; with the tablets of stone for the Decalogue, 275; with the disappearance of the *Evil Yezer* in the Messianic time, 291 (*bis*); with the atoning power of the righteous, 310; with Pharaoh's hardened heart, 332.

Extermination, penalty for adultery, 224.

"External" books. *See* Apocalyptic; Apocryphal.

Eye, term for the relation between God and Israel, 47.

Eye, the evil, causes death, 245.

Eye of the world, epithet for God, 26.

Eyes, the, cause sin, 208, 214; agents of sin, 258.

Ezekiel, the visions of, and God's heavenly abode, 28–9.

Ezekiel, the Book of, cited, in connection with the pride of Hiram, 38–9; with Israel's relation to God, 44; with the kingdom of God, 71, 88; with imputed sin, 187, 196; with robbery, 228; with the *Evil Yezer*, 243–4; with the sinning soul, 261; with the *Evil Yezer* regarded as *stone*, 275; with the grace needed to conquer the *Evil Yezer*, 281; with the punishment of sinners, 293; with repentance human and Divine, 328.

Faith, the Rabbis quoted on, 14; the reason for Israel's election, 59–60.

Faithfulness, the, of God, 38.

Family, the, and the doctrine of imputed sin, 192.

Family of God, Israel, 200.

Fasting, a sacrificial atonement, 308; cannot replace repentance, 335; with repentance, 339–40.

Fasts, public, the *Zachuth* of pious ancestors invoked at, 172.

Father, term for the relation between God and Israel, 46, 49, 50–6; as used in the liturgy, 155.

Father of the world, epithet for God, 26.

Fatherhood of God, the, to be acknowledged by Israel, 50–1; Luther on, 51 n.; an unconditional relation, 51–6; in the liturgy, 54–6; changed by apostasy, 55 n.

*See also* Reciprocal relation.

Fathers, the, in the sense of the three patriarchs, 171; imperfections and distinctions of, 173–4.

*See also* Patriarchs, the.

"Fathers, the, the Chapters of," character of the contents, 2.
Fathers, the, the merits of. See *Zachuth*.
Fear, an expression for love with the Rabbis, 72; a constituent of the Torah, 146.
Fear of God, the, not in the power of God, 285.
*Fiend*, name for the *Evil Yezer*, 243.
First-born son, term for the relation of Israel to God, 46.
Flock, term for the relation of Israel to God, 49.
Folly, a description of sin, 236–7.
*Foolish old king*, name for the *Evil Yezer*, 244, 254.
Forbidden food, causes impurity, 206–7.
Forgetfulness, the commandment on, illustrated, 149.
Forgiveness, for sins, attained through repentance, 293–4, 335; resides with God alone, 294–5; through suffering, 309; five classes not subject to, 328–30; granted three times for the same sin, 332.
*See also* Atonement; Reconciliation.
Freedom, attained through the yoke of the kingdom of God, 70.
Free will, and the *Evil Yezer*, 284–9.
Future world, the. *See* World, the future.

Gabriel, angel, not a mediator, 45, 67; may not approach Moses, 238.
Galgalim, the, surrounding God, 32.
Gamaliel the Second, Rabban, alluded to, 176.
Gehazi, ruled by the *Evil Yezer*, 271; urged to repent, 333.
Gehenna, children save parents from, 197; repentance in, 341 n.
Gemara, the. *See* Talmud, the.
Genesis, the Book of, cited in connection with the dignity of men, 120; value of, 121; cited in connection with the protective power of the *Zachuth*, 190; with the imitation of God, 202; with the *Porek ol*, 221 (*bis*); with bloodshed, 226, 251; with the Tetragrammaton, 240; with the *Evil Yezer*, 242, 243, 264, 265 (*bis*), 266; with overcoming the *Evil Yezer*, 270, 283; with the *Evil Yezer* as *stone*, 274.
Gentiles, the, transitory character of opinions on, 9–10; magnify God, 58; God's relation to, 62–4; of the kingdom of God, 106; refuse the Law, 131–2; refuse to share in the Law with Israel, 133; rebellious under suffering, 310.
*See also* Kingdom of God, the universal.
Geonic Responsa, quoted, on prayers for the dead, 198.
Geonim, the, and the visible universal kingdom of God, 95–6; and the national kingdom of God, 97.
Gluttony, incompatible with holiness, 211–12; auxiliary to the *Evil Yezer*, 277.
God, man's relation to, treated by the Agadah, 3; epithets for, 21–2, 26–8, 34, 35–6; man's nearness to, determined by his conduct, 33; an *imitatio hominis*, 37–8; attendant at the wedding of Adam and Eve, 37, 203; as used by the Hellenists, 43 n.; the unity of, emphasised, 43–4; worship due to him alone, 44–5; relation of, to the world, 21–45; relation of, to Israel, 46–56; terms for the relation of, to Israel, 46–7; applies his own attributes to Israel, 47; and the angels, 49; before the creation of the world, 80–1;

removed from the world by sin, 83; teaches Israel how to pray, 157; to be imitated by men, 201–5; the denial of, the essence of sin, 233; name given to the *Evil Yezer* by, 243; responsible for the existence of the *Evil Yezer*, 266, 280–3; regrets the creation of the *Evil Yezer*, 284.

*See also under* Forgiveness; Kingdom of God; Transcendentalism.

Gods, a term applied to Israel by God, 47, 49.

Golden calf, the, indicative of Israel's rebelliousness, 86; the sin of, counteracted by the *Zachuth* of the Fathers, 174 (*bis*), 180; and the doctrine of imputed sin, 189; the sin of, permitted, to teach repentance, 317.

Good inclination, the. See *Good Yezer*, the.

*Good Yezer*, the, in the Book of Chronicles (I), 243; term of a late date, 243; the heart the seat of, 255, 256, 257, 259; represented by men, 262; a creature of God, 264–5; preferred by the righteous, 271; to be stirred up against the *Evil Yezer*, 272–3; prayers for, 279–80; in the Messianic time, 291.

Goodness, the law of, akin to holiness, 214; defined by Nachmanides, 214–5; and insisting upon strict justice, 215.

Goodness of God, manifested in the creation, 80.

Goodness of the world, epithet for God, 26.

Gomorrah, and the doctrine of *Zachuth*, 190; the people of, rebels, 219, 222; the people of, cause pain to God, 219–20.

Government, a corrupt, incompatible with the kingdom of God, 106–9.

Grace, Rabbi Akiba on justification by, 15–16; the reason for Israel's election, 61–2; the revelation an act of, 133–5; needed in connection with the Torah to conquer the *Evil Yezer*, 278; prayers for, 278–9; prayers for, in the liturgy, 279–80; the need for, implies God's responsibility for the existence of the *Evil Yezer*, 280–2; needed to subdue the *Evil Yezer*, in the world to come, 282–3; granted to Abimelech, 283–4; man must show himself worthy of, 289–90; Akiba on, 306; reserved for this world, 307; repentance an act of, 324.

Graciousness of God, the, to be imitated by man, 201–2.

Guilt offering, the, ensures forgiveness, 293; accompanied by repentance, 296.

Habakkuk, the Book of, cited, in connection with the *Mizwoth*, 140; with bearing witness, 247.

Hagiographa, the, sometimes excluded by the term *Torah*, 118; included in the term *Torah*, 121–6; frequently quoted by the Rabbis, 122; included in the Scriptures, 123; benediction for, 123; how cited in Rabbinic literature, 124–5.

*See also* Wisdom.

Halachah, the, not subject to miraculous proof, 7.

Halachic discussions, epithet for God in, 34.

Hallam, quoted, 39.

Hallevi, Judah. *See* Judah Hallevi.

Hamnuna Zuta, on the contemplation of death, 276.

Hananiah, justified in rebelling against Nebuchadnezzar, 107.

Harnack, on Pauline Epistles, 18.
Hatred, a greater sin than the cardinal sins, 227; causes death, 245.
Hausrath, disparages the Jewish Sabbath, 153.
Heart, the, causes sin, 208; in Jewish literature, 255 n.; as the seat of the *Yezers*, 255–61; the agent of sin, 258; not equivalent to the *Evil Yezer*, 258–9; good, 259; accused of inconsistency, 259; equivalent to the soul, 260–1; in the righteous and the wicked, 270.
*See also* Soul, the.
Heaven, as the abode of God, 28–9, 30–1, 32; notion as such leaves Rabbinic theology uninfluenced, 30.
Heaven, epithet for God, 21, 28; does not imply remoteness, 46.
Hegelianism, and the Rabbis, 19.
Height of the world, epithet for God, 28.
Hell, endowed with pre-mundane existence, 128.
Hellenism, and the Rabbis, 39–40, 42–3; and its use of God, 43 n.
Heresy, akin to adultery, 225–6.
Herod, king, alluded to, 93.
Hezekiah, king, alluded to, 177.
*Hidden-One*, name for the *Evil Yezer*, 244.
High One, epithet for God, 28.
High priest, the, the vestments of, have atoning power, 300.
Higher criticism, the, on the literature produced under the predominance of the Law, 116.
Hillel, Rabbi, not a miracle-worker, 7; as a modern altruist, 18–19; on the resurrection, 102 n.; on the oneness of the material and the spiritual life, 145; on material uses of the Torah, 154, 159; on individual righteousness, 182; worthy of the Divine Presence, 238.
Hillel, the school of, on the creation of man, 8; on the atoning power of the burnt offering, 299.
Hiram, of Tyre, reproved for pride, 38–9.
Holiness, the Law a source of, 168; a motive for the performance of the Law, 168–9; the culmination of the Law, 199; grows out of the kingdom of God, 199; an *Imitatio Dei*, 199–200, 201–5; divisions of, 201; and separateness, 205; destroyed by impurity, 205–9; abstention from things superfluous, 211–12; abstention from things permitted, 212–13; and the law of goodness, 214; and communion with God, 218.
See also *Kedushah; Chasiduth.*
Holiness, a name for God in Rabbinic literature, 199.
Holy, applied to the patriarchs after their death, 173; attribute applied to Israel by God, 47.
Holy Land, the, talk of the people in, called Torah, 126.
Holy One, the, epithet for God, 21; most frequent name for God in Rabbinic literature, 199.
Holy Spirit, the, dictates the Torah, 120–1; *Chasiduth* leads to communion with, 217–18.
Hope, term for the relation between God and Israel, 46.
Hosea, rebuked for excessive zeal, 53.
Hosea, the Book of, cited, in connection with God as a man of war, 36; with God's love for Israel, 61; with the manner of performing the Law, 161; with *Zachuth*, 178; with man's worthiness of grace, 289; with repentance for many sins, 325; with confession of sins, 338.

Hoshayah, Rabbi, on wisdom, 127.
Humanising of God, 37–8.
Humanity, the essential principle of, in the Book of Leviticus, 120.
Humbleness, the reason for Israel's election, 60.
Hushai, the Archite, reproves David, 212–13.
Hypocrisy, detrimental to belief in the unity of God, 68–9.
Hypocrites, excluded from the Divine Presence, 232.

Idolater, the, animosity to, dates from the revelation, 131; a *Porek ol*, 220; names for, 222–3; compared to the unmerciful, 231–2.
Idolatry, laws on, not a practical consideration, 141; a cardinal sin, 205; transgression of the dietary laws leads to, 207; consequences of, 223; pride, a form of, 223–4; anger, a form of, 224; a contamination, 233; described as folly, 237; and the *Evil Yezer*, 244, 250; the cause of sin, 291–2.
*See also* Polytheism.
Idols, defined, 67.
*Imitatio Dei*, holiness is an, 199–200; particularised by Abba Saul, 201–2.
Immorality, dirties the Torah, 234.
*See also* Adultery; Sexual immorality.
Immortality, treated by the Agadah, 3.
Impurity, in the sense of sexual immorality, 205–6; of body, 206–7; caused by a disgusting act, 267; caused by a transgression of a Biblical law, 208–9; of thought, 210–11, 232.
*See also* Levitical impurity.
Imputed righteousness. See *Zachuth*.
Imputed sin, the doctrine of, a counterpart of *Zachuth*, 170; Biblical authority for, and against, 185–7; and the sin of Adam, 188; and the sin of the golden calf, 189; through contemporaries, 191–5; and secret sins, 194; and the revelation, 195; through posterity, 195–7.
Incest, laws on, not a practical consideration, 141.
Inclination, the evil. See *Evil Yezer*, the.
Inclination, the good. See *Good Yezer*, the.
Incontinence. *See* Sexual immorality.
Individualism in religion, 76–9.
Informer, the office of, performed by the *Evil Yezer*, 252.
Inheritance, regulated by the Mishnah, 2.
Initiative, in repentance, 324, 327.
Isaac, God condoles with, 37.
*See also* Fathers, the; Patriarchs, the.
Isaac, Rabbi, on the Prophets, 124.
Isaiah, the condition of his prophetical call, 52; the mouthpiece of the Mosaic revelation, 124.
Isaiah, the Book of, cited, in connection with separation from God, 33; with the intimate relation of God to Israel, 47, 50; with the rebelliousness of Israel, 52; with Israel's filial relation to God, 54 (*bis*); with Abraham, 59; with God's relation to the Gentiles, 62; with the glorification of God through creation, 80; with universalism, 106 (*bis*), 131; prophetical portion for the Day of Atonement from, 119; cited, in connection with the *Mizwoth*, 140 (*bis*); with humility, 223; with robbery, 228; with nearness to God, 233 (*bis*); with the attribute of mercy, 240; with the *Evil Yezer*, 243; with the heart,

258; with remedies against the *Evil Yezer*, 277; with grace to conquer the *Evil Yezer*, 281; with free will and the *Evil Yezer*, 287, 288; with man's worthiness of grace, 290 (*bis*); with the atoning power of the righteous, 310; with things that prevent repentance, 331.

Ishmael, Rabbi, on the pre-mundane existence of repentance, 314.

Israel, God teaches Torah to, 37; attributes of God applied to, 47; higher than the angels, 49; prayer by, acceptable, 49, 50–1; high responsibility of, 51–2; prophets and patriarchs, atone for, 53; attributes of, qualifying it for election, 59–60; elected by God as the first-born, 62; establishes the kingdom of God, 85–6, 88–9; rebellious against the kingdom of God, 86–8; connected in the liturgy with the kingdom of God, 97; suppresses the evil inclination to acknowledge the kingdom of God, 97–8; the redemption of, and the kingdom of God, 98–103; the depository of the kingdom of God, 105; what constitutes it a nation, 105–6; mission of, to destroy a corrupt government, 108–9; the kingdom of God dependent on, 114–15; endowed with pre-mundane existence, 128; the Torah pleads for, and against, 129; wedded to the Torah, 130; why made the bearer of the Torah, 131–2; to share the Torah with the Gentiles, 133; its view of the Torah, 137; commended for joy in the Law, 149–50; taught by God how to pray, 157; holy through the commandments, 168–9; lives through the *Zachuth* of the Fathers, 175; the solidarity of, 191–5; the holiness of, 199–200; dietary laws the special privilege of, 207; delivered to the sword by idolatry, 223; the sanctuary of, destroyed by bloodshed, 226; redeemed from Egypt to fulfil the commandment of justice, 230; redeemed from Egypt on condition that it obeys the commandment on usury, 230–1; purified by the Day of Atonement, 234; the sin of, removes the Divine Presence, 236, 238; weakened by sin, 239; apostasy of, due to the *Evil Yezer*, 242; needs grace to extenuate its guilt, 282; and the disappearance of the *Evil Yezer*, 291; rewarded for subduing the *Evil Yezer*, 292; the solidarity of, and the atoning power of sacrifices, 300–1; repentance of, 304; to be punished in the future world, 307; humble under suffering, 310; the righteous and the children atone for, 310–11; given opportunity for repentance, 316; made to sin, as an example of repentance, 317; encouraged to repent for great sins, 326; met halfway by God, 327; must confess sins, 336.

*See also* Election of Israel, the; Kingdom of God, the.

Israel, the kingdom of, identified with the kingdom of God, 103; safeguards the conception of the kingdom of God, 104; adds the feature of material happiness to the kingdom of God, 109–14.

*See also* Israel; Election of Israel, the; Kingdom of God, the national; Kingdom of God, the visible universal.

Israel, the relation of God to, 46–56; terms for, 46–7; reciprocal, 47–9, 50–1; paternal character of, 51–6; changed by apostasy, 55 n.; indicated by election, 57.

*See also* Israel; Election of Israel, the.

Jacob, and the kingdom of God, 84; chooses the world to come as his portion, 100.
*See also* Fathers, the; Patriarchs, the.
Jealousy, and the imitation of God, 204; Elijah rebuked for, 204–5.
Jehoiachin, the repentance of, acceptable, 326.
Jehoiakim, spites God, 220.
Jeremiah, the Book of, cited, in connection with reward for proper zeal, 53; with the election of Israel, 58; with God's relation to the Gentiles, 63 (*bis*); with the kingdom of God, 99; with joy of the Law, 151; with prayer, 156; with the attachment of Israel to God, 200; with the Shechinah, 225; with the inconsistent heart, 259; with the study of the Torah as a weapon against the *Evil Yezer*, 274; with the grace needed to conquer the *Evil Yezer*, 281, 282; with the justice to prevail in the future world, 307; with repentance human and divine, 327.
Jeroboam, the division of the kingdom under, rebellion against God, 87; urged by God to repent, 319–20.
Jerusalem, identified with the kingdom of God, 99; cause of the destruction of, 215; a resident of, and the continual burnt offering, 300.
Jesus, the son of Sirach, on wisdom, 70.
Jethro, illustrates the attitude of a proselyte, 25.
Job, Satan's good intentions concerning, 268; argues with God regarding the *Evil Yezer*, 273, 280.
Job, the Book of, cited, in connection with man's rebelliousness, 83; with the spiritualisation of Scriptures, 103; with adultery, 214, 224–5; with heresy, 226; with the justice of God, 305.
Jochanan, Rabbi, on robbery as a capital sin, 227–8.
Jochanan ben Sakkai, as a modern altruist, 18–19.
Joel, the Book of, cited, in connection with man's direct relation to God, 44–5; with being called by the name of God, 201; with the *Evil Yezer*, 244; with fasting and repentance, 339.
Jonah, the Book of, quoted, in connection with efficacious repentance, 335.
Jose, Rabbi, quoted on the reward of the righteous, 14.
Jose ben Chalafta, Rabbi, on the qualities of God's chosen ones, 61.
Joseph, rules over the *Evil Yezer*, 271; the brothers of, defended by the Rabbis, 281.
Joseph Askari, on the joy of the Law, 151.
Joshua, Israel under, accepts the kingdom of God, 87.
Joshua, the Book of, cited, in connection with Rahab's acknowledgement of God, 26.
Joshua ben Levi, Rabbi, and the law of saints, 216; enumerates seven names for the *Evil Yezer*, 243–4; on repentance in Gehenna, 341 n.
Joy of the Law, an essential element in the understanding of the Law, 146, 148; illustrated in the commandment of forgetfulness, 149; Israel commended for, 149–50; Scriptural and Rabbinical quotations on, 150–1; mediæval writers on, 150–1; a modern illustration of, 151–2; illustrated on the Sabbath, 152–4; illus-

trated in the prayers, 154–9; a motive for the performance of the Law, 168–9.

*See also* Law, the; Torah, the.

Judah, the princes of, rebellious against God, 87–8.

Judah, the Saint (Rabbi), on the time when the *Evil Yezer* takes possession of man, 253–4; prays for grace to conquer the *Evil Yezer*, 279.

Judah (Judan), Rabbi, on man's direct relation to God, 44–5.

Judah ben Ezekiel, Rabbi, defines *Chasiduth*, 209.

Judah ben Ilai, Rabbi, limits the paternal relation between God and Israel, 54; on the imitation of God, 203.

Judah Hallevi, on the inclusiveness of the Torah, 146. *See also Kusari.*

Judaism, and individualism, 76–9; to convert the world, 77; aims to establish the visible kingdom of God, 79; teaches a universal kingdom of God, 93; views of, on poverty, 110; view of, on suffering, 111; insists upon man's happiness on earth, 111.

*See also* Rabbis, the; etc.

Judges, the Book of, cited, in connection with the administration of justice, 229.

Justice, in God, 38; the execution of, conditions the Torah, 143; and the imitation of God, 204; bad administration of, a form of bloodshed, 229–30; superior to sacrifices as a means of atonement, 296; God's attribute of, evoked by sin, 239–40; the Rabbis on, 304–6; prevails in the future world, 307; and repentance, 322.

Kaddish, the, and the kingdom of God, 95.

*Kedushah*, holiness within the limits of the Law, 201, 209; original meaning of, 205; the reward of, 217–18.

*See also* Holiness; *Chasiduth.*

Kiara, Simon. *See* Simon Kiara.

King, epithet for God, 21.

Kingdom of God, the, defined by the Rabbis, 65; conception originates in the Scriptures, 65; divisions of, 66; universal in its aims, 93; conception narrowed and enriched by national aspect, 103–4; bad government incompatible with, 106–9; material features of, 109–14; dependent upon Israel, 114–15; confers authority upon the Law, 116; holiness grows out of, 199; the yoke of, thrown off by the *Porek ol*, 220–1; the yoke of, thrown off by the respecter of persons, 230.

Kingdom of God, the invisible, how to receive the yoke of, 66–7; not a burden, 70–2; and the dangers of quietism, 78.

Kingdom of God, the national, in the liturgy, 97, 105; connected with the redemption of Israel, 98–101, 114–15; opposed to the kingdom of Rome, 101; the features of, 104; the spiritual features of, 104–6; penitents and proselytes in, 106; and material happiness, 109–14.

Kingdom of God, the universal, in the *Shema*, 64.

*See also* Gentiles, the.

Kingdom of God, the visible, the aim of Judaism, 78–9; divisions of, 80.

Kingdom of God, the visible universal, dates from the creation of man, 81, 82; impaired by sin, 83; restored by Abraham, 83–4; taught by Jacob, 84; established by Israel, 84–6, 88–9; Israel rebellious against, 86–8; received by Israel under Joshua, 87; in this world, 89; terms for, 89; established by man conscious of God's nearness, 89–90; an ethical concept, 90–1; and the Torah, 91–2; not political, 92, 93; in the liturgy, 93–6; and the unity of God, 96; connected with the kingdom of Israel, 104–6, 114–15.

*See also* Israel, the kingdom of.

Kingdom of heaven, the, defined, 65–6, 89.

*See also* Kingdom of God, the.

Kings (I), the Book of, cited, in connection with God's closeness to the earth, 29; with Elijah's excessive zeal, 52–3; with jealousy, 204 (*bis*).

Kings (II), the Book of, cited, in connection with Naaman's acknowledgement of God, 26; with imputed sin, 187; with sin as rebellion, 219; with the repentance of Manasseh, 318, 319.

Kingship, the, of God, and his abode in heaven, 31–2; begins with the creation of man, 81, 82.

*See also* Kingdom of God, the.

Kneading, forbidden on the Sabbath, 153.

Korah, alluded to, 222; given opportunity for repentance, 316.

*Kusari*, the, by Judah Hallevi, quoted, 146.

Lamb, term for the relation between God and Israel, 47.

Lamentations, the Book of, cited, in connection with Jeremiah's proper zeal, 53; with the kingdom of God, 67; with the weakening influence of sin, 239; with the attribute of justice, 240.

Law, the, not connected with hardness, 34; the allegorising method directed against, 40–2; fulfilment of, easy to a child of God, 55; derives its authority from the kingdom of God, 116; not a correct rendering of Torah, 117; holiness the highest achievement of, 199; relation of *Kedushah* and *Chasiduth* to, 201; overruled by God, for the sake of repentance, 322.

*See also* Joy of the Law; Legalism; Leviticalism; Mosaism; Torah, the.

Leaven in the dough, the, the *Evil Yezer*, 262–3; identified with the *Evil Yezer* in a prayer, 265–6; God takes the responsibility for, 266, 282; good purpose of, 266–8.

*See also Evil Yezer*, the.

Legalism, charged to be the predominant element in Jewish theology, 23–4; misunderstood, 117.

*See also* Law, the; Leviticalism; Mosaism; Torah, the.

Legends, on the revelation, 130–5; universalistic tendency of, 131–2.

Levitical impurity, sacrifices intended for, 296; the Day of Atonement concerned with, 301.

Leviticalism, not antagonistic to Prophetism, 119.

Leviticus, the Book of, cited, in connection with binding laws, 13; with the election of Israel, 58; with the sanction of the Law, 116; Scriptural portion for the Day of Atonement from, 119; contains the essential principle claimed by Christianity and humanity, 119–20 (*bis*); cited, in connection with the intention to underlie sacrifices, 160; with God's covenant with the patriarchs, 172 (*bis*); with the doctrine of imputed sin, 192 (*bis*); with the holiness of Israel, 200; with holiness through separation, 205, 211; with sexual immorality, 206; with relations between man and his fellow, 215; with love of neighbour, 226–7; with justice, 230; with spiritual corruption, 235; with unintentional sins, 241 (*bis*); with the good heart, 259; with the removal of the *Evil Yezer*, 292; with the punishment of sinners, 293; with the limited efficacy of sacrifices, 295; with the size of the sacrifice, 297; with the scapegoat, 301; with encouraging sinners to repent, 321.

Liars, excluded from the Divine Presence, 232.

Libertinism, and the observance of the Torah, 211.

Life of the world, epithet for God, 26.

Light, the, of the first day, concealed by sin, 237.

Light of the world, epithet for God, 26.

Limitation theory of the Cabalists, 128.

*Lishmah*, defined as single-mindedness in the performance of the Law, 159–61; attained through the performance of the Law, 161; excludes the idea of reward, 162–3.
*See also* Reward.

Liturgy, the, a source for Rabbinic theology, 3, 9–11; as a theologic test for the Talmud, 10; early origin of, 11; in the Talmud, 11; free from alien epithets for God, 44; the fatherhood of God in, 54–6; the election of Israel in, 57; the kingship prayers in, universal in tone, 93–6; the kingdom of God in, 97, 105; on the Torah as a source of joy, 147; and the doctrine of *Zachuth*, 184; and prayers for the dead, 198; on holiness, 218; prayers for grace to conquer the *Evil Yezer* in, 279–80; daily prayer for repentance in, 341.
*See also* Prayer; Prayer Book, the; Prayers, the, of the synagogue.

Lord of the World, epithet for God, 21, 26.

Lost things, keeping, prevents repentance, 330.

Love of God, the, the reason for Israel's election, 61; defined, 67–70; unconditional, 68; incompatible with love of self, 68–9; a longing for God, 69–70, 73–6; must be disinterested, 72, 74; and the visible kingdom of God, 78–9; a constituent of the Torah, 146, 147; the only proper motive for the worshipper, 163; the motive for performance of the Law, 167–9.

Lovingkindness, works of, a weapon against the *Evil Yezer*, 273; have atoning power, 312.
*See also* Charity.

Lust, corresponds to the *Evil Yezer*, 246; in the soul of man, 260; the world based on, 267.
*See also* Sexual immorality.

Luther, quoted, on the intimate relationship of God and man, 51 n.

Luzzatto, Moses Chayim, on love of God, 69–70; on the joy of the Law, 151; on *Chasiduth*, 209 n.

Lydda, alluded to, 216.

Maacah, mother of Absalom, alluded to, 213.

Maimonides, and Israel's election, 57; on the *Mizwoth*, 141; on the Sabbath, 152; on the fulfilment of the *Mizwoth*, 165; on repentance, 331; on the nature of repentance, 335; on prayer and repentance, 339.

*Makom*. *See* Space.

Malachi, the mouthpiece of the Mosaic revelation, 124.
Malachi, the Book of, cited, in connection with the greatness of God, 58; with purity of motive in performance of the Law, 160–1; with heresy, 226; with God as judge and witness, 247; with the encouraging of repentance in sinners, 321; with repentance human and Divine, 327.
*Malady*, the name for the *Evil Yezer*, 244.
Man, the creation of, and God's kingship, 81, 93; a free agent, 81–2; the centre of creation, 82; in rebellion, 83; effect of his consciousness of God, 89–90; the master of his inclinations, 270–3.
Manasseh, a *Porek ol*, 221; his repentance acceptable to God, 318–19, 326; his repentance not the highest degree, 320.
Manners, good, God a model of, 203.
Marcion, Harnack on, 18.
Marriage laws, in the Mishnah, 2.
Martyrdom, enjoined to prevent the commission of the cardinal sins, 222.
*Mashal*, the. *See* Allegoric interpretation of Scripture.
Master of all Creation, epithet for God, 22, 34.
Masters, slights put upon, prevent repentance, 330.
Material, term not used in Rabbinic literature, 144.
Material happiness, a feature of the national kingdom of God, 109–14; and religion, 111.
*Mechilta*, the, censures Israel for deferring the kingdom of God, 86; numerous citations from the Prophets and Hagiographa in, 122.
Mediatorship, denounced by the Rabbis, 21, 45.
Meekness, the reason for Israel's election, 60.
Meir Ibn Gabbai, quoted, on love of God, 69, 75–6.
*Memra*, epithet for God, 35; (Word) as used by the Rabbis, 39, 43 n.
Men of the Great Assembly, and the *Evil Yezer*, 246–7, 250.
Menelaus, high priest, alluded to, 92.
Merciful One, epithet for God, 34.
Mercy, God's attribute of, turned into justice by sin, 239–40; and repentance, 322–4; represented by the "right hand" of God, 323.
Mercy of God, to be imitated by men, 201, 202; in the interpretation of the Law, recommended, 215–16; lack of, equal to a denial of the law, 231–2; the world based on, 267.
Merits of the Fathers, the. See *Zachuth*.
Messiah, the, pre-mundane existence of the name, etc., of, 13 n., 59, 128; and the kingdom of God, 100, 101–3; poverty delays the coming of, 114; exalted beyond the patriarchs, 174; the advent of, to banish the *Evil Yezer*, 290–2.
Messianic aspirations, treated by the Agadah, 3.
Messianic time, the, and the unity of God, 96.
Metatron, read into the Book of Exodus, 41.
Micah, the Book of, cited, in connection with the *Mizwoth*, 140; with the grace needed to conquer the *Evil Yezer*, 281; with the atoning power of the burnt offering, 299.
Michael, angel, not a mediator, 45, 67; may not approach Moses, 238.
Midrash, the, on the narratives of the Bible, 120.

Midrashic works, theologic sources, 3.
Midrashim, the. *See* Rabbis, the; Rabbinic literature, the.
Ministering angels, surrounding God, 28, 32.
Miracles, in Rabbinic literature, 5–8.
Mishael, justified in rebelling against Nebuchadnezzar, 107.
Mishnah, the, character of the contents, 2; drawbacks as a theologic source, 3–4; liturgical passages in, 11; on the *Evil Yezer*, 245, 246.
Missionary enterprises, and the Rabbis, 132.
*Mizwoth*, the, complementary to the Torah, 117–18; the number and divisions of, according to R. Simlai, 138, 141–2; denounced as a burden, 138–9; the number of, interpreted homiletically, 139–40; which were obsolete in the time of the Rabbis, 141; which were restricted in their application, 141; character of, 142; inclusiveness of, 142–4; how considered by Israel, 148; salvation not dependent on the number fulfilled, 164–6; a source of holiness, 168–9; doctrinal value of, 231.
"Modernity," and the Rabbis, 19–20.
Moloch, laws on sacrifices to, not a practical consideration, 141.
Mommsen, on the cruelty of the Roman government, 108–9 n.
Montaigne, quoted, 39.
Moral principles of the revelation, unacceptable to the nations, 132.
Mosaism, not antagonistic to Prophetism, 119.
*See also* Law, the; Legalism; Leviticalism; Torah, the.
Moses, form of his acknowledgement of God, 26; appearance of God to, a proof of God's omnipresence, 29; buried by God, 37; offers himself as an atoning sacrifice, 53, 310; exalted place of, as a prophet, 118, 124 n.; captures the Torah from heaven, 130; instructed in all the deductions from the Torah, 134–5; and the appointment of judges, 143; invokes the *Zachuth* of the tribes, 172–3; invokes the *Zachuth* of the Fathers, 174; the meekness of, 223; the effect of sin on, 237–8; name given to the *Evil Yezer* by, 243; reproaches God for the *Evil Yezer*, 283; prays for the regeneration of the sinner, 316.
Moses Loeb, of Sasow, on scepticism, 111.
Mother, term for the relation between God and Israel, 47.
Mothers, the, in the sense of the wives of the three patriarchs, 172.
Murder, and the doctrine of imputed sin, 196; a cardinal sin, 205; different kinds of, 213; unknown, sacrifice for, 301; not subject to repentance, 333.
*See also* Bloodshed.
Mystic, a, on repentance, 334.
Mysticism, and God's abode, 28–9, 32; in Judaism, 76; defined by De Wette, 77; and law, 78.
Mystics, the, on the reciprocal relationship of God and Israel, 47–8; on the love of God, 68–70, 72–6; on the creation of the world, 128; and combinations of letters, 129; their view of the Torah, 135; on unintentional sins, 241; on the heart as the seat of the *Yezers*, 256.

Naaman, illustrates the attitude of a proselyte, 25–6.
Nachmanides, on imputed sin, 186 n.;

on *Chasiduth*, 211–12; on the law of goodness, 214–15.
Narratives, the, of the Bible, how regarded, 120.
Nationalism, and the Torah, 105–6.
Nazarite, a, cuts off hair to subdue the *Evil Yezer*, 277.
Nazir, the, the holiness of, 211–12.
Nebuchadnezzar, justified rebellion against, 107.
New Testament, the, the Prophets and Hagiographa called Law in, 125.
New Year, the, the kingdom of God, in the liturgy of, 93–4, 105.
*Nezikin*, Talmudic tractate, attention to, identified with *Chasiduth*, 209.
Nimrod, a rebel, 219.
Nineveh, the repentance of the men of, 326.
Noah, and the doctrine of imputed sin, 195; saved for the sake of his children, 196; the dietary laws distinguish Israel from the descendants of (*see also* Gentiles, the), 207.
Nomism. *See* Legalism.
*Nomos*, not a correct rendering of Torah, 117; applied to the Prophets and Hagiographa, 125.
Numbers, the Book of, cited, in connection with the faithfulness of Israel, 59; with the superiority of the Torah, 118; with the joy of the Law, 150; with the holiness of fulfilling Biblical commandments, 208; with the *Porek ol*, 221; with humility, 223; with the weakening influence of sin, 239; with the Nazarite, 249; with free will and the *Evil Yezer*, 287; with the intention underlying sacrifice, 298; with the atoning power of the continual burnt offering, 299.

Oaths, administration of, in the Mishnah, 2.
Obadiah, the Book of, cited, in connection with the kingdom of God, 100.
*Olah*, the. *See* Burnt offering, the.
Old Testament, the, the economic ideal of, 112.
Only One of the world, epithet for God, 26.
Ophanim, the, surrounding God, 28, 32.

Palestine, laws on the conquest of, obsolete, 141.
Pantheistic notions in Jewish writers, 27–8, 30.
Pappos, on the arbitrariness of God, 305.
Paradise, endowed with pre-mundane existence, 128.
Pardon. *See* Forgiveness.
Patriarchs, the, atone for Israel, 53, 310; teachers of the kingdom of God, 92; have dominion over the *Evil Yezer*, 271.
*See also* Fathers, the.
Paul, apostle, antinomian influence of, 4; attitude of commentators on Epistles of, 18.
Penitence, qualifies for the kingdom of God, 106.
*See also* Repentance.
Pentateuch, the, often equivalent to Torah, 118; sometimes considered higher than the prophets, 118; contains more than law, 121; importance of, in the Messianic time, 124 n.; the Prophets depend on, 124.
*See also* Law, the; Torah, the.
People, term for the relation of Israel to God, 46.
Persecution, the reason for Israel's election, 60.
Personification of the Torah, 129–30.

Perushim, those who abstain from things superfluous, 211.
*Petra*, an epithet for Abraham, 173.
Pharaoh, type of man deified, 39; why God hardened his heart, 332.
Phenomena, natural, warn men to repent, 315.
Piyutim, fictions, term applied to the narratives of the Bible, 120.
Pledge, taking the, of the poor, prevents repentance, 330.
Ploughing, forbidden on the Sabbath, 153.
Polytheism, disguised, detrimental to belief in the unity of God, 68–9.
*See also* Idolatry.
Poor, plundering the, prevents repentance, 331.
*Porek ol*, defined, 220–1.
Poverty, inconsistent with the kingdom of God, 110; the Rabbis on, 112–13; a remedy against the *Evil Yezer*, 278.
Power, the, of God, 38.
Prayer, heard instantaneously by God, 31; defined by a mediæval Rabbi, 42; by Israel, acceptable to God, 49, 50–1; characterised by the Rabbis, 156–7; devotion indispensable in, 156–9; proper motive for, 162; renders the *Zachuth* of the Fathers efficacious, 180; invalidated by robbery, 228–9, 234; accompanying repentance, 338–9.
Prayer, a, by a girl regarding the *Evil Yezer*, 265; by a Rabbi regarding the leaven in the dough, 265–6; by a Rabbi regarding the *Evil Yezer*, 277.
Prayer Book, the, and the charge of a transcendental God in Rabbinic theology, 22–3, 29; term for the kingdom of God in, 89.
*See also* Liturgy, the; Prayer; Prayers, the, of the synagogue.
Prayers, by Rabbis, for grace to conquer the *Evil Yezer*, 278–9.
Prayers, the, of the synagogue, illustrate the joy of the Law, 154–9; composed by the Rabbis, 155.
Pre-mundane existences, 13 and n., 59–60, 80, 127, 128–9, 135, 314.
Presence, the Divine. *See* Shechinah, the.
Pride, a form of idolatry, 223–4.
Profanation of the name of God, caused by idolatry, 223; a sin not subject to repentance, 328, 329.
Prohibitive laws, the number of, 138.
Property laws, in the Mishnah, 2.
Prophecy, equivalent to holiness, 217; on the punishment of sinners, 293.
Prophetism, not antagonised by Mosaism, 119.
Prophets, the, atone for Israel, 53, 310; plead with God for Israel, 53–4; demand punishment by death, rather than repentance, 323.
Prophets, the, the books of, sometimes excluded by the term *Torah*, 118; sometimes considered less than the Pentateuch, 118; included in the term *Torah*, 121–6; lessons from, accompany the Pentateuch portions, 122; frequently quoted by the Rabbis, 122; benediction for, 123; dependent on the Pentateuch, 124; how cited in Rabbinic literature, 124–5.
Proselytes, transitory character of opinions on, 9–10; inclined to transcendentalism in acknowledging God, 25–6; and epithets for God, 46; in the kingdom of God, 106.
Proverbs, the Book of, cited, in connection with the wisdom of God, 38; with the glorification of God through Creation, 80; with

wisdom, 127, 129; with the ways of the Torah, 143; with the *Zachuth* of a pious contemporary, 190; with the doctrine of imputed sin, 193; with the *Zachuth* of a pious posterity, 197; with the strict interpretation of the Law, 216 (*bis*); with pride, 223; with the contamination of sin, 234; with unintentional sins, 240; with the *Evil Yezer*, 243; with sin as the cause of death, 247; with free will and the *Evil Yezer*, 287 (*bis*); with the punishment of sinners, 293; with the limited efficacy of sacrifices, 296; with atonement through suffering, 309; with death-bed repentance, 340.

Psalms, the, cited, in connection with Araboth, 28, 31; with the abode of God, 32, 36; with the wealth of God, 38; with Israel forsaken by God, 43; with the title applied by God to Israel, 47; with the election of Israel, 58; with the unity of God, 69; with longing for God, 70; with the kingship of God, 82, 90, 97, 98, 99; and the Law, 116; cited, in connection with the power of God's work, 121; with the extent of the Torah, 122; with the Torah as the bride of Israel, 130; with the *Mizwoth*, 140; with the inclusiveness of the Torah, 144; divested of individualistic tendency, 155; cited in connection with devotion in prayer, 156, 157; with performing the Law without reference to reward, 162–3 (*bis*); with the essential commandments, 164; with negative and positive virtue, 167; with the *Zachuth* of a pious ancestry, 183; with revenge, 204; with exaltation, 204; with pride, 223; with the weakening influence of sin, 239; with the *Evil Yezer*, 242, 243, 244 (*bis*), 245; with sexual intercourse, 253; with the clean heart, 258; with the study of the Torah as a weapon against the *Evil Yezer*, 274; with grace to conquer the *Evil Yezer*, 78 (*bis*); with free will and the *Evil Yezer*, 286; with the punishment of sinners, 293; with pardon granted by God, 294–5 (*bis*); with the intention underlying sacrifice, 298; with humility in suffering, 310; with the act of revelation, 311; with mercy through repentance, 313; with God's instruction in repentance, 314–16; with repentance human and Divine, 327 (*bis*), 328.

Pseudo-Jonathan, on the *Evil Yezer*, 242.

Punishment, the, of the sinner, 293, 294, 304.
*See also* Reward and punishment.

Queen, epithet of the Sabbath, 154.

Rab, and the strict interpretation of the Law, 215–16.

Rabba, defines *Chasiduth*, 209.

Rabba Bar bar Chana, and the strict interpretation of the Law, 215–16.

Rabbinic literature, as a theologic source, 2–9, 11–16.
*See* Rabbis, the.

Rabbis, the, supposed characteristics of, 2; as miracle-workers, 7; on faith, 14; on sin, 14; on the closeness of God to man, 24–8, 29–30, 31, 33; epithets for God used by, 26–8, 34; and the doctrine of a personal God, 30; their view of the Law, 34; on the names of God, 35–6; on corporeal terms applied to God, 36–7; delight in humanising God, 37–8; object to deifying man, 38–9; and the allegorising method, 39–44; reverence of, for the Scriptures, 42–3; substitute the Tetragrammaton for the epithets for God, 46; terms applied by, to the relation between God and Israel, 47; on the reciprocal relation between God and Israel, 48–9, 50–1; on the fatherhood of God, 51–6; on the election of Israel, 58–64; define the kingdom of God, 65; on love of God, 66–8, 79; on freedom in the kingdom of God, 70–2; on the character of the reward of the righteous, 78; on the creation of man as a free agent, 81; on the kingship of God, 82; on Israel's establishing the kingdom of God, 85–6, 88–9; on man's righteousness and the kingdom of God, 89–91; on the Torah and the kingdom of God, 91–2; on the form of government, 92; on the national kingdom of God, 100, 101–3, 105, 114–15; on what constitutes Israel a nation, 105–6; on the Roman government, 107–9; on material happiness connected with the national kingdom of God, 109–14; on poverty, 110, 112–13; the economic ideal of, 112; object to speculation, 112–13; on the relation of employer to employee, 113; on the connection between Israel and the kingdom of God, 114–15; on the sanction of the Law, 116; on the relative value of Moses and the other prophets, 118; on the books of the Prophets, 119, 124; on the Torah as the word of God, 120–1; on the Book of Genesis, 121; on extralegal elements in the Torah, 121; frequently quote the Prophets and Hagiographa, 122; include the Hagiographa in the Scriptures, 123; extend the use of Torah beyond the Scriptures, 126; on the Torah as wisdom, 127; attitude toward missionary enterprises, 132; on the pregnant meaning of the Torah, 134; on the Torah as God's will, 136–7; *Mizwoth* obsolete in the time of, 141; on the inclusiveness of the Torah, 142–4; make no division between material and spiritual, 144–6; the Torah a source of joy to, 146–7, 150–1; on the Sabbath, 152–4; accused of mechanical tendencies, 155; the composers of the liturgy, 155; on prayer, 155–7; on purity of motive in the performance of the Law, 160–1; on reward and punishment, 162–3; on negative and positive virtue, 166–7; on love as the motive for the performance of the Law, 167–9; on the ancestors whose *Zachuth* is invoked, 172–3; on the Fathers, 173–5; on the *Zachuth* of a pious ancestry, 176–7, 181–5; limit the *Zachuth* of the Fathers, 177–8; impute unlimited efficacy to it, 178–81; on imputed sin, 186–9; on the *Zachuth* of a pious contemporary, 189–90; on the solidarity of Israel, 191–5; on imputed sin through posterity, 196–7; on the *Zachuth* of posterity, 197–8; on holiness as an *Imitatio Dei*, 199–200; on the imitation of God by man, 201–5; on sexual immorality, 205–6; on the dietary laws, 207; on acts provoking disgust, 207; on *Chasiduth*, 209–10; on the law of goodness, 215–16; on communion with God, 217–18; define sin as rebellion, 219–20;

on usury, 230–1; on separation from God, 232–3; on the contamination of sin, 233–6; on sin as folly, 236–7; on the blighting influence of sin, 237–40; on unintentional sins, 240–1; on the two *Yezers*, 243; give various names to the *Evil Yezer*, 243–4; on the activity of the *Evil Yezer*, 244–7; on the period in which the *Evil Yezer* takes possession of man, 252–5; do not consider man corrupt, 262; keep to the golden mean, 264; on the leaven in the dough, 266; on weapons against the *Evil Yezer*, 273; on the uses of the study of the Torah against the *Evil Yezer*, 275; on ascetic remedies against the *Evil Yezer*, 277; on grace to conquer the *Evil Yezer*, 278–84; on the punishment of sinners, 293–4; on the intention underlying sacrifices, 297–8; on the Day of Atonement, 301–4; on the justice of God, 304–6; offer themselves as an atonement for Israel, 311; on God's instruction of men in repentance, 314–15; on relapsing into sin, 339.

Rahab, illustrates the attitude of the proselyte, 26.

Reaping, forbidden on the Sabbath, 153.

Rebellion, against God, the first sin, 83; the sin of Israel, 86–8; definition of sin by the Rabbis, 219–22, 233.

Reciprocal relation between God and Israel, 47–9, 50–1.

Reconciliation with God, through sacrifices, limited in efficacy, 295–7; through death and suffering, 307–8; through confession of sin, 338.
  *See also* Atonement, Repentance.

*Regulations of Chasiduth*, by Eliezer of Worms, quoted, 210.

Religion, place of material happiness in, 111.

Remnant, the, of Israel, establishes the kingdom of God, 88–9.

Renan, quoted, 155.

Reparation, a condition of acceptable repentance, 333.
  *See also* Restitution.

Repentance, treated by the Agadah, 3; accepted instantaneously by God, 31; endowed with premundane existence, 128, 314; restores efficacy to the *Zachuth* of the Fathers, 180–1, 185 n.; ensures forgiveness for sins, 293–4; ways of achieving, 294; must accompany sacrifices, 294, 296–7, 313; on the Day of Atonement, 302–3; for the *Evil Yezer*, 304, 313; prayer for, 313; the only means of atonement, 313; urged by God himself, 314–16, 319; possible for the greatest sins, 317, 318, 325–6, 333–4; Manasseh an extreme instance of, 318–19, 320; through fear, of a low order, 320; and restitution, 320; encouraged through intercourse between saints and sinners, 321; opposed by the angels, 321–2; and God's attributes of justice and mercy, 322–4; the good portion assigned to this world, 324; an act of grace, 324; depends on the initiative of man, 324, 327, 334; false shame not to stand in the way of, 324–5; need not be public, 326; a mutual relation between God and man, 327–8; inefficacious in five cases, 328–30, 333; prevented by twenty-four things, 330–1; Maimonides on, 331, 335, 339; inefficacious after three warnings, 332; must be accompanied by reparation,

333; a mystic's view of, 334; the nature of, 334; consists of acts, 334–5; must be accompanied by confession of sin, 335–8; and prayer, 338–9; and fasting, 339–40; on the death-bed, 340–1; daily, 342; during the Ten Penitential Days, 342; not limited to special seasons, 342–3.
*See also* Penitence.
Restitution, a condition of atonement for moral sins, 296, 303; and repentance, 320.
*See also* Reparation.
Resurrection, controversy about the Scriptural authority for the belief in, 124–5.
Reuben ben Astrobolis, Rabbi, on the time when the *Evil Yezer* takes possession of man, 252.
Revelation, the, indispensable to the existence of the world, 128–9; the day of, in Rabbinic literature, 130–1; universalistic feature of, 131–2, 133, 135; moral features of, unacceptable to the Gentiles, 132; an act of grace, 133–5; due to the *Zachuth* of the Fathers, 174; and the doctrine of imputed sin, 195; the act of, made dependent upon the children of the Israelites, 311.
*See also* Law, the; Pentateuch, the; Torah, the.
Revenge, and the imitation of God, 204.
Reward, the, of the righteous, R. Jose on, 14; not the motive for the performance of the Law, 167, 169.
See also *Lishmah.*
Reward and punishment, in the Rabbinical system, 162–3.
'Right hand," the, of God, represents the attribute of mercy, 323.
Righteous, the, reward of, 14; compose the kingdom of God, 106; how they differ from the wicked, 270–1; and the appearance of the *Evil Yezer*, 290; the atoning power of, 310.
Righteous One of the world, epithet for God, 26.
Righteousness, imputed. See *Zachuth.*
Righteousness, treated by the Agadah, 3; establishes the kingdom of God, 89–90, 93; culminates in holiness, 199; and the *Zachuth,* 176, 180, 189–90; of God, to be imitated by man, 202.
Ritual observances, attacked by the *Evil Yezer*, 251.
Robbery, a form of bloodshed, 227–9; invalidates sacrifices, 228; invalidates charity, 228; invalidates prayer, 228–9, 234; not subject to repentance, 333.
Rome, identified with the enemies of the kingdom of God, 99–101, 106–9; obedience to, enjoined upon Israel, 107; objection to the government of, 107–8; considered corrupt by the Rabbis, 108–9.

Saadya, Rabbi, on what constitutes Israel a nation, 105; defines the worshipper, 164; on relapsing into sin, 339.
Sabbath, the, man the lord of, 152; attacks upon, 152–3; illustrates the joy of the Law, 153–4; celebrated by the observers of it, 153–4; epithets given to, 154; profanation of, due to the *Evil Yezer*, 246.
Sacrifices, invalidated by robbery, 228; accompanied by repentance, 294, 296–7; limited in efficacy as a means of atonement, 295–7; charity superior to, 296; efficacy depends upon the intention, 297–8; atoning power as-

signed to, by the Rabbis, 300–1; suffering compared to, 308–9; death compared to, 310; the Torah and charity compared to, 312; demanded by the Torah, 323.
Safety, term for the relation between God and Israel, 46.
Saintliness. See *Chasiduth.*
Saints, associate with sinners to encourage repentance, 321.
"Saints, The, Chapters of," miracles reported in, 6.
Salvation, not dependent on the number of commandments fulfilled, 164; secured by the fulfilment of one commandment, 165–6; secured by negative virtues, 166–7; depends upon the actions of man, 182, 189.
Salvation, term for the relation between God and Israel, 46.
Samael, identified with the *Evil Yezer,* 246, 262.
Samaritans, the, on what is to be included under Torah, 122.
Samuel (I), the Book of, cited, in connection with the foundations of the world, 173; with the *Zachuth* of posterity, 197.
Samuel (II), the Book of, cited, in connection with Israel in rebellion, 87; with the righteous as the pillars of the spiritual world, 89.
Samuel de Ozedo, quoted, on disinterested love of God, 72 n.
Samuel Hakaton, worthy of the Divine Presence, 238.
Satan, identified with the *Evil Yezer,* 244–5, 251–2, 268; harbours good intentions concerning Job, 268; cannot enter the Beth-Hammidrash, 274.
Scapegoat, the, the atoning power of, 301.
Scepticism, reason for, given by Moses Loeb, of Sasow, 111; due to the *Evil Yezer,* 251–2.
Scoffers, excluded from the Divine Presence, 232.
Scoffing, prevents repentance, 331.
Scriptures, the, the conception of the kingdom of God in, 65–6; included in the term *Torah,* 121–6; knowledge of, required of the Talmid Chacham, 122.
*See also* Law, the; Pentateuch, the; Prophets, the; Torah, the.
Secret sin. *See* Sin, secret.
Sectarianism, how dealt with in Rabbinic literature, 10 and n.; opposed by the Rabbis through Scriptural interpretations, 36–7.
*Seder Elijah,* the, term for sin in, 233.
Seducing, the function of the *Evil Yezer,* 248; others, prevents repentance, 329, 330, 333.
*See also* Tempting.
Self, love of, incompatible with love of God, 68.
Self-aggrandisement at the expense of others, prevents repentance, 330.
Separateness, and holiness, 205; Nachmanides on, 211–12.
*See* Holiness.
Separation between God and man, caused how, 232–3.
Seraphim the, surrounding God, 28, 32.
Serpent, the, identified with the *Evil Yezer,* 246, 262, 282.
Sexual immorality, denounced by the Rabbis, 205–6; due to the *Evil Yezer,* 246; affects the minority of men, 250.
*See also* Adultery.
Sexual intercourse, subject to restrictions, 211; tainted with sin, 253.
Shame, not to stand in the way of repentance, 324–5.

Shammai, not a miracle-worker, 7.
Shammai, the school of, on the creation of man, 8; on the atoning power of the burnt offering, 299.
*Shechinah*, epithet for God, 35.
Shechinah, the, as used by the Rabbis, 39; removed by idolatry, 223; removed by pride, 223; not respected by a violent man, 224; removed by adultery, 224–5; removed by murder, 226; removed by slander, 227; removed by the bad administration of justice, 229–30; removed by disrespect, 232; removed by sin in general, 232–3, 238; classes of persons excluded from, 232; revealed upon the removal of the *Evil Yezer*, 292.
Shedding of blood. *See* Bloodshed; Murder.
*Shema*, the, and the universal kingdom of God, 64; and the kingdom of God, 65, 66–7, 71; Israel's confession of faith, 119.
Shepherd, term for the relation between God and Israel, 46, 49.
*Shirah* (Song), the, and the kingdom of God, 85.
*Shofar*, the sound of the, an invitation to repentance, 342.
Simlai, Rabbi, on the *Mizwoth*, 138–40.
Simon, Rabbi, on Israel's connection with the kingdom of God, 98.
Simon ben Jochai, on the responsibility of God for the existence of the *Evil Yezer*, 281.
Simon the Just, on the *Evil Yezer*, 248–9.
Simon Kiara, on the *Mizwoth*, 141.
Simon ben Lakish, Rabbi, on the abode of God, 30–1; sums up the activity of the *Evil Yezer*, 244, 245.
Sin, treated by the Agadah, 3; the Rabbis on, 14; separates man from God, 33; has no effect upon the paternal relation between God and Israel, 54; angels incapable of, 81; disfigures man and the world, 83; counteracted by the *Zachuth* of the Fathers, 174; caused by the heart and the eyes, 208; defined by the Rabbis as rebellion, 219–22; causes the separation of man from God, 232–3, 241; various equivalents for, 233–5; a symptom of corruption, 235–6; described as folly, 236–7; has a blighting influence upon the world, 237–40; man persuaded to, by the *Evil Yezer*, 245, 260; death the consequence of, 245, 247; children immune from, 254; the agents of, 258; sways the soul, 260–1; relapsing into, 339–40.
See also *Evil Yezer*, the; Imputed sin; Sins; Sins, the cardinal, etc.
Sin, imputed. *See* Imputed sin.
Sin, secret, and the doctrine of imputed sin, 194; classified with blasphemy, 222.
Sin, unintentional, held in abhorrence like others, 240–1; a sign of carelessness, 240–1; Nachmanides on, 241; sin offering for, 296.
Sin offering, the, accompanied by repentance, 296.
Sins, the number of, not to stand in the way of repentance, 325; the character of, not to stand in the way of repentance, 325–6, 333–4; repentance for, inefficacious if repeated, 328–9, 330.
Sins, the cardinal, enumerated, 205–6; sins of rebellion, 222–32; have appurtenances, 223; exceeded by hatred, 227; called evil things, 232.

*See also* Adultery; Bloodshed; Idolatry.
Sins, the confession of. *See* Confession of sins, the.
*See also* *Evil Yezer*, the; Sin; Sins, the cardinal.
Sister, term for the relation between God and Israel, 47.
Skinning, forbidden on the Sabbath, 153.
Slander, a form of bloodshed, 227; called an evil thing, 232; a common sin, 250–1; habitual, prevents repentance, 330.
Slavery, describes the relation of Israel to God, in certain conditions, 55 and n.
Social misery, inconsistent with the kingdom of God, 110.
Sodom and the doctrine of *Zachuth*, 190; the people of, rebels, 219, 222; cause pain to God, 219–20; warned to repent, 315.
Solidarity, of Israel, and the doctrine of imputed sin, 191–5.
*See also* Community, the.
Solomon, throws off the yoke of God, 87; name given to the *Evil Yezer* by, 243.
Solomon, The Psalms of, not useful as a source of Rabbinic theology, 4–5.
Song of Songs, cited, in connection with the sweetness of the Law, 137; with the contamination of sin, 134.
Soul, the, the mystics on, 241; equivalent to the heart, 260–1.
*See also* Heart, the.
Sowing, forbidden on the Sabbath, 153.
Space of the world, epithet for God, 26, 34; does not imply remoteness, 34, 46.
Spinning, forbidden on the Sabbath, 153.
Spiritual, term not used in Rabbinic literature, 144.
Spite towards God, 220.
*Spoiler*, the, name for the *Evil Yezer*, 244.
Statutes, the, observance of, undermined by the *Evil Yezer*, 251.
Stay of the world, epithet for God, 26.
*Stone*, name for the *Evil Yezer*, 243; allegory on, 274.
*Strange God*, name for the *Evil Yezer*, 244.
Strength, epithet for God, 34.
"Stretching the hand into the root," blasphemy, 222.
"Strong hand," the, equivalent to the "right hand," 322.
Students, and the doctrine of imputed sin, 193.
*Stumbling-block*, name for the *Evil Yezer*, 243.
Suffering, treated by the Agadah, 3; inconsistent with the kingdom of God, 110–11; the punishment of the sinner, 293, 294, 304; an atonement, 304, 307–10; to be accepted submissively, 309–10.
Supreme, epithet for God, 21.
Suspicion of the upright, prevents repentance, 331.
*System der Altsynagogalen Palästinensischen Theologie*, by Weber, charges Jewish theology with excessive legalism, 23–4.

Taanith, Talmudic tractate, miracles reported in, 6.
Tabernacle, the laws about the, obsolete, 141.
Talmid Chacham, the, knowledge of the Scriptures required of, 122.
Talmud, the, as a theologic source, 5–6, 9–11; composite character of, 9–11; liturgical elements in, 11.
Talmud, the Babylonian, epithet for God in, 34.

Talmudical works, theologic sources, 3.
Tanna, the, of the School of Elijah, on Israel's election, 61–2.
Tannaitic times, origin of the liturgy in, 11.
Tanning, forbidden on the Sabbath, 153.
Targum, the, on the *Evil Yezer*, 243.
Targumim, the, epithets for God used in, 35; commentators on, not systematic theologians, 15–16.
*See also* Rabbis, the.
Tempting, the function of the *Evil Yezer*, 248.
*See also* Seducing.
Ten Penitential Days, a call to repentance, 342; ascetic practices connected with, 342.
Tetragrammaton, the, applied to the God of mercy, 36, 239; connected with the Scriptural description of the sacrifices, 45; ordered to be pronounced, to guard against heresies, 45; substituted for epithets for God, 46; a pre-mundane existence, 80.
Theocracy, a, the only form of government known to the Rabbis, 92, 93.
Theology, Rabbinic, sources of, 2–6, 9–11; not a formal system, 12–17; impulsive character of, 12–13; lacks logicality, 13–15, 30; difficulty of systematising, 16–17; Jewish attitude of author to, 17–18; attitude of author to, not apologetic, 18–20; exalted character of, 20; charged with having a transcendental God, 21–2, 23; not influenced by mystical and pantheistic notions of God's abode, 30.
*See also* Rabbis, the.
Theosophy, and the Torah, 135.
Thieves, partnership with, prevents repentance, 330.
Throne of glory, the, 28, 32.
Tochachoth, the, make the Book of Deuteronomy an *Imitatio Dei*, 119.
Torah, the, and the creation of the world, 81; and the kingdom of God, 91–2; makes Israel a nation, 105–6; forced denial of, absolves from obedience to Rome, 107; the term misunderstood, 116–17; not correctly rendered by Law, etc., 117; what it conveys to the Jew, 117, 125; *Mizwoth* complementary to, 117–18; often equivalent to Pentateuch, 118; Scriptural warrant for the superiority of, 118; the Prophets a commentary on, 119; dictated by the Holy Spirit, 120; legal part of, begins in Exodus, 120–1; not always confined to the Pentateuch, 121–6; name applied to the Prophets and Hagiographa, 125; extends beyond the Scriptures, 126; as a revelation and a promise, 127; identified with wisdom, 127–8, 129, 135; endowed with a mystical life; 129–30; wedded to Israel, 130; captured from heaven, 130; refused by the Gentiles, 131–2; intended for the Gentiles as well as Israel, 133; potentialities of, 134–5; the Rabbinical view of, 136–7; character of the laws in, 142; inclusiveness of, 142–4, 146; based on the execution of justice, 143; the *Kusari* on, 146; a source of joy to the Rabbis, 146–7; how considered by Israel, 148; joy an essential element in the understanding of, 148; material uses of, deprecated, 154, 159; disinterested performance of, 159–69; occupation with, a positive virtue, 167; love the motive for the performance of, 167–9; a

source of holiness, 168, 208; observance of, and libertinism, 211; correctives of, 212–16; a merciful interpretation of, recommended, 215–16; with holiness brings communion with God, 217; how regarded by the *Porek ol*, 220–1; denied by the usurer and the unmerciful, 231–2; defiled by immorality, 234; the study of, a weapon against the *Evil Yezer*, 273–5; how it operates, 275; grace needed for efficacy of, 278; on the punishment of sinners, 293; the atoning power of, 312; demands sacrifices rather than repentance, 323; and God's attribute of mercy, 323.

*See also* Joy of the Law; Law, the; Legalism; Leviticalism; *Mizwoth*, the; Pentateuch, the; Rabbis the; Revelation; Scriptures, the.

Torah, the, yoke of. *See* Kingdom of God, the.

Torath ha-Adam, the Torah in its universalistic aspect, 133.

Tosephta, the, on the commandment of forgetfulness, 149.

Tower, generation of the, rebels, 219; conceal the light of the first day, 237; warned to repent, 315.

Transcendentalism, charged against the God of Rabbinic theology, 21–2; disproved by the Prayer Book, 22–3, 29; disproved by the Rabbinic sources, 24–8, 29–30, 31, 33–4; a failing of proselytes, 25–6.

*See also under* God.

Treasure, term for the relation of Israel to God, 46.

Tribes, the, the *Zachuth* of, invoked by Moses, 172–3.

*Tumah*, term applied to the cardinal sins, 205, 206.

*See also* Adultery; Sins, the cardinal.

Ula bar Koseheb, and the law of saints, 216.

Unchaste thoughts, equivalent to adultery, 214.

Unchastity, included under adultery, 225.

*See also* Adultery; Sexual immorality.

*Uncircumcised*, name for the *Evil Yezer*, 243.

*Unclean*, name for the *Evil Yezer*, 243.

Uncovering of faces, the, and the *Porek ol*, 220–1.

Unintentional sin. *See* Sin, unintentional.

Uniqueness of Israel, 48.

Unity, the Song of, quoted, 27–8; 158–9.

Unity of God, the, emphasised, 43–4; declared by Israel, 48; things detrimental to the belief in, 68–9; and love of God, 75; to be realised in the Messianic time, 96.

Universal character of the kingdom of God, 93.

Universalism, repugnant to the Rabbis, without the Torah, 105–6.

Universalistic features of the Sinaitic revelation, 131–2, 133.

Usury, fulfilment of the commandment on, a condition of the Exodus, 230–1; a sin equal to murder, 231; a denial of the Law, 231–2.

Vanity, exposes one to the *Evil Yezer*, 248–9; the *Evil Yezer* chiefly representative of, 276.

Vile language, incompatible with holiness, 211–12.

Vine, the, a symbol for Israel, 175.

Vineyard, term for the relation of Israel to God, 49.

Watcher, term for the relation of God to Israel, 49.

**Wealth**, the, of God, 38; desire for, not counted among the great passions, 250; in the soul of man, 260; auxiliary to the *Evil Yezer*, 277.
Weaving, forbidden on the Sabbath, 153.
Weber, charges Jewish theology with excessive legalism, 23-4.
Wicked, the, forfeit the *Zachuth* of the Fathers, 179-80; how they differ from the righteous, 270-1; and the appearance of the *Evil Yezer*, 290; association with, prevents repentance, 330.
Widows, plundering, prevents repentance, 331.
Will of God, manifested in creation, 80.
Wine-drinking, restricted, 211.
Winnowing, forbidden on the Sabbath, 153.
Wisdom, the, of God, 38; Jesus, the son of Sirach, on, 70; the yoke of, a glory, 70; equivalent to the Torah, 127, 129, 135.
Wisdom (Hagiographa), on the punishment of sinners, 293.
Wisdom literature, the, and the Law, 116.
Wise, attribute applied to Israel by God, 47.
Women, looking at, prevents repentance, 330.
Word. *See* Memra.
Work, thirty-nine kinds of, forbidden on the Sabbath, 153.
Workmen, treatment of, urged by the Rabbis, 113-14.
Works, Rabbi Akiba on the justification by, 15-16; and the love of God, 75.
World, Lord of the, epithet for God, 21, 26.
World, the, relation of God to, 21-45; epithets describing God's relation to, 26-8; fate of, may depend on a single action, 189-90; chosen as his portion by Esau, 100; the seat of the kingdom of God, 104; purpose of the creation of, 80-1; plunged into chaos by sin, 83; is the kingdom of God, 89.
World, the future, chosen as his portion by Jacob, 100; persons destined for, 165-6; the *Evil Yezer* subdued in, 283; justice to prevail in, 307.
Worship, due to God alone, 44-5.
Writing, forbidden on the Sabbath, 153.

*Yezer*, the, equivalent to the *Evil Yezer*, 262.
*Yezer Hara*. See *Evil Yezer*, the.
Yoke of the kingdom of God, the. *See* Kingdom of God, the; Kingdom of God, the invisible; Kingdom of God, the visible; Kingdom of heaven, the.
Yoke of the Torah, the. *See* Kingdom of God, the.

*Zachuth*, acquired through the commandments, 164; place of the doctrine in Judaism, 170; etymology, etc., of the word, 170-1; divisions of the subject, 171-3; and individual righteousness, 176, 189-90.
See also *Zachuth*, the, of the Fathers, etc.
*Zachuth*, the, of a pious ancestry, 171, 175-7, 181-5; defined, 175-7; individual righteousness and, 176; extension of, 181-3; does not relieve the individual from responsibility, 183-5; in the liturgy, 184; and trust in God, 184-5.
*Zachuth*, the, of a pious contemporary, defined, 189-90; and Sodom and Gomorrah, 190.

*Zachuth*, the, of a pious posterity, 195, 196–7; limited, 197; and the dead, 198.
*See also* Children.

*Zachuth*, the, of Israel, and the kingdom of God, 98.

*Zachuth*, the, of the Fathers, in relation to the patriarchs, 171–5; called a rock, 173; historical events attributed to, 174–5; limited, 177–8; unlimited, 178–81.

*Zachuth*, the, of the Mothers, in relation to the wives of the three patriarchs, 172; invoked at public fasts, 172.

Zadok, Rabbi, prayer by, regarding the Sabbath, 153; on material uses of the Torah, 154, 159.

*Zebaoth*, God in war, 35.

Zechariah, the Book of, cited, in connection with God's relation to the Gentiles, 64.

Zephaniah, the Book of, cited, in connection with God's relation to the Gentiles, 64.

Zerachya ben Shealtiel, on the spiritualisation of the Scriptures, 103.

*Zohar*, the, on the *Evil Yezer*, 246.

# Contents

*List of figures and tables* *vii*
*Preface* *ix*
*List of abbreviations* *xi*

**Part 1: Sport media foundations** **1**

1 Sport and the media: a defining relationship 3

2 The evolution of the nexus: understanding the game 17

**Part 2: Sport media landscapes** **41**

3 The sport and media industries: meeting the global players 43

4 Broadcast rights and revenue: putting up big numbers 68

5 Sport media regulation: making the rules 98

**Part 3: Sport media professionals** **123**

6 Sport journalists: friend or foe? 125
*David Lowden*

7 Sport media relations practitioners: inside the team 145

**Part 4: Sport media strategies** **163**

8 Sport media planning and promotion: the foundations of coverage 165

9 Sport media communications: feeding the media 183

10 Sport media interactions: working with the media 201

11 Sport and social media: keeping up with the tweets, posts and links 218

12 Major sport event media management: controlling the chaos 244
*Chris Gottaas*

13 Managing crises, scandals and reputations: not all publicity is good 263

*References* *284*
*Index* *299*

# Figures and tables

## FIGURES


1.1 Sport typology 4
1.2 Elite and competitive sport levels 5
1.3 Media forms and types 6
1.4 Sport media nexus 7
1.5 Sport media nexus II 8
2.1 Local media to global media 26
3.1 Media industry organization 51
3.2 Media integration and cross promotion 52
4.1 Commercial dimensions of the sport media nexus 69
5.1 Joint selling 104
8.1 Media planning and strategy flow chart 169
11.1 The traditional access model in sport 221
11.2 The new access model in sport 221
13.1 Crisis management phases 270


## TABLES


3.1 World's largest media companies (2014) 45
3.2 FIFA membership by confederation, 1904–2013 54
3.3 Most valuable sport team brands (2014) 55
4.1 Olympic Games broadcast rights 84
4.2 Percentage contribution of US broadcast rights fees to the total broadcast rights fees for the Summer and Winter Olympic Games 85
4.3 Percentage contribution of broadcast rights fees to the total broadcast fees for the Summer and Winter Olympic Games 85
4.4 Television sport audiences in 2012 (United States) 87
4.5 2013 Deloitte Money League 94
8.1 Mock media list 172
8.2 Mock media grid 174
11.1 Draft social media plan for the South Bay Pirates, in the American national crocodile wrestling championships 233

12.1 IOC media accreditation categories 249
13.1 Sport organization crises and scandals 272

# Preface

We live in a world immersed in sport media, yet it has become so much part of our daily lives that it often goes unnoticed. Sport media has become an important part of the ways in which people and nations construct individual and collective identities, as well as understand their place in the world, yet it is often left unquestioned. This book was born out of a desire to write a text for students that provided a detailed examination of sport and the media, as well as provided them with the skills to engage in sport media management. It is hoped that through reading the book the world of sport media will not only be noticed, but understood, and that questions will not only be asked, but answered.

The book has primarily been written for first and second year university students studying sport management and sport studies courses. It is particularly suited to students studying sport management within business-focused courses, as well as students studying human movement or physical education courses who require a more detailed understanding of the skills required to manage the media in a variety of sport contexts. The book is divided into four parts. The first part sets the foundations, the second explores the contexts of the nexus, the third introduces students to sport media professionals and the fourth examines the skills of sport media management.

This second edition differs significantly from the first edition that was published in 2007, which is entirely appropriate given the rapid pace of change in the sport media industry. Like new mobile phones and computer operating systems, it seemed as if the first edition was obsolete as soon as it was printed, such have been the changes in the industry, particularly the development of social media. Thankfully, the instructors who have used the book over the years have managed to update material and make the core principles underpinning the book relevant to each new group of students. Hopefully this new edition will be useful and will not date as quickly, although notably absent from this edition is a chapter on sport media futures, because in part I think it would be foolhardy to predict what is likely to happen in the next decade if the changes in the last ten years are any indication. The first edition of this book was very much a solo effort, whereas this second edition has been a collaborative partnership, which has resulted in a better book. Anthony Kerr and Merryn Sherwood have been invaluable in writing new material and updating essential chapters from the first edition, while David Lowden and Chris Gottaas have contributed new chapters that have ensured the second edition is something that we can all be proud of. The second edition contains a new section on sport media professionals and new chapters on major event media management and social media management, which were missing from the first edition and are necessary for the contemporary sport media professional.

To assist students, teachers, instructors, tutors and lecturers, all chapters include a set of objectives, an overview of core principles and practices, a set of review questions or suggested exercises, two In Practice examples and a case study. The chapters in the sport media professionals section do not have In Practice examples or a case study, but instead have two interviews, each with respected professionals in their respective industries.

I would like to thank Simon Whitmore at Routledge for his friendship, care and support over the last few years, and for his support for the second edition of this book, as well as the sport management series more generally. My thanks go also to Will Bailey at Routledge, particularly for his patience, which was tested in 2014. I would also like to thank Professor Russell Hoye, for his friendship and for editing the world's best sport management textbook series. My thanks also go to Angela Osborne, whose tireless work ensured a much improved final product. Finally, all the co-authors and contributors would like to thank our respective partners and families, for providing us with support and understanding as we sought to bring the second edition of this book to fruition. We are indebted to you.

# Abbreviations

| | |
|---|---|
| AAP | Australian Associated Press |
| ABC | American Broadcasting Company |
| ABC | Australian Broadcasting Corporation |
| ACMA | Australian Communications and Media Authority |
| AFL | Australian Football League |
| AP | Associated Press |
| ARL | Australian Rugby League |
| ASADA | Australian Sports Anti-Doping Agency |
| ASP | Association of Surfing Professionals |
| ATP | Association of Tennis Professionals |
| BBC | British Broadcasting Corporation |
| BCS | Bowl Championship Series |
| BFL | Brazilian Football League |
| BSkyB | British Sky Broadcasting |
| BWWT | Big Wave World Tour |
| CADE | Brazilian Competition Agency |
| CBS | Columbia Broadcasting System |
| CCTV | China Central Television |
| CoSIDA | College Sports Information Directors Association |
| DFL | German Football League |
| EPL | English Premier League |
| EPO | erythropoietin |
| ESPN | Entertainment and Sports Programming Network |
| F1 | Formula 1 |
| FCC | Federal Communications Commission |
| FFA | Football Federation Australia |
| FIBA | Fédération Internationale de Basketball |
| FIFA | Fédération Internationale de Football Association |
| HD | high definition |
| HTML | HyperText Markup Language |
| IBC | International Broadcast Centre |
| ICC | International Cricket Council |
| IOC | International Olympic Committee |
| IPC | International Paralympic Committee |

| | |
|---|---|
| IPL | Indian Premier League |
| IPTV | Internet Protocol Television |
| IRB | International Rugby Union Board |
| ITU | International Triathlon Union |
| LOCOG | London Organising Committee for the Olympic Games |
| LPFP | Portuguese Football League |
| LPGA | Ladies Professional Golf Association |
| MEAA | Media Entertainment and Arts Alliance |
| MLB | Major League Baseball |
| MLS | Major League Soccer |
| MMA | mixed martial arts |
| MMC | main media centre |
| *MNF* | *Monday Night Football* |
| MUFC | Manchester United Football Club |
| NASCAR | National Association for Stock Car Auto Racing |
| NBA | National Basketball Association |
| NBC | National Broadcasting Company |
| NBL | National Basketball League |
| NCAA | National Collegiate Athletic Association |
| NESN | New England Sports Network |
| NFL | National Football League |
| NHL | National Hockey League |
| NMa | Netherlands Competition Authority |
| NOC | National Olympic Committee |
| NRL | National Rugby League |
| NSWRL | New South Wales Rugby League |
| NUJ | National Union of Journalists |
| PDF | portable document format |
| PGA | Professional Golfers' Association |
| QRL | Queensland Rugby League |
| SANZAR | South African, New Zealand and Australian rugby unions |
| SD | standard definition |
| SDE | Secretariat of Economic Law |
| SID | sports information director |
| SPJ | Society of Professional Journalists |
| UCI | International Cycling Union |
| UCL | UEFA Champions League |
| UEFA | Union of European Football Associations |
| UFC | Ultimate Fighting Championship |
| USADA | US Anti-Doping Agency |
| WADA | World Anti-Doping Agency |
| WCT | World Championship Tour |
| WRC | World Rally Championship |
| WTA | Women's Tennis Association |
| WWE | World Wrestling Entertainment |

PART 1

# Sport media foundations

CHAPTER 1

# Sport and the media

## A defining relationship

## OVERVIEW

This chapter provides an overview of the nexus between the sport and media industries and outlines why sport and the media is an important field of study. It also defines sport, the media and the sport media nexus. The study of sport and the media is placed within a management context in order to explain its relevance to students of sport management, as well as sport managers and administrators in professional settings. This chapter also discusses the core drivers and major features of the sport media nexus in order to contextualize the material in subsequent chapters. Finally, this chapter provides an outline of the structure of the book.

## LEARNING OUTCOMES

After completing this chapter the reader should be able to:

- identify the core features of the sport media nexus;
- explain the core features of the sport media nexus and what underpins the relationship between the sport and media industries;
- understand the environment in which sport media is produced and consumed; and
- identify and explain the impact of each core driver of the sport media nexus.

## DEFINING SPORT AND THE MEDIA

Prior to discussing the sport media nexus in detail, it is important to clarify what is meant by the terms sport and media. Although sport seems a superficially simple concept, it can be difficult for players, policy makers, managers, marketers and media alike to define. Depending on the context, sport might be interpreted in different ways, which will in turn influence whether and how it is mediated. Sport is best understood as having three core dimensions (Guttmann, 1978). First, it has a physical dimension. Second, it is competitive. Third and finally, it must be structured and rule bound. These dimensions might appear

self-evident, but are worth noting because mediated sport is almost exclusively highly structured, highly competitive and very physical. In fact, sports such as football that emphasize, if not exaggerate, sport's tripartite definition tend to dominate media coverage generally and television coverage in particular. On the other hand, sport that has low or non-existent levels of competition, structure and physicality are typically not attractive media products.

Figure 1.1 graphically represents a sport typology that illustrates different types of sport (Stewart *et al.*, 2004). Spontaneous sport includes 'pick-up' sport that occurs by chance, which is often formalized as recreational sport. Recreational sport also includes extreme sport activities, as well as informal exercise. Exercise sport typically occurs in formalized settings, such an aerobics class or a gym workout. These first three categories, represented at the bottom and sides of Figure 1.1 are minor components of the sport media nexus. By contrast, competitive sport, which includes competitions below the elite level, receives media coverage and uses it to increase participation and financial capacity. This category includes sport played by amateurs at the community level through to high level school and university (college) sport. The final category, elite sport, is a major player in the sport media nexus. It comprises professional and semi-professional competitions and major

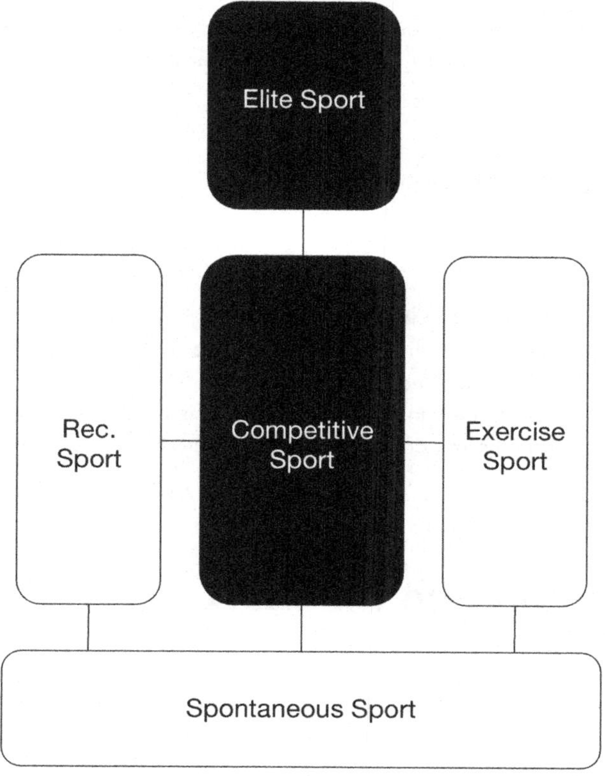


**FIGURE 1.1** Sport typology

Source: adapted from Stewart *et al.* (2004).

Global Events (Olympic Games, FIFA World Cup)

Global Circuits (Formula One, World Rally Championship, Tennis, Golf, Surfing)

Global Events (Asian Games, Commonwealth Games, World Championships, Euro Football)

Regional Leagues (European Champions League, Super 14 Rugby)

National Leagues (NFL, English Premier League, NBA, La Liga, J-League, Bundesliga)

Regional and State Leagues and Competitions

Local Community Sport – Clubs, Associations and Schools

**FIGURE 1.2** Elite and competitive sport levels

events, from state and national championships through to the Olympic Games and FIFA World Cup.

The final two categories of competitive and elite sport can be segmented further to demonstrate various tiers of activity, which are graphically represented in Figure 1.2. Figure 1.2 illustrates that competitive and elite sport cover the spectrum from local community level sport through to major global events. However, the diagram should not be interpreted as a hierarchical model of media interest or influence, as national leagues are often the most valuable sport media properties in the world.

Definitions of media are likely to make people think of vastly different and distinct occupations, people, organizations, texts and artefacts. The word media has come to mean a variety of things, in a similar fashion to sport, but in far greater complexity and breadth. According to Briggs and Burke (2005), ancient Greeks and Romans considered the study of oral and written communication important, as did scholars during the Middle Ages and the Renaissance. It was not until the 1920s, however, that people referred to the concept of 'the media'.

In contemporary usage the term media typically applies to two separate yet related elements. First, media refers to the means of mass communication, such as television, radio, newspapers or the internet. The various forms of communication and its types are

illustrated in Figure 1.3. Importantly, within one form, such as television, there are many different types, such as commercial, public, independent and community. Furthermore, these types also have various levels. For example, a commercial media organization might own national television networks through to local stations that service a city or town. Second, media refers to those people employed within an organization such as a television station or newspaper, such as journalists and editors.

It is important to note that these two definitions span a variety of meanings that are context specific. In reference to broadcasting regulation, the media might be interpreted as the entire industry, which in turn might be national or global. In a discussion focusing on mergers and acquisitions, media might refer to a transnational corporation such as the Walt Disney Company. If the issue relates to the sale of broadcast rights, media might refer to different forms such as pay television, free-to-air television or the internet. Referring to the way in which a telecast of a game uses metaphors of war, the media might refer to the commentators. Finally, if the issue relates to the reporting of a scandal or crisis, media might refer to the specific article or broadcast in which it was first announced.

Television (Commercial, Public, Independent, Community)

Newspapers (Commercial – Major Dailies, Tabloid, Local – Independent, Community)

Radio (Commercial, Public, Independent, Community)

Magazines (Commercial – General, Sport, Lifestyle, etc.)

Film (Major and Minor Studios, Independent)

Music (Major and Minor Studios, Independent)

Internet (Commercial, Non-Profit, Public, Personal)

Social Media (Commercial, Non-Profit, Public, Personal)

**FIGURE 1.3** Media forms and types

## THE NEXUS

The word nexus has its etymological roots in Latin and is a derivation of the word *nectere*, which means to bind. In essence a nexus is a connection, bond or tie between two or more things. The use of the word nexus in the subtitle of this book is deliberate. It is meant to signal that sport and the media are not two separate industries that have been juxtaposed coincidently. Rather, their evolution, particularly throughout the twentieth century, has resulted in them being inextricably bound together. Furthermore, the word nexus can refer to the core or centre. In this respect the use of the word nexus is meant to illustrate that the relationship between sport and the media is at the core of contemporary sport. Whether in reference to the way in which children are socialized through sport, the power of player associations and unions, or the use of talent identification programmes to foster elite development, the relationship between sport and the media is likely to reside at the very centre of the issue or problem. Thus, the sport media nexus refers to the relationship between sport and the media industry generally, the relationship between sport and specific media institutions such as television, the relationship between sport and media employees such as journalists and finally, the ways in which sport is presented in specific media texts, such as a radio broadcast or newspaper article.

Figure 1.4 represents the sport media nexus in its most basic form. In this diagram the sport and media industries are represented as two equal partners and the nexus is the point at which they intersect. Although simple, Figure 1.4 also illustrates that not all of sport is part of the nexus. Rather, a proportion of sport is mediated. Similarly, not all media is sport related. However, this diagram does not represent the reality of much elite, professional and competitive sport, nor does it represent the importance of the media in daily sport consumption. In this respect the nexus is more accurately represented in Figure 1.5. Elite and professional sport is enveloped by the media. In this case sport might

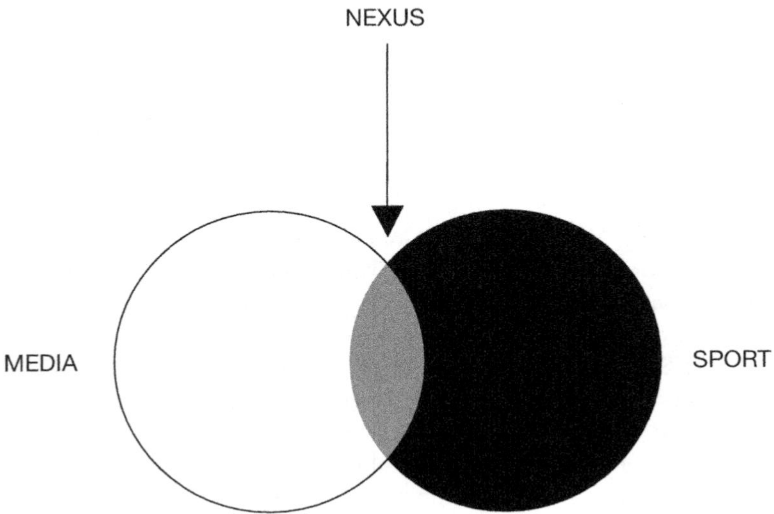


**FIGURE 1.4** Sport media nexus

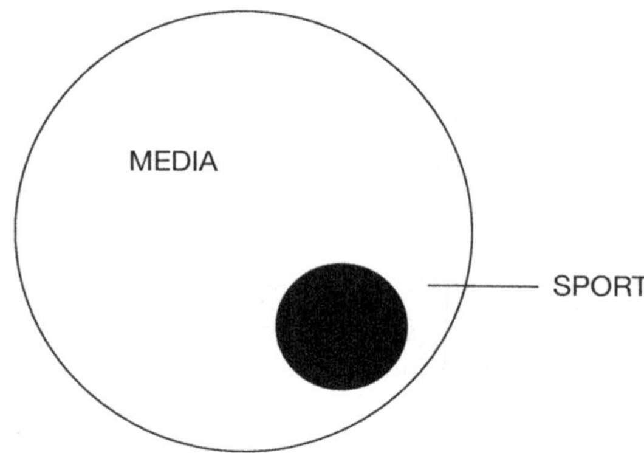


**FIGURE 1.5** Sport media nexus II

accurately be described as media sport because without the nexus or bond between the two the product would not exist. Consumers of sport must necessarily consume a mediated product. As the sport media nexus develops, the amount of sport consumed by the media increases (the circles in Figure 1.4 move closer together), as does the commercial importance of sport to the media (the black circle in Figure 1.5 grows larger).

## SPORT MEDIA SATURATION

Every four years the world stops to watch football teams compete for a trophy called the World Cup. The final of the 2010 tournament in South Africa between Spain and the Netherlands was watched by 909 million people, while the number of viewers who watched a minimum of 20 consecutive minutes during the tournament was 2.2 billion throughout 214 nations, equivalent to nearly a third of the world's population. The world also tunes in on a four year cycle to watch athletes strive to go higher, faster and stronger at the Summer and Winter Olympic Games; approximately 2.7 billion people watched at least 15 consecutive minutes of the London 2012 Olympic Games, while a total of 27.9 billion hours of London 2012 coverage was consumed by viewers worldwide. These mega-events compete for the attention of media consumers with year-long sport circuits, such as Formula One Racing, the Professional Golfers' Association (PGA) European Tour and the Women's Tennis Association (WTA) Tour. These events and circuits, in turn, compete with national sport competitions that take place over the course of a season, with games played between one and four times per week. In the United States the nation stops every year for the Super Bowl, the championship game of the National Football League, when families and friends gather around television sets for what equates to a secular holiday. In 2013 the television audience was large enough for the television broadcaster to command US$4 million for each 30 second block of advertising time. It is clear from the examples above that there are large numbers of people watching sport on television, that there is a significant amount of sport broadcast on television and that televised sport is a primary vehicle for advertising. However, it is not only the major sport events and

leagues that are broadcast by television, and television is not the only media form that is saturated by sport. In fact, from even a cursory examination of the media available in a single city or nation, it is readily apparent that sport has a significant presence across all media forms. Moreover, the media coverage of sport saturates daily life (Rowe, 1999), a phenomenon clearly illustrated by the way in which News Corporation sees itself in the following annual report excerpt.

> Virtually every minute of the day, in every time zone on the planet, people are watching, reading and interacting with our products. We're reaching people from the moment they wake up until they fall asleep. We give them their morning weather and traffic reports through our television outlets around the world. We enlighten and entertain them with such newspapers as *The New York Post* and *The Times* as they have breakfast, or take the train to work. We update their stock prices and give them the world's biggest news stories every day through such news channels as FOX or Sky News. When they shop for groceries after work, they use our SmartSource coupons to cut their family's food bill. And when they get home in the evening, we're there to entertain them with compelling first-run entertainment on FOX or the day's biggest game on our broadcast, satellite and cable networks. Or the best movies from Twentieth Century Fox Film if they want to see a first run movie. Before going to bed, we give them the latest news, and then they can crawl into bed with one of our best-selling novels from HarperCollins.
>
> (News Corporation, 1999; cited in Law *et al.*, 2002)

The relationship between sport and the media has become the defining commercial and cultural connection for both industries at the beginning of the twenty-first century. The media has transformed sport from an amateur pursuit into a hyper-commercialized industry, while sport has delivered massive audiences and advertising revenues to the media. The coverage of sport on television in particular has created a product to be consumed by audiences, sold by clubs and leagues, bought and sold by media organizations and manipulated by advertisers.

Throughout the latter half of the twentieth century and into the twenty-first, the relationship between the media and sport industries intensified, to the point that they have become so entwined it is difficult to determine where one ends and the other begins. In an attempt to identify this process, as well as inform public and academic discourse, authors have combined the words sport and media in a variety of permutations. The common theme has been the creation of a new word or phrase that is representative of the nexus between these two commercial industries. In the 1980s and 1990s the sports/media complex and the media/sport production complex were both used to frame academic analyses of sport and the media (Jhally, 1984, 1989; Maguire, 1993, 1999). At the end of the twentieth century an edited collection was published with the title *MediaSport* (Wenner, 1998). Whether the words are juxtaposed, jammed together to create a new word, or separated by 'and the', it is clear that there is an imperative to characterize the process by which 'sports, and the discourses that surround them' became, as Boyd (1997: ix) suggested, 'one of the master narratives of twentieth-century culture'.

The importance of this master narrative has been enhanced by the growing globalization of media corporations and the use of sport to consolidate established markets and

exploit new ones, as well as the ways in which mediated sport is used to construct individual and collective identities. The extent to which this master narrative has become an assumed part of global, cultural, commercial and personal discourses is illustrated by Rowe's (1999: 8) assertion that 'a trained capacity to decode sports texts and to detect the forms of ideological deployment of sport in the media is, irrespective of cultural taste, a crucial skill', and 'an important aspect of a fully realized cultural citizenship'. In other words, the mediation of sport has become so pervasive that in order to live within the cultural and social world you must necessarily be able to understand the sport media nexus.

## SPORT MEDIA TEXTS

At the end of the twentieth century Real (1998: 15) noted that ignoring sport media in contemporary society 'would be like ignoring the role of the church in the Middle Ages or ignoring the role of Art in the Renaissance'. In other words, sport media is an omnipresent feature of contemporary societies and without the ability to analyse sport media we cannot hope to understand the societies in which we live. Real also argued that the saturation of media sport makes it difficult to analyse. Thus, the paradox is that understanding sport media is crucial to an understanding of broader society, but its place in society makes it almost impossible to do so. Because we are bombarded with images and sounds from sporting events and contests of the past, present and future, we are in a difficult, if not impossible place from which to establish a reference point. Often, and this is particularly true for people engaged in the study of sport or who are employed within the sport industry, people grow up immersed in sport and have been inculcated into sport's particular and peculiar rituals and routines from an early age, by family, friends and peers. For many, sport and sport media have become important vehicles for creating and understanding a series of individual and collective identities. These identities make it difficult to analyse sport media, but all the more important to develop the skills to understand sport media texts.

A sport media text is not just the written or printed word, although a text can be a book, such as the one you are currently reading. Rather, a text is anything in audio or visual form that presents or represents sport to an audience. Thus, a sport media text could be a billboard on a freeway advertising a particular brand of deodorant used by a well-known athlete, a live radio broadcast of a rugby union game, a pop song performed by the wife of a footballer or a tweet from a coach of a rival team. In each of these examples the audio or visual text can be understood differently by different people. The interpretive possibilities of sporting texts are infinite because they refer to a wide variety of people and events, were constructed by journalists, editors, producers, commentators and photographers with particular personal and professional agendas, and are able to be examined in a variety of contexts by readers, viewers, listeners and users who have unique ways of reading the text.

As a result of these different contexts in which sport media texts are created and experienced, the way in which sport texts are understood can vary markedly. For example, one person driving their car past the advertising billboard may subconsciously believe their performance in a social basketball game later that evening will be improved because their

choice of deodorant is that of the well-known athlete, while another may experience self-loathing because they discover they use the same brand as an athlete from a team they hate.

In developing an understanding of the ways in which the media represent sport, it is important to note that texts 'foster specific ways of seeing the world, hinder other ways, and even structure ways of relating to the text itself' (Dahlgren, 1992: 13). In other words sport media texts can influence the way in which people understand the world around them. For example, an emphasis on male sport within media coverage may encourage young men and women to see the world as a place where men are rewarded for being active and women are passive. Sport media texts might also prevent people from interpreting or understanding the world in particular ways. For example, an emphasis on nationalism and patriotism may encourage division and combativeness, which prevents or limits a view of the world as one without borders. Finally, the ways in which a text is constructed may influence the way it is interpreted. For example, a newspaper article might consist of a story, a headline, a photograph and a caption. The boldness of the headline and the angle of the photograph might arouse anxiety in the reader, which will affect any reading of the story.

In daily life we use sport media texts to make sense of sport, the world and our place in it. These texts are not neutral and objective. Rather, they are infused with political, cultural, commercial and social ideologies. These ideologies influence our readings of the texts consciously and subconsciously. In order to understand how we make sense of sport, the world and our place in it, it is essential to develop the ability to decode or deconstruct sport media texts, which is facilitated by a deep understanding of the sport media nexus.

## MANAGING THE NEXUS

Over the course of the twentieth century, sport was transformed from a typically ad hoc unregulated amateur activity to one driven by professional standards and accountability at all levels. This transformation has resulted in the proliferation of and demand for sport management training in related areas such as human resource management, financial management, event management and organizational behaviour. The broad transformation from amateur to professional and the need for professional sport management, particularly at the elite or major league level, is directly related to the extent and breadth of the sport media nexus. Whereas sport organizations were once guarded and cautious about the role of the media and the impact that broadcasting might have on live attendance, they are now engaged in a media partnership that delivers a majority of revenue through broadcast rights and associated sponsorships. The corollary of the importance and significance of the nexus is that it requires management. This notion is compounded by the competitiveness of the media industry generally and the sport media industry more specifically. An examination of a major daily newspaper will reveal that national, state and local governments, entertainers from television, film and music, business corporations, tourism destinations, not to mention sport stars, teams and leagues are some of the people and institutions vying for media coverage. Media space, despite the proliferation of types and forms, is limited. As such it is a valuable commodity because it can generate awareness and revenue, as well as confer status, prestige and credibility.

Without athletes sport cannot exist. Hence, player management has expanded exponentially in professional and elite sport since the 1960s in particular. Player welfare programmes have been developed, as have talent identification schemes, elite pathways, player associations and unions. In other words, the importance of players and athletes to the sport enterprise has been matched by administrative and management systems designed to protect and enhance sport as a product. It is too much to say that without the media sport cannot exist. In this respect those who play the game are more important than those who watch or report on it. However, it is clear that professional sport in particular would cease to exist in its current form without the media. Thus, like the development of player management, the management of the media also requires systems and strategies to ensure the success of sport organizations.

Sport teams are not only competing against other teams for coverage, but against other sports, against other leisure options and against a myriad of other newsworthy events and announcements. This competitive environment cannot be left to chance, whereby a sport team or league conducts its business in the hope that it will receive media coverage. Rather, like other aspects of the sport business, where individuals, teams and leagues seek to obtain a competitive advantage, media coverage is enhanced by effective planning and management.

The media coverage that a sport receives is directly proportional to the amount of revenue that individuals and organizations are able to generate from its broadcast or reporting. A large organization, such as the National Football League in the United States is able to generate massive revenues through broadcast rights fees because of the audiences it is able to deliver to media organizations. It is also able to generate revenue through commercial sponsorship, which is proportional to the amount of media coverage. Throughout the last quarter of the twentieth century and the early part of the twenty-first professional sport in particular has become dependent on the media. It is clear that in order to be successful in the competitive arena of professional sport, a team, league or event must not only have official media partners, but also be able to attract general media coverage that illustrates a broad interest or awareness among the population. In order to remain successful, teams, leagues and events must manage their ongoing relationship with the media, while teams, leagues and events that are not as successful as they would like to be must develop systems and apply strategies to either begin the relationship or enhance it. This book is designed to provide prospective and practising sport managers with the knowledge and skills to engage in effective sport media management and successfully navigate the sport media nexus.

## WHAT IS DRIVING THE SPORT MEDIA NEXUS?

The relationship between sport and the media is defined by change. Neither sport nor the media are static industries and their relationship has enhanced both the rate of change and the fluidity of each at the beginning of the twenty-first century. The following discussion identifies a series of drivers that influence sport, the media and the relationship between the two: technology; commercialization; convergence; and globalization. These drivers provide the context for much that follows in subsequent chapters.

## Technology

Technological change has been a key driver in the relationships between the media and all aspects of society, not to mention the nexus between sport and the media. In simple terms, the transition from newspapers to radio, to television, to the internet and now to a multitude of social media platforms and social networks, illustrates a rapid development in communication technology. In turn this development has had an impact on access for consumers, as well as power and influence for owners and operators.

As a result of technological change, in a relatively short period of human history, a transformation has occurred. People who were previously limited to information that related to their local surrounds now have access to information on a global scale. The currency of this information was previously bound or constrained by the lack of technological development. Whereas information might have taken days or weeks to reach its audience, through advances in mobile technology in particular, this information is now effectively immediate. In addition, changes in technology have meant that people can now be both consumers and producers of sport media content, often simultaneously. These developments within the context of the evolution of the sport media nexus will be addressed in more detail in the following chapter.

## Commercialization

The relationship between sport and the media is not predicated on benevolence or generosity. The media does not report on sport as a function of public service, nor does sport provide the media with access merely to increase public awareness. Rather, the sport media nexus is driven by commercial forces.

Since the late 1960s sport has become a commercial vehicle for media organizations, sponsors and advertisers. As a result, professional sports in particular have become increasingly wealthy, as well as dominant. Professional athletes and teams are often referred to as products, properties, commodities or businesses. Professional football teams in Europe such as Manchester United in England, Real Madrid in Spain and AC Milan in Italy are estimated to have annual revenues of between US$300 million and US$600 million. By any measure these are significant businesses. Importantly, their wealth has been driven by the media. Where their revenue was once derived primarily from match or gate receipts, they are now dependent on broadcast rights or commercial sponsorship that is directly proportional to the amount of media coverage they generate. Professional sport is now a commodity that can be bought and sold by the media, as well as a vehicle through which other businesses can promote and sell their products.

## Convergence

Convergence remains a buzzword in media studies and to a lesser extent within sport media studies (Turner and Cunningham, 2002). Convergence refers to a multitude of drivers in the sport media landscape.

First, convergence refers to technological change, whereby the means of delivery are becoming integrated. For example, where a household might previously have had an antenna to receive a television signal, a telephone to place and receive calls and a radio to

receive transmissions, these might now be available through a single cable that also delivers pay television and internet access.

Second, convergence refers to the phenomenon of increasing cross media ownership. For example, a newspaper or television station might previously have been owned independently of any other media interests. In the late nineteenth and early twentieth century it was usual for a newspaper to be a family business. At the start of the twenty-first century this is the exception rather than the norm. It is now far more likely that a single media organization will have commercial interests in television, print media, film and internet. In short, this means that media organizations are able to promote a single product, such as a sport team or league, across multiple media forms for commercial advantage.

Third, convergence refers to the increasing national and global domination of large media organizations, otherwise known as media conglomerates or transnational media corporations. The rise of media organizations such as News Corporation or the Walt Disney Company has resulted in an increasing lack of diversity. Rather than a variety of small media organizations, the global media landscape is dominated by massive media organizations that continue to acquire smaller organizations, increasing both their reach and economies of scale. Furthermore, it is increasingly likely that these conglomerates will have mutual commercial interests, which further increases the industry's complexity and lack of diversity.

Fourth and finally, convergence refers to the ownership of content and the means of distribution. For example, in the United States of America, many sport teams are owned by media organizations. In these cases the commercial interests of previously independent entities have converged.

## Globalization

It could be argued that globalization is the most important driver of the sport media nexus; however, it is more useful to view technological change, commercialization and convergence as drivers that have all led to the increasing globalization of media and sport media. Without advances in technology and increases in access to information, globalization would not have occurred to the extent that it has. The commercial imperative behind the sport media relationship has driven sport and media organizations to find and then reach new markets, often on the other side of the world, while the rise of media conglomerates has facilitated, not hindered, globalization. It should be noted that there are other important factors that have had an impact on globalization, such as economic trade, labour migration and the ease of international travel. However, the media remains the most important driver of globalization in the world today. The media is both an essential feature of daily life and the most tangible indicator of globalization.

At one level globalization has driven and accelerated changes in the relationship between sport and the media, while at another level sport and its media partners have played an important role in the globalizing process. Sports such as cricket and rugby union created World Cups to determine a world champion in the sport every four years, despite the fact that only a handful of nations are proficient at an international level. World championships such as these are the direct result of the global appeal of sport, as well as the increasing amounts of revenue available to sports through broadcast rights agreements.

On the other hand, sport has been used as a conduit of globalization. The popularity and appeal of the FIFA World Cup and the Olympic Games are examples of the impact of sport and sport media in the globalizing process.

## THE STRUCTURE OF THE BOOK

This book is divided into four parts. Part 1, 'Sport media foundations', of which the current chapter forms the first half, consists of two chapters that are designed to introduce the reader to the concepts that underpin the sport media nexus and examine its evolution. The premise of the book's second chapter is that an understanding of the history and development of the sport media nexus is essential to participating in the contemporary sport media management landscape. In other words, without a clear sense of the ways in which the relationship between sport and the media evolved, it is difficult to understand its current status and contexts.

Part 2, 'Sport media landscapes', is a detailed examination of the sport media nexus. The chapters in this section are intended to provide a comprehensive examination of the way in which the sport and media industries interact. More specifically, the chapters provide: an overview of the sport and media industries; an examination of the way in which broadcast rights are bought and sold and how sport and media organizations leverage sponsorship and advertising revenue from the media coverage of sport; and an analysis of sport media regulation and government intervention in both industries.

Part 3, 'Sport media professionals', contains two chapters. The first chapter examines sport journalists, while the second chapter examines the sport media practitioners employed with sport organizations. In essence, this section of the book presents two perspectives of the sport media nexus, one from the media and one from sport, two sides of the same coin. This section is designed to develop an understanding of the working conditions and pressures on both sets of sport media professionals.

Part 4, 'Sport media strategies', is a detailed examination of the key strategies used to manage media communications and interactions within the sporting context. The chapters in this section are not designed for those people who produce media, as there are numerous textbooks that examine the role, functions and skills of journalists, editors and associated media professionals. Rather, the chapters in this section are designed to develop the knowledge and skills of those people who will be engaged in managing the media, communication and public relations activities of sport organizations, which include clubs, leagues, associations and event organizers. The sport media strategies section contains six chapters that examine specific components of sport media management. First, the process by which sport media managers plan for media coverage and what strategies they use to promote their organization. Second, media communications such as media releases, fact sheets and media guides. Third, media interactions such as media conferences and interviews. Fourth, the management of social media platforms and networks. Fifth, the management of media at major events. Sixth and finally, managing crises and scandals to ensure the reputation of the organization is maintained. Upon completing this section of the book the reader should be able to apply skills, strategies and techniques to the planning, acquisition and management of media coverage within a variety of sport organizations.

## SUMMARY

This chapter has introduced the concepts of sport and the media, as well as the nexus between them. Importantly, it has highlighted that we live in a world that is saturated by sport media, the result of a defining cultural and commercial relationship between these two massive industries. The extent of these commercial and cultural connections is such that the sport media nexus demands management, a theme that will be reinforced throughout the following chapters. The chapter also contained discussion of a series of key sport media drivers – technological change, commercialism, convergence and globalization – each of these drivers or contexts informs both the evolution of the sport media nexus, as well as its continued development. Finally, the chapter concluded with an outline of the structure of the book and the chapters that follow. Review questions and exercises are listed below to assist with confirming your knowledge of the core concepts and principles introduced in this chapter.

## REVIEW QUESTIONS AND EXERCISES

1. What are the key features of sport?
2. Should card games and similar activities be considered sport, and does media coverage of the World Poker Tour indicate that only two of the three sport dimensions are required for media coverage?
3. What is media?
4. List the media that you interact with on a daily basis. To what extent is your day saturated by media in general and sport media more specifically?
5. What sustains the sport media nexus?
6. Why does the sport media nexus require management?
7. What is the most important driver of the sport media nexus? Why?
8. Compare a major daily newspaper from today with one from the 1950s. Is the sport being reported local, global or international? Are there any differences?
9. Identify the most popular newspapers, television stations and magazines where you live and find out who owns them. Is there any convergence?
10. Choose a professional sport or league and find out what percentage of the revenue is directly or indirectly related to media coverage.

CHAPTER 2

# The evolution of the nexus

## Understanding the game

### OVERVIEW

This chapter examines the evolution of the sport media nexus, including developments in newspaper, radio, television and the internet. In particular, it explores the way in which each industry uses the other as a commercial stimulus, particularly in the United States and Great Britain. This chapter provides an historical perspective on the sport media nexus in order that contemporary practices and relationships are able to be contextualized and understood more completely.

### LEARNING OUTCOMES

After completing this chapter, the reader should be able to:

- explain how the sport media nexus has evolved over time;
- describe the ways in which each of the key media forms influenced the development of sport and used sport to drive its popularity;
- generalize about the types of sport coverage provided by each media form throughout the history of the sport media nexus; and
- contextualize the contemporary sport media nexus by referring to its evolution and history.

### INTRODUCTION

As the previous chapter illustrated, the contemporary world we inhabit is saturated with media sport, in which both commercial industries, media and sport, engage in a symbiotic relationship of mutual benefit. McChesney (1989) suggested that this concept of symbiosis is not only a way of interpreting the present, but is also an ideal lens through which we might view the history of the relationship between sport and the media. Writing about the sport media nexus in the United States, McChesney (1989: 49) argued that 'virtually every

surge in the popularity of sport has been accompanied by a dramatic increase in the coverage provided to sport by the media'. Furthermore, he also argued that this symbiotic relationship has not developed by chance, but rather is determined by the way both institutions have operated as commercial entities (McChesney, 1989). In other words, the history of the sport media nexus is characterized by organizations driven together in search of greater profits, audiences and resources.

The impact of sport news on the popularity and profitability of media outlets has only been equalled by the transformation that sport has undergone, as a result of its interplay with the media. If it was possible in the 1890s to conceive of an image of sport without reference to the media, by the 1990s the task was impossible. Now 'one is literally unthinkable without the other' (Rowe, 1999: 13). Sport and the media have been fused together at a number of levels. On the one hand, the media's involvement in sport has created the context for sport's increased commercialization and globalization and, on the other, it has supplied a multitude of formats with which to mediate the game and its immediate aftermath. The media has also been an instrument to foster and promote phatic discourse, or 'sports chatter' (Eco, 1986). It is clear that an understanding of the evolution of the complex relationship between sport and the media is an essential component of any analysis of sport media's contemporary structure and practices.

## THE BEGINNING

The dominance of television in the media coverage of sport often leads to the false conclusion that the sport media relationship began in the middle of the twentieth century with the advent of television. In fact, the sport media nexus has a much longer and more complex history. It began at the end of the eighteenth century with the establishment of a sporting magazine industry in Great Britain and the United States (Boyle and Haynes, 2000; McChesney, 1989), which developed throughout the nineteenth century. The commercial opportunities of gambling in particular influenced the development of these magazines, which generally focused on sports such as horse racing and boxing and the publication of results. The way in which sports were covered in high circulation magazines often had a significant bearing on their popularity. For example, in the United States William Porter attempted to popularize the game of cricket in the 1840s in his *Spirit of the Times* periodical, which had a circulation of 100,000, but by the 1850s he had turned his attention to baseball. The *New York Clipper*, a new sporting weekly in the 1850s, soon took over from the *Times* in popularizing the sport of baseball, and employed a full-time sportswriter (McChesney, 1989). While baseball became America's national pastime, the sport of cricket remains almost non-existent in that country. In Great Britain, the sporting press began to contribute to the widespread dissemination and organization of sport from the 1820s and 1830s (Harvey, 2004). Beginning in 1824, *Bell's Weekly Messenger* employed expert writers for specific sports and provided extensive and detailed coverage of boxing. The sporting press during the middle of the eighteenth century in Great Britain and the United States were important in creating an audience for sport, propelling it toward a commercial outlook and operation.

Throughout the 1830s and 1840s the newspaper industry generated its income through the combination of advertising space sales and circulation. This commercial emphasis laid

the foundation for the exploitation of sport as a form of entertainment that could generate both sales and advertising revenue. Sport was covered by newspapers throughout the middle of the nineteenth century; Boyle and Haynes (2000) have noted that the establishment of regular fixtures and seasonal events greatly contributed to the steady flow of news for the sporting press.

In 1883 Joseph Pulitzer purchased the *New York World*, an American metropolitan daily newspaper with a circulation of approximately 15,000, and immediately set about creating a product that we now recognize as the modern mass-circulation newspaper. He lowered the paper's price, changed the layout and look to focus on more visual elements, developed editorial and news gathering functions, took a sensationalist approach to news, and sold advertising space on the basis of circulation. Pulitzer was also the first to use headlines in a concerted effort to capture the attention and stimulate the curiosity of audiences. By 1892 the *New York World* had increased its circulation to two million readers and it was clear that Pulitzer had set a new standard for the newspaper business (Schudson, 1978; Hughes, 1981).

The *New York World*, according to Oriard (1993), was also a pioneer in sports coverage throughout the 1880s and early 1890s. One of Pulitzer's first initiatives as publisher was to establish a sports department with its own sporting editor. The subsequent increase in the amount of space devoted to sport was a significant factor in the increased circulation of the *New York World*. By the end of the nineteenth century, most newspapers had their own sport editor and, in 1895, Pulitzer's competitor, William Randolph Hearst, introduced the first sport section in the *New York Journal* (McChesney, 1989). The period spanning the late nineteenth century and early twentieth century was a boom time for the print media coverage of sport across the world; in many instances this coverage helped to popularize and nationalize a variety of sports. Only 12 journalists covered the first modern Olympiad in Athens in 1896, however, by the 1920s dedicated sport sections were features of most major daily newspapers in the United States.

The sport media nexus throughout the print media era was characterized by localized coverage and a slow growth in sport's popularity. Newspaper reporting of sport typically took the form of a colourful, exciting, factual description of the event. Newspapers and magazines used sport to increase sales and advertising revenue, while sport used the media to increase attendances and subsequent revenue. During the print media era, both sport and the media enjoyed a relationship of mutual benefit through which they were able to increase their audiences. They did this through associating their respective 'products', rather than engaging in an overtly commercial relationship.

## RADIO WAVES

In 1893, Hungarian inventors, Theodore Puskas and Nikola Tesla, offered subscribers in Budapest what has been described as the world's first broadcasting system, a Telefon Hirmondo service (Briggs and Burke, 2005). The service, which had over 5,000 subscribers by the end of the century, offered a daily schedule that included sport news. In 1897, Italian Guglielmo Marconi established the Wireless Telegraph and Signal Company, but it was not until the 1920s that radio was introduced and became established globally. From the start the symbiotic relationship between sport and media was

evident, as sporting events on radio were popular in most countries (Briggs and Burke, 2005) and sport was used to popularize the new medium. Unlike daily and weekly newspaper reporting, however, early radio coverage of sport was limited to events, such as the baseball World Series in the USA.

In Great Britain, the British Broadcasting Corporation (BBC) developed the scope of sport broadcasting on radio throughout the 1920s, 1930s and 1940s. By 1930, broadcasts of cricket test matches, Wimbledon, the Football Association Cup Final, the Grand National and the Derby (both horse-racing events) were annual broadcast events, with trained commentators and established commentary conventions (Whannel, 1992). These events were nationally significant and radio helped to increase their popularity and appeal (Boyle and Haynes, 2000). In 1934, the Australian Broadcasting Corporation's (ABC) coverage of the cricket series between England and Australia, the Ashes, coincided with large increases in the sale of radio sets, and marked a break from routine programming. In the same year, the Ford Motor Company paid US$100,000 to sponsor the World Series on the National Broadcasting Company (NBC) and Columbia Broadcasting System (CBS) in the United States, illustrating the popularity of radio sport programming and the increasing connection between sport, money and the media (McChesney, 1989). In 1948, the BBC introduced the *Sports Report*, which attracted more than 12 million listeners and included reports from towns throughout Great Britain and, in some cases, from other countries (Boyle and Haynes, 2000).

The development of new technologies had an impact on the existing formats for sport reporting. The immediacy of radio and its capacity to broadcast to large audiences were a challenge to newspapers, if not a threat to their livelihood. Newspapers relied on being able to provide accounts of games and matches and, in the late nineteenth and early twentieth centuries, newspaper reporting of sport was extremely colourful and detailed. Newspaper reporting was seen as the next best thing to attending the event, but radio brought sport consumers a step closer to the action, in the same way that television would bring them even closer in the 1950s and 1960s. The introduction of radio and then television meant that newspaper reporting changed from typically factual reporting to include a greater emphasis on opinion and analysis. Similarly, the introduction and then development of television presented a challenge to radio, although in many cases the companies and corporations involved in broadcasting radio became major players in television.

Radio altered the sport media nexus by regionalizing and, in some cases, nationalizing the audience for sport. Where newspapers were limited to previewing and reviewing games and matches, radio created immediacy through live coverage. Radio allowed geographically distant audiences to consume sport at the same time as those in the stadium. The notion of a simultaneous audience was enhanced by the broadcast of events that were of national importance. For example, a complex short wave system saw 40 countries receive radio broadcasts of the Berlin 1936 Olympic Games while Australian listeners were able to tune into the BBC for commentary each night (McCoy, 1997). Both radio and sport enjoyed an association that provided increased audiences and financial returns; however, like the era dominated by print media, the relationship was one of mutual benefit rather than primarily commercial outcomes.

## SMALL SCREEN, BIG IMPACT

According to Whannel (1992), television came second to radio as the popular broadcast medium throughout the 1930s and 1940s in Great Britain, although broadcasts of events such as the London 1948 Olympic Games provided publicity and stimulated ticket sales. The 1940 and 1944 Games were cancelled as a result of the Second World War but television coverage of the London 1948 Olympic Games was available in both the United States and Great Britain. Although the audience was small, the London 1948 Olympic Games – the world's first large-scale multi-sport outside broadcast – helped to popularize the new medium and kick-start *BBC Sport*, a landmark programme.

It was not until the 1950s that television started to become the most popular broadcast medium. In 1950, only 9 per cent of American homes and approximately 5 per cent of British homes contained television sets, yet by 1965 the figures had increased considerably to 93 per cent, and approximately 80 per cent, respectively (Chandler, 1988). This increase in the ownership of television sets was both a factor and a result of the increase in sport programming. The 1960s in the United States were characterized by robust competition between the major television networks to secure broadcasting rights; in particular, massive battles occurred over the right to broadcast football. One of the key results of these battles was the merger of the National and American Football Leagues, to form the National Football League (NFL), while the national passion for the sport was entrenched with the establishment of *Monday Night Football* on the ABC.

The 1970s were a boom period for US professional sport leagues. Baseball, basketball, ice hockey, college football and college basketball all secured network broadcast contracts, while the annual number of hours of sport broadcast on television increased from 787 to 1,356 throughout the decade (McChesney, 1989). In 1977, NFL commissioner Pete Rozelle, amidst intense competition to secure the rights to premium sport leagues and events, negotiated a four-year US$656 million broadcast rights deal (Rader, 1984). According to Barnett (1990), ABC's approach to sport broadcasting in the US in the 1970s and 1980s, where sport represented entertainment value, influenced sport programming around the world. Boyle and Haynes (2000) claimed that those decades were 'golden years' for sport broadcasting in Great Britain, with the BBC and ITV providing extensive sport coverage. In 1985, Britons were able to enjoy the first live telecast of a league soccer match. Contemporary sport broadcasting is evidence of the connection between sport and entertainment, with dramatic introductions, detailed analysis of off- and on-field activities, instant and slow motion replays and interviews before, during and after games. The half-time show at the NFL Super Bowl and the opening ceremony of the Olympic Games are further examples of the centrality of entertainment to sport broadcasts.

As previously noted, many have viewed the relationship between sport and television as the central component of the sport media nexus. This view has been shaped by three central themes: globalization, commodification, and modification. First, television globalized sport. Events such as the Olympic Games and the FIFA World Cup have become global spectacles, while national sports have crossed geographical, cultural and language boundaries that were previously impenetrable (Barnett, 1995). While some national events, such as the Tour De France cycling race, are celebrated through their television coverage, Barnett (1995) noted that some nationally popular sports, such as cricket in the West Indies, have been threatened by the transmission and popularity of American sports

## IN PRACTICE 2.1

### Roone Arledge and *Monday Night Football*

The National Football League's *Monday Night Football* (*MNF*) has become a beloved institution for millions of Americans since it began in 1960. But while many football fans around the world look forward each week to their regular football 'fix', few would be aware of the man who brought the concept to life. In 1960, Roone Arledge joined the fledgling ABC television network primarily to cover college football yet his vision was much grander. As Arledge explained:

> When I got into it in 1960, televising sports amounted to going out on the road, opening three or four cameras and trying not to blow any plays . . . the marvel of seeing a picture was enough to keep people glued to their sets.

Although contemporary sports broadcasting brought the game to the viewer, Arledge soon broke with tradition and instead brought the viewer to the game. In short, he claimed that ABC Sports was 'going to add show business to sports!'.

It was also at this time that NFL Commissioner Pete Rozelle was looking to expand the league's television audience by having a weekly game on Monday nights on one of the three major networks, NBC, CBS or ABC. Arledge immediately saw the potential of the new show to boost its ratings and forever changed the face of sports broadcasting. He ordered twice the usual number of cameras to cover the game, used a three-person broadcasting booth, scene-setting story lines, bold graphics and 'close-ups of everyone from angry coaches to nervous mothers to face-painted drunks' to create compelling television. Within a year, *MNF* had a weekly audience of nearly 30 million; it would become the longest running prime time show in US television history.

During his nearly four decades at ABC, Roone Arledge won many Emmy Awards and went to great lengths to make whatever event ABC Sports was covering – from track and field to the Olympic Games, from *Wide World of Sports* to *Monday Night Football* – an interesting spectacle for viewers. Derided as gimmicks at the time, Arledge introduced instant replay, slow motion, freeze-frame, field microphones, cameras in blimps, and under water vision; these features are now considered almost mandatory in televised sport events. In 1994, *Sports Illustrated* ranked Arledge third behind Muhammad Ali and Michael Jordan as the most significant individual in US sport since *Sports Illustrated* was first published. As ESPN columnist Ralph Wiley explained, 'he dreamt a world. He's the Mark Twain of TV sports. The greatest storyteller there ever was, at least in this country. The author of the book from which all other American sports TV are made' (Wiley, 2002).

*Monday Night Football* was seen on ABC for 35 years before moving to ESPN and remains a weekly staple for pay television viewers worldwide in English, in Spanish on ESPN Deportes and in Portuguese on ESPN Brasil. ESPN and the National Football League have also agreed to a deal that will keep *Monday Night Football* on the cable network through 2021 which will see the iconic franchise survive 50 years in an increasingly competitive and fragmented television universe.

Sources: Meserole (2002); Wiley (2002).

such as basketball. This tension between global appeal and local traditions is as prevalent today as it was when television was introduced.

Second, through broadcast rights and sponsorship revenues, television has transformed sport from an amateur pursuit into a highly commercialized activity. It is important to note this is a relatively recent phenomenon. Prior to television, and then throughout the early years of television into the 1960s, sport was a commercial enterprise, but the vast majority of revenue was derived from gate receipts and memberships. For example, only two years after the end of the Second World War in 1947, Americans were spending approximately US$250 million on entry to sporting events annually, which increased to US$650 million by 1965 (Chandler, 1988). In 1962 the National Football League signed a national broadcast rights deal worth just US$4.7 million annually. In Europe, the annual broadcast rights fees for premier football leagues did not reach the equivalent of US$5 million until the 1980s. In the last quarter of the twentieth century, however, broadcast rights fees and sponsorship revenue increased exponentially, to the point that for many sport organizations they now represent the majority of overall revenue. The ubiquity of television and the capacity for sport organizations, advertisers and sponsors to capitalize on the mass television market resulted in the refinement and expansion of commercial processes, to the point that television is now viewed as the key agent in the selling, buying and re-selling of sport.

Third, sports have been modified to better suit the needs of broadcasters and to appeal to mediated, rather than live, audiences. Modifications vary, depending on the sport, the country and the commercial and cultural contexts. Football as it is played in Europe and South America has largely remained unchanged, with 45 minute halves uninterrupted by advertising. By contrast, some football codes in the US and Australia have created special breaks or have elongated natural stoppages to provide more time for advertising messages during television coverage. For example, in 1958 the NFL commissioner permitted the use of television time-outs, specifically designed to facilitate advertising and increase associated revenues (McChesney, 1989). In Great Britain, the half time break in football was extended from ten to 15 minutes in the 1980s in order to provide advertisers with more time to promote their products (Barnett, 1995). At the other end of the spectrum, new events, such as the X-Games, and new versions of old sports, such as Twenty20 cricket, have been created primarily as television products. For example, Twenty20 cricket is a shortened version of the traditional game, with each team playing an innings of just 20 overs, and concludes in just three hours. It features bright clothing, big hitting and plenty of wickets, incorporating more action in less time than longer formats of the game. Television networks have also played an influential role in determining the scheduling of events that suit their broadcast needs but that, in the worst cases, has resulted in athletes playing or competing at inappropriate times. Examples include scheduling football games for the middle of the night, Olympic swimming finals for the morning or marathons in the heat of the day, in order to enable broadcast in prime time in large commercial markets.

## PAY TELEVISION

Although technically not a new medium, the development of pay television (this term will be used throughout the book to denote television content that a viewer pays for, rather

than receives via free-to-air television) has had distinct implications for the sport media nexus. Prior to the introduction of pay television, spectators were able to attend the event and pay the sport organization directly, or might have been able to watch the event on free-to-air television. The introduction of pay television created the opportunity for spectators to pay to watch sport without attending a live event. The requirement to pay to watch a sporting event on television has entrenched the notion that sport is a product to be bought and sold. As an example, in 2006 the Commonwealth Games were held in Melbourne, Australia, and sport watchers were able to view a selection of events on free-to-air television. On pay television, a service was available on Australia's Foxtel whereby, for A$49.95, a viewer was able to access seven separate channels, with over 1,100 hours of coverage, including 650 hours of live coverage. A viewer could switch between sports or watch a channel dedicated to the best performances and moments of the 2006 Melbourne Commonwealth Games. Fast-forward to the London 2012 Olympic Games, and Foxtel offered residential subscribers free access to eight dedicated channels in both high definition (HD) and standard definition (SD), with 3,200 hours of coverage, including 1,100 hours of live events. In addition, for the 17 days of competition subscribers were able to stream all the action to their tablet device. Throughout the history of televised sport, sport organizations have been concerned by the relationship between mediated and live attendance. Although the Olympics is an event that most consumers are unable to attend live, the ability to access 3,200 hours of coverage, which is impossible via a single free-to-air channel or by attending the event, illustrates the ongoing tension between live and mediated sport.

The impact of pay television has yet to be fully realized. Although pay television is an accepted component of the sport media nexus in North America and Europe – where sport consumption and disposable incomes are high – it still has limited penetration throughout the rest of the world. In North America and Europe the introduction and entrenchment of pay television has altered the consumption of sport media. Whereas viewers were once able to consume televised sport through free-to-air channels and programmes, they are now required to pay to access the product. Indeed, sport has even been referred to as 'a battering ram' that can be used to build market share in the competitive pay television industry (Came, 1998).

In each of the previous sport media nexus developments (print media, radio and television) a return on investment was achieved by media organizations through advertising revenue. Newspapers, radio stations and television stations received income from commercial organizations seeking to access the audiences generated by sport programmes. Pay television has created a direct commercial relationship between the media organization and the consumer. In addition, the rapid pace of technological change has serious implications for sport organizations and the ways in which free-to-air and pay television networks mediate the sport product. Pay television broadcasters have led the development of the mediated audience experience. Pay television viewers can now watch the latest in sport action in HD, increasingly in three dimensions, can switch between events or even track a favourite player via a dedicated camera. For example, in 2012 Australian pay TV channel Foxtel added a Del Piero Hero Cam to its A-League football broadcast. Fans were able to press a particular button and launch a dedicated camera to follow Alessandro Del Piero, Sydney FC's marquee player, during one match. According to the Fox Sports promo, 'one camera, one hero, every pass, every run, everything Del

Piero does on the pitch, you'll see it first with the Fox Hero Cam' (Fox Sports, 2014). This example illustrates that networks are increasingly trying to offer more value for their consumers, via broadcasting innovations, which in turn leads sport and media organizations to adopt and adapt new technologies.

## INTERNET

While television continues to be the dominant medium for following sport, the internet is a significant competitor to traditional sport media and has become a disruptive technology that seriously threatens existing sport media business models. In much of Europe and Australia, more than one in two fans consume sport online. This rises to two out of three in Spain, the US and Russia, while online sport consumption in Brazil and China continues to grow rapidly (up 12 per cent and 20 per cent respectively) where eight out of ten fans consume sport online (Perform, 2012). In the context of the evolution of the sport media nexus it is important to discuss six key themes in relation to the internet.

First, like radio and television before it, the internet is a medium that provides consumers with immediacy. If a consumer wants to access the results of a match, the internet is often the quickest option. Just as the immediacy of radio and television caused newspapers to begin to change the way sport was covered, the internet has exacerbated the trend, so that hard copy newspapers now provide even more analysis and opinion and rely less on providing a record of events. Declining circulation and advertising revenue has seen the newspaper industry in the US shrink by 43 per cent since 2000 (Mitchell and Rosenstiel, 2012) and has forced the industry to dramatically rethink how it delivers its product in order to remain viable. Almost all major daily newspapers now have an online version that includes analysis and opinion, but also provides breaking sport news. Newspapers have also begun to charge for online content. Rupert Murdoch argued that, 'I think we've been asleep. They're very happy to pay for it when they buy a newspaper. And I think when they read it elsewhere they're going to have to pay' (Speers, 2009). By 2014 however, the introduction of paywalls had limited success.

Second, the internet provides greater access to a greater variety of sports than any other media form. Despite technological developments that enhance consumers' experiences of televised sport, the depth and breadth of sport coverage online is unrivalled. An internet user is able to access information about almost any sport in the world at any time of the day, and in some cases, watch it live. The International Olympic Committee (IOC) provided free live streaming of the London 2012 Olympic Games to 64 territories across Asia and Africa, while surfing fans have access to live web casts of all Association of Surfing Professionals (ASP) World Tour events.

Third, the internet is global. Newspapers and radio are necessarily local, regional or national in their content and audience; however, it must be noted that as these media develop an online presence their reach is undeniably much larger. While television has had an important role in globalizing sport, most free-to-air television coverage of global events still exhibits a parochial nationalism. For example, in Australia an Olympic Games broadcast will focus almost exclusively on Australian athletes. Pay television often offers a more global outlook, because it sometimes takes overseas broadcasts of a certain event,

such as FoxSports in Australia that broadcasts the NBA's feed direct from American broadcasters. But, in most cases, such as Premier League football and American professional codes, television broadcasts are produced for a limited set of consumers within a certain geographical area. By contrast, the internet is a truly global medium in that it allows users to follow a sport on the other side of the world, which has led to most sport organizations developing websites to meet this need. This is reminiscent of radio's ability to allow geographically distant audiences to consume sport at the same time and has fuelled the rise in the numbers of satellite fans for many sport teams (Kerr and Gladden, 2008). According to Murillo and Murillo (2005: 322), FC Barcelona considers that the internet plays 'an essential role in the process of diffusion, in generating new resources, and transmitting the "Barça" feeling'. The progression from local to global and from newspaper to the internet is represented in Figure 2.1. Larger sport organizations are also capitalizing on the global nature of the internet by providing a range of language options for their websites. The Texas Rangers (Major League Baseball) has a Japanese version of its website to capitalize on the popularity of pitching sensation Yu Darvish, while Barça's online video channel is available in Spanish, English, Arabic, French, Chinese and Japanese and has subscribers in more than 50 countries (Portet and Ortiz, 2008).

Fourth, the internet is personal. Although this seems to contradict the previous feature of the global medium, the internet has allowed consumers to personalize their sport

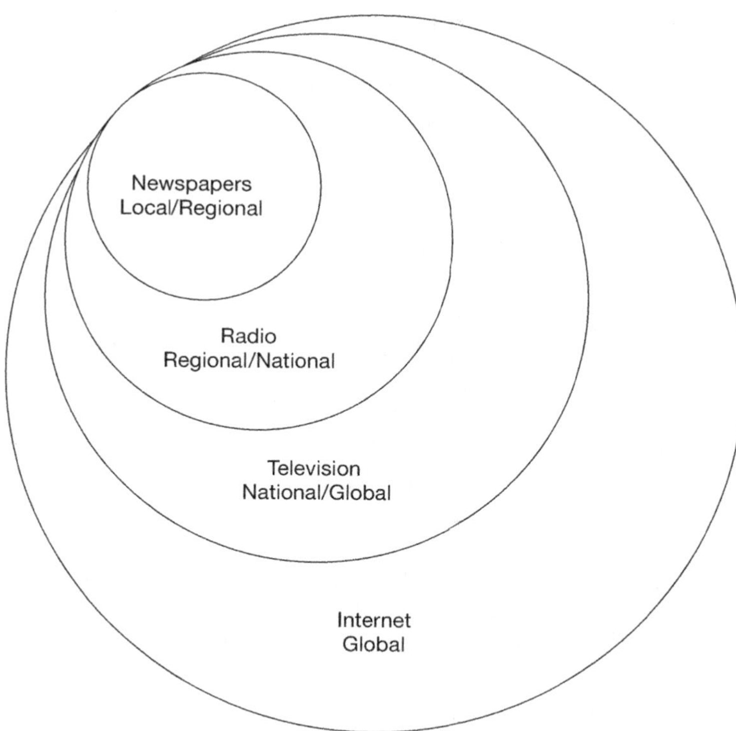


**FIGURE 2.1** Local media to global media

preferences and experiences. Whereas television is dominated by sports that are able to attract a mass audience, the internet allows consumers to not only choose from a greater range of sport options, but also to become members of sport communities that cross cultural and geographic boundaries. In particular, the internet has enabled sport fans to 'talk' and share experiences in virtual online communities, as well as participate in fantasy leagues. As a result, many of the world's most famous teams, such as Liverpool FC, have virtual communities where supporters connect with fellow fans and share consumption experiences (Kerr and Emery, 2011). For example, a Liverpool supporter club in Norway boasts more than 54,000 followers on social media and has its own app available from iTunes. By contrast, analogue television did not allow for any audience interaction, while radio and newspapers traditionally had limited audience interaction in the form of talk-back callers and letters to the editor.

Fifth, the internet provides sport organizations, advertisers and sponsors with direct access to consumers. While television, radio and newspapers are able to sell advertising space and time, it is rare for consumers to be able to interact with sponsors or purchase products while they are accessing sport media through those channels. By contrast, consumers of internet sport media are able to click through to sponsor or advertiser websites and products. In the example referred to previously, FC Barcelona fans can visit the club's website in order to watch game highlights, download applications for their mobile device, buy merchandise or buy tickets to see their heroes in person. In short, some sport organizations websites are now interactive multimedia portals that service all the sport media needs of consumers, including the ability to watch live games, listen to audio commentary, bet on the results of games and purchase the products and services of sponsors and advertisers.

Sixth and finally, the internet is a converged medium that has the potential to create a brave new world for the sport media nexus. The internet has the capacity to provide consumers with the products or services offered by newspaper, radio and television – all at once. Text based information and photographs provide a basis for many websites, like newspapers, while many publishers, such as News Corporation that owns Australia's most widely read newspaper *The Herald Sun*, now offer digital passes that 'unlock a world of news, sport and entertainment – online, on your phone, and on your iPad' (*Herald Sun*, 2012 in ABC, 2012). As more traditional media content moves online, we have also seen established media companies partnering with social networks. For example, video portal YouTube funds news agency Reuters to produce original news shows and social networking site Facebook has partnered with major newspaper brands (Mitchell and Rosenstiel, 2012). Websites are also able to stream radio broadcasts and live video which sport organizations increasingly offer to fans worldwide, sometimes at a cost. However, this brave new world of media convergence is likely to result in increased government oversight and regulation.

## MOBILE TECHNOLOGIES

Although relatively new, communication technologies such as the 'smartphone' or other mobile devices are already having a significant impact on the sport media nexus. The Walt Disney Company refers to mobile phones as the 'third screen', following television and the

## IN PRACTICE 2.2

### Adding to the broadcast – app style

The Oxford Dictionary defines an app as 'A self-contained program or piece of software designed to fulfil a particular purpose; an application, especially as downloaded by a user to a mobile device'. In the twenty-first century, there are mobile apps to help monitor blood pressure, measure your IQ, combat anxiety and pay bills. Increasingly, sport organizations, sport events and sport broadcasters are developing apps to help connect with sports fans and improve their experience of the sports product.

In 2014, Australian network SBS introduced an app to complement its Australian free-to-air coverage of the 2014 FIFA World Cup. Developed by FIFA's own production contractor Host Broadcasting Services, and supported by SBS through technology company Akamai, which provided video streaming, security and analytics (Cowan, 2014), the app was downloaded over 400,000 times during the tournament.

The app included the ability to watch every match live, with six camera angles to choose from including the actual host broadcast television feed, a tactical camera, two focused player cameras and two focused team angles. It also offered highlight clips of goals and other major moments, seconds after they appeared, pre and post match interviews and a highlights package at the end of each match, as well as a daily five minute wrap. The app was free, though included advertisements to watch before the live feed started.

The app received rave reviews from some technology writers, such as Campbell Simpson of *Gizmodo* stating:

> Whether I was watching matches replayed on TV in the office, from under the bedcovers at 5AM on my tablet, or on my phone on the train through a Wi-Fi hotspot, the video coverage was top-notch – no match-breaking glitches, no drop-outs, and adaptive streaming that actually worked. Youtube could learn a thing or two from SBS.
>
> (Simpson, 2014)

The 2014 SBS FIFA World Cup app is a good example of delivering extra content to sport fans – allowing fans to watch whichever game they chose, wherever they happened to be. The app was just one part of a myriad of mediated content that SBS offered fans in 2014, including through television, online, radio, mobile tablet and social media, but helped to draw some of the biggest engagement numbers. While SBS reached 10.7 million Australians through their TV broadcast, there were 13 million video streams viewed through the app and website (SBS, 2014).

Sources: Cowan (2014); SBS (2014); Simpson (2014).

internet (Walt Disney Company, 2005). Through ESPN's digital centre, the company claims to have created a 'technological interface in which producers of television, internet, radio and wireless content work literally or virtually side by side to produce sports content that is delivered in ways that were unimaginable just a few years ago' (Walt Disney Company, 2005). Mobile television promises to create new business opportunities for media companies and telecommunications providers (Bayartsaikhan *et al.*, 2007). As a result, ESPN subscribers can now download the WatchESPN app and access video on demand on their mobile device.

Within a year of third party developers being given access to the iPhone nearly 2,000 sport-related applications had been launched. The surge in popularity caught many off guard and mobile media has quickly changed the game. When Apple launched the iPad in 2010 it soon sold nearly 14 million of the devices (Scot Johns, 2011), and the new technology has fuelled the popularity of many sport-specific apps. The London Organising Committee for the 2012 Olympic Games (LOCOG) created a number of apps to allow fans to make the most of the Games experience: they could keep track of the Olympic Torch Relay, the latest news, schedules and results or visit the IOC's Olympic Athlete's Hub, a directory of verified athlete social media accounts. As LOCOG Chair Sebastian Coe explained, 'we encourage people everywhere to share their Olympic experience with the world, whether they have tickets for a sporting event or not' (LOCOG, 2012).

These developments have prompted some of the world's top clubs to develop strategic partnerships with telecommunications providers. Manchester United (MUFC) has partnered with telecommunication providers in Asia, the Middle East and Europe to offer subscribers exclusive Manchester United news, interviews and special content. It has also been predicted that telecommunication providers will become key players in the sport media nexus and will hold the rights to major sport events in the future (Perform, 2012).

While it may be true that fans will tend to watch sport on the biggest, highest quality screen available to them, there continues to be significant growth in the number who follow sport on a mobile device (Perform, 2012). Sport on mobile phones has so far proven to be a complement to, rather than a substitute for, the television experience (Savage and Savage, 2009). Yet it must be noted that mobile media relies on other media, such as television and the internet, for content and format. In other words, these technologies have not yet evolved into a separate media form that presents or represents sport in new or radically different ways. Rather, these communication technologies are able to access internet websites or receive live coverage or highlight packages from television broadcasters. In this respect, these technologies enable a greater personalization of sport media coverage in the sense that it is available on demand, when and wherever the consumer wants to access it. As a result, media and sport organizations, as well as advertisers and sponsors, will also have greater access to consumers, a theme that will be discussed further in an analysis of the commercial dimensions of the sport media nexus in Chapter 5.

## SOCIAL MEDIA

The availability of high-speed internet and the ubiquitous nature of the mobile phone have fuelled the growth and popularity of social media, the group of internet-based applications that allow the creation and exchange of user-generated content (Kaplan and

Haenlein, 2010). Social media has become a powerful tool to find, connect, inform, engage with, and develop a community around fans. According to Oldenburg (2001), all great societies provide a 'third place' such as the neighbourhood pub or coffee shop where people can relax in an informal meeting place outside home and work. Although new applications constantly emerge, Kaplan and Haenlein (2010) argued that there are six different types of social media: collaborative projects (e.g. Wikipedia), blogs (e.g. Twitter), content communities (e.g. YouTube), social networking sites (e.g. Facebook), virtual game worlds (e.g. World of Warcraft) and virtual social worlds (e.g. Second Life). Although these are the dominant players in the social media space, other players include Google+, Bebo, Pinterest, LinkedIn, MySpace, Flickr and China's RenRen. A number of these warrant further discussion, especially as social media might serve as a virtual 'third place' (Soukup, 2006; Rao, 2008), and will be discussed at length in future chapters as sport media professionals use social media extensively to promote their organizations and connect with fans.

## DIGITAL TELEVISION

At the end of the twentieth century the face of television broadcasting changed dramatically when digital television was introduced in France and the United Kingdom, through Canalsatellite and SkyDigital, respectively (Griffiths, 2003). By 2006, both these companies also offered HD television channels and had been joined by BT Vision, the hybrid digital television and Internet Protocol Television (IPTV) service owned by British Telecom. By 2012, many European countries had made the switch from analogue to digital television and were soon followed by Australia, New Zealand, South Africa and much of Asia. The United States is due to complete the transition by 2015 and, by the time it welcomes the world for the Rio 2016 Olympic Games, Brazil will also have made the changeover.

Digital technology offers many additional benefits for viewers, such as better picture and sound quality. The technology also provides more bandwidth, allows more channels, enables video on demand, allows interactive entertainment such as games and gambling and provides more sophisticated pay-per-view capacities (Griffiths, 2003). There has been a concerted effort by sports broadcasters to bring the game to life for subscribers. In 2010, Fox Sports, BSkyB and ESPN all introduced dedicated sports channels in 3D and both the BBC and NBC experimented with 3D coverage of the London 2012 Olympic Games. Later that year, emerging players in the sport media nexus, China and Latin America, introduced 3D television channels. The emergence of HD as a global standard for sport broadcasting, coupled with the number of events now broadcast in 3D, has made the televised sports experience more immersive and compelling than ever before; a case can be made that television now offers a better sport experience than can be found at the stadium (Levy, 2011).

In many respects, the impact of digital television, like the internet and, to some extent, pay television, is not yet clear. For many years, NBC's line-up of hit shows such as *Seinfeld*, *Friends* and *ER* dominated US television ratings as millions of Americans tuned in at the same time to watch 'Must See TV'. The implications for television's traditional business model – in the light of the capacity of personal video recorders (PVRs, such as

TiVo or Foxtel's IQ) to allow viewers to access programmes whenever they want, rather than being bound by a television schedule – remain to be seen. Furthermore, consumers are now able to instantly bypass commercials, 'timeshift' programmes and access the latest content on mobile devices. As a result, digital television has ushered in a commercial shift to the consumer meaning viewers can now use the remote control to purchase products, access the internet and send and receive emails (Griffiths, 2003).

There is intense competition in the sector and almost limitless choice for consumers: TV-enabled internet devices, pay-per-view services such as Netflix; the evolution of YouTube; internet-enabled TV sets (so-called smart TVs); as well as the entry of major technology companies such as Google and Apple into the market. By 2017, there will be 800 million smart TVs worldwide and IPTV will reach a penetration level in Australia equivalent to pay television (Healey, 2012; PWC, 2012). Tech giant Apple launched Apple TV in 2007, a small digital console that connects the user's computer and Apple account to their TV. It acts as a hub for the user to buy content via their Apple account and stream content to their television set. Its major bonus for sports fans includes integration with many major sports digital channels, for example international users with a subscription to a US league digital channel – such as the NBA's League Pass or the NHL's GameCenter – can use Apple TV to stream a HD match broadcast directly to their TV, footage that is often not otherwise available in local markets on either free-to-air or pay television. Google TV was first launched in the US in late 2010 as a platform to turn a user's TV into a browser, however it was rebranded and reshaped to become Android TV in 2014 (Kahn, 2013). Both services now aim to offer a way for consumers to easily find and buy entertainment online and stream it directly to their chosen devices, including HD TV, whenever and wherever they like. Telecommunication providers have also promoted their own IPTV services, such as Telstra's T-Box or BT Vision. As a result, the traditional 'network' model is likely to break down and be replaced with 'libraries' of content, such as Netflix, iTunes, Amazon or Hulu (Blodget, 2012). Hulu is a joint venture between the major US networks that offers streaming video of television shows, movies and behind-the-scenes footage from NBC, FOX, ABC and CBS.

Hutchins and Rowe (2009) explained that online sport content distribution has created 'digital plenitude'; where once there was comparative scarcity in terms of content and channels, there is now a number of ways that media companies, sport organizations and individual athletes can produce and share content for fans to consume. The programming options available to consumers, as promised by the proliferation of television channels and IPTV, provide a dilemma for those who manage the sport media nexus. The value attributed to live sport events, as 'perishable' products, should see significant competition for broadcast rights, and will feature heavily in later chapters of this book, but there is pressure for broadcasters to maximize their expensive investment in sport. Given the propensity for viewers to skip advertisements, television executives may turn to product placement, where advertisements are overlaid during a telecast and are only visible to the television viewer, in order to capture audience attention and substantially boost revenues (Turner and Cusumano, 2000). For example, Kellogg's Nutri-Grain co-funded *Football Superstar*, an Australian reality television series that saw contestants compete for a spot on the A-League's Sydney FC, and its logo was omnipresent throughout the series. Ultimately, broadcasters will provide consumers with a comprehensive package of news, information, statistics and even betting opportunities across a wide range of devices in

order to maximize their return on investment. How digital television changes the sport media nexus is unclear, but given its range of new features, it is likely to shift the emphasis towards the consumer and away from the traditional television model of advertising revenue supported by mass audiences.

## CONCLUSION

The sport media nexus has been steadily evolving since the eighteenth century. It is clear from the information contained in this chapter, which is necessarily brief and selective, that sport has been irrevocably changed through its relationship with the media. However, it is important to note that the sport media nexus continues to evolve and does not end with the maturity of the internet, the growth and popularity of social media, the ubiquitous nature of mobile communications or the evolution of television. The pace of technological change means that any attempt to accurately forecast the future of the sport media nexus is foolhardy to say the least; the convergence of the media and sport industries and the increased globalization and commercialization of sport will undoubtedly produce unforeseen developments. Furthermore, the evolution discussed in this chapter is uneven. For the United States and Europe, the evolution of the nexus has been comparatively rapid, yet in other countries some of the phases described in this chapter have yet to be fully experienced. Despite massive audiences and recent technological developments, the sport media nexus in Africa, China, India and much of Latin America and the Middle East is still in its relative infancy; many of the world's poorer countries have only sporadic access to television and the internet.

## SUMMARY

This chapter has examined the history and evolution of the sport media nexus. In particular, it has examined the impact that various media forms, such as television and the internet, have had on sport. It is clear from the information and discussion presented in this chapter that sport has influenced the development of the media, while the media has transformed sport, particularly at the elite and professional levels. Review questions and exercises are listed below to assist with confirming your knowledge of the core concepts and principles introduced in this chapter.

## REVIEW QUESTIONS AND EXERCISES

1 When did the relationship between sport and the media begin?
2 How did sport contribute to the creation of the modern mass circulation newspaper?
3 Were the early days of radio broadcasting characterized by regular or sporadic sport coverage?

4 What are the three major themes that can be used to describe the relationship between sport and television?

5 Identify any examples within your country that illustrate the tension between global appeal and local traditions in sport broadcasting.

6 Beyond those identified in the chapter, identify three examples of the modification of sport or scheduling as a result of the mediation of sport.

7 Will pay television increase or decrease live sport attendance in the future? Why?

8 Choose a professional sport league and identify the fees paid by television broadcasters over the past decade. Have the fees increased or decreased during this time and what might account for the change in rights fees paid?

9 Which of the six key themes or features referred to in the discussion about the connection between sport and the internet will be most important in its future development? Why?

10 Has the internet become a disruptive technology that will destroy traditional business models in the sport media nexus or will it instead open up new revenue streams? If so, how?

## FURTHER READING

Boyle, R. and Haynes, R. (2009) *Power Play: Sport, the Media and Popular Culture*. Edinburgh: Edinburgh University Press.

Chandler, J. M. (1991) Sport as TV product: A case study of 'Monday Night Football'. *The Business of Professional Sports*, 48–60.

Colman, M. (1996) *Super League: The Inside Story*. Sydney: Pan Macmillan Australia.

McCoy, J. (1997) Radio sports broadcasting in the United States, Britain and Australia, 1920–1956 and its influence on the Olympic Games. *Journal of Olympic History, 5* (1), 20–25.

Pegoraro, A. and Clavio, G. (2010) Look who's talking – athletes on twitter: A case study. *International Journal of Sport Communication, 3* (4), 501–514.

Rowe, D. (1996) The global love-match: Sport and television. *Media, Culture and Society, 18*, 565–582.

Sanderson, J. (2011) *It's a Whole New Ballgame: How Social Media is Changing Sports*. New York: Hampton Press.

Scherer, J., Falcous, M. and Jackson, S. J. (2008) The media sports cultural complex local–global disjuncture in New Zealand/Aotearoa. *Journal of Sport and Social Issues, 32* (1), 48–71.

Williams, J. (1994) The local and the global in English soccer and the rise of satellite television. *Sociology of Sport Journal, 11*, 376–397.

Zimmerman, M. H., Clavio, G. E. and Lim, C. H. (2011) Set the agenda like Beckham: A professional sports league's use of YouTube to disseminate messages to its users. *International Journal of Sport Management and Marketing, 10* (3), 180–195.

# RELEVANT WEBSITES

## Americas

National Football League – www.nfl.com
'Monday Night Football' –www.espn.go.com/nfl/mnf
*Sports Illustrated* – www.sportsillustrated.com
ESPN *Deportes* – www.espndeportes.com
National Basketball Association – www.nba.com
Texas Rangers – www.texasrangers.com
Washington Redskins (on Twackle) – http://files.redskins.com/twackle
Portland Trail Blazers (Pinterest) – www.pinterest.com/pdxtrailblazers
Red Bull (YouTube) – www.youtube.com/user/redbull
Hulu – www.hulu.com

## Australia and New Zealand

Foxtel – www.foxtel.com.au
National Rugby League – www.nrl.com
A-League – www.footballaustralia.com.au/aleague
*Herald and Weekly Times* – www.heraldsun.com.au
Australian Football League – www.afl.com.au
Netball Australia – http://netball.com.au/

## Europe

BBC Sport – www.bbc.co.uk/sport
British Sky Broadcasting Group (BSkyB) – www.sky.com
English Premier League – www.premierleague.com
European Super League – www.superleague.co.uk
London 2012 Olympics – www.london2012.com
FC Barcelona – www.fcbarcelona.com
Liverpool FC – www.liverpoolfc.com
Liverpool FC Supporter Club Scandinavian Branch – www.liverpool.no
Leeds Rhinos – www.therhinos.co.uk

## Global

World Cup – www.fifa.com
Olympics – www.olympic.org
Association of Surfing Professionals – www.aspworldtour.com

## CASE STUDY

### Murdoch's millions – sport as pay television's 'battering ram'

This case examines the importance of pay television in the creation of a global media empire; it explores how News Corporation, owned by Rupert Murdoch, used football to build market share and increase subscribers for his fledgling pay television services in England and Australia. Murdoch has famously argued that sport overpowers all other forms of entertainment as a means to generate a television audience and, as a result, he often uses sport 'as a battering ram and a lead offering in all . . . pay-television operations' to break into new markets (Came, 1998: 56).

For more than a century, some of the biggest football clubs in England had been fighting for a greater share of the game's revenue; since the 1980s there had been talk about forming a 'super league' in order to bring this about. In 1983, the television rights to broadcast five live matches each year for two years were sold for £5.2 million and for many years the big clubs heavily subsidized smaller ones. However, by 1991, pay television company BSkyB – the majority owner of which is News Corporation – determined that English football was the only sport capable of attracting a sizable number of new customers to satellite television. In February 1992 the top clubs broke away from the old Football League to form the FA Premier League or, as it is better known by millions of fans around the world, the English Premier League (EPL). The new league had commercial independence and was able to negotiate its own broadcast and sponsorship deals. The new arrangement saw BSkyB, backed by Murdoch's millions, trump its rivals with a £304 million bid to broadcast the league for the next five years on Sky Sports, its dedicated sports channel.

The infusion of cash into the English game guaranteed each Premier League club at least £1 million in the first year (Ball, 1992) and allowed the shareholder clubs (based upon promotion and relegation) to spend more money on players and better compete with cashed-up European rivals. At the same time, the BSkyB monies boosted the coffers of the smaller clubs in the league; however, there were concerns that the gap between the lower division clubs and the Premiership contenders had continued to widen. It was around this time that the Premier League began to become a global powerhouse, especially when the European Court of Justice ruled that domestic football leagues in its jurisdiction could not impose quotas on the number of foreign players a club fielded. As a result, overseas stars such as Dennis Bergkamp and Ruud Gullit arrived to ply their trade in England while Arsene Wenger took the reins at Arsenal. The presence of high quality foreign players is a key reason for the popularity of the EPL among global television audiences (Duguid, 2004). Yet not everyone was happy with the events that had transpired and some expressed concerns over the loss of tradition and accessibility to the English game. For example, in a bid to get back in the black, BSkyB did away with the traditional three o'clock kick-off on Saturday afternoons and launched a glitzy advertising campaign – 'It's a whole new ball game' – in a bid to sign up armchair football fans. At the time in his role as a Conservative MP Sebastian Coe argued, 'I think it is wrong that only

two million [satellite] dish owners get access to such major sporting events' (Rodrigues, 2012). That said, as a partner in the BSkyB bid, the BBC received a highlights package of all the EPL action in order to revive the popular *Match of the Day* programme.

BSkyB had taken an all-or-nothing gamble by paying more than six times the existing free-to-air television rights deal. Failure would mean:

> [being] caught inexorably in a ghetto of cheap and unattractive programming. However, if the new relationship with soccer succeeds, as predicted, in eventually selling more than three million sports channel subscriptions in Britain, it is likely to secure the long-term future of the entire BSkyB network.
>
> (Williams, 1994: 384–385)

Although rivals thought Murdoch had overpaid for the rights to the new football competition – a charge that was also levelled at the Australian media mogul when his fledgling FOX television network acquired the rights to the NFL – the gamble helped to establish BSkyB as a major media player in Europe. The pay television operator easily recouped its initial investment in the EPL television rights when nearly two million homes paid £144 per year for the Sky Sports Channel. Although BSkyB will spend £2.3 billion to keep the crown jewels of English football – a total of 116 live Premier League matches per year until 2015–16 – the deal means that for its ten million television customers, 'Sky Sports remains the home of Premier League football'. Clearly, its decision 20 years ago has proved to be a profitable one for News Corporation (British Sky Broadcasting Group, 2012).

Perhaps emboldened by his success in England, Murdoch then turned his attention to the land of his birth and the popularity of rugby league football. Pay television had only arrived in 1995 and, reflecting the popularity of sport to many Australians, the inaugural programme was dedicated to sport (Rowe, 1997).The Australian Government had ensured that locals had free access to the country's most popular sporting events. There is no annual licence fee paid by viewers for free-to-air television, as there is in Britain, and Australian free-to-air broadcasters are given the first rights to acquire sporting events of national importance. However, unlike Murdoch's operation in Britain, which delivered the product to subscribers by satellite dish, pay television in Australia was delivered by the rival telecommunication companies, Telstra and Optus. Both companies had spent more than a billion dollars rolling out cable and had launched pay television services; Telstra joined forces with Murdoch's News Corporation to launch Foxtel, while Optus Vision had tapped the financial resources of Australian media magnate, Kerry Packer (Rowe, 1997).

Rugby league has been very popular in Australia since 1908 when nine clubs were established in Sydney under the auspices of the New South Wales Rugby League (NSWRL). At the same time, the Queensland Rugby Football League (QRL) began to build its own club competition, and at the end of the 1908 season the first national representative side, the Kangaroos, toured England. In 1982, the first non-Sydney clubs joined the competition and by 1995 there were 20 teams, including the

Auckland Warriors in New Zealand, in the now Australian Rugby League (ARL) national competition. A rugby league match was televised for the first time in Australia in 1961 and for the next few years the rights to broadcast the NSWRL competition were shared between the local television networks. However, by 1994 rugby league games, including the very successful annual series between New South Wales and Queensland, were consistently some of Australia's most watched television programmes. Kerry Packer recognized the value of rugby league as a media product and locked up the television rights to the game, both on his free-to-air Channel Nine and Optus Vision, until the end of the century. Murdoch likewise understood its value and tried to persuade Packer to on-sell the pay television rights, rights he had acquired for free, but there was to be no agreement. News Corporation's inability to secure these rights ultimately paved the way for the Super League war.

There had been speculation concerning a rebel Super League as early as March 1994 and Kerry Packer was intent on safeguarding his financial investment. At a meeting in February 1995, Packer reminded the ARL and its club representatives that he had a contractual agreement to broadcast the competition and threatened legal action should he not be allowed do so. Despite this threat, by March of that year News Corporation had decided to sign up ARL players and coaches in order to stage a rival Super League. Rupert Murdoch had a vision to take the game 'to the world' and the Super League concept was seen as valuable sports programming, not only for his Australian Foxtel operation, but also for StarTV (Asia), BSkyB (Europe) and FOX Broadcasting (US). In April 1995 News Corporation paid the Rugby Football League in Britain £87 million for a five-year television deal on BSkyB; the move isolated the Australian Rugby League while strengthening News Corporation's bargaining position. Murdoch had created a European Super League and had persuaded the game's administrators to break with a hundred years of tradition, to merge teams, include teams in London and Paris and, most amazing of all, to switch the competition to the summer months where it would run parallel to the southern hemisphere's winter season.

Reminiscent of their Premier League experience, local British fans were now being asked to watch games spread out throughout the week rather than the traditional Sunday afternoon, and historic teams were adopting commercially motivated nicknames. For example, Castleford Glassblowers became the 'Tigers', Bradford Northern became the 'Bulls' and Leeds became known as the 'Rhinos'. The European Super League served to promote other products in the Murdoch media empire, such as when a figure in a Bart Simpson costume roamed the sidelines of a London Broncos game promoting *The Simpsons* cartoon, another BSkyB product. Murdoch's worldwide commitment to Super League was estimated to be worth around £300 million and he soon did exclusive deals with rugby league administrators in New Zealand, France, USA, Papua New Guinea, Western Samoa, Tonga and Fiji. Furthermore, those behind Super League argued that only News Corporation and Super League had the organizational capacity to successfully take the product to the world. For example, John Ribot, initial Chief Executive of the Australian Super League, extolled the virtues of the concept: 'when Manfred from Germany is watching Canberra [Raiders] versus London [Broncos] on pay-TV, he'll be able to

pick up his phone and order Ricky Stuart's number seven jumper there and then' (*Open Rugby* magazine, January 1996 in Falcous, 1998: 13).

Although an Australian Federal Court judge had originally forbade News Corporation from staging a Super League competition in Australia until 2000, Murdoch ultimately prevailed upon appeal and the Super League Telstra Cup began in March 1997. The ten-team Super League, with new clubs Adelaide Rams and Hunter Mariners, ran parallel to the 12 Australian Rugby League teams who fought for the Optus Cup. Despite this, record crowds turned up to see the Brisbane Broncos and Newcastle Knights win the Super League and ARL competitions respectively, and rugby league continued to win the ratings war in Sydney. While this served to highlight the importance of the game to pay television, the court victory was a pyrrhic one as rugby league in Australia had suffered serious damage and both competitions faced heavy losses. Ultimately, sanity prevailed and the two warring parties agreed to run a merged competition the following year and reduce the number of teams to 14 by 2000. The new National Rugby League (NRL) would be a 50:50 joint venture and would comprise eight Super League clubs, eleven ARL clubs and the new Melbourne Storm franchise.

The breakaway competition was supposed to have cost News Corporation A$60 million, yet the true cost proved to be much closer to A$560 million (Chenoweth, 2005). Rugby league was a prized asset that Foxtel, News Corporation's Australian pay television channel, desperately needed in its bid to capture market share, and its willingness to invest A$100 million a year to broadcast the NRL until 2017 highlights the importance of the game to News Corporation (Chessell and Holgate, 2012). As Fox Sports Chief Executive Patrick Delany explained, 'Rugby league is a part of Fox Sports' and Foxtel's DNA and we are delighted to be able to continue bringing the live action to households [through Super Saturday and Monday Night Football] across Australia every week' (NRL, 2012). Yet while nearly 2.5 million homes subscribe to Foxtel's Fox Sports channels at A$61 per month (Fox Sports, 2014), only 26 per cent of Australian households, compared with 40 per cent in Britain, subscribe to pay television (White, 2012). While the Super League saga ultimately delivered Murdoch the prize he coveted, and is consistent with his use of sport as 'a battering ram', it came at a hefty price that alienated many traditional fans forever.

## CASE STUDY QUESTIONS

1 Why do you think the threat of a breakaway league worked so well for News Corporation in Britain but not in Australia?
2 English football and rugby league were important building blocks in Rupert Murdoch's bid to create a sustainable business model for BSkyB and Foxtel, yet News Corporation also has significant pay television assets in Asia and North America. What sports leagues might the media giant have its eye on as it seeks to develop those businesses?

3 Can you think of some examples in your country where pay television has changed the way a sport is broadcast, the scheduling of its games or perhaps made the sport product less accessible to its fans?

4 News Corporation made a significant investment in order to build market share for its pay television services. Indeed, it has even been suggested that sport may simply be a 'loss leader', positioning the company to make money from other channels or perhaps telephonic services in the future. Was Murdoch's investment in securing exclusive broadcast rights ultimately worth the price he paid and, perhaps more importantly, was it good for the game?

Sources: Williams (1994); Rodrigues (2012); McGaughey and Liesch (2002); Falcous (1998).

# PART 2

# Sport media landscapes

CHAPTER 3

# The sport and media industries

## Meeting the global players

## OVERVIEW

This chapter examines the sport and media industries at a global level. Specifically, it explores the major players of the media industry and the structure and extent of their business operations. The major sport players are also examined, such as the major football organizations and leagues, major events and sport circuits. An examination of the media and sport industries reveals the role of both in creating the sport media nexus.

## LEARNING OUTCOMES

After completing this chapter, the reader should be able to:

- contextualize the sport media nexus within a broader knowledge of the media and sport industries;
- identify the key players in both media and sport industries in order to explain their place in the sport media nexus; and
- understand the interactions between media organizations and how sport is used to forge these links and commercial relationships.

## INTRODUCTION

Viewed in isolation, the media and sport industries are two massive commercial systems. But as the first two chapters illustrated, it is increasingly difficult, if not impossible, to disentangle these systems. At a macro level their spheres of influence include the processes of globalization, the flow of trade and the ways in which nations seek status on the international stage. At the micro level their influence might include the ways we choose a particular product to quench our thirst or communicate with friends. Our everyday

experiences and actions are 'mediated' as we watch, read and download on a daily basis. Our knowledge of the world around us, either at a local or global level, is very much dependent upon the media. Similarly, we learn, adopt and reject a variety of values and behaviours through our participation in, and viewership of, sport events. When viewed together, sport and the media are a powerful combination.

It is likely that a cursory examination of the ways in which sport and the media interact will reveal a jumble of images, messages, replays and action shots and, as a result, it will be difficult to determine the major players – those media and sport organizations that have influence at national and global levels. In order to understand the sport media nexus more completely it is necessary to dig down beyond the pastiche of sport celebrity, sponsors' products and mega events to examine how the sport and media industries operate as a series of organizations. In terms of the media, this means examining the major players in various locations across the globe, although examination of only a sample is possible because of the diversity and size of the industry. In terms of sport, a similar investigation means examining those sports and organizations that dominate the media landscape and involves a discussion of those sports and global events that capture the lion's share of audience attention.

## ENTERTAINMENT AND PROFIT DRIVEN

It has often been noted that the media perform three essential functions: information, education and entertainment (Briggs and Burke, 2005). Sometimes education is substituted with interpretation (Coakley, 2003), but there is general agreement that information and entertainment are the most prominent functions of any media form or outlet. It is typically a relatively simple exercise to distinguish what role the media is playing at a particular time in a particular context, although for some events the categories can easily become blurred. For example, at times when a disaster causes suffering and loss of human life, such as a flood or an act of terrorism, the media provide a service by disseminating information. However, it is also clear that the media often structures coverage of these events as entertainment to be consumed by an audience, blurring the distinction between media as information and media as entertainment. In the case of sport these distinctions are usually far clearer and a significant majority of all sport media is entertainment driven.

As the previous chapter demonstrated, as the sport media nexus has deepened and become more complex, sport leagues and clubs have sought to make their product more entertaining in order to appeal to the media and consumers. This appeal is required by both the sport and the media industries to drive profits. The next chapter will examine the commercial dimension of the sport media nexus in more depth, but in order to contextualize a discussion about the two industries and their connections, it is important to recognize that a commercial imperative is at the heart of the nexus. This chapter discusses how profit motive has driven the growth in the sport and media industries, the way in which the nexus has developed and the size and influence of the major players in the current market.

## KEY MEDIA PLAYERS

There are several major media players at a global level. Because of the importance and value of sport, these companies are also important sport media players. Table 3.1 shows the five largest media companies in the world based on 2014 sales and profits, current assets and market value. These companies are based in either the United States or Europe, but have global reach through subsidiary companies and by on-selling sport programming content.

It is important to note, however, that designated media companies are not the only companies to have media or sport media interests. In recent years, telecommunication companies such as British Telecom or Canada's Rogers Communications, and technology giants such as Google and Yahoo, have made significant investments in sport and media assets. For example, Google, the world's fifth most powerful brand with a market value of US$203.2 billion, acquired YouTube in 2006. Since then Google has made a concerted effort to transform the video-sharing website into a viable alternative to mainstream television networks. In 2010, Indian cricket's Indian Premier League (IPL) became the first sport event to be broadcast live on YouTube and Google has since acquired the rights to stream more than 350 National Basketball Association (NBA) Development League games live to basketball fans worldwide.

### Comcast

Although Comcast is the world's largest media company, its commercial operations lack the international diversity of most of its major rivals. In its 2012 Annual Report, CEO Brian Roberts stated that Comcast is committed to innovation and operational excellence. As a result, the company 'can innovate faster, developing and bringing to life products that excite and delight' (Comcast, 2013: 1). Comcast's revenue comes from two primary segments – cable communications and NBC Universal. Its cable communications division

**TABLE 3.1** World's largest media companies (2014 – all figures in US$ billion)

| *Company* | *Position in top 2000 global companies* | *Sales* | *Profits* | *Assets* | *Market value* |
|---|---|---|---|---|---|
| Comcast | 57 | 64.7 | 6.8 | 158.8 | 130 |
| The Walt Disney Company | 100 | 46 | 6.6 | 83.2 | 142.9 |
| Twenty-First Century Fox Inc* | 152 | 32 | 4.9 | 53.3 | 74.6 |
| Time Warner | 156 | 29.8 | 3.6 | 69.9 | 58.9 |
| Vivendi | 548 | 31.6 | –1.3 | 67.8 | 37.3 |
| News Corporation* | 922 | 8.8 | .5 | 16 | 10.1 |

* Twenty-First Century Fox was created in 2013 when News Corporation split into two companies.
Source: www.forbes.com.

dominated corporate earnings and delivered nearly two-thirds of its 2012 revenue. Comcast Cable provides cable television, broadband Internet and telephone service to customers in 40 states across the US, while NBC Universal is one of the country's four major television networks serving more than 200 affiliated stations.

NBC Universal is the result of a partnership between General Electric's NBC and Vivendi Universal Entertainment. In January 2011, Comcast acquired a controlling interest in the merged entity and two years later assumed full ownership. According to Comcast's CEO, the acquisition gives Comcast scale in content and distribution and creates additional value for the company (Comcast, 2013). The acquisition enables Comcast to reach a wide audience through a portfolio of 15 national cable networks, 11 regional sports and news networks that reach 39 million subscribers in key markets such as Boston, Chicago and San Francisco, the Spanish-language broadcast network *Telemundo* and more than 60 international channels. The company also owns and operates motion picture companies and branded theme parks.

Comcast engages in sport programming through its cable television networks, although its investment and commitment to sport is less than its US rivals. However, there are exceptions. NBC, a Comcast subsidiary, has held the American broadcasting rights to the Summer Olympics since Seoul 1988; NBC also paid US$4.38 billion for the rights to the 2014–2020 Olympic Games, making it the most expensive television rights deal in Olympic broadcast history (Crupi, 2011). The deal enables Comcast to leverage the Olympic Games as a valuable brand across its stable of television channels – channels as diverse as CNBC, Bravo, *Telemundo* and the NBC Sports Network – and means that NBC can proudly boast that it is 'America's Olympic Network'. NBC replicated this strategy in the acquisition of the exclusive English- and Spanish-language rights to the English Premier League and the Spanish-language rights to the FIFA World Cup. As a result, American soccer fans are able to tune into NBC, or NBC-owned subsidiaries, for all the live action.

## The Walt Disney Company

The Walt Disney Company (Disney) brand is synonymous with the image of Mickey Mouse. The company is famous for its theme parks in the United States, Europe and Asia, and as Law *et al.* (2002: 285) have noted: 'Disney entertainment products are rooted in American values and tradition'. These theme parks might be what Disney is associated with globally, however like the other major media players, Disney also has successfully diversified its business interests.

In his letter to shareholders as part of the Disney 2012 Annual Report, Chief Executive Officer Robert Iger referred to the company's three key strategic priorities: high-quality creative content, global expansion and application of new technology. These priorities are achieved through five primary business segments: media networks; parks and resorts; studio entertainment; consumer products; and interactive. According to Disney these collectively represent an 'amazing collection of some of the world's best media brands – Disney, ESPN, ABC, Pixar, Marvel, and now Lucasfilm – that provide enormous opportunities for us to continue to create high quality content and unparalleled experiences' (Walt Disney Company, 2013: 1).

According to the company's 2012 annual report, media networks are the largest driver of the company's performance and ESPN, the company's cable sports channel, is a key element of its success (Walt Disney Company, 2012). Media networks represented 46 per cent of the company's 2012 revenue, compared with 31 per cent and 14 per cent respectively, for parks and resorts and studio entertainment. Sport media content is distributed throughout the world by Disney's ESPN networks in Europe, Latin America and Asia. Sport programming through ESPN is one of the most important ways that Disney achieves its strategic priority of global expansion. Through ESPN, Disney has purchased the rights to a number of major sport properties, including the National Football Leagues (NFL), Major League Baseball (MLB), the National Association for Stock Car Auto Racing (NASCAR), the UEFA Champions League, the Wimbledon Championships and college football and basketball.

## News Corporation and Twenty-First Century Fox

News Corporation evolved from humble beginnings in Adelaide, Australia, to become a global media giant under the leadership of Rupert Murdoch. Along the way he acquired the Twentieth Century Fox movie studio, became an American citizen in order to establish the FOX Broadcasting Company, that country's fourth television network, and used sport to break into new markets. In News Corporation's 2005 Annual Report, Murdoch explained how the company had 'learned how to integrate our content and distribution assets into a seamless whole that allows us to get the most out of each individual asset – an attribute that further distinguishes us from our peers' (News Corporation, 2005: 5). This operational capacity – to engage in cross promotion so that no single product is isolated from its commercial siblings – is facilitated by media diversity. Many of the major players' operations feature a similar approach to media diversity.

News Corporation has historically divided its business into six corporate segments: filmed entertainment; television; cable network programming; direct broadcast satellite television; publishing; and 'other'. This last segment includes its digital media properties, education technology business and its investment in local sporting properties, such as the National Rugby League's (NRL) Brisbane Broncos. However, in a response to the changing media landscape, the company chose to split its assets into two publicly traded companies which would 'unlock more value for our stockholders and enable each company to better deliver on its promises to its customers across the globe' (News Corporation, 2013: 5). News Corporation now focuses on news, publishing and education, while the new Twenty-first Century Fox, with Rupert Murdoch at the helm, holds the media and entertainment properties.

Like Time Warner and Disney, News Corporation's filmed entertainment segment is important to its business; however, it differs substantially in its significant publishing holdings, which include more than 110 newspapers in Australia where the company began. According to News Corporation's 2012 Annual Report, publishing represented 24 per cent of consolidated revenue in 2012, behind filmed entertainment and television (36 per cent), and cable network programming (27 per cent). Despite the move to split its assets, News Corporation continues to place an emphasis on sport and it invests significant amounts through its FOX television network in the United States, BSkyB in the United

Kingdom, Sky Italia and Sky Deutschland in Europe, Fox Sports in Australia and STAR in Asia. In the US, News Corporation has rights agreements with the NFL, MLB and NASCAR that will last at least until 2021, while in the United Kingdom it holds the rights to one of the world's most valuable sport properties, the EPL. At the same time, it continues to invest aggressively in pay television, both in its battle with ESPN to be America's dominant sports network and for global growth. For example, in 2012 News Corporation acquired full control of Fox Sports Australia. Fox International Channels emerged as 'a major player in the global sports-rights market' (Sports Business, 2012) when it acquired pan-Asian sports broadcaster ESPN Star Sports, took a minority stake in Setanta Africa and launched Fox Sports Brasil.

## Time Warner

Like many of the world's largest media companies, Time Warner has diverse business interests across the media sector. In 2000, it announced plans to merge with America Online, the country's top internet company, to form AOL Time Warner, Inc. Media analysts celebrated the marriage between new media and old media, suggesting the merger was the ultimate in media convergence. Steve Case, then Chairman of AOL Time Warner said, 'we will lead the convergence of the media, entertainment, communications and Internet industries, and provide wide-ranging, innovative benefits for consumers' (Time Warner, 2001), yet within a decade the dot-com bubble had burst and the company had lost tens of billions of dollars in market value. Time Warner had spun off AOL and its cable communications division to focus on three core segments: networks, film and television entertainment and publishing.

According to Time Warner's 2012 Annual Report, networks contributed almost half of the company's total revenues in that year, followed by film and television entertainment at 42 per cent and publishing at 12 per cent (Time Warner, 2013). Time Warner achieves global distribution through all three segments; sport features most prominently in the networks and publishing segments. Time Warner publishes almost 100 magazines worldwide and all of Time Inc.'s US magazines, such as its signature sport publication, *Sports Illustrated*, are available as tablet editions. Time Warner's networks include TNT and TBS, which feature the NBA, MLB, the NCAA's March Madness and NASCAR in the United States, as well as CNN, a global news network.

In March 2013, Time Warner followed News Corporation's lead and announced plans to spin-off Time Inc., the nine-decade-old publisher of *Time*, *People* and *Sports Illustrated*. According to Chairman and CEO, Jeff Bewkes, the proposed move 'provides strategic clarity for Time Warner Inc., enabling us to focus entirely on our television networks and film and TV production businesses, and improves our growth profile' (Hagey and Peers, 2013). It is hoped that the move, like the spin-offs of Time Warner Cable and AOL, will create additional value for stockholders. As a result, Time Warner now divides the company into two distinct corporate segments: networks; and film and television entertainment. While sport still remains an important vehicle for Time Warner, its investment in sport media and sport broadcasting, in particular, is far less than either Disney or News Corporation.

### Vivendi

Vivendi is a French multinational media and telecommunications company that can trace its roots back to the mid-eighteenth century when it was a regional water utility that supplied Lyon, Venice and Paris. In 2000, Vivendi made headlines when it merged with the Canal+ television networks and acquired Universal Studios to become Vivendi Universal. The Universal assets were later sold to General Electric's NBC and Comcast. Vivendi now focuses on four core activities: television and cinema; music; telecommunications; and games. The television and cinema segment includes the Canal+ Group, which is the largest pay television provider in France, selling its services in 30 countries, including Africa, Poland and Vietnam; the segment also includes Studiocanal, a major film producer and distributor in Europe. Vivendi's Universal Music Group is the world leader in recorded music, music publishing and merchandising. Vivendi also owns telecommunication companies in France, Morocco and Brazil, and Activision Blizzard, Vivendi's games publishing arm, makes a significant contribution to the bottom line through best-selling franchises such as *Call of Duty* and *World of Warcraft*. In 2012, Vivendi's telecommunication activities delivered 54 per cent of consolidated revenue, followed by television and cinema, 17 per cent, music, 16 per cent and games, 13 per cent. These figures highlight the importance of the emerging market: 6 per cent of the company's 2012 revenue was derived from Vivendi's Brazilian telecommunications company, GVT, selling telephone, broadband and pay television services to customers in more than 119 Brazilian cities (Vivendi, 2013). Through Canal+, Vivendi enjoys the exclusive French rights to the English Premier League and Formula 1, while it shares the rights to the French National Football League, Ligue 1, with Al Jazeera's BeIN Sport.

## COMPARISONS AND CONNECTIONS

Television assets contributed at least 40 per cent of revenues for the top four media players, while media networks were critical in overall business strategy and development. Disney and News Corporation invest heavily in sport, as will be revealed in more detail in the following chapter, while sport is far less important for companies such as Comcast or Vivendi, in which telecommunications drive a significant proportion of overall revenue. As previously noted, Disney's parks and resorts business segment is unique; similarly, Vivendi's Music and Games are unique segments for that company within this cohort of key global media players.

Although these major players are in direct competition with one another, in particular in terms of network and cable television, publishing and filmed entertainment, there are often commercial partnerships that make the media landscape even more complex. For example, ESPN Star Sports used to be a 50:50 joint venture between Disney and News Corporation, and Yahoo has partnered with Comcast to collaborate on major sports news events and to jointly develop original sports programming for online distribution. According to Mark Lazarus, Chairman of NBC's Sports Group, such a complementary partnership 'dramatically expands the digital reach of NBC Sports around the biggest sporting events' (Strange, 2012).

## OTHER MEDIA PLAYERS

The major media players have a significant global presence, yet there are a host of other media companies that also have a significant role in the sport media nexus. Bertelsmann in Germany, Fininvest in Italy, CBS Corporation and the Fenway Sports Group in the United States, Rogers Communications in Canada, the Al Jazeera Media Network in Qatar, Comunicação e Participações S.A. (Globo) in Brazil and ITV in the United Kingdom are all important players in their respective sport media markets. Bertelsmann owns 92 per cent of the publicly listed RTL Group, which in 2012 comprised 54 television channels and 29 radio stations in ten countries throughout Europe. In 2012, RTL used these media outlets to broadcast 9,200 hours of television programming such as the European Football Championships. The Fininvest Group owns a number of media assets, including a digital television broadcasting network and television channels in Spain; in addition to its media properties it also owns the Serie A's A.C. Milan. CBS Corporation has more than 200 television stations in the US and through its CBS Sports Network televises 350 live games per year, as well as managing a network of websites for 215 university athletic departments. The Fenway Sports Group owns a majority stake in major regional cable television network, the New England Sports Network (NESN), and also owns MLB's Boston Red Sox and the Liverpool FC. Toronto-based Rogers Communications owns significant television, radio and telephone assets, as well as a stake in all of the city's sports properties. Al Jazeera began as an Arabic news channel in 1996 and over the years has expanded into sport, including the launch of the beIN Sport brand in France and the US in 2012. South America's largest media company, Globo, has been a FIFA broadcast partner since 1970. Al Jazeera and Globo have both secured the rights to broadcast the 2018 and 2022 FIFA World Cups to their respective markets: the Middle East and Brazil.

## THE MEDIA INDUSTRY

Profiling the ways in which the key media players are organized and structured is useful for developing a more generalized understanding of the media, as well as identifying the points at which sport and the media intersect. Figure 3.1 graphically represents the core business dimensions of the media industry: communication services, distribution and products. As the profiles of the major media players illustrate, typically, not all segments are fully represented in a single organization. The first dimension is providing communication services, such as telecommunications or internet/broadband access. In the case of internet/broadband access, the service enables consumers to access other products and services. Some of these products and services may be contained within websites owned or operated by the same media organization providing the communication service.

The second dimension is distribution, which comprises television, newspapers, radio, magazines and internet websites. These are the means of distributing media content. For the purposes of providing clarity in relation to the sport media nexus, this content is divided into two sub-sets: sport and non-sport. Sport content is the games, matches and events that media organizations bid for the rights to broadcast on television, radio and the internet, as well as cover in newspapers and magazines. Typically, sport content is

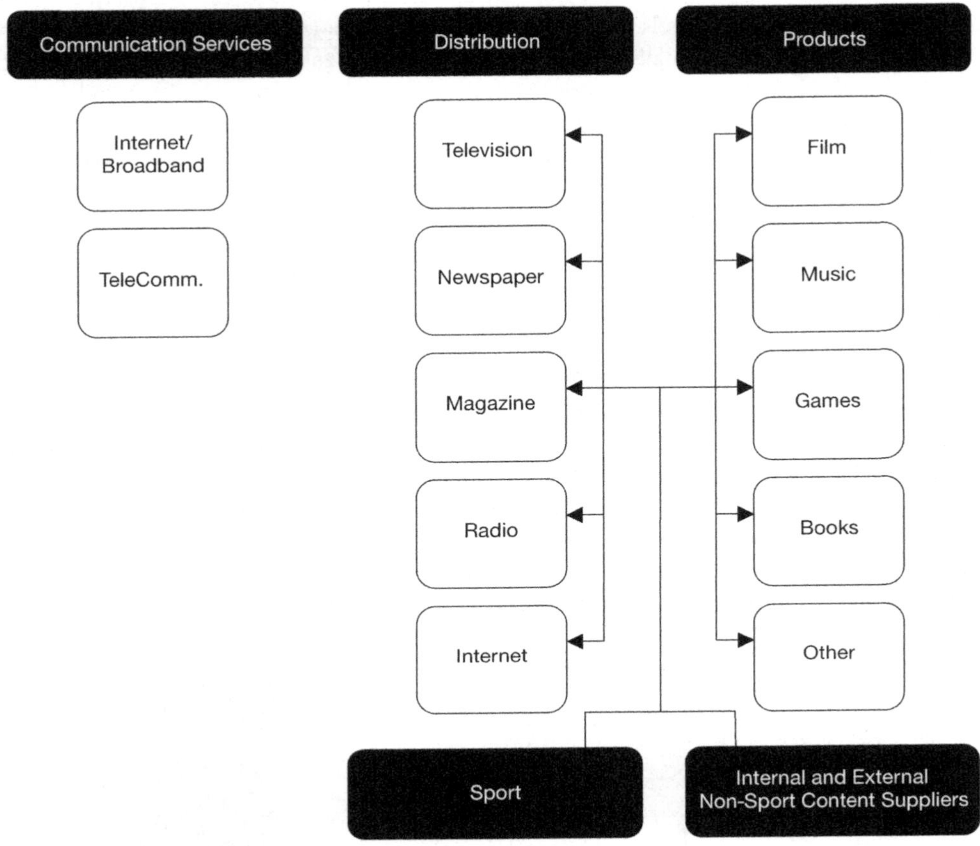


**FIGURE 3.1** Media industry organization

provided by an external party, or in other words, the sport organization providing the content is an independent entity. Sometimes, although not very often in the contemporary nexus, a sport organization is owned by a media organization that then plays a role in broadcasting it. Rosner (2010) explained that corporations see sport 'franchises' as entertainment assets that can generate revenue through media rights and allow ownership to exploit a wide range of synergies. For example, the Fenway Sports Group owns one of the most valuable brands in sport and a regional cable network allowing it to distribute valuable sport content to millions of fans. Although this strategy has worked to great effect for smaller players, some global media players have had less success in adopting the approach. For example, Manchester United was identified as a valuable asset for BSkyB but the acquisition was ultimately blocked by the British regulators. Many global media players have been unable to unlock these synergies and have sold down their investments in sport teams.

The third core business dimension of the media industry is its products. Products consist of film, music, games, books and 'other', which includes parks, resorts and

associated consumer products. The content associated with each can be produced via internal and external channels. For example, a media organization may produce films or studio entertainment internally for external distribution and sale, or it might contract external authors to provide manuscripts in order to produce books. Similarly, television drama might be produced internally by the media organization or it might be purchased from an external, independent production company. Sport content also services the products dimension, such as with licensed games or books, although it is a minor contributor relative to non-sport content.

Sport attracts audiences to the media's modes of distribution, but its importance is more clearly illustrated in Figure 3.2, which highlights horizontal and vertical integration as a way of producing a web of promotion. In Figure 3.2, a single media organization owns multiple distribution outlets. Sport content can be utilized by any distribution outlet in the web, and coverage of sport in one outlet in turn promotes the coverage via another outlet. Sport coverage in one outlet can also promote another outlet that does not cover sport, or non-sport content on the same outlet. Sometimes this occurs on the same horizontal plane – the same type of outlet, such as two television stations or programmes – and sometimes it occurs on the same vertical plane – two different outlet types, such as a newspaper and a magazine. In some countries media ownership laws restrict the amount of vertical and horizontal integration a media organization can achieve, as this can lead to a lack of media diversity. For example, if a media organization owns all the newspapers in a single city,

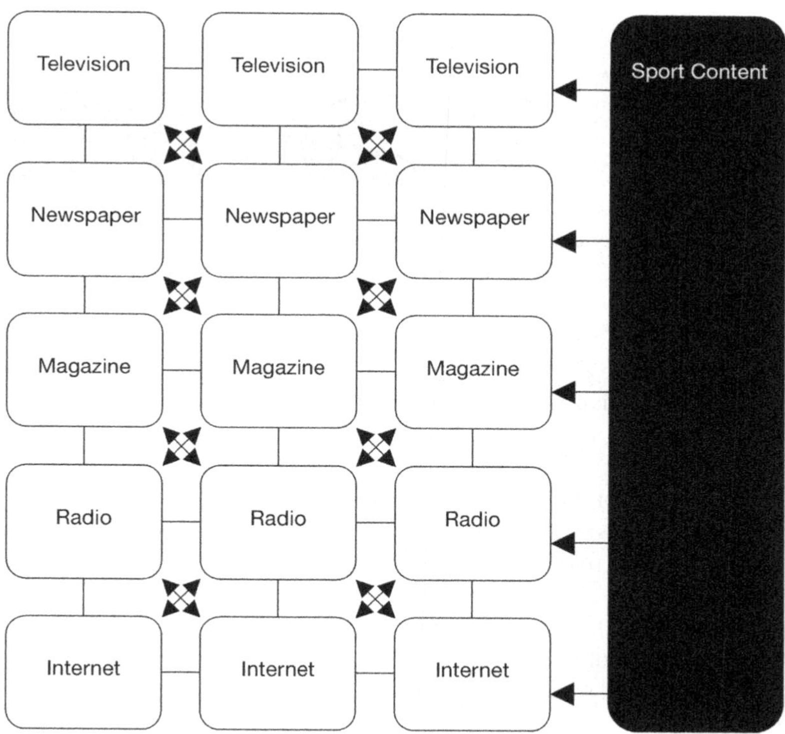


**FIGURE 3.2** Media integration and cross promotion

then it could cross-promote its activities, raise prices or use its news gathering infrastructure to service all its publications. The products represented in Figure 3.1 can also be promoted through horizontal and vertical integration. For example, a film produced internally within the media organization could be promoted during sport coverage on one of its television stations, or in one of its magazines.

## KEY SPORT PLAYERS

Like the media industry, there are also key players that dominate the sport industry and the sport media nexus. These sport organizations and their competitions have become valuable commercial properties; however, they are not spread evenly throughout the world and some sports have been more successful at capitalizing on the media's need for content and desire to increase audiences and revenue. The following sections provide thematic discussions of the key players in the sport industry.

## KING FOOTBALL

Depending on where you are in the world, the phrase football can take on a different meaning. In the southern states of Australia, it might mean Australian Rules football, in the United States of America, NFL (gridiron), or in most European and South American countries, it literally means football (soccer). Whatever the type, and wherever it is played, football in its various forms is a leader in the sport media nexus. Globally, football is considered by many fans to be a *lingua franca*, a shared language despite their cultural and linguistic differences. Different forms of football are played in more than 200 countries and in many of those it is the most popular spectator sport, for both live and mediated audiences. In some countries, such as the United States, New Zealand, Australia, South Africa, Canada and parts of the United Kingdom, an indigenous code is the dominant sport. For example, in Australia, Australian Rules football competes with rugby league, rugby union and soccer. Each of these football codes has a professional league and some are the top sports in Australia in terms of media revenue and overall popularity. Globally, each of these different football codes has an organization charged with governing it.

### FIFA

The Fédération Internationale de Football Association (FIFA) is the world governing body for football (soccer) and consists of six football confederations that span the globe: Africa, Asia, South America, North and Central America and the Caribbean, Europe, and Oceania. The history of FIFA's membership (countries), demonstrated in Table 3.2, illustrates the growth of the sport and the growing awareness of the sport outside Europe (FIFA, 2013). It is also indicative of FIFA's increasing political, economic and cultural power. FIFA's mission is to 'develop the game, touch the world, build a better future'; furthermore, it seeks to use the power of football 'to support local communities in the areas of peacebuilding, health, social integration, education and more' (FIFA, 2013). FIFA has more member states than the United Nations and recognizes non-sovereign states such

**TABLE 3.2** FIFA Membership by Confederation, 1904–2013

| | *1904* | *1925* | *1950* | *1975* | *1990* | *2013* |
|---|---|---|---|---|---|---|
| Europe | 8 | 28 | 32 | 35 | 36 | 53 |
| South America | 0 | 6 | 9 | 10 | 10 | 10 |
| North/Central America | 0 | 3 | 12 | 22 | 27 | 35 |
| Asia | 0 | 1 | 13 | 33 | 38 | 46 |
| Africa | 0 | 1 | 1 | 35 | 48 | 54 |
| Oceania | 0 | 0 | 1 | 4 | 8 | 11 |
| Total | 8 | 39 | 68 | 139 | 167 | 209 |

Source: www.fifa.com.

as Palestine and Denmark's Faroe Islands. The organization is responsible for one of the two biggest sporting events in the world, the FIFA World Cup, staged every four years.

As far as its media presence is concerned, FIFA has embraced multimedia in order to engage and communicate with football fans worldwide. During the 2010 FIFA World Cup more than 220,000 people followed FIFA on Twitter, while FIFA.com registered seven billion page views during the month-long tournament. The World Cup final was seen live by an estimated 700 million people and the in-home television coverage of the competition reached more than three billion worldwide. According to FIFA, the 2010 World Cup was:

> shown in every single country and territory on Earth and with an unprecedented level of TV production geared to serve screens of all shapes and sizes, it was also the first major sports event to be distributed globally across all platforms, namely TV, radio, mobile, broadband as well as in 3D.
>
> (FIFA, 2011)

In 2014, FIFA extended its multimedia offering and reported that 24 million unique users watched 15 million hours of content through FIFA's multimedia streams (FIFA, 2014). The FIFA World Cup mobile phone app was downloaded ten million times (FIFA, 2014). The event was also embraced on third-party channels such as social media sites Facebook and Twitter; Facebook claimed there were 3.5 billion interactions around the event via 350 million people, while Twitter reported 672 million tweets related to the 2014 FIFA World Cup, including 35.6 million for a single game (Frier, 2014).

## UEFA

Of all FIFA's confederations, Europe is the oldest and most powerful. The Union of European Football Associations (UEFA) is the governing body for football in Europe. Its core mission is to promote, protect and develop European football at every level of the game. The promotion component of its mission is largely achieved through the annual UEFA Champions League and the European Championship, held every four years in

between FIFA World Cups. A global television audience of 299 million viewers saw Spain defeat Italy in the Euro 2012 final (UEFA, 2012). As a result of massive television viewership, these events are valuable media properties; UEFA derives 75 per cent of its income from television revenue (UEFA, 2011).

## National football leagues

National football leagues are among the most powerful players in the sport media nexus, consistently providing regular content that secures a loyal audience and a price premium. The relative importance of the different forms football can be seen in Table 3.3 where

**TABLE 3.3** Most valuable sport team brands (2014)

| *Rank* | *Team* | *National league* | *Team value US$ billion* |
|---|---|---|---|
| 1 | Real Madrid | La Liga | 3.44 |
| 2 | Barcelona | La Liga | 3.2 |
| 3 | Manchester United | EPL | 2.81 |
| 4 | New York Yankees | MLB | 2.5 |
| 5 | Dallas Cowboys | NFL | 2.3 |
| 6 | Los Angeles Dodgers | MLB | 2 |
| 7 | Bayern Munich | Bundesliga | 1.85 |
| 8 | New England Patriots | NFL | 1.8 |
| 9 | Washington Redskins | NFL | 1.7 |
| 10 | New York Giants | NFL | 1.55 |
| 11 | Boston Red Sox | MLB | 1.5 |
| 12 | Houston Texans | NFL | 1.45 |
| 13 | New York Knicks | NBA | 1.4 |
| 14 | New York Jets | NFL | 1.38 |
| 15 | Los Angeles Lakers | NBA | 1.35 |
| 16 | Arsenal | EPL | 1.331 |
| 17 | Philadelphia Eagles | NFL | 1.314 |
| 18 | Chicago Bears | NFL | 1.252 |
| 19 | Baltimore Ravens | NFL | 1.227 |
| 20 | San Francisco 49ers | NFL | 1.224 |
| 21 | Chicago Cubs | MLB | 1.2 |
| 22 | Ferrari | Motorsport | 1.2 |
| 23 | Indianapolis Colts | NFL | 1.2 |
| 24 | Green Bay Packers | NFL | 1.183 |
| 25 | Denver Broncos | NFL | 1.161 |

Source: www.forbes.com.

21 of the sport teams with a market value of US$1 billion play football in one of its forms. The English (Premier League), Spanish (Liga Nacional de Fútbol Profesional or La Liga), Italian (Serie A) and German (Bundesliga) leagues are the most popular football leagues and the National Football League in the United States has also been a dominant player in the sport media nexus since the 1950s. The J-League and K-League are prominent in Japan and South Korea, respectively. In South Africa and New Zealand, rugby union's dominance is partly achieved through the successful Super Rugby (Super 15) competition, which includes teams from each of the countries and Australia. The northern hemisphere also has a Six Nations rugby union tournament that is popular as a live and mediated product, while rugby league is a popular product on both free-to-air and pay television in parts of England, New Zealand and Australia.

## OTHER SPORT PLAYERS

Although football in all its various forms remains the undisputed leader, there are other sport players that have a significant global presence or are developing considerable interest worldwide. For example, popular team sports such as basketball, cricket, baseball and softball have a role to play in the sport media nexus.

### FIBA

The Fédération Internationale de Basketball (FIBA) is the world governing body for basketball and has 213 national federations as members from five zones: Africa, Americas, Asia, Europe and Oceania. Although it has been developing and promoting the game since 1932, FIBA's mission was expanded in 2011 to 'bring people together and unite the community' (FIBA, 2013). FIBA organized the first World Championship in 1950 and now holds these events every four years, alternating with the Olympic Games. In 1989, the decision was made to allow professional players to participate in Olympic competitions and subsequently the US Dream Team, featuring the likes of Michael Jordan, Magic Johnson, Larry Bird and Charles Barkley, won gold at Barcelona '92. According to FIBA, over 450 million people play the game and it has the potential to surpass football worldwide (FIBA, 2013). The National Basketball Association (NBA) in the US is the world's most prominent basketball league and drives much of the sport's popularity internationally. As such, the case of basketball is interesting because the promotion of the sport is shared by a dominant national league and an international governing body.

### ICC

The International Cricket Council (ICC) is the world governing body for cricket. Although membership was originally limited to the governing bodies of cricket in countries within the British Empire to which cricket teams were sent, or which sent teams to England, the ICC now has 106 members from Africa, the Americas, Asia, East Asia-Pacific and Europe (ICC, 2013). There are ten full members, including England, Australia, New Zealand, India and Pakistan, which are qualified to play official Test matches, with associate and affiliate members limited to other forms of the game.

## IN PRACTICE 3.1

### Surf's up! The ASP world tour goes online

Surfing is a sport that is heavily dependent upon the natural conditions; in this respect it is unlike many other sports that are able to specify a broadcast date and time and are able to play despite the conditions, for example, a football match where the players will play in any conditions or basketball where the conditions are static. Most major surfing competitions are scheduled over approximately ten days, a time frame which is necessary to allow for highly variable conditions. In these competitions it is not unusual for competitors and event organizers to spend a number of days waiting for the waves to reach an acceptable height to start, resume or finish the competition. This unpredictability means that a surfing competition is not an ideal product for live broadcasting.

Live television broadcasting relies largely on predictability, as sport programmes need to go to air when they are scheduled and viewers have come to expect programming to reliably conform to their expectations of a mediated sport experience. A season based on weekly competition, where teams play in all types of weather, fair or foul, means that football is an excellent television product that suits rights holders and broadcasters very well. On the other hand, surfing is more problematic and has had to develop a broadcast strategy that is in line with the unpredictable nature and length of its competition format, as well as the commercial and cultural environment in which surfing consumers and sponsors operate.

The Association of Surfing Professionals (ASP) has been the governing body for surfing since 1983 and, among its functions, manages the world tours for men, women and juniors. Like tennis and golf, surfing is a global circuit; the men's and women's tours visit places such as French Polynesia, Fiji, Indonesia, Brazil, Portugal, Hawaii, Australia and France. Highlights of the competition are shown throughout the world on news and sport programmes, while highlight programmes are produced following the tournament and broadcast to a global audience on television.

The unusual aspect of surfing circuit's place in the sport media nexus is that it used to rely to a large degree on sponsors, not media organizations, to broadcast its product. Up until the 2014 season, the title sponsor of the event would host a webcast of each event. In 2014 the ASP Tour underwent significant change, when it was bought by US independent media company Zo-Sea. With some sponsors undergoing difficulties in the wake of the global financial crisis, it was seen as the best way forward to ensure the future of the sport. The new owners helped to establish a new media distribution deal. American broadcaster ESPN would be the exclusive US broadcaster, but the major announcement was that all events would be streamed live and free on YouTube. The ASP World Tour stated:

> The ASP YouTube channel, along with the rebuilt ASP website which will embed this content via the YouTube player, will exclusively provide fans with more than 3,000 hours of programming, including 26 live streamed events annually across the men's ASP World Championship Tour (WCT), the women's

> ASP WCT and the ASP Big Wave World Tour (BWWT). For the first time in the sport's history, the ASP YouTube channel will enable fans around the world to go to one global destination to view surfing digitally.

The ASP World Tour also announced that they would work with Facebook, and its other social media network Instagram, to ensure a new level of connectedness to fans. While the ASP World Tour is not one of the major players in the sport media nexus in terms of rights value, its process of broadcasting its own events – and how it moved to ensure this would still happen despite the transition away from sponsor hosted webcasts – shows that it is one of the most innovative.

Source: www.aspworldtour.com.

Unlike other sports that have a single format, cricket has a number of variations (Stewart, 1995). The oldest version is 'Test' cricket, which sees countries compete for five days in daylight, with approximately six hours of play each day, depending on weather conditions. In one-day cricket, which began in England in the early 1960s, teams are each allowed an innings of 50 overs (six balls are bowled per over), games are often played at night under lights, and players wear coloured clothing instead of the traditional all-white. In the twenty-first century, another form of cricket emerged in England: Twenty20. In this format of the game, teams are allowed only 20 overs each and games last about three hours bringing them more in line with other team sports. Although the equipment and number of players is the same in each of the three variations of cricket, there are differences in the rules, ostensibly to make the two shorter versions of the game more attractive to spectators.

As part of the ICC's mission, the global game is promoted and 'major' events are delivered across these three formats (ICC, 2013). As a result, the body is responsible for the game's major international tournaments, including the Test Championship (to be held for the first time in 2017), the Cricket World Cup and the World Twenty20. Furthermore, the popularity of the shortened game has seen many ICC members introduce domestic Twenty20 competitions, such as India's IPL or Australia's Big Bash League, and some have called for its inclusion in future Olympic Games. In the last decade, the ICC has set up new headquarters in Dubai and continues to combat such issues as match-fixing, player conduct, the use of floodlights in Test matches, and the challenge of balancing three diverse forms of the game so as to 'inspire people of every age, gender, background and ability while building bridges between continents, countries and communities' (ICC, 2013).

# MAJOR EVENTS

## Olympic Games

The Olympic Games, organized and managed by the IOC, is one of the most recognizable global events. The American and European markets continue to be the most profitable, as will be demonstrated in the following chapter, and its worldwide popularity has

historically been fuelled by the principle that broadcasting agreements are based on free-to-air coverage. For example, members of the European Broadcasting Union have shown the Olympics on free-to-air television since 1956 in part because its 75 members reach the most viewers (Gilmour, 2008). This has resulted in more than US$10.5 billion in broadcast rights deals from 1998 to 2012 alone, but has also meant that the majority of the world's population has been able to access the event for free. The inability to gain additional revenues through pay television rights deals has been offset through significant sponsorship deals with global brands such as Coca-Cola, General Electric, Proctor & Gamble, McDonalds and Visa. These brands and products have further contributed to the increased global awareness of the Olympic Games. However, the IOC has begun to maximize revenue from broadcast rights and bypass free-to-air television in favour of more lucrative bids by pay television operators.

Although not as popular or as profitable as the Olympic Games, events such as the Asian Games, the Pan-American Games and the Commonwealth Games also generate significant media attention in the countries competing in the events. Annual events, such as the Tour de France, are also attractive as global media events. Some national leagues, such as the NFL in the US, are so popular that the championship game can be considered a major event. The NFL's Super Bowl has been played since 1967 and is the most-watched annual sports event in the United States. The past few years have seen more than 100 million viewers tune in to the spectacle and it attracts premium advertising rates as a result.

## Sport circuits

Sporting circuits are another segment in the collection of sport's major players. Tennis, golf and surfing are prominent examples of global or regional circuits that attract significant media coverage. For example, in 2013 the Association of Tennis Professionals (ATP) World Tour for men held 62 tournaments in 32 countries (the Grand Slams are not ATP events), while the Women's Tennis Association (WTA) Tour held 54 events in 33 countries. The WTA tour is the most prominent professional sport for women in the world and in 2012 more than 2,500 players, representing 92 nations, competed for more than US$100 million in prize money (WTA, 2013). In addition, the events that make up tennis' Grand Slam – the Australian Open, French Open, Wimbledon and the US Open – are major events that capture significant media coverage.

Similarly, the global circuits for golf and surfing are also popular media properties. Male and female golfers compete on both the American and European tours, which have affiliated events throughout the world. For men, the US Open, US PGA, US Masters and British Open are the major events that attract significant media coverage. Professional surfers compete in the Association of Surfing Professionals World Professional Tour (ASP World Tour) sanctioned events in exotic locations all over the world. Because of the prominence and popularity of individual tennis players, golfers and surfers, these circuits are popular global products and feature on both free-to-air and pay television. The insatiable appetite for sports programming has even seen the emergence of global circuits in mixed martial arts and so-called 'extreme' sports with the expansion of ESPN's popular X Games concept.

## IN PRACTICE 3.2

### FOX enters the cage with the Ultimate Fighting Championship

The Ultimate Fighting Championship (UFC) started in the US in 1993 as a competition to determine the most effective martial art for unarmed combat situations. With minimal rules – fighters must either knock out their opponent, get their opponent to submit, or fight the best they can to be judged the victor – the UFC is a battle of various fighting styles, including karate, jiu-jitsu, boxing, kickboxing, wrestling and other combat sports. This blend of fighting styles and skills, known as mixed martial arts (MMA), sees contenders in weight classes from flyweight to heavyweight enter the field of battle, a 70 square metre cage known as 'The Octagon'.

As the sport implemented rule changes to better protect fighters, the UFC evolved into a more fan-friendly television product. In 2005, Spike TV unveiled a new reality television series, *The Ultimate Fighter*, to help the UFC generate exposure for mixed martial arts. The show introduced MMA to millions of Americans who were unfamiliar with the sport, helped fuel its popularity and made household names of fighters such as Randy Couture and Tito Ortiz. The UFC also pioneered the use of social networking site Facebook to give fans free access to selected fights and to connect with its audience.

In 2011, the UFC burst into the mainstream with a landmark seven-year broadcast agreement with the FOX network. The UFC deal saw the mixed martial arts series carried on FOX, with thousands of hours of programming on its subsidiaries, FX and Fuel TV. According to UFC President Dana White, 'We're excited to be part of the FOX family. I've always said that the UFC will be the biggest sport in the world, and with this relationship it will become a reality' (Fox Sports, 2014). The decision was soon taken to extend the agreement to its Fox Sports 1 sports network and to other markets through Foxtel in Australia and Fox Sports Latin America.

The deal will deliver FOX the much coveted young male demographic, a market that is typically difficult to reach. For example, FOX's sixth Ultimate Fighting Championship 'delivered a knock-out blow to the network's prime time competition' (Fox Sports, 2014) and won the battle for the nation's adult male viewers when 5.2 million Americans tuned in to see flyweight Demetrious 'Mighty Mouse' Johnson defend his title (Fox Sports, 2014). In early 2013, the UFC made history when two-time Olympian Ronda Rousey took on Liz Carmouche to become the first women to fight in The Octagon. After becoming the UFC's first female champion, Rousey defended the sport against those who question the MMA's meteoric rise: 'It's not some barbaric spectacle, it really is an art, and that's why the word 'art' is in it' (UFC, 2013).

In the early days critics labelled the UFC 'human cockfighting', and the major cable companies refused to carry its events; however, the UFC is now the fastest growing sport organization in the world. It has its own line of licensed DVDs, video games, merchandise, trading cards, and streams live event broadcasts and video on demand. The UFC hosts more than 30 fights each year in locations as diverse as London, Stockholm, Tokyo and Rio de Janeiro and is the largest pay-per-view event provider in the world, accessible to nearly one billion homes worldwide.

Sources: www.ufc.com; www.mmawild.com.

### Motor sport

Although most of the world's major motor sports operate as sport circuits, it is worth considering them as a specific segment in order to establish their importance in the sport media nexus. Formula 1 (F1) racing is one of the most popular television sports in the world, in part because it travels to a significant number of countries. The F1 circuit includes Grand Prix events in Australia, Malaysia, Bahrain, China, Spain, Monaco, Canada, Austria, Great Britain, Germany, Hungary, Belgium, Italy, Singapore, Japan, Russia, US, Mexico, Brazil and Abu Dhabi. Formula 1 is broadcast in Europe on RTL, Canal+ and Sky Sports, on the BBC and Sky Sports F1, a dedicated F1 channel, in Great Britain and NBC Sports in the US.

The World Rally Championship (WRC), the second most prominent motor sport circuit, also holds events across the globe: Monte-Carlo, Sweden, Mexico, Argentina, Portugal, Italy, Poland, Finland, Germany, Australia, France, Spain and Great Britain. Both the WRC and F1 are centred in Europe, but events are increasingly being held in emerging markets such as Asia, Latin America and the Middle East. A domestic circuit, the NASCAR, comes in second in television ratings in the United States, beaten only by NFL. NASCAR manages 36 races across the country, including the iconic Daytona 500, in the NASCAR Sprint Cup Series, the premier competition. Telecast on major television networks, NASCAR claims it has a fan base of 75 million people and is seeking to increase its popularity in international markets with an increase in the number of foreign drivers and exhibition races in Japan and Canada.

## THE GLOBAL SPORT MEDIA INDUSTRY

Profiles of the major sport players in the sport media nexus reveal that media organizations value content that can deliver large national and global audiences. Recalling the three dimensions of the media industry – communication services, distribution and products – this chapter has shown that sport content that is able to secure widespread distribution is valuable. However, even more valuable sport content is that which can be effectively utilized through vertical and horizontal integration across distribution outlets and between distribution and products. The most valuable sport content, such as the FIFA World Cup, the Olympic Games or national football leagues, is able to draw large audiences into a web of media consumption, rather than an isolated mediated sport experience.

## SUMMARY

This chapter has examined the sport media nexus at global and national levels by examining the special characteristics of the media and sport industries. In particular, this chapter profiled key media and sport players, which facilitated generalizations about the way in which both industries operate. This chapter also highlighted the dominance of particular sports and their importance to the media as content that is able to penetrate and leverage new markets around the world. Review questions and exercises are listed below to assist with confirming your knowledge of the core concepts and principles introduced in this chapter.

## REVIEW QUESTIONS AND EXERCISES

1 Does the media provide entertainment, information or education in its coverage of sport?
2 Why is sport an important asset for the world's largest media organizations?
3 Which organization is the most important sport media player in the world? Why?
4 Which media organizations are dominant in your country of origin? Are there many major players or only a few? What is the impact of this diversity or lack thereof?
5 Which business segments are important to these organizations? How important is sport to these segments?
6 What proportion of the major television stations and newspapers in your city or nation are owned by one of the major media players profiled in this chapter?
7 What impact does the ownership referred to in the previous question have on content?
8 Do any of the media organizations in your nation have commercial interests as owners or part owners of professional sport teams? If so, what impact does this have on content?
9 What proportion of all sport broadcast rights fees in your nation are paid to the football codes?
10 Were the highest rating sport broadcasts in your nation or state last year local or global? Were they based on the seasonal, circuit or event model?

## FURTHER READING

Andrews, D. L. (2003) Sport and the transnationalizing media corporation. *The Journal of Media Economics, 16* (4), 235–251.

Falcous, M. and Maguire, J. (2006) Imagining 'America': The NBA and local–global mediascapes. *International Review for the Sociology of Sport, 41* (1), 59–78.

Frost, L. (2004) Globalisation and the future of indigenous football codes. *Economic Papers, 23* (4), 355–368.

Gerrard, B. (2006) Media ownership of pro sports teams: Who are the winners and losers? *International Journal of Sports Marketing and Sponsorship, 2*, 199–218.

Klein, A. (2003) *Stealing Time: Steve Case, Jerry Levin, and the Collapse of AOL Time Warner.* New York: Simon & Schuster.

Law, A., Harvey, J. and Kemp, S. (2002) The global sport mass media oligopoly: The three usual suspects and more. *International Review for the Sociology of Sport, 37* (3–4), 279–302.

Rowe, D. and Gilmour, C. (2008) Contemporary media sport: De- or re-westernization? *International Journal of Sport Communication, 1*, 177–194.

Rumford, C. (2007) More than a game: Globalization and the post-Westernization of world cricket. *Global Networks, 7* (2), 202–214.

Smith, A. F. and Hollihan, K. (2009) *ESPN the Company: The Story and Lessons Behind the Most Fanatical Brand in Sports.* Hoboken, NJ: John Wiley & Sons.

Wertheim, L. J. (2009) *Blood in the Cage: Mixed Martial Arts, Pat Miletich, and the Furious Rise of the UFC*. New York: Houghton Mifflin Harcourt Publishing.

# RELEVANT WEBSITES

## Americas

Comcast – http://corporate.comcast.com
The Walt Disney Company – www.thewaltdisneycompany.com
ESPN, Inc. – www.espn.com
News Corporation – www.newscorporation.com
Time Warner – www.timewarner.com
National Collegiate Athletic Association – www.ncaa.org
X Games – www.xgames.com
Super Bowl – www.superbowl.com

## Australia, New Zealand and South Africa

Super Rugby – www.sanzarrugby.com/superrugby
Big Bash League – www.bigbash.com.au

## Asia

J-League – www.j-league.or.jp
Indian Premier League – www.iplt20.com

## Europe

Vivendi – www.vivendi.com
Union of European Football Associations – www.uefa.com
English Premier League – www.premierleague.com
Liga Nacional de Fútbol Profesional – www.ligabbva.com
Serie A – www.legaseriea.it
Bundesliga – www.bundesliga.com

## Global

Fédération Internationale de Football Association – www.fifa.com
International Olympic Committee – www.olympic.org
Fédération Internationale de Basketball – www.fiba.com
International Cricket Council – www.icc-cricket.com
International Baseball Federation – www.ibaf.org
International Softball Federation – www.isfsoftball.org
Association of Tennis Professionals World Tour – www.atpworldtour.com
PGA Tour – www.pgatour.com
Association of Surfing Professionals World Tour – www.aspworldtour.com
Ultimate Fighting Championship – www.ufc.com
Formula 1 – www.formula1.com
National Association for Stock Car Auto Racing – www.nascar.com

CASE STUDY

## The Evolution of ESPN, the 'Worldwide Leader in Sports'

This case examines the evolution of ESPN from a regional sport channel to a multimedia, multinational sport and entertainment brand worth nearly US$12 billion. A tale stranger than fiction – in which a father and son team maxed out their credit cards to launch a network that would one day entertain viewers in more than 200 countries – is worthy of a *SportsCenter* special all of its own.

Early in 1978, Bill Rasmussen was fired as the communications director for the New England Whalers, now the Carolina Hurricanes in the NHL. Although discouraged by this turn of events, Rasmussen saw this as an opportunity to explore a new dream, the creation of a regional cable television network that would cover Connecticut sports. Together with his son, Scott, and insurance salesman Ed Eagan, Rasmussen created the Entertainment and Sports Programming Network (ESPN).

Cable television was well established in the US, yet satellite technology had emerged as a new alternative to transmit programming to cable operators. RCA had successfully launched satellites in Europe and was eager to promote the technology in America. On discovering that satellites could transmit ESP's signal across the entire country, and that it was cheaper to rent satellite time for an entire day, the decision was made to offer 24/7 sport programming on a national basis. Rasmussen used his remaining credit; the trio scraped together the funds to hire sportscasters and bought a parcel of land in Bristol, Connecticut, which would become the network's spiritual home. Rasmussen decided that a four letter acronym would help to distinguish the channel from its rivals and help it to attract more sponsors, and so 'ESPN' was born. For Bill Rasmussen, ESPN was no longer a dream.

History was made on the night of 7 September 1979 when an estimated 30,000 viewers tuned in to the launch of ESPN and the debut of *SportsCenter*; since then ESPN's signature show has logged more than 50,000 episodes. On that night, courtesy of a satellite uplink over Hawaii, Anchor Lee Leonard welcomed 'sports junkies' across the nation with the words, 'If you love sports . . . if you really love sports, you'll think you've died and gone to sports heaven' (Rasmussen, 2010: 15). Such enthusiasm is consistent with the company's mission statement today: 'To serve sports fans wherever sports are watched, listened to, discussed, debated, read about or played' (ESPN, 2013). Anheuser-Busch, a major brewing company in the US and owners of the Budweiser brand among others, saw how a channel devoted to sport could reach beer drinkers and bought US$1.4 million worth of advertising, a record at the time for cable television.

Despite its early success, ESPN struggled to fill the 8,760 hours per year required to realize Rasmussen's dream of a 24/7 network. As a result, the channel served up a motley assortment of sports programming from around the world, including hurling from Ireland, tractor pulls and Australian Rules football. The latter were simply tapes of Australian broadcasts that helped to fill the schedule. Yet there were hints of the greatness yet to come as ESPN televised several New England Whaler and

Washington Capitol games and the NFL Draft on ESPN was born. Although ESPN was not in a financial position to compete for the rights to the major US professional leagues, it reached a two-year deal with the National Collegiate Athletic Association (NCAA) to broadcast a wide range of collegiate sports, including lacrosse, baseball, football and basketball. Every game of the NCAA's March Madness in 1980 not televised by NBC was on ESPN, catching the attention of sports fans nationwide. This contract was instrumental in the success of the network, especially as many viewers called their cable operator to find out how they could get 'that channel that has all the basketball' (Miller and Shales, 2011: 23).

Although ESPN was well on its way to becoming an established sports network, the fledgling brand had gone through US$25 million in only its first seven months of operation and desperately needed additional revenue streams beyond advertising. An innovative solution was proposed: rather than provide programming for free, which was then standard practice in the industry, cable operators were charged a small monthly fee per subscriber. ESPN management was able to convince the major cable companies that without this fee the network would not survive. As a result, ESPN received six cents per subscriber that gradually increased to 10 cents by 1985 (and US$5.13 by 2013). The practice still exists today and can be seen in pay television bills around the world, especially when ESPN announces a major rights extension and passes along some of the increased costs to cable and satellite operators that carry its channel.

Not only did ESPN survive, it prospered, and by the end of 1983 it was cable's largest network with nearly 30 million households; it was acquired by the American Broadcasting Company (ABC) in 1984. This development provided the financial foundation for the network's growth. ESPN began broadcasting Thursday and Saturday night college football games; in 1987 ESPN began the first of nearly 20 years of *Sunday Night Football* and televised the NFL draft to the masses. The US$153 million deal enabled ESPN to become the first cable network to achieve 50 per cent penetration in the US television market and it was able to add an additional 'NFL surcharge' to cable operators. It was during this time that ESPN also landed major contracts with the NHL and MLB, but the network only truly became part of the national psyche when it broadcast the 1986–87 America's Cup finals, which saw Americans host parties and gather in bars to cheer on Team USA's Stars & Stripes 87.

During this period, ESPN also underwent international expansion. The company began distributing programming overseas in 1983 and launched a redesigned Eurosport in partnership with local broadcasters TF1 and Canal+. The company created ESPN International five years later in order to launch networks in foreign markets; it introduced ESPN Latin America in 1989 and ESPN Asia in 1992. This period of international expansion was consolidated with aggressive investment in the domestic market. In 1991, the ESPN Radio Network was launched and featured 16 hours of programming per week; two years later, ESPN2, a second sports channel, which targeted a younger demographic, began transmission. However, as ESPN became part of the global Disney empire, it was in the mid 1990s that it made perhaps its most innovative move: the creation and development of the Extreme Games.

Disney, under the leadership of Michael Eisner, became a major player in the sport media nexus during the 1990s. In 1995, the company acquired Capital Cities/ABC for US$19 billion and, by doing so, took control of 'the worldwide leader in sports'. ESPN's inaugural Extreme Games event drew 200,000 fans, provided more than 60 hours of content for ESPN and ESPN2 and went a long way towards legitimizing action sports and enhancing ESPN's brand appeal. A year later, the event had changed its name to the Summer X Games and delivered more than 35 hours of content for ESPN. Such was its success, the Winter X Games was introduced in 1997, spawning a range of successful merchandising tie-ins; all advertising inventory for the events – events that often featured new tricks such as Tony Hawk's '900' – soon sold out.

The late 1990s saw Disney further integrate ESPN and ABC Sports into its business empire, although both brands would remain distinct and separate divisions. Disney created *Sports Night*, an ABC sitcom modelled on ESPN's *SportsCenter*, which ran for two seasons from 1998–2000. The company committed to new long-term contracts with the NFL: ABC retained *Monday Night Football*, while ESPN expanded its Sunday night coverage. Disney also acquired the Classic Sports Network with its four million subscribers as well as launching *ESPN: The Magazine* and a chain of ESPN Zone restaurants to complement the ESPN family that by now included ESPN, ESPN2 and ESPNEWS.

However, all was not right in the Magic Kingdom, as Disney (and ESPN) was by now facing serious competition from Murdoch's News Corporation (and Fox Sports). By the late 1990s, Disney had made two significant sport property investments in southern California – the Mighty Ducks of Anaheim in the NHL and MLB's Anaheim Angels – while continuing ESPN's tradition of innovation. The network developed the 'Skycam' in 1998, followed that up with the yellow 'First and Ten Line' which is now ubiquitous in American football broadcasts, and won an Emmy Award for its *Sunday Night Baseball* K-Zone in 2001. Not to be outdone, News Corporation bought the Los Angeles Dodgers and introduced innovations such as FoxTrax, a specially designed ice hockey puck that had a comet-like trail to help television viewers keep track of the action. Fox Sports also adopted a regional approach to sports programming in which it customized its broadcasts for each local market, giving ESPN significant competition for advertising dollars.

As we fast forward, it appears not much has changed. According to Disney's annual report, most sports fans in America are watching ESPN and whether they are consuming the product on television, online via a computer or on a hand-held device, the brand remains the world's undisputed leader in sports programming. ESPN has become a multimedia, multinational brand that operates eight 24-hour domestic television sports networks including ESPN, ESPN2, ESPNEWS, ESPN Classic, ESPN Deportes and ESPN 3D; it also owns 27 international sports networks in more than 200 countries and has won nearly 150 Emmy Awards for excellence.

Despite ESPN's dominance in many of the markets in which it operates there remain significant obstacles to overcome, namely the high cost of rights fees and News Corporation's ambitions for a national sports network. At least for now, ESPN welcomes the competition: 'we like our position and the fact that others recognize

what we've known for a long-time, which is the power of live sports' (Cohen, 2013). ESPN has evolved from one man's dream to become, arguably, the 'worldwide leader in sports' with significant brands such as SportsCenter and the X Games. Whatever the future may hold, Bill Rasmussen has forever changed the way we watch sport.

## CASE STUDY QUESTIONS

1 ESPN was the brainchild of an out-of-work hockey announcer who had a dream of a 24/7 cable sports network. Given the global sport media nexus, is it likely that we will ever see another company like ESPN emerge?

2 News Corporation has announced plans for a national sports channel designed to rival ESPN. Given what you have read in this case, do you see News Corporation as a viable threat?

3 The Walt Disney Company has established three strategic priorities designed to position the company for future growth and deliver value to shareholders. How might the ESPN brand contribute to Disney's strategic direction for the future?

4 ESPN is formally known as the Entertainment and Sports Programming Network and provides a daily fix for 'sports junkies' in nearly 200 countries. Although it televises such popular events as the ESPY Awards, an event created by ESPN to recognize for Excellence in Sports Performance yearly, is the network true to its name?

Sources: Rasmussen (2010); Miller and Shales (2011); www.espn.com.

CHAPTER 4

# Broadcast rights and revenue

## Putting up big numbers

## OVERVIEW

This chapter examines the commercial relationship between the sport and media industries and the ways in which money drives the sport media nexus. The right to broadcast sporting events is an extremely valuable asset for media companies and, increasingly, non-traditional players such as telecommunication providers. This chapter will explore how companies secure the broadcast rights for these properties. This chapter also investigates the ways in which sport and media organizations attempt to leverage their audiences in order to achieve greater revenues, primarily through advertising and sponsorship.

## LEARNING OUTCOMES

After completing this chapter, the reader should be able to:

- identify and explain the commercial relationships between sport, the media, sponsors, advertisers and consumers;
- describe the process by which sport and media organizations sell and purchase the rights to broadcast sport via media;
- understand why media organizations and, in some instances, non-media rivals, seek to acquire the rights to broadcast sport; and
- explain the rationale behind segmenting rights in order to maximize revenue and how sport and media organizations use each other to increase revenue through advertising and sponsorship.

## INTRODUCTION

The evolution of the sport media nexus, its strength, and the global power and influence of both of its component industries, has largely been driven by money. The media coverage of sport has become the central means by which sport organizations obtain revenue, while sport has become one of the most valuable properties for media organizations.

The importance of sport is such that major national broadcasters almost always bid for the rights to high profile sports (Hoehn and Lancefield, 2003). In fact, the rights to broadcast premium sports have become such an important commercial asset that not having them can adversely impact a media organization's bottom line or, in extreme cases, lead to the demise of the company. The way in which the commercial dimension of the sport media nexus operates can be divided into five interrelated components, which are represented in Figure 4.1.

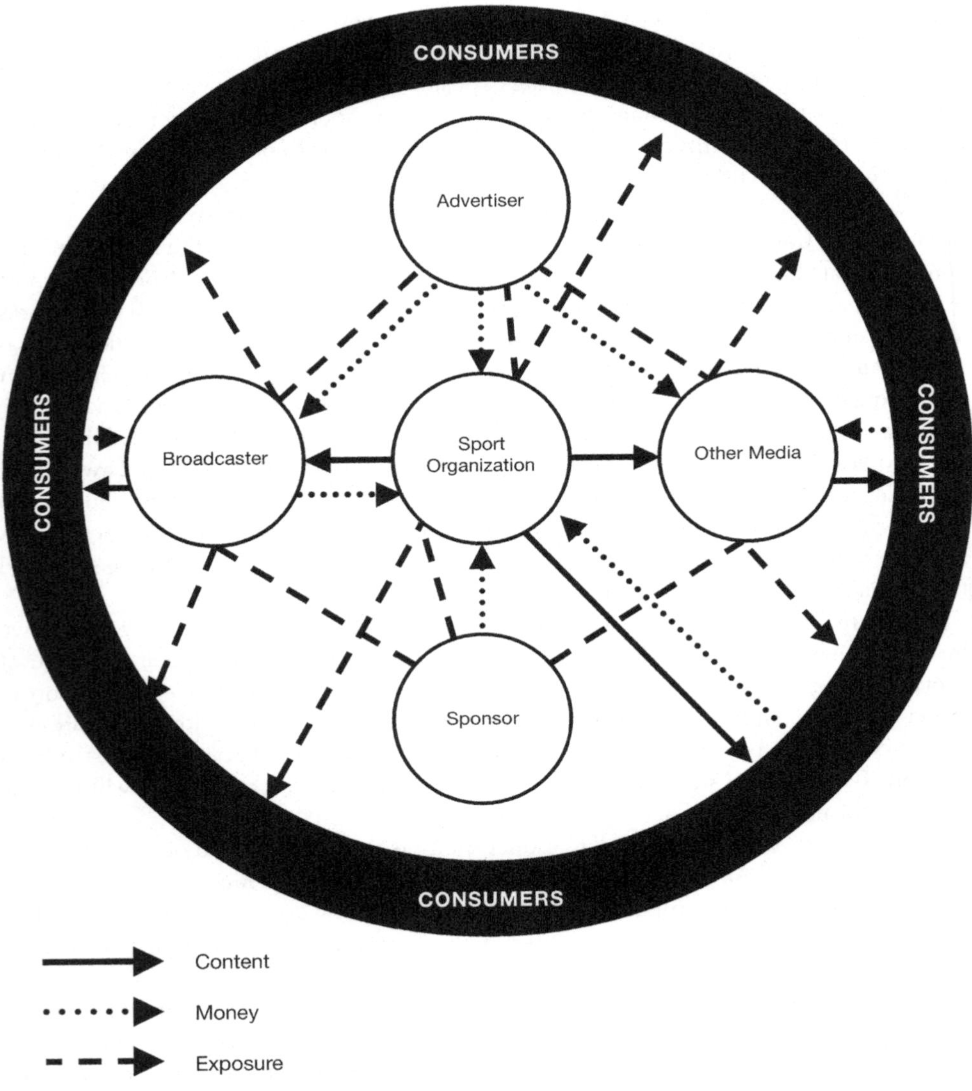


**FIGURE 4.1** Commercial dimensions of the sport media nexus

First, media organizations pay for the right to broadcast a sport event, season or series of games. These broadcast rights are typically limited to free-to-air television, pay television, radio, the internet and mobile (handheld devices); of these five the two television forms are by far the most lucrative for sports organizations. In Figure 4.1, this is demonstrated by the sport organization providing the official broadcaster with content and in return the broadcaster pays a rights fee. The print media typically reports on sport as news or to serve the public interest, rather than in a promotional capacity via an exclusive contract or arrangement. As a result, and in contrast to most forms of electronic media, no fees are collected by sport organizations for print media content.

Second, media organizations that purchase the rights to broadcast a sport event, season, or series of games seek to secure a return on investment. On free-to-air television this is primarily achieved through the sale of advertising space and time. In Figure 4.1, this is represented by the advertiser acquiring exposure to the consumer via the broadcaster. The number of people watching the sport is directly proportional to advertising revenue and to the broadcast rights fee paid. On pay television, a return on investment is achieved by the sale of advertising space and by attracting subscribers who, in general terms, are prepared to pay for a particular service, dedicated sport channels or pay-per-view events. In Figure 4.1, this relationship is represented by the consumer paying the broadcaster for content that has previously been purchased by the broadcaster from the sport organization. Increasingly, through developments in digital technology, television networks are also able to generate a return on investment through interactive revenue, such as gaming and gambling. In the case of pay television, the number of people watching sport and, more specifically, those who are prepared to pay, is directly proportional to the broadcast rights fees. The popularity and appeal of sport also means that acquiring the rights to broadcast sport events and games can increase the broadcaster's brand awareness, which in turn might increase the demand for other non-sport related content (Hoehn and Lancefield, 2003). The positive impact on brand is likely to be greater if a broadcaster has held the rights for an extended period of time and consumer loyalty to both the sport and the media products has been established.

Third, media organizations, such as print media outlets, that do not have exclusive broadcast rights will also seek to attract advertising revenue through their coverage of sport. For example, a sport magazine or newspaper will invest in the coverage of sport in a non-exclusive, and typically a non-official capacity. This is represented in Figure 4.1, where consumers pay media providers for non-exclusive, supplementary sport-related content. Based on the size and demographics of the readership, advertisers will pay the magazine or newspaper to access consumers.

Fourth, sport organizations seek to attract sponsorship revenue based on the popularity of the sport, which, in turn, is proportional to the amount of media coverage achieved. In this way, sport organizations secure additional revenue via the broadcaster, as well as via the media coverage provided by other media outside the exclusive rights agreement. The consumer might pay for the content by purchasing a newspaper or magazine, or may receive the content for free through an internet or radio news programme. These relationships are represented in Figure 4.1, where the sponsor receives exposure to consumers via the broadcaster and other media, and the sport organization receives a direct financial benefit. Thus, sport organizations must not only maximize media coverage that results from exclusive broadcast rights agreements, but must also seek to maximize

general media coverage, thereby increasing exposure, awareness, interest and audience share.

Fifth and finally, sport organizations are able to provide mediated sport content directly to consumers. In Figure 4.1, this is represented by consumers paying the sport organization for the product. In this scenario, an organization might offer fans live game footage, highlights of past matches and behind-the-scenes access to players through its own online subscription service. If the product is free, the sport organization is able to increase their revenue through sponsorship or advertising sales. For example, a sport organization provides content on its website, through which sponsors and advertisers are able to gain access to consumers. Again, the preparedness of sponsors or advertisers to pay is primarily dependent on the size of the audience. In most situations where a sport organization is increasing its revenue in this way, the relationship is with an official sponsor of the club or league. The situation of an advertiser paying a sport organization, as represented in Figure 4.1, is becoming increasingly prevalent as content produced by sport organizations gains popularity, particularly among football clubs with large fan bases. Developments in technology mean that entrepreneurial sport organizations are increasingly able to maximize club or league revenues using this approach.

It is clear from an analysis of the core commercial dimensions of the sport media nexus represented in Figure 4.1 that sport and the media generate revenue by attracting the greatest number of viewers, listeners, readers and users. The media are attracted to sport because a large number of people are interested in a variety of sport products, while sport is attractive to the media because it can generate interest and ultimately increase audiences, both live and mediated.

## BROADCAST RIGHTS

Sport and sport broadcasting rights are extremely valuable national and global commodities that have special features not exhibited by other media products. Sport events are ephemeral products or perishable goods, which means that they last for a very brief period of time (Tonazzi, 2003; Sandy *et al.*, 2004). Although sport is available via delayed coverage or through highlight packages, the value of these is far less than live sport because of the intense consumer interest in the result of the game, match or event as it is taking place. There are very few non-sport related events that are ephemeral or perishable in the same way. Occasions of state and crisis events might exhibit similar features, but they are either too infrequent or too sudden to warrant legitimate comparison. Sport is also unique in that there are very few products that consumers are able to satisfactorily substitute (Tonazzi, 2003). In other words, a consumer who wants to watch televised games of a football league has little option but to view the product offered by the broadcaster who has secured the rights. It is unlikely that the consumer will consider watching tennis or golf on another network a viable substitute. By contrast, a consumer interested in watching a legal or medical drama is likely to be able to substitute a variety of products on a variety of networks and stations. In essence, each sport is a relatively unique product, which means that it is of more value than a product with multiple variants or imitations. Moreover, premium sport leagues and events are even more scarce, which results in even greater competition to acquire the broadcast rights. Unlike the

multitude of news and drama that is available to television networks in particular, the amount of professional sport available for broadcast is finite (Tonazzi, 2003).

Professional sport has always been about the production of a live sport event, a commodity to be sold at a profit (Dart, 2014). The limited ability consumers have to substitute this commodity for a suitable alternative and the desire of consumers to view these events 'as they happen' makes sport a highly valuable asset. As discussed in the previous chapter, News Corporation has exploited these unique qualities of sport in order to gain entry into new markets and consolidate existing markets for pay television services. Sport is a lead offering because it overpowers everything else (Andrews, 2003). The fact that sport is viewed as a key driver of direct and indirect revenues for media organizations – and increasingly telecommunication and technology companies – has significant impact on the size of broadcast rights, the competition to secure them, the ability of sport organizations to maximize revenue through sponsorship and the service that these media partners demand from the sport organization.

As discussed in Chapter 2, telecommunication companies are increasingly moving into the media landscape to become key players in the sport media nexus. Given that there is a limited amount of high quality sport content, these new entrants have the potential to generate higher media fees and offer effective sponsorship opportunities for rights holders. For example, an aggressive bid by British Telecom for English Premier League rights saw the league secure an additional £1.25 billion for the rights until 2015–16, a 70 per cent increase on the previous deal; at the same time, BT Vision was positioned as a viable competitor in the local pay television market. This example demonstrates the increasing importance of telecommunications organizations in the development of the sport media nexus.

## BYPASSING THE TRADITIONAL BROADCAST MODEL

Hutchins and Rowe (2009) explained that the distribution of online sport content has restructured the media sport content economy. Whereas in the past there was comparative scarcity – in terms of content and channels – sport organizations, individual athletes and media companies can now produce and share content for fans to consume in many different ways. As a result, athletes are well placed to monetize new media technology in order to promote themselves and their sport or team (Dart, 2014) and have been quick to embrace the commercial advantages of social media. At the same time, significantly lower barriers of access and cost have allowed sport organizations to challenge the established order and hegemony of television networks and, at least in part, act as their own broadcaster.

For some time now, the major sport properties have catered directly to an increasingly international fan base through online subscription services such as NFL Game Pass, MLB.TV, NBA League Pass or UFC.TV. These services allow subscribers to watch games live or on-demand, online and in HD. In addition, many of the world's most popular team brands control or have launched television channels. Examples include the Los Angeles Dodgers (SportsNet LA), Boston Red Sox (NESN), Toronto Maple Leafs (Leafs TV), FC Barcelona (Barça TV) and Manchester United (MUTV). MUTV is available on BSkyB in England, as well as various other TV broadcasters, and for £6 per month subscribers

receive exclusive interviews, documentaries and live pre-season, reserve and academy games. A complementary service, MUTV Online, allows subscribers to access highlights and to listen to live radio commentary on match days. Because the league negotiates the sale of broadcast rights for its member clubs – a topic covered in more detail in the next chapter – MUTV does not currently deliver live Premier League action to subscribers, yet its existence hints at a future where clubs bypass the traditional broadcast model. Online sport content distribution allows a sport organization to take a more hands-on approach to the distribution of its product and, in this case, enables the Red Devils to 'enhance [their] media proposition and distribution capabilities in the years to come' (Sawers, 2013).

The shift towards digital media has also empowered smaller rights holders, such as Australia's National Basketball League (NBL) or Minor League Baseball in the United States, to broadcast and market a television product directly to the consumer. For example, when NBL.TV was launched in 2012, basketball became the first sport in Australia to which fans had comprehensive digital access to live sports content. According to the NBL, the initiative was a landmark deal in Australian sport that provided 'a major new revenue stream, as well as an attractive new proposition for sponsors' (Ward, 2012). Although the move to 'go it alone' is a risky proposition – the organization receives advertising and subscription revenue but is also responsible for absorbing the costs – it has increasingly become a practical solution to generate awareness and exposure, ultimately leading to increased sponsorship revenue. For example, the Russian Premier League launched its own television channel to show live football matches to its domestic fans after rejecting offers from commercial broadcasters; further, it has incentivized pay television operators to carry the channel by offering to split subscription revenues equally. In a competitive media landscape, it is difficult for many smaller sports to sell their rights and so, unless they 'come up with some new solutions, smaller sports that cannot bring in large audiences are going to face serious challenges' (Wilson, 2009). Exploiting the revenue generating opportunities offered by digital media represents one such solution for smaller sports to combat the lack of exposure through traditional broadcast channels.

Broadcast rights fees and sponsorship revenue now represent the major income streams for many sport organizations, notwithstanding the fact that some properties have chosen to bypass the traditional broadcast model and sell content directly to fans, either to maximize the value of their rights or in the absence of viable alternatives.

As the battle to maximize value for rights holders intensifies, it is important to further examine the ways in which sport organizations in the sport media nexus capitalize on their worldwide popularity and determine the value of these broadcast rights.

## SELLING RIGHTS

A sport organization has a number of factors that need to be considered in negotiating a broadcast rights agreement with a media partner (Foster *et al.*, 2006). The size of the bid is generally the most important: if all other elements of the bid are equal then the highest will be chosen. The size of the bid is even more important to sport organizations for which broadcast revenues represent a majority of total revenue or for those organizations that seek to maintain the exponential growth experienced since the 1990s. For example, in 1983 the annual rights to broadcast English football cost just £2.6 million; the birth of

BSkyB saw that figure rise to £60 million in 1992, £367 million in 2001 and more than £1 billion in 2012 (Williams, 1994; Andrews, 2003; O'Halloran, 2012). Despite the escalation in domestic rights fees, the sale of overseas rights will soon eclipse domestic rights (Harris, 2010). In Europe alone the broadcast rights fees have increased enormously during the past 20 years. For example, fees to secure rights to broadcast the English Premier League have risen by 1000 per cent, while fees to broadcast the FIFA World Cup have risen by 900 per cent and those for the Summer Olympics by 400 per cent (Hoehn and Kastrinaki, 2012). For most sport organizations the size of the broadcast rights deal is the overriding factor, often to the detriment of other considerations, such as how much coverage they are able to provide or the financial solvency of bidders.

The ability of the broadcaster to provide broad coverage is an important consideration for most sport organizations in accepting or rejecting a bid. Broad coverage is a factor, whether the organization is seeking to build its profile or to further enhance the cross-promotional purposes made possible by a large audience and national or global sponsors. This consideration appears to differ between sports and between countries. Some sports will opt to sign broadcast rights deals that offer no free-to-air television coverage, thereby limiting their reach to pay television subscribers only, while others will seek to capitalize on the commercial opportunities provided by increased audience awareness. For example, Rule 49 of the Olympic Charter decrees that the IOC's broadcasting policy 'takes all necessary steps in order to ensure the fullest coverage by the different media and the widest possible audience in the world for the Olympic Games' (IOC, 2014). However, it is often the case that coverage of the sport and the amount of money available to rights holders as part of a broadcast rights agreement are competing factors in determining the best bid. Broad coverage requires significant financial investment, thereby reducing the potential revenue for the media organization.

The financial solvency of potential bidders is also a consideration: a high bid from a media company that cannot afford the price is as useful as no bid at all. This consideration is important in situations where there is a third party or broadcast rights agent involved in the process. For example, FIFA sold the rights to the 2002 and 2006 World Cup competitions to Kirch, a German media and marketing company that negotiated rights deals with individual broadcasters (Sandy *et al.*, 2004). In 2002, Kirch declared bankruptcy, causing FIFA and other European sport properties to rethink their broadcast rights strategies. Similarly, in 2009, the collapse of cash-strapped Setanta Sports caused a number of Scottish Premier League clubs severe financial distress. Although BSkyB and ESPN subsequently picked up the rights, clubs were forced to settle for half of the amount previously negotiated with Setanta. Financial solvency is less of a concern for high profile sport organizations that negotiate directly with large national or multi-national companies with diversified commercial interests.

Broadcast rights can also be used to develop new markets and to influence regional preferences in a landscape characterized by satellite television, 24/7 programming and broadband internet. In the absence of an international market for media rights, leagues have sometimes had the strategic vision to give the broadcast rights away so as to grow an audience and cultivate future fans. For example, in 1989 NBA Commissioner David Stern visited China hoping to use the star power of Larry Bird, Magic Johnson and Michael Jordan to break into a new market. He offered China's state operated television provider free NBA programming. 'It dawned on me', Stern explained, 'that the combination of the

global appeal of our game and the growth of television markets around the world meant that NBA games were going to be seen everywhere' (Larmer, 2005: 71). A year later, China Central Television (CCTV) began to air the NBA finals and millions of Chinese marvelled at the athleticism of the 'Space Flier', Michael Jordan, a development that fuelled the growth of the league and the emergence of future NBA stars such as Yao Ming. Likewise, the Australian Football League (AFL), a domestic league with limited opportunities for expansion, struck a deal with China's Shanghai Media Group to broadcast its product live each week, along with a pre-match programme that explains the rules, recent events and historical rivalries to local viewers (Silkstone, 2010). While the deal will not bring any financial benefit to the league, it is critical to the AFL's long-term approach to the Chinese market and complements its Mandarin language website.

## BUYING RIGHTS

The attractiveness of broadcast rights for a prospective buyer is dependent on the audience the broadcaster is able to capture by broadcasting the match, game or event. A large audience pool should equate to a willingness to pay a significant amount of money, while a small audience will generally make the acquisition of the rights package far less appealing, equating to a reduced willingness to pay large sums for the product. In a similar way that money is the overriding factor for the vendors of the rights, the size of the audience is invariably the overriding factor for the buyers. However, for media organizations, the quality of the audience is also a major consideration, and in this respect sport is a particularly good product. Sport usually attracts male viewers aged between 16 and 35 years of age, who typically have high disposable incomes, and have been historically difficult to reach (Hoehn and Lancefield, 2003). Sports such as golf or yachting have the capacity to attract a different demographic, such as older males, who also have high disposable incomes. In other words, both the size and the quality of the audience are key variables in calculating the worth of rights to media organizations and advertisers.

The vast majority of sport rights sales, particularly for major sports and events, are negotiated on a fixed revenue basis. There are cases in which sport and media organizations enter into commercial relationships where the revenue is shared or the sport organization assumes the financial risk, as mentioned in previous discussion, however, a fixed revenue arrangement is far more common. What this means in practice is that the media organization agrees to pay a fee for the duration of a contract, which might be anything from one event to ten seasons long. The media organization makes the offer based on what it predicts it can recover primarily through advertising and subscription sales. In the event that the audience ratings for the sport product that has been purchased are less than expected, then it follows that the advertising revenue will also be less than expected, particularly if the ratings decline significantly over a four- or five-year period. In this situation, the broadcast rights deal may result in a net loss for the broadcaster.

The value of sport rights increases in proportion to the exclusivity, scope and duration of the rights (Hoehn and Lancefield, 2003). If the rights are non-exclusive then the broadcaster must not only concern itself with maximizing its investment through advertising and subscription sales, but must also compete against rival broadcasters that are

seeking to do the same. This non-exclusivity is likely to reduce advertising and subscription sales, as well as lessen the additional benefit of consumer loyalty. Non-exclusive rights are likely to increase, rather than reduce, 'churn' – the process in which consumers switch from one provider to another to access preferred programmes. Similarly, it is to the broadcaster's commercial advantage to have access to the greatest number of games for the longest time. Although a long-term broadcast rights agreement shifts a significant amount of risk from the sport organization to the media organization, the trade-off is that the media partner is able to build long-term viewer loyalty.

News Corporation provides a succinct summary of the sports rights marketplace and the pros and cons of buying in:

> Sports programming rights contracts between the company, on the one hand, and various professional sports leagues and teams, on the other, have varying duration and renewal terms. As these contracts expire, the company may seek renewals on commercial terms; however, third parties may outbid the current rights holders for such rights contracts. In addition, professional sports leagues or teams may create their own networks or the renewal costs could substantially exceed the original contract cost. The loss of rights could impact the extent of the sports coverage offered by FOX and its affiliates, and the company's regional sports networks ('RSNs'), and could adversely affect its advertising and affiliate revenues. Conversely, if the company is able to renew these contracts, the results could be adversely affected if escalations in sports programming rights costs are unmatched by increases in advertising rates and, in the case of cable networks, subscriber fees.
>
> (News Corporation, 2005: 43)

In 1998, President of NBC Sports, Dick Ebersol, in response to a new NFL broadcast deal, famously declared that 'the dollar figures have reached an insane level' and 'it is a foolhardy economic venture' (Higgins, 2005: 18). The network that had shaped television broadcasts of football for six decades ultimately couldn't make the numbers work, and lost its rights to televise the NFL. Although the rights for major sport properties have continued to rise, in part because of the fears expressed above by News Corporation, the damage caused by losing the rights to broadcast premium sport properties seems to be an overwhelming concern among media organizations. For example, BSkyB was forced to pay more than it wished for the rights to broadcast the EPL until 2015–16, and 'we had to make some tough choices', because losing the rights would have 'put into question the whole future of Sky' (O'Halloran, 2012).

That the future of the television network was potentially jeopardized by the loss of the rights to broadcast EPL is indicative of the value of these rights to the holder and of the integral position that broadcast rights occupy in the media organization's business model.

In the face of escalating rights fees and a sporting public with an insatiable appetite for quality programming, some media organizations have decided to develop their own sport properties as valuable content. While some of these have become iconic brands, such as ESPN's X Games, others – like the ill-fated XFL – have been far less successful. The XFL football league, the brainchild of wrestling personality Vince McMahon, was a joint venture between NBC – which had recently lost its coveted NFL rights – and the World

## IN PRACTICE 4.1

### Australian broadcasters' billion dollar battle for the pigskin

Australia, a relatively small market, has two major recipients of broadcast rights income: the Australian Football League (AFL) and the National Rugby League (NRL). Both competitions are very popular and can trace their roots back more than a hundred years, the AFL in Melbourne and the NRL in Sydney. This popularity has seen media companies continue to aggressively bid for the rights to these premium properties.

In 2001, after a 43-year association with the Seven network, one of Australia's three commercial free-to-air broadcasters, the AFL awarded the broadcast rights to the 2002–06 seasons to a consortium headed by News Corporation. The consortium split the rights, valued at A$500 million, between free-to-air networks, Nine and Ten, and pay television's Foxtel. In 2005, the Seven and Ten networks announced that they were preparing a joint bid for the rights to broadcast the 2007–11 AFL seasons. In late 2005 the Nine network, in conjunction with Foxtel, submitted a bid of A$780 million. However, recognizing the value of the Australian football as an asset, the Seven network had signed an agreement that gave it first and last rights at the negotiating table until the end of 2011. As a result, the Seven and Ten networks were able to match the rival bid and secure the AFL rights for A$156 million per year for five years, a record at the time. Although Seven's Director of Corporate Development, Simon Francis, said 'we will let our heads and not our hearts make the final decision' (Barrett, 2005), it is debateable whether the successful networks were forced into a deal that significantly overvalued the rights. The rights to the 2012–16 AFL seasons were later sold to the Seven network and Fox Sports for A$1.25 billion, the richest deal of its kind in Australian sporting history.

A similar situation took place in Sydney, where the NRL signed an A$500 million deal with the Nine network and Fox Sports for the rights to broadcast the 2007–12 seasons, a 60 per cent annual increase on its previous rights fees. The contract continued the Nine network's longstanding relationship with the sport, ensuring that two free-to-air games would be shown each week on the Nine network, and Monday Night Football became a popular addition to the Fox Sports rugby league schedule. The Nine network, which had negotiated its own first and last rights of refusal, and Fox Sports secured the rights to the 2013–17 seasons for A$1.025 billion. According to Nine network's Chief Executive, David Gyngell, 'We've had the NRL for 20 years. It's part of our core brand strategy, we own rugby league' (White and Davidson, 2012: 19).

In the Australian context, the AFL and NRL represent valuable programming assets that broadcasters are willing to invest heavily to acquire. Although the rights continue to escalate for the Seven and Nine networks (and Foxtel as it seeks to maintain subscriber numbers), the sports are an integral component of their brand appeal and failure to secure the rights was almost unthinkable. However, the highly competitive nature of the negotiations has led some analysts to conclude that the rights were significantly over-priced and that this will lead to increased financial pressure on the successful media partners as they endeavour to derive a satisfactory return on their investment.

Sources: Read and Honeysett (2005); Stapleton (2005); Grigg (2006); White and Davidson (2012).

Wrestling Federation (Willoughby and Mancini, 2003). Designed to build upon the success of the NFL and professional wrestling, XFL was positioned as aggressive and innovative. In 2001, eight teams – with names as colourful as the Orlando Rage, Las Vegas Outlaws and New York/New Jersey Hitmen – took to the field in its inaugural season. The league did away with penalties for roughness, abolished the 'fair catch' rule that protected punt returners and teams had to either run or pass the ball into the end zone in order to receive the extra point after a touchdown (Willoughby and Mancini, 2003). Although the season began with sold-out crowds, television ratings soon plummeted and the XFL folded at the end of its first season, having reportedly cost NBC US$35 million.

In contrast, other organizations have had phenomenal success in creating and modifying events; Red Bull's Stratos and Crashed Ice properties have been very successful (see In Practice 4.2), as have ESPN's X Games. In the early 1990s, ESPN realized that there was a large segment of America that wasn't watching *SportsCenter* and so the X Games was born. ESPN spent US$10 million on the first X Games in Newport, Rhode Island in 1995, which saw skateboard legend Tony Hawk come out of retirement, and the event quickly became a hit. Two years later, the success of the event billed as 'sheer unadulterated athletic lunacy' had given birth to the Winter X Games and it is 'easy to see the parallels between those who watch "Big Air" skateboarding and motocross and the bloodthirsty crowds at the Colosseum of Ancient Rome' (Pickert, 2009). By 2013, the X Games had evolved into a series of six events in locations all over the globe – Los Angeles, California; Aspen, Colorado; Tignes, France; Foz do Iguaçu, Brazil; Barcelona, Spain; and Munich, Germany – and has become a lucrative franchise for ESPN. The creation of intellectual property such as the X Games or the XFL has many advantages as the parent media company can modify the rules whenever it pleases. Furthermore, it can control the marketing and licensing of the franchise, or control the distribution of the product, choosing to fill holes in its programming schedule or instead on-sell the rights for additional revenue. The case of the XFL though shows the importance of creating a sporting event with rules and modifications that are attractive to consumers. While the X Games has become a hit, mostly because it created something that did not exist – a competitive major games environment for edgy street and extreme sports – the XFL's modifications on the sport of NFL were not embraced by fans.

## A COMPETITIVE ARENA

Competition, as previously alluded to, is an important element of the broadcast rights process for both sellers and prospective buyers and has three primary dimensions. First, leagues prefer to limit competition between clubs by entering into joint or collective selling arrangements. The government regulation of this practice will be discussed in more detail in the following chapter, but it is sufficient in this context to note that for sport organizations it is important to minimize internal league competition in order to maximize external competition for the product. A broadcaster that is able to secure the rights also wants to limit competition within the league to maximize the benefits that flow from exclusivity. However, more competition between clubs within a league might benefit a range of broadcasters, particularly where high profile football rights are concerned.

## IN PRACTICE 4.2

### Red Bull soars to greater heights

Although Red Bull is now a household name and dominates the multi-billion dollar energy drink market, its founder Dietrich Mateschitz is largely unknown outside his native Austria. Despite this, he has become one of the most innovative people in the sport media nexus. Inspired by a visit to Thailand in the early 1980s where he stumbled upon a local energy drink, Krateng Daeng ('Red Water Buffalo'), Mateschitz modified the flavour and carbonated the beverage to suit the European market. According to the company's marketing, Red Bull 'gives wings to people who want to be mentally and physically active and have a zest for life' (Red Bull, 2013). The product was launched in Austria in 1987, by 1997 it had entered the North American market and by 2004 Red Bull had spread its wings globally.

A key strategy in the early success of the company was to engage action sport athletes to embrace and endorse the caffeinated beverage. As part of this strategy, Red Bull created new and innovative sport properties, such as Red Bull Crashed Ice, the Red Bull Air Race and Red Bull X-Fighters. Crashed Ice is a daredevil combination that sees four competitors at a time skate in a man-on-man battle down an ice track with chicanes, jumps and hairpin turns. Red Bull Crashed Ice was the first in a long line of signature events, each with its own branding and rules, designed to reach its core market of young men. In 2013, Red Bull performed one of the most audacious extreme sports events, Red Bull Stratos, which saw Felix Baumgartner freefall 24 miles through space and was worth millions of dollars in global exposure for the brand. Not only has Red Bull supported action sport athletes for more than two decades, but its cameras have been there to capture every death-defying moment. As Red Bull's Werner Brell explained, 'whenever we did any event, or signed an athlete or executed a project, everything has been put on film or photographed. Stories have been told, it's part of the DNA of the brand' (Iezzi, 2012).

Red Bull Media House was launched in Austria in 2007 and brought to the United States four years later. The media company's goal is to establish a global network to distribute Red Bull related content across television, mobile, print, music and new media; the company allows Red Bull to leverage its media assets for growth and to solidify its position as an action sports leader. As Brell argued, 'in content, everything has to do with rights ownership [but with Red Bull Media House] we own the lifecycle from beginning to end' (Jessop, 2012). Through events such as Stratos and Crashed Ice, Red Bull has been able to leverage its brand via magazines, music publishing, social media, television shows and video games, such as Red Bull Crashed Ice on Xbox 360 Kinect.

Red Bull has recognized the power of sport to engage with consumers and now spends US$300 million per year to build a brand ubiquitous in popular culture. 'Everything we do pretty much pays back and powers the brand' explained Brell, as ultimately 'the brand is why we do the things we do' (Jessop, 2012).

Sources: Gorse *et al.* (2010); Jessop (2012); www.redbull.com (2013).

Second, in order to maximize broadcast rights fees, a league, or in some cases a team, must maximize the competition between prospective buyers. In other words, if there is only one legitimate buyer then it is likely that the fee will be low, whereas if there are many broadcasters willing to bid for the rights then the competitive process is likely to considerably increase the fees. Media organizations, however, want to create the opposite scenario, in which competition, and therefore cost, is minimized. In essence, the effect of a broadcaster engaging in long-term exclusive agreements in a limited and finite market could be a reduction in competition, whereby the dominance of a single broadcaster might limit the entry of rival broadcasters or the profitability of existing operators.

Finally, sport leagues and teams are engaged in competition with other sports at national and international levels. In his second term as President of FIFA, Sepp Blatter described the final competitive dimension as follows:

> The act of tendering and selling rights for mammoth sporting events boils down to a battle for the available capital. International sports federations are consequently compelled to deal in the manner of commercial corporations—in direct competition with one another—and other institutions (especially cultural ones) to procure this precious commodity.
>
> (FIFA, 2004: 7)

The highly competitive nature of sport broadcasting invariably means that smaller sport leagues and teams have to attempt to make their product as attractive to broadcasters and advertisers as possible, while larger sport events, leagues and federations have the ability to demand more from broadcasters because of their superior product and audience.

## SEGMENTING THE MARKET

Segmenting the market refers to two primary approaches by sport organizations in selling broadcast rights to sport events and major games: segmentation by platform or region. The first approach is to offer broadcast rights to multiple providers, rather than offer all broadcast opportunities to a single media provider, which would create an exclusive relationship. In practice this means that broadcast rights might be split between free-to-air television, pay television, radio, the internet and mobile (handheld), while maximizing exclusivity within each of the media forms. For example, Australia's AFL and NRL struck billion-dollar deals for their broadcast rights when they were split between a free-to-air network, Fox Sports, and the country's largest telecommunication provider, Telstra. Broadcast rights might also be split on the basis of live, delayed or highlights of coverage, but the prominence of live coverage means that this segmentation has a finite ability to raise revenue. As previously noted, in segmenting the rights there is a trade-off between exclusivity and competition; however, in the case of segmenting the rights based on media platform, exclusivity can be maintained by offering separate broadcast packages.

The second way in which sport organizations might be considered to segment the market is where they offer the broadcast rights to multiple broadcasters across different territories or geographic areas. In a national context this might mean selling the broadcast rights to a television network that broadcasts into a state or region and, at the same time, selling the

rights to a second or third broadcaster that operates in a different market; in this arrangement, broadcasters are not engaged in direct competition with one another. In an international context the segmenting of rights might manifest in an organization selling to individual countries, rather than to a third party independent agent that then on-sells the rights to media organizations. For example, the 2016 UEFA European Championship broadcast rights were sold on a market-by-market basis, rather than to Europe as a whole, offered on a platform neutral basis, staggered throughout Europe. UEFA claimed that the European Championship of football is the third biggest sport property in the world, with only the Olympic Games and the FIFA World Cup as more valuable sport events. The UEFA Champions League is also sold on a market-by-market basis, resulting in the following broadcasters securing contracts for their respective territories for the period 2012–15:

- Brazil – Globo TV, Esporte Interativo and ESPN;
- Canada – Rogers Sportsnet;
- China – CCTV, QQ and Sina Corporation;
- France – Al Jazeera Media Network and Canal+;
- India Sub-Continent – TAJ TV;
- Italy – Sky Italia and RTI Spa (Mediaset);
- Latin America (except Brazil) – ESPN, Fox Sports Latin America and OTI;
- Middle East and North Africa – Al Jazeera Satellite Network;
- US and Caribbean – Fox Sports US;
- United Kingdom – ITV and BSkyB.

## THE VALUE OF RIGHTS

The rights paid to broadcast premium sport properties underscore the importance of the football codes in their respective markets. In Europe, more than a quarter of the time devoted to watching sport on television is spent watching football; in Spain this figure is as high as 59 per cent (Nielsen, 2012). The continued popularity of football has driven bidders to raise the stakes in pursuit of the broadcast rights: the EPL saw its domestic rights increase by nearly 70 per cent to €1.35 billion per season from 2013–14 (EFPL, 2008), nearly double the rights paid to the French Ligue 1. In the United States from 2014, the NFL rights were worth US$5.9 billion per year to the league, which dwarfs those in any other sport (Futterman *et al.*, 2011). The broadcast rights for Latin America's six leading football leagues, dominated by Brazil's Campeonato Brasileiro Serie A with 57 per cent, broke the US$1 billion barrier for the first time in 2012 (Soccerex, 2013).

In Europe, four-fifths of the US$8.5 billion invested in sport television rights in the big five European markets in 2011 went to football (soccer), especially the rights to the top domestic league (Dunne, 2011). In a smaller market such as Australia, the football codes absorb more than 73 per cent of expenditure by media organizations on sport broadcast rights. Similarly, in the United Kingdom, 71 per cent of total broadcast rights fees are devoted to football and in Italy, a staggering 90 per cent of total rights paid went to acquiring broadcast rights for football (Dunne, 2011). In order to gain further clarity about the extent of the rights market, it is useful to examine a range of media and sport perspectives at an organizational level.

## MEDIA PERSPECTIVES

An examination of the contractual agreements and liabilities of some of the world's major media organizations reveals that a significant amount of money has been allocated to securing the broadcast rights to sport events and leagues. It also reveals the extent to which sport has become the major property for global media organizations.

For example, News Corporation's 2012 Annual Report states that as of 30 June 2012 the company is contractually committed to spend US$36,309 million, including US$3,367 million in 2012–13 and US$7,295 million in 2012–15 for sports programming rights (News Corporation, 2013). In 2012, revenue from its cable network programming – which includes the Regional Sports Networks – and television business segments, contributed 27 per cent and 14 per cent of News Corporation's consolidated revenues, respectively. The company's cable network programming revenue grew by 14 per cent during this period due to higher RSN subscriber fees, increased advertising revenue in the US, Latin America and Asia and an improved performance by STAR in India. The NBA lockout resulted in fewer NBA telecasts and News Corporation's cable network programming costs increased with the acquisition of rights to the Ultimate Fighting Championship. These two factors – reduced number of telecasts and an increase in acquisition costs – have the potential to negatively impact revenue derived from programming and yet the company reported an increase in programming revenue. In contrast, television revenue decreased marginally when compared with the 2010–11 financial year when FOX held the rights to Super Bowl XLV, at the time the most-watched television show in US history with 111 million viewers. This decline was despite News Corporation receiving additional advertising revenue as a result of FOX broadcasting two extra post-season games in MLB and increased television ratings during this period (News Corporation, 2013). The 2011 post-season campaign, with the marketing tagline 'Legends are Born in October', saw the St Louis Cardinals defeat the Texas Rangers in seven games. The 2011 World Series averaged 16.6 million viewers and the final Game Seven was the most-watched baseball game since the Boston Red Sox broke their World Series drought in 2004.

The Walt Disney Company signed a US$15.2 billion agreement for the rights to broadcast *Monday Night Football* for eight seasons commencing in 2014; it also continued ESPN's long-standing relationship with MLB when it signed a US$5.6 billion deal for a package of television, digital, radio and international rights until 2021. In addition, ESPN agreed to a 12-year deal worth US$5.64 billion with the NCAA to broadcast the College Football Play-off, a four-team tournament to replace the Bowl Championship Series (BCS) (Horlock, 2013).

The Walt Disney Company, through ESPN and ABC, also holds the rights to the NBA, NASCAR, the Wimbledon Championships, US Open Tennis and the US Masters. As a result of acquiring these sport properties, The Walt Disney Company claims that approximately 100 million Americans regularly turn to ESPN every week for their sports viewing and news. The Walt Disney Company's 2012 Annual Report states that as of 29 September 2012 the company, as part of contractual agreements, was committed to US$40,700 million for sports programming rights, including US$4,798 million for 2013, US$9,349 million in 2014–15 and US$8,020 million in 2016–17. The sums of money that organizations like Walt Disney Company are willing to pay underscore the central place that sport occupies in media organizations' business activities.

Similarly, Time Warner's 2012 Annual Report states that as of 31 December 2012 the company, as part of contractual agreements, was committed to US$17,334 million, including US$2,682 million in 2013, US$4,179 million in 2014–15 and US$10,473 from 2016 onwards. Time Warner's figures are not directly comparable with those of News Corporation or the Walt Disney Company as they include licensing arrangements with movie studios for movies on theatrical release; however, Time Warner's commitment to premium sports rights dominates its contractual liabilities. For instance, Time Warner is contractually committed to pay a further US$9.4 billion over the next 12 years to the NCAA.

Finally, Vivendi's 2012 Annual Report states that as of 31 December 2012 contractual obligations for sports rights amounted to €1,715 million, comprising €612 million in 2013, €1,103 million in 2014–17 but, as yet, no commitments exist beyond 2017 (Vivendi, 2013). Viviendi's subsidiary, Canal+, acquired the rights to the 2012–16 seasons of the French professional football Ligue 1 for €1,708 million but the competition for domestic rights has intensified with the arrival of new media players, such as Al Jazeera.

It is clear from the information presented above that sport rights represent a significant investment for the world's major media companies, further emphasizing the commercial foundations of the sport media nexus. The following section examines this relationship from the perspective of sport organizations and similarly illustrates that sport organizations are heavily dependent on media revenue.

## SPORT PERSPECTIVES

The allocation of sport rights fees is not even. Rather, the revenue that a sport organization is able to achieve through the sale of broadcast rights depends on the size and demographics of the market. An examination of a variety of broadcast rights deals reveals that rights fees are usually proportional to the size of the national and global audience that a sport event or league is able to attract.

Globally, the Olympic Games and the FIFA World Cup are the largest sporting events in the world and capture the greatest amount of interest and hence media coverage. The Summer and Winter Olympic Games each consist of approximately two weeks of sporting competition held every four years in which all countries can compete; the FIFA World Cup is likewise held every four years but consists instead of four weeks of competition for the 32 teams that qualified for the finals. The Olympic Games are an ideal case study in the growth of broadcast rights, the importance of the US and European markets to international events and the proportion of revenue that is acquired through broadcast rights agreements.

Table 4.1 illustrates the growth in broadcast rights fees paid to the IOC by international broadcasters. The figures demonstrate the enormous growth in broadcast rights fees since 1960 when US$1.2 million was paid for the rights to broadcast the Summer Games in Rome, and only US$50,000 for that year's Winter Games in Squaw Valley, California. By the 2009–12 quadrennial period, broadcast rights accounted for approximately half of all Olympic Games revenue. Table 4.1 also shows that since the 1984 Olympic Games in Los Angeles, which marked the birth of a highly commercialized Olympics, the broadcast rights fees have increased by in excess of 500 per cent. A more detailed examination of the figures demonstrates that the majority of broadcast rights revenue has been generated by

**TABLE 4.1** Olympic Games broadcast rights (in US$ million)

| *Summer Games* | | *Winter Games* | |
|---|---|---|---|
| Rome (1960) | 1.2 | Squaw Valley (1960) | 0.05 |
| Tokyo (1964) | 1.6 | Innsbruck (1964) | 0.937 |
| Mexico City (1968) | 9.8 | Grenoble (1968) | 2.6 |
| Munich (1972) | 17.8 | Sapporo (1972) | 8.5 |
| Montreal (1976) | 34.9 | Innsbruck (1976) | 11.6 |
| Moscow (1980) | 88 | Lake Placid (1980) | 20.7 |
| Los Angeles (1984) | 286.9 | Sarajevo (1984) | 102.7 |
| Seoul (1988) | 402.6 | Calgary (1988) | 324.9 |
| Barcelona (1992) | 636.1 | Albertville (1992) | 291.9 |
| Atlanta (1996) | 898.3 | Lillehammer (1994) | 352.9 |
| Sydney (2000) | 1331.6 | Nagano (1998) | 513.5 |
| Athens (2004) | 1494 | Salt Lake (2002) | 738 |
| Beijing (2008) | 1739 | Turin (2006) | 831 |
| London (2012) | 2635.1 | Vancouver (2010) | 1279.5 |

Source: Olympic (n.d.) www.olympic.org.

the US market. Table 4.2 shows that although this dominance has abated somewhat – indeed, the 2013–16 period will see the US contribution to total IOC television revenue fall below 50 per cent for the first time (Mickle, 2012) – broadcast rights revenue for the Olympic Games is still largely dependent on westernized countries.

Table 4.3 breaks down the contribution that each region represented in the Olympic movement has made to the total IOC broadcast revenues for the past four quadrennial periods, beginning with the Nagano 1998 Winter Olympic Games. During this period, USA and European television markets contributed at least 75 per cent of total broadcast rights revenue for the Olympic Games. This highlights the fact that beyond westernized countries, in which advertising markets are strong and provide broadcasters with opportunities to maximize a return on their investment, broadcast rights fees have been of nominal value. While the rights fees paid by smaller markets to broadcast Vancouver 2010 and London 2012 were dominated by Canada and Oceania (largely driven by Australia) with 3.91 per cent and 3.27 per cent, respectively, the importance of regions such as Latin America, the Middle East and Africa continue to increase. For example, a Brazilian consortium led by TV company Globo paid US$170 million for the rights to broadcast the 2014 and 2016 Olympic Games – a dramatic increase on the US$9 million paid for Olympic television rights in 2009 (Mickle, 2012). At the same time, Mexico's America Movil acquired the broadcast rights to the Sochi and Rio Olympic Games for the rest of Latin America, from Mexico to Uruguay, ensuring that there will be free Olympic Games television coverage not only across the region, but also across all other media platforms. The commercial growth of these markets suggests that the dominance historically shown by western economies might not be the case in the future.

**TABLE 4.2** Percentage contribution of US broadcast rights fees to the total broadcast rights fees for the Summer and Winter Olympic Games

| *Summer Games* | *(%)* | *Winter Games* | *(%)* |
|---|---|---|---|
| Montreal (1976) | 72 | Innsbruck (1976) | 86 |
| Moscow (1980) | 99 | Lake Placid (1980) | 75 |
| Los Angeles (1984) | 78 | Sarajevo (1984) | 89 |
| Seoul (1988) | 75 | Calgary (1988) | 95 |
| Barcelona (1992) | 63 | Albertville (1992) | 83 |
| Atlanta (1996) | 51 | Lillehammer (1994) | 85 |
| Sydney (2000) | 53 | Nagano (1998) | 73 |
| Athens (2004) | 53 | Salt Lake (2002) | 74 |
| Beijing (2008) | 51 | Torino (2006) | 74 |
| London (2012) | 45 | Vancouver (2010) | 64 |

Sources: Olympic (n.d.) www.olympic.org.

**TABLE 4.3** Percentage contribution of broadcast rights fees to the total broadcast fees for the Summer and Winter Olympic Games (in US$ million)

| *Quadrennium* | *US (%)* | *Europe (%)* | *Asia (%)* | *Other (%)* |
|---|---|---|---|---|
| 1997–2000 | 59 | 23 | 11 | 7 |
| 2001–2004 | 60 | 23 | 10 | 7 |
| 2005–2008 | 59 | 23 | 11 | 8 |
| 2009–2012 | 51 | 24 | 14 | 11 |

Source: Olympic (n.d.) www.olympic.org.

As regular global events, the Olympic Games and the FIFA World Cup are able to acquire significant revenues through broadcast rights. For example, the London 2012 Olympic Games and the 2010 FIFA World Cup in South Africa delivered approximately US$2.5 billion in broadcast rights for their governing bodies. In September 2013, the IOC's television and marketing director Timo Lumme told IOC members that the sum raised from broadcasting rights for the 2013–16 cycle was expected to top US$4.1 billion (Owen, 2014). During the course of the twentieth century, FIFA experienced massive revenue growth, largely due to the broadcast rights generated by the World Cup. In 1930, match levies and subscriptions from its members accounted for 85 per cent of FIFA's revenue, yet by 2011 only 0.4 per cent of revenue was from the same source. According to FIFA, its finances are dependent upon successfully staging the World Cup: during the four-year cycle between 2007 and 2010 the sale of television rights to the South African edition delivered 57 per cent of the organization's total revenue (FIFA, 2013).

Although the Olympic Games and the FIFA World Cup dominate the sport media nexus, the rights to national leagues and global circuits are also significant. For example,

NASCAR signed a US$2.4 billion broadcast rights deal for the 2015–22 seasons with News Corporation. In deals that both segmented the rights and maintained exclusivity, FOX and Fox Sports 1 have committed to broadcast the first half of the NASCAR season, including the famous Daytona 500, while ESPN and Time Warner's TBS hold the right to the remainder of the schedule (Saward, 2013). In this scenario, the broadcasters are compelled to work together to ensure that consumers, sponsors and advertisers enjoy a level of continuity that would not normally be apparent with two or more competing broadcasters.

In 2010, the South African, New Zealand and Australian rugby unions (SANZAR) signed a broadcast deal with News Corporation and Africa's Supersport. The agreement includes the rights to Australia, New Zealand, Africa and the United Kingdom and was worth US$437 million over five years (Warren, 2010). The previous deal was US$323 million for the same period; the increase is a result of expanding the Super Rugby competition to include a fifteenth franchise that has seen the number of matches available to broadcast increase from 94 matches to 125. In other words, News Corporation was prepared to pay more money for more content and with Argentina joining the Rugby Championship – the southern hemisphere's equivalent of the Six Nations – and Rugby Sevens' inclusion in the Rio 2016 Olympic Games schedule, future rights deals could mirror those of its rival football codes in Australia.

Rights agreements are not limited to free-to-air or pay television: radio, the internet and mobile (handheld) devices also feature in broadcast agreements between sport and media organizations. For example, in 2005, XM Satellite Radio signed a US$100 million agreement to be the exclusive satellite radio network for the NHL over ten years, beginning with the 2007–2008 season (Consoli, 2005). Its rival at the time, Sirius Satellite Radio, made a similar investment with NASCAR. The now merged entity, Sirius XM Radio, offers listeners a wide range of sports programming, including the NFL, NHL, PGA Tour and the MLB Network. In addition to its satellite radio services, Sirius XM offers 30 play-by-play channels with live radio broadcasts of every MLB game broadcast on smartphones, mobile devices and online. At the same time, the online sports universe continues to expand. In 2010, Time Warner's Turner Sports and the NCAA announced a 14-year digital rights deal that complements its March Madness broadcasts on TBS and TNT. According to Lenny Daniels, Chief Operating Officer of Turner Sports, 'the long-term television world is going to change, and we think everything is, eventually, going to be interconnected. We want this to become the place you go to for college sports' (AP, 2010).

## RECOVERING RIGHTS FEES AND MAXIMIZING EXPOSURE

The way in which free-to-air television recovers the money it expends on acquiring the rights to broadcast sport is primarily by selling advertising space and time. Advertisers are charged a rate based on expected ratings. These rates are calculated based on prior ratings for similar programmes, and the expected demographics of the television audience. Previous audiences that watched similar programmes can also be used in the calculation (Foster *et al.*, 2006). Sport is a popular product with television audiences that generates high ratings and, therefore, commands high advertising rates. In 2012, there were nearly

60,000 hours of sports programming shown in the US and 23 per cent of television advertising expenditure was committed to these programmes (Nielsen, 2012). Table 4.4 illustrates the popularity of the major sport events with that country's 315 million viewers. It demonstrates the importance of regional preferences, the attraction of elite sport properties and their value to media organizations.

The Walt Disney Company's explanation of the connection between expenditure on rights and return on investment through advertising is expressed in the following excerpt from its 2012 Annual Report:

> Even if these contracts [contractual commitments for the purchase of television rights for sports and other programming] are renewed, the cost of obtaining programming rights may increase (or increase at faster rates than our historical experience) or the revenue from distribution of programs may be reduced (or increase at slower rates than our historical experience). With respect to the acquisition of programming rights, particularly sports programming rights, the impact of these long-term contracts on our results over the term of the contracts depends on a number of factors, including the strength of advertising markets, effectiveness of marketing efforts and the size of viewer audiences. There can be no assurance that revenues from programming based on these rights will exceed the cost of the rights fees plus the other costs of producing and distributing the programming.
>
> (Walt Disney Company, 2012: 20–21)

The amount that advertisers spend on sport is relative to the size of the audience, but is often also dependent on cultural context. In many cases this means that football is a

**TABLE 4.4** Television sport audiences in 2012 (United States)

| *Event* | *Audience (million)* |
|---|---|
| NFL Super Bowl XLVI | 111.35 |
| Opening Ceremony, London 2012 Olympics | 40.65 |
| NCAA BCS Championship Game | 26.38 |
| NCAA March Madness Championship Game | 20.87 |
| NBA Finals | 16.86 |
| NASCAR's Daytona 500 | 13.67 |
| The US Masters | 13.49 |
| MLB World Series | 12.66 |
| UFC on FOX (Evans vs Davis) | 4.66 |
| UEFA Euro 2012 Final | 4.07 |
| NHL Stanley Cup | 3.01 |
| UEFA Champions League Final | 1.98 |

Source: Nielsen (2012).

dominant media product in terms of advertising revenue; however, there are some special cases. For example, cricket has long been the dominant sport property in India, capturing 90 per cent of the nation's advertising revenue, which is primarily spent on the Indian Premier League.

In 2014, the Seattle Seahawks defeated the Denver Broncos 43–8 at Super Bowl XLVIII, the NFL's annual championship game. Off the field, companies competed with each other to advertise their products in the most creative and appealing ways on television network CBS. The broadcast drew an average of 111.5 million viewers, the highest total in US television history (CBS Sports, 2014). In addition, 2.3 million unique visitors streamed the game live and watched the half-time performance from Bruno Mars and the Red Hot Chili Peppers, and there were 24.9 million tweets (CBS Sports, 2014).

Advertising rates averaged US$4 million for 30 seconds during the 2012 Super Bowl – almost double the US$2.5 million charged to advertise a decade before. The top five Super Bowl advertisers between 2003 and 2012 were Anheuser-Busch InBev, Pepsico, General Motors, Coca-Cola and Walt Disney; they accounted for 37 per cent of total Super Bowl advertising revenue during this period (Kantar Media, 2013). However, General Motors declined to advertise during Super Bowl XLVII, citing the high costs. A number of advertisers of major consumer products and brands did accept the cost, often for more than one commercial:

- Audi (1)
- Axe (1)
- Beck's (1)
- Best Buy (1)
- Blackberry (1)
- Bud Light (2)
- Budweiser (4)
- Calvin Klein (1)
- Cars.com (1)
- Century 21 (1)
- Coca-Cola (2)
- Doritos (2)
- E-Trade (1)
- Gildan Activewear (1)
- GoDaddy.com (2)
- Got Milk? (1)
- History Channel (1)
- Hyundai (2)
- Jeep (1)
- Kia (2)
- Lincoln (2)
- M&M's (1)
- Mercedes-Benz (1)
- Mio Fit (1)
- Oreo (1)
- Paramount Pictures (2)
- Pepsi (1)
- Pizza Hut (1)
- Ram Trucks (1)
- Samsung (1)
- Skechers (1)
- Sodastream (1)
- Speed Stick (1)
- Subway (2)
- Taco Bell (1)
- Tide (2)
- Toyota (1)
- Universal Pictures (1)
- Volkswagen (1)
- Walt Disney Pictures (1)
- Wonderful Pistachios (1)

Not including those commercials that promoted the NFL or a network's television series, companies spent nearly US$300 million during the broadcast of the Super Bowl to promote their products to more than 160 million consumers – one in every two Americans – throughout the broadcast (Zeidler and Richwine, 2013). Anheuser-Busch InBev, the company that owns the Budweiser and Beck's beer brands, spent US$28 million on seven commercials. The Super Bowl has been a key piece of the brewery's strategy in introducing new products; Super Bowl XLVII was used to roll-out the Budweiser Black Crown and Beck's Sapphire brands. As Paul Chibe, Vice President of US Marketing, explained,

'The Super Bowl is the ultimate beer occasion and it was extremely critical because [with] over 100 million viewers it gives you an instant shot of awareness' (Rotunno, 2013).

For pay television and associated media forms that are able to sell video or highlight packages on demand, a return on investment is achieved via direct sales to consumers. The most prevalent is the purchase of pay television, in which consumers gain access to live broadcasts. These broadcasts may be available as part of a standard package of pay television programmes, a specialized sport service or as pay-per-view events. Pay-per-view broadcasting has historically been dominated by boxing and, to a lesser extent in the US, by World Wrestling Entertainment (WWE) events; however, the UFC has quickly moved into this space and earns more from pay-per-view events each year than it does from its rights deal with the FOX network. In addition, media organizations are increasingly examining and utilizing pay-per-view to ensure a return on expensive football rights deals around the world.

## SPORT SPONSORSHIP AND MEDIA

As illustrated in Figure 4.1, sport organizations derive revenue from sponsors based on the exposure to consumers through exclusive (official) and non-exclusive (unofficial) media coverage. Similar to the relationship between advertisers and media organizations, sponsors are prepared to pay sport organizations to promote their products and services depending on the number of consumers they will be able to access.

For example, the extent of NASCAR broadcast rights deals referred to previously is reflected in the level of the organization's sponsorship revenue. In this respect, broadcast rights and additional sponsorship revenue are proportional to the same variable: the number of spectators and fans of the sport. Sponsorship deals, like broadcast rights, represent increasingly large investments for sponsors. For example, in the early 1960s, sponsorship of a car for the entire season was approximately US$6,000. In the current context, companies can pay between US$5 million and $35 million for a primary sponsorship for a NASCAR team (NASCAR, 2013). The massive increase in NASCAR sponsorship is due to companies gaining increased access to more than 75 million Americans who now follow the sport through media organizations, as well as those fans' loyalty (Hunter, 2005). A *Sports Illustrated* poll found that 81 per cent of NASCAR fans make an effort to purchase the products of their favourite team sponsors; after Coca-Cola began sponsoring NASCAR, it sold an additional 55 million bottles of soft drink per month (Hunter, 2005). In 2011, Sprint Nextel extended its sponsorship of NASCAR through to 2016, a long-term agreement that began in 2003 when Nextel Communications agreed to pay the sport US$700 million over 10 years (NASCAR, 2011). According to CEO Dan Hesse, the US telecommunication provider was pleased to continue its association with the sport because 'NASCAR fans are great customers who reward us with their loyalty' (NASCAR, 2011).

An extension of sponsorship arrangements is the ownership of teams, although this is a relatively limited phenomenon. Major League Soccer (MLS) has been a professional football league in the United States since its inception in 1994, and the New York/New Jersey MetroStars was one of the league's original teams. In 2006, however, the team was

purchased by Red Bull Energy Drink, was renamed Red Bull New York and the uniform, colours and logo were changed to reflect the team's new ownership. Red Bull also owns other sport properties, including FC Red Bull Salzburg and Red Bull Brasil, football teams in Austria and Brazil, respectively, a number of Red Bull branded events and a racing team in Formula 1. The purchase of these sport properties is predicated on the ability of the purchaser to gain a return on investment through increased exposure and sales of its products.

Because of the constant exposure during games, uniform sponsorship is a particularly significant method of capitalizing on media coverage. General Motors' Chevrolet signed a seven-year, record-breaking agreement with Manchester United in 2014 worth £53 million per season. This amount is roughly double the deals its European rivals FC Barcelona (Qatar Airways), Bayern Munich (Deutsche Telekom), Real Madrid and Arsenal (Emirates) have been able to negotiate.

Sport betting has become an increasingly prevalent part of the sport media nexus, with public awareness and revenue associated with betting on sport increasing dramatically. Major betting operations have become household names, largely due to their sponsorship of major brands in the world's football codes. Gambling has become an increasingly important source of sponsorship revenue, especially for smaller and lower profile clubs that struggle to find major brands as partners. Sport's exposure in the media has enabled sport organizations to secure additional revenue via association with sport betting providers, either as sponsors or via revenue sharing agreements. In Australia sport betting is the fastest growing form of gambling, having doubled since the industry was de-regulated in 2008, with revenues predicted to be more than A$500 million by 2015. As a result, the Australian government turned its attention to the rapid growth in the industry in a bid to address the 'enormous level of community disquiet' (Kruger, 2013) concerning the symbiotic relationship between gambling and Australian sport, especially evident in popular sport broadcasts.

As an example of the importance of sponsorship revenue generated through and via media coverage, the National Rugby League (NRL) in Australia has a sponsorship agreement with Australian telecommunication provider Telstra, which pays A$100 million for naming rights to the league and exclusive new media rights for the sport in Australia. The five-year deal enables Telstra to stream eight NRL games a week, plus the finals series, State of Origin and Test matches and is similar to the deal it struck with the rival AFL. Telstra makes NRL content available to fans on any mobile network, but non-Telstra subscribers are charged an extra fee that is shared with the League. In this case, the sponsor is paying for exposure as well as paying for content as a broadcaster. The partnership is critical to the NRL's plans to nearly double its income by 2017 and it also enables Telstra to move towards a more media-centric platform. According to the League, 'Telstra's proud history in supporting rugby league and its fans . . . is at the heart of its commitment to providing the investment and latest technology for a digital network that is changing the ways fans connect with the game'. Further advances in mobile communication technologies are likely to encourage this trend towards partnerships between telecommunication providers and sport organizations.

## SUMMARY

This chapter examined the commercial relationship between sport and media organizations. In particular, the process by which sport broadcast rights are bought and sold was discussed and the amount of money expended on broadcast rights was examined from both media and sport perspectives. It was clear from an analysis of the world's major professional sport organizations that broadcast rights are now a significant component of overall revenue and, in many cases, represent the majority of income. Media and, increasingly, telecommunications companies continue to sign multi-million dollar, multi-year deals for the rights to broadcast premium sport properties. Importantly, it is also clear from this chapter that money is the most important driver of the sport media nexus, especially in the highly commercialized world of professional sport. Review questions and exercises are listed below to assist with confirming your knowledge of the core concepts and principles introduced in this chapter.

## REVIEW QUESTIONS AND EXERCISES

1 What is the role of a sport organization in the commercial dimension of the sport media nexus? Do they access consumers directly, or via media organizations?

2 What is the role of an exclusive broadcaster in the sport media nexus? How do they ensure a return on investment?

3 What is the role of non-exclusive media, such as magazines and newspapers, in the sport media nexus?

4 How do sponsors access consumers within the sport media nexus?

5 How do advertisers access consumers within the sport media nexus?

6 What factors do sellers consider in the broadcast rights process?

7 What makes a broadcast rights deal more valuable for a prospective purchaser?

8 Choose a sport organization not referred to in this chapter and find out the amount paid for the rights to broadcast the sport. Is it an exclusive agreement? Are the rights segmented between free-to-air and pay television and is there provision for radio, the Internet and mobile (handheld) rights? Have the media rights fees increased or decreased in the past five years?

9 Choose a sport organization not referred to in this chapter and find out the amount paid to become a major sponsor of the organization. Is the sponsor visible or mentioned frequently in media coverage of the league or team?

10 Access a major sport organization's website. Are sponsors or advertisers featured on the site? Do you believe that this is an effective way to access sport consumers?

## FURTHER READING


Chadwick, S. and Arthur, D. (2012) Més que un club (more than a club): The commercial development of FC Barcelona. In S. Chadwick and D. Arthur (eds) *International Cases in the Business of Sport* (1–12). Oxford: Butterworth-Heinemann.

Cobbs, J. (2011) Legal battles for sponsorship exclusivity: The cases of the World Cup and NASCAR. *Sport Management Review, 14* (3), 287–296.

Evens, T., Lefever, K., Valcke, P., Schuurman, D. and Marez, L. D. (2011) Access to premium content on mobile television platforms: The case of mobile sports. *Telematics and Informatics, 28* (1), 32–39.

FitzSimons, P. (1996) *The Rugby War*. Sydney: HarperSports.

Gorse, S., Chadwick, S. and Burton, N. (2010) Entrepreneurship through sports marketing: A case analysis of Red Bull in sport. *Journal of Sponsorship, 3* (4), 348–357.

Hill, D. (2010) A critical mass of corruption: Why some football leagues have more match-fixing than others. *International Journal of Sports Marketing and Sponsorship, 11* (3), 221–235.

Hutchins, B. and Rowe, D. (2012) *Sport Beyond Television: The Internet, Digital Media and the Rise of Networked Media Sport*. New York: Routledge.

Magdalinski, T. and Nauright, J. (2012) Commercialisation of the modern Olympics. In Trevor Slack (ed.) *The Commercialisation of Sport* (185–204). London: Routledge.

St John, A. (2009) *The Billion Dollar Game: Behind the Scenes of the Greatest Day in American Sport – Super Bowl Sunday*. New York: Doubleday.

Willoughby, K. A. and Mancini, C. (2003) The inaugural (and only) season of the Xtreme Football League: A case study in sports entertainment. *International Journal of Sports Marketing and Sponsorship, 5*, 227–235.


## RELEVANT WEBSITES

### Americas

National Football League – www.nfl.com
Major League Baseball – www.mlb.com
National Basketball Association – www.nba.com
Toronto Maple Leafs – www.mapleleafs.com
X Games – www.xgames.com
Campeonato Brasileiro Serie A – www.cbf.com.br
Sirius XM Satellite Radio – www.siriusxm.com
NCAA March Madness – www.marchmadness.com
Super Bowl – www.superbowl.com
World Wrestling Entertainment (WWE) – www.wwe.com

### Australia, New Zealand and South Africa

National Basketball League – www.nbl.com.au
Australian Football League – www.afl.com.au
National Rugby League – www.nrl.com.au
Fox Sports Australia – www.foxsports.com.au
Super Rugby – www.sanzarrugby.com/superrugby

## Asia

Indian Premier League – www.iplt20.com

## Europe

English Premier League – www.premierleague.com
Manchester United (MUTV) – http://mu.tv.manutd.com
Union of European Football Associations – www.uefa.com
Liga Nacional de Fútbol Profesional – www.ligabbva.com
Serie A – www.legaseriea.it
Bundesliga – www.bundesliga.com
Real Madrid FC – www.realmadrid.com
FC Barcelona – www.fcbarcelona.com

## Global

Ultimate Fighting Championship – www.ufc.com
Federation Internationale de Football Association – www.fifa.com
International Olympic Committee – www.olympic.org
Red Bull – www.redbull.com
National Association for Stock Car Auto Racing – www.nascar.com

## CASE STUDY

### Making the grade: the Deloitte Football Money League

This case examines the highest earning clubs in the world's most popular sport, and further highlights the importance of football in the sport media nexus. Each year the Sports Business Group at Deloitte in the United Kingdom ranks the top European football clubs – based on an analysis of the clubs' relative financial performance, including broadcast rights revenue, sponsorship, merchandise, ticket and hospitality sales – and the result is the Deloitte Football Money League (Table 4.5). Real Madrid's Jose Angel Sanchez once famously argued that many consumers now 'support a local side, and one of the world's big six [football team brands]' (Frost, 2004: 367); for a club such as Manchester United, some 130 million satellite fans follow the Red Devils as their second or third team (Manchester Evening News, 2010). While all of the top 20 clubs represented in the 2013 Deloitte Football Money League come from the EPL, Serie A, Bundesliga, la Liga, Ligue 1, clubs such as Ajax from the Netherlands, Turkey's Galatasaray and Brazil's Corinthians are all in the top 30 and may soon challenge for one of these 'big six'.

Despite the tough economic conditions that buffeted the world economy in the wake of the global financial crisis, the Money League clubs generated over €4.8 billion in 2011–12, an increase of 10 per cent on the previous year. As a result, these Money League representatives contribute more than a quarter of the total revenues

**TABLE 4.5** 2013 Deloitte Money League

| *No.* | *Team* | *Country* | *Revenue (€ million)* | *% from Broadcasting* | *% from Commercial* |
|---|---|---|---|---|---|
| 1 | Real Madrid | Spain | 512.6 | 39 | 36 |
| 2 | FC Barcelona | Spain | 483.0 | 37 | 39 |
| 3 | Manchester United | England | 395.9 | 32 | 37 |
| 4 | Bayern Munich | Germany | 368.4 | 22 | 55 |
| 5 | Chelsea | England | 322.6 | 43 | 27 |
| 6 | Arsenal | England | 290.3 | 37 | 22 |
| 7 | Manchester City | England | 285.6 | 38 | 49 |
| 8 | AC Milan | Italy | 256.9 | 49 | 38 |
| 9 | Liverpool | England | 233.2 | 34 | 42 |
| 10 | Juventus | Italy | 195.4 | 47 | 37 |
| 11 | Borussia Dortmund | Germany | 189.1 | 32 | 51 |
| 12 | Internazionale | Italy | 185.9 | 60 | 27 |
| 13 | Tottenham Hotspur | England | 178.2 | 43 | 29 |
| 14 | Schalke 04 | Germany | 174.5 | 22 | 53 |
| 15 | Napoli | Italy | 148.4 | 58 | 26 |
| 16 | Olympique de Marseille | France | 135.7 | 52 | 35 |
| 17 | Olympique Lyonnais | France | 131.9 | 54 | 32 |
| 18 | Hamburger SV | Germany | 121.1 | 19 | 48 |
| 19 | AS Roma | Italy | 115.9 | 55 | 32 |
| 20 | Newcastle United | England | 115.3 | 59 | 15 |

Source: Deloitte (2013).

of the European football market. This situation highlights the growing disparity between the richer and poorer clubs in world football, yet there were substantial revenue differences even among these 20 Money League clubs. For example, Real Madrid earned almost €200 million more than fifth-placed Chelsea, and double that of eighth-placed AC Milan. Indeed, the European Union has even called for a luxury tax, as seen across the Atlantic in the NBA and MLB, to be levied on Europe's top football clubs in order to introduce more financial equality into the game (Deloitte, 2013). Participation in lucrative European club competitions, such as the UEFA Champions League (UCL) or Europa League, significantly boosted the balance sheets of most of the Money League clubs. This was predominately due to large and loyal supporter bases enabling clubs to deliver large broadcast audiences, in both domestic and international markets. As discussed in this chapter, sport is a very popular television product and advertisers and sponsors alike are willing to invest substantial amounts in order to promote their products and services. Europe's elite football

clubs are extremely attractive to corporate partners as diverse as gaming, airlines, motor vehicles, telecommunications and electronics. The top six clubs dominated the Deloitte Football Money League rankings for a fifth successive year: Real Madrid, FC Barcelona, Manchester United, Bayern Munich, Chelsea and Arsenal.

The Spanish powerhouses, Real Madrid and FC Barcelona, took out the top two spots in the Deloitte Football Money League for the fourth consecutive year. Both clubs have superstars that are recognized around the world and contribute to on-field success and off-field exposure. Real Madrid not only maintained their position at the top of the Money League for an eighth consecutive season, a record held by Manchester United, but they also became the first club to generate €500 million in annual revenue. The club's revenue has grown over the past 15 years at a compound rate of 13 per cent, largely in line with the growth of its international fanbase.

Nearly 40 per cent of the club's €513 million revenue came from its lucrative broadcast rights deal with Mediapro. Real Madrid's ability to negotiate its own individual broadcast rights provides the club with a valuable advantage not available to many of its rivals who instead are bound by the collective selling found in other European markets. On the field, 'Los Merengues' took out its 32nd La Liga title and made the UCL semi finals under the reign of the enigmatic Jose Mourinho; the success drove merchandise sales and saw global brands keen to align themselves with the world's most successful football club. Other examples of incredibly lucrative deals are found within the Deloitte Football Money League. For example, although FC Barcelona was unable to repeat its success of the previous year when it won the Champions League and La Liga, the Catalan giants generated a healthy €483 million in revenue. The club receives €30 million per season from Qatar Sports Investments that saw the logo of Qatar Airways adorn Barça's famous strip from the 2013–14 season in a deal that was, at the time, the most lucrative in world football. While FC Barcelona also benefits from being able to individually negotiate its own broadcast rights, broadcast revenue fell slightly as a result of its semi-final exit in the UCL. Plans to re-develop historic Nou Camp and average crowds of 75,000 ensure that FC Barcelona is well-positioned to battle Real Madrid for continued dominance in the Deloitte Football Money League for some time to come.

Three of the next four in the Football Money League – Manchester United, Chelsea and Arsenal – come from the highly popular English league, while Bayern Munich sits in fourth place on the rankings. Manchester United retained third place despite declining revenue, which was largely as a result of early exits in the Champions League and FA Cup. Indeed, failing to progress beyond the group stage of the UCL saw the club's broadcast revenue decline by 11 per cent. During this period, however, the Red Devils were able to leverage the global brand to secure lucrative deals with Chevrolet, Bwin and a range of telecommunication providers across Europe and the Middle East, which saw commercial revenues make the largest contribution to its bottom line. An improved on-field performance, especially in Europe, combined with the Chevrolet deal and the new, improved EPL broadcast rights deal should see Manchester United mount a strong challenge to the dominance of its Spanish rivals. Despite freezing ticket prices for the 2011–12 season, Bayern

Munich's match-day revenue increased by 19 per cent. This increase was largely because the Bavarian giant continued to play to sell-out crowds at Allianz Arena and hosted the Champions League final, ultimately losing on penalties to Chelsea; the event was watched by 167 million worldwide (UEFA, 2012). Although its UCL run saw the club's coffers rise by nearly €44 million, its place in the Money League table is largely due to its relentless commercial growth. Bayern Munich signed an eight-year, €25 million per season extension with German equipment supplier, Adidas, and on the back of its new deal with Deutsche Telekom the club may be able to hold off the charge of its London rivals.

While Chelsea had a memorable Champions League run and secured an additional €15.4 million as a result, they finished a modest sixth place in the EPL, far short of its owner's and fans' expectations. Although commercial revenue remained strong, courtesy of long-term deals with Samsung and Adidas, capacity constraints with Stamford Bridge mean that the club is overly reliant on its on-field success to maintain its edge over Arsenal and Manchester City in the Money League. In contrast, Arsenal maintained its proud tradition in Europe and qualified for the Champions League for the fifteenth consecutive season. The quality facilities at Emirates Stadium and its loyal fan base, coupled with additional UCL fixtures, saw match-day and broadcast revenues remain stable. However, Arsenal remained the only club in the Money League for which match-day revenue was its largest revenue source; the club attracts only half of the commercial revenue Manchester United is able to command. In response to this, and in a bid to reclaim its top five spot, Arsenal secured new commercial partnerships with Bharti Airtel and Malta Guinness and has signed a multi-year, multi-million pound extension with Emirates Airlines.

Representatives from the Italian Serie A join the EPL's Manchester City and Liverpool to round out the Football Money League's top 10. Manchester City rocketed into seventh spot as a result of its fairytale finish to the season, winning the English title for the first time in 44 years and its inaugural participation in the Champions League. As a result, broadcast revenue rose by 28 per cent, commercial revenue almost doubled, largely due to its new partnership with Etihad Airways, the United Arab Emirates airline, and the club played before almost sell-out crowds. In contrast, although AC Milan saw broadcast revenue increase by 17 per cent as a result of reaching the quarter-finals of the Champions League and almost winning the Serie A title, its average league attendances continued to decline. AC Milan struggled to generate sufficient match-day revenue from an ageing San Siro stadium and, together with Juventus, had the lowest match-day revenue of any of their top ten rivals. Although Liverpool and Juventus failed to qualify for European competition and will need to improve in this area to consolidate their position in the Money League, both clubs have reason for optimism. An unbeaten Serie A season, and a new €150 million stadium, saw match-day revenue almost treble and commercial revenue dramatically increase for the famous Italian club. Liverpool remains committed to a redeveloped Anfield and has signed lucrative commercial partnerships with Standard Chartered, Chevrolet and Irish bookmaker, Paddy Power, to fully leverage its global brand.

This case explores the top 20 football clubs in the 2013 Deloitte Football Money League and the reasons for their financial success. Many of the clubs represented here

have been in the Money League for the past decade and the top six have remained in the same order for the past five years. The fact that very few new clubs have entered the Money League and that the same clubs dominate the top of the table demonstrates that the commercial dimensions of the sport media nexus benefit the largest sport organizations the most and make it difficult for smaller and less popular sport organizations to establish themselves as media properties worthy of investment.

## CASE STUDY QUESTIONS

1 Examine the most recent Deloitte Money League. Which clubs have moved up or down from the 2013 League presented in this case study? What are the reasons for these moves – refer specifically where possible to media and sponsorship revenue and the drivers of these revenue streams.
2 Think about your favourite European football club – did it make the Football Money League? If so, what elements drove its financial success in its most recent season? If not, what changes would need to occur for its media and sponsorship revenue to increase? Is this likely or realistic?
3 Why do the clubs represented in this edition of the Deloitte Football Money League have such an advantage? What common elements drive revenue for the highest earning clubs and ensure that they continue to participate in the Money League and boast impressive financial records?
4 What was so special about the two Spanish heavyweights, Real Madrid and FC Barcelona, that enabled them to dominate the Deloitte Football Money League rankings?

Source: Deloitte (2013).

CHAPTER 5

# Sport media regulation

## Making the rules

## OVERVIEW

This chapter examines the regulation of the sport media nexus and, in particular, the broadcasting of sport on both free-to-air and pay television. The chapter explores the rationale for government involvement in the regulation of sport broadcasting, government objectives and the regulatory mechanisms applied to govern sport broadcasting in different national contexts. This chapter also examines the impact of sport broadcasting regulations on the sport and media industries and their respective operations.

## LEARNING OUTCOMES

After completing this chapter, the reader should be able to:

- understand why governments seek to regulate sport broadcasting;
- describe how government regulation might protect the interests of consumers and prevent anti-competitive behaviour;
- evaluate the impact of sport broadcasting regulation in a number of geographic, cultural and national contexts; and
- speculate on the impact of changing sport broadcasting regulation in terms of: the interests of consumers; the profitability of sport organizations; the place of sport in society; and the competition between and within media organizations.

## INTRODUCTION

The sport media landscape, outlined in the first four chapters, is both complex and dynamic. It has also altered dramatically, marked by the advent of television, the hyper-commercialization of sport since the 1970s and the evolution of pay television, the internet and mobile technologies in the past three decades. The increasingly commercial

nature of the sport media nexus and the relationship between sport and television in particular has presented a series of challenges for governments throughout the world. These challenges have included ensuring that its citizens have reasonable access to sport broadcasting on television and that media and sport organizations do not engage in practices or behaviour that are anti-competitive. Governments have responded to these challenges by regulating sport broadcasting, albeit in different ways, depending on cultural, national and geographical contexts. The regulatory mechanisms and their impact are indicative of both the special social significance of sport and the commercial power of the media.

The regulation of sport broadcasting attempts to ameliorate the problems that result from the often divergent interests of audiences, broadcasters, sport organizations and governing bodies. Hoehn and Lancefield (2003: 566) noted:

> The pre-eminent position of sports programming in a channel's offering and as a key driver of a TV delivery/distribution platform has forced governments to intervene in media merger proposals, sports-rights contract negotiations, and disputes among TV distribution systems over access to content.

This government intervention has had a significant impact on the way in which sport is broadcast, the products that are allowed to be promoted via an association with sport, the amount of sport that audiences have access to via free-to-air television, the ways in which sport organizations are able to sell broadcast rights and, in some cases, the ownership of sport teams. Like the sport media industry generally, the regulation of sport broadcasting is not static, but rather has evolved dynamically, especially since the introduction of pay television. This process has been exacerbated by a shift from an industry paradigm in which content, such as sport, was competing for broadcast time on media outlets that were scarce, to one in which a multitude of outlets and forms are competing for scarce content (Cowie and Williams, 1997).

## GOVERNMENT INTERVENTION

In market driven economies, resources are allocated through the interaction of demand, supply and prices. There are occasions where the full benefit of the market is not realized because of an under supply of socially desirable products or an oversupply of less desirable products (Cooke, 1994). This situation is known as market failure, in which the market does not deliver the best outcome possible and where the allocation of resources is distorted (Michael, 2006). In this instance, the market does not operate in the best interests of the community or nation, and a government may intervene if it believes that it can engineer a better outcome. This intervention can take the form of market participation, market regulation, financial intervention or economic intervention (Michael, 2006).

In market participation interventions, governments provide goods or services in competition with private providers, which often serves to keep prices low. Market regulation typically refers to enacting legislation in order to dictate the way in which an industry operates and, in particular, the way specific companies are able to do business.

Financial intervention is where a government allocates financial resources to specific industries. This might occur through investment in infrastructure or awarding grants. Finally, economic intervention is where governments implement tariffs and subsidies to stimulate production, protect markets or alter the costs of a product or service.

Sport broadcasting on free-to-air television, as demonstrated in the previous chapter, is subsidized by advertising revenue. Aside from the cost of a television set and an antenna to receive a broadcast signal, sport broadcasts are available to consumers at no cost. In this case, the consumption of the product by one consumer does not adversely impact the consumption of other consumers as the service or product has a non-excludable feature. The number of consumers simply raises or lowers the revenue that can be generated through the broadcast, either from the sale of advertising time or the sale of additional goods and services being advertised. In the case of free-to-air sport broadcasts therefore, the benefits of watching sport, an activity that often has considerable social and cultural significance to the public, can be enjoyed by a substantial majority of the population.

In contrast, sport broadcasting on pay television is predicated on the notion that consumers will pay to consume the product. In this case, the migration of sport matches and events from free-to-air television to pay television transforms sport from an essentially free consumer product subsidized by advertisers to one that requires payment. This migration of the product has the potential to cause market failure, as the cost imposed on a product that was previously delivered at no cost is likely to result in significantly fewer people being able to access the product. The same is likely to occur if a single broadcaster is able to secure sufficient sport rights to reduce competition in the market place and subsequently increase costs above market value. Many governments regard sport events of national and international significance to be merit goods. Merit goods are commodities or services for which community demand is high because of social benefits, 'but the normal market cost would be intolerable for an individual consumer' (Michael, 2006: 63). Convergence and the emergence of new media markets have created 'considerable uncertainty' (Productivity Commission, 2000: 31), to the extent that it is unclear whether sport will remain available to all or whether it will become restricted to only to those with sufficient funds to 'enjoy the extensive range of consumer technologies and digital content required to experience the excitement of media sport spectacle' (Hutchins and Rowe, 2012: 183). In order to avoid such an outcome, governments often intervene where merit goods are concerned to ensure that a wide public distribution of the product is achieved, in order to maximize the number of people able to receive a social benefit from the product or activity.

Of the four intervention strategies referred to previously, governments that are seeking to avoid or limit the extent of market failure in sport broadcasting prefer market regulation. For example, many governments around the world have regulated the migration of sport matches and events to pay television by legislating that events of national and international significance are broadcast on, or offered first to, free-to-air television. This is referred to variously as anti-siphoning legislation or the 'listing' of sport events.

Broadcasting regulation generally, and sport broadcasting regulation more specifically, is an attempt to balance social, cultural and economic objectives (Productivity Commission, 2000). All three objectives can be achieved, but it is rare that a government does not make compromises to ensure that one objective does not dominate or overwhelm

## IN PRACTICE 5.1

### The sky's the limit: government denies BSkyB's bid

On 29 October 1998 the British Secretary of State referred the proposed acquisition of Manchester United by British Sky Broadcasting (BSkyB) to the United Kingdom's Monopolies and Mergers Commission. In its final report, the Commission noted that BSkyB was

> a vertically integrated broadcaster that buys TV rights, including those for sporting events, makes some of its own programmes, packages programmes from a range of sources into various channels, and distributes and retails these channels to its subscribers using its direct-to-home satellite platform, as well as selling them wholesale to other retailers using different distribution platforms.

It also noted that Manchester United by any measure was the strongest club in the English Premier League.

In considering the competitive effects of the proposed £623 million take-over bid, the Commission determined that the merger would increase the market power of BSkyB, given that it was essentially the only provider of premium sport channels on pay television and that new market entrants relied upon an ability to secure rights to live sport events. Furthermore, there were insufficient rights to sustain a significant number of channels and its market share meant that BSkyB had considerable market power. Given this market power essentially represented a monopoly, the acquisition of the Red Devils was likely to contribute to the pay television broadcaster's ability to raise prices above competitive levels with impunity.

The Commission noted:

> [B]ecause of its financial strength, the size of its supporter base and recent sporting success, Manchester United has greater influence within the Premier League than any other club and that, in the event of the merger, it would use this influence to persuade other members of the Premier League to support the sale of rights to BSkyB. Many parties felt that it would be objectionable if BSkyB, or indeed any other broadcaster, bought any Premier League club, because it would give it a seat on both sides of the table when rights sales were being negotiated. For BSkyB, the incumbent broadcaster of Premier League football, to acquire the most influential club was widely seen as particularly detrimental.

The notion that BSkyB could be both a club owner and a bidder for the broadcast rights was just one of the anti-competitive impacts of the proposed merger that led the Commission to conclude that it should be prohibited.

The Monopolies and Mergers Commission concluded that the proposed take-over of Manchester United by the United Kingdom's primary pay television sports channel provider would result in BSkyB acquiring a significant advantage in the market place at the expense of competitors. In particular, it would have an advantage in gaining the

broadcast rights to the EPL and rivals would be at a competitive disadvantage in establishing sport channels on pay television. The Commission noted in their final report that its public interest conclusions were based mainly on the effects of the merger on competition between BSkyB and other broadcasters. However, it also believed the merger would adversely affect football by reinforcing 'the existing trend towards greater inequality of wealth between clubs, thus weakening the smaller ones' and would also give BSkyB 'additional influence over Premier League decisions relating to the organization of football, leading to some decisions which did not reflect the long-term interests of football'. In both instances the Commission believed this would damage the quality of British football.

Ultimately, the Monopolies and Mergers Commission argued that it was unable to identify any public interest benefits from the proposed merger and was therefore likely to act against the public interest. As a result, after four and a half months of deliberation, the Commission recommended that the acquisition of Manchester United by BSkyB be prohibited, which it duly was. Disappointed in the decision, BSkyB's chief executive, Mark Booth said, 'this is a bad ruling for British football clubs who will have to compete in Europe against clubs who are backed by successful media companies' (Larsen and Grice, 1999). Many of the EPL's major team brands are now in foreign hands, including Manchester United, which was acquired by American Malcolm Glazer, owner of the NFL's Tampa Bay Buccaneers, for £790 million. The take-over bid was not referred to the Commission since it was not considered to have any adverse impact on competition and hence it was not detrimental to the public interest.

Sources: Competition Commission (1999); Larsen and Grice (1999).

the others. In the case of sport broadcasting, government, sport and media organizations often disagree on the balance between the three. Not surprisingly, sport and media organizations often argue that broadcasting regulation is skewed in favour of social and cultural objectives and does not allow them to maximize the economic returns available through the transaction of sport products, such as the sale of broadcast rights or the purchase of access to pay-per-view events. The regulation of sport broadcasting is dependent on commercial, cultural and geographic contexts. In other words, governments apply a different set of regulations depending on the country, the importance of sport, the historical relationship between free-to-air and pay television, the access of consumers to pay television and the proximity of different national and regional markets.

Sport broadcasting regulation may be divided into three distinct components as governments seek to protect the 'viewing rights' of citizens. First, government regulation attempts to prevent sport events migrating from free-to-air television to pay television exclusively. Second, government regulation attempts to ensure that sport and media organizations do not engage in anti-competitive behaviour when buying and selling the rights to broadcast sport. In particular, monopolies created through the sale of broadcast rights are to be avoided, especially as media companies can 'hoard' mediated sport content, as this restricts supply and raises prices to a level that exploits consumers (New and Le Grand, 1999; Hutchins and Rowe, 2012). Third and finally, government regulation attempts to limit or prevent any negative consequences that arise from the vertical

integration of the sport and media industries, such as the purchase of a sport team or league by a media organization. The following sections outline the regulation of sport broadcasting in various regions and nations in order to contextualize the impacts of regulation on the sport and media industries.

## EUROPE

The European Union considers sport one of the key areas that can bring its citizens together and help forge an identity. In recognition of its cultural significance, in December 2009 the European Commission adopted the Lisbon Treaty (and Article 165) to provide the European Union with a framework to support, coordinate and supplement sport policy actions by its members. By early 2011, the European Commission began to implement the new Treaty provisions and put in place measures to enhance the societal, economic and organizational dimensions of sport (European Commission, 2011). With respect to sport broadcasting regulation, the European Commission seeks to ensure that sport leagues, clubs and broadcasters do not engage in anti-competitive behaviour. In particular, the Commission regulates the practice of joint, or collective, selling, which the Commission describes as a situation where sports clubs assign their media rights to their association, which sell the rights on behalf of the clubs (Toft, 2003).

The European Commission has noted that as a result of joint selling, leagues and associations have traditionally packaged all media rights and sold them to a single broadcaster in each territory. European regulators recognize that the licensing of sport media rights should be responsive to different cultural preferences and market demands and, as such, collective selling may be allowed under certain circumstances. Nonetheless, the European Commission strongly recommends sport associations establish mechanisms for the collective selling of media rights that ensure revenues are adequately shared yet remain fully compliant with EU competition law (European Commission, 2011). This practice enables the league or association to control the sale of the broadcast rights and maximize the exclusivity of the contract; however, the Commission believes that joint selling is a horizontal restriction of competition, whereby clubs are unable to compete for broadcast rights fees on an individual basis. This lack of competition creates an additional lack of horizontal competition between broadcasters that, in turn, limits public access. The process and implications of joint selling are graphically represented in Figure 5.1.

The European Commission acknowledges that the collective selling of sport broadcasting rights is accepted practice and in many instances facilitates exclusivity that, in turn, maximizes the return that sport leagues and clubs can achieve. However, joint selling also facilitates long-term contracts and if the broadcaster is dominant in the marketplace, this can lead to market foreclosure. The practice of joint selling long-term exclusive rights packages also results in a minority of media organizations being able to afford the rights. In other words, the act of selling the rights can be anti-competitive, while long-term exclusive contracts can result in a lack of competition between broadcasters, which might result in an increase in prices and a further reduction in competition between broadcasters. It is because of these concerns that the European Commission saw fit in the early 2000s to intervene in the sale of broadcast rights by UEFA, the German Bundesliga and the English Premier League.

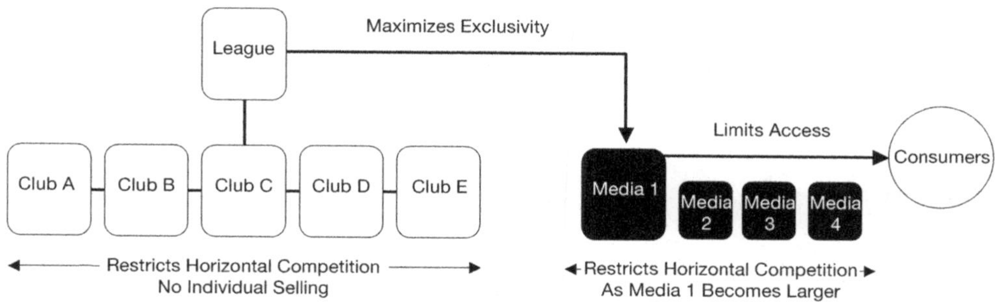


**FIGURE 5.1** Joint selling

In 2001, the European Commission objected to UEFA's proposed joint selling arrangement for UEFA Champions League games, especially since it sold these rights as an exclusive contract to a single broadcaster for up to four years at a time. As a result of these arrangements not all games were seen live on television, while internet and telephone operators were denied access to the rights. The European Commission's statement of objections concluded that these arrangements prevented individual clubs, participating in the Champions League, from 'taking independent commercial action in respect of the TV rights and excluded competition between them in individually supplying TV rights to interested buyers' (European Commission, 2003: 30). Therefore, in the opinion of the Commission, this situation restricted competition between broadcasters, as well as hindered the development of new technology, which was regarded as a disadvantage to broadcasters, individual clubs and spectators.

UEFA's amended joint selling arrangement, which was approved by the European Commission in 2003, consists of UEFA centrally selling the rights to live television transmission of mid-week night matches in two separate packages. These packages cover 47 matches of the total 125 played during the UEFA Champions League competition and give the broadcaster the right to select the best of the available matches, while UEFA has the exclusive right to sell the remaining matches. If UEFA does not manage to do this, then individual clubs are given the opportunity to sell the rights to matches themselves. In response to the Commission's additional concerns, the amended rights arrangement also allowed the sale of internet, radio and mobile Champions League content to different third parties. UEFA also has the exclusive right to sell a highlights package covering all 125 Champions League games (European Commission, 2003). Finally, as a way of counteracting the potentially negative effects of long-term broadcast rights agreements, UEFA agreed to limit contracts to a period no longer than three years. The UEFA case has proved particularly significant because it has guided the European Commission's approach to future joint selling arrangements and many leagues have decided to adopt joint selling of broadcast rights, especially as alternative arrangements are often seen to favour the stronger teams.

The European Commission has adopted legal measures to ensure that major sport events do not migrate exclusively to pay television and that events of major importance are available on free-to-air television, thereby maximizing public access and attempting to avoid market failure. In member states of the European Union these legal measures

became enshrined in the Television Without Frontiers Directive (henceforth referred to as 'the Directive'). The Directive was established in 1989 and amended in 1997, with the aim to create an effective single European market for emerging audiovisual media. Reflecting the increased convergence of the sport media nexus, the Directive evolved into the Audiovisual Media Services Directive in 2007. The legislation was designed to regulate all broadcasts – via traditional television or video-on-demand within new media technologies, such as the internet or mobile phone.

Article 3j of the Directive stated:

> Each Member State may take measures in accordance with Community law to ensure that broadcasters under its jurisdiction do not broadcast on an exclusive basis events which are regarded by that Member State as being of major importance for society in such a way as to deprive a substantial proportion of the public in that Member State of the possibility of following such events by live coverage or deferred coverage on free television. If it does so, the Member State concerned shall draw up a list of designated events, national or non-national, which it considers to be of major importance for society. It shall do so in a clear and transparent manner in due time. In so doing the Member State concerned shall also determine whether these events should be available by whole or partial live coverage, or where necessary or appropriate for objective reasons in the public interest, whole or partial deferred coverage.
>
> (European Union, 2007)

The European Commission noted that events such as the FIFA World Cup, the Olympic Games or the European Football Championship are of major importance to society; article 3j of the Directive is designed to prevent instances whereby such events are broadcast exclusively on pay television.

As a result of article 3j, individual member states are able to construct a list of events that they believe should be available on free-to-air television. These lists are formulated using different criteria and reflect different national sporting and cultural preferences. For example, the Austrian listed events feature the Olympic Games, football and skiing. In Austria the following events are listed:

- the Summer or Winter Olympic Games;
- FIFA World Cup matches, if the Austrian national team is involved, as well as the opening match, the semi-finals and the final of the football World Cup;
- European Championship football matches if the Austrian national team is involved, as well as the opening match, the semi-finals and the final of the football European Championship;
- the final of the Austrian Football Cup;
- FIS World Alpine skiing championships;
- World Nordic skiing championships.

By contrast, in Belgium 18 sporting events are listed as being either popular, culturally or nationally significant or have traditionally been broadcast on free-to-air television. Of these events, five are related to the broadcast of football at national or international level and

eight are cycling events. This Belgian preference for cycling events is not reflected in any of the other European lists, unlike football, which dominates many of the European lists. For instance, in Germany the following significant events are listed:

- the Summer and Winter Olympic Games;
- all European Championship and FIFA World Cup matches involving the German national football team, as well as the opening match, the semi-finals and finals, irrespective of whether the German team is involved;
- the semi-finals and final of the German FA Cup;
- the German national football team's home and away matches;
- the final of any European football club competition (UEFA Champions League or Europa League) involving a German Club.

The notion that the listing of events is dependent on the national importance and heritage of particular sports and events is confirmed by Ireland's list, where, unlike central European countries, the Winter Olympics has been excluded. Instead the Irish list includes hurling and horse racing. The Irish list is as follows:

- the Summer Olympics;
- the All-Ireland Senior Inter-County Football and Hurling Finals;
- Ireland's home and away qualifying games in the European Football Championship and the FIFA World Cup Tournaments;
- Ireland's games in the European Football Championship Finals Tournament and the FIFA World Cup Finals Tournament;
- the opening games, the semi-finals and final of the European Football Championship Finals and the FIFA World Cup Finals Tournament;
- Ireland's games in the Rugby World Cup Finals Tournament;
- The Irish Grand National and the Irish Derby;
- The Nations Cup at the Dublin Horse Show;
- each of Ireland's games in the Six Nations Rugby Football Championship.

Like the German list, the Italian list is relatively short and is dominated by football, but also includes two events of national importance, the Tour of Italy (Giro d'Italia) cycling competition and the Italian Formula 1 Grand Prix. The most complex regulation in Europe is in the United Kingdom, where the list is divided into Group A and Group B events. The Broadcasting Act 1996, as amended by the Television Broadcasting Regulations of 2000, states that Group A events must be made available for acquisition by a free-to-air broadcaster whose channel is available to at least 95 per cent of the UK population. By contrast, Group B events are those that may not be broadcast live on an exclusive basis unless adequate provision has been made for secondary coverage. The minimum acceptable service for Group B events is edited highlights or delayed coverage of at least 10 per cent of the event's duration subject to a minimum of 30 minutes of coverage for an event lasting one hour or more, whichever is greater. An event may be listed because it is of 'national' interest within England, Scotland, Wales or Northern Ireland separately, and this accounts for the inclusion of the Scottish FA Cup Final. The United Kingdom Group A listed events are as follows:

- Olympic Games;
- FIFA World Cup Finals Tournament;
- European Football Championship Finals Tournament;
- FA Cup Final;
- Scottish FA Cup Final (in Scotland);
- Grand National;
- The Derby;
- Wimbledon Tennis Finals;
- Rugby League Challenge Cup Final;
- Rugby World Cup Final.

## AUSTRALIA

The Australian Broadcasting Services Act 1992 and its amendments are the primary mechanisms by which the Australian Federal Government has regulated Australian broadcasting generally, and sport broadcasting more specifically. The Act included the following aims: to promote the availability of a diverse range of radio and television services offering entertainment, education and information to audiences throughout Australia; to provide a regulatory environment that will facilitate the development of a broadcasting industry in Australia that is efficient, competitive and responsive to audience needs; to promote the role of broadcasting services in developing and reflecting a sense of Australian identity, character and cultural diversity; and to encourage providers of commercial and community broadcasting services to be responsive to the need for fair and accurate coverage of matters of public interest and for an appropriate coverage of matters of local significance.

Part seven of the Act described how the responsible government minister may protect the free availability of certain types of programmes. In practice, these programmes are sporting events that are considered to be nationally significant. In 1994, the Minister for what is now Broadband, Communications and the Digital Economy, was given the power to list in a formal notice, known as the anti-siphoning list, which sporting events are to be available on free-to-air television. This list, which was designed to be periodically reviewed, gives free-to-air broadcasters the first option to purchase the rights to these events and sports, but does not compel them to do so and, in the event that no free-to-air broadcaster wishes to purchase the rights, they are offered to pay television. The anti-siphoning law is designed to prevent pay television operators from exclusively siphoning off the rights to broadcast events of national importance and cultural significance (Department of Broadband, Communications and the Digital Economy, 2009). In short, the legislation protects the interests of commercial free-to-air broadcasters to ensure that sport is available to the Australian population at little or no cost. An investigation into Australia's sport broadcasting regulation by the Australian Broadcasting Authority (2001) concluded that 'Australia's anti-siphoning scheme and its list of events are both more extensive and restrictive than those in operation overseas'. However, as a result, the Australian Government has placed pay television operators at a commercial disadvantage, largely in response to the concerns of free-to-air television networks that feared pay television rivals would capture the rights to most of the popular sports and cost them

advertising revenue. In 2012 free-to-air advertising exceeded A$1,993 million, in comparison with pay television advertising revenue worth approximately A$440 million.

Australia's anti-siphoning scheme had been largely unchanged since its introduction in 1994; however, a number of developments – notably the proliferation of digital television channels, the introduction of IPTV services such as Telstra's T-Box, and the expiration of the 2006–10 list – necessitated a major review by the Minister for Broadband, Communications and the Digital Economy. The result was the Broadcasting Services Amendment (Anti-Siphoning) Bill 2012 that introduced a two-tier scheme, similar to the legislation passed in the United Kingdom, where the list is divided into Tier A and Tier B events. The new scheme is designed to allow greater use of multi-channels, especially as Australians switch to digital television. The legislation states that Tier A events, nationally iconic events, such as the Melbourne Cup and the finals matches of major international and domestic competitions, must be shown first on a free-to-air broadcaster's main channel (with some consideration to allow coverage for overlapping events or where an event overlaps with the news). In addition, Tier A events must be shown live to all parts of Australia, as the event actually happens. By contrast, Tier B events, regionally iconic and nationally significant events, such as the round and preliminary matches of international and domestic competitions, can be premiered on a free-to-air broadcaster's multi-channel, either live or with a delayed starting time of not more than four hours. The Australian 2011–15 Tier A and Tier B listed events are as follows:

## Tier A

- each event held as part of the Summer Olympic Games, including the Opening Ceremony and the Closing Ceremony;
- each running of the Melbourne Cup (Horse Racing);
- the Grand Final of the Australian Football League Premiership;
- the Grand Final of the National Rugby League Premiership;
- the final of the Rugby World Cup;
- each International Test Match involving Australia played in Australia (Cricket);
- each International Test Match between Australia and England played in the United Kingdom (Cricket);
- each One-Day and Twenty20 Cricket Match involving Australia played in Australia;
- each match in the semi-finals and the final of the International Cricket Council One Day International World Cup;
- each match of the International Cricket Council One Day International World Cup involving Australia;
- the final of the International Cricket Council Twenty20 World Cup;
- each match of the International Cricket Council Twenty20 World Cup involving Australia;
- each match of the FIFA World Cup tournament involving Australia;
- each match in the quarter-finals, semi-finals and the final of the FIFA World Cup;
- the men's and women's singles finals of the Australian Open (Tennis);
- each match in a final round tie of the International Tennis Federation Davis Cup World Group tennis tournament involving Australia;

- each race in the Formula 1 World Championship (Grand Prix) held in Australia;
- each race in the Moto GP held in Australia;
- the Bathurst 1000 race in the V8 Supercar Championship Series.

## Tier B

- each event held as part of the Summer Olympic Games, including the Opening Ceremony and the Closing Ceremony (excluding those on Tier A);
- each event held as part of the Winter Olympic Games, including the Opening Ceremony and the Closing Ceremony;
- each event held as part of the Commonwealth Games, including the Opening Ceremony and the Closing Ceremony;
- each match of the Australian Football League Premiership competition, including the Finals Series, played after 1 January 2017 (excluding those events on Tier A);
- each match of the National Rugby League Premiership competition, including the Finals Series (excluding those on Tier A);
- each match in the State of Origin Series (Rugby League);
- each international Rugby League Test Match involving Australia, played in Australia, New Zealand or the United Kingdom;
- each match of the Rugby League World Cup involving Australia;
- each match in the quarter-finals and semi-finals of the Rugby World Cup;
- each match of the Rugby World Cup involving Australia (excluding those on Tier A);
- each international Rugby Union Test Match involving Australia, played in Australia, New Zealand or South Africa, or as part of the team's 'Spring Tour';
- each match in the Australian Open tennis tournament (excluding those on Tier A);
- each match in the men's and women's singles quarter-finals, semi-finals and finals of the Wimbledon (the Lawn Tennis Championships) tournament;
- each match in the men's and women's singles quarter-finals, semi-finals and finals of the United States Open tennis tournament;
- each match in each tie of the International Tennis Federation Davis Cup World Group tennis tournament involving Australia (excluding those on Tier A);
- each round of the Australian Open (Golf);
- each round of the Australian Masters (Golf);
- each round of the United States Masters (Golf);
- each international netball match involving Australia, played in Australia or New Zealand;
- each match in the semi-finals and finals of the International Federation of Netball Associations World Championships involving Australia;
- the English FA Cup Final (Football);
- each match of the FIFA World Cup tournament (excluding those on Tier A);
- each match in the FIFA World Cup Qualification tournament involving Australia;
- each race in the V8 Supercar Championship Series (excluding those on Tier A).

The revised anti-siphoning list is intended to protect sporting events that occupy an important place in Australian society. As a result, the list includes events from 12 sports,

and ensures that the public is able to enjoy matches from the highly popular AFL and NRL competitions. For instance, the government is confident that the existing AFL broadcast rights agreement has sufficient safeguards in place and so did not see the need to include weekly matches nor the Finals Series in the 2011–15 anti-siphoning list. However, despite the popularity of the football codes, it is clear from the above list that there are some inconsistencies, particularly if the strict criterion of national importance is applied. For instance, the final of a football competition held in the United Kingdom is considered to be of national significance to Australians; further, the US Masters golf tournament is on the list but the US Open, British Open and the USPGA are not, despite recognition that these competitions comprise golf's four 'majors'. Furthermore, the final three rounds of Wimbledon and the US Open tennis tournaments are listed, but in each case would only be of national interest and social significance if an Australian was successful in the early stages of the tournament, while the French Open, arguably of equal importance, is noticeable by its absence.

The regulatory framework is designed to protect the availability of sport on Australian free-to-air television. As a result, there are a number of key provisions in the revised legislation that will see the Australian Communications and Media Authority (ACMA) enforce penalties for non-compliance by free-to-air broadcasters. For instance, free-to-air broadcasters will face a 'use it or lose it' provision if they do not agree to televise an event on the anti-siphoning list to which they hold the rights and will instead be forced to offer those rights to rivals, with the first option given to free-to-air networks. Furthermore, IPTV or other online service providers are unable to acquire exclusive access to listed events, and events will be 'delisted' for that year, and made available to pay television rivals, should no free-to-air broadcaster acquire the rights within 26 weeks of the event taking place.

Australia's anti-siphoning laws are an example, by international standards, of extreme government regulation in the area of sport broadcasting. For instance, Australia's trans-tasman neighbour New Zealand does not currently operate an anti-siphoning scheme, although the government has investigated how to ensure greater free-to-air access to nationally significant sport events in a way that has only minimal impact upon the commercial revenue available to sporting bodies. The high level of Australian regulation has been sharply criticized by some of Australia's largest sporting bodies, and even the International Olympic Committee, as it threatens their primary revenue source. According to the IOC, Australia's anti-siphoning laws are 'inherently and self-evidently anti-competitive, operate to the commercial detriment of sporting organizations and the declaration of all events in the Olympic Games as anti-siphoning events is overboard and excessive' (Hepworth, 2012).

Such criticism serves to highlight the challenge governments face when seeking to balance the social, cultural and economic objectives of all stakeholders. While it is true that the Australian Government has prevented market failure, it has also provided sustained assistance for more than 20 years to one set of commercial providers in preference to another. Often government regulators see a need to intervene in order to serve the public's interest, prevent market failure and engineer a better outcome for viewers, administrators and fans. For instance, consider the Australian Government's response to public concern over the relationship that has developed between sports betting agencies and the broadcasting of Australia's favourite sports (see In Practice 5.2).

## IN PRACTICE 5.2

### Don't bet against sports betting regulation

Australia deregulated sports betting in 2008 and it was soon the country's fastest growing form of gambling, much to the concern of sport administrators, viewers and fans. In 2011, representatives from Australia's biggest sports called on the federal government to introduce new laws to protect the integrity of their sporting contests and target bookmakers who seek to corrupt the nation's athletes. At the same time, the Australian Senate launched an enquiry into online gambling and gambling advertising, largely in response to the gambling industry's increasingly symbiotic relationship with Australia's most popular sport properties. According to Senator Richard di Natale, an inquiry was necessary because 'not only do we risk undermining the integrity of sport, we risk creating another generation of problem gamblers' (Kruger, 2013).

Government regulators were increasingly concerned about the long-term effects of gambling advertising on children, that sports betting is becoming 'normalized', and 'that the boundaries between sports betting advertising and the game are being blurred' (Lunn, 2011). This blurring occurs through the promotion of live odds on television, within the match or game play, and through branding opportunities provided by the sponsorship of sport teams by betting agencies. These companies had been able to exploit a loophole in current laws that gave sport broadcasters a special exemption to include gambling advertising and live odds, even during the day when children are most likely to watch television. A joint select committee on gambling reform received information that included 'worrying stories of children who no longer talk about their team's form, but their team's odds' (Lunn, 2011). The Minister for Broadband, Communications and the Digital Economy even threatened to ban the promotion of live odds if the networks did not voluntarily agree to curtail the practice. According to the National Rugby League, it was 'a sensible opportunity for the industry to self-regulate in relation to the more aggressive promotional aspects of sports betting' (Lunn, 2011). As a result, in June 2012 broadcasters agreed to a new code of practice, which included a ban on commentators mentioning live odds, and banned all live odds promotions during play.

The issue again dominated headlines in the early rounds of the 2013 NRL competition when bookmaker Tom Waterhouse appeared alongside Channel Nine's commentary team, updating the betting odds and offering his opinion on the rugby league action. Waterhouse had paid to secure partnership deals with the NRL, AFL, Australian Rugby Union, Cricket Australia and Tennis Australia and so had become a well-known figure to sports fans around the country, yet there was a public backlash to the bookmaker's on-air appearances. The NRL was also concerned over the integration of sports betting into Nine's early season broadcasts of its product, especially as 'the lines were a little blurred' (Conway, 2013) between what the viewer might perceive as commentary and the promotion of sports betting; steps were taken to ensure there was a clear distinction between the two parties. According to the NRL, while gambling was legal, 'the integrity of the competition is our utmost priority for the game [and] we would not allow any arrangement to threaten that' (Conway, 2013).

Legislation was designed to curb the role of bookmakers as commentators, and the Senate Committee remains concerned about the sponsorship of sporting clubs by betting agencies, especially as sports betting turnover is worth A$4.5 billion per year. It has called for a total ban on the display of gambling companies' logos on playing uniforms and merchandise. Understandably, the NRL and the Nine Network, like other major players in the Australian sport media nexus, have serious reservations about further regulation of gambling sponsorship and promotion. Despite their reservations, and if history is a guide, further intervention and subsequent regulation are a 'sure bet'.

Sources: Lunn (2011); Conway (2013); Kruger (2013).

## UNITED STATES OF AMERICA

Cave and Crandall (2001: F13) have noted that 'throughout the modern history of sports broadcasting in the United States, there has always been controversy over the ability of leagues or sports associations to limit individual members' rights to broadcast their games'. For instance, the Sherman Antitrust Act 1890 prohibits unreasonable restraints of competition such as those that might be seen when a league collectively sells its broadcast rights, therefore reducing competition for those rights. Although there is no government body that directly regulates professional sports in the US, court rulings in 1953 and 1960 determined that league-wide television contracts that benefited the collective at the expense of the rights of individual teams violated Section 1 of the Sherman Act. The courts understood that league clubs must compete as hard as they can on the field, but there was also an understanding that the same intense competition off the field was likely to see the strongest teams 'drive the weaker ones into financial failure [and] eventually the whole league' and without a league no team can operate profitably (Mitten, 2010: 7). In response, the NFL successfully lobbied the US Congress for a limited antitrust exemption that would allow them to maximize television broadcast revenue yet also maintain the league's competitive balance, integrity and existence (Mitten, 2010). In 1961, the federal government enacted the Sports Broadcasting Act 1961 and allowed leagues to offer rights as a package to a national network on the grounds that it was in the interest of spectators and the leagues' health and competitive balance (Cave and Crandall, 2001; Sandy *et al.*, 2004). Before this legislation was passed, sport leagues were unable to do so and, as a result, the NFL signed its first national television contract in 1962, which was worth US$4.7 million annually.

The Sports Broadcasting Act has allowed the National Football League to offer collective rights to national networks since 1962. Cave and Crandall (2001) have demonstrated that no other professional sports league in the United States relies solely on national rights and that the NFL has the highest proportion of total revenue derived from broadcast rights. Although the Sports Broadcasting Act legalized collective selling, it did not legalize other forms of restrictive practices by sport leagues and associations in the sale of broadcast rights. Mitten (2010) referred to the Supreme Court's ruling that the National Collegiate Athletics Association's (NCAA) plan to control the broadcast rights to all college football games was unlawful, since it fixed the price of televised college

football games and artificially limited their total number without an economic justification, such as maintaining on-field competitive balance. As a result, individual colleges were able to break from national broadcast rights contracts and sign their own rights agreements.

A league or association's capacity to limit or prevent the individual sale of rights by teams to local and regional broadcasters is related to the league or association's ability to make the argument that it is necessary to maintain competition within the league. In reality, this is a difficult argument to sustain and almost all basketball, baseball and hockey teams in the United States sell broadcast rights individually. The concerns that surround joint selling in Europe are also partly ameliorated in the US by the segmentation of rights deals in order to maximize revenue, which in turn increases competition, as well as consumer choice and access. For example, the NFL's rights until at least 2021 are shared by ESPN, CBS, FOX and NBC, and the league-owned NFL Network can be seen on major cable networks such as Comcast or Time Warner Cable. In addition, although the Federal Communications Commission (FCC) investigated sport programming in the early 1990s, it found no evidence to suggest that government intervention was needed to protect the public's access to sporting events of national significance. As a result, the FCC – a government agency perhaps best known for its crackdown on perceived indecency on American airwaves in the wake of Janet Jackson's 'wardrobe malfunction' during the halftime show of Super Bowl XXXVIII – saw no need for an anti-siphoning scheme that can be found in many other countries.

## CHINA

Until the beginning of the 1980s, state-funded monopoly broadcasters generally dominated European broadcasting and, as such, there was very little competition (Tonazzi, 2003). The impact of the entry of commercial broadcasters into the marketplace was increased competition, as well as the increased importance of sport properties. For instance, there was no live football on French television until Vivendi obtained the country's first ever pay television licence and secured the broadcast rights to Ligue 1. Unlike most of Europe and the United States of America, China is yet to experience the impact of commercial broadcasting, as it is almost exclusively controlled by the central government; however, sport is an important feature of national and state broadcasting. For instance, millions of Chinese were first introduced to Michael Jordan when CCTV screened the 1996 NBA finals. CCTV began in 1958 and is effectively a government department that has a network of 22 free-to-air and pay television channels, of which most are available to all Chinese people who own a television, and a range of other specialist stations that are available at a cost. Although there is a financial return to the government, the key tenets underpinning broadcasting are public and political benefits. In other words, broadcasting in China is not a commercial enterprise in the same way as it is in westernized countries, despite the fact that advertising revenue is significant. Despite this, in recent years China has slowly welcomed overseas television networks such as BBC World, Eurosport and STAR TV and is expected to have made the switch to digital television by 2015.

The Chinese broadcasting system is further complicated by the fact that there are a multitude of Chinese states that also provide public broadcasting in the form of free-to-

air and pay television stations for the citizens of that state. Pay television networks usually carry all of the CCTV channels but may also offer additional channels from metropolitan stations, such as Shanghai Media Group. In both the case of CCTV and state run television networks, sport is available on both forms, depending on the sport and its importance. The majority of major international events, such as the Olympic Games or the FIFA World Cup, are broadcast on one of CCTV's satellite stations, in order to provide public access. In this way CCTV regulates the broadcasting of events of global or national significance, in much the same way as the listing of events does so in other countries. CCTV-5, China's sport channel established in 1995, broadcasts sport, such as the UEFA Champions League, the Chinese Basketball Association and the Asian Games, 24 hours per day, seven days per week to 700 million people, while CCTV also controls external access to Chinese sporting events. Finally, the purchase of sport events by state-run networks is ad hoc, where different states purchase rights based on particular interests or historical anomalies. For example, one state-run cable station may elect to purchase the rights to the EPL, while another in a different part of the country might have purchased the rights to the Serie A in Italy, while CCTV might purchase the rights to the Bundesliga. The regulation of these broadcasts is inconsistent, however, as citizens of one state can often receive sport broadcasts from stations in other states.

## BRAZIL

Latin America, especially Brazil, is also emerging as a major player in the sport media nexus. For instance, in 2013 Brazil hosted ESPN's X Games in Foz do Iguaçu and Rio de Janeiro hosted the Chicago Bulls in a NBA pre-season game. However, Brazil remains inextricably linked with football; the Brazilian national team has won the FIFA World Cup a record five times, has produced footballers such as Pele, Ronaldo, Ronaldinho, Kaka, Neymar and Marta, while Brazil hosted the 20th FIFA World Cup in 2014. Football is a national passion and public access to the Brazilian Football League, and the highly popular Serie A and Serie B, has received greater attention in recent years by government regulators.

Since the mid 1980s, Globo has been the sole broadcaster of the country's most important competition, the Brazilian Football League (BFL). Globo is the dominant media player in the country and secured the broadcast rights to Euro 2016, the FIFA World Cup until 2022 and the Sochi 2014 and Rio 2016 Olympic Games. In 2002, Brazil's Secretariat of Economic Law (SDE) heard a complaint against Globo regarding its exclusive broadcasting rights contract with the BFL. The SDE was concerned that the country's largest free-to-air television broadcaster held the exclusive rights to Brazilian football across a range of commercial media and that Brazil's biggest football clubs (the 'Club of 13') had acted as a cartel to jointly sell these rights (Mattos, 2012). The SDE's concerns were further exacerbated because this cartel represented the interests of the most powerful football clubs in Brazil – such as Corinthians, Santos, Flamengo and Fluminense – and that Globo earns 75 per cent of all advertising expenditure on free-to-air television in Brazil, as well as owning the country's most popular sport channel on pay television. In addition, the contract had granted Globo the free-to-air, pay television, pay-per-view, internet and mobile rights, and the broadcaster had a preference clause for renewal of the

2012–14 rights. After concluding its investigation, the SDE proposed a ban on the sale of exclusive rights, the creation of two separate free-to-air television packages and that the five media platforms should be unbundled and sold separately (Mattos, 2012). This would offer greater access to the Brazilian public, especially as only 5 per cent of households have pay television. However, the Secretariat ruled that the joint sale of rights by the 'Club of 13' was an efficient mechanism and recommended its continuation.

In 2010, the Brazilian Competition Agency (CADE) reached an agreement with the two parties on a three-year deal for the exclusive broadcast rights to all BFL games spanning the five principal media platforms (Mattos, 2012). A key point of SDE's earlier analysis was that the bundling of these rights favoured Globo as the conglomerate owned a wide range of media assets. For instance, in 1997 the 'Club of 13' decided against a bid by the television network SBT, because it was not able to offer a pay television package. However, as the Brazilian market has matured, potential bidders are now able to consider partnerships with pay television operators, such as ESPN, or telecommunication providers in Latin America. Moreover, although the SDE had recommended a ban on exclusivity, CADE instead ruled that such a measure would threaten the economic value of the BFL, especially as the sale of broadcast rights accounts for nearly 40 per cent of revenues. The settlement ultimately saw the removal of the preference clause in current and future broadcast rights deals and a commitment made to offer separate packages for the five relevant media platforms to facilitate entry and provide greater competition in the Brazilian rights market (Mattos, 2012). In early 2011, Corinthians left the 'Club of 13', while Botafogo, Flamengo, Fluminense and Vasco also decided that they would no longer negotiate television rights as part of the cartel and would instead sell broadcast rights to the 2012–14 seasons on an individual basis. The announcement should provide greater competition in the sale of football broadcast rights and go a long way towards appeasing government regulators in an increasingly important sport media market.

## SUMMARY

This chapter has examined the regulation of sport broadcasting. In particular, it has examined the ways in which governments regulate the broadcasting of sport on free-to-air and pay television, the vertical integration of sport and media organizations and the practice of anti-competitive behaviour by sport and media organizations in the sale and purchase of broadcast rights. This chapter has demonstrated that governments, sport organizations and media organizations are engaged in a complex activity, where it is often difficult to achieve a balance between social, cultural and economic objectives.

Governments throughout the world are attempting to achieve parity between the public interests of citizens and the commercial interests of sport and media organizations at a time when broadcast rights represent an increasing proportion of overall revenue for sport teams and leagues. It is unlikely that these competing forces will abate, as live sport is a highly sought after product by broadcasters and consumers alike. As pay and digital television providers achieve greater market penetration, it remains to be seen whether the concept of national significance will be able to sustain the practice of listing

events in an increasingly globalized sport market. Finally, it is also likely that cases of vertical integration will confront governments more often in the future as the convergence of the sport and media industries continues. Review questions and exercises are listed below to assist with confirming your knowledge of the core concepts and principles introduced in this chapter.

## REVIEW QUESTIONS AND EXERCISES

1 Why do governments regulate sport broadcasting?
2 What is market failure and how does it relate to sport broadcasting in particular?
3 What are the ways in which government can intervene and what is the preferred method of intervention where sport broadcasting is concerned?
4 What are the three main areas in which governments seek to regulate the practice of sport broadcasting?
5 What are anti-siphoning legislation and listed events designed to avoid and what are they designed to achieve?
6 What is joint (or collective) selling?
7 How does the practice of joint or collective selling restrict horizontal competition in sport and media?
8 What is a potential impact of the vertical integration of sport broadcasters and sport teams? Is it sufficient to warrant legislation?
9 Are there any sport teams in your region, city or nation owned by media organizations? If so, do these media or sport organizations have any advantages, as a result of this ownership?
10 Identify whether your country of origin has any legislation that enables the listing of events of national significance. If so, what are these events and why have they been chosen by government regulators? If not, what is the proportion of major sport events on pay television?

## FURTHER READING

Evens, T. and Lefever, K. (2011) Watching the football game: Broadcasting rights for the European digital television market. *Journal of Sport and Social Science, 35* (1), 33–49.

Kennedy, P. and Kennedy, D. (2012) Football supporters and the commercialisation of football: Comparative responses across Europe. *Soccer and Society, 13* (3), 327–340.

Lefever, K. (2012) Sports/media complex in the new media landscape. In Katrien Lefever (ed.) *New Media and Sport: International Legal Aspects* (7–30). The Hague: T.M.C. Asser Press.

Lefever, K. and Van Rompuy, B. (2009) Ensuring access to sports content: 10 years of EU intervention. Time to celebrate?, *Journal of Media Law, 1* (2), 243–268.

McNamee, M. (2013) The integrity of sport: Unregulated gambling, match fixing and corruption, *Sport, Ethics and Philosophy, 7* (2), 173–174.

Paolino, R. C. (2009) Upon further review: How NFL network is violating the Sherman Act. *Sports Law Journal, 16*, 1.

Scherer, J. and Sam, M. P. (2012) Public broadcasting, sport and cultural citizenship: Sky's the limit in New Zealand? *Media, Culture and Society, 34* (1), 101–111.

Turner, P. (2012) Regulation of professional sport in a changing broadcasting environment: Australian club and sport broadcaster perspectives. *Sport Management Review, 15* (1), 43–59.

Turner, P. and Cusumano, S. (2000) Virtual advertising: Legal implications for sport. *Sport Management Review, 3* (1), 47–70.

Zagrosek, R. and Schmieder, S. (2004) Centralized marketing of sports broadcasting rights and antitrust law, *Seton Hall Journal of Sports and Entertainment Law, 14*, 381.

## RELEVANT WEBSITES

### Americas

National Football League – www.nfl.com
Federal Communications Commission – www.fcc.gov
Campeonato Brasileiro Serie A – www.cbf.com.br
Globo – www.redeglobo.globo.com
Corinthians FC – corinthians.com.br/en

### Australia

Department of Broadband, Communications and the Digital Economy – www.dbcde.gov.au
Australian Communications and Media Authority – www.acma.gov.au
National Rugby League – www.nrl.com.au

### Asia

China Central Television – http://english.cntv.cn

### Europe

Monopolies and Mergers Commission – www.competition-commission.org.uk
European Commission – www.ec.europa.eu/index_en.htm
Union of European Football Associations – www.uefa.com
Bundesliga – www.bundesliga.com
English Premier League – www.premierleague.com
Serie A – www.legaseriea.it
Italian Competition Authority – www.agcm.it/en
Juventus FC – www.juventus.com
AC Milan FC – www.acmilan.com

Inter Milan FC – www.inter.it/en
Liga Nacional de Fútbol Profesional – www.ligabbva.com
Spain's National Competition Commission – www.cncompetencia.es
FC Barcelona – www.fcbarcelona.com
Real Madrid FC – www.realmadrid.com
Mediapro – www.mediapro.es/eng/tvchannels.php
French Football Ligue 1 – www.ligue1.com
Dutch Football Eredivisie – www.eredivisie.nl
Netherlands Competition Authority – www.acm.nl/en
Portugal Football Primeira Liga – www.lpfp.pt
Audiovisual Media Services Directive – www.europa.eu/legislation_summaries/audiovisual_and_media
British Office of Communications – www.ofcom.org.uk

## CASE STUDY

### Collective selling bankrolls Europe's 'Big Five'

The European Commission's decision on the collective selling of UEFA Champions League rights provided a template for other leagues, most notably the German Bundesliga and the English Premier League. However, while the collective selling arrangements in place for the elite clubs in German and English football have been highly lucrative for many of its participating clubs, the adoption of such a rights process has historically faced stern opposition from major European rivals in Italy, Spain, the Netherlands and Portugal.

Teams from Europe's 'big five' football leagues – England, Germany, Italy, Spain and France – dominate the Deloitte Football Money League (referred to in the previous chapter's case study) largely due to the substantial revenue they generate from match-day, commercial and broadcasting sources. However, the approach government regulators and league administrators have taken in the sale of broadcast rights and the distribution of revenue between member clubs has been a cause of concern, especially as debate continues about the financial stability of European football and the growing disparity between football's haves and have-nots. Although broadcast rights remain the main driver of revenue growth for the 'big five', there are clear differences between the national leagues and how they choose to share the €13 billion-plus they receive in broadcast rights sales.

In 2005, the German Football League (DFL) agreed to an amended arrangement to sell the rights to Bundesliga matches after European regulators expressed concerns that existing deals restricted competition and exacerbated trends in media concentration. The amended rights process allowed joint selling, with the proviso that individual football clubs regained their rights to sell the match if the DFL was unable to do so. The rights to the Bundesliga first and second division matches were divided into nine different packages according to distribution markets – television, new media and mobile – and the nature of the rights – live or highlights. In 2012, with the blessing of the European Commission, the Bundesliga went back to the market and sold the broadcast rights for the 2013–17 seasons for €2.5 billion, an increase of 50 per cent

on the previous rights deal. Sky Deutschland held off telecommunications provider Deutsche Telekom to acquire the pay television, IPTV and mobile rights, while free-to-air broadcaster ARD retained the rights to broadcast game highlights and a seven-game package of live broadcasts. While a good outcome for German football, some saw the €485 million per season paid by the News Corporation subsidiary as a risk:

> [W]ith these rights, the Bundesliga is definitely on Rupert Murdoch's financial drip. If the moody czar fails with his ambitious TV plans in Germany, it will throw professional football into crisis. Paying for the multiple channels [television and new media] before knowing the extent to which people will ultimately use the new technologies is a gamble.
>
> (Warner, 2012)

The European Commission also investigated the joint selling of broadcast rights by the EPL and found that individual clubs were prevented from selling rights, even to matches that were not included in the collective package. The result of this situation was that approximately 25 per cent of matches were broadcast live and that these matches were limited to a single broadcaster. As a result of discussions between the Commission and the EPL, an amended agreement was reached on the sale of rights for the 2007–09 seasons. Essentially, the EPL agreed to offer six balanced packages of rights, with the additional clause that no single bidder would be allowed to buy all six. This amendment effectively ended BSkyB's monopoly of the live rights to EPL football; BSkyB secured four of the packages and pay television rival, Setanta, acquired the other two, with a weekend highlights package made available on free-to-air national broadcaster BBC. The arrangement meant that at least two broadcasters would televise EPL matches, ensuring greater competition and consumer access. In 2012, BSkyB and British Telecom (BT) signed a three-year deal worth €4 billion for the rights to broadcast live English Premier League matches until 2015–16. BSkyB retains the lion's share of the rights (with five of the seven packages on offer) while, in a surprise move, BT outbid ESPN for two packages, or a quarter of the 154 live matches to be shown each season. BT will pay £246 million per season and, after acquiring the rights to Serie A, Ligue 1, Brasileirao and Major League Soccer with ESPN's exit from the UK market, plans to launch a new football-focused channel and offer fans EPL content across its fibre network and other platforms. The broadcast rights deal saw the league secure an additional £1.25 billion, a 70 per cent increase on the previous deal, and will see each club in the EPL receive an additional £20–30 million per season. As a result, the additional revenue from broadcast rights is likely to mean that English clubs dominate the Deloitte Football Money League in the future. Despite this financial windfall and the relative strength of clubs in the EPL, some club bosses believe that EPL clubs should be able to sell their own foreign television rights and thus capitalize on the millions of 'satellite supporters' they have worldwide.

In Italy, collective selling had been commonplace for many years, with the Italian Football League selling the television rights to all first and second division football – the Serie A and Serie B – and re-distributing the revenue between its members.

In 1999, the Italian Competition Authority decided that this arrangement was a restrictive practice and, as a result, individual selling of broadcast rights replaced centralized selling. However, concerns over the financial plight of many smaller clubs saw the Melandri Law passed which re-introduced collective selling to Italian football from 2010. The legislation stipulated that 40 per cent of media rights revenue be divided equally between the 20 Serie A clubs, with 30 per cent distributed according to the club's supporter base and 30 per cent based on the club's sporting results since 1946–47 when the modern league was founded. While the return to collective selling delivered revenue growth, and helped balance the revenue more evenly among clubs, the gap between Italy's Money League representatives and the bottom Serie A clubs has dramatically reduced. The Serie A clubs share €849 million per annum in a three-year deal with pay television's Sky Italia and free-to-air broadcaster RAI that expires after the 2014–15 season. Although 16 of the top-flight clubs agreed to the new revenue sharing arrangement, the Italian Competition Authority remains concerned about the current revenue distribution model, especially as it gives an unfair advantage to big-city teams over rivals from smaller urban areas; it wants instead to reward clubs for current on-field performance, rather than historic results. This proposal would prove detrimental to the likes of Juventus, AC Milan, Internazionale, AS Roma, SS Lazio and Napoli and is likely to face stern opposition from their supporters.

In contrast, the Liga Nacional de Fútbol Profesional (La Liga) in Spain allows each of its member clubs to sell its own individual broadcasting rights in a system that was introduced in the mid 1990s when the market was deregulated with the emergence of satellite television. As a result, Real Madrid and FC Barcelona consistently dominate both off and on the field as they secure around half of the league's broadcast rights revenue. For example, Mediapro pays FC Barcelona around €160 million per season for control of Barça TV and the rights to broadcast all of the club's league, cup and exhibition matches until June 2015. In 1997, government regulators passed legislation in line with the European Commission's demand that member states could protect sporting events of public interest and so one match per week was made available to Spanish viewers on free-to-air television. In 2012, the broadcast rights for La Liga were sold for €731 million per season through until 2014–15. The agreement saw free-to-air channel La Sexta, owned by Mediapro, pick up one game per week and a highlights programme, while Mediapro and Canal+ shared the pay television rights with a first-choice match of the day, usually featuring Real Madrid or Barça, and will each show one of the two highly-popular 'Clásico' matches between the two heavyweights.

Dissatisfaction with the television deal saw 13 disgruntled clubs threaten to postpone the start of the 2012–13 season. In December 2012, the National Competition Commission found that deals entered into between three La Liga football clubs and Mediapro had restricted competition. Despite this, pay television still has its eyes on the weekly La Liga match that remains on free-to-air and league administrators would welcome the additional revenue its sale would deliver. Although Real Madrid and FC Barcelona brokered an agreement to share some of the broadcast revenues from 2015, many of Spain's less profitable clubs approached the European Parliament to force the league to adopt the 'fairer' system of collective selling. While clubs such

as Atletico de Madrid and Sevilla fight for change, even clubs that benefit from the current arrangement, such as Barça, understand its importance:

> [T]he Spanish league is the second most popular (in Europe), but some [of the La Liga clubs] are in a very bad position and I don't think they will come back . . . [we are] the only league where TV rights are negotiated individually and sometime in the next three or four or five years we have to put it all in one pot and make the distribution the way it is in Serie A and the Premier League.
>
> (Soccerex, 2011)

The French Football Federation was granted legislative protection as the sole authority responsible for the sale of broadcast rights to Ligue 1 football. However, unlike in many other European countries, matches played in the domestic football league were never considered sufficiently important to be 'listed' and, as such, have always been unavailable on free-to-air television. In 1984, Vivendi launched its first pay television channel, Canal+, and it held the exclusive rights to broadcast all Ligue 1 football matches until Orange, a division of France Telecom, also started broadcasting the league in 2008. The French league was the only one of the top five to experience a decline in the value of its broadcast rights in the last round of negotiations, largely due to the decision by France Telecom to focus on its core telecommunications activities rather than pursue the rights to expensive sport properties. Canal+ will pay €457 million per season through 2016 and shares the pay television rights to the league with Al Jazeera, which will pay €150 million to acquire two packages for its beIN Sport service. While Al Jazeera had taken a 'considerable economic bet on France', Ligue 1 President Frederic Thiriez said, the broadcaster would 'need at least five years to succeed' and so is expected to participate in the subsequent 2016–20 rights cycle (McManus, 2012).

Although small when compared with the revenues of Europe's five largest football markets, the Eredivisie in the Netherlands and the Primeira Liga in Portugal have also debated the merits of collective selling. In 1996, the Dutch Football Association sold exclusive broadcast rights to the league to the newly established Canal+ yet consumers were only able to see 44 of the 306 matches played each season live and most matches featured the top three clubs. As a result, Rotterdam's Feyenoord took the Dutch league to court over the sale of television rights as it wished to be able to sell the rights to its own matches. In 2002, the Netherlands Competition Authority (NMa) ruled that the current arrangement disadvantaged consumers and unnecessarily restricted competition between clubs and, upon review a year later, prohibited the joint sale of broadcast rights. Ultimately, however, the NMa decided not to intervene since it believed that individual selling would financially damage the majority of Dutch football clubs and it approved a proposal by the Eredivisie to offer six rights packages to the market that would promote competition between broadcasters and, in the event the rights to a particular game did not sell, would see these rights revert to the individual club. In 2012, the NMa approved the sale of a controlling interest in pay television channel, Eredivisie Live, to Fox International

Channels which will see each Eredivisie club receive €80 million per season Fox and broadcast the Dutch league until 2025. A highlights package will continue to be screened on NOS, one of the major Dutch free-to-air networks, until at least July 2014. The Portuguese Football League (LPFP) has also expressed frustration with the current broadcast rights model that allows individual clubs to sell their own broadcast rights. Like neighbouring Spain, this system has seen a handful of clubs – FC Porto, Benfica and Sporting Lisbon – receive half of the €75 million that pay television company SportTV pays for the rights to broadcast Primeira Liga football. Despite opposition from Benfica and Porto, the league also plans to petition the European Union to make the LPFP the sole negotiator for Liga rights and hence adopt collective selling for its member clubs.

While collective or joint selling is the most prevalent system adopted in European football to sell broadcast rights, government regulators continue to be vigilant in a bid to best serve the interests of the media, sport organizations and the public and to ensure that these commercial arrangements do not unnecessarily restrict competition or reduce consumer choice. However, as is evident from the information presented with this case study, not all parties can agree about how to balance the social, cultural and economic objectives of the respective stakeholders.

## CASE STUDY QUESTIONS

1 Although collective or joint selling is common in many of Europe's largest football markets, regulatory watchdogs remain concerned that this system of selling broadcast rights can lead to anti-competitive behaviour and market foreclosure. What are the key advantages and disadvantages of this practice and how might it lead to a reduction in competition?

2 Do you believe that collective selling is the best mechanism for the sale of domestic broadcast rights? What evidence exists to support your conclusion and whose perspective have you taken?

3 Based on the developments outlined in this case, which clubs do you think in the near future will move up or, conversely, move down in the Deloitte Football Money League rankings?

4 The European Commission objected to UEFA's proposed collective selling arrangements for UEFA Champions League football, and intervened in the sale of broadcast rights by the English Premier League and Bundesliga. Both Spain and Portugal are considering how collective selling might strengthen the Iberian football leagues, but how might these rights be best packaged so as to appease competition watchdogs and European regulators?

Sources: Iosifidis and Smith (2011); McManus (2012); Deloitte (2013); Lelyukhin (2013).

PART 3

# Sport media professionals

CHAPTER 6

# Sport journalists

## Friend or foe?

*David Lowden*

## OVERVIEW

The commercial and social connections between sport and the media have been defined by the relationships between people employed within organizations from both industries – sport journalists on one side and the people (athletes, coaches and administrators mostly) who the public want more information about on the other. Sport journalists have been a central cog in the machine of the sport nexus, and this chapter examines some of the key issues that define the role of sport journalists in the contemporary sport media industry, such as the beat model of reporting and the changes to access brought about by the advent of social media and a diverse range of content distribution platforms. The chapter also reveals the ways in which sport journalists operate, which is essential information for staff employed within sport organizations, particularly within media management roles.

## LEARNING OUTCOMES

After completing this chapter, the reader should be able to:

- identify what a 'beat reporter' is;
- assess the impact of social media on sport reporting;
- appreciate a sport reporter's view regarding their work, in particular access to sport organization employees; and
- identify the different types of external media opportunities via an understanding of the way in which sport journalists work.

## INTRODUCTION

The sport media nexus is a significant field of employment, within both sport and media organizations, and in many countries sport is the largest journalism specialty. During the latter half of the twentieth century both print and broadcast sport journalism were transformed from mostly fun and games to serious journalism. However, inherent contradictions still exist, such as the popularity of sport journalism versus credibility within the broader profession and the seriousness of work versus the fun of sport. Perhaps the most significant barrier to professional credibility is the notion that sport media producers are more likely to promote sport through their coverage, 'go easy' on a story to curry future favour or even turn a blind eye to a story to maintain necessary daily working relationships.

## THE BEAT SYSTEM

One of the criticisms of sport journalism, and a reason for low credibility that has resulted in its slightly poor reputation within the broader field of journalism, is that the frame often utilized by sport media producers is an uncritical and promotional discourse. In other words, unlike other more serious elements of the media that engage in objective investigative journalism, sport media producers have often been accused of adopting work practices and routines that institutionalize the promotion of sport and its related activities. The intimate connection between sport and the media and their reliance on each other for commercial success – perhaps less so today than in the past – has resulted in the development of particular professional codes and work practices.

The 'beat' is a particular method that media organizations use to prioritize their time, resources, personnel and money, as well as the way in which they ensure that there is enough news to publish or broadcast. In essence, a media organization creates a beat by assigning personnel to cover an institution or area of human endeavour full-time. The beat reporter's job is to provide news about the people, businesses, issues, events and controversies on that beat, in order that the media outlet can establish a regular feature or section in the area. The beat is essential to the manufacture of news and is not limited to sport news production. Beat reporters can cover crime, politics, sport, religion, science, weather, foreign affairs, or a whole range of other topics, depending on the interests of the audience, or the specific nature of the region, city, state or country.

Unlike other beats, however, the sport beat has particular and peculiar implications for the management of sport. Whereas politicians might vary what they say or do because of the media coverage, they rarely have to consider the impact of the way in which news is manufactured. For sport organizations the reality is very different. The routines and ideologies that underpin the beat reporting model mean that some sports receive coverage while others do not. The beat model of sports reporting also has specific implications for sport reporters and editors, as it relies on the reporter or journalist maintaining very close relationships with people at the heart of their beat.

The beat model of sport reporting places media professionals in a precarious position, and although this is true of all beat reporters, it is particularly true in sport because of the inextricable commercial link between sport and the media. On the one hand they need to

satisfy their audiences, who demand interesting and at times provocative/controversial stories. On the other hand they need to keep their sources (their beat) onside. Without the audience they have no job and without the sources they have no job. In other words, it is sometimes difficult to determine the more powerful master.

Similar to other news departments, the sport news work environment, suggested by Lowes (1997; 1999), is one in which there are daily pressures to produce a sufficient amount of quality copy as well as constraints within which the sport journalists must operate, such as time, money and resources. In response to these conditions and to cope with the demands placed on them, sport journalists have institutionalized their work routines. The major component of this institutionalization is the beat system, whereby a reporter is assigned to cover one or more sports on a full-time basis. The large commercial spectator sports could have several journalists working their beat, depending on the size of the sport, the newspaper and the market. As Theberge and Cronk (1986) noted, journalists must have ready and frequent access to reliable news sources in order to do their work. The beat is a way of both formally and informally organizing a journalist's access to information, in order that the information is regular, newsworthy and is attributable to credible news sources.

Lowes (1999) explained that the beat system is a huge investment of the financial and human resources of a media organization. As such, beat reporters must produce copy, regardless of the newsworthiness of the story or the quality of the writing. The result is that only the major commercial spectator sports are assigned beats, because they are seen to attract the greatest audience share.

Lowes (1999) identified two primary categories of sources for the sports reporter: first, major commercial sport organizations; and second, the journalist's clubs and personal contacts on the beat. These routine sources could be athletes, coaches, administrators or managers, player agents, team doctors, trainers, equipment managers, administrative staff, or in some circumstances, other sports reporters. Lowes (1999) noted that over a period of time a reporter would more than likely develop affection for the players or for the team as a whole. These sentiments he argued, are precisely what sport organizations seek to exploit. However, the intimacy of this relationship means that sport journalists must be careful not to offend their routine sources, thereby cutting themselves off from a reliable and constant source of information. Lowes (1999) suggested that in the most extreme cases sport reporters can be subjected to physical intimidation and violence as a result of a negative story, however, the more likely consequence of overt criticism is that the reporter will be cut-off or ostracized. It is important to note that Lowes (1999) conducted his research in North America, where typically cities have only one professional team in any one sport. In other contexts where teams are not so geographically disparate, a beat might refer to a league or teams from a league based in the same city. It is possible that this might change the nature of the beat reporting relationships, because a reporter will necessarily have more sources and contacts at their disposal, yet the need to establish strong and intimate links with the respective teams is unlikely to be obviated.

## CUTTING OUT THE 'MIDDLE MAN'

At the beginning of the twenty-first century, sport journalists have entered a new world, one in which they are not as important as they once were. In fact, some owners and

executives involved in professional sport would go so far as to say the sport journalist is redundant. There are now well-resourced sport organizations run by individuals who are convinced they can achieve their goals without ever needing to talk to a sport journalist. What is even more troubling for the sport journalist is they may be right. The previously symbiotic and mutually dependent relationship between sport journalists and sport organizations has been eroded by the introduction of social media and highly skilled strategic communicators.

There is still a role for the sport journalist, because they perform the same function as other journalists do; that is, they hold people and organizations to account, accurately and dispassionately relate the details of an event and pursue the truth. But, the advent of social media has given sport fans direct access to the clubs they follow and the stars they idolize (see the social media chapter for more information regarding the old and new sport media access model). In addition, the widespread popularity of the World Wide Web and the development of new technologies have provided sport organizations with the ability to communicate directly with the public and disseminate content and information, a role that was once the sole preserve of the sport journalist. Some sport organizations believe that this is preferable to entrusting sport journalists to convey information to the team's fans, given the perceived danger of being misunderstood or misrepresented.

There have always been athletes, coaches and administrators involved in high performance sporting organizations around the world that have had to be convinced to conduct an interview with a journalist. Many of these sport organization employees take pride in the fact they 'give nothing'. The athlete will comply with the rules that compel them to grant a media outlet an interview, or participate in a routine media conference, but will be deliberately bland or non-committal with his or her answers. What has changed since the introduction of Facebook, Twitter and other social media platforms, is the individual athlete can have a one-to-one or one-to-many conversation with his or her fans without the need to talk to a sport journalist. They know they won't be misquoted, they can answer direct questions from their fans and can even commercialize their 'likes' and 'follows'.

Manchester City, a football (soccer) club in the English Premier League, is an example of a professional club that prefers to use its own channels, such as the club's official website, its own television channel and YouTube, to engage with its fan base rather than court external media. The club sees community engagement as vital to its growth and has 28 people in its media team, ensuring that its fans can access news and information across a range of media platforms at any time of the day, any day of the year. Yet despite a declared desire to connect with its global fan base, Manchester City all but ignores reporters working for external or traditional media outlets. The 2013/2014 premier league champions are not regarded as hostile to the media; the club continues to allow the manager and players to appear at media conferences but City does not pursue media attention in the way its cross town rival Manchester United does. The Red Devils try to manage the message the media reports, but unlike City they believe publicity underpins the huge commercial returns the club enjoys worldwide. The club has had its own television channel, MUTV, for more than a decade, which is now just one of the direct marketing channels open to the club. For United, there remains a lucrative reason to solicit publicity, but this has not come at the expense of external media's access to key newsmakers. It is unclear in the future whether the City or United model of 'media interaction' will prevail, and what the impact on sport journalists will be, particularly if the City model is preferred.

## ACCESS

Experienced sport journalists have witnessed a gradual decline in the amount of access they have to newsworthy athletes, coaches and administrators within sport organizations. At the beginning of their careers, these sport journalists would most likely have had direct contact with coaches and players. They might have been able to ring a player at home or the coach at the club's headquarters, and it would have been up to the player or coach to decide whether to grant an interview and what responses they would give to questions posed. Nothing was vetted. There were no briefing notes and no 'company (read club) line'. What changed these relationships was the introduction of media managers, particularly at well-resourced professional sports organizations, whose job was to proactively seek media coverage, ensuring maximum exposure for sponsors in the process. Media managers have been willing facilitators of media requests during a time in which sporting organizations and media outlets needed each other equally. In this context it is perhaps not surprising that many of today's experienced sport journalists are indignant at being told by media staff who they are 'putting up' (which athlete, coach or official will represent the sport organization), where and when that interaction will take place and what may or may not be asked. Their ire is raised even further when access is withdrawn altogether or rules are put in place preventing the dissemination of newsworthy information. For example, the current television contract in the Australian Football League includes a clause where the free-to-air host broadcaster is given exclusive access to team changes. Clubs are contractually banned from providing team changes to other journalists before it has been broadcast by the news service of the rights holder.

It is interesting to note that this reduction in access has been most prevalent in countries such as Australia and the United Kingdom, but that in the US there has not been a noticeable reduction in access. The unique culture of journalists being able to conduct interviews in the players' locker rooms remains intact. Journalists from rights holder media outlets are sometimes granted exclusive interviews and special access, but non rights holder journalists are not obstructed from gaining the access required to write their stories.

Social media and the internet have made it possible for sporting organizations to cut out the 'middle man' – the sport journalist – between country/club/competitor and the sport fan. To make matters worse for sport journalists, almost everywhere in the world, circulation is declining of the product to which many sport journalists contribute, the printed newspaper. In other words, from the journalist's point of view, not only is it harder than ever to get a story, but when they do, fewer people read it. Journalists tell themselves that they are caught in a transition from the old revenue model of cover price and classifieds to a new model of digital page impressions, click-throughs and eyeballs for ads. It remains to be seen whether commercial journalism will make the transition.

In Australia in 2015, Michael (Mick) Malthouse broke a record that many had always presumed would never be broken when he coached his 715th game in the AFL, surpassing the mark set by the legendary Collingwood coach Jock McHale between 1912 and 1949. Malthouse was a premiership player and after suffering a career ending injury took up coaching at the age of 28. He has coached four different clubs, two of them to the ultimate prize of an AFL premiership. In the mid 1990s he was the senior (head) coach of the West Coast Eagles, a Perth based professional football club in the AFL. Malthouse

was one of the first, if not the first, to restrict journalists' access to interview players and to the filming of training. By contrast, many of the other AFL clubs at that time had a relaxed attitude to contact between journalists and players. Malthouse is often portrayed in the Australian media as 'anti media' and it is true that he has had a tempestuous relationship with journalists over his record breaking career. However, for Malthouse it is rarely personal. He believes in the wartime decree that 'loose lips sink ships' and sees media coverage as something that could interfere with his players' single-minded pursuit of success. At the Eagles, Malthouse produced a rule book for the players, a pocket-sized pamphlet containing a list of individual behaviours or acts he thought were vital for team success. One of those rules was titled 'Media. Enemy'. Malthouse wanted to control the flow of information out of the club and, by and large, he did. The club did not have a designated media manager at the time and was so popular with the West Australian public (as it remains today) that it did not need to proactively court publicity. In fact, if anything, it did the opposite. Malthouse literally locked reporters out of training sessions, long before it was fashionable. After being allowed to film or take photos of players warming up for ten minutes from behind the boundary line of the vast oval (where if players were on the other side of the ground it was difficult to identify individual players), members of the media would be escorted to the exit. A club official would, in what became a television news ritual, padlock the gates to Subiaco Oval.

Closed training sessions are now commonplace in elite sport and the desire for professional sporting clubs to control information has become far more sophisticated than padlocks and club rule books. The introduction of the internet and social media, combined with the employment of professional media managers within sport organizations, have given clubs more control of information and access than would ever have been contemplated two decades ago. Damian Barrett, former newspaper-turned-broadcast and website sport journalist, has won multiple awards for his reporting of the most popular sport in Australia, the Australian Football League. Barrett agrees that it is getting more difficult for sports journalists to do their job because of restrictions on access and a desire by sporting organizations to control what is written and said about them:

> Every player has got so much protection around him now and it's actually very hard to get through to the key players, be they players or officials. If you go back to the late '80s and early '90s, you could actually just walk into the (locker) rooms and I recall you could go up to [former AFL star player] Gary Ablett [Senior], you could actually walk up to him when he was getting changed for training and it was just a done deal. I still recall being able to go up to [former Geelong Cats key position player] Barry Stoneham and he would stop and chat for 15 to 20 minutes and just give you everything he had and talk quite open and honestly. That's only early '90s and you fast forward 20 or so years and to get an interview with a Barry Stoneham equivalent these days, you'd need to be going through, obviously the football club and then his manager and then there would be discussions how they would do it; and who would do it; and the club would be thinking, 'well we should do it on our own platform' and that's probably been the big change I reckon. The clubs now have got very smart about the ownership of the main ingredient in this game, the players. They pay the players. They control them. Every single action of the player is going to impact on that footy

club, be it positively or negatively. They set up a structure now where they make it very difficult for access. It's all about controlling the messaging now, be that a positive message or a negative message, but they can control it and they've got their own abilities to do that now. It's almost now where you just cannot get access to the people you need when you want them.

(Personal communication)

## HOW SPORT JOURNALISTS OPERATE

Sport journalists are the same as other journalists in that they are – or should be – in pursuit of the truth. What a sport journalist actually wants is a good story that will sell newspapers or magazines, get website hits or attract eyeballs and ears to a screen. Despite the cynicism of much of the general public, most sport journalists want to inform the public through the presentation of facts, but they also want to write or produce a story that will be entertaining and attract attention. The contemporary sport journalist is interested in what is really going on behind the wall of the sport organization and is naturally wary and suspicious of media management professionals (sometimes called public relations spin-doctors) who seek to shape and frame a story to suit the objectives of their sporting organization.

Sport journalists are also, in a paradoxical way, on the side of the employees of sport organizations. The sport journalist, like the people they report on, loves sport. They differ from other journalists in this respect. The police reporter, political reporter and most other reporters on a specialist 'round' or 'beat' will develop close working relationships with those at the 'coal face' of their profession, but they are unlikely to be passionate supporters of that profession. They might be dedicated to their work and even personally committed to a cause – for example, lowering violent crime – but they are not 'fans' in the same way sport journalists are. In fact sport journalists can sometimes feel like they are in a 'no man's land'. They love sport, but are mistrusted by athletes and officials, while at the same time are often derided by their colleagues who regard sport journalism as frivolous and lacking significant public utility.

Sport journalists are just as likely, perhaps even more likely, to be loyal to their contacts at a sport organization, rather than to colleagues at their media organization. One senior journalist, who wished to remain anonymous, said of his colleagues in the general news department of his newspaper:

> I would never give a news journalist a phone number. I wouldn't tell my desk that . . . I don't trust them. News journalists are hit and run. They do the story and they never see those people again. We have got to nurture relationships.

Many sport journalists cover a single sport and some cover a single team. They know they will see the people they are writing about week after week and cannot afford to compromise these relationships.

Some sport administrators consider sport journalists to be untrustworthy, but this is a perception that is unfair. Rather, sport journalists learn to perfect the art of convincing someone to talk to them on the record – this is part of their job and good sport journalists

do it very well. Unlike the police, journalists can't employ a line of questioning that threatens incarceration if you don't talk – 'Tell me which position Jones is playing this week or you're going to jail'. Instead, sport journalists, like most other journalists, understand the value of striking up an amiable conversation. They might ring once a week and be quite prepared to hang up the phone without a story, in order to build a relationship.

Building a rapport with a journalist can be advantageous to the sport management professional. There are occasions when someone from a sport organization would like to be able to have a conversation with a sport journalist without it being reported. It can be important for them to understand the wider context of a current issue or why a seemingly appropriate course of action is not being pursued. Sport journalists, like all journalists, have contact with a lot of people and are in possession of vast amounts of information, some of which may be useful to the sport manager. It might take years to develop a trustworthy relationship, but some executives in professional sport organizations like to have one or two sport journalists 'on side' to provide a 'sounding board' or informed (read friendly) reporting of decisions taken by their organization. However, no credible journalist is going to act as a quasi public relations representative. Sport journalists still need to write a news story, but there is always more than one way to write it.

Even if someone in sport management gets to the point where he or she has a strong relationship with one or two journalists, there may come a time when that person gets 'burned'. In other words, the journalist writes a story the sport management professional would rather was not published. This can happen for a variety of reasons but most usually it is because there is a 'scoop' or exclusive available and the journalist has decided the public utility in publishing the story outweighs the loyalty to their contact. Sometimes the lure of an exclusive story and its associated kudos proves irresistible.

For those who intend on a long career in sport management there will be numerous interactions with sport journalists. The actual process of speaking to a journalist is more complicated than it might first seem. In Australia, the Media Entertainment and Arts Alliance (MEAA) Code of Ethics states that a journalist must identify himself or herself before asking questions on the record. There are 12 standards that make up the MEAA code. The standard that relates to identification states: 'Use fair, responsible and honest means to obtain material. Identify yourself and your employer before obtaining any interview for publication or broadcast. Never exploit a person's vulnerability or ignorance of media practice' (MEAA, 2014). There is no specific equivalent in the SPJ (Society of Professional Journalists) Code of Ethics for journalists working in the United States or in the NUJ (National Union of Journalists) in the United Kingdom. However, it is standard practice for journalists in these countries to identify themselves to all prospective interviewees. The sport management professional should be in no doubt as to the identity of the journalist he or she is speaking with and the purpose of the interview. It is also useful to understand what mediums and format the interview will be published in. For example, is the interview to be played in full on radio or television? If it is to be edited, will an extended version be available to the audience? It is worth noting that newspaper interviews may well be used to publish an article but also to provide content for the media outlet's website. If the interview is for television then the interviewee should ask even more questions about the purpose of the interview. Facial expressions, body language and pauses can provide the audience with a lot of information, without the interviewee saying a word. In this day and age of 24-hour news channels, what is said once in an interview

may be replayed several times in a day and be shared with other programmes or even other networks. Television and radio interviews for news bulletins are typically fairly short, usually only several minutes, but interviews for magazines, newspapers and online articles run much longer, even as long as an hour.

Although some people will find television interviews more nerve-wracking, there can be a false sense of security with the seemingly lengthy but pleasant 'fireside chat' with a print journalist. The journalist may have identified himself or herself correctly and made it clear they wanted to ask some questions on the record for a story, but keeping track of the myriad of topics and responses can be problematic for the interviewee. Unless the journalist is in a rush, the interview is being broadcast or published in full or the journalist is being deliberately confrontational, the journalist will rarely ask the questions they really want the answers to at the start of an interview. Standard practice, time permitting, is to ask a couple of friendly questions that act as an 'ice-breaker', before asking more pertinent questions.

Prospective interviewees ought to be cautious even when conducting a phone interview for print and online journalism. Unlike a television interview where there is a heightened sense of awareness of its purpose, having a phone conversation is a common everyday occurrence. Those unfamiliar with an inquiry from a journalist on the phone would be entitled to think the conversation might commence like this:

*Charlie*: Hi Annie Administrator, this is Charlie Chatter from the Daily News. I am writing a story/looking into a story about a specific issue and I was wondering if I could ask you a few questions about it?

*Annie*: Okay Charlie, what do you want to know?

*Charlie*: Well I was wondering if it was true that . . .

What actually happens is not necessarily designed to deceive, but it may not be as clear-cut to the interviewee that an interview on the record has commenced. Journalists trying to get information over the phone will keep their request as informal as possible. They will use conversational language, talk about a range of topics (some of which may not directly relate to the interviewee's organization) and often cultivate an impression they are 'on side' and sympathize with the prospective interviewee's position. Sport journalists will almost always identify themselves because they will have said their name and the name of their organization at the start of the phone call. However, unless we know someone well, nearly everyone we deal with on the phone commences a conversation by saying their name and the organization they represent. Think about the people you call who do not already have your number in their phone. When they say 'hello', you probably respond with, 'Hi it's [your name] from [your organization] . . .'. You might then inquire how they are going. When a journalist rings and identifies him or herself an alarm bell won't go off in your head to remind you that everything you say after they have identified themselves as a journalist – and whom they are working for – is 'on the record' and can be legitimately reported unless you specifically stipulate that your conversation is 'off the record'. The following fictional example of a telephone conversation between a journalist and a sport management professional is admittedly far-fetched, but is designed to clearly illustrate the point that it can be difficult to discern the difference between an on the record interview and a normal telephone conversation. The fictional Charlie Chatter works for a national

newspaper and makes a telephone call to Annie Administrator, the CEO of the governing body of a professional sport.

*Charlie*: Hi Annie Administrator? Charlie Chatter here from the *Daily*.
*Annie*: Hi Charlie.
*Charlie*: Much happening down your way?
*Annie*: No not really, steady as she goes.
*Charlie*: Not like the other mob, sounds like they've got their hands full.
*Annie*: I did hear something about that.
*Charlie*: I'm hearing . . . (Reporter provides useful details that keep you up to date with industry developments).
*Annie*: That's interesting.
*Charlie*: Do you get a break soon?
*Annie*: Yes I do actually, straight after the finals.
*Charlie*: Where are you going?
*Annie*: Yuppie Beach for a week, I'm looking forward to it. It's been a long year.
*Charlie*: I know what you mean. I've got another couple of weeks of work after the grand final and I'll then get some sun too. If you're like me, your partner will be glad to actually see you.
*Annie*: I'm pretty lucky in that respect, I have an understanding partner but you do have to make time for them. We're off to the opera on Friday night because my husband likes that sort of thing and it has been ages since we've gone to a function together that wasn't related to my work.
*Charlie*: Yeah right. By the way, are there any developments with Sally Superstar's contract? I understand a rival code is trying to poach her.
*Annie*: Well that's a matter for her club but my understanding is negotiations are proceeding well and she has been an excellent ambassador for our sport in a developing market.
*Charlie*: Good to hear. And with finances, I'm hearing some clubs are running a bit tight for money at the moment.
*Annie*: That's true but nothing out of the ordinary for this time of year. Here at Central HQ we monitor each club's cash flow and they will actually get their distribution of money from ticket sales about two weeks earlier this year due to improved efficiencies from our venues.
*Charlie*: Well sounds like you're on top of the finances. And I guess with the finals, everything is organized by the operations team so you don't actually have to go to them all?
*Annie*: That's right. We have a great team and I trust them to put on a great show. They don't need me at every game but of course I get along to as many of the finals as I can.
*Charlie*: Should be a great series. Thanks for the chat and I hope you enjoy your holiday.
*Annie*: Thanks Charlie.

It is a fictional conversation and sport journalists rarely set out to 'trap' or 'catch out' people who work for sport organizations. The idea of asking some friendly questions at the start of an interview is a genuine attempt to make the interviewee feel more comfortable. On most occasions the journalist will have a preconceived idea of what they want to get out of the interview and it is a good idea to find out what this is, whether directly or through the use of a communications professional. It is similar to any normal business conversation, where there is some small talk before someone gets to the point. In this case, the structure of the conversation was general sport industry chat (other mob's troubles), some seemingly unobtrusive personal questions (holiday plans and work/life balance) and then some more direct questions about specific topics (Sally Superstar's contract and competition finances). The first two topics prepared the ground for questions about the specific topics that the journalist hoped may have resulted in a story. However, sometimes the story can come from the earlier innocuous questions too. Out of his conversation with Annie Administrator, Charlie Chatter could conceivably write a front-page story for the *Daily News*' sport section the next day that reads as follows:

> *Opera Annie gives finals the boot*
>
> The CEO of Professional Sports League, Annie Administrator, will be at the opera on Friday night instead of the blockbuster final of the country's most popular sport. Despite confirming several clubs are strapped for cash and are yet to be paid, Administrator and her partner will be hob-knobbing with the city's social set at the opera, where tickets cost up to $300 each. 'We have a great team and they put on a great show, they don't need me at every game,' Ms Administrator said. Central HQ is also yet to ratify Sally Superstar's new contract. That might get done by the pool at a resort on Yuppie Beach because Administrator will be on the first plane out of town after the grand final. 'I'm looking forward to it. It's been a long year.' Administrator described the ongoing problems with her rival sport as 'interesting'.

Once that article is published the talkback radio hosts will be asking whether it is right that Annie Administrator chooses to go to the opera instead of the final. Social media will light up, the phones will ring and Annie will have a PR crisis on her hands. Annie will not be able to claim she was misquoted although she might argue her comments were taken out of context. To the fans of her league, that may look like a lame defence for choosing the opera over the finals.

It is important to point out that the Charlie Chatter article example is far-fetched and unlikely. As outlined earlier, sport journalists understand and appreciate that their career will be short lived if they were to 'burn' their contacts in such a way. They are aware that many of the people they interview today will be the same ones they interview tomorrow. However, those who follow the Australian Football League may recognize the fictional interview between Charlie Chatter and Annie Administrator and that the hypothetical sensationalist article was based on a true story. In 2004, AFL chief executive Andrew Demetriou and AFL chairman Ron Evans were forced to defend a decision to attend the opera with their wives instead of going to an AFL final. It was front-page news in Melbourne and the 'issue' ran for several days.

There will be times when the sport management professional or athlete may wish to speak to a journalist 'off the record'. However, different journalists have different opinions about what the term 'off the record' actually means. What it is supposed to mean is that anything that is said to the journalist cannot be published. In practice, some journalists confuse 'off the record' with 'anonymous source'. An anonymous source is when a journalist is told something that the interviewee knows will be published but does not want attributed to them personally. Watergate is the most famous example in journalism, but there are numerous examples in sport journalism where it has been appropriate to quote an anonymous source. Off the record, by contrast, is when the interviewee tells a journalist something that they do not want published. It is extremely rare for a journalist to be told something off the record and then publish the information and attribute the source by name. The protection of a contact's identity is taken extremely seriously by journalists the world over and many have been in contempt of court or gone to jail to protect the identity of a source. However, some journalists will publish some or all of the information – given to them on the basis it was off the record – and attribute it anonymously using phrases such as 'a well placed source', 'someone close to negotiations' or an 'industry insider'. Quoting a source in such a way is to misuse off the record information. It is legitimate to ask why someone would talk to a journalist if they did not want it reported. The answer is that there are occasions when it is useful to provide information to a journalist that is not to be published in order to prevent harm or the distortion of the narrative of a story. For example, an elite athlete misses training; sport journalists note the absence and ask the club why. If the reason is a personal and private matter, such as a health issue, the club may decide to share enough information about the matter with the journalists to prevent further stress on the player at a difficult time. If the player was unable to represent his or her team when the team is announced, the club might list the player as 'ill' or in some sports simply 'rested' or 'did not dress – coaches decision'. The journalists would know there was more to it, but can only report what the club releases on the record and respect that the off the record information given to them was not to be reported. Journalists reporting on crime and police matters deal with this issue constantly. The journalist may through their own inquiries discover information that the police do not want released at a particular time because it would harm the chances of catching a criminal. The police might have an off the record conversation with a trusted journalist to detail the progress of the investigation, to ensure the journalist is aware of why it would be irresponsible to publish.

The problem for sport management professionals is there are many issues that are of great interest to the public that are far less sensitive than undermining a police investigation. Sport journalists regard health issues such as mental illness as private and requiring the player's consent to report. However, there are many other issues that the journalist will view in the public interest and likely to cause proportionally less harm. For example, if a journalist is told off the record how much a player gets paid, he or she is more likely to publish that information by attributing it to an anonymous source.

One forum where there is no doubt what is said is on the record is the media conference (alternatively called a news conference or a press conference). The major purpose of a media conference is to release information to as many journalists as possible at the same time. Media conferences can be used to announce something new or to stipulate a

person or organization's position in reaction to an event. From the journalist's perspective, they have usually been *invited* to the media conference. They regard it as an opportunity to ask about almost anything that might relate to the people holding the media conference. It does not matter to the journalist that the media conference was called for a specific purpose. If, in their mind, there is a better story to chase then that is the story they will pursue.

In sport, individuals and organizations are often compelled by governing bodies to hold a weekly media conference before competition and one directly after. There is a time and a place for a certain line of questioning. For example, haranguing a coach about industry wide issues moments before the start of a match would be considered by most journalists to be inappropriate timing. It is also reasonable for the sport organization to advise journalists to speak to the person responsible for the matter they have raised and not address questions to someone from the club with little knowledge of the issue (which doesn't mean they won't). However, 'stone-walling' or being deliberately evasive will raise the ire of those employed within the media.

It is in the interests of both the sport management professional and the sport journalist to build strong mutually beneficial relationships. While it is true that technology and social media have provided an opportunity for athletes and sport organizations to 'cut out the middle man' in their conversation with athletes, sport journalists perform an important role for the sport loving public in interpreting, questioning and analysing information. Whether they have access to the main players or not, journalists will continue to report on the drama that is modern professional sport.

## SUMMARY

The proliferation of social media has changed the game for sport management professionals and the journalists they deal with. Gone is the necessity for the sport organization to engage with sport journalists in order to communicate and grow their fan base. Strategic communicators are now able to restrict access to the key actors in sport and even use access as an element of media rights negotiations. They do this safe in the knowledge that there are now direct channels of communication with their fans, or in other words, it is now possible to cut out the 'middle man', the sport journalist. At the same time, sport journalists – like other journalists – are being asked to provide more content with fewer resources. Failing to come up with a story will ultimately render the media outlet they work for redundant. Chasing stories is therefore not just in the public interest but in their own interest. The sport management professional must decide whether this desire for news represents an opportunity or an unnecessary intrusion. Review questions and exercises are listed below to assist with confirming your knowledge of the core concepts and principles introduced in this chapter.

## REVIEW QUESTIONS AND EXERCISES

1 What are the reasons that sport journalists might be considered less credible or professional than their non-sport colleagues?

2 In your experience as a media consumer, is sport media generally more positive or negative? Why?

3 Choose a series of sport related articles from the newspaper and identify the source of the article. Is there more than one source and does the article contain opinion or fact or both?

4 What is a beat?

5 Why might a sport journalist be reluctant to report negative aspects about people on their beat?

6 Examine articles in the sports section of a major daily newspaper. How many relate to events on the field of play and how many relate to events off field. For example, an update of an injured player would be related to 'on field' while an update on a player's social life would be 'off field'.

7 How has social media affected the relationship between the sports organization and their fans?

8 What is meant by the term 'off the record'?

9 Most professional sports organizations employ communications professionals or 'media managers'. What is their role? Include in your answer the perspective of the sport organization and the sport journalist.

10 What are the potential advantages for sport management professionals to build rapport with sport journalists?

## FURTHER READING

Andrews, P. (2013) *Sports Journalism: A Practical Introduction*. London: Sage.

Aris, S. (1990) *Sportsbiz: Inside the Sports Business*. London: Hutchinson.

Boyle, R. (2006) *Sports Journalism: Context and Issues*. London: Sage.

Nicholson, M., Zion, L. and Lowden, D. (2012) A Profile of Australian Sports Journalists (Revisited). *Media International Australia, Incorporating Culture and Policy*, 140 (Aug 2011), 84–96.

Stofer, K. T. (2009) *Sports Journalism: An Introduction to Reporting and Writing*. Maryland, MD: Rowman & Littlefield Publishers.

Wilstein, S. (2001) *Associated Press Sports Writing Handbook*. New York: McGraw Hill.

## RELEVANT WEBSITES

Australian Media, Entertainment and Arts Alliance – www.alliance.au

National Union of Journalists (UK) – www.nuj.org.uk/home

Society of Professional Journalists (US) – www.spj.org
Sport Journalists Association (UK) – www.sportsjournalists.co.uk/
National Sports Journalism Centre (US) – http://sportsjournalism.org/
National Sportscasters and Sportswriters Association – http://nssafame.com/

## INTERVIEW WITH A PRACTISING SPORT JOURNALIST, PART 1

### Sam Farmer, columnist and writer, *Los Angeles Times*

Sam Farmer, three-time finalist for the California Sportswriter of the Year award (2012–14), is in his twentieth season covering the NFL. Because he works for the *Los Angeles Times* and is in a city that doesn't have an NFL team, he's had unique assignments such as travelling with an officiating crew, spending a week behind the scenes with Pete Carroll and the Seattle Seahawks, spending a Sunday watching games with John Madden, sitting next to Al Michaels in the 'Monday Night Football' booth, and climbing Mount Rainier – or at least 11,000 feet of it – with NFL Commissioner Roger Goodell. Farmer, a 1988 graduate of Occidental College, began his career at small papers in the Pacific Northwest, before moving onto the *San Jose Mercury News*, where he was an Oakland Raiders beat writer for five seasons. At various times, he has also been a beat writer covering the NBA, PGA Tour, and college football and basketball.

*What does a typical day look like for you?*
It really depends on the time of year, the day of the week, and what news is breaking. That's part of the appeal of the job – the variety. As an NFL writer, my week begins on Sunday, when the vast majority of games are played. Say I'm in New England, covering a Patriots game that kicks off at 4:30 p.m. ET. I'll likely get to the stadium around 2 p.m. I don't like to get to games too early because I tend to burn out, creatively, if the day is too long. Before kick-off, I'll talk to fellow reporters, touch base with team officials, maybe stop in to see the owner and collect what pre-game information and 'colour' I can. I'm always looking for information/scenes/anecdotes that a) the public doesn't know and couldn't have access to, and b) other reporters don't have. I always want to take advantage of the added value of me being on site.

When I cover a game, I keep my own play-by-play, written in the shorthand chicken scratch that I've developed over the past 25 years and that only I can decipher. I'll file a story (without quotes) as soon as the game ends.

When the game is over, I'll head down to the locker room(s) to talk to coaches and players, staying down there maybe a half-hour, less if I'm on a tight deadline. I then rush back to the press box and file a second, typically better story, with quotes. Again, depending on deadline, I might have between 30 and 60 minutes to write this one. Sometimes, I might have as little as five minutes to write it, so that means smoothing over the first version and pumping in a few relevant quotes. It might be midnight on the East Coast at this time, so I'll continue to mine my notebook for my day-after

story, and assemble some blog posts for the next morning. Then, I'll leave the press box, drive back to the hotel, and sleep a couple of hours – with one foot on the floor, which helps me not oversleep for my early-morning flight to the next city, where I'll do it all over again for the Monday night game.

*What is the most challenging part of your job?*
The most challenging part is constantly pushing the limits of creativity to keep your writing and topics fresh and interesting, avoiding the rut of sameness that is so tempting, as it's the path of least resistance.

*What types of pressures are you under on a daily and weekly basis?*
There's constant time pressure. Everything you need to have done needed to be done yesterday. Especially early in your career, the hands of the clock spin so quickly you'd think they'd break off their hinge. As you get more experience, you can almost slow time and do much more with less. There's the pressure of accuracy, of course. Mistakes you make are on display for the world to see/laugh at/deride you for, so you need to get it right as much as humanly possible. If you're like me, you're more critical of yourself and your own failings than your harshest readers are. You need to do your job well. That means building a trustworthy and informed network of sources, getting good information from those people, making astute observations yourself, asking smart (and a lot of dumb) questions, and then assembling it in a cohesive, understandable and artful way. And then getting up and doing it again the next day.

*What type of articles do you regularly write?*
All types. News stories, game stories, columns, features . . .

*What are the characteristics of sport organizations that are best to work with?*
It starts with honesty. You'd like to cover an organization that's honest, and – rarest of rarities – realistic about its shortcomings and failures. That second part isn't mandatory, as you'll be able to discern that information yourself, but if we're talking ideals . . . You want an organization that gives you access to the players, coaches, management and owner(s). Some teams are much better about that than others.

*What are the characteristics of sport organizations that are worst to work with?*
Lying organizations that severely limit your access.

*What can sport organizations do to get better coverage?*
Win.

*Have you had more or less difficulty in the last five years getting access to athletes? How does access impact on your work?*
The glut of media outlets means press boxes are much more crowded, and players are more loaded down with requests. What's more, players typically are more guarded, largely because people are not as accountable when they write and electronically publish stories.

*Are sport organizations more worried about their image and brand in the social media age? If so, why do you think this is the case and are their fears warranted?*
Sports is entertainment. It's a business. So, yes, a team's fears about maintaining a positive image are warranted. Social media and web coverage cuts both ways – it can broadcast the good, and shine a spotlight on the bad.

*What advice would you give to athletes, coaches or administrators being interviewed by the media?*
If you're a player, coach or executive speaking to a reporter who covers your team on a regular basis, address that reporter by his/her first name, as opposed to 'Hey you' or 'Dude' or 'You guys'. That goes a long way.

*Has the fans' ability to access the club/players via social media (and the club to access fans) had an impact on your role?*
Readers understand what's fluff and PR, and what's credible information coming from a credible source. If you were planning a vacation, would you rather read about a hotel by perusing that hotel's brochure, or by reading honest reviews on a travel website by people who actually stayed at the hotel?

*Given you frequently see the people you write about, how do you manage your relationship with players, coaches and front office? Do they ever get mad at something you wrote and tell you so?*
Of course. You face them, you listen to what they have to say, and you just might get your next day's story.

## INTERVIEW WITH A PRACTISING SPORT JOURNALIST, PART 2

### Ian Murtagh, north-east football correspondent, *Daily Star*

Ian Murtagh has been covering football in the north-east of England since 1986. He grew up in the area, attended Newcastle University and was awarded an Arts degree in history and politics, but always wanted to be a sport journalist. For many years the 50 year old wrote for a regional broadsheet and now writes for the UK national tabloid *The Daily Star*, which has a circulation of 750,000 per day. The most popular professional sporting competition in the United Kingdom is the English Premier League (EPL). In fact, 25 years after it was spawned from the former Football Association first division, the EPL has become one of the most watched sporting competitions in the world. There are 20 teams in the English Premier League including global brands such as Manchester United, Manchester City, Liverpool, Chelsea and Arsenal. There are two teams in the EPL based in England's north-east, Newcastle and Sunderland. Murtagh's daily mission is to inform the paper's readers

about the team news from those clubs. He must write at least one story every day. Some of them can be as few as 300 words while others can be 1,000 word features.

*What does a typical day look like for you?*
I suppose the typical day is a lot less glamorous than people would imagine. Years ago, when Kevin Keegan and Peter Reid were the managers of Newcastle and Sunderland, they had two press conferences a day, every day. One for the evening papers and one for the 'dailies'. So a typical day back then would be going to press conferences. Now with all the restrictions, a typical day is working from home and trawling the net, seeing what's happening, ringing contacts – you can't ring players – not officially anyway because you've got to go through press officers – so a typical day can be quite tedious.

*The fans' desire for information about the game is increasing but do you think the journalists' ability to get that information is getting harder and harder?*
The journalist's ability to get the information can be harder and harder. The fans' ability to access the information gets easier and easier so that is a paradox because if a player on international duty, say a Frenchman, talks to the French press, that gets on the web instantly and the fans find out about that as quickly as the journalist.

Newcastle United have become quite an unpleasant club because of the owner and his anti-media campaign. They will only give access to players to rights holders such as Sky and the BBC and so they get players to interview and we don't. We have to scramble around to try and get interviews, etcetera, so there are an awful lot of obstacles in the way compared to 20 years ago when you could pick up a phone and just ring a footballer at home.

*And why does he (the owner of Newcastle United) do it?*
His argument would be: 'why should they get something for nothing?', because he says, well, Sky and BBC pay millions, newspapers don't. Our argument would be if it wasn't for newspapers, football 120 years ago would never have got off the ground. Newspapers have given football a free advert for decade upon decade. So yes it is changing, the landscape is changing.

*Television isn't a 'journal of record'. I know the* Daily Star *probably doesn't consider itself a journal of record either, but as a journalist you would still take the view that you are writing the truth and you have got to put that down in print.*
You've got rolling news on Sky, you've got *Match of the Day* on BBC, but what newspapers do I think is set the agenda, they fuel the soap opera that is football and you can give opinion far more easily in newspapers than you can maybe on television when you are just commentating on a match.

*What is the most challenging part of your job?*
Well there are two. The most challenging part is access, obtaining access. On a more dynamic level I would say when you are writing a match report of an evening and after 85 minutes – take the Arsenal game away at Anderlecht in the Champions

League on Wednesday night – now they were 1–0 down with two minutes to go and they won 2–1. Now that's a huge re-write for a journalist who's ready to press the button on the whistle. It's the one thing sportswriters – football writers – do which maybe news journalists can't do, [which] is just turn things around in an instant. It's hard, it's challenging, it's fun – you've got to have the adrenalin pumping but that is challenging and you've just got to get used to it.

*What are the characteristics of sport organizations that are best to work with?*
I think clubs have a basic misunderstanding of the media. They'll always claim that if we give you players you'll just stitch them up. The opposite happens. With Newcastle the two players we have managed to get at away matches have been giving their support to Alan Pardew saying we want Pardew to stay. We're saying to the club well surely that's a positive. They don't get it. Press officers are there – should be there – to help the press. Even though we get on with them they are there really to put barriers up. And I do believe you know the more access you get the better it is for all sides not just the media side. If you take American football in the States, the press are allowed in the locker room, it's a way of life. When I do Wimbledon tennis, players are fined if they don't talk to the press, it's an ATP rule. I think football is sometimes over protective of itself.

*What are the characteristics of sport organizations that are worst to work with?*
Ones that are very sceptical or very mistrusting and see the press as a pariah (i.e. Newcastle United).

*Has it has got progressively worse in terms of access in the last five years?*
Oh it has, absolutely, especially Newcastle. In the last 12 months they've had this policy of rights holders only.

*And how does this impact you? Does that mean you have got to break their rules? They want you to go through the media officer, but you've got to find a way around that?*
You do. You've got to be proactive. You've got to keep in touch with journalists and get translations of pieces that are written in France or Germany. When teams are on international duty you'll ring a [foreign journalist], I rang a Dutch journalist saying 'Could you ask Tim Krul (Newcastle United goalkeeper) these questions?' So you know the world's become a smaller place, so you're probably a bit more proactive in that respect.

*And do you have insiders in the club, people that you can call inside?*
You try to yes, of course.

*Has the club's official access policy hindered your ability to even lean on those contacts?*
Yeah it can do, yeah. At Newcastle I rang somebody about five weeks ago and he said, 'Ian, don't ring me, don't ring me on my mobile, they check, it's a club mobile'. He was so paranoid, he reckons that they would know that I rang him and he told me to ring him on his landline.

*Are sport organizations more concerned than they need to be about their image and brand in the social media age?*
Good question. Yes, because I think profile is a natural thing, it doesn't necessarily have to be worked on. I think, you know, they will get publicity good and bad whether they want it or not, so really what they should do is channel the positive and try and justify all of the negative. It should be a two-way relationship.

*Do you think if sport clubs formed strong relationships [with you] it would be beneficial?*
Oh yeah. We got a Christmas hamper from Newcastle 20 years ago. It's funny, when we were travelling around Europe with Newcastle and there was a lot of players that were suspicious of the press and yet if you see them at an airport waiting for your baggage return and just have a natural conversation, they suddenly realize you're friends. There's a lot of players I know who were suspicious of the press who become friends because they do radio work and they suddenly realize they're part of the media.

*What advice would you give to athletes, coaches or administrators about being interviewed by the media?*
Be natural. Be as truthful as you can be. I appreciate they can't always wear their heart on their sleeve all the time. Be friendly and open up as much as you can. Of course I would say that wouldn't I? If they want a good piece written about them, don't speak in monosyllabic tones, give a few stories, let them see your inner self almost.

*Do you think they are justified in feeling that if they open up too much you'll misuse the information?*
Can be. I think you've got to examine individual cases. I think that will happen sometimes but sometimes, it can work both ways can't it. It depends who the journalist is, it depends on who the sportsman is and what the article is.

CHAPTER 7

# Sport media relations practitioners

## Inside the team

### OVERVIEW

The relationship between sport and the media has become the defining commercial and cultural connection for both industries. In the late twentieth century, broadcasters' billion-dollar bids for television rights financed the move from an amateur pursuit into a hyper-commercialized one. In turn, sport provided television broadcasters with a highly marketable product. Professionalism developed not only on-pitch, but off it. Business functions, such as human resource management, started to appear within sport organizations and staff were employed in IT support, legal services and marketing. Given the increasing dependence of sport on media and media on sport, it is not surprising that a new addition has been a public relations position, designed to help facilitate and frame sport coverage from within. This chapter tracks the historical development of the public relations worker within sport organizations, from the initial role of a press agent, to a media relations specialist and beyond. It explores the role of public relations within sport, the importance of the media relations function, effective media relations, research that explores those who practice sport media relations and the impact of digital and social media. It also features discussion on the future of communication roles within sport organizations. This chapter also includes in-depth interviews with media relations practitioners from English Premier League Club Manchester City and the governing body of women's professional tennis, the Women's Tennis Association.

### LEARNING OUTCOMES

After completing this chapter the reader should be able to:

- identify why media relations has become an integral role in sport organizations;
- understand the major job functions of media relations staff members within sport organizations;
- understand how social and digital media have impacted on traditional media relations roles and organizational structure; and
- understand the skills required to gain a job in the industry.

## THE HISTORY OF SPORT PUBLIC RELATIONS

The year was 1919 and Notre Dame's American football coach Knute Rockne, already lauded for his innovative tactics on and off the field, had become distraught with how the local newspaper was reporting on his college programme. As Francis Wallace detailed in his autobiography of the coach, 'the writing had become more fanciful and there were times when inaccurate stories antagonized other schools and endangered the Rockne job of schedule-building' (Wallace, 1960: 21). Rockne's answer to this was to appoint an official correspondent, a move taken from the playbook of Hollywood press agents (Wallace, 1960). Sportswriter Archie Ward's new role was to help shape what journalists wrote or said about Rockne. Littlewood (1990) reported his brief was to 'see to it that the football news from Notre Dame was what Knute Rockne wanted it to be – no more, no less'. According to Littlewood's (1990) history, Ward travelled with the team and fed match reports from the road back to journalists, but only after Rockne had given his approval. This created a style that 'had its chief objective as the glorification of a man and an institution' (Littlewood, 1990: 25). Ward's appointment as an in-house journalist is thought to be the first example of a communications specialist working for a sport organization and attempting to frame the message, perhaps the world's first public relations practitioner in sport (Stoldt, 2013).

While US college sports were the first sport organizations to hire in-house public relations practitioners, professional leagues in the United States soon followed suit. Anderson (2003) reported that baseball's National League started a press office in 1922, followed by the American League in 1928, with the St Louis Cardinals the first team to hire a full-time staff member in 1931. Eugene (Gene) Karst's role occasionally included bagging fan mail for the Cardinals' star player Pepper Martin, driving general manager Branch Rickey to spring training and dealing with his correspondence, but mostly his tasks were those that modern-day media relations practitioners still practise:

> My job included singing the praises of the Cardinals to newspaper editors, sports writers and announcers . . . It also included writing and editing *The Cardinal News*, the first fan publications. I dug up statistics, made them available for sport writers . . . *The Sporting News* used our material occasionally, as did some of the sportswriters for New York and other metropolitan dailies.
>
> (Karst, 1992: 153–154)

In basketball, Howie McHugh was one of the earliest NBA public relations practitioners, and was one of just four members of the Boston Celtics front-office team in their inaugural 1946 season. McHugh was an All-American University ice hockey player who knew little about basketball, but developed a strong media following for the Celtics due to personal relationships. McHugh once told sport broadcaster Jonny Most:

> Considering I don't know much about basketball, I'm doing ok . . . We're friends, so you know I'm not bragging about myself when I tell you that there are writers coming to our games, not because they want to cover the Boston Celtics, but because they want to say hello and bullshit a little.
>
> (Carey and Most, 2003: 49)

While McHugh was an exception, most public relations staff were recruited from a sport journalism background. In the US, the first public relations specialist to be added to baseball's Commissioner office in 1965 was Joe Reichler, described by *Sports Illustrated* as 'The Associated Press's most knowledgeable baseball writer' (Anderson, 2003: 13). By the 1970s to 1980s, it had become common for professional sport teams and other major sport organizations in the US to have a public relations specialist on their staff.

While the role was initially designed to attract and facilitate media attention through interaction, as practised by Karst and McHugh, public relations practitioners in sport developed more strategic ways to attract attention. Fortunato (2000) detailed how the NBA media relations department in the late 1990s used various strategies to make it easier for media to cover the league. In addition to supplying the media with traditional information such as media releases, season guides, statistics packs and events such as press conferences, the NBA also created pre-packaged video news and even a radio hotline. Journalists could call this hotline and record a statement from an NBA official, which played on a loop, to then play on news bulletins (Fortunato, 2000: 485). More strategic initiatives were also planned to ensure that even when matches were not being played, there was a focus on basketball. In his 30 years of service at the NBA, current NBA Commissioner Public Relations advisor Brian McIntyre is credited with initiatives such as the Sixth Man Award, the Defensive Player of the Year, the Most Improved Player, White House visits by NBA championship teams, and a range of other strategies (NBA, 2012). These initiatives confirm Fortunato's observation that a key function of the NBA media relations department is to set the media agenda, illustrated by the following quote from then NBA President of Television Ed Desser: 'It's not just the media deciding on their own: "oh well, let's focus on the NBA today"' (Fortunato, 2000: 484). This focus on setting and shaping the sport media news agenda has become common in sport public relations practice, not just in the US, but globally.

Public relations roles within sport clubs and organizations in the United Kingdom only became widespread in the 1990s. Arsenal, a prominent club in the English Premier League, only introduced a media officer as late as 1999. Instead 'for most clubs, up until the 1990s, a PRO dimly meant an ex-player who would be around on match-days to speak to some of the supporters and the corporate sponsors' (Boyle and Haynes, 2006: 223). However, these roles have quickly moved from basic media relations that focused on facilitation, to more strategic decision making centred on access, spurred by the increasing focus of clubs to deliver their own media content. Chris Tate, managing director of Digital Media at EPL club Chelsea, stated in 2002, 'Why should we give access to certain newspapers really, who are trading on our name, our football players, our brand to sell their newspaper?' (Boyle and Haynes, 2006: 228).

In Australia, the Australian Football League's Corporate Affairs department listed in the AFL annual report in 2012 that a key function of its weekly news list was to set the agenda:

> In addition, over at least the past 14 years, the AFL has issued a weekly news list for up to 32 weeks each year to all accredited media that highlights upcoming milestones and issues of interest in our code. Not only does this assist many reporters but it also helps to set the agenda and is an initiative that other sports are starting to adopt.
>
> (AFL, 2012: 101)

The power of the sport public relations practitioner is also evident in Canada, where Lowes (1999) found that sport journalists work to a routine that is not just centred around a match, but also defined by what the sport media relations manager's schedule is. Lowes contended, because 'major-league sports organizations and individual athletes institutionalize contacts with reporters' (Lowes, 1999: 96), sport public relations practitioners can control the sports beat. Whereas Eugene Karst of the St Louis Cardinals simply supplied journalists with information in the 1930s, sports public relations practitioners are now active participants seeking to set the media agenda, and as such are now influential actors with the sport media nexus.

At the start of the twenty-first century, public relations has become a key business function for sport organizations. The scope of the role has widened from simply facilitating access and producing packs of information, to setting strategic direction, dealing with internal and external affairs, and the production of content in-house, delivering directly to fans through digital channels. This has led to an increase in the amount of roles available within sport, which is evident, for example, in the current NBA communications structure. At the start of the 2012/2013 season, the NBA listed 14 staff members in the Basketball Communications Department within their head office. A further nine staff members were listen within the International Communications Department, including a Spanish department in New York, a London office targeting Europe and an Asian office based in China. The communications department also encompasses marketing, which includes another 12 staff. The department lists its scope as the NBA, the WNBA and the NBA Development League (D-League), setting policies and procedures for each of these leagues and their teams, as well as business communication for all three leagues on a global basis, developing and implementing strategic plans to oversee global marketing, merchandising, media, community relations, production and programming initiatives. As sport organizations have developed commercially, so too have the media and communication departments of these organizations, to the point that these roles and their functions have spawned an entire industry, which necessitates specific training, skills and expertise.

## PUBLIC RELATIONS AND SPORT MEDIA

While there is ongoing debate surrounding an appropriate public relations definition among global public relations associations (CIPR, n.d.), a widely accepted definition is from Broom's *Effective Public Relations* that stated 'Public relations is the management function that establishes and maintains mutually beneficial relationships between an organization and the publics on whom its success or failure depends' (Broom, 2009: 2). The emphasis on mutual benefit is a useful starting point, but this definition still doesn't answer the question 'what type of work do public relations practitioners actually do?' According to the PR Universal Accreditation Board (Sha, 2011) there are 12 different work functions that public relations practitioners engage in, as noted in the following list:

- account/client management
- strategic planning
- PR programme planning
- stakeholder relations
- issues management
- crisis management

- project management
- media relations
- social media relations
- internal and employee relations
- special events, conferences and meetings
- community relations.

In a further analysis, Sha (2011) conflated these functions into four overall work categories: public relations management; issues management; corporate communications; and media relations. A public relations practitioner may practise one of these, a selection, or perhaps even all depending on their particular role and particular organization.

*Public relations management* activities are focused on management tasks, such as strategic planning, client and account management and project management. In sport public relations, activities might include setting strategic communications objectives for a particular sport organization, managing the department's budget, or working with external companies to deliver certain communications or public relations campaigns.

Tasks that fall within the *corporate communications* category include special events, conferences and meetings, internal relations, employee communications and community relations. In particular, internal relations and community relations are important elements of sport public relations. For example, Football Federation Australia (FFA) is the governing body for football in Australia. As well as supporting its elite teams to qualify and play at FIFA World Cups and managing Australia's professional football leagues, the A-League and the W-League, the FFA is also responsible for the governance of soccer in Australia. This includes developing junior players, coaches, and supporting the sport at the community level. Communications and public relations efforts should be focused not only on securing media attention, but on communicating to all members. For the FFA, the change in an interpretation of a rule that may affect refereeing at the community level is important to communicate to all stakeholders of the game, not just media. Internal relations activities are also important in sport, with common tasks such as producing in-house publications, training guides, annual reports, and developing web content.

The *issues management* category includes not just the short-term management of crisis communications, but also long-term planning focused on potential problems in order to prepare for crisis. The fact that modern-day athletes are considered celebrities and role models means that sport public relations practitioners need to be competent in various aspects of crisis management, as the reaction to player indiscretions often receive widespread media attention. For example, Tiger Woods is one of the most successful golfers in the sport's history, but his image was tarnished when it was revealed he had cheated on his wife multiple times, with multiple women. Writing crisis management plans, providing strategic counsel to clients or stakeholders, and resolving conflicts are all important elements of issues management. Specifically, crisis management focuses on reacting to immediate problems, including executing a crisis management plan, coordinating the release of information, understanding reactions, briefing spokespeople and monitoring and analysing media coverage.

The most important public relations work category within sport organizations is *media relations*. Media relations has been defined as 'the ongoing facilitation and co-ordination of communication and relationships between an individual, group or organization and the news media' (Johnston, 2012: 6). The intense media focus on sport, as well as the number of journalists assigned to sport or sport organizations, requires a staff member to facilitate media access and deal with media enquiries. In many large sport organizations this role is

performed by multiple staff members because of the intense media interest and the volume of media requests for access and information. For example, the AFL accredited more than double the number of journalists relative to players in the 2012 season – more than 2,000 journalists, editors, broadcasters, photographers and producers were accredited to cover the exploits of 700 players (AFL, 2012). With the role and number of sport journalists continuing to expand, the media relations function of sport public relations practitioners is essential in connecting the media with the producers of sport, the athletes and coaches.

Effective media relations is also focused on guaranteeing that a team, organization or sport receives media coverage in a crowded media environment through employing strategic planning and objectives. Within sport organizations the range of media relations activities includes preparing and issuing media releases, keeping media lists, dealing with media enquiries and facilitating access through one-to-one interviews or media conferences. It also involves producing information packs such as statistical guides, match previews or review notes. A key function of media relations is to ensure that journalists can cover a particular event. This includes managing a media accreditation process, and match-day media operations, such as set-up and operation of the media box, facilitating the mixed zone, moderating media conferences and ensuring that broadcaster and other media requirements are fulfilled. The perception of these standard functions and the apparent ease with which they are performed has led to media relations being labelled the 'soft' side of public relations (Johnston, 2012). This is an unfair characterization of the role, particularly as media relations can be a complex process that requires an understanding of the media, the ability to build relationships, and the capacity to interpret and deliver information effectively.

## EFFECTIVE INFORMATION SUBSIDIES: THE KEY TO MEDIA RELATIONS

Press-agentry is an outdated practice that was the domain of Hollywood press agents in the early 1900s, but is essentially the basis for labelling public relations as 'spin', a deceptive and dishonest practice, where practitioners feed the media with information designed to exclusively portray their client in a positive light. Modern-day media relations practised by ethical professionals is much more than Hollywood spin. In defining a theory for media relations practice, Zoch and Molleda (2006: 264) stated:

> Becoming proficient in media relations is a complex process involving a deep understanding of media routines, interpersonal relations, and message construction, a savvy regard for timing, organizational factors and news values, good research, both internal and external, awareness of current and potential holders, publics and interest groups.

The basic building blocks of media relations in everyday work can be described as creating pre-packaged information for use by media. These could come in the form of media releases, media advisories, media conferences, photographs or, in the twenty-first century, social media posts. These packaged pieces of information were first labelled

'information subsidies' by Gandy (1982: 8), who described them as 'the effort to reduce the prices faced by others for certain information in order to increase its consumption'. It is important to note here that 'price' may refer to time or difficulty of access rather than pure costs. For example, a media relations manager travelling with a team on an overseas trip may now send a media release complete with an audio or video file back to media in their home country. For a print journalist in Rio seeking a quote to add to a story on a Brazilian mountain bike rider who has won a World Championship in Russia, this means they will not need to travel to Russia to cover the event, or even track down an athlete on the phone to gain a quote to add to their story. This type of information subsidy reduces both time and cash costs, and means the journalist is more likely to cover this story, particularly when information is easily accessible.

However, there is a difference between providing an information subsidy, and providing an *effective* one. Sending a media release to a newspaper journalist 48 hours after a match is not likely to be effective; if the media release is not filed before the newspaper deadline directly after the match, then it becomes old news. As Turk (1985: 3) explained, media seek information that is useful to them in constructing news and 'sources who make this information quickly and inexpensively available to journalists through . . . "information subsidies," increase the likelihood that the information will be consumed by the journalist and used in media content'. For example, at many major sports events, communications staff will produce 'television packs' with pronunciation guides, statistics, career highlights and player profile information for television and radio commentators to use within their commentary for the match. This reduces preparation time for sport commentators, ensuring that they have the correct information at their disposal, while at the same allows the sport organization to direct what type of information is referred to in commentary. An effective pack should include a basic profile, all previous head-to-head matches, and interesting and relevant personal information, such as 'this player just became a father for the second time, with son Roger born in July'. But a poorly formatted pack, that only contains a selection of matches, or is too text-heavy and hard to read, will not make it easier for a commentator to understand and use. As such, the sport organization will relinquish the ability to influence the type of information referred to during the commentary or broadcast.

Another important type of information subsidy is the media transcript. Major sport tours such as the WTA, ATP, LPGA, NASCAR and others use a professional transcription service for all their media conferences, so all media conferences are transcribed and delivered via email to selected journalists shortly after the media conference has finished. This service reduces the time that journalists would have spent transcribing the quotes, while also acting as an official record or source, ensuring that reports can be filed quickly and accurately. In addition to the basic toolkit of media releases, press conferences, media advisories and audio and vision clips, specialist information subsidies such as detailed season media guides and statistics reports can be produced by sport media practitioners within sport organizations (Hall *et al.*, 2007; Pedersen *et al.*, 2007; Stoldt *et al.*, 2012). In the US in particular, these detailed season media guides have become huge undertakings, with those in professional sports such as the NBA, NFL, NHL and MLB running into hundreds of pages, with historical records and individual player statistics. They perform an important function as the go-to guide for any statistics questions throughout the year.

## SPORT MEDIA RELATIONS PRACTITIONERS

Despite media relations roles within sport organizations reaching back to the 1930s in the US, there is little research exploring who they are and how they work. One small cohort of sport public relations practitioners that has been a focus of research is those working in American college sport, the sports information director (SID). The College Sports Information Directors Association (CoSIDA) was formed in 1957 and in 2013 had a membership of 2,800 media relations, public relations and sport information and communications staff from across America (CoSida, n.d). In surveys of SIDs, McCleneghan (1995), Neupauer (1999) and Hardin and McClung (2002) stated that the average SID in US college sport is male, in his mid thirties, university educated and with a low to medium salary range. More often than not, the SID had come to their role through a journalism degree, not public relations. Hardin and McClung noted that SIDs were different from the general population of PR workers in America; while women had started to outnumber men in PR at a ratio of 2:1 in 2001 in the US SIDs were overwhelmingly male at 9:1 (Hardin and McClung, 2002: 38). An average salary was 55,000 US$ yet only 26.5 per cent of SIDs earned more than this. Hardin and McClung (2002) proposed that this showed a profession still very much in development, comparing it to print and broadcast journalism in its formative years. Whiteside and Hardin's (2010) updated profile took a gendered approach and found that while the percentage of women in SID positions had increased, women were more likely to be in assistant roles than directors, reported lower levels of job satisfaction and had shorter tenures than men. Importantly, Whiteside and Hardin also found that the representation of racial minorities within sport information positions is very low.

As the media relations role has developed within sport organizations, two differing viewpoints on its status have emerged – the idea of a 'dream job' versus a profession in 'crisis'. McCleneghan (1995: 14) asked SIDs what the biggest challenge in their work was and found the most common answer was 'lack of respect'. He contended that 'the SID business today is not practicing what public relations wants all of its practitioners to do – advise and counsel management'. Stoldt (2000) found that 20 per cent of SIDs wanted to be managers but only 7 per cent actually were. Battenfield and Kent's (2007: 248–249) most significant finding in their ethnographic study of the culture of sport information was 'that SIDs no longer operate as communicators, but are now mere producers of information' and SID culture is that of 'virtual anonymity'. This concept of anonymity can be seen in Battenfield's (2013: 449) description of the production of a media guide:

> Nameless, faceless people spent countless days, weeks and months at a keyboard producing a highly anticipated artifact that thousands clamber for each August when the printed version is delivered. Yet credit for this astonishing piece of journalistic work is limited to a one-inch square box on page one of the guide.

Whiteside and Hardin (2010) also found job satisfaction among SIDs was not high. When presented with the statement 'I have considered leaving my career', 76 per cent of women and 64 per cent of men ticked 'yes'. Collectively, this research does not paint an attractive picture of the media relations role, yet at the same time it is clear that these positions are highly sought after. The director of media relations at the Carolina

Hurricanes NHL team, Mike Sundheim, said he received over 300 resumés for the position of Media Relations Co-ordinator in a matter of days, despite it being a job that would require an additional salary and has irregular hours (Sundheim, 2013). On the surface media relations managers enjoy many perks, such as regularly attending major sporting events, negotiating daily with high-profile athletes and members of the media and seeing the outcome of their work in major news outlets. However, they must also juggle these perceived benefits with the downside of long hours, less pay than their general PR counterparts and a lack of recognition. Perhaps the answer to this divide between the 'dream job' and the 'profession in crisis' is best summed up by respondents to Hardin and McClung's (2002: 38) survey, on advice to those seeking a career in media relations: 'Plan on a career with little pay and little appreciation, but also plan on it being a lot of fun'.

## SPORT MEDIA RELATIONS IN THE TWENTY-FIRST CENTURY

The twenty-first century's communication revolution has had an impact on those working within media roles within sport organizations in two main ways: first, the ways in which media relations is practised; and second, the organizational structure of the media department. Social and digital media have both complicated and simplified different areas of media relations work. Gibbs and Haynes (2013) found that the micro-blogging website Twitter made the job more demanding in terms of time, due to constantly monitoring the social network's collective views, in particular those of athletes, media and fans. But, Twitter has also allowed some other tasks to be more direct. For example, this NHL team media relations staff member explains how he now posts information publicly that relates to journalists:

> In some cases it reduces face-to-face dialogue with reporters. Instead of me going around to 25 reporters spread throughout the arena watching practice to relay an item of information, I can just send out a tweet. . . . So, it does take away the face-to-face dialogue (Informant #12 – team media relations, NHL).
>
> (Gibbs and Haynes, 2013: 403)

There is no doubt that social and digital media channels have also had an impact on the access model in sport media. While fans once relied on traditional media such as television, radio or newspapers to receive news about their favourite team, they can now gain this directly from that team's website, Facebook page or YouTube channel. In turn, there are now staff employed in sport organizations to produce this content in-house. While there may only be two to three media relations roles within major sport organizations, these new digital content production roles offer potential new forms of employment within the media departments of sport organizations. The 'journalistic' nature of these roles suggests that it could be a place for sport journalists to gain employment; however, they must be aware of the different organizational constraints. Scherer and Jackson (2008) found in a case study of the production of www.allblacks.com, the official website of the New Zealand Rugby Union, that their production values were very much guided by commercial imperatives, which is the complete opposite of journalism's mission to deliver an unbiased

truth. Yanity (2013) detailed the case of a former newspaper beat writer who had moved to become a writer for a US college sport team. Gregg Bell stated that he still practised journalism, but that constraints were evident – he was not allowed to write certain stories based on what management of the athletics department said and was asked to write stories that were clearly promotional. While journalists seemingly have the perfect skills to take on these types of roles within sport organizations, 'in-house' journalism does have a different set of purposes and constraints.

## THE FUTURE OF SPORTS MEDIA RELATIONS

While many traditional media organizations are struggling in the era of free news via the internet, sport organizations have still been able to leverage sport's attractiveness into record breaking television rights deals. The media demand for sport will ensure that media relations roles will still be crucial within a sports organization, but now they are likely to be just one element of a revamped media department. This department is likely to now include an in-house video production team, a social and digital media manager and perhaps a graphic designer. Balancing organizational needs with media demands (such as whether or not to break news through the organization's own channels rather than work with the media), is likely to be one of the crucial issues for media relations managers within sport organizations in the next ten years.

## SUMMARY

This chapter has explored the history of public relations roles in sport organizations, where a slow trickle in the early to mid 1900s led to a global flood of practitioners in the twenty-first century. It suggested that while traditional public relations encompasses a range of activities, the main function in sport organizations is media relations. However, this function has changed over time from simply facilitating coverage to now being more strategic about influencing the news agenda. This chapter has emphasized the importance of providing effective information subsidies to the media in order to accomplish this. This chapter has also illustrated that social and digital media has had a significant impact on traditional sport media relations roles, in particular adding additional channels of communication to monitor and implement, and the addition of new content production staff within the media department. Review questions and exercises are listed below to assist with confirming your knowledge of the core concepts and principles introduced in this chapter.

## REVIEW QUESTIONS AND EXERCISES

1 How did the media relations role in US sport change from Archie Ward's initial role under Knute Rockne to Fortunato's study of the NBA?

2 List Sha's four main areas of PR work. How is each area different? Use the different work practices in each to help illustrate this.

3 Why does sport public relations focus more on media relations than other functions of PR?

4 What are the basic building blocks of media relations work? And why are they so important?

5 Why is it important to think about the effectiveness of information subsidies? Use examples of effective and ineffective subsidies to explain your answer.

6 Identify the two areas of media relations work that social and digital media have affected.

7 How does Simon Heggie, head of media relations at Manchester City, describe the approval process for media requests? Explain the strategic thinking behind this.

8 What kind of skills do Simon Heggie and Eloise Tyson mention are important for those pursuing a career in sports PR?

9 Look up your favourite team in a major league and try to find out the structure of their media department. How does this compare to other areas of the organization? Compare with a smaller team and discuss the differences.

10 Find some sport media relations managers on Twitter. What sort of things do they tweet? Do they use it as a work resource or a personal one? What are the benefits and risks of each?

## FURTHER READING


Battenfield, F. L. and Kent, A. (2007) The culture of communication among intercollegiate sport information professionals. *International Journal of Sport Management and Marketing, 2* (3), 236–251.

Boyle, R. and Haynes, R. (2006) The football industry and public relations. In J. L'Etang and M. Pieczka (eds), *Public Relations: Critical Debates and Contemporary Practice* (221–240). Mahwah, NJ, London: Lawrence Erlbaum Associates.

Fortunato, J. A. (2000) Public relations strategies for creating mass media content: A case study of the National Basketball Association. *Public Relations Review, 26* (4), 481–497.

Gibbs, C. and Haynes, R. (2013) A phenomenological investigation into how Twitter has changed the nature of sport media relations. *International Journal of Sport Communication, 6*, 394–408.

Hardin, R. and McClung, S. (2002) Collegiate sports information: A profile of the profession. *Public Relations Quarterly, 47* (2), 35–39.

L'Etang, J. (2013) *Sports Public Relations*. Dorchester: Sage.

McCleneghan, J. S. (1995) The sports information director: No attention, no respect, and a PR practitioner in trouble. *Public Relations Quarterly, 40*, 28–32.

Pedersen, P. M. (2012) Reflections on communication and sport: On strategic communication and management. *Communication and Sport, 1* (1–2), 55–67.
Stoldt, G. C., Miller, L. K. and Vermillion, M. (2009) Public relations evaluation in sport: Views from the field. *International Journal of Sport Communication, 2*, 223–239.
Yanity, M. (2013) Publishing for paydirt: A case study of an athletic department writer. *International Journal of Sport Communication, 6*, 478–489.

## RELEVANT WEBSITES

College Sports Information Directors of America – www.cosida.com
Sports PR Summit – www.sportsprsummitt.com
Public Relations Association of Australia – www.pria.com
Chartered Institute of Public Relations (Great Britain) – www.cipr.co.uk
Public Relations Society of America – www.prsa.org
Canadian Public Relations Society – www.cprs.ca
Global Alliance for Public Relations and Communication Management – www.globalalliancepr.org

## INTERVIEW WITH SPORT MEDIA RELATIONS PRACTITIONER A

### Eloise Tyson – Director, Communications at the Women's Tennis Association (WTA)

The Women's Tennis Association (WTA) is the global leader in women's professional sport. More than 2,500 players representing 92 nations compete for $129 million in prize money at the WTA's 55 events and four Grand Slams in 33 countries. Close to 5.4 million people attended women's tennis events in 2014 with millions more watching on television and digital channels around the world. Further information on the WTA can be found at www.wtatennis.com; facebook.com/WTA and twitter.com/WTA.

Eloise Tyson is Director, Communications at the WTA. After completing a Bachelor of Arts in Public Relations at RMIT University in Australia, she took a four-month contract as a media operations assistant at the 2002 Australian Open. After a stint at a PR agency, working across accounts in education, charity and IT, she joined Tennis Australia as Media and PR Co-ordinator one week before Australia defeated Spain in the 2003 Davis Cup final in Rod Laver Arena. She moved to London in 2008 to take on the role as Manager, Communications, at the WTA.

*Working in sports communications quite often means that no two days are the same, but could you describe what an average work day might include?*
When I'm working on-site at an event, a large part of my role is to manage the various requests for the players from the tournament, media and sponsors. I work with the players and their agents to negotiate, schedule and execute activities such as post-match press conferences, 1:1 interviews, photo shoots, autograph sessions, sponsor

meet and greets, kids' clinics and player parties. We only have a limited amount of time with each player, so it's crucial to prioritize requests and be as organized as possible in order to get maximum value from each activity. We are also on-site to help media with any questions they may have about the sport and our players, and provide briefing notes filled with statistics and information about the featured matches of the day. As with any event work, the hours are long, but the opportunity to work with world-class athletes, travel to various countries around the world, and be part of a great team is very inspiring.

*Working in sports communications often means liaising with some of the world's most high-profile athletes, their managers, corporate sponsors and international media, as well as liaising across different departments within your own organization. How important is developing relationships in your role? Do you have any tips or tricks for developing and maintaining strong relationships?*
No matter which career path you choose, building and maintaining strong relationships is absolutely crucial. In sports communications, so many jobs are filled through referrals from contacts in the industry. While at university, try to work as many events as you can. You'll build your experience, expand your network, and you never know who might take note of your performance and recommend you for a job in the future. Sports communications is connected to a variety of event stakeholders, each with their own set of priorities, challenges and pressures. Empathy is really important: journalists are working under highly stressful conditions, while athletes are dealing with emotional highs and lows tied to their performance. Adapt your approach according to the person and the situation, and don't take it personally if someone is having a bad day!

*What are some of the biggest challenges of your job?*
One of the biggest challenges is the unpredictable nature of sport, which is also what makes the job so interesting! All the best laid plans can be thrown into disarray by an unexpected loss or injury. Managing the expectations of media, tournaments and sponsors is also very important, as many of our players receive more requests for their time than they can possibly fulfil. It's essential to keep up with the latest news and social media updates to ensure the players are well briefed on issues before they go into a press conference. Whenever possible, we try to avoid a situation where one of our players is taken by surprise by a contentious issue.

*Could you tell us a few of your favourite memories from your time working in sports communications?*
Starting at Tennis Australia the week of the Davis Cup final in 2003 was an incredibly exciting moment, and I have some wonderful memories from travelling as press manager with the Australian Fed Cup team. Working with first-time Grand Slam winners is very special: it's such a rare accomplishment and something the player has worked towards and dreamed of their whole life. But my best memories have come from working with so many talented and dedicated colleagues who've become close friends. It's such a privilege to have a job where most days don't feel like work.

*What are the most important skills someone needs to have if they want to work in sports communications?*

Start with outstanding written and verbal communication skills, a keen interest in sports news and current affairs, and a thorough understanding of social media. Then look to build up your CV with practical events experience, which shows potential employers you are committed to a career in the industry. It sounds basic, but demonstrating enthusiasm, being a team player, and having a strong work ethic really goes a long way. Learn how to build and maintain effective working relationships with colleagues and other stakeholders, develop exceptional time management skills, and thrive in high-pressure environments. Be results-focused and always think about how you can add value to an organization. Lastly, if you are working with professional athletes, it's important to understand all the demands on their time, and how media and sponsorship commitments must be scheduled around training, conditioning and recovery.

## INTERVIEW WITH SPORT MEDIA RELATIONS PRACTITIONER B

### Simon Heggie, Head of Media Relations at Manchester City

Manchester City is one of the world's largest football clubs. Founded in 1880 as St Marks, they became Manchester City in 1894. After a successful period in the 1960s and 1970s, Manchester City hit a period of decline, culminating in their relegation from the English Premier League in 1998. After regaining Premier League status in 2002–03, the club was purchased in 2008 by the Abu Dhabi United Group and has gone from strength to strength. Manchester City won the FA Cup in 2011 and the Premier League title in 2011–12 and 2013–14. In the 2012/2013 financial year, they turned over £271million, the sixth-highest club total in Europe, and spent £233 million on player wages.

Simon Heggie is Head of Media Relations at Manchester City. After completing a sports studies honours degree at Northumbria University in the UK, his experience writing for the university newspaper led him to a cadetship at his local newspaper on the sports desk. He then moved to London to work at the *South London Press*, where he covered premier league football, Wimbledon, athletics, boxing and county cricket. He moved into PR in 2003, taking up a role at the football club Wimbledon, just before the club became Milton Keynes. He then spent two years at EPL club Reading, before moving to Manchester City in 2009.

*Working in sports communications quite often means that no two days are the same, but could you describe what an average work day in your current role at Manchester City might include?*

Every day is different and I guess at different points in the year I'll be finding that I do different things, different audiences. One day might be a PR event with a player attending, conducting a wide range of media interviews, another might be a pre-match press conference with our manager and a player, previewing a standard premier league game – or occasionally a massive champions league game. There are the match-days of course, home and away, very busy days not just in terms of the media that takes place but when it comes to planning that as an event, accreditation for the event. In between that there is a lot of liaising on the phone with journalists, a steady stream of enquiries about rumours, transfer rumours, injury rumours, general stories around the club and formulating responses in conjunction with players and senior officials. A lot of weekly work is done at the stadium but I'll also spend time at the training ground briefing and liaising with players, about many and varied media bits. Obviously we have a number of paid rights-holders, it's one of the most profitable sports leagues in the world, and all of those companies that pay for those rights have an entitlement to player access within that contract. So we have to find a way to juggle that demand along with all the other requests that come in to the department or the club for players' time. But we as the media relations and communications department tend to be the one department outside of the football department that have more face-time with the players, they recognize us, whereas they wouldn't recognize a lot of people here at the stadium – so it tends to be that because we know, we have the relationships with players, a lot of requests that the players have to do will be filtered through us.

*So that must be a challenge, working in a media relations role when players don't think they have to do media? How do you negotiate and work with them to fulfil requests?*
Over time it's a case of trying to create a culture. We have some individuals in our squad who are better than others, we've got a mix like every other club. We just try and make sure they are aware of contractual demands. First and foremost, we have to make sure that, those who have contracts, that those are honoured. We have a lot of demand on players and we try to make sure it's structured evenly so it's spread across the squad. Beyond the contracts, we filter other requests, and decide whether we are going to do them based on the importance of the journalist, based on the eyeballs that are going to be on that interview, based on whether it's an interview to be seen in a part of the world that is a target market, a target audience for the business. They are the three main criteria we use in the media relations department, every now and then there is something else that comes in that carries huge commitment that falls outside those parameters that we look at. But generally that's it. We always explain to players, we try to pick the best player for that piece of media and explain to them why they have been chosen, what the benefit to the club is.

*Manchester City is one of the world's premier football clubs. Could you give us some insight into the media attention the club receives, i.e. how many different media requests are you likely to receive each day?*
Difficult to put a number on it. I think we did a piece of work at the club some time ago. I think we worked out that we had delivered 1,500 pieces of media in the course

of the season. Very roughly speaking. Including pre-match media conferences and then the post-match media commitments, depending on the level of the game. So yesterday for instance (the potentially league deciding match against Liverpool on 13 April 2014) we delivered 13 post-match interviews for rights holders TV. We then did the post-match press conference, we also did two pre-match interviews and we did some interviews for our own internal website. We also have a mixed zone, outside each stadium and quite often we don't see how many players deliver interviews in those mixed zones, because they are walking through and they could be interviewed by five or six people through there. So if we don't count that we delivered about 15 or 16 pieces of media yesterday. That was a couple of seasons ago, I think we'd easily be getting up to 2,000 a season because we've got so many partners now that have access to players now. I don't often clock some of these things that players do, so it might be an old number. And it also doesn't take into account the work we do on our pre-season tour which can actually end up being the busiest time of our year these days. Four years ago our tours were very low key, we'd do the media on the ground at the games, whereas now our tours pre- and post-season are global and there is a lot of media that takes place on the road now that didn't used to happen three to four years ago.

*What are the best parts of your job?*
We get to see the world really with this club. I'm very biased but I think in world football there are not much more exciting places to be than Man City. There are a lot of big clubs out there, but there is no club that is growing as quickly as Manchester City. We were listed last year as fifth in terms of the size of the club now, which is unbelievable considering where we came from five years ago. So there are some really exciting projects around the corner, we are touring Abu Dhabi in a few weeks time and then we go to America for three weeks in the summer. So some of the football that Manchester City play now is breathtaking to watch. I'm not a Manchester City fan, I'm a Nottingham Forest fan, and every now and again I'll go back to watch Forest play and it's like watching another sport. So I'm getting to watch some of the best players in the world play every week and getting to know them and work with them. There have been some amazing highlights – I was there in the tunnel managing the media operation on the day that we won the league, which was one of the most dramatic endings to a season ever. So to have that on your CV and the excitement around the new projects we are working on in New York and Melbourne, it's a privilege to be part of it.

*Overall what is the main role of the Manchester City media relations and communications department?*
I guess we are here to ensure that Manchester City is represented in the best way, every club will have its own strategy for ensuring that it's represented correctly. I guess we are often represented in the media as being the wealthiest club in the world and everything that comes with that. The challenge for us is to make sure that we are still connected with our fans, not just fans in Manchester, but fans globally and to make sure that the myths of the club just being the richest club in the world and

throwing money around and not having a strategy for that . . . That's something from the last few years – people are starting to see that the plans for the club are very wide ranging and thought through and I think that's probably one of the biggest challenges in everything that we do. I think that's one of the biggest challenges, that the messages from the clubs are put through in the best way.

*Working in sport is often tough on work/life balance. How do you manage this?*
If you are working in a role, that essentially, the *raison d'être* of which is to play football on the pitch. There is a lot that goes on around it but we are all here to support a team playing football on the pitch essentially. Some of those games are played on a Saturday and they are played in the evening and midweek. So there are roles within a club that mean you don't have to be there on a match-day to work but the media relations role, or the football media relations role that I work in, you have to be there to oversee the media on all of the match-days. Home and away, I've probably missed five games this season. So that's European games, home and away mid-week trips to Europe, pre-season trips to the States, that's three weeks. I have an eight-year-old daughter and a three-year-old son that I miss when I'm away, but that's the job that I do and I wouldn't change that. You find a way of working out work/life balance. I make sure that I try and take a day in a week to compensate the fact that I've not been around on the weekend, I take a chunk of time off during the season when perhaps players are on international duty. That's usually a cue for many people within the football department or who work with the footballers to take time off as well. That's always been the case and I guess if it's something you aren't comfortable with you wouldn't be doing the job.

*Looking more broadly at your career, how have you seen the communications role within sports organizations change since you started?*
The role I did then at Wimbledon is completely unrecognizable to the work that I do now, but that's partly to do with the fact that I work for a much much bigger club than I did then. When I started out at Wimbledon, the internet was only just really taking off. The club had the bare bones of a website, compared with what you see now. I think even Milton Keynes now would have four or five people now doing what I was doing, I was doing everything, the match-day magazine, the programme, the press officer work and everything else that goes with the press office work. Our department here at City, just in PR, does not even touch our website, our magazine, any of the social media content we have, just purely communications and media relations bodies – we are currently nine strong. If you added in the people that do our website, our social media, our magazines, all of our other output – it's triple that. It's a huge department. It's commensurate with what you would get at the other big club in Manchester, the two big clubs in London, we are all operating on that level. But if you are taking it back essentially, there might be more people doing that role but the actual role hasn't changed too much.

*What do you think are the most important skills for someone to develop if they wish to work in a sports communication or media relations role?*

I think the first thing is to have a good command of English. I think quite often people come to me and say, should I do a sports journalism degree? And my advice is often not to do that – only because those degrees can narrow your field so much. It's such a tremendously competitive industry, there are so many people vying for these jobs. If it doesn't come off and you are left with a sports journalism degree, it doesn't really translate to helping you in another field beyond that. My love of journalism just came from me doing lots of writing, I did do a sports degree – so I'm not really practising what I preach, but to me it's about your love of journalism. If you are going to manage a media department then really you need to know media, so it's about versing yourself in media, enjoying reading and enjoying writing and essentially doing what I do, I do it because I love football too and I have always loved football. So with all of these things together, the determination and being a people person really. It's all about building relationships and being politically savvy when you are in the role.

# PART 4

# Sport media strategies

CHAPTER 8

# Sport media planning and promotion

## The foundations of coverage

## OVERVIEW

This chapter examines the importance of media planning and the specific tools and strategies that a sport media manager can use for effective and consistent media coverage for a sport organization or individual athlete over the course of a year or season. In particular, this chapter will discuss media lists, media plans and tools that can be used to plan and evaluate media coverage, such as the media grid. This chapter also provides practical information related to promotional strategies and campaigns, including the necessity to create a visual hook to obtain media coverage in a highly competitive market. It includes examples of two different media events that gained extensive media coverage, as well as a case study that explores some of the extensive media activities planned and executed at the London 2012 Olympic Games.

## LEARNING OUTCOMES

After completing this chapter the reader should be able to:

- devise media planning goals for a sport organization, event or season;
- generalize about the differences between advertising and publicity;
- use media planning tools and strategies to ensure that a sport media organization or individual athlete is well positioned to acquire media coverage;
- evaluate the success of media planning and promotion strategies in order to implement improved practices and systems; and
- structure an event or media opportunity to maximize the potential for media coverage.

## INTRODUCTION

It is often said that those who fail to plan, plan to fail. When this saying is applied to the sport media nexus, it simply means that those who fail to plan get no media coverage. As previous chapters have illustrated, the sport media nexus is highly competitive. Sport organizations compete to acquire mass audiences, increased revenue and media coverage, while media organizations compete to acquire premium sport content and access to its consumers. In this context failure to plan will have three important implications. First, the sport organization that fails to plan will surrender any promotional advantages to its competitors. Second, a failure to plan will result in an organizational mindset in which the essential sport media relationship will be subsumed by other management functions that are perceived to be more important and pressing. Third and finally, these organizations will be reactive, rather than proactive, and therefore at the mercy of the media with respect to the amount and quality of the media coverage they receive. Media planning and strategy are essential for sport organizations, whether small or large, that want to operate effectively and competently within the sport media nexus.

## ADVERTISING AND PUBLICITY

In sport media and the media generally there is a distinction between advertising and publicity. In general, advertising is media coverage that an organization pays for, either in cash or in kind. Advertising is necessarily defined by the commercial relationship between the media outlet and the organization or individual purchasing space (in the case of print media and the internet) or time (in the case of broadcast media). By contrast, publicity is free. In essence, publicity is the coverage that media outlets devote to an organization or individual in the form of news, whether positive or negative. The distinction between advertising and news based publicity often appears superficially simple, but can be far more complex. In a newspaper or television broadcast, advertisements are generally very clearly delineated from news. On television, advertisements are generally grouped together or occur in single units during breaks in a sport broadcast, while in a newspaper the distinction between advertisement and news type is usually obvious. The confusion arises when media news is infused with advertising content, either consciously or unconsciously. For example, there have been cases in which prominent radio broadcasters have been paid by commercial organizations to talk positively about particular products under the guise of news. In these cases the media consumer has no way of distinguishing between advertising and news based publicity as the distinction between the two is unclear.

Publicity has the advantage that it is considered a credible source by consumers. In other words, consumers might ignore advertising because it has a blatantly commercial dimension, but be attracted to or at least influenced by publicity because it is typically viewed as news. The distinction between advertising and publicity means that competition for publicity is fierce, because of the cost benefit and because of the status and credibility conferred by the coverage. Sport is atypical in this respect, because professional high profile sports in particular already have interest value as news. This high interest value means that sport organizations are readily able to generate regular free publicity through television broadcasts or newspaper reports on forthcoming events or past games. This

publicity might in turn lead to an increase in the number of fans at the game and subsequent gate revenue, or an increase in interest from sponsors wishing to purchase naming rights, thereby increasing total revenue. A telecommunications company, by contrast, might be able to generate free publicity sporadically, from the launch of a new product for example, but the media are unlikely to report on the daily or weekly activities of the company. Thus, the telecommunications company is more likely to advertise

## IN PRACTICE 8.1

### USA Swimming's viral video: 'Call me maybe'

A sport team lip-syncing to a popular music video might not seem like a sure-fire way to gather major mainstream media attention, but that is exactly what the USA swim team managed to do with their catchy clip ahead of the London 2012 Olympic Games. Following an already popular trend, USA Swimming's media team helped direct a video that included Olympic gold medallists Michael Phelps, Ryan Lochte and the soon to be star Missy Franklin, lip-syncing to Carly Rae Jepson's 'Call me maybe'. The video was uploaded to USA Swimming's YouTube channel on 26 July 2012 with a note that said:

> It's no secret that members of the US Olympic swimming team work hard, but there's also a little bit of downtime during training camp. In an attempt to blow off a little steam during that spare time, Alyssa Anderson, Kathleen Hersey and Caitlin Leverenz spearheaded this video project, which Leverenz says incorporates about 95 percent of the team.
>
> (YouTube, 2012)

Initially the video was shared mostly by the athletes who were part of it through their own social media networks. But as the interest started to grow, it was picked up by major news outlets, reaching a total of 7 million views by the end of the London Games. However, the video's success wasn't just as a result of promotion through these regular channels, for part of its 'viral' pathway was a strong response from influential web-based news sites such as *Mashable*, the *Huffington Post*, *Live Leak* and *The Daily Beast*. These websites helped push the content out to new audiences, ones that were unlikely to find their way to USA Swimming's official website to watch the clip. As of early 2014, the video had reached over 12 million YouTube views. This example is not the traditional way in which most sport organizations would aim to attract widespread media attention, but it does illustrate the power of new digital channels and how they can potentially by-pass traditional media gatekeepers. The video was extremely cost and time effective, and, as it was driven by the team and supported by the media department, ensured enthusiastic participation. While it is impossible to tell exactly what will go 'viral' on the internet, this example illustrates that social and digital channels can be used to show a different side of your sports organization, team or athletes, and yet can still have an impact on traditional media.

Source: YouTube (2014).

through the media and use sport as a vehicle for promotion because of the publicity it receives.

The value of publicity as a generator and barometer of wealth and public perception means that it is highly sought after. High profile professional sport organizations might engage in advertising to increase ticket sales, merchandise sales and public awareness, but mostly, sport organizations are desperate to acquire publicity. In even the smallest markets this is difficult because there is simply not enough media space and time to report on every event, match or achievement. As discussed earlier in the book, the media are constantly required to make decisions about what constitutes news. The reality is that only a minority of sport organizations and athletes achieve media coverage, and they are competing for media space with a wide variety of organizations and individuals from sport and non-sport fields such as politics, the financial markets and the arts. Organizations that engage in media planning and promotion have a better chance of acquiring media publicity. Furthermore, the publicity they acquire is usually better quality and better positioned and they are able to evaluate the success of the media activities more effectively, having set targets and strategies against which to measure their success.

## SETTING MEDIA GOALS

Prior to beginning the media planning required to achieve consistent media coverage for a sport organization, it is important to understand the distinction between strategy and planning. Strategy can be defined 'as the process of determining the direction and scope of activities of a sport organization in light of its capabilities and the environment in which it operates' (Hoye, *et al.*, 2015). In this context the amount and quality of media coverage is dependent on factors such as the level of the sport organization (national, state, regional or local), the team or individual's performance, as well as its location. In other words, the strategic direction of the Beijing Dolphins under 14 girls softball team to gain international media coverage for its championship season in B division is unrealistic. But regular coverage in a local newspaper, with the specific goals of one article published per month and a feature article on the best player, is achievable. By contrast, planning is the process by which the organization makes the strategy or direction happen, by documenting what has to be done, by whom, with what resources, within a specific timeframe.

Prior to media planning, a sport organization must set goals for the organization or athlete. These goals will be most useful and relevant when they are tied directly to the sport team or league's strategic plan. In other words, an organization's media goals do not exist in isolation. Rather, the media performance of the organization should be intimately connected to its overall vision and objectives. The entire media strategy planning process is graphically represented in Figure 8.1.

The overall role of Cricket Australia's public affairs department is 'as the face and voice of Cricket Australia, with the mission to generate positive interest and media attention in cricket' (Cricket Australia, 2014), which is directly related to the overall goals of the organization. This is further illustrated in Cricket Australia's 2011 to 2015 Strategic Plan, with 'Share of all sports media voice' highlighted as one of seven key areas where cricket aspires to be No. 1 (Cricket Australia, 2014). The media are one of Cricket Australia's key stakeholders and importantly, are able to influence other stakeholders through their

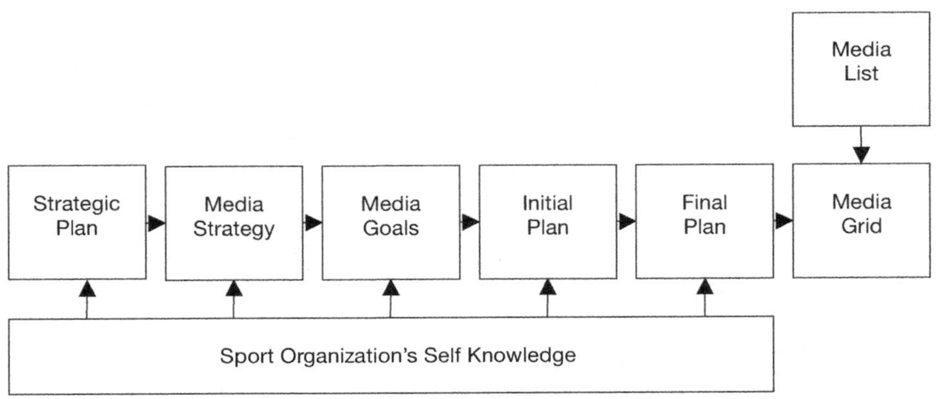


**FIGURE 8.1** Media planning and strategy flow chart

coverage of the game. The International Rugby Union Board's (IRB) 2010–20 strategic plan illustrates how strategy informs everyday media and communication work practices. In the detailed plan, each specific communication objective is linked directly back to one or several of the overarching seven strategic IRB goals. For example, the first strategic objective for communications is 'ensure the IRB communicates effectively with key partners and stakeholders'. This is directly related to goals 1 and 7 of the strategic plan: 'Protect and Promote Rugby, its values, ethos and spirit' and 'to provide strong and effective leadership'. Another communication strategy, 'drive global promotional strategies that optimize exposure in existing and developing markets' is directly related to the overarching IRB goal to 'increase global participation'. The IRB strategic plan goes one step further and also details the steps that will be taken by communications staff to deliver this strategy. For example, for 'ensure the IRB communicates effectively with key partners and stakeholders', the plan states:

> We will do this by: Implementing a comprehensive media services programme, developing strategy based communications programmes to promote all IRB and Rugby activity, delivering a proactive and comprehensive global Rugby issues management policy, delivering world class websites, delivering quality promotional publications and delivering media training for key IRB staff.

In this case, each of the overall IRB strategic goals provides guidance for the IRB's communications staff in their daily work practices and interactions with media (World Rugby, 2011).

Media strategy and specific goals for a season or event will differ from organization to organization, but whatever the size and type of sport organization, it is essential that the goals are as realistic and specific as possible. A goal for a large sport organization might be to increase the number of major daily newspaper articles published about the team by 10 per cent. On the other hand a small sport organization might set a goal of six local newspaper articles throughout the course of the season. In both cases the goal will

determine the media planning and in particular the types of media opportunities the organization attempts to create. The larger sport organization might set the goal of increasing the number of spectators through media coverage, which might mean that a major focus of media planning is to create regular media opportunities prior to matches. By contrast, the smaller sport organization might seek to attract participants to the organization, which means that the media planning focuses on creating stories that illustrate how much fun the sport is to play, as well as its social benefits.

## GETTING TO KNOW THE MEDIA

One essential planning and promotion tool is getting to know the media on a personal level. Getting to know journalists by name and treating them as individuals rather than cogs in the media machine are ways of establishing a sound professional relationship. This relationship will strengthen the already essential connection between media and sport personnel referred to in previous chapters. A strong personal connection may minimize harsh criticism at a time of crisis, or may simply enable the sport organization to have their perspective of an issue more easily heard.

The first chapter in this book highlighted that the term media can be used to describe institutions, people and the texts we interact with on a daily basis. For the purposes of media planning, it is essential to dig deeper and discover that the media is a multilayered set of institutions and outlets (Johnston, 2012). Media planning and promotion relies on being able to target ideas, stories and events so that specific media respond by providing positive media coverage. Planning will be hindered, however, if the media is viewed as an homogenous entity, where each institution or outlet will respond in the same way. This thinking will result in wasted opportunities, time, resources and money. Rather, it is important to view local, regional and national media organizations as having different needs. Similarly, television will have distinctly different needs to the internet, a newspaper, radio or a magazine. For example, a television news bulletin may require a 30 second story that is highly visual with a concise ten second interview sound bite, whereas a radio station may require an athlete, coach or manager to participate in a ten minute live interview.

The formal component of the process of 'getting to know the media' is the formulation of a media list (Helitzer, 1999). A media list, as the term suggests, is a list of all media organizations and contacts that are likely to cover the activities of the sport organization throughout the course of an event or season. For most sporting leagues and events, a media accreditation process is the major mechanism by which a sport organization develops a working media list, as well as determining who is authorized to cover the event. Major sporting events such as Wimbledon or sporting circuits such as F1 have online accreditation systems, whereby journalists, editors, camera operators, commentators and photographers are able to register. Once accepted, the media employee will have access to specific media facilities and resources. The 2015 Rugby World Cup in England estimated it would accredit more than 3,000 members of the media, while the summer Olympic Games accredits more than 20,000 media personnel in total. As a result of the accreditation process, a necessary step to be able to provide accreditation to members of the media to cover the event, a sport organization will have a comprehensive list that can be used to disseminate information.

Similarly, large sport organizations that participate in major leagues, such as the NFL, the EPL in England or the AFL in Australia, also have accreditation processes to determine the eligibility of media personnel and provide access to media events, games and special media facilities. In a relatively small country such as Australia, the AFL accredits in excess of 2,000 media personnel for a single season, which is almost three times the number of players on combined club lists. As is the case with a large event, the accreditation process enables the AFL to determine whether an individual is employed by a media organization in an official capacity, or whether they are attempting to gain access to the league, teams or players by deception. At the conclusion of the accreditation process, which occurs prior to the start of the season, the league has acquired a comprehensive list of media personnel, which may then be used throughout the season. This process is not limited to the major football codes, as many sport organizations and events provide media access and use an online system to register potential media attendees. Some organizations have even developed online media workrooms that are a way to give event and athlete information through their websites, as well as develop an effective media list. For example, the International Triathlon Union website has a section reserved for the media that contains press releases, high-resolution images and audio clips from various events. To gain access, media personnel must register through the website and provide details of their organizational affiliation. Once again, the end product of the process is that the sport organization has vetted the media and developed a useful resource for future use, while in this case also providing a useful resource for the media.

For smaller sport organizations that do not have the resources to implement an accreditation process or design and service a website that requires media registration, a media list must be developed manually. Essentially, a media list must include all media personnel and organizations that the club or league is likely to have contact with during an event or season. In practice, when the media manager wants to send out a media release about the captain of the team breaking the league's goal or point scoring record, they are able to send it to all the media on the list. Without the list, the process of communicating with the media would be slower, which would result in wasted time and resources, as well as less media coverage.

For a media list to be an effective tool for a sport organization it must exhibit two key features. First, it must be updated constantly. The media is a fluid industry, in which media personnel switch employers. So it is essential that sport organizations, through their media manager, keep track of the location of key journalists, producers, editors and commentators. New media outlets will also need to be added to the list as they are developed, launched or released. In this respect some media forms are more easily monitored than others. Major television networks and daily newspapers remain relatively stable, but at the other end of the spectrum new internet sites are launched often, making it difficult to keep the list current.

Second, the media list must be segmented. In other words, a media list must be divided into the various media types, such as television, newspapers, magazines, radio and online, and sizes, such as local, regional, national and international. This segmentation is essential to ensure that news items or story ideas are pitched at the appropriate media. If the media list is not segmented, then news items and story ideas will go to all media outlets, which runs the risk of putting media outlets off-side if for example you are holding a media opportunity for a UEFA Champion's League match in Germany but send the information

to your global media list, many of whom cannot attend. Sport organizations need to be more strategic in their media communications and the media list is an important way of organizing and prioritizing differing media contacts and information.

Constructing a media list is achieved primarily by examining the media outlets and identifying the journalists that cover a sport on a regular basis (Helitzer, 1999). For major sport organizations, this will include beat reporters and general sport reporters. For minor sport organizations, which may not have beat reporters assigned to the league or team, this will be general sport reporters only. Other personnel such as newspaper editors and sub-editors, magazine editors, television producers, radio producers and internet site editors should also be included. Broadening the media list beyond major media organizations requires a considerable amount of research, in order to locate appropriate outlets, their employees and their contact details. Fortunately, in most major media markets, media

**TABLE 8.1** Mock media list

| | | |
|---|---|---|
| *Newspaper* | | |
| Fred Reports | Email | f.reports@mchronicle.com.ru |
| Journalist | Mobile | 555 6666 777 |
| *Moscow Chronicle* | Landline | 334 556 667 |
| | Fax | 334 556 668 |
| | Address | 6 Main Street, Moscow |
| | Twitter | @ReporterMan |
| | | @MosChronow |
| *Television* | | |
| Julie Anchor | Email | j.anchor@S2S.com.ca |
| Producer | Mobile | 0770 663 425 |
| S2S Broadcasting | Landline | 61 944 45676 |
| | Fax | 61 944 45678 |
| | Address | 345 Puck Drive, Calgary |
| | Twitter | @TheAnchor |
| | | @S2SBroadcast |
| *Magazine* | | |
| Chuck Stevens | Email | chuck@bigwave.com |
| Editor | Mobile | 932 008 7650 |
| *Big Wave Monthly* | Landline | 4378 996 553 |
| | Fax | 4378 996 550 |
| | Address | 6/88 Coral Reef Road, Hawaii |
| | Twitter | @GoofyChuck |
| | | @BigWaveMon |

guides and directories have been developed for commercial purposes. These guides and directories contain lists of media organizations and personnel, usually segmented by media type, size and topic (sport, business, finance, travel, politics, etc.). From these guides and directories, a sport organization should be able to construct a working media list; however, it is advised that small sport organizations do not make their media list too large. The size of the media list should be proportional to the size of the organization and its audience. Table 8.1 is a mock media list, which illustrates how one might be formatted.

## MEDIA COVERAGE OPPORTUNITIES

Once the organization's media goals have been set and a media list developed, the organization must decide which of its activities it wants the media to cover. Importantly, for most sport organizations the media will not be able to cover everything, nor is every activity likely to be attractive to media, and activities must be prioritized. Helitzer (1999) suggested that the most effective way to do this is for the organization to construct an initial and final plan prior to the season or event. The initial plan is essentially a list of ideal media opportunities in an ideal world. The final plan is arrived at by sifting through the ideas contained in the initial plan and prioritizing them based on the media strategy, the size of the events required to attract media coverage, the organization's budget, availability of the players or athletes, likelihood of attracting media coverage, health and safety considerations and competition from other teams, leagues and sports.

For example, the initial plan might include the team conducting its annual pre-season training camp at a military base, where the players will skydive from an aeroplane and do some white water rafting. This event will probably attract significant media coverage because it contains visual elements necessary for television, newspapers and magazines. However, not all sport organizations will have the resources to fund such an activity and the safety risks might outweigh the benefits. In a case like this, the organization might exclude the risky idea from the final plan, but retain the idea of securing media coverage of pre-season training by staging a less hazardous activity, such as a weightlifting competition that a selection of fans can participate in by entering a competition on a radio station. This event will be extremely low cost, but will still provide good media opportunities. Similarly, the initial plan might contain a family day with players dressed as clowns interacting with circus animals. Again, the media are likely to cover the event, but the cost might be exorbitant and the chance of an elephant trampling a fan too great. Thus, in the final plan the family day might be excluded but the clown theme retained in a visit to a local children's hospital by some of the players.

The final plan is not an end point. Rather, it requires execution. In evaluating the constitution of the final plan and constructing smaller action plans for each of the items on the final plan, it is advisable to consider the following:

- Are the media opportunities well spaced throughout the course of the season or event?
- Is there a mix of stories prior to, during and after the event or season?
- If the final plan is for a season, are there regular media opportunities in the lead up to games or matches?

- Are there any competing demands at any stage of the season or event that would reduce the coverage or impact of the story?
- How will information be communicated to the media for each of the story ideas (media release, media conference, media event, etc.)?
- How much will each media opportunity cost (keeping in mind that ideas that were over budget were excluded from the final plan)?
- Which players or athletes will be required?
- What logistical planning is required for each media opportunity (location, time, props, staff, resources, etc.)?
- Are there enough human interest stories?
- How can the visual element of the story be enhanced to generate greater television and print media coverage?

## MEDIA GRIDS AND CHARTS

Media grids, or flow charts as they are sometimes referred to, are a media planning and evaluation tool. Helitzer (1999: 234) referred to the media grid as a 'visible and ever-changing document' that allows large organizations to check their daily media progress and small organizations to check their progress over weeks, months or an entire season. At its core, the media grid is a way of organizing and allocating news items and story ideas to specific media outlets. Table 8.2 is an example of what a media grid might look like at the end of an event. Media organizations or individuals are listed across the top and news items and story ideas are listed down the side (from the final plan). The news items or story ideas are listed as published/broadcast or rejected, but during the season or event, other terms might be included, such as 'discussed' or 'reworking', in order to indicate that the story still has a possibility of being published or broadcast.

**TABLE 8.2** Mock media grid

| *Story idea/ Media outlet* | *USA Today* | *BSkyB* | *Sports Illustrated* | *STAR* | *CNN* |
|---|---|---|---|---|---|
| Dodgem (Bumper) cars driven by star players | Rejected | Broadcast | Rejected | Broadcast | Broadcast |
| Launch of trophy tour | Rejected | Rejected | Rejected | Broadcast | Rejected |
| Hot air balloons in team colours | Rejected | Broadcast | Published | Broadcast | Rejected |
| First training at major tournament | Published | Broadcast | Published | Broadcast | Broadcast |

## IN PRACTICE 8.2

### LeBron James makes 'The Decision'

A major new signing is a significant announcement for any team, but one that would usually be catered for with a media release and press conference, to allow a photo opportunity with the athlete in new uniform and for the media to ask questions of all relevant individuals. NBA star LeBron James took a dramatically different approach when he became an unrestricted free agent in 2010, taking part in a one-hour television special on US TV network ESPN. The story of where James would go, after spending seven years at the Cleveland Cavaliers, was covered widely from all angles as several teams courted him.

Freelance sportscaster Jim Gray initially pitched the idea to James' management team and ESPN for a one-hour special where James would announce his 'decision'. On 8 July 2010, ESPN then aired the live special *The Decision* over 75 minutes. Almost 30 minutes into the broadcast James announced he would be moving to the Miami Heat in the 2010–11 season. A unique part of the broadcast was that ESPN offered James and his management team the air time for free. Advertising space was then sold, but all profits went to charity. While almost ten million US viewers tuned into the decision, most in Cleveland, it was roundly lambasted as a flop due to the quirky interview questions, delay in announcement of team and general self-promotion. In particular, Cleveland fans and most media outlets were not impressed with the self-serving way that LeBron acted. Cavaliers majority owner Dan Gilbert even released a statement that said in part: 'This was announced with a several day, narcissistic, self-promotional build-up culminating with a national TV special of his "decision", unlike anything ever witnessed in the history of sports and probably the history of entertainment' (Gilbert, 2010).

There is no debate that the unique way LeBron announced he was changing teams generated mass publicity, even though most of it was negative, and continued to do so months afterwards. In an interview with ESPN in July 2011, James admitted if he had his time again he wouldn't have engaged in the TV special:

> I can now look and see if the shoe was on the other foot and I was a fan, and I was very passionate about one player, and he decided to leave, I would be upset too about the way he handled it.

In July 2014, James stayed true to this word, announcing he was returning to Cleveland through a simple letter published on *Sports Illustrated's* website, reinforcing he was doing things differently with statements such as 'I'm not having a press conference or a party. After this, it's time to get to work'. While the initial example of James' television spectacular is not replicable for the vast majority of sport organizations, it is an interesting lesson in how the opportunity to create a huge media event may not actually be the best strategy to create positive media coverage.

Sources: Gilbert (2010); James (2014).

The media grid can be used as a planning tool that matches stories with organizations, a cue for action or an evaluation tool. At the end of a month, event or a season, a sport organization can examine the grid to discover which types of stories were successful or unsuccessful, which media outlets published or broadcast many stories and which published or broadcast none, and which stories were suited to particular media types and sizes. For example, the grid might reveal that throughout the course of the season the organization achieved significant media coverage in newspapers and on radio, but none on television. This might indicate that the stories or events did not have a strong visual element. The grid might also reveal that one media outlet published almost all the organization's news items or stories, but another media organization of the same type and size (such as two newspapers) published very little. This might indicate that personal and institutional relationships need to be fostered and improved prior to the next season. Finally, a sophisticated grid might reveal that media releases were a successful communication tool for some media outlets, with others responding to more personal communication.

## KNOWING YOURSELF

To undertake successful media planning and promotion a sport organization must have a well developed knowledge of the media industry, media outlets and individual media personnel. Equally so, the organization must have an excellent knowledge of itself. On the surface this seems to be self-evident, for an organization should know itself better than anyone. However, in terms of media planning, promotion, communication and interaction, this means having detailed information about the league or the team and its players. This detailed information enables any organization to respond quickly and effectively to media questions. Some small to medium sport organizations have been caught out when one of their athletes or teams breaks a record or wins a tournament unexpectedly. A lack of detailed information can result in the organization being viewed as unprofessional, losing potential media coverage, or not capitalizing fully on the benefits of a good news story. In order to assist the media planning and communication processes, sport organizations should have:

- an up-to-date detailed history of the sport organization or event, including key milestones and achievements, such as season by season champions and major award winners;
- current profiles of athletes, including their history and significant achievements, as well as interesting facts that could be used in a feature story;
- detailed sport-specific statistics, such as the point-scoring record for a particular basketball league or individual goal-scoring records for a netball competition; and
- current photographs and/or generic vision of athletes that can be provided to media organizations as part of a news item or story idea.

This information will be used in responding to the media, or included in media communications such as fact sheets and media releases, which will be examined in greater detail in the following chapter.

## STRATEGIES SPECIFIC TO SMALL TO MEDIUM SIZED SPORT ORGANIZATIONS

Professional sport organizations that operate at the elite level typically have sophisticated media planning and promotion departments and strategies. However the vast majority of sport organizations have limited budgets, a small staff and are constantly searching for ways to increase their media management capacity. Small state or national sport organizations might only have one to three staff employed, with each staff member allocated a wide range of tasks and responsibilities across the organization, while a local or regional sport organization will likely be managed exclusively by volunteers. In these sport organizations media planning and promotion are often critical, particularly for smaller state and national sport organizations seeking greater profile and resources. Strategies must be simple, targeted and well-timed in order to be effective. If there are complex plans that lack strategic focus then they will be abandoned in favour of other business activities such as financial management or athlete development.

The following are a range of strategies that can be applied in small to medium sport organizations to achieve increased media management capacity (adapted from Phillips, 1996):

- identify a hook that might create media interest in your sport, event or players. This will require the organization establishing a greater knowledge of the personalities within the sport, as a human interest story is often most appealing for the media;
- develop a one-page profile of each member on the national, state or representative team. Use these profiles at championships or events, when records are achieved or when the media enquires about an athlete;
- make the media employee's job as easy as possible by providing timely results and information in electronic format;
- divide your media communication into three phases (pre-event, event and post-event) and focus on one story from each that the media might be interested in;
- select a media officer from among the best volunteers within the organization and make them responsible for communicating with the media and generating publicity. If possible, allocate funding for this person to receive basic training in media skills and management; and
- utilize students studying university level sport management, media or marketing courses in the role of media officers or as part of short-term projects, such as events or championships. These students will be learning on the job, so there may be mistakes, but the long-term investment will be worth it.

## SUMMARY

This chapter has examined specific strategies and tools that sport organizations can use to plan for media coverage. In particular, the chapter discussed setting goals, differentiating media types and outlets, developing media lists, creating media coverage opportunities and using evaluation tools. The chapter also examined the ways in which sport organizations can promote themselves by adopting creative visual and event based strategies to attract media attention. Review questions and exercises are listed below to assist with confirming your knowledge of the core concepts and principles introduced in this chapter.

## REVIEW QUESTIONS AND EXERCISES

1. What is the difference between advertising and publicity?
2. Do large sport organizations need to plan more or less than small organizations for media coverage? Why?
3. Choose a small sport organization in your local area. Identify five key media coverage goals.
4. Choose a large sport organization in your region, state or nation. Identify five key media coverage goals.
5. How do the goals of the small and large sport organization developed in the previous two exercises differ in terms of quantity, type of media and audience awareness? Do you need to alter the goals as a result of considering these factors?
6. Choose a small sport organization and develop a media list. Organize the list by media type (television, radio, newspaper or Internet) and size (local, regional, state, national).
7. Based on the five key media coverage goals, create a list of 20 media coverage opportunities throughout the course of the season that would be included in an initial plan.
8. Using the 20 items from the initial plan, choose five that would form the final plan and expand each of the ideas to make them functional.
9. Use the five media coverage opportunities identified in the previous exercise and ten journalists or organizations from your media list to create a media grid.
10. Explain how the media grid can be use to evaluate media coverage acquired by a sport organization.

## CASE STUDY

### The London 2012 Olympic and Paralympic Games

The Olympic Games are the largest multisport event on earth, with 10,000 athletes competing over two weeks across 38 different sports. At the London 2012 Olympic Games, over 20,000 media were accredited to cover the sporting part of the Games. But even a large sporting event such as the Olympics requires media planning and a series of events to stimulate public interest and awareness. Throughout the lead-up and during the event, media opportunities and publicity stunts were conducted. The following are some of the examples that the London 2012 Olympic Games Organising Committee (LOCOG) and associated partners used to help spread the messages of the Games even further than those who could attend events in London.

#### *The Olympic Torch Relay*

The Torch Relay is a requirement of each Olympic host, but aside from the fact it must be lit at the birthplace of the Games in Athens and then used to light the Olympic Flame on the night of the Opening Ceremony, the route is up to each organizing committee to decide. Some of the unique features of the London 2012 Olympic Torch Relay were:

- 95 per cent of the UK population was within 10 miles of the Flame;
- 8,000 inspiring Olympic Torchbearers, travelling 8,000 miles to over 1,000 communities, villages, towns and cities;
- on each day of the 70 days of the relay there was an average of 110 Torchbearers who carried the Flame an average of 110 miles;
- 66 evening celebration towns and cities;
- the Olympic Flame visited all 33 London Boroughs; and
- 4 Paralympic Flame Festivals, with a 24-hour relay from Stoke Mandeville to the Olympic Stadium.

The media campaign for the London 2012 Torch Relay included regular updates on the official Olympic website, which highlighted the involvement of noted public figures, such as British tennis champion Andy Murray running with the Flame when it visited Olympic venue Wimbledon, meeting the Queen, and other quirky stories, including one torchbearer who used the opportunity to propose to his girlfriend.

#### *The London 2012 Festival*

The Cultural Olympiad is also another condition of hosting an Olympics, with a point in the Olympic Charter stating that 'The OCOG shall organise a programme of cultural events which must cover at least the entire period during which the Olympic Village is open'. The London 2012 Cultural Olympiad went beyond this, running over four years and culminating in the London 2012 festival, a two month

programme that ran alongside the 2012 Olympic and Paralympic Games (Arts Council, n.d.). According to LOCOG, the festival was based on the history of the Games in Ancient Greece, where art was an Olympic event. Artists were even awarded medals up until the London 1948 Olympic Games. The 2012 Festival invited artists from all over the world to create events across the UK, and offered ten million free tickets to the public. It included events ranging from comedy, film, dance, poetry and storytelling, theatre and performance and music. Some of the highlights included:

- US choreographer Elizabeth Streb and her team of 'extreme action' dancers who completed 'one extraordinary day' around London landmarks. The team of stunt dancers played on some of the city's most famous buildings, including dangling off the Millennium Bridge and abseiling down the side of City Hall;
- the biggest ever Radio 1 live music event with BBC Radio 1's Hackney Weekend 2012, which was free to an audience of 100,000 and broadcast nationally;
- let the music flow at BT's River of Music, which included six stages with artists from five continents beside iconic landmarks on the River Thames;
- displaying potentially the world's longest artwork, with an installation of pulsating LED lights across 73 miles of 2,000-year-old Hadrian's Wall; and
- artist Martin Creed's Work No. 1197, which aimed to have all the bells in the country ring as loudly as possibly for three minutes. At 8.12am on 27 July 2012, Creed led the performance piece that included London's iconic Big Ben pealing 40 times in the three minutes. It was believed to be the first time the strike of Big Ben has been rung outside its normal schedule since 15 February 1952.

### *Live sites*

The London 2012 Olympic Games provided every UK nation and region with an official live site, where spectators could gather and watch Olympic events on big screens. It was estimated that 500,000 people attended the live sites during the Olympic Games. As well as big screens, each live site had try-a-sport events, food and music. The biggest, in London's Hyde Park, also hosted concerts on the night of the opening and closing ceremonies, where British band Blur made a comeback three years after their last comeback tour to play on the closing ceremony night.

### *London Prepares test events*

Test events are another crucial part of hosting an Olympic Games, as sports and venues are given a chance to test the field of play, results, scoring and timing systems, as well as key operational procedures and functions. In London the significance of these events with regard to the Olympics was highlighted in the London Prepares Series. Unlike Olympic events, where tickets are secured by ballot, entry to these events was on a first-come, first-served ticket basis and allowed spectators to catch many of the Olympic events, in soon to be Olympic venues, before the Games had started. The test events included a mix of one-off special events, such as the Hadleigh

Farm Mountain Bike Invitational and the London Canoe Slalom Invitational, as well as events that were part of an international series or World Championship, such as the 2011 World Triathlon Series London event and the 2011 FISA World Rowing Junior Championships.

### *Sponsor activation*

As well as LOCOG activity, Olympic sponsors pay a premium to be associated with the Olympic Games and therefore they also maximize their opportunity by creating events or products that attract more media attention. Some examples from London included the following.

The Coca-Cola Company's 2012 Campaign titled 'Move to the Beat', which Coca-Cola stated aligned with the vision of the London 2012 Games, to inspire youth. It consisted of an anthem by Grammy award-winning producer Mark Ronson and chart-topping vocalist Katy B, which aimed to fuse the sounds of Olympic sports with the beat of London music. Ronson travelled the world meeting young athletes to record their sounds, which provide the beat of the song. Throughout the Games, Coca-Cola also broadcast 'The Beat of London', a live TV show highlighting the social side of the Olympic Games. Broadcast worldwide, the show featured Olympic athletes, celebrities and musical performances, giving fans insight into the social side of the Games. In addition to the song, Coca-Cola's 'Move to the Beat' also had an interactive component, where visitors could 'play' the company's pavilion in the Olympic Park like a musical instrument, pushing different elements of the building to remix the sounds that Ronson had gathered into a new track.

McDonalds' 'Champions of Play' programme involved selecting 200 children to experience the Olympics first-hand, including a behind-the-scenes look at select venues, such as the athletics stadium, velodrome and BMX track, and special access to where the athletes were due to compete. Dara Torres, five-time US Olympic swimmer and mother, was the global ambassador of the programme. In addition, many of the children were also youth correspondents, sharing their experiences with their hometown media.

Overall, these are just a small selection of some of the many events put on by LOCOG or their partners in the lead up to and during the London 2012 Olympic Games. Most of these events were designed to engage the London and wider British community, but would not have been successful if not for successful media engagement. The media helped to spread the stories of these events, ensuring their success. LOCOG's communications and public relations team were recognized for their work, with respected Public Relations publication *prweek* awarding them 'Campaign of the Year' in 2012:

> The campaign was highly focused and meticulously planned. From the Opening Ceremony's creative display of British eccentricity, to managing public transport expectations, to quickly responding to minor grievances, the comms team was highly prepared, well briefed and responsive. It displayed shrewd use of internal comms to make sure the sizeable freelance workforce

was on-message. It also deftly handled the additional pressure of social media that no other organizing committee had faced on such a scale.

(Magee, 2012)

## CASE STUDY QUESTIONS

1 The scope of different promotional activities listed above is wide – why is it important for an event such as the London 2012 Olympic Games to have a variety of different activities and stunts that will attract media attention?

2 What are the particular features of the London 2012 Festival events listed here that were likely to attract media coverage?

3 The Torch Relay for London 2012 stated that it offered 8,000 inspiring Olympic Torchbearers, travelling 8,000 miles to over 1,000 communities, villages, towns and cities. What implications does this have for media coverage opportunities?

4 If you were promoting a London Prepares test event, what would be your three key media coverage goals? What three different media opportunities would you use to meet these goals?

5 Why would it be important for the LOCOG media and communications team to have an up to date and detailed media list?

Sources: Olympic.org (n.d.); Arts Council (n.d.); *The Telegraph* (2011); Coca Cola (n.d.); McDonalds (n.d.).

CHAPTER 9

# Sport media communications

## Feeding the media

## OVERVIEW

This chapter is the first of two chapters that examine the specific tools used by professionals who manage the media, public relations or promotional activities of a sport organization. Each of the chapters focuses on sport organizations or individual athletes receiving as much media coverage as possible, with strategies and approaches tailored to their particular level and context (elite or community and profit or non-profit are two major distinctions that impact the type of media coverage being sought in a particular context). This chapter provides practical information related to media releases, fact sheets, media advisories and media guides.

## LEARNING OUTCOMES

After completing this chapter the reader should be able to:

- use a set of guidelines or rules to write a media release;
- use a set of guidelines or rules to write a fact sheet;
- use a set of guidelines or rules to write a media advisory;
- use a set of guidelines or rules to develop a media guide; and
- evaluate the quality of media communications using a range of criteria, in order to improve the quality and impact of media communications.

## MEDIA COMMUNICATIONS

There are a variety of ways that sport organizations can manage their media communications. The last chapter demonstrated that an organization's media planning will determine when and how the organization communicates or interacts with the media. However simple or complex the plan, it is likely that a sport organization will need to use media releases, fact sheets, media advisories and media guides as the basis of all its

communications. A large professional sport organization will use these communication strategies repeatedly throughout the course of a season or circuit, particularly media releases and fact sheets. By contrast, a small sport organization may only use these communications infrequently and might never compile a media guide. However, it should be noted that, while a small sport organization may not use media guides because they are perceived to consume vital resources that could be used in the operational side of an event or competition, a media release and two or three fact sheets might form the basis of an embryonic media guide. It might be useful to release this information in a package, even to local media in a small town. It is important to be aware that these forms of communication can be hard copy or electronic. In other words, a media guide can be provided to media organizations as a printed document, or a version of the document can be sent via email or uploaded to a website in HyperText Markup Language (HTML) or portable document format (PDF). In each instance, hard copy or electronic, the same principles of communication apply, even if the end product or format differs. Furthermore, improvements in technology – from desktop publishing software to the storage capacity of hardware – have meant that the differences between hard copy and electronic versions are small, and in fact, electronic copy may be more cost-effective for the organization and useful for media.

## RELEASES

Media releases (sometimes referred to as news or press releases) are a direct and effective way for a sport organization to communicate with the media. They are often considered as a way of disseminating information to the media in ready-to-publish form (Johnston, 2012), central to media communications to the point that Straubhaar and LaRose (2008: 311) refer to them as the 'workhorse of public relations'. By following set formats and guidelines, they can be written with relative ease after some practice. Because of this ease and apparent simplicity, organizations often assume that bombarding the media with releases is a sure fire way to get media coverage and thus valuable publicity for their organization. These organizations are working on the principle that if they fire off enough shots, at least one will hit the target. Unfortunately, in hitting the target once, the organization will not only have wasted valuable time and energy, but in all likelihood will have damaged its credibility in the eyes of the media. Like the boy who cried wolf, these organizations are constantly crying 'news', when the reality is that very few people outside the organization would be interested in the story they are pitching. When they finally have a story that the public would find interesting and newsworthy, the media aren't interested because they have spent too much time wading through releases filled with tedium. A better approach is to focus on quality rather than quantity and continually ask whether the issue will interest people outside the organization, in fact a good test to apply might be to consider whether you would read the release if you were not employed within the organization (Johnston, 2012). Sport organizations do have an advantage over generic business organizations because of an overwhelming interest among the general public, but applying stringent newsworthiness criteria to media communications is likely to result in better long-term quality coverage and better media relations, rather than taking this media interest for granted.

A media release should follow a series of rules or guidelines, so it conforms to media expectations and so that media releases from a single organization are consistent over time.

- The *headline* of the media release should summarize the most important information in the release. A good headline is often plain, precise and informative. A common mistake that media release writers make is to imagine that they are a sub-editor and provide a headline that will appear in a newspaper. The reality is that this is unlikely to happen and people involved in sport media communications should not waste their time creating catchy headlines. It is true that the headline should attempt to capture the attention of the journalist, but the journalist is likely to be struck by the newsworthiness, rather than a clever headline. Furthermore, clever headlines that appear in newspapers often obscure the content of the story that follows and the meaning of the headline only becomes apparent if the reader reads on. The media release writer cannot take the chance that the media might not read on.
- A media release must have a date. If the media release is clearly dated then journalists and editors know when it was sent and are able to assess its worth accordingly. Without a date a journalist or editor has no way of knowing when it was written, when the release was received by the media organization or whether another media organization might have covered the story in the intervening period. Timeliness is an integral factor of newsworthiness, and therefore a simple inclusion like the date holds huge importance for the media.
- The media release must contain a summary of the most important information in the *lead* paragraph. If this information is 'buried' in the body of the media release and is not readily apparent to the reader, then the media are unlikely to search for it, particularly with tight deadlines and an abundance of competitor releases. The lead paragraph must contain the who, what, when, where and why of the release and must be confirmed prior to writing the release. The first paragraph should act as the 'hook', to get media interested in the story, which is why it is crucial to include the five 'Ws' most commonly used in news writing. The following is an example of the details that are included in the example media release (see In Practice 9.1), from the Aegon Championships tennis event confirming that British player Ross Hutchins has been appointed as a new tournament director.

  Who: Ross Hutchins, a British player who has also beaten cancer
  What: Signs as new tournament director of the Aegon Championships
  When: Dated 05.03.2014
  Where: Aegon Championships, an annual grass court tournament at the Queens' Club in London, England
  Why: To increase the success of the Aegon Championships event

- An effective media release invariably includes a high level of *statistical and factual information*. This information has the twofold benefit of improving the credibility of the release and increasing the chances of it resulting in media coverage. In the Ross Hutchins media release (see In Practice 9.1), this information is contained within the second and third paragraphs, including his exact role with the tournament and history. One of the significant story 'hooks' is Hutchins' personal history, including a cancer diagnosis and his subsequent recovery, as well as a past with the tournament.

This included the success of a 'Rally Against Cancer' tennis event he organized there in 2013, which raised more than £300,000 for the hospital where he received treatment. This release is also supplemented with a video feature on Hutchins, a short interview and a biography to provide additional information.

- A media release, wherever possible, should be no more than one page in *length*. The essence of most stories should be able to be conveyed in one page. Follow up contact from either the sport or media organization should result in further information being distributed, or an interview or series of interviews being arranged. If the complexity of the story is such that it demands more than one page, the pages prior to the final page should clearly say 'continued' on the bottom of the page. The final page of the media release (whether this is the first or the third) should include the word 'END' at the bottom to denote that there is no more information to follow. Even if the media release is delivered online, these elements must still be included for clarity.
- The release should form what is known as an *inverted pyramid*, where the bulk of the information is found in the base or the foundations of the pyramid. In this way the information in the lead is the foundation of the release. The least important information is at the point of the pyramid. If the release is structured like an inverted pyramid the media can assess the newsworthiness by scanning the foundations and should they want to investigate further they can delve deeper towards the point. A good way of reviewing a media release and checking that it has the shape of an 'inverted pyramid' is to omit the last two or three paragraphs, then re-read the release. If it still has all the important details and could be sent without those paragraphs, then the chances are that your release is well structured. If, on the other hand, you discover essential information in the deleted paragraphs, then you should edit your release so that any essential information is included in the lead paragraphs, not buried in the body of the release or at the end. Another method of ensuring the release is well structured is to assume the media will not read beyond the first two or three paragraphs. This should provide a necessary focus. The Ross Hutchins media release (see In Practice 9.1) is a good example of how a release should be structured, with the most attention grabbing elements in the lead. Additional information, such as the quotes and biography in this example can easily be included further down. This structure also ensures that your media releases are easy to use for sub-editors who may need to cut for space.
- A media release should contain *quotes*, particularly if the release features the achievements, exploits or activities of an individual. The Hutchins example contains quotes from Hutchins himself, the former Tournament Director and the Chief Executive of the Lawn Tennis Association. The media will usually contact an organization for further information and in particular for quotes that can be used in a published article. For broadcast media (radio and television) the quotes will serve as a guide for an interview that will result from the release.
- It is imperative that a media release contains a complete list of *contacts*, so that the media are able to contact the sport organization for further information. Releases without current contact details are useless and a waste of the journalist's time. In fact, a release without the necessary information will lower your credibility with the journalists, thus making it harder when you next send out a release or pitch a story idea. The names of at least two people should be included with their landline phone

number, mobile phone number and email address. If the media release is being distributed by a large sport organization, then it is likely that there are enough people in the media, communications or marketing department to include at least two contacts on the release. Ensure that you only include a person's contact details if they have been briefed and pre-approved to speak to the media.

- A media release should conform to a range of *formatting* conventions. The release should be printed on A4 paper with substantial margins for the media to make notes in. It should also be double spaced and the media should be able to quickly and easily distinguish between sentences and paragraphs. In this respect each sentence might equate to a paragraph, the beginning of each paragraph might be indented or a line break might be included after each paragraph. It is not necessary to be overly prescriptive here, but it is important to recognize that the approach needs to be consistent.
- Media releases vary in the type and quality of *header*. Some organizations prefer to use a complex header, which is similar to an organizational letterhead. The use of an organizational logo or letterhead can convey credibility and status, but the header shouldn't overwhelm the release. In this respect, organizations that include logos of major (and sometimes minor) sponsors on the release can often produce media releases that are cluttered to the point that the text and the message it is attempting to convey are lost. An organizational logo or a letterhead that incorporates the logo is sufficient. This is particularly important if the release is being distributed electronically, as too many logos or photographs embedded in the file may result in it being too large to be of practical use.
- *Embargos* are to be used only when they cannot be avoided. An embargo is a way of a sport organization stipulating a date and time that the media are able to use the information contained in the release. Because the media is a highly competitive industry, embargos may not be adhered to, or the media might legitimately make a mistake and use the information prior to its release date. In general it is better if the majority of media releases are marked 'for immediate release', which is a clear and unambiguous sign that the information can be disseminated from the time the release is received. If this is not the case, then a phrase such as 'Embargoed, for release 25 March, 10:00am' should be included.

## Improving the media release

A media release should not be distributed to media personnel and outlets until it has been critically reviewed, either by the writer or a third party within the organization. The following checklist is a useful starting point for conducting the review (adapted from Tymson and Lazar, 2002):

- Are you certain that all of the information contained in the release is correct (in the cases where a public relations or communications firm has been subcontracted to produce media releases and other communications, it is wise that the release is checked internally prior to distribution)?
- Is it newsworthy (try to be as objective and critical as possible)?

## IN PRACTICE 9.1

### Media release

ROSS HUTCHINS NAMED QUEEN'S TOURNAMENT DIRECTOR

London

by AEGON CHAMPIONSHIPS 05.03.2014

British tennis player Ross Hutchins has been appointed the new Tournament Director of the Aegon Championships, the annual grass court tournament at The Queen's Club in London.

Hutchins, who returned to the court this year with partner Colin Fleming after recovering from Hodgkins Lymphoma last year, joins the tournament's managing director Stephen Farrow in taking on the responsibilities of Chris Kermode, who recently became the Executive President and Chairman of the ATP. Hutchins will be responsible for tennis decisions and player/ATP relations during the tournament week, advising on tournament strategy throughout the year, and speaking publicly on behalf of the tournament. He will report to Farrow, who has overall responsibility for the event.

Last year at the Aegon Championships, Hutchins led the organization of Rally Against Cancer – a charity tennis match played on finals day which featured Andy Murray, Ivan Lendl and Tim Henman, as well as London Mayor Boris Johnson, Jonathan Ross and Michael McIntyre – to raise money for the Royal Marsden, the hospital that had treated him. The event set out to raise £100,000, and eventually brought in more than £300,000.

Michael Downey, Chief Executive of the LTA, said:

> Ross is a very impressive young man and he is the perfect fit to be the new Tournament Director of the Aegon Championships. He has the respect of his peers, is well known and liked throughout the tennis world, and brings with him current, direct experience of the ATP World Tour. Ross will work closely with the tournament's outstanding team, led by managing director Stephen Farrow, and I am confident that under their stewardship the tournament, which was recently voted ATP 250 Tournament of the Year, will go from strength to strength.

Hutchins said:

> I am honoured to have been given this opportunity. The Aegon Championships is one of the longest running and best tournaments on the ATP World Tour, and I will do everything I can to make it even better. It has always been a special event for me as a player because it was the first main tour tournament I ever played, but my appreciation for the event grew further last year when I had the chance to work with the fantastic tournament team on the Rally Against Cancer charity match. I was fascinated by how much work went on behind the scenes, and I loved being involved with it. Chris Kermode invited me to join him in meetings, I was able to work alongside Stephen Farrow and the team,

> and I embraced the opportunity to learn from them. When Chris moved on to head the ATP, I knew that this was a role I wanted. I have the same passion and desire to succeed at this as I have in my tennis career, and I think my experience on the tour will equip me well. I know and understand what matters to players, I've spent a lot of time with Tournament Directors, sponsors and the media, and I think I have a good understanding of what makes a great tournament.

Chris Kermode said:

> I worked with Ross on the Rally Against Cancer last year, and with Stephen Farrow and the rest of the tournament team for many years, and the tournament is in safe hands. The way Ross threw himself into organizing the charity match last year at a time when he was going through chemotherapy was an inspiration. Everyone likes Ross, and his drive, determination, passion and positive attitude will ensure he is a huge success in this role.

Aside from not competing in the Aegon Championships, Hutchins will continue his tennis playing-career as normal.

The release also included a short player biography of Ross Hutchins, a link to a video feature, and a short interview with Hutchins.

Source: ATP World Tour (2014) www.atpworldtour.com.

- Is it truthful (if it isn't then it shouldn't be distributed, not only because it is unethical, but it will damage the organization's credibility)?
- Do you have enough factual information to interest the media (is there enough detail to write a newspaper article)?
- What is the hook and is it strong enough to sustain media and audience interest?
- Does the first paragraph contain who, what, where, when, why and how (if it doesn't, re-write the release and start the checklist again)?
- Has the release been spellchecked and proofread (not just by the writer, but by a fresh set of eyes)?
- Is the media release objective or subjective in tone (keep in mind that the media will not be able to write a subjective article)?
- Can you make the language stronger, more precise or more colourful?
- Can you shorten any sentences in order to make the writing tighter?
- Can you shorten the media release (if it is more than one page and the story is relatively simple then you must shorten it)?
- Does the media release need to be checked by the legal department (this might be necessary in crisis situations, when the organization is involved in a legal dispute or might be, or when an employee is being discharged)?
- Does it contain unnecessary jargon (most sports journalists are familiar with individual sports jargon, but it's always a good idea to review your release to see if a non-sport fan could understand it. Clarity is always a great attribute in a media release)?

## Why didn't the release make the cut?

There are likely to be a variety of reasons why a media release was not used by the media and why no coverage in either print, online or broadcast media was secured. The above checklist is a good starting point for working out where a media release might have been structurally deficient. On the other hand, the following reasons are more contextual and should be considered as part of both the planning and evaluation processes.

First, the media release was competing against other media releases for media attention. More to the point, the organization was competing against other sport organizations for media coverage. On the particular day or week when the media release was distributed, a major announcement might have been made by another club within the league, or by another league or sport within the city or nation. Or, the media release was distributed on a sport-rich media day rather than a sport-poor media day. Put simply, the media release might have been distributed on a Friday afternoon when journalists were busy putting the finishing touches on their previews for the weekend's games, instead of a Tuesday or Wednesday morning, when the opportunities for coverage are greater, particularly for smaller sports. In other words, the story might have been newsworthy, but was swamped by other stories that were more newsworthy. In this respect, the media manager within the organization needs to be aware not only of his or her own club, league or association, but also of other clubs, leagues and associations. For example, it makes no sense to distribute a media release on a topic that has marginal newsworthiness value the week prior to the start of the season of a major league sport. This can be moderated by good planning, but the media manager must still have a good awareness of the local sport landscape in order to pitch media releases at the right time.

Second, the media release might have been newsworthy, but didn't have a strong enough hook to convert the story from interesting to must-cover, such as a human interest or visual element. Although in part these are structural issues referred to in the checklist, the broader issue of newsworthiness relates to planning. In this respect, rather than pitching a story about increases in seat size and leg room at the club's renovated stadium as one of advances in plastics technology, it might have been better to illustrate how long-time supporter 'BIG Max' can now be accommodated in comfort, rather than being restricted to the 'standing room only' section at the back of the grandstand. The human interest story, visual element and newsworthy development can be incorporated to secure valuable media coverage. The story that emphasizes technological development could probably be pitched (via a media release) very quickly by the media manager, while pitching the story that incorporates a strong human interest angle or a visual hook would invariably require more development and more time, but could result in significantly better coverage.

Third, the media release might have been pitched at the wrong level of media. In their examination of newsworthiness Galtung and Ruge (1981) propose that an item must be 'meaningful' in order to be newsworthy, which relates to its cultural and geographic proximity. In other words, the story must be meaningful to the audience, otherwise it is not newsworthy and the media will not be interested. At a practical level this means that the recruitment of a new player to the local handball team will be meaningful to those living in the local area and surrounding districts. Therefore, it is likely to be considered newsworthy by local print and perhaps local broadcast media. The same story is not meaningful for a regional, city, state or national audience. For these audiences the story is

not newsworthy and the media release, no matter how well written, will not result in media coverage. On the other hand, a story about a junior basketball player making the national training squad might be meaningful for national audiences, or even local audiences from the area in which she grew up, but has little or no meaning outside these contexts. The challenge is for local sport organizations to pitch their media releases and stories at the appropriate media level and for large national or international sport organizations to localize their media releases and content.

Fourth, the sport organization needs to make an assessment of whether the media release is to undergo macrodistribution or microdistribution (Wilcox *et al.*, 2000). In macrodistribution the media release is distributed as broadly as possible, to as many media outlets and sources that resources and time will allow. In microdistribution the media release is distributed to targeted media organizations. Both these methods have potential negatives and positives. In terms of assessing why a media release did not make the cut, the type of distribution might provide some answers, which in turn will improve efficiency and use of limited resources. It is likely that only the most significant stories about large organizations will require macrodistribution. In the majority of sport organization media communications, microdistribution – which relies on an awareness of which media outlets are appropriate for specific issues and within particular contexts – should be the typical approach. The extreme of microdistribution is to provide a single journalist or media organization with an exclusive media release. This has the potential benefit of gaining coverage because the media organization might be attracted to the notion of gaining a competitive advantage. However, the exclusive might also create resentment among the media organizations that did not receive the exclusive, which might in turn mean that future media releases are ignored.

## FACT SHEETS

Fact sheets are another effective, yet simple, way of communicating information to the media. In general they are used to present some of the information contained within a media release in a different format and are typically suited to sport events, rather than issues. Where a media release might announce that Coca-Cola have been signed as the naming rights sponsor for the World Darts Championships from 2010 to 2015 and might include some information about the event to give context to the story, the fact sheet would focus on the World Darts Championship and would mention that Coca-Cola is the major sponsor, but only as one of a range of facts provided.

Similar to the lead paragraph of a media release, a fact sheet should include items that address the questions of what, who, where and how. It is not necessary to answer the question why. There are no hard and fast rules that determine the content of a fact sheet, but the following headings are a useful starting point for an event, which could be a single game in a season, a single race in a sporting circuit or a major event, such as world championships.

- *Event overview* – this section might include information about when the event is being held, the history of the event, previous winners and its place in the international profile of the sport.

- *Event location* – this section might include information about where the tournament is being played and how media and spectators can access the facility (such as public transport, distance from the closest airport, etc.). It might also include special features of the location and how it is being used for any complementary activities, such as cultural activities or landmarks to be used for photographic opportunities with star players, as well as any specific media facilities that can be accessed.
- *Event athletes* – this section might include information on the players or teams who will be competing, such as the key players or teams and their international ranking or special characteristics. Players or teams that have won the event previously might be included, as might the star players who could attract media interest.
- *Event statistics* – this section might include a range of event and game statistics that the media might be able to use in an article or broadcast, such as the number of spectators that attended last year's event, the record number of spectators at the event, the longest and shortest games played at the event, or the biggest winning margin by an individual or team.
- *Event partners* – this section might include information on major sponsors and media partners. Key details about the naming rights sponsor could be included, as might information about the broadcast partner and the way in which spectators can access a mediated version of the event.

The event's context, as well as the level of media for which the fact sheet is being written, will determine the type of information that is included in each of the sections.

## IN PRACTICE 9.2

### FIFA fact sheet

The Fédération Internationale de Football Association (FIFA) is the world governing body for football, and as such, plays a key role in the organizing of not only one of the world's biggest events – the FIFA World Cup – but a significant number of other FIFA sanctioned tournaments. Each of these has a unique history and different elements that need to be conveyed to media. Due to the huge volume of tournaments and matches under FIFA's guidance, they regularly use fact sheets as a quick and effective way to communicate important information. For example, FIFA's fact sheet on the history of World Cup host countries from 1930 to 2022 is a simple three-page document with colour-highlighted tables that allows media to quickly see which countries have hosted major FIFA World Cups, from the elite men's tournament to the futsal event and the Under-17 Women's World Cup, and in which global region that host nation sits in. It is an easy one-stop shop for media seeking to clarify say, how many different European nations have hosted World Cup events, the last time a World Cup was in Asia or whether or not the Oceania region has hosted any at all. All of FIFA's fact sheets are available online at www.fifa.com, making them easily accessible for the global media base following football.

For example, a fact sheet released by an international sport federation about a world championship might highlight that the event is being broadcast in 130 countries and identify specific broadcasters in some of the key markets, whereas one distributed by a minor sport league, promoting its championship game, might highlight some local businesses that have donated products to be auctioned at the game as part of fundraising activities.

Like the media release, a fact sheet can be presented in hard copy or electronic format. Whatever the format, the fact sheet should be presented clearly and simply. Bolded headings are an effective way to organize a fact sheet, as well as present the information. Furthermore, the nature of the information lends itself to bullet point presentation, rather than the sentence structure that is typical of media releases, although the information need not be presented in this way. Like a media release, a fact sheet is often more effective when kept short and sweet, and many of the formatting rules that apply to a media release also apply to a fact sheet. The fact sheet should include an organizational logo and contact details if it is presented in hard copy format or if it is designed to be printed; however, it need not be dated as the information is likely to be far less time-dependent than that contained within a media release.

## MEDIA ADVISORIES

A media advisory is a way of alerting the media to a potential media opportunity. Like a fact sheet it outlines some basic facts, but unlike a fact sheet is not intended as a stand-alone document that is able to provide the media with sufficient background information about an event or individual. Rather, a media advisory, also called a media alert, outlines interview prospects, as well as opportunities for photographic and video coverage (Wilcox *et al.*, 2000). Media advisories are usually much shorter than media releases and fact sheets and are essentially a way of making contact with the media in order to make them aware of a forthcoming event, media conference or when particular athletes, coaches or administrators will be available for interviews. The what, when, where, who and why elements, which also form the basis of media releases and fact sheets, may also be included in media advisories. Furthermore, these categories can be used to provide a critical review of the media advisory prior to distribution. In other words, assess the advisory to ensure, for example, that the time of the media conference or the names of the athletes scheduled to provide interviews are included.

The information in In Practice 9.3 was included in a media advisory sent by Cricket Australia to media organizations ahead of the 2013 Ashes Series in the UK, for a mock training session held on a floating barge on London's River Thames. Importantly, after a brief introduction, information in the advisory focused on four key areas: attendees, schedule, location and contacts. Email addresses and mobile telephone numbers were included for Cricket Australia's media manager, and a UK based public relations officer. The sections on attendees and schedule illustrate that brief information is sufficient to attract media attention. The training session on the specialized floating cricket pitch in front of the iconic Tower Bridge provided a good visual opportunity, which resulted in significant media coverage of the event.

## IN PRACTICE 9.3

### Media advisory – Australia's cricketers float on the River Thames

LONDON – Members of the Australian Ashes squad will participate in a unique training session on the River Thames to help remind Aussie fans to join the Australian Cricket Family for their chance to obtain priority access to tickets for the Commonwealth Bank Ashes Series, Carlton Mid One Day Series and KFC T20 Internationals in Australia this Summer.

The ACF Thames Cricket Pitch will be positioned on a barge in front of the iconic Tower Bridge, creating a great backdrop for training before the Australian team begin their quest to return the urn.

Michael Clarke, Shane Watson, Chris Rogers, James Faulkner and Mitchell Starc will come together on the floating pitch for a brief training session under the shadows of Tower Bridge. Michael Clarke and Chris Rogers will be available for a media stand-up opportunity following the media event.

**WHEN:** 3.30pm for 4.00pm start, Thursday 20 June 2013 (London time)

**WHERE:** Butler's Wharf Pier, Shad Thames, London SE1 2YE

**WHO:** Michael Clarke, Shane Watson, Chris Rogers, James Faulkner and Mitchell Starc

The Media Advisory also contained an RSVP request and an email address for doing so at the end of the advisory, as well as two media contacts.

Source: Businesswire (2014).

## MEDIA GUIDES

Media guides, sometimes referred to as press kits, are an ideal way to provide the media with information they need to produce content, particularly for large sport organizations. Rather than have each individual reporter or editor approach staff for facts and statistics related to the organization or the event, a media guide should be produced that contains information about the history and context of the event, team, club or league. The media guide will provide the media with essential background information they need to conduct their jobs and therefore lead to greater and better quality coverage, while it will also free up communications and publicity staff to generate targeted media coverage. The question of whether a sport organization should produce a media guide is typically answered by a simple cost–benefit analysis. For larger sports and organizations, a media guide is a useful way of gaining publicity, ensuring accuracy of information and providing the media with significant help. Thus, the benefit outweighs the cost. For smaller sports and organizations

that do not attract significant media coverage and are constrained by limited resources the production of a media guide is a questionable enterprise. Often, the cost outweighs the benefit. In order to produce a media guide, the sport or organization must receive enough regular coverage to make it worthwhile. In other words, for smaller sports and organizations, the time, energy and money spent on a media guide might better be directed at strategic opportunities or events, where media coverage is more likely.

The content of media guides will vary depending on the events and the audience they aim to serve. For example, the New York Yankees listed their 2015 Media Guide for purchase via their official website, either a limited edition bound hard copy, regular hard copy or a digital guide with the tagline:

> Typically available only to sportswriters, broadcasters and Yankees front office staff, the 440-page New York Yankees 2015 Official Media Guide and Record Book is the ultimate insider's resource and collectible. It contains stats and biographies of every player in the Yankees organization, hundreds of photos of Yankees past and present, and the definitive history of the club since its inception in 1903. The experts agree that the Yankees 2015 Official Media Guide and Record Book is the best and most comprehensive book about the Yankees anywhere.
>
> (New York Yankees, 2015)

But for most sport organizations and events, the media guide will not be a commodity but a simple one-stop shop for all media seeking information about the event, team or sport. The ANZ Championship is the world's premier netball competition, played between five teams in Australia and five in New Zealand. The 2014 ANZ Championship Media Guide was made available through its website (ANZ Championship, 2014) and contained the following:

- key contacts;
- table of contents;
- welcome letters from the General Manager and title sponsor;
- media information, including accreditation, guidelines and online resources;
- The 2014 ANZ Championship season draw;
- individual venue information;
- league format and rules;
- player overview, including player movements and import players;
- umpire information;
- detailed statistics section, including all-time statistic leaders, championship MVPs and previous season highlights; and
- detailed team profiles, including player profiles, team specific statistics and a media contact for each franchise.

While media guides can be provided in hard copy or electronic format, increasingly more sport organizations are moving towards solely publishing online. The Professional Golfer's Association (PGA) of America's online media guide is a good example of the way in which

a large professional organization, responsible for a multitude of tournaments, is able to compile its history, statistics and profiles into a manageable and informative resource for the media (PGA, 2014). Constructing an online media guide means that the PGA does not have to continually produce a hard copy media guide for each of the tournaments the organization is involved with, which would essentially reproduce much of the information. The UEFA Champions League media centre is also a good example of this, as their detailed game press-kits, which contained masses of detailed information, are more cost-effectively and efficiently distributed online.

## VIDEO RELEASES

A video release is essentially a media release in video format. A sport organization will produce a video, or in some cases an audio file, in which one of the employees of the organization will be recorded, then supply the video to television stations for broadcast (Fortunato, 2000). A video release will provide the media with broadcast quality content at no expense; however, the video release is usually used to communicate a particular point of view on an issue of sensitivity, rather than act as an advertisement. While initially an expensive strategy, advancements in technology now mean a video release is a viable option for many sports organizations, with many mobile phones now offering quality that is suitable for online broadcasts. A video release may also have the advantage of ensuring the sport organization's point of view is broadcast faithfully, in contrast to an interview or media conference. It is important when issuing a video release to include any relevant information broadcasters may need to pull together a story, as well as any relevant broadcast restrictions. The International Triathlon Union issues a television news feed after each of its major races or events, and the release always includes a link to the file, a notice that informs non rights-holders of the restrictions on video use and a short three to four paragraph written description of the event or news story to provide context.

## FOLLOW UP

Each of the media communications introduced above can be improved by a simple action called the 'follow up'. The next chapter deals in greater detail with media interactions, but it is worth noting that, within the context of media communications, tools such as media releases, in particular, are more effective when they are supplemented by personal communication, which usually takes place via the telephone, and in some cases in-person. The 'follow up' will typically establish whether the journalist or producer requires more information or requires interviews with key personnel to complete the article or broadcast segment.

## SUMMARY

This chapter has examined a variety of media communication tools. When used well, each of these communication tools has the ability to not only capture media attention, but acquire media coverage for a sport club, league or association. The media release, media advisory and media guide are the key tools used by sport organizations in the daily media communications. The chapter also provided criteria and checklists to both assess and improve the quality of media communications produced by sport organizations. Review questions and exercises are listed below to assist with confirming your knowledge of the core concepts and principles introduced in this chapter.

## REVIEW QUESTIONS AND EXERCISES

1 What is the purpose of media communications?
2 What are the key rules for writing a media release?
3 Acquire a media release from a semi-professional or professional sport organization. Evaluate the release using the rules outlined in this chapter. Can the release be improved? How?
4 Use the media release writing rules and guidelines to write a release on one of the following topics: the team has just signed a new major sponsor; the team has just signed a new star player; a celebrity will be opening the cultural festival that complements a major sport event; the team captain will be celebrating a milestone in the forthcoming game; a legend of the sport will be making a comeback at a forthcoming event after being in retirement for a year; or the forthcoming game, match or event has a special feature to attract more spectators.
5 After writing the media release, critically evaluate the chances of it resulting in media coverage, considering both structural and contextual issues.
6 Produce a fact sheet for a local sport event you are involved with or have attended.
7 Write a media advisory for a forthcoming sport event (such as a conference or season launch) and outline which athletes will be available for interviews (as well as when, where and for how long).
8 Identify the elements you would include in a media guide for a sport organization or sport event in your local area.
9 Identify the elements you would include in a media guide for a sport organization or sport event in a major city.
10 Identify the elements you would include in a media guide for a national sport organization or sport event.

## CASE STUDY

### Media guides: The Tour de France versus The Tour Down Under

The UCI World Tour is an initiative from the Union Cycliste Internationale (or International Cycling Union), to create one cohesive banner for the world's leading road cycling events. Under the World Tour banner 18 UCI teams are carefully selected according to ethical, financial, administration, but above all sporting criteria, to participate in all the events on the calendar. Organizers can also invite UCI Professional Continental Teams of their choice according to the number of places still available. Three rankings (individual, teams and nations) are calculated at the conclusion of each UCI World Tour event and then released publicly, making it a system that enables recognition of the most consistently successful cyclists, teams and nations at the end of each season.

While the UCI World Tour provides an overarching banner, the events under its banner are quite different, ranging from the world's three premier stage road races, the Tour de France, the Giro d'Italia or the Vuelta a España, to the world's premier one-day classics, such as Paris–Nice. The UCI's aim to develop cycling in new regions has also seen it add more races to the World Tour calendar recently, most notably in Oceania, America and Asia. One of those events is the Santos Tour Down Under, a race scheduled in the Australian city of Adelaide since 1999 and that became the first race outside Europe added to the UCI World Tour in 2008. Over its history this Australian event has attracted some of the world's best cyclists, including Tour de France's winners Oscar Pereiro, Alberto Contador, Carlos Sastre and Australia's own Cadel Evans. The Santos Tour Down Under cannot compete with the world's premier cycling event, the Tour de France, which is broadcast worldwide to an audience of millions and an estimated five million people turn out across France to spectate, but these two events have many things in common and provide a useful comparison for the purpose of evaluating media guides. Both Tours are multi-stage road cycling events on the UCI World Tour, but their differing locations and history have an impact across most event operations functions, including media. While many of the same media operations standards apply for each event, including facilities for journalists to file, media accreditation and accommodation, others need to be different. Some of these differences are apparent in the respective media guides, the contents of which are listed below.

The Santos 2014 Tour Down Under Media Kit is 27 pages long and includes:

- a contents page;
- a fact sheet titled '16 years of cycling milestones' that lists major achievements for the Santos Tour Down Under event in year order such as '*2006* – The hottest race in the Santos Tour Down Under's history with four consecutive days over 42 degrees (Celsius) and melting bitumen in Yankalilla';
- contact details – names, email addresses and phone numbers for two media contacts;

- a section on media accreditation and a separate contact for media accreditation;
- a one-page article on the Santos 2014 Tour Down Under, including some statistics on spectatorship from previous events and some of the major highlights for 2014;
- key dates;
- individual stage maps – each stage has a full stage map in the guide, that marks out details such as the hills where King of the Mountain points are obtained, the start, finish and the direction riders will cycle in, as well as start time, total stage distance and a short description of the day's course;
- the jerseys – a section with descriptions and images of the six race jerseys up for grabs at each stage of the event;
- team and rider information – a short section that directs media to visit the event website closer to the event start date for full lists of teams competing;
- Santos Tour Down Under statistics – includes statistics such as attendance figures, economic impact and accredited media, from 2010 until 2013;
- honour roll – lists all holders of each jersey in all years of the Tour;
- Santos Tour of Cycling – includes a note about the public presentation of the 2014 professional teams and a short story on the BUPA challenge ride, the mass participation event of the Tour Down Under, where recreational riders can ride the same course as the professionals. It also includes short blurbs on other events such as the legends night, the Adelaide City Council Tour Village and Bike Expo and the BUPA mini ride for kids;
- events in South Australia – a rundown of what to expect in each season in South Australia;
- travel information – includes official hotel, links to specialist travel packages and coach transfers;
- South Australia destinations, which details major tourist destinations near Adelaide such as the Barossa Valley and Kangaroo Island;
- Adelaide, a detailed tourist guide to the city; and
- One day in Adelaide – an hourly itinerary of how to spend a perfect day in Adelaide.

The 2013 Tour De France Media Guide, which was also the hundredth year of the Tour de France, is written in both English and French, is 58 pages long and contains:

- a table of contents;
- an introduction from Tour director Christian Prudhomme;
- a history of the Tour, described in bite-sized pieces with interesting facts from ten different Tours, for example: 1936 states 'Coinciding with the adoption of the first week of paid holidays by the Front Populaire Government, the Tour de France becomes synonymous with holidays, and crowds flock en masse to cheer on the champions';
- an overall 2013 route map, and two to three paragraph route descriptions;
- the 100th Tour – a user's guide. This includes a short overview of the stages and some of the major points of interest for the 2013 tour, including where the tour starts, the two stages that take in the famous Alpe Du Huez climb, the ten new

city stages. There is also an explanation that in 2013 there will be no time bonuses allocated for sprints and stage finishes, an explanation of point allocation and information about each of the different jerseys. It also includes information about the individual and team time trial events;

- two pages dedicated to the race's start in Corsica, stating how in the previous 100 years of the tour it had never visited this area;
- pages 17 to 51 include detailed descriptions of each of the 20 stages. Each stage has three main components: a description from race director Christian Prudhomme, a brief blurb that describes the stage – including any other historical Tour de France results – and a fact box on the town or area that includes its name, number of residents and links to any relevant websites. As well as these stage descriptions, this section also includes a detailed section on 'Tour Summits' with specialist maps that show exactly the elevation that riders will face over each stage;
- a statistics section that lists some of the major highlights, such as most number of wins, days in yellow, stage wins, the most times of participation, the most number of white, green, polka dot jerseys and the number of wins per nation. This section also includes one statistic that shows the largest and smallest gap between the first and second riders of the Tour de France, the oldest and youngest competitors and some statistics on the number of spectators; and
- a full list of all Tour de France winners.

Each media guide contains many of the features required to make it an informative and useful guide for media, including detailed statistical information, and route maps, but they also remain different. It is useful to examine these differences and understand why each event has included, or not included, certain information in its media guide.

## CASE STUDY QUESTIONS

1 Why do you think the Tour Down Under media guide has more elements focused on tourism in South Australia and events scheduled alongside the actual race information?

2 Why do you think the Tour de France media guide has less specific media information details within it?

3 What are some of the key elements in each media guide that you would expect to find in all UCI World Tour media guides?

4 How would a professional sports team media guide differ from these specific event guides?

Sources: Tourdownunder.com (2014); Tour de France (2014).

CHAPTER 10

# Sport media interactions

## Working with the media

## OVERVIEW

This chapter is the second of two chapters that examine the tools of the trade for professionals who manage the media, public relations or promotional activities of a sport organization. It builds on the previous chapter that examined written media communications by examining face-to-face media interactions. In particular, the chapter provides practical information on conducting interviews, media conferences and media events.

## LEARNING OUTCOMES

After completing this chapter the reader should be able to:

- apply a set of guidelines to prepare for and structure an interview for an employee of a sport organization;
- apply a set of guidelines to prepare for and conduct a media conference; and
- apply a set of guidelines to prepare for and conduct a media event for a sport organization.

## INTRODUCTION

The previous chapter examined a range of communication tools available to sport organizations. These communications, both in hard copy and electronic form, are designed to generate media coverage and in some cases are also intended to generate media interactions, which in turn lead to greater and better quality coverage for the organization. These media interactions might be as simple as a journalist contacting the media manager of a sport organization for more information in response to a media release. Or, they might be as complex as a media conference or event to launch a new product or competition. This chapter examines the major types of media interactions that are likely to occur between sport and media organizations at a formal level, such as interviews, media

conferences and media events. This chapter is not intended to specify how sport organization personnel should conduct informal interactions with journalists, editors and producers. These are often the result of a relationship built over time and also directly related to the personal qualities and preferences of the individual.

Coverage on network television stations is the most competitive of all the media environments. Newspapers, radio, magazines and online outlets all have more time and space to devote to news. This has three important implications. First, non-television media forms are able to provide more coverage to a single story, leading to potentially more in-depth features, which means that sport organization employees must be able to participate in lengthy interviews if required. Second, the time and space available to non-television media forms results in greater opportunities for smaller sports to gain media coverage. This means that even in smaller sports the members of a sport organization must be competent in the field of media interactions. Finally and most importantly, because television is also the most visual of the media forms, sport media management must ensure it delivers content that has visual appeal. For the purpose of managing media interactions, in practice, this means sport organization employees appear competent in front of a camera and behind a microphone and media interactions are conducted in a professional environment.

## MEDIA CONFERENCES

Planned events are a way of attracting media coverage for a newsworthy story or event and the most common is the media conference, also referred to as a press or news conference. Media conferences are an effective way of disseminating essential information to a wide variety of media. Rather than distribute a media release and then field questions from a range of media organizations, it is often more effective to gather the media organizations at a single venue for a media conference. Journalists will also have access to a range of sport organization employees, which will in turn facilitate the media coverage of the event or issue.

As indicated in the previous chapter, media are typically alerted to the staging of a media conference via a media release or media advisory. This communication will notify the media of the following:

- issue or event for which the media conference is being staged;
- venue;
- date and time;
- sport organization personnel who will be present; and
- opportunities for interviews, questions, photographs, vision, etc.

Prior to sending out a media advisory or release it is essential to consider three key elements: value, timing and site. A media manager needs to assess whether the issue or event has enough value to warrant a media conference (the newsworthiness criteria discussed in previous chapters is a good starting point). For larger professional sport organizations, the amount of media interest is likely to be significant enough to regularly hold media conferences. Media conferences are a rarity for small sport organizations, as they are unlikely to attract enough media attention to warrant the time and resources that

will be expended. A targeted media release and follow-up contact is likely to be a more effective strategy. In this respect the same cost–benefit analysis that was referred to in the previous chapter regarding media guides should be applied.

Whatever the size of the organization, the media conference must be valuable to the media. As such, the sport organization must critically assess whether calling a media conference will be an effective use of the media's time and resources. Inviting the media to conferences in which the information is either trivial or could have been disseminated through a media release is a bad strategy. In the worst case, the resentment at being called to a media conference in which there is little or no valuable information might adversely affect their willingness to provide media coverage of future events. Thus, the question 'should a media conference be held' must be the first question any sport organization asks (Wilcox *et al.*, 2000).

Wilcox (2008) identified six scenarios where it is appropriate for an organization to call a media conference. First, an announcement of significant public interest warrants holding a media conference, such as the appointment of a new national team captain in a high profile sport or the addition of a new team or franchise to a league. Second, when an issue arises of significant public concern, such as a new stadium having problems with spectators getting access to the ground in time for the start of popular games. Third, where there have been a significant number of media requests and it is important to provide access equity. For example, there might be speculation about the retirement of a key player, which is leading to media requests for interviews. In this case it might be easier and more time effective for all concerned to hold a media conference. Fourth, a new product, facility or service is being announced, such as the construction or upgrade of a sporting facility or the installation of new technology to assist referees and umpires. Fifth, when a person of importance visits, such as the head of the International Olympic Commission conducting a site visit, or a high profile athlete participating in an international event. Sixth and finally, a complex issue where the media are likely to need further information may require a media conference, such as the announcement of new anti-doping regulations. While it is good to note that there often needs to be a newsworthy reason to hold a media conference, most professional sport clubs will hold them regularly, with no specific reason other than to preview an upcoming game. In this case, the league or club precedent should be followed if this is what the media expect, but the newsworthiness criteria should be applied to the talent selected to appear.

A media manager must also consider the timing of the media conference. Similar to the evaluation criteria applied to media releases in the previous chapter, staging the media conference at the right time is an essential element of its success. In this context success is measured by the amount of media coverage that results from the conference, which in turn is directly proportional to the number of external media personnel who attend. A media conference may fail because the value or newsworthiness of the conference is considered low relative to other conferences, events or incidents that take place at the same time. No matter how well planned the conference is in terms of timing and positioning relative to the work demands of journalists and competing events and sports, a story may break that will result in the media conference being abandoned for a news item with greater immediacy, interest or impact. Wilcox *et al.* (2000) suggested that a media conference be scheduled at a time that accounts for the deadlines of various media outlets. If the media conference is scheduled at a time that allows print media, but not

television, to cover the story then the sport organization risks offending television journalists. Importantly, a media manager within a sport organization must have a good working knowledge of local media deadlines (Johnston, 2012).

Finally, the media manager must ensure that the venue or site is appropriate for the size of the conference and the expected number of media personnel attending. A standard media conference may be held at the club, team or league head office if there is a space big enough, or at an indoor venue that has the necessary facilities. For a non-standard media event the venue could be staged anywhere, although consideration will need to be given to the facilities required by the organization and the media, as well as contingencies – such as weather if the event is being staged outdoors. Consideration should also be given to the amount of time it will take for media to travel to and from the venue. A venue that is central and accessible to most media outlets is preferable (Wilcox *et al.*, 2000).

If the conference value, timing and site have been arranged and media advisories or invitations distributed, the conference set-up must be attended to. The following is a guide to the key elements of media conference delivery.

- *team or league logo* – it is important that the logo and name of the organization (team or league) is visible in any media coverage that results from the conference. For major professional sports it is often necessary that a sponsor's logo is also visible. Set or background dressings, such as banners or posters, should be designed so that logos, names and website addresses are visible in newspaper photographs and television broadcasts. A background banner should have many small logos, so that the entire logo or logos are visible when one or more people are sitting or standing in front of the banner. A large logo, which may look impressive to those attending the conference, will in all likelihood be partly obscured when the interviewee is filmed or photographed. It is important to remember that the conference backdrop is for media coverage, rather than the aesthetic pleasure of those attending the event.
- *models and props* – if the media conference is announcing a new facility, product or uniform then models and props may be a useful visual addition (Helitzer, 1999). Hence, if the media conference is announcing the development of a new stadium, a giant scale model of the facility would be appropriate, whereas if the media conference is designed to launch the season and unveil a new uniform, a fashion parade of the new uniforms may be a way of acquiring television coverage.
- *the room* – in order to maximize media coverage, all media must have an unimpeded view of the media conference and its participants. Television cameras should be allocated space at the rear of the venue, on the sides of the room or on a specifically placed platform that gives them a clear shot of the stage and the speaker. Journalists will usually be seated in front of a panel table or podium, which means that television cameras can be located behind the journalists, assuming that the venue does not have tiered seating and the view of the speakers is not impeded. Whatever the size of the room and the audience, it is likely that the media will need to set up microphones in front of the speaker to ensure high audio quality. The time and space required for this should be allowed for in the overall conference plan. If it is a particularly large interview room, then an audio system linked up to a microphone that will be passed around to journalists is a good system to ensure all questions and answers are captured on audio recordings.

- *panel table or podium* – a table for the spokesperson or panel should sit on a slightly raised platform to ensure a clear view for photographers and camera people. The speakers should not be sitting at the same level as the reporters, as they will need to be able to see the journalists three or four rows deep. Alternatively, a single podium may be appropriate if there are only two or three speakers who are able to approach the podium one after the other. A panel table is usually preferred as it enables the speakers to deliver prepared statements and the entire panel to field questions that follow. The table must also be covered to ensure that the legs of the panellists are not visible to the media.
- *identifying the speakers* – if there is only one speaker who is well known to the journalists then a name plate is not necessary. However, if the media conference is conducted by two or more people then it useful to have name plates in front of media conference speakers, and for the media manager to introduce the speakers to the media prior to the commencement of the conference.

It is usual that the media conference will begin with a welcome to the media and an outline of the conference format, which will be followed by one or more of the speakers reading a prepared statement. In media conferences that deal with a sensitive issue, which is either part of or likely to cause a crisis or scandal, the end of the prepared statement may be the end of the conference. In this case, the prepared statement will be used to clarify the issue, present factual information or to dispel rumours. In this case the media conference's particular purpose is to provide footage for television networks and audio for radio stations. Most media conferences, however, will also include a question and answer period. In these instances it is typical that little or none of the prepared statement will be aired, as the question and answer period with journalists usually provides the best sound bites (White, 2005). However, it is usual that the media are provided a copy of the statement, in order to ensure accuracy. It may also be useful to provide the media with a fact sheet that includes names, titles and brief biographies of the speakers. If the statement has been prepared well in advance then it is useful to conduct a conference rehearsal, which will give the speakers an opportunity to familiarize themselves with the text of the statement and acclimatize to the venue.

As noted previously, the question and answer period is an important component of most media conferences. Although the question and answer period cannot be rehearsed as effectively as the reading of a prepared statement, it is useful for the media manager and speakers to anticipate difficult questions and prepare answers. At worst, a mock question and answer period may eliminate any awkward pauses by the speaker and make them appear more fluid. At best, it may prevent the speaker from revealing confidential information, becoming angry in response to a particular line of questioning or becoming flustered as a result of being taken by surprise. For more experienced media performers a written or verbal briefing that includes potential difficult questions may suffice.

In many professional sport leagues it is a requirement for coaches, managers or players to participate in a media conference soon after the conclusion of a match. These conferences are typically question and answer sessions that allow journalists to elicit quotes for publication in newspaper articles or to provide television footage with sound bites to accompany highlight packages. Often these conferences are available on club or league websites, and in some leagues streamed live online. These conferences are potentially

## IN PRACTICE 10.1

### Press conference conduct: NASCAR's teleconference

This following excerpt is a transcript from a NASCAR teleconference held on 12 November 2013, with driver Trevor Bayne and Steve Newmark, President of Roush Renway racing. This transcript illustrates several features of media conference conduct, including an introduction, a welcome by a moderator and an introductory statement to give context, an introduction of the panellists, and an initial statement from each of the participants.

THE MODERATOR: Thank you, good morning, everyone, and welcome to today's NASCAR teleconference. Our guests are Trevor Bayne, driver of the No. 6 Roush Fenway Ford Mustang, and Steve Newmark, president of Roush Fenway Racing.

Trevor, it was announced today that you've been diagnosed with Multiple Sclerosis and have been cleared by doctors at the Mayo Clinic and NASCAR to continue to compete in NASCAR. Can you talk about the announcement and your mindset moving forward with the goals of winning races and championships?

TREVOR BAYNE: Yeah, for sure. First of all, I appreciate everyone's concern and their willingness to call and to want to find out more and all their support. But the art of today to make this announcement comes because we didn't want to keep everybody in the dark about things once we got information and got a diagnosis. I wanted to let everybody know what's going on.

More than anything, I appreciate the support of my team and our sponsors here. They've been unbelievable. Obviously, at first, when I found out, I didn't know how it would be taken, and the more I talked to them, the more support I got. Obviously, I feel great. I've had no symptoms and everything's going really well. But the biggest thing we want to figure out is how to keep winning races and championships and keep this thing going.

THE MODERATOR: Steve, can you talk about the organization's support and confidence in Trevor as he competes full-time for the NASCAR Nationwide Series Championship next season?

STEVE NEWMARK: Absolutely. I think that the diagnosis is a refreshing one for Trevor to understand the situation. But it absolutely has no impact on the support and the way that we view Trevor going forward. I mean, he is one of our premier race car drivers and we fully expect him to be competing for wins and championships well into the future.

We have a lot of respect and admiration for the fact that he wanted to come out and make this known publicly. It was not something that he had any obligation to do, and quite frankly I don't think most 22-year-olds would have the maturity that he does to be able to deal with this. So we're completely supportive of all of his efforts, and quite frankly, we'll turn very quickly to try to figure out how to get our cars faster and put him in a position to win a championship next year.

THE MODERATOR: We will now open up for questions for Trevor or Steve.

Source: ASAP Sports (2013).

positive and negative. A winning coach or manager is more willing to answer questions from journalists, while their losing counterpart is more likely to make disparaging remarks about the standard of officiating and be unwilling to engage in meaningful conversation with journalists. It is essential that these conferences are also rehearsed, in order that the performance of coaches and managers is maximized.

The media manager or conference moderator must make a decision to draw a media conference to a close. The conference may reach its natural conclusion when there are no more fresh questions, when the time limit has expired or when the speakers require a break from media questioning. Importantly, a speaker should never walk out of a media conference in anger or as a way of demonstrating power. This is only likely to exacerbate the issue and provide the media with sensational footage for the evening news. In order to draw the media conference to a close the media manager can announce that there is time for one last question. At the conclusion of the answer to this question the media manager can thank the media for attending and provide details of whether individual interviews are able to be conducted and if so where they will be located and how much time is available. If there are no interviews to be conducted the media manager can make themselves available for further questions or requests.

Some reporters will call prior to the conference to arrange an interview with one of the people involved in the media conference prior to it commencing, in order to save time and get ahead of other broadcast and print competitors. Agreeing to the interview can ensure media coverage, particularly if there is a concern that the issue might not attract a large crowd. In this case agreeing to the interview is insurance against other media outlets not participating in the conference. The downside to this strategy is that a degree of control will be surrendered to the media, as the conference format, with a prepared statement followed by questions and answers, is controlled by the sport organization. In the interview situation the media will have more control, with the question and answer component likely to be favoured in place of a prepared statement. For an issue that is likely to attract significant media interest, agreeing to an interview prior to the conference is a risky strategy. First, other media outlets might perceive that there is a degree of bias or favouritism towards one media outlet. Second, if the interview is held prior to the conference and runs over time, the interview could turn into a mini conference as other broadcast journalists and their camera people arrive and start filming (White, 2005). Finally, if the broadcast media get what they need in terms of sound bites prior to the conference, the conference may be delivered to the print media alone, for the broadcast media are unlikely to stay if the chance of capturing more valuable footage is minimal.

## MEDIA EVENTS

Media events are another way of generating coverage through media interactions. They may include a media conference, will often provide opportunities for interviews and typically have an unusual theme or visual element that will ensure additional media coverage. The theme or visual element might be as simple as two surfers swimming in a shark tank, or a day of golf at a luxury course to promote a forthcoming competition. However, some media events are designed simply to help facilitate media access in the quickest and most effective way possible. Each year the championship match in the NFL,

the Superbowl, will stage a 'media day' in the host city of the event. For the 2014 Superbowl final in New York City this consisted of the Seattle Seahawks and Denver Broncos coming together at the stadium for a set time of all-in media interviews and photographs. Media events for some less mainstream sports may also include a chance to take part in the event to help expand journalists' knowledge, as well as gain a different angle for coverage. For example, a media day at the 2013 America's Cup sailing event in San Francisco included a media briefing, as well as an opportunity for media to sail on the yachts that would be raced in the event's final.

Media events differ in size and scope. As noted in the previous chapter, in the lead up to the London 2012 Olympic Games, one of the media events included 'action dancers' performing on some of London's landmarks as part of the London 2012 Festival that ran alongside the Games. Not all organizations have the resources or the intense media interest to ensure these events are successful. But, not all media events need to be large and complex. A successful event might simply consist of a state, regional or national team being presented with their uniforms in a public place, such as shopping mall. At the other end of the scale, the announcement of the host city for the FIFA World Cup or Olympic Games has become such an important public media event that it is broadcast live and watched by millions of people. This is unlikely to be achieved by all but the largest international sport organizations. Whatever the event, it is important that it contains a visual element or a special feature to attract the media.

Another form of event is often referred to as a media briefing (Wilcox *et al.*, 2000). This function or reception usually consists of breakfast, lunch or dinner and may also include the media being presented with gifts, although this practice is ethically and strategically dubious. For instance, if the media briefing is to announce the signing of a major electronic goods manufacturer as the major sponsor of a league, the media might be presented with digital radios at the end of the night, but the sport organization should be aware that this will not ensure positive media coverage. The primary purpose of a media briefing is to allow representatives from the media to socialize with employees from the sport organization, although the explicit reason for the briefing might be to introduce the media to a development or issue of importance to the team, club or league. In the Australian Football League teams have organized media briefings to discuss negative media coverage of a team or particular issue, or to discuss the strategic development of the league. Thus, a media briefing might be used as either a promotional strategy, or a defensive strategy in which the media is gathered so that the organization can clarify their position on a contentious issue. At a base level the media may be prepared to attend a briefing in order to establish or develop contacts that are essential to conducting their work, as demonstrated in previous chapters.

## INTERVIEWS

The interview is a key point of interaction between sport and the media and one of the key forms of communication between individuals within sport organizations and the general public. In radio and television broadcasts in particular, the public get to hear information direct from the sport organization, rather than moderated through a secondary source. Thus, the interview can be a powerful tool for sport organizations, but just as easily it can

## IN PRACTICE 10.2

### Media event: the LPGA puts a spin on media day

Most media days are a chance for media to quickly and effectively interview various relevant athletes, officials and organizational representatives ahead of a major event. However, sometimes a new angle can pay off. In 2013, the RR Donnelley LPGA Founders Cup media day had a different spin. Golfers Amanda Blumenherst, Paige Mackenzie and Wendy Ward were on hand to launch the tournament a month from the start date, but instead of sitting at a podium and answering questions, they flipped the script on the media and challenged them to a closest-to-the-pin contest – from the rooftop of the JW Marriott Desert Ridge Resort and Spa. Following a quick introduction by Tournament Director Chris Garrett and RR Donnelley representative Director of Marketing Rick Ryan in the resort's main lobby, Mackenzie appeared and challenged all in attendance to a closest-to-the-pin contest from atop the sixth floor roof down to the ninth hole of the tournament course. 'This is nothing within my imagination that I would see myself ever doing while playing golf', Mackenzie said, 'but it was a lot of fun out here today and hopefully this will help create some buzz about the tournament'.

A 12 × 12 platform was built with a hitting mat, and the media and sponsors in attendance all got two shots to see whether they could best the LPGA professionals: 'We just wanted to do something fun and something a little different, and based by the reaction from everyone out here, I think we accomplished that,' Garrett said. This is a clear example of the organizers realizing that regular media days have only limited appeal, but a chance to engage in a fun, different activity was likely to secure available media and also put a positive spin on subsequent coverage. An approach such as this that situates the event as fun and different when it comes to media interaction straight from the launch can also help ensure that all available media return to cover the actual event.

Source: LPGA (2013) www.lpga.com.

prove dangerous. The athlete skilled in media relations might be able to charm the media and the public in equal measures, but the athlete, coach, manager or administrator who is uncomfortable in the media spotlight has the potential to look aloof, stupid, clumsy or incoherent.

Some interviews are spontaneous, while others are planned. In general, it is best if interviews with athletes, coaches and administrators are planned, in order to give the subject time to prepare. There will be some occasions where spontaneous interviews are conducted, such as on the field after a game, but even these interviews will have been arranged in advance by the broadcaster as part of an agreement with the league or team. Thus, it is very rare for a situation to arise where a representative from the sport organization is unprepared. If they are it is the fault of the media manager or the result of an overzealous media organization.

Not all interviews will produce the same outcome and not all interviews will produce news (White, 2005). Different interview styles will result in different outcomes. The types of questions a journalist will ask the chief executive officer or general manager of a club or team after the sacking of the head coach because of poor on-field performance will be very different from those asked of a 16-year-old star who has just won her first professional tennis tournament. Similarly, an interview with a magazine or newspaper reporter is likely to be longer and more in-depth than a television or radio interview in which the questions are straightforward and designed to elicit a specific response. The implication of the variety of outlets, styles and possible outcomes is that a media manager must be able to prepare interviewees for a range of possible media interactions. The media manager should:

- if possible, select the type of media that is appropriate to conveying the message or executing the media plan;
- be aware of the style of most media outlets and prominent journalists and educate interviewees accordingly;
- rehearse interviewees with mock questions and answers for both routine and extraordinary situations;
- encourage interviewees to avoid sport specific jargon or insider language in order to appeal to a broad spectrum of the public;
- encourage interviewees to be enthusiastic, as there is nothing worse than watching an athlete or coach who does not want to be interviewed and appears bored and/or tired;
- ensure the timing of the interview is positive for the interviewee, i.e. not scheduling a long feature piece immediately after they have been knocked out of a major event;
- instil an organizational culture in which media training (particularly in interview skills) is an accepted part of professional development;
- review the interviews of athletes, coaches and administrators as a way of improving performance;
- exploit those athletes that have natural media skills; and
- establish a set of general media interview guidelines.

Interview set-up is important for creating an environment in which the subject feels comfortable and the organization is able to represent itself in the best possible manner. In short, the media manager needs to consider the site, date, subject matter, amount of time required/available, props or visual aids required and uniform/dress for the interviewee. The date and the amount of time available are simple logistical issues to be dealt with, while the subject matter will determine what and how much preparation the interviewee should complete. The site, props, visual aids and uniform or dress code are all essential if the interview is being conducted for television broadcast, or if the interview is part of a newspaper or magazine article that will include photographs. The site and any props required can be handled by the media manager, while the image of the athlete or coach is a little more problematic. It is particularly important to have policies and procedures within the league or team that govern player dress codes. In many instances this will be covered as part of a collective bargaining agreement. For example, in the National Hockey League (NHL), the collective bargaining agreement states that 'Players are required to wear jackets, ties and dress pants to all Club games and while traveling to and from

such games unless otherwise specified by the Head Coach or General Manager' (NHL, 2013).

Because of the amount of space available to them, newspaper and magazine journalists are likely to conduct more in-depth interviews, while radio and television journalists will necessarily make their interviews more targeted, specific and compressed because they have limited air time. This difference will alter the way journalists approach their interviews and the types of questions they ask. Similarly, the type of answers and approach of the subject will need to be altered if the media coverage received is to be of good quality. If the athlete, coach or administrator being interviewed wants to get their message across, then the answers they give will need to be appropriate to the media outlet that will be printing or broadcasting the results of the interview. Short concise answers that will make good sound bites will be appropriate for television and radio, while longer more considered answers will be appropriate for newspaper and magazines, particularly if the latter are preparing a profile or feature article on a player or coach.

Prior to an interview, journalists will have researched the subject, in order to find out as much information about it or them as possible. In order to make the interviewer's job as easy as possible, the sport organization should provide a detailed fact sheet on the subject to be interviewed. It should not be assumed that this will be the only information that the media will consider. In fact, ease of access to the internet and the amount of information available means that the media will be able to gather far more information than you are able to give them in one fact sheet, however detailed. Thus, the fact sheet in this instance is a way of providing a range of standard information about the subject, so that the journalist will be able to crosscheck their information and sources if necessary. This type of information is freely available, lacks controversy, but is likely to be mentioned in any media coverage, particularly print media.

## INTERVIEWEE CHECKLIST

The following checklist is a good starting point for providing interviewees with practical skills to negotiate their media interactions. It applies specifically to interviews, but could be broadened to provide athletes, coaches, managers and administrators with more general media skills training.

### Interview context

- What is the topic of the interview? This might seem obvious, but being prepared is a key to producing a good media image in interview situations. Athletes, coaches, managers and administrators will perform best when they are most comfortable, which is more likely if they have been adequately briefed on the topic or subject.
- Is there an angle or perspective to the interview? The interviewee may be aware of the topic or subject matter, but it is essential that they also consider what angle the reporter might be taking, and what role they might be asked to play in constructing the story.

## Interviewer

- Who is the interviewer/what is the media outlet? It is essential that interviewees are aware of who will be interviewing them, and what media outlet they work for. Both of these points will have a bearing on how the interviewee might prepare, and what they can expect. Furthermore, the interviewer might be familiar to the interviewee, which might relax them, or alternatively lead to them saying things they wouldn't normally divulge.
- Does the interviewer have an established position on the discussion topic? This is an important question to consider if the topic or subject matter is sensitive, or the interview forms part of a broader debate that the reporter has been a part of, or was an instigator of.
- What is the interview style of the reporter or media personality? Being prepared for a particular style might often be just as important as the subject matter itself. In this respect the interviewee's image might be determined by how they are perceived to have handled the interviewer.

## Purpose

- Who is the audience I want to reach by giving this interview? All interviewees must have an audience in mind. Identifying the audience will help to focus the interviewee's answers.
- Where do I fit in the overall story? This is important if the issue is sensitive and others are likely to be interviewed on the same topic. For example, a range of athletes might be interviewed on their response to new anti-doping regulations. In this case it is essential to consider what the views of others might be and how the interviewee's opinion might be presented.
- What is my primary theme for the interview? It is useful if each interview has a central theme running through it. Identifying this theme can help an interviewee answer difficult questions or continue to answer if they lose their train of thought or become flustered.
- Can I develop one concise sentence that captures the reason for doing the interview and the message I wish to convey? Clearly identifying a concise reason for conducting the interview will give the interviewee purpose. This will help to focus responses to questions and influence the overall tone of the interview by allowing the interviewee to be more proactive.
- What are three major points that I wish to make? If the interviewee is able to convey three major points to the audience in a coherent manner then it is likely the interview will be successful. Identifying these points prior to the interview will improve the interviewee's responses and overall performance.

### Maximizing performance

- Have I said too much? It is important to remember that the average attention span of people listening to interviews is about 15 to 30 seconds. Therefore, simple, short and straightforward answers will avoid diluting the message. Identifying an audience, interview focus and key points will facilitate more concise and direct answers.
- What are the three most obvious or difficult questions I might be asked? While obvious questions might be easy to identify, as well as answer, it is still useful to rehearse a response. More difficult questions are both harder to identify and harder to answer; however, anticipating these difficult questions will improve an interviewee's preparation and in doing so they are less likely to be surprised or caught off guard in an interview.
- Do I have any appropriate anecdotes, analogies or examples to help reinforce my position or provide an interesting angle to the interview?

## OFF THE RECORD?

Media communications, by their very nature, are on the record (see the previous chapter on the way in which sport journalists operate for more information on this issue). Media communications, through media releases, media fact sheets, media guides and media advisories, represent the official views of individuals and organizations; impromptu or unscripted media interactions on the other hand are less constrained. Because media interactions involve personal verbal communication, the potential for an individual to express views that are not representative of the organization is far greater. It is generally accepted that employees at all levels of a sport organization should restrict themselves to on the record media interactions. In other words, they should assume that anything they say could be reported by the media and modify their comments accordingly. Off the record communications and interactions in which the employee divulges information that she or he would prefer not to see in print should be avoided.

## SUMMARY

This chapter has examined three major forms of formal media interaction: the media conference, interview and media event. The chapter has provided guidelines to prepare for and conduct each of these three interactions. With practice, a media manager should be able to use these guidelines to conduct successful media interactions and provide basic training for employees within the organization in interview skills in particular. Review questions and exercises are listed below to assist with confirming your knowledge of the core concepts and principles introduced in this chapter.

## REVIEW QUESTIONS AND EXERCISES

1 When should a major professional sport organization stage a media conference?
2 When should a minor sport organization stage a media conference?
3 What are the three key factors to consider prior to announcing a media conference?
4 Why is it important that the media conference background incorporate small logos?
5 When will a prepared statement be broadcast by media organizations?
6 Should a sport organization agree to media interviews prior to a media conference?
7 Should interviewees be rehearsed or is it better to have them give 'natural' answers? Why?
8 What are the three most important items of the interviewee checklist? Why?
9 Stage a mock media conference, either live or recorded. Make sure that both the speakers and media are briefed on the issues in order to make the conference as realistic as possible.
10 Stage a mock interview (either a conversational interview, or a direct to camera interview). Make sure that both the interviewer and interviewee are briefed on the issues in order to make the interview as realistic as possible.

## CASE STUDY

### Caroline Wozniacki's kangaroo attack: a study in good interview etiquette

As illustrated within this chapter, the interview is a key point of interaction between sport and the media, and one of the key forms of communications between those who work within sport and the general public. Giving a good interview can be the difference in gaining widespread media coverage, and those who build a rapport with journalists can often be more successful in securing sponsorships and other endorsements. This case study illustrates an interesting interview strategy taken by Danish tennis player Caroline Wozniacki at the 2011 Australian Open tennis tournament, a subsequent negative experience and how she recovered journalists' trust. Wozniacki entered the 2011 Australian Open as the World No. 1 and one of the sport's most marketable players. But after hearing rumours within media circles that her press conferences had become boring, Wozniacki decided to tackle the issue head on and at the start of the post-match press conference on 21 January 2011 made a statement.

CAROLINE WOZNIACKI: Well, yesterday I got the question by the media, they said that my press conferences were kind of boring. Yeah, that I always gave the same answers.

You know, I find it quite, you know, funny because I always get the same questions. So I'm just going to start. I know what you're going to ask me already. So I'm just going to start with the answer.

I felt great out there today on the court. You know, I think I played a pretty good match. I am happy I got the revenge since I lost to her in Sydney last week. It was not an easy match. She went out there, she was really on fire.

You know, I'm happy to be through to the next round. I don't know who I'm playing, so maybe you can ask me that afterwards. But I'm really looking forward to playing my fourth round. It's the second time in a row that that's happened.

I mean, what I do need to do to win this tournament, if I feel like I played too defensively today. I actually feel like I had to do that. I had to run a lot of balls down today because, I mean, she was playing really aggressively, trying to hit from the first point.

Uhm, if I deserve to be No. 1. If this was maybe another proof that I belong there. Again, I don't feel any pressure to be No. 1. I really enjoy myself. I think I've had a great year and a great tournament so far. So I'm just happy to be in the next round, and hopefully I can pull a win through.

My racquet feels really good (laughter). I feel like the racquet is really helping me out. I feel like there is no problems. I really, uhm, enjoy playing with it. So I feel like, uhm – yeah, I'm just happy to be here. Hopefully this was a little bit different than usual, and now you can maybe, yeah, give me some questions that are a little bit more interesting, a little bit different than what I usually get.

Wozniacki was then swamped with questions about everything but tennis, including her visit to an Australian cricket match, her opinion on the appointment of Kenny Dalglish to coach English Premier League team Liverpool, how to solve global warming and then to more personal questions, like whether she wanted to get married and how many children she wanted to have. The press conference transcript is peppered with laughter from both journalists and Wozniacki, as they were clearly unused to such a playful and upfront athlete. This off-kilter tact gathered much more media attention than a normal post-match press conference; however, Wozniacki perhaps went a little too far in her next time in front of the media. After winning her next match, the first question asked of Wozniacki was: 'What is the most exciting thing you've ever done? If it's illegal, we promise not to tell anyone.' Wozniacki then launched into a detailed story of why she was wearing a bandage on her shin, from when she approached a kangaroo within a local Melbourne park.

CAROLINE WOZNIACKI: Well, the other day I went to the park and I saw this kangaroo lying there. If you've seen, I'm playing with the thing on my shin here. It was lying there. So I wanted to go over and help it out. As I went over to it, it just started to be aggressive and it actually cut me. So I think that's pretty exciting. But I learned my lesson and I just started running away.

The media continued to grill Wozniacki about the kangaroo for a further six questions, including whether or not she went to the doctor, why she went to help it out and where the incident occurred. The problem lay in the fact that Wozniacki was joking about the entire incident, something which some members of the media did not pick up on. Various media outlets, including some of the world's leading news wires, went out with the story that Wozniacki had actually been attacked by a kangaroo. Due to this media reaction Wozniacki decided to hold another press conference, a few hours later in the day, in order to clear up the confusion.

THE MODERATOR: Everyone, thanks for coming back. Caroline just wanted to say a few words, and also make a clarification. So she's going to start out and then we'll take questions.

CAROLINE WOZNIACKI: Well, I want to come back, because I just wanted to clarify and say I'm sorry if I've caused any harm or made your job a little bit more difficult. But the kangaroo story, I made it up because it sounded better than what actually happened. I walked into the treadmill so that wasn't really – you know, that's my blonde. Sometimes that happens.

I'm sorry if I caused an inconvenience. I really didn't mean to. I didn't think you would believe it because I already told the Danish press and they know. I thought it was out there already. So I just wanted to apologize and that's why I'm here. I'm hoping that the press conferences in the future will still be funny. I promise if I make a joke like this, I'll make sure to clarify it before I leave. Again, I didn't think that it was going to, yeah, spin this way.

The media coverage of Wozniacki's subsequent apology was even larger than the initial take-up of her joke story, and generally labelled with headlines that were unfavourable, such as 'Wozniacki tricks media with story of kangaroo attack' and 'Caroline Wozniacki Plays Joke on Media, Lies About Leg Scratch'. Wozniacki's failed joke could have meant a quick turnaround from one of the media's favourites to one of their least liked athletes. Journalists who had run with the story were embarrassed that they had filed something that turned out to be entirely fake. However, Wozniacki's approach to the situation did help regain journalists' trust. She was quick to hold another press conference to clarify and apologized to media straight away. A question at the end of her second clarifying press conference also illustrates that perhaps the kangaroo story had not damaged her relationship with journalists, as there was no doubt her press conferences were definitely not routine and filled with clichés anymore.

Q. Your press conferences are definitely not boring anymore. Are you happier with that?

CAROLINE WOZNIACKI: You know, definitely think that this shows more of my personality. I think also the journalists are asking me fun questions. I think it's a bonus for all of us. You don't find me boring, I don't find it boring sitting here. We all gain from it.

Another example of how Wozniacki turned this potentially damaging situation into a positive one was playing off it during publicity for the following year's Australian Open. A common press opportunity at the Asia/Pacific Grand Slam event is to have players pose with baby Australian animals; Wozniacki was quite happily paired with a joey (a young kangaroo) and used it as a space to talk about her failed joke again. And later in the tournament, after a question about an increasing number of bugs on the Australian Open courts, happily answered another kangaroo question.

Q. Are they more dangerous than kangaroos?

CAROLINE WOZNIACKI: I actually had a small kangaroo – and I'm not kidding this time. (Laughter.) I was holding a small kangaroo, baby kangaroo, trying to show me that actually it was very nice to me this time.

Do you know what it did afterwards? I gave it some milk, and it just spit it all over me. I was like, 'Is this a thank you for just being nice and petting the kangaroo?' I got milk all over myself. I guess I deserved that from the story last year.

Wozniacki's self-deprecating nature, which shines through in the answers 'and I'm not kidding this time' and 'I guess I deserved that from the story last year', show an athlete happy to poke fun at themselves and engage with the media on what could have otherwise been a negative media experience.

## CASE STUDY QUESTIONS

1. What do you think of Wozniacki's strategy of calling out journalists for always asking the same questions? Is this a good tactic?
2. If you were moderating the press conference, would you have done anything differently when Wozniacki detailed the kangaroo attack?
3. What kind of briefing notes do you think would have been given to Wozniacki before her 'clarifying' press conference? Would you have changed anything about her apology message?

Sources: ASAP Sports (2011 a,b,c); ASAP Sports (2012).

CHAPTER 11

# Sport and social media

## Keeping up with the tweets, posts and links

## OVERVIEW

As discussed in previous chapters, the primary function of communication staff members within sport organizations has traditionally focused on media relations. This was largely because until the late 1990s the only way that sport organizations, athletes and coaches could communicate directly with their fans beyond the field of play was through traditional media outlets. The main role of communication staff members within sport organizations was to facilitate access for newspaper journalists, television broadcasters and radio commentators. In the twenty-first century, however, sport fans can navigate directly to a team's website, which offers a wide variety of news and information in different multimedia formats. Sport fans can also access news directly from their social networks, by liking a team's page on Facebook or following an individual athlete on Twitter. Not surprisingly this has led to more media related roles within sport organizations such as writers, editors, video producers and social media managers. These professionals are now employed within sport organizations to mirror some of the roles previously performed only by media organizations. Sport organizations no longer seek to solely facilitate content for the media, but also to create it. This chapter seeks to explore what impact these developments have had on the traditional access model in sport media. It then provides a detailed examination of the social media networks and platforms that have developed as ways of distributing this content. This chapter explores the adoption of social media by sport organizations, as well as implementing strategy and developing social media guidelines and policy. It concludes with a brief discussion on the future of social and digital media in sport.

## LEARNING OUTCOMES

After completing this chapter the reader should be able to:

- understand how social and digital media has changed the traditional access model in sport media;
- understand the major social media networks and be able to draw upon best practices for different platforms;
- develop, action and measure a social media strategy for an organization; and
- develop a social media policy for an organization.

## THE NEW CONTENT PROVIDERS

The NFL's New England Patriots claim to be the first professional sport team to launch their website, in 1995 (patriots.com). An early screen shot of that website, in 1996, shows an already comprehensive list of content, with links to the following:

- press releases
- Foxboro Stadium
- personalities
- features
- 1996 media guide
- cheerleaders
- behind the scenes
- express yourself
- fantasy forecast
- pats links
- trivia
- feedback
- 1996 season review.

A visit to the patriots.com website in 2014 reveals a comprehensive multimedia experience, with content and interactivity that was unimaginable 20 years ago. The front page links to similar sections as it did in 1996, but underneath each header – 'News', 'Schedule and statistics', 'Multimedia', 'Fan zone', 'Cheerleaders', 'Gillette stadium' and 'Fantasy football' – there are drop-down menus that link to even more detailed content and information. In addition to the media available on their own website, which includes in-built videos, audio and photo galleries, there are also links to the Patriots' pages and handles on Facebook, Twitter, Instagram, Pinterest, Google Plus and three separate mobile device applications.

Delving a little deeper into one part of Patriots' website, the 'News' menu, uncovers a link to three different columnists, an official newspaper of the New England Patriots, *Patriots Football Weekly*, and eight different news categories, including latest news, blogs and analysis, press releases, transcripts, from the NFL, an Associated Press wire feed, *Patriots Football Weekly* and an ASK PFW section, where readers submit questions for *Patriots Football Weekly* to answer. Not surprisingly, the incredible amount of content uploaded on these various channels takes a small army of staff to create. In the official 2013 Patriots media guide staff directory, there were three members in broadcast production, a senior executive producer, a director and supervising producer and a director of event presentation and broadcast distribution. In the section titled *Patriots Football Weekly* (the Patriots in-house newspaper) and patriots.com, there are five staff – a publisher and vice president of content, a director of digital services, two art directors and an editor. The media relations department lists just three members – a vice president of media and community relations, a director of media relations and an assistant director of media relations (Salkin and Jurovaty, 2013). Patriots' publisher and Vice President of Content Fred Kirsch explained early in 2014 that his team produces about 60 minutes of on-demand video every day and another 30 minutes of streaming video per day during the season. His main problem isn't struggling to fill that time,

but limiting it: 'Sometimes the problem is doing too much, we are a content brand, more than a company like Proctor & Gamble, which is a product brand,' he said in an interview with CMSwire.com. 'The meat of what we do is content. Even then, we have a lot of different departments that want to do a lot of different things, the challenge is not to do too much stuff that confuses our fans' (Raynovoich, 2014). The changes that have occurred within professional sport teams and leagues over the last 20 years since the popularization of the internet mean that the media department in professional sport organizations no longer simply facilitates access for media, but creates their own media content. This has had a profound impact on the traditional sport media access model.

## THE IMPACT ON THE ACCESS MODEL

Since Joseph Pulizter put the first sports pages in the *New York Post* in 1883, sport has been a valuable media commodity. The hyper-commercialization of sport in the 1990s was driven by television broadcasters engaging in bidding wars to win the rights to host sport on their channel. In turn, broadcasters sold advertising spots, or cable subscriptions, to recover their investment. This is still evident in the Superbowl advertising market, where a 30 second spot during the 2014 match cost US$4 million (Farhi, 2014). The major income source for professional sport today is still television rights, as discussed in one of the earlier chapters. Historically, the media have retained power in the production of sport news and controlled what content fans could access, as well as how, where and for how much. The financial models that underpin the relationship between sport and the media and sport media industry are predicated on content control, most particularly through the sale of exclusive broadcast rights. In this context it is perhaps not surprising that the development of technologies and media networks that have enabled sport organizations and athletes to communicate directly with consumers (fans) has threatened traditional media networks and their operating model. This change in access is represented by the models shown in Figures 11.1 and 11.2.

In the traditional access model, journalists had direct access to athletes, coaches and administrators and were able to speak to them in order to write a story or analysis, which was then published or broadcast to the public (Figure 11.1). In this model the journalists (the media) were the mediator between the employees of the sport organization and their fans. There was also little or no chance for feedback in this model, other than when athletes, coaches or administrators came into contact with reporters and were able to provide private feedback regarding their opinions or when the public wrote letters to the editor of the newspaper. In the new access model, a set of professionals have been added who moderate the relationship and contact between the employees of the sport organization and the journalists (the media) – media relations managers. The media relations manager provides sport organizations with more control over their players, coaches and administrators as it relates to media coverage, while at the same time giving them more control over their public image and media message. At the same time, the development of new technologies and social media platforms in particular has allowed sport organizations and their employees, including media managers, to bypass the media and communicate directly with the public (this is represented in Figure 11.2 by the arrows at the top and bottom of the flow chart). This has provided sport organizations and their

employees with more control, allowing them to deliver content and messages directly to fans, but social media has also meant that the public is able to continuously offer feedback. Sport fans have more access to the sport organizations they follow than ever before, but the media, the traditional gatekeepers of sport information, are now only one of a number of sources.

An early indication of how the sport media reacted to this new model of access was when pitcher Curt Schilling was traded to the Boston Red Sox in 2004. Poor (2006) detailed that during trade negotiations Schilling visited a fan website, created a profile and started to chat. After hearing from a fan on a forum that he was being bad-mouthed by a sport radio station, Schilling called in. Responding to a comment that he should have spoken to traditional media first, Schilling said 'it was [their] job to get the story', and 'not our job to give it to you'. *The Boston Globe* reported that local media were 'irked', but there were some who noted the positives. Baseball fan and *Slate* columnist Seth Stevenson found Schilling's appearance on the forum surreal – 'As a fan,' he wrote, 'this is the dream. Shooting the breeze with the star from your favourite team' (Stevenson, 2003). Fast-forward to 2014 and there are an incredible number of high-profile athletes with accounts on social network sites such as Twitter and Facebook, where they often engage directly with fans. As well as regular Q&As where players ask fans for questions and answer them, it is a chance for fans to see what was once the athlete's private side. Czech tennis player Tomas Berdych had projected a rather a dour personality on court, but he joined Twitter

**FIGURE 11.1** The traditional access model in sport

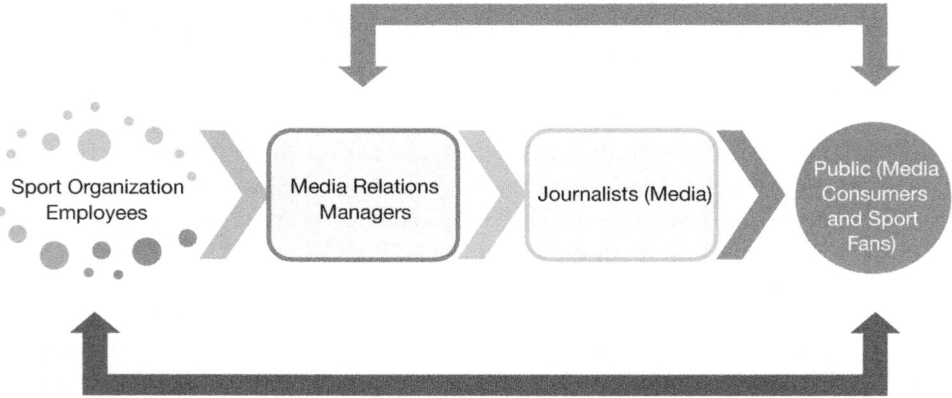


**FIGURE 11.2** The new access model in sport

in 2013 and through quirky text posts and pictures managed to change the public perception of him (Pearce, 2014). In an ultimate act of fan interaction, Oklahoma City fan Charlie Wright decided to contact NBA player Russell Westbrook to ask if he would help him propose to his girlfriend, Rachel Haycraft (Dwyer, 2013). After an initial Facebook conversation, Westbrook tweeted the proposal in June 2013, and then re-tweeted a follow-up picture from the pair with the caption 'I said yes'.

> @rachelhaycraft, @chuuuuck1 loves u, he wants to know if u would spend the rest of ur life watching thunder games w/him. #marryhim #Whynot
>
> (Russell Westbrook (@russwest44) 21 June 2013)

Aside from conversations with fans, high-profile athletes and sport organizations are now using social media networks as a place to break news, which is further eroding the traditional access model and the position of the media. Multiple Grand Slam champion Novak Djovokic announced his engagement via Twitter (Whitcomb, 2013), while British Olympic diving medallist Tom Daley came out in a YouTube video in December 2013 (Hart, 2013). The United States National Women's Soccer team announced via Instagram that Jill Ellis was their new coach in May 2014 (Daniels, 2014). Whereas sport journalists and media organizations were previously the sole gatekeepers in the sport media nexus, controlling which stories made it through to the public, fans can now hear news from their favourite athletes and sport organizations, chat to them, and even ask them to be involved in their lives. The traditional sport media access model has been turned on its head via the development of new communication technologies and platforms. What is written and posted to social media now often becomes the sport media's story. This is illustrated in In Practice 11.1, which examines the social media profile of Los Angeles Lakers star Kobe Bryant.

## THE SOCIAL NETWORKING REVOLUTION

Social media networks have become one of the most influential ways to distribute content and engage with sport fans on the internet, as well as the starting point for subsequent media coverage. They have become a non-negotiable part of working in a modern-day media environment. In the most widely accepted definition, Boyd and Ellison (2007: 211) describe a social network as:

> a web-based service that allows individuals to (1) construct a public or semi-public profile within a bounded system, (2) articulate a list of other users with whom they share a connection and, (3) view and traverse their list of connections and those made by others in the system.

While the nature of the connections referred to by Ellison and Boyd change from network to network, these three elements are common to all social networks. The first recognized social media networks started in the late 1990s, with both AOL messenger and sixdegrees.com allowing users to create a profile, share conversations and connect with others. But it wasn't until the early to mid 2000s that social networking became a

## IN PRACTICE 11.1

### Twitter, Facebook, Instagram and Kobe Bryant

The Los Angeles Lakers and Team USA guard Kobe Bryant is one of the world's most recognizable sports stars. As of 2014, Bryant was the youngest basketball player to reach 28,000 points in NBA history, a five-time NBA champion, a two-time Olympic gold medallist, a two-time NBA MVP and the Lakers' all-time leading scorer (NBA, 2013). Bryant was a latecomer to social media, only joining Twitter on 4 January 2013. His first tweet, 'the antisocial has become social #blackmamba' was re-tweeted over 50,000 times. He has since become one of the most engaging and entertaining athletes and as of November 2014, he had 5.85 million followers. Shortly after joining the micro-blogging network he live-tweeted a broadcast of his 81-point game against the Toronto Raptors. One US sport columnist wrote afterwards 'Looking back, watching the performance this time around was just as incredible as watching it live. Why, you ask? Because we got to watch it with the 81-point man himself, Kobe Bryant' (Favale, 2013). But possibly Bryant's most interesting use of social networks was to post about his season-ending Achilles injury in 2013. Straight after the injury, instead of talking to media, Bryant took to his Facebook page:

> This is such BS! All the training and sacrifice just flew out the window with one step that I've done millions of times! The frustration is unbearable. The anger is rage. Why the hell did this happen?!? Makes no damn sense. Now I'm supposed to come back from this and be the same player Or better at 35?!? How in the world am I supposed to do that?? I have NO CLUE. Do I have the consistent will to overcome this thing? Maybe I should break out the rocking chair and reminisce on the career that was. Maybe this is how my book ends. Maybe Father Time has defeated me. . . . Forgive my Venting but what's the purpose of social media if I won't bring it to you Real No Image?? Feels good to vent, let it out.
>
> (Bryant, 2013)

In his next social media move, Bryant joined photo-sharing network Instagram and posted photos of his MRI, him in his hospital bed, teammates visiting, and finally the stiches being taken out. One month post surgery Bryant posted a graphic photo of his ankle cut open mid Achilles-operation. In July 2013, he posted a video of his surgeon talking about his progress. Bryant's use of social media is successful because he provides his fans with never before direct access, and lets them access parts of himself and his story that the mainstream media previously did not have access to. By posting private shots from his hospital bed and real, honest messages, Bryant not only bypasses the media as the way of distributing his message, but he ensures that these posts actually become the stories the media report on.

mainstream phenomenon. Friendster was the first version of the 'new' social network to achieve prominence; it launched in 2002 and reached three million users it its first year. MySpace launched the year after, before what has become the world's biggest social network, Facebook, launched in 2004 and in doing so launched the social networking revolution. Sport organizations and professional teams have been early adopters of social media and a social media manager is now a common position within many sport organization's media departments. These social media managers must utilize a wide range of different platforms, each of which is unique and requires different types of content and strategies for engagement.

## Facebook

The first major social media network to be adopted by the mainstream was founded in 2004 by Harvard student Mark Zuckerberg. Originally designed as a network for university students to share experiences (posts), photos and 'like' the posts of others on the network, it went global in September 2006. Facebook's final quarter reports for 2013 re-affirmed it is the world's largest social network with 1.2 billion active monthly users. While Facebook was initially about connecting people, it quickly built a business case for connecting users with brands and organizations. Facebook 'pages' were introduced in 2007, which allowed individual users to 'like' a page and posts from that page will then appear in the individual user's newsfeed. Some of the largest Facebook pages are sport organizations; in February 2014 FC Barcelona became the first sport team to reach 50 million Facebook fans (facebook.com/fcbarcelona), closely followed by Real Madrid, with 47 million. While each post can vary in terms of engagement, an example week from February 2014 shows that each post on Real Madrid's Facebook page received between 100,000 and 700,000 likes (facebook.com/realmadrid), which means millions of individual views.

Facebook is the largest social network in the world by far, which makes it an obvious online venue for sport organizations and individual athletes. However, Facebook's algorithm driven newsfeed makes it one of the more frustrating social networks to master for organizations. For example, Joe Smith, an average citizen, uses Facebook to keep up to date with his friends and family. When Joe logs in to Facebook, the different posts in his newsfeed do not appear in chronological order. Instead, a photo from a friend's wedding on the weekend might be the first post that appears when he looks at the page on Tuesday morning. Because of the complex nature of this algorithm, individuals and organizations cannot determine why the post appears when it does; it is likely driven by the fact that a number of Joe's friends have engaged with the post by 'liking' and 'commenting'. Therefore, sport organizations should avoid using Facebook to post live-score updates, as there is no guarantee those posts will appear in a user's feed in chronological order. Facebook's nature means that an organization wants fans to engage with its post, through liking, commenting or sharing. The more fans engage, the better the post will perform. Most sport organizations post a range of content on Facebook, such as links to website stories, videos and photo galleries. During the week after winning the premier league title in 2014, Manchester City's Facebook page included a photo gallery of the Champions Parade around Manchester, as well as photos and links to stories on their upcoming tour of Abu Dhabi, updates of the Manchester City women's team, a 'City in the Media' post

## BREAKOUT BOX 11.1 – FACEBOOK

### Pros

- The world's largest social media network. Therefore, largest pool of potential fans.

### Cons

- Posts do not appear in chronological order, so not ideal for posting live updates.

### Features and uses

- Engagement is based on how many people like your individual page, and then individual posts on the page, through liking, sharing or commenting.
- Use a mix of content, links to web articles, videos, photos and photo galleries.
- Use Facebook analytics to see where your fans are based, what time they are online, what language they are using and what posts get the most engagement.

with links to media stories, competitions to win a signed shirt and a new pair of football boots, and a birthday post for Yaya Toure. On the day Manchester City won the premier league, Facebook content consisted of different photo galleries including pitchside, match and dressing room, which provided exclusive access to Manchester City's behind the scenes celebrations.

## Twitter

Twitter is a microblogging service launched in July 2006 that has grown to be one of the world's largest social-networking sites. It allows users to send messages of up to 140 characters. Users follow other users to create a personalized newsfeed, and interact by tagging others using their handle (e.g. @Twitter) or hashtags. By placing a hash in front of a word, it makes the term searchable on Twitter (e.g. #Twitter), and is used as a way of linking tweets on a single event or idea. Twitter also allows users to embed photos and videos within tweets. Since it started, sport has been one of the biggest successes on Twitter as it is a platform that thrives on live events. Super Bowl XLII in 2008 broke the then record as the most tweeted event with 27 tweets per minute. In February 2013, Super Bowl XLVII generated 231,500 tweets per minute, the busiest period coming during a power outage in the stadium during the third quarter (Ashtari, 2013). The biggest moment in Twitter sport history so far is Spain's win against Italy in the 2012 Euro competition. It peaked at 15,384 tweets per second around the fourth goal, a total of 267, 200 tweets per minute (Rios, 2012).

As a time-based newsfeed, Twitter is particularly suited for live sport. This means that a leveraging strategy *during* matches is particularly important to grow overall follower numbers. In October 2013, Twitter conducted a study with five Major League Baseball clubs to determine which types of tweets and content were most successful on game days.

With the aim to help boost follower engagement and grow each team's audience, five teams were chosen to utilize five different live-tweeting formats.

The five teams in the analysis were: the Cleveland Indians (@Indians), Oakland Athletics (@Athletics), Los Angeles Dodgers (@Dodgers), Seattle Mariners (@Mariners) and Texas Rangers (@Rangers). The live-tweeting formats examined as part of the study were:

1 play by play: tweeting each play of the game in real time;
2 takeover: turning over a team's Twitter account to a high profile fan or expert (for example, the Dodgers asked long-time announcer Vin Scully to tweet his thoughts and reactions during a game);
3 Vine (a short-looped video sharing site) videos: using Vine to post six-second clips of action during the game, or in the stadium, to complement the TV coverage;
4 behind-the-scenes photos: tweeting out pictures from the locker room, the dugout, and other spots to give fans access to parts of the game-day experience they rarely see; and
5 fan engagement in-game conversation: responding directly to fan tweets during the game, engaging fans in ongoing conversations in real time.

The study found that Twitter takeovers resulted in the most followers (up 125 per cent on the average three-month follower growth), that tweets that contained Vine videos gained the most re-tweets, mentions and favourites, and that the official hashtags were most used in the play by play discussion. The study also found that any effort to engage with fans led to an increase in followers and engagement. One of the interesting parts of the study was that fan engagement is not necessarily driven by winning. There were an average of 41 tweets per day for a winning team, compared with 32 per day for each losing team –

## BREAKOUT BOX 11.2 – TWITTER

### Pros

- Tweets appear in chronological order, so it is perfect for commentating on live sport.

### Cons

- Content can get lost in a feed that updates so often.

### Features and uses

- Each post has only 140 characters, but you can embed multiple photos, tag individuals or add in longer web story links without going over the limit.
- Use Twitter to update from your live sport event, with an event specific hashtag which you have promoted pre-game.
- Complete an analytics report post game to see the most popular tweet, your reach and what type of content was best.

a 56 per cent to 44 per cent split. Only one team tweeted more when they were losing, the Rangers. While they lost eight games of 11 during the period Twitter measured, they still gained more followers than any other team, an increase of 16 per cent on the control week.

## Instagram

Instagram is a photo and short-video sharing network launched in October 2010, where users directly follow other users to create a customized news feed of photos. Instagram's difference lies in the fact it offers an easy, quick and free way to edit photographs. Offering a menu of photo filters, as well as the ability to crop, highlight and adjust exposure means that Instagram quickly found a following with those interested in high-quality images. As of March 2014, Instagram had 200 million monthly users. In April 2012, Instagram was purchased by Facebook for US$1 billion. Since then, Instagram's compatibility with Facebook has increased. Most sport organizations use Instagram as a place to share great imagery of sport and give behind the scenes access. The NBA's newest team, the Brooklyn Nets, have used their Instagram account to live out their specific team values. Many of the posts have a black and white filter applied to them, in keeping with the Brooklyn Nets' colours. Brooklyn's Instagram feed is also unique in that it is sponsored by local Brookyn photography and video store B&H photos.

## Google+

Google is one of the world's largest and most successful tech companies, but the company behind the world's most utilized search engine has had to wait for growth on its own social network. Launched in 2011 by private invitation, Google+ had similarities to Facebook in that it was about creating profiles and connecting with friends. While its growth was slow compared with some other networks, Google+ reached 300 million monthly active users

### BREAKOUT BOX 11.3 – INSTAGRAM

#### Pros

- Great way to show high-quality behind the scenes pictures and short videos.

#### Cons

- Not as easy as other social networks to gauge, manage and encourage interactivity.

#### Features and uses

- Can post extended text with each image.
- Use Instagram filters to make your images appealing.
- Tap into already established hashtags.

## BREAKOUT BOX 11.4 – GOOGLE+

### Pros

- Offers features that other social networks don't have, including the innovative Google+ Hangout, and the ability to attach multiple types of content in the one post.

### Cons

- Still not quite as many users as other social networks, and sport organizations so far typically have smaller follower numbers here.

### Features and uses

- Multiple content in the same post, i.e. photos, videos and web links.
- Use Google+ to host a hangout, where fans can ask their favourite athletes questions from wherever they are in the world.

in October 2013. One specific Google+ feature that has been used by sport organizations is the hangout. In collaboration with YouTube, Google+ Hangouts allow a number of users to be pulled together in one virtual room. For example, FC Barcelona kicked off their Google+ Hangout program with star striker Gareth Bale in April 2014. Eight fans won the chance to 'hangout' with Bale through Google+, albeit virtually. In the Google+ Hangout video, the fans' webcam images were broadcast across the bottom of the larger window focused on Bale. When it is was their chance to ask a question of the English superstar, each fan took centre stage on the screen before hearing and seeing Bale answer their question live. Manchester United took the Google+ Hangout technology one step further in March 2014, with their 'Front Row' competition to allow international fans the chance to watch a game at Old Trafford. While logged into Google+ Hangout during the match against Liverpool on 16 March 2014, their images were streamed onto the pitchside advertising screens (Manchester United, 2014).

## YouTube

YouTube is by definition a social network, although often not considered as such. The video-sharing website was founded in February 2005; its 2014 statistics state that more than one billion unique users visit each month and that over six billion hours of video are watched each month – almost an hour for every person on Earth, and 50 per cent more than the previous year (YouTube, 2014). YouTube is also the second largest search engine in the world, behind Google.

Sport's greatest value lies in the unpredictability of live sport, and the number one use of YouTube by sport organizations is to provide video highlights. The NBA is the top subscribed YouTube channel in sport, with just over 5.5 million subscribers and provides

## BREAKOUT BOX 11.5 – YOUTUBE

### Pros

- The No. 1 destination for anyone searching for video (and second biggest search engine behind Google), which means that it makes sense to upload highlights.

### Cons

- Requires video footage.

### Unique features

- Its function as a search engine.
- Use YouTube as an official place to store video highlights of your sport, or exclusive interviews.

its followers and fans with a mix of content such as game highlights, exclusive interviews, career player highlights, instructional videos and behind-the-scenes locker room vision. Because of its emphasis on video, YouTube allows sport organizations to convey a 'personality' to fans. Australia's first professional tour cycling team, Orica GreenEdge, has been active on YouTube since its start in 2011. As of May 2014, Orica GreenEdge cycling had over six million video views with a quirky mix of content that includes a regular Backstage Pass that goes behind the scenes with the team, how-to videos such as 'how to ride over cobblestones' and 'top 5 coffee tips'. In May it released a series of team Orica versus Team Sky (another professional team) videos, where members engaged in contests that included staring without blinking, rock-paper-scissors and a supermarket sweep competition to see who could find a series of items quickest. Their most popular video is the team lip-syncing to pop song 'Call me maybe'. This YouTube channel allows the team to keep fans updated on results and get cycling expertize, but does so in a humorous and light-hearted way.

## HASHTAGS – HOW TO NAVIGATE SOCIAL NETWORKS

As of May 2014, Twitter, Instagram, Google+ and Facebook use hashtags as a way to search for information. A hashtag is when a # symbol is before a word, making it a clickable, searchable term within that network. Introduced first by Twitter as a way to identify 'trending' or popular topics that users were discussing, hashtags are a way to join a conversation without tagging each user involved in the conversation directly. Importantly, hashtags work slightly differently on each social network. Twitter was the first platform to use hashtags and they remain a crucial element of the network. Instagram uses hashtags as a way to search other photos on the same topic. While Facebook and Google+

are latecomers to the function, adding them in 2013, they are mostly used as a search function on both – to find posts on a related topic. Hashtags are important across all forms of social media as they are a way to link posts and conversations, as well as a way for a social media manager to collect fans' posts and conversations. Choosing an appropriate hashtag is crucial, particularly as hashtags now appear on event signage, team uniforms and the playing surface.

In the Australian Football League, the league mostly mandates game hashtags – the short nickname of both clubs playing, preceded by AFL. For example, #AFLSwansHawks refers to the Hawthorn Hawks versus the Sydney Swans. But teams have also introduced their own specific hashtags for fans to show their support for the club, not just talk about the game. While Sydney have opted for a more generic #goswans in recent seasons, Hawthorn's tag in 2013 was #always, a shortened version of the #alwayshawthorn tag it started with in the 2012 season. The hashtag is used widely by fans, but also by many other users on generic posts. For example, a search for the hashtag #always brings up many more results other than just tweets related to Hawthorn. If you are wishing to engage with fans and followers by searching the hashtag, then a non-generic hashtag can make this harder to do. Before deciding hashtags for a team, a season or even a competition, it is important to do a search to determine whether that hashtag has previously been used for something else.

## SOCIAL MEDIA GLOBALLY

One of the biggest benefits of social media is its ability to instantly connect sport organizations to the global marketplace. Manchester United's Front Row Google+ Hangout captured this perfectly, as fans from South Africa, Ethiopia, Mexico, Malaysia, the US and Namibia were given a 'virtual' front row seat at Old Trafford for a match against Liverpool, with their images beamed onto pitchside advertising screens. Whereas in the past fans may have had to find a venue with international cable TV to watch a game, they can now watch the games on demand and interact with their team on a variety of social media networks and platforms. The globalization of sport through online social media networks has added a layer of complexity to media management, because not all social media platforms are culturally and geographically relevant. For example, China is one of the world's biggest growing economies, but has an entirely different network of social media platforms. One of the largest sites is Sina Weibo, which was launched in 2009 and has commenting and reposting status functions similar to Facebook's share and comment. Cognizant of the importance of the Chinese market, the International Olympic Committee was an early adopter of Sina Weibo and in 2011 then IOC President Jacques Rogge hosted a live Q&A with fans through their official Weibo page; the IOC reported after the event that 'in less than 24 hours following the interview, the video of the Q&A session had been viewed over one million times, while the Olympic site on Weibo welcomed over 40,000 new fans over the same period' (IOC, 2011). According to a 2014 report by marketing firm Mailman, the NBA has the best following on Sina Weibo with 27 million followers, in addition to 25 individual team accounts. With an active audience of 144 million monthly active users, sport organizations that view China as a potential market must add Sina Weibo to the suite of social media platforms they are engaged with.

In addition to the actual platform, the other key issue that sport organizations and social media managers need to consider in a global marketplace is language. While many major sport leagues and teams are based in English speaking countries, many fans are not. Some teams have already met this demand, such as English Premier League club Liverpool that has 12 different official language accounts outside its main English handle of @LFC, including Thai, Indonesian, Malaysian, French, Arabic, Spanish, Turkish, Bengali, Korean, Portuguese, Greek and Norwegian. It also has five other localized accounts that tweet English news to their regions in India, Pakistan, Australia and New Zealand, the USA and South Africa (Liverpool FC, 2014). FC Barcelona has adopted the strategy of multiple language posts on its Facebook page. For example, a post in May 2014 to announce the retirement of long-time Captain Carlos Puyol was captioned in English, Spanish and Catalan. The move towards different platforms and multiple languages has been driven by the development of social media networks and the acknowledgement by sport organizations that they are content providers for a global fan base.

## DEVELOPING A CONTENT AND SOCIAL MEDIA STRATEGY

At the beginning of this chapter we introduced the case of the New England Patriots, in which Director of Content John Hirsch noted that an overload of content on social media platforms is the biggest challenge facing sport organizations. In this context a content and social media strategy is essential to ensure that each piece of content is utilized and leveraged for the benefit of the organization. As with all forms of planning within an organization, a content and social media strategy does not exist within a vacuum, but rather is connected to a broad set of goals and activities. Importantly, the content and social media strategy should be aligned with the overall strategic objectives of the organization. As such, the first basic step when it comes to planning a social media strategy is to use available social media platforms as an extension over the overall strategic plan or goal of the organization or department.

Once an organization has identified its strategic objectives, it is imperative to determine the target market, what kind of content they like and where they like it. Asking who, what and where is essential to an effective content strategy. Some of these questions will require market research, in particular what type of people are current or potential fans of your organization, what type of content they want via social networks and what type of social networks are best suited to your fans and your content. An important internal analysis is also required as part of the content and social media strategy, which involves determining what 'tone of voice' a particular organization might use on social media channels. As a reflection of the organization and brand, the wording of different social media posts can have a significant influence on public perception. Boston Celtics director of content Pete Stringer stated in an interview with Brian Solis:

> I take great care in managing our social media properties to be sure that they reflect our team and brand in the right way. The Boston Celtics have a reputation built on 17 championships and 60 years of history. I don't want to tarnish that with one poor tweet that doesn't hit the mark or sends the wrong message. It can

> be tempting to try to be funny, sarcastic, or irreverent, but risk usually far outweighs the reward.
>
> (Solis, 2012)

By contrast, the Los Angeles Kings NHL team has built a loyal following on their social media channels by being quirky, different and not afraid to stand out (see the Case Study in this chapter for more details of the Kings' social media strategy).

It is important to consider how social media can help an organization achieve goals in other areas of its operations. For example, the Australian Open Grand Slam tennis event created an @AOSOS handle in 2012 and encouraged anyone with questions about the Australian Open (as varied as where to find statistics or which door to enter Rod Laver arena), to use the hashtag #aohelp. The benefits of using social media as a customer service function, such as @AOSOS and #aohelp, can be more satisfied consumers. This social media strategy works particularly well for large organizations that have staff able to answer questions 24 hours a day through an event, but for small organizations this might not be possible and social media might be used to assist other operational areas. At the 2014 Australian Open, the digital team also introduced the social shack, a place designed to create opportunities for both on-site and virtual fans. The social shack was a good example of using social media within a sport organization or event to drive fan engagement, both at the venue and online and included the following features:

- a virtual tug of war between social media juggernauts, with fans tweeting support to get their favourite player over the line;
- a Social Scoreboard to determine who rules on Twitter, Facebook, Instagram, with a player crowned No. 1 at tournament's end;
- World No. 1 Rafael Nadal judged the Kia Greatest Fan competition, with the winner taking home a new Kia Soul car. Fans onsite and worldwide dressed up in true Aussie Open style and uploaded video and photo evidence of their enthusiastic support for their favourite players;
- an on-site12-metre LED screen of @australianopen coverage;
- an on-site larger-than-lifesize 3D #AUSOPEN hashtag for novelty selfies and photo opportunities;
- an on-site multimedia studio for player visits and live tweet-ups;
- live Q&As with players and special guests; and
- a daily AO Radio social show between day and night sessions.

## DEVELOPING A CONTENT PLAN

A content plan is required to operationalize the content and social media strategy. A content plan or editorial calendar should include a weekly (daily for some organizations) content schedule that includes key responsibilities and content production roles. For most sport organizations the content schedule will be driven by the match schedule, which is driven by an accepted routine. It is important to remember, however, that sport is inherently unpredictable and sometimes the best social media moments are those that are unexpected. Brian Srabian, from the social team at the San Francisco Giants, has stated:

> Baseball is different from other sports because of the frequency of games (almost every day during the season), so that means there is new information to push out to fans almost every day, as well: time and place of the game, the lineup, sponsored messages, photos or videos, ticket availability, and updates within the game. The editorial calendar is loosely based around the planned games and events at the stadium, but then a lot of content updates are based on what happens in the moment, both on and off the field.
>
> (Baer, 2013)

In addition to identifying who is responsible for creating and posting content, the content plan should also include a short description of the type of content, which platform it is scheduled for and any particularly important key messages that need to accompany it. Another important part of the content plan is detailing the behind the scenes logistics needed to ensure that each activity can occur as planned. For example, tweeting each play of the game in real time will require a staff member with a secure internet connection, probably situated in front of a TV rather than watching in the stands.

**TABLE 11.1** Draft social media plan for the South Bay Pirates, in the American national crocodile wrestling championships

| *Date* | *Post* | *Platform* | *Author* | *Notes* |
|---|---|---|---|---|
| 26/07/2015 | New sponsor announcement | Facebook | Sam | Announce new boot sponsor, take picture of player X wearing the boots at training. Link to website story. |
| 26/07/2015 | Team announcement | Twitter | Sally | Team announcement on Twitter first, then link to website story. Confirm team announcement with coach post training. |
| 27/07/2015 | Training | Instagram, Twitter | Sam | Photos from final pre-match training. |
| 28/07/2015 Match-Day (Pre-Match) | Twitter takeover | Twitter | Sally & currently injured star player | Twitter takeover Q&A with star player, to give insights into the ahead game. Confirm this two days beforehand, promote on Twitter once confirmed. |
| 28/07/2015 Match-Day | Match-Day, Live Coverage | Twitter, Facebook, Instagram, YouTube | Sam | Live tweets during the game for score updates. Facebook, update pre and post event. Instagram, update pre and post event, with excusive behind the scenes footage. Upload highlights to YouTube post event. |

A Twitter takeover would require liaising with the talent for a suitable time frame, and perhaps training them on the logistics of the platform, or having someone to read out the questions and dictate answers. Posting behind the scenes videos and photos would require the relevant accreditation to gain access to these areas, as well as briefing those who may be photographed. Table 11.1 provides a very brief example of a fictional editorial calendar for a fictional team.

## LIMITING SOCIAL MEDIA RISK – DEVELOPING A SOCIAL MEDIA POLICY

So far this chapter has dealt with how sport organizations can use social media to directly engage with fans, and change the traditional access model in their favour. Yet it is important to also acknowledge and account for the risks evident in using social media; the increased power of athletes to speak unfiltered and directly to an audience, the potential clashing of sponsors or commercial agreements, and the actual administering of the accounts themselves all have inherent risk. Athletes speaking directly to fans and the media without a filter has been particularly challenging for sport organizations, often with negative implications for athletes. Australian Olympic swimmer Stephanie Rice lost her sponsorship deal with Jaguar after tweeting a homophobic slur after an Australian Wallabies win over the South African Springboks (Byrnes, 2010), Australian cricketer David Warner was fined A$5,750 after an angry Twitter exchange with an Australian cricket journalist in 2013 (Otto, 2013), while Greek athlete Voula Papachristou was expelled from Greece's Olympic team for her comments on Twitter mocking African immigrants and expressing support for a far-right political party (Spits, 2012).

Social media has been used by sport organizations and athletes for commercial gain, particularly via sponsorship, and the commercial implications of social media use have quickly become an area that requires risk management. At the Sochi 2014 Winter Olympics, Skeleton racer Noelle Pikus-Pace had deals with Deloitte, Kelloggs, TD Ameritrade and Under Armour that stipulated social media requirements, such as mentioning some brands a minimum of 25 times on Twitter and six times on Facebook before the 2014 Games. This ability to dictate what appears on athlete's social media feeds can take away from the authenticity that was the reward of using it in the first place, particularly if sponsors dictate exactly how messages appear. Skateboarder Tony Hawk reportedly lost sponsorship deals because he refused to tweet sponsors' words as his own 'If I have a sponsor requirement to tweet, I tell them I'm not gonna put it out verbatim, because there's no heart in it' (Gray, 2011). Another risk of sponsorship and social media is that it can potentially damage lucrative commercial arrangements, such as when an athlete tweets they are consuming or using a particular product that is in direct competition with an official sponsor, partner or supplier.

Allowing one or multiple people control over all an organization's social media channels also carries significant risk. For example, in 2012 a rogue employee at MLB Advanced Media, who had access to all teams' social media accounts, created multiple, bizarre posts across a number of major league teams' Facebook pages, such as 'Just a note: Although the handicapped are allowed to watch Padres games at Petco Park their attendance is STRONGLY DISCOURAGED.' These posts created outrage and were damaging to

## IN PRACTICE 11.2

### Social media guidelines and policy – the International Paralympic Committee

The International Paralympic Committee (IPC) is the global governing body of the Paralympic Movement. Its purpose is to organize the summer and winter Paralympic Games and act as the International Federation for nine sports, supervising and coordinating World Championships and other competitions. The vision of the IPC, run by 200 members, is 'To enable Paralympic athletes to achieve sporting excellence and inspire and excite the world' (www.paralympic.org, 2014). Ahead of the London 2012 Paralympic Games, the IPC's Director of Communications Craig Spence stated that one of their objectives for London 2012 was to raise the profile of leading athletes. The IPC's social media policy for accredited persons at the Games emphasized this, stating 'The International Paralympic Committee (IPC) would like to actively encourage all athletes and Accredited Persons to use Social Media to share their experiences of the Paralympic Games through Social Media in London'. The six-page document included 14 different sections which are briefly outlined below.

*1 Introduction*

Signals the purpose of the policy, that all accredited persons at the London 2012 Olympic Games need to operate within the guidelines of this document.

*2 Definition of social media*

Outlines what social media is, including blogs, microblogs, social network services (i.e. Facebook) and Wikis.

*3 Postings*

Encourages all Accredited Persons to post, in the first person and only personal opinion or views, from their own personal Paralympic experience. Posts should be polite, courteous and respectful, and shall not be obscene, profane, vulgar, sexually explicit, defamatory, or use abusive language. This section also outlines that posts should not disclose private information, or be used for commercial or advertising purposes.

*4 Sound or moving images of the games*

Due to broadcast rights agreements, no video or audio is allowed to be posted from venues.

*5 Still pictures*

Still pictures are allowed, but not in any back of house areas, for personal use.

*6 Media*

Accredited media can freely use social media for bona fide reporting purposes.

*7 Paralympic marks*

Accredited persons are not allowed to use the Paralympic Symbol on any social media.

*8 Advertising and sponsorship*

Clearly states that accredited persons must not include any commercial reference with any Paralympic posts, except when it is an IPC partner, NPC partner or Games sponsor.

*9 Domain names/URL/page naming*

Domain names with the word Paralympic or Paralympics are not allowed.

*10 Links*

Includes links to all official IPC platforms.

*11 Liability*

Reminds accredited persons that they are responsible for personal commentary on social media platforms.

*12 Responsibility and further restrictions*

States that LOCOG, the National Paralympic Committees and International Federations are in charge of ensuring their respective delegations are informed of those guidelines and agree to fully comply with them.

*13 Prior or subsequent agreements entered into by the IPC*

This states that nothing in these guidelines shall be interpreted as amending or superseding the terms and conditions set forth in any agreement entered into, or to be entered into, by the IPC.

*14 Infringement of guidelines*

States that violation of these guidelines by an accredited person may lead to the withdrawal of such person's accreditation. The IPC reserves the right to take any and all other measures it deems fit.

Importantly, the policy clearly states what accredited persons can do – posts in the first person, still images only – and cannot do – film moving vision, or act like a journalist or reporter. Liability is clearly explained – social media users can be held personally liable for any commentary deemed to be defamatory, obscene or proprietary. It is also clear that infringements of the guidelines could lead to the withdrawal of accreditation, which would mean expulsion from the Games. Overall, the IPC's policy is guided by one of the most widely used guidelines in social media: 'The IPC encourages all Accredited Persons to post updates on Social Media sites during the Games, whilst at all times using common sense' (IPC, 2011).

Post-event, the IPC's emphasis on social media turned out to be a great success, with statistics showing that over the period of the London 2012 Paralympic Games:

- nearly two million people visited www.paralympic.org;
- close to nine million views of videos featuring London 2012 action or ceremonies on youtube.com/paralympicsporttv;
- 130 per cent growth of IPC's official Facebook group;
- four figure growth of athlete Facebook fan pages;

- 50 per cent increase in followers of Paralympic Twitter; and
- over 300,000 views of behind the scenes videos provided by athlete Samsung Bloggers.

The IPC social media policy is an example that clearly sets the boundaries and restrictions surrounding social media, without discouraging social media use. The success of the policy was demonstrated by the successful growth of the number of people following various platforms during and immediately after the Games.

each sport organization's brand. While initially claiming that these accounts were hacked, Facebook later released a statement stating they were the work of one employee that had written them as a 'stunt' and had not intended them to go public. Website Deadspin stated that the staff managing these pages were often young, and were paid well below the average wage – 'MLBAM runs all the teams' web and Facebook pages. That's a lot of responsibility – and power – put in the hands of people who apparently aren't being paid very much'. Such incidents indicate the false economy of handing over a social media page to a lowly paid intern. Pages or accounts on social media networks now constitute an important part of the brand of a sport organization and the people in charge of them are an important aspect of ensuring that the risks are limited.

The risks inherent in allowing athletes a direct voice to the world and the potential legal implications of sponsorship breaches make constructing a social media policy important. The aim of these policies and guidelines is to give both organizations and the individuals working within them a frame of reference when it comes to social media, as well as a reference point for disciplinary action. In Practice 11.2 in this chapter outlines a best practice social media policy from the International Paralympic Committee; an effective social media policy encourages the use of social networks to engage potential fans, but also ensures rules and regulations designed to protect organizational members are adhered to.

## THE FUTURE OF SOCIAL MEDIA AND SPORT

Social media networks have changed the way in which sport organizations and athletes communicate with fans, with each platform's specific features driving the way content is delivered and consumed. As new social networks are developed, we can expect sport organizations to be some of the first to engage given their history of early adoption. Two new platforms to create waves in sport at the end of 2013 included Reddit and Snapchat. Snapchat is a photo-sharing mobile application that was originally for users to send photos to other users, which would then expire after ten seconds. Sport organizations that started to use Snapchat in late 2013 included the Cleveland Cavaliers and the Philadelphia Eagles (App, 2013), while the ASP World Surfing Tour became active users in 2014, using it to send 'autographed' photographs to fans. Reddit markets itself as the 'front page of the internet' and is a form of community where users vote on content. One of its most popular features is the AMA, or Ask Me Anything, where anyone can apply to host, which has been the site of some of the most interesting celebrity discussions in recent years. In conjunction with a promotion to launch a new social command centre, NASCAR driver

Dale Earnhardt Jnr conducted a Reddit AMA in December 2013 (Ryan, 2013). The proliferation of new networks and platforms presents one of the biggest challenges for all sport organizations, as each team, athlete or coach weighs up which ones they should use. With so many different options to distribute content, deciding which platforms are the best to communicate your organization's message will be a crucial decision for anyone working within the social and digital media space within a sport organization.

Perhaps the biggest issue that will face sport organizations in the future of social and digital media is how far they go in establishing themselves as content generators. While this chapter has dealt mostly with the mechanics of social media management, the overarching issue of sport organizations' transition to content 'broadcaster' is an important one. As social and digital media has changed the access model, sport organizations will increasingly need to acknowledge and understand the responsibility they assume as primary content providers. In 2014, no professional sport organizations have cut off media access entirely, as television media rights are still a major source of revenue and facilitating access for major media organizations is an important part of delivering on the rights contract. However, some of the world's most popular sport organizations are aiming to perform more of the role typically provided by traditional media, as they develop their own distinct channels, such as Manchester United's TV station (MUTV) available on Sky, which includes:

- exclusive access to everything United – the players, the manager, the Club;
- all the match-day build up, including exclusive interviews with the players and manager, and live commentary;
- live coverage of U21 and U18 matches – see the future of United in action;
- all the United news first with hourly bulletins from Old Trafford and Carrington; and
- the opportunity to join the debate in live studio shows with legends such as Paddy Crerand, Nicky Butt, David May and Andrew Cole.

In addition to MUTV, the club now also offers MUTV Online, a highlight service available online throughout the world, with interviews, news, features, match highlights and live radio commentary on match days. It is priced at £4 per month or an annual fee of £40 per year. Initially started as a three-way partnership between the club and broadcasters ITV and SKY, Manchester United bought out both these partners to take 100 per cent control in 2013. The official press release sent by the club stated that 'This latest acquisition is a natural progression and is indicative of the club's desire to have full control of the content generating and distribution capabilities across all of its businesses'. MUTV has a staff of 60, based in offices in central Manchester, Old Trafford, with a studio at the Carrington training ground. MUTV not only allows the club to source revenue directly from fans, but also allows them to constantly set the media agenda. By conducting exclusive player interviews on this channel, the club has complete control over the editorial agenda.

The future of sport media is often unclear because of the rapid technological developments, but what appears certain is that sport organizations will continue to create and drive their own content, and use this content to set the sport media agenda. It is unclear if or when they will displace traditional media as the primary content providers, but the change to access models created by online and social media networks will be one of the defining features of the sport media nexus in the next decade.

## SUMMARY

This chapter has established that digital and social platforms have dramatically impacted the traditional access model in sports media. While sports organizations previously needed the media to disseminate their stories to their fans, social and digital media allow sports organizations to communicate *directly* with these fans. The chapter briefly described the major social media networks that have been adopted by sports organizations – Facebook, Twitter, YouTube, Instagram and Google+ – with a focus on their strengths, weaknesses and best practice for each. After reading this chapter participants should be able to prepare a social media strategy and social media content plan. This chapter also illustrated some of the inherent risks in using social media, for both sports organizations and individual athletes, and finished with an examination of the future of social and digital media in sport. Review questions and exercises are listed below to assist with confirming your knowledge of core concepts and principles introduced in this chapter.

## REVIEW QUESTIONS AND EXERCISES

1. Describe how social media has changed the sport media access model.
2. Why is it important for social media strategy to take into account the location of fans? What kind of initiatives might organizations take to ensure content is delivered to all fans?
3. What is the role of a content plan in delivering social media strategy?
4. Compare the major social media networks discussed in this chapter. If you could only pick one to use with your sport team or organization, what would it be and why?
5. What are some of the advantages and the disadvantages of a social media policy?
6. Access your favourite sport team's social media accounts, and measure how often they post, what kind of content they distribute and the amount of engagement they get. Do they have a particular tone they employ across posts and do they show 'personality'? Or, is there no evidence of an overriding strategy?
7. Pick an upcoming sport event near you and construct a content plan for that event, focusing on the detail needed behind the scenes to ensure the plan can be executed.
8. The New England Patriots have a vast amount of content on their own website. Pick a sport team in your local town or city and take a look at their website. What kind of content do they deliver? How much? How many staff do they have to deliver this content?
9. Sport organizations have been enthusiastic adopters of new social media platforms, in particular adopting Snapchat in 2013 and 2014. What are some of the elements to weigh up when deciding whether or not your organization should start an account on a new social media platform?
10. Manchester United's MUTV points to a future where sport organizations control the sport content we see. What implications will this have for fans and wider sport consumers?

## FURTHER READING

Billings, A. C. and Hardin, M. (2014) *Routledge Handbook of Sport and New Media*. London: Routledge.

Boyle, R. (2012) Reflections on communication and sport: On journalism and digital culture. *Communication and Sport, 1* (1–2), 176–187.

Hambrick, M. E., Simmons, J. M., Greenhalgh, G. P. and Greenwell, T. C. (2010) Understanding professional athletes' use of Twitter: A content analysis of athlete tweets. *International Journal of Sport Communication, 3* (4), 454–471.

Hipke, M. and Hachtmann, F. (2014) Game changer: A case study of social-media strategy in big ten athletic departments. *International Journal of Sport Communication, 7* (4), 516–532.

Hull, K. and Lewis, N. P. (2014) Why Twitter displaces broadcast sports media: A model. *International Journal of Sport Communication, 7* (1), 16–33.

Hutchins, B. (2011) The acceleration of media sport culture: Twitter, telepresence and online messaging. *Information, Communication and Society, 14* (2), 237–257.

Hutchins, B. and Mikosza, J. (2010) The Web 2.0 Olympics athlete blogging, social networking and policy contradictions at the 2008 Beijing Games. *Convergence: The International Journal of Research into New Media Technologies, 16* (3), 279–297.

Sanderson, J. (2011) To tweet or not to tweet: Exploring Division I athletic departments' social-media policies. *International Journal of Sport Communication, 4* (4), 492–513.

Sanderson, J. (2011) *It's a Whole New Ballgame: How Social Media Is Changing Sports*. Creskill, NJ: Hampton Press.

## RELEVANT WEBSITES

### Twitter

Twitter sports handle – twitter.com/twittersports
Twitter blog – blog.twitter.com/media
Kobe Bryant – twitter.com/kobebryant
LA Kings – twitter.com/LAKings
Australian Open Help – twitter.com/AOHelp
Tomas Berdych – twitter.com/tomasberdych

### YouTube

YouTube – Youtube.com
Orica GreenEdge – www.youtube.com/user/GreenEdgeCycling
NBA – www.youtube.com/nba

### Facebook

Facebook blog – https://newsroom.fb.com/
FC Barcelona – www.facebook.com/fcbarcelona

## Instagram

Instagram blog – http://blog.instagram.com/
Brooklyn Nets – http://instagram.com/brooklynnets
Kobe Bryant – http://instagram.com/kobebryant

## Google+

Google blog – http://googleblog.blogspot.com.au/
Manchester City – https://plus.google.com/+mcfcofficial/posts

## Other relevant websites

Social in Sport (case studies) – http://socialnsport.com
SportsGeek (case studies) – http://sportsgeekhq.com/
Play by the Rules – www.playbytherules.net.au/toolkits/social-media-toolkit
Manchester United – www.manutd.com/en/MUTV-New.aspx
International Paralympic Committee – www.paralympic.org
Association of Surfing Professionals – www.asp.com

## CASE STUDY

### Risk versus reward in social media – the LA Kings Twitter strategy

Sport organizations globally were quick to realize the power of social media and use it as another way to distribute key information and engage their fans. However, many sport organizations simply use these new platforms, such as Twitter, Instagram, Facebook and YouTube, to deliver content that already existed in other channels in a very straightforward way. The Los Angeles Kings Ice Hockey team in North America's National Hockey League (NHL) took a decidedly different Twitter strategy in their 2011–12 Stanley Cup play-off run. The LA Kings have played in the NHL since 1967, collecting two conference championships (1992–93 and 2011–12), and were on their way to claiming their first Stanley Cup title when their digital team went viral, all based on just one tweet. The following tweet was posted after beating the Vancouver Canucks in the first of a seven game series, in the first round of the 2011–12 play-offs:

> 'To everyone in Canada outside of BC, you're welcome'
>
> (LA Kings (@LAKings) 11 April 2012)

The tweet was crafted by Pat Donahue, second in charge of LA Kings digital media. The Club's head of digital, Dewayne Hankins, stated afterwards:

> We were so excited about the first game being won, and I see that tweet, and I'm thinking, 'OK, no matter how this ends up, this is going to be a Hall of Fame tweet' . . . We knew right away we had enraged an entire province,

> we were starting to get worried. And then they started asking the players about it.

That tweet enraged many Canucks fans, who called the LA Kings 'classless', while Vancouver newspaper journalist Cam Cole retweeted the message with the comment 'Seriously? This is a professional hockey club?'. In Canada it received negative media attention, with *The National Post* deciding on 'LA Kings troll Canucks Fans' for its headline, but elsewhere the tweet was viewed as a masterpiece of Twitter marketing. While none of their other play-off tweets gathered quite so much attention, the social media team continued to score goals throughout the post-season. One such opportunity was a stunt with actor Rainn Wilson, who played Dwight Schrute in the US version of the television comedy *The Office*. In response to his request for play-off tickets, they replied to say only if they could be delivered in a bowl of jello – a reference to an *Office* skit from the pilot episode.

> *@rainnwilson* We can give you tickets – if you let us deliver them to you in a bowl of jello.
>
> (LA Kings (@LAKings) 16 May 2012)

The LA Kings delivered on their promise, which led to widespread media coverage of the initial ticket delivery, which was done by LA Kings legend Luc Robitaille. Wilson's live-tweeting of the subsequent match against the Phoenix Coyotes helped to create even more Twitter engagement. In a world in which sport organizations typically repeat the status quo, technology website Mashable stated:

> The NHL's Los Angeles Kings, however, are tearing that playbook to bits—and it's working. The Kings' Twitter account and social media team have an unabashedly biased voice, regularly poke fun at opposing teams' fans and hometowns and pull comedic stunts other pro sports teams would likely deem too lively.

The @LAKings went on to win the Stanley Cup and the Twitter ratings. Across the play-off series, there were 1.4 million @LAKings mentions – almost 800,000 more than the any other Stanley Cup play-off team – and 146 per cent growth (100,000 followers) in two months.

As Hankins explained to ice hockey journalist Greg Wyshynski, the LA Kings' unique position in the market – as the fourth or fifth choice team in a city bursting with the LA Lakers, LA Clippers, LA Dodgers and Anaheim Angels, as well as MLS team the LA Galaxy, and the fact that ice hockey isn't a usual choice of sport for California's sunny climate – meant they could afford to do something different. Hankins said:

> Part of the deal for me coming in was that if we're going to do this, we're going to go all-in. Be different. Be unique. In LA, you can do that. We're the little brother of the other four or five teams here, so we gotta do something

> to be entertaining. If you're a different team, you can't do this. The Lakers can't. Not to the extent that we can.

But this doesn't mean that the LA Kings' social media posts, in particular via Twitter, were off the cuff. While the Vancouver tweet went down as one of the biggest sport social media wins in 2012, Hankins revealed it was actually crafted on the back of Canadiens, who were not Canucks fans, tweeting them. 'You go back to the Vancouver tweet, and that doesn't happen if we didn't have Oilers fans and Flames fans and Canadians fans all tweeting us and telling us that we're "Canada's team" in the play-offs,' said Hankins (Wyshynski, 2012).

Yet the Kings' use of social media hasn't always been positively received. Another key engagement strategy used by the Kings has been to have Twitter takeovers, where star guests would take control of the handle for a period of a game. In 2013 this backfired when local radio shock jock Kevin Ryder, a co-host of LA radio station KROQ's *Kevin and Bean* show, took to the helm. He took over the Kings' Twitter page as a promotion during its play-off matchup against the San Jose Sharks and compared a tackle to sexual assault. The tweet was quickly deleted and the LA Kings issued an apology later.

> We apologize for the tweets that came from a guest of our organization. They were inappropriate and do not reflect the LA Kings
>
> (LA Kings (@LAKings) 21 May 2013)

While Hankins has since moved on to the Portland Trailblazers in the NBA, Donahue still likes to keep the LAKings Twitter account edgy, as emphasized by their profile tagline. In May 2014, the Kings Twitter account stated 'Just a quick note, we apologize for any future tweets that might offend you'.

## CASE STUDY QUESTIONS

1 What are some of the elements that made the @LAKings Twitter account so popular?
2 The LA Kings digital director DeWayne Hankins stated that the LA Lakers couldn't use the same strategy. Why is this? Are there any benefits to an established and popular team taking an edgier social media strategy?
3 Could anything have prevented the incident with the Kevin Ryder Twitter Takeover?
4 Why is strategy and research so important in delivering effective social media posts?

Sources: Laird (2012a, 2012b); LA Kings (2012a, 2012b, 2013).

CHAPTER 12

# Major sport event media management

## Controlling the chaos

*Chris Gottaas*

## OVERVIEW

This chapter examines the facilities and services provided to media working at international major sporting events. Specifically, the chapter explores the types of workspaces that need to be made available to journalists and the role they play in assisting media to effectively report on sport. This chapter also examines the role of the media liaison and the various positions pre, during and post event that contribute to the overall success of media operations.

## LEARNING OUTCOMES

After completing this chapter the reader should be able to:

- understand the various facilities and services available to media at major sport events;
- understand the significance of well-planned and operated services and facilities to deliver effective and efficient media operations;
- devise a media operations plan for local, national and international sport events to maximize the potential for media coverage; and
- evaluate the success of media operations following an event.

## INTRODUCTION

The Olympics are the biggest sporting event in the world and attract more than 10,000 athletes from more than 200 National Olympic Committees (NOCs), competing in 26 sports, every four years. As noted in previous chapters in this book, interest in the Olympics goes far beyond athletes, coaches, support staff and their respective NOCs;

the Olympics reaches out through its media and broadcasting to more than two-thirds of the world's population. Along with the FIFA World Cup, the Olympics is a global mega-event. Over the last hundred years and the since the 1980s in particular, the Olympics has evolved to meet public and media interest and is now a major exercise in planning and logistics. For example, at the London 2012 Olympic Games there were 18,600 media and broadcast personnel accredited to cover the 17 days of competition, nearly twice the number of athletes competing. A total of 5,600 media were represented, from a record breaking 172 nations, while 13,000 broadcasters provided more than 100,000 hours of Games coverage to 4.8 billion people around the world. The media and broadcast personnel at events such as the Olympics require specialized and sophisticated facilities, operational practices and support in order to be successful.

Intricate planning, preparation and delivery of major sport events ensures event media are able to work effectively and efficiently, delivering live coverage, editorial stories and images to all corners of the globe. The needs of media personnel working at major sport events are the same regardless of whether the event is a major international multi-sport competition (such as the 2016 Olympic Games in Rio, Brazil or the 2018 Asian Games in Jakarta, Indonesia), world championship event (such as the 2015 FINA World Championships in Kazan, Russia) or domestic competition (such as the 2016 NFL Super Bowl in Santa Clara, California, US). While the level and detail of services provided to the media and broadcast personnel will vary between these events and tournaments, working media will require a minimum of access, appropriate workspaces, access to talent and the ability to file a story in order to adequately perform their job. It is essential that the media operations at major sport events take these needs into consideration in undertaking planning and implementation of an event. During the planning process consideration must be given to how many media will attend the event, because this will dictate the size of media centres, the number of accreditations and the services available through the media operations team. For example, the World Men's Curling Championship in Basel, Switzerland in 2016 shouldn't plan spaces and services for 10,000 media representatives based on previous experiences at the 2014 Championships in Beijing or the 2015 Championships in Halifax, while the 2016 Summer Olympic Games in Rio *must* prepare to service double that amount based on experience of previous events such as the London 2012 Olympics or the 2014 FIFA World Cup, also held in Brazil. The importance of media operations extends beyond the services provided to journalists, for its success, or lack of, can have a significant impact on relationships with media organizations, which in turn can have an impact on the public perception of an event. Well-executed media operations can positively promote a sporting organization's image while a poorly delivered plan can be damaging to the brand and image of the organization.

An example of how press operations can directly affect the brand or image of the organization is detailed in Gratton (1999), who explained the shambolic press operations at the Atlanta 1996 Olympic Games. Some of the problems included:

- a Main Press Centre (MPC) too small to accommodate the number of media. At just 27,000 square metres it was smaller than Barcelona (51,000) and Seoul (35,000). News agencies that would normally have space were denied access;
- the Main Media Centre (MMC) was across two buildings, and the media were not the sole occupants, meaning it was hard to regulate accredited people;

- the fit-out was lacking, with aluminium framework three metres high supporting panels of composite that were four millimetres thick. They were not strong, not secure and had very poor sound quality;
- the venue hosted an event up to three days beforehand, which gave event staff only 66 hours to bump in;
- the much touted new information system failed to provide the promised flow of results and INFO computer terminals to the MPC from competition;
- IBM feeds to agencies were initially non-existent, and in some cases inaccurate;
- the pigeonhole system didn't work because there was no notification system;
- there were issues with cabling, networking and phone installation;
- the TV feed in the MPC had no sound;
- the sound feed from on-site news conferences was of poor quality;
- the main workroom had tabled 600 work stations, but there was only room for about 500 and the lines of tables were too close together;
- there were complaints about the food from the only in-house café;
- the MPC was too far to walk to venues and also too far from the free shuttle bus hub, which created further logistical issues: 'the media usually took a shuttle bus from the MPC to the hub in order to take another bus to a competition venue . . . Journalists told of how they were not allowed to leave buses outside the MPC, even when it was their ultimate destination, because the bus in question had to deliver them to the notorious hub, where they would then have to catch another bus back to the MPC';
- and finally, media were housed in nearly 40 different accommodation venues.

Gratton, the Main Media Centre manager of the Sydney Olympic Games, emphasized that media reports from Atlanta helped to cement its status further as the worst modern Olympics, because 'the international media, more than any other group, help to define the reputation of an Olympics in the short term'. Newspaper headlines included 'IBM's Atlanta Games becomes Olympic Debacle', 'Tin-pot organisation wins Atlanta the wooden spoon', and 'Welcome to the nightmare', while Roy Eccelston of the *Australian* newspaper stated, 'Remember the fact that while the Games is about the athletes and spectators, it is the journalists whose impressions will form world opinion. Atlanta treated journalists down the scale of importance and got universal criticism'. Gratton detailed how the Sydney Olympic media operations team, led by respected former foreign correspondent Richard Palfreyman and a team of staff with news backgrounds, learned from these mistakes to deliver press services that were widely praised and helped contribute to the Sydney 2000 Olympic Games' reputation as one of the best in the event's history. In doing so, they created a blueprint for modern day press operations.

Media operations and their various services and facilities have three distinct phases: pre-competition, in-competition and post-competition. The pre-competition phase, which includes planning and preparation, includes detailed research in order to understand the event, competition or tournament, as well as establishing the media's requirements, including scoping services, facilities and accreditation procedures. During the in-competition phase, media work spaces, including tribunes and media centres, are operational, while media personnel require access to official scoring, timing and results. During the post-competition phase journalists conduct interviews and source quotes from athletes, coaches and administrators via media conferences and mixed zones, often as soon as possible after

the end of the games to ensure media meet deadlines. All three of the phases are crucial to successful media operations at a major sport event. Each of these phases and the different elements that comprise successful media operations at a major sport event will now be discussed in the following sections.

## ACCREDITATION

A media accreditation system ensures that appropriately qualified and eligible media have secure and reliable access to facilities, resources and event personnel, in order to perform their professional roles. Accreditation, which is granted free of charge, is a tool to manage a large number of people, while facilitating their movement in a secure fashion. The success of a media accreditation system depends on the planning, execution and management of the accreditation process. Successful implementation of a media accreditation process requires consideration of time frames, scoping the quota of accreditations, production of passes and distribution of accreditation passes. The event size, venues, security and number of media are all factors that influence the type and scope of the accreditation system, which can vary between a basic process for local events to complex systems for international major events. For smaller community events, the accreditation process may simply be a list of names on a guest list and the presentation of an identification tag upon arrival. For major global events such as an Olympic Games, accreditation includes a headshot and comprehensive security features. An accreditation system requires a series of connected stages to be well managed, as outlined below:

1. *Scoping the workspace capacity*. This is to establish how many media can be expected, and accommodated. For example, it would not be an effective use of resources to accommodate for 50 journalists when only five are expected to attend, or vice versa, when 5,000 journalists are expected making accommodations for 50. There are some ways to determine how many media are expected, including examining similar events, examining previous years' events and working with international or national federations to establish how many media are likely to attend (particularly to events such as a world championship).
2. *Developing an application process*. In the twenty-first century, this mostly happens online, with an online form sent to media organizations. An important step is ensuring you collect the correct information, such as name, media organization, contact details, type of media (i.e. broadcast, print, magazine), and event specific information such as days of an international series they will actually attend. For example, Cricket Australia control the accreditation for Australian matches but, given the geographic distance between venues, not all journalists are likely to travel with the team to cover all matches. Often accreditation passes are for a series, not match specific, which makes it important to identify what matches journalists will attend in order to accommodate them. It is important at this stage to also ask for the journalist's media organization and contact details for an editor. In the past, paper applications usually included a written letter from an editor to support a journalist's accreditation, to ensure that only qualified journalists from recognized media organizations were able to obtain accreditation. In the new media world, some high-profile blogs may be

granted media accreditation. Generally, the aim of media operations is to facilitate as much media coverage as possible, and the number of media accredited is determined by the size of the media facilities available.

3 *Approving accreditations*. Decisions to approve or deny accreditation applications are based on a number of factors, illustrated by the previous discussion, such as how many journalists can be accommodated and which media organizations they represent. However, it is important to note that at some major events the media operations manager will not directly approve accreditation. For example, National Olympic Committees determine the allocation of media accreditation for each Olympic Games. The National Olympic Committees are granted a quota of media accreditations and it is their responsibility to allocate and approve media accreditation applications within their country. In the event that demand exceeds capacity, applications need to be prioritized based on readership, reach, profile, rights holders and working media. For example, a major metropolitan newspaper should be given priority over a small blog.
4 *Production of accreditation passes*. At some smaller events, a generic accreditation pass may be produced by the media team, which simply states a category of accreditation (i.e. media, photographer or broadcaster). For major events such as a FIFA World Cup or Olympic Games, the accreditations include photo identification, full names and sometimes passport information, and security measures (to ensure they cannot be counterfeited), and are produced by a centralized department that takes care of all accreditation pass production, including those for athletes, coaches and officials. Accreditation pass security measures usually include barcodes, holographic elements and security chips. These measures are taken because of the complex nature of accreditations and security needed at a major event. At these major events passes will be digitally scanned upon entry to each venue to manage access. At a major event accreditations may be segmented into specific categories that make it clear what role each specific accredited individual is performing. The different needs of various media need to be taken into account when determining access to media workspaces. For example, a print journalist does not require access to photo positions, while rights-holding broadcasters' privileges need to be protected.
5 *Distribution of passes*. The distribution of accreditation passes is an important process to consider, because while some accreditations might be available for collection once media personnel arrive at the location, at other major international events the accreditation will also act as a visa for entry into the country. For the Nanjing 2014 Youth Olympic Games, accreditation passes for international media were shipped approximately two months before the Games and acted as a visa for media attending. This allowed media to bypass the usual visa application process. This type of distribution obviously has implications for the planning process, as the accreditation applications must be submitted, approved, produced and shipped months before the event start date. This process also involves the cost of distributing accreditation passes, as they must be sent by courier and tracked appropriately. For events where media are predominantly local, accreditation collection points may be provided for media to collect their accreditation pass and as such production can be completed in the days prior to the event.

6 *Access control at events*. Controlling access at major events is important for media who require access to venues and for media who require access to media workspaces, such as photo positions. Event and security staff need to be briefed on the appearance of accreditation passes and the various accreditation access categories, in order to control and facilitate access. For example, photographers may be allowed on the sidelines of an English Premier League game in order to undertake their work, but print journalists will only have access to the press workspaces. Constant monitoring of access is particularly important in major high-demand events, in order to monitor capacity and maintain the quality and availability of media workspaces.

International events such as the Olympic Games offer a variety of accreditation categories to assist with the management and access of media (Table 12.1). These different categories enforce what different types of media are allowed to do within the event's official spaces. For example, ENRs are non-rights holding broadcasters and cannot record any action or interviews from within official competition venues, with the only exception being the main media conference room at the main media centre. This is to protect the broadcast rights of those organizations who have paid for the right to broadcast the event. As such, the accreditation of media is important for ensuring not only reliable and secure access for media personnel working at the event, but also that the policies, practices and commercial regulations of the event are adhered to.

**TABLE 12.1** IOC media accreditation categories

| *Code* | *Description* |
|---|---|
| **E** | Journalist: journalist, editor, photographic editor, employed or contracted by a world news agency, a national agency, a general daily newspaper, a sports daily, a sports magazine or sports internet site, a periodical or independent/freelance journalist under contract. |
| **Es** | Sport specific journalist: journalist specializing in a sport on the Olympic Games programme, meeting the same criteria as those defined for category 'E'. |
| **EP** | Photographer: photographer, meeting the same criteria as those defined for category 'E'. |
| **EPs** | Sport specific photographer: photographer specializing in a sport on the Olympic Games programme, meeting the same criteria as those defined for category 'E'. |
| **ET** | Technician: technician, meeting the same criteria as those defined for category 'E'. |
| **EC** | Support staff: support staff (office assistant, secretary, interpreter, driver, messenger). Access to the MPC only. Assigned only to media groups, newspapers/magazines and NOCs that have reserved a private office area at the MPC. |
| **ENR** | Non-rights holding broadcast organization: member of a non-rights holding radio and/or television organization. ENR accreditations are only allocated by the IOC. It is strictly prohibited for an NOC to grant a member of an ENR organization any type of E accreditation. |

Source: IOC website at www.olympic.org.

## MEDIA CENTRE

A media centre is a physical space reserved for media personnel. For large global sport events, such as the Olympic Games or the FIFA World Cup, a media centre is likely to be constructed specially for media organizations and personnel, based on technical specifications. During a major sport event the media centre is a dedicated space in which media personnel such as journalists and photographers can work 24 hours a day, acting as a hub of vital resources and services necessary to allow media personnel to successfully compile and transmit their coverage from a major event. The size, services and facilities of media centres are dictated by the nature of the event and number of accredited media. It is not uncommon for media personnel to cover major sport events without leaving the media centre. This illustrates the importance of the media to major sport events, the ways in which advances in technology have allowed the media coverage of major sport events to become more 'remote' and the significance of a well-organized and resourced workspace for media personnel at major sport events.

### Main media centre

The primary venue dedicated to accredited media located in event host cities, the main media centre offers organizations and individuals a central location from which to cover the major event. The main media centre not only provides journalists with workspaces, but it also has media services such as transport and accommodation help-desks, photography services, tourist information, IT support, lounge areas, lockers, cafés and restaurants, and retail outlets including a post office, pharmacy, telecommunications providers and souvenir shops. For large-scale organizations, the main media centre should offer a location at which they can set up remote offices for editorial teams, including chiefs of staff, editors, sub editors, picture editors, journalists and photographers. These office spaces are typically hired by major news organizations. For example, the 2014 Commonwealth Games in Glasgow had offices for AAP, NewsCorp, BBC, Fairfax, Reuters, AP and Getty Images located within the main media centre. For individuals, the main media centre provides a dedicated workspace, including desks, power and an internet connection, but these spaces are provided on a first come, first served basis in contrast to the dedicated spaces available to major media organizations. The main media centre at the London 2012 Olympics was a 24-hour hub catering for 5,600 journalists and photographers. Depending on the event, the main media centre can include media conference facilities, interview rooms, televisions with live feeds, official scoring, timing and results. Not all major events feature a main media centre, however, as these facilities are often reserved for events with multiple venues across cities and countries.

### Venue media centre

Depending on the nature of the event, a venue media centre can serve as the main media centre, particularly for events that are hosted at a single primary venue within the host city, such as the Netball World Cup. Regardless of the event, venue based media centres serve the same purpose as the main media centre, offering similar facilities and services for accredited media personnel, but often on a smaller scale. The primary advantage of a

venue based media centre for working journalists and photographers is to be able to file directly from the venue. Instead of watching the 100m final at an Olympic Games and having to make the journey back to the main media centre, journalists, photographers and broadcasters can deliver their stories, pictures and packages directly from the venue, ensuring a faster workflow, which means that the stories, images and footage of the events can reach the world faster.

### International broadcast centre

For large scale international major events, such as the Olympics and FIFA World Cup, a dedicated venue is provided to host broadcasters, typically referred to as the International Broadcast Centre (IBC). Often mirroring the facilities and services offered at the main media centre, the IBC is the temporary hub for rights holding broadcasters during major events. Conference centres are converted into broadcast studios, where the host broadcaster provides live video and audio feeds from every venue, along with colour shots and transmission facilities. In most cases, the IBC needs to cater for even larger media staff than a main media centre, due to the size of broadcast crews. For example, the London Olympics catered for approximately 5,600 journalists and photographers, and around 13,000 broadcast staff.

## TRIBUNES

Media personnel often require a place from which to view the game, match or contest at the same time they are working, which has led to the development of tribunes. Tribunes are media workspaces with uninterrupted view of the field of play and other important information (such as the scoreboard). Tribunes come in two forms – 'tabled' or 'untabled'; a tabled tribune is an active workspace from which media are able to file stories and images, whereas an untabled tribune is simply a space for accredited media to view the event. Located either next to the field of play, such as courtside in basketball, or further up in the grandstand for sports such as rugby union or football, tabled tribunes provide accredited media personnel with a desk, power and internet connection, so that they are able to cover the event more easily. In order to create a tabled tribune for a major event, grandstand seating usually reserved for paying spectators is removed and replaced with purpose built tables to facilitate the requirements of the media. In addition to power and internet, which are necessary to compile and transmit media coverage, tabled tribunes may also feature televisions with a host broadcast feed, providing replays and statistics to media personnel. In some instances, media organizations or outlets will organize for dedicated phone lines to be installed, via the rate card service, at a dedicated tribune seat, in order to provide their journalists with a dedicated phone line to file copy or speak with editorial staff.

In addition to providing the media with a workspace, tabled tribunes can also feature host broadcast commentary positions, where existing venue broadcast facilities may not cope with the demand. The tribunes also house the primary broadcast positions. These positions are located in the last rows of the tribune, are separated by fibreglass screens and feature the necessary equipment to commentate the event, including a live broadcast feed from the host broadcaster and a feed of live statistics.

## IN PRACTICE 12.1

### The city as a field of play – media operations for triathlon

Most sport events take place in a stadium, where the field of play is in view for the entire duration of the sporting event. In these cases, the media operations is usually fairly static, such as for an English Premier League match, an NBA game, a Grand Slam tennis tournament or even an Australian Rules football match. At these events the media box (a location for a tabled tribune) will be in the same location for every match, the photo positions will not change, and the flow of journalists to the rooms for the post-match media commitments will be predictable. However, there are a number of international sports where the field of play is not static. Events such as major marathons, road cycling events and triathlons all fall within this category, in which there are no purpose-built spaces where the event takes place; instead these events make use of public roads, parks and even lakes. As such, the media operations at these types of events require detailed planning, which sets them apart from standard venue-static sports. For example, in almost all stages of the Tour de France (other than time trials), the stage will start and finish in a different location. At each location there must be a dedicated media centre, and usually there is transport provided for media, in the form of a media bus, to get journalists and photographers from one end to the other, as well as media bikes for broadcasters to capture footage of the race.

The media operations for a major International Triathlon Union event are complicated further because of the fact that triathlon is made up of three disciplines, and has two transitions where athletes switch from the swim to the bike, and then the bike to the run. Provisions must be made for photographers on each 'stage' to have access to the course. In the swim stage this is usually in the form of a media boat, while on the bike and run stages this could include a dedicated motorbike for pool photographers, photo positions on the course for other accredited photographers, and media transport for photographers and journalists to get to these positions. Usually most of the action happens in transition, so a dedicated media lane is positioned between the racks of bikes, allowing broadcasters and photographers to easily transmit the action.

A final further complicating factor is that photographers and broadcasters must often share the same pathways on course, so enforcing protocol is an important part of triathlon media operations. For example, the swim start is often from a pontoon in a lake. The number of photographers the pontoon can hold needs to be assessed beforehand, and then enforced, so that risk is mitigated. After the swim start, photographers then have the option to stay on the pontoon to shoot the swim exit, or walk up the shared athlete pathway to the first transition. If photographers miss this opportunity, they are unable to get to transition.

Media tribunes may include additional untabled seating, or overflow, for accredited media not requiring the need to file directly from the tribune. Located in close proximity to the tabled tribunes and the venue media centre, an untabled tribune still requires an uninterrupted view of the field of play, access to power and internet. When planning a tribune, proximity to the mixed zone, media workroom, media conference and other venue-based media facilities must be taken into consideration.

## MIXED ZONE

An official media conference usually doesn't take place until at least half an hour after the game, match or competition has ended, which means that any emotion that is present directly afterwards is often lost. For coaches and athletes who have lost an important contest this is probably a good thing, but the time between the end of the game or match and the start of a media conference present a problem for media personnel. Media deadlines will have passed during this 'dead' media time, newspapers may have gone to print, a story may have appeared online and live television broadcasts will have finished. At major events, the 'dead' media time between the end of the competition and the start of the media conference has been solved by the creation of what is called the 'mixed zone'. The mixed zone is essentially a highly controlled physical space in which athletes and the media are able to interact immediately after the conclusion of competition. At major sport events these mixed zones are located as close as possible to the finish line or field of play exit, ensuring an efficient exit for athletes and as much as possible access for media. Importantly, the mixed zone provides media personnel with an opportunity to capture and document the emotion of the event directly after an athlete has left the pool, track or pitch.

The location and size of the mixed zone are the most important elements that contribute to whether it will be considered as useful or successful for athletes and media. The mixed zone at a major sport event must offer sufficient space for athletes to pass through in a safe and controlled manner. It is important to note that athletes at major championships are not required to speak to the media, but rather are given the option or opportunity to do so. Although many will be happy to engage with the media in the mixed zone, some will want to proceed directly to the warm down facilities or the change-rooms. The mixed zone must be big enough for athletes who do not wish to speak to the media to pass through without feeling threatened or pressured by the physical presence or proximity of the media. In most major sport event mixed zones athletes and media personnel are separated by a barrier, such as bollards or temporary fencing; athletes pass by on one side of the mixed zone, not accessible to the media, while the media conduct their interviewing, filming and recording from the other side within designated areas. At international major sport events, the media side of the mixed zone is divided into broadcast and print sections with interviews conducted in that order. Rights holding broadcasters are allocated broadcast pens, complete with appropriate lighting, to conduct live or pre-recorded interviews with athletes. The media section of the mixed zone is typically separated into two further sections, with world news agencies and the event news service given priority access to athletes for interview before accredited media and photographers in the remaining section. The following list shows the mixed zone order of access at the Olympic Games, based on the IOC technical manual (IOC, 2005):

*Broadcast section*

1 host broadcaster;
2 live unilateral television and radio rights-holders;
3 electronic News Gathering rights-holders;

*Media section*

4 IOC-recognised world news agencies;
5 host national news agency;
6 press;
7 photographers.

Important factors in designing and implementing a mixed zone at a major sport event include athlete and media flow, proximity to spectators, proximity to broadcast and print workspaces, noise interference and broadcast background. These factors will all contribute to an effective mixed zone, which will encourage athletes to engage with the media. According to Olympic and Commonwealth Games guidelines, all athletes must pass through the mixed zone when leaving the field of play. While athletes are strongly encouraged to participate in interviews, they are not obligated to stop and answer questions. It is clear that the mixed zone is a potential flashpoint for problems between athletes and the media, but can be very successful if media personnel respect the athletes, who may be experiencing extreme emotion or fatigue immediately following competition, and competitors respect the media's role in covering the event and providing publicity for the athletes and their sport. At Olympic Games this process is managed by a mixed zone supervisor, whose job is to make sure the mixed zone operates efficiently, with assistance from teams' media managers.

Additional provisions should be considered for the management of high-profile athletes in the mixed zone, including a dedicated space, risers, elevated platforms or amplifying devices to ensure the athlete can be seen and heard. Additional services that may be included depending on the size and scope of the event are televisions in sections of the mixed zone that don't have sight of the field of play or finish line, power, a Wi-Fi internet connection and competition information screens. Mixed zones may be operational at training venues under the same conditions.

## MEDIA CONFERENCE FACILITIES

In addition to mixed zones, media conference facilities provide another designated area in which media personnel can interview athletes and officials. Depending on the size of the sport event, dedicated media conference rooms may be located at the main media centre, the athletes' village and competition venues. Although the way in which media conference facilities are set up remains constant, the size, capacity and services of media conference rooms vary based on event type, the number and type of accredited media and the capacity of the venue's media facility. It is important to recognize that media conference facilities differ from mixed zones on the basis of their formality. While mixed zones can, to the untrained eye, appear as organized chaos governed by few rules, a media conference

## IN PRACTICE 12.2

### Solutions to extreme demand at the Olympics

As of 2014, Michael Phelps is the greatest Olympian of all time, with a total of 18 gold medals, two silver medals and two bronze medals. At the Beijing 2008 Olympic Games the American made his mark, winning an Olympic record eight gold medals and breaking seven world records. ESPN columnist Pat Forde wrote then that 'Michael Phelps single-handedly saved the Olympics. These Beijing Olympics, and perhaps those to come. The entire enterprise has new life' (Forde, 2008). But Phelps' record-breaking performance also exposed an issue for the media operations, as the demand for access to Phelps meant that only a small portion of the journalists that wanted to get a quote from Phelps post-race were able to do so. While the media crammed into the mixed zone, only a very limited number could get close enough to hear and record what was said. The solution was to have a portable microphone and speaker placed near Phelps when he came to the general media section of the mixed zone, which would amplify his voice (and therefore the valuable quotes) to the journalists out of earshot. This simple solution meant that while journalists couldn't ask a question, they could still hear what was being said, which gave them valuable access to content required to perform their jobs. The solution put in place to cater for the demand for Phelps is now a standard procedure in most major event mixed zones.

The Olympics are the single-largest sport media event in the world and the demand sometimes, as with the Phelps example, leads to creative solutions to problems. For example, at the London 2012 Olympic Games, the main media conference room was designed to accommodate 700 journalists; however, during the US men's basketball pre-Games media conference an additional breakout session was held immediately after. While the media conference satisfied most journalist needs, the breakout session was required to facilitate additional interviews with individual athletes. A selection of players, including NBA superstars Kobe Bryant, LeBron James and Kevin Durant, were initially available on stage for the media conference. But after the formal media conference proceedings, all players were made available and to avoid congestion, were put in different areas of the room. Some remained on stage while journalists gathered below, while others moved to smaller broadcast platforms and others stood in separate corners. The examples of Michael Phelps at the 2008 Olympics and the US men's basketball team at the 2012 Olympics illustrate that media operations at major sport events must conduct planning and forecast demand, but must also be prepared to be flexible and implement creative solutions to ensure the media and athletes are satisfied with the experience.

by contrast is a formal gathering of media personnel. Media conferences typically consist of a raised table and chairs for athletes, coaches and administrators and sufficient seating for media organized in rows. Media conference facilities can range from a basic set-up, with tables and chairs arranged in a standard room, to complex mini-events conducted in a theatre with broadcast integration and audio splitters, Wi-Fi and language services.

The largest media conference room at a major sport event can typically be found at the main media centre (MMC), where accredited journalists, rights-holding broadcasters and non-rights holding broadcasters have access in order to record audio and video. According to the IOC's Technical Manual on Media, the primary media conference room at the MMC should include the following: seating capacity for at least 700 journalists; raised podium or stage for athletes, coaches and administrators, including table, chairs, microphones and headsets for 15 people; separate platform for photographers and broadcasters with direct sightlines, broadcast lighting; and simultaneous interpreters. At a summer Olympics it is mandatory that interpretation services include English, French, Arabic, Chinese, Korean, German, Italian, Japanese, Portuguese, Russian and Spanish. The largest media conference room is complemented by small media conference rooms at the MMC that feature a raised platform for athletes, coaches and officials and a separate platform for broadcasters, in addition to microphones and audio splitter for broadcast, branding and chairs. A moderator is responsible for the conduct, duration and order of media conferences. At an Olympics, media conferences, typically held following the mixed zone and warm down, at the conclusion of events and require the attendance of the three medallists. Additional media conferences may be held at other times during the competition, for example following round robin and semi-final matches in team events, should the media's demand for athletes and coaches warrant an additional opportunity.

## NEWS SERVICE

A news service is essentially the official communications channel of the event organizer and has become a standard fixture of all major events in the twenty-first century. The event news service provides accredited media with up-to-date information, results, news, flash quotes and statistics, as a way of helping them effectively report on the event and its activities. The news service at an Olympic Games is available to all accredited media at the main media centre, the IBC, the venue media centres, the village and increasingly online via a remote web portal. The Olympic News Service, which provides unbiased, balanced coverage, is mostly staffed by professional writers and editors. The news service documents every event, all media conferences that occur at the main media centre and highlights from mixed zones. It provides support for media personnel who are unable to be in every venue at the same time, as well as providing the official record of the Games. The news service is also typically used as a portal for the organizing committee to issue official communications. In the case of the Olympics this is from the IOC, NOCs or the international sport federations.

There are various types of information and content provided by the news service:

- scoring, timing and results – the news service serves is the source for all official scores, times and results from the event;
- flash quotes – quotes collected from athletes in the mixed zone immediately following competition. Collected by flash quote reporters, these quotes are usually recorded by listening to the interviews with the official rights holding broadcasters;
- previews and reviews – sport specific previews and reviews for each event and game. These are always independent and tell the story of the event;

- media conference highlights – similar to flash quotes, these are quotes from athletes, coaches and officials, recorded at official media conferences;
- colour stories – these are human interest colour feature pieces that do not focus on the event but on personal stories that might be of use to media personnel covering the event;
- general news stories – non-sports specific news from the event;
- biographies – profiles of all athletes, coaches and teams competing at the event; and
- historical results – facts, figures and results from previous events.

Some news services have recently provided content for the official event website, for example the 2011 Rugby World Cup news service wrote stories for use by media but these also appeared on the website at rugbyworldcup.com.

## RATE CARD

The 'rate card' at major sport events is essentially the opportunity for media organizations and rights holding broadcasters to rent furniture, equipment and services essential to their coverage of major events. The rate card, organized by the media operations division in conjunction with broadcast operations, is predominantly available at international major events such as Olympic and Commonwealth Games. The goods and services, which come at a cost to organizations, are made available to facilitate the media and broadcasters' ability to cover the event at a high standard, ensuring maximum exposure for the event. Rate card facilities and resources range from the ability to rent dedicated and private office spaces at the main media centre, international broadcast centre or venue media centres, to telecommunications equipment, technology, office equipment, vehicles and parking permits.

The rate card service provides media organizations with a one-stop shop to rent all the necessary equipment and services at cost price, which would otherwise be costly and difficult to coordinate for visiting outlets. Organized years in advance, rate card purchases, such as office space, can have a significant impact on the planning of media facilities, including the layout of the main media centre, and require temporary building, delivery and setup.

## ACCOMMODATION AND TRANSPORT

Media operations at a major sport event often encompass more than ensuring the media personnel have access to the venues and media facilities and facilitating the interactions between media personnel and athletes. At almost all international major sport events, media operations also include accommodation and transport. It is the responsibility of the organizing committee to ensure there is enough suitable accommodation for all accredited media, provided at a reasonable cost and in close proximity to major venues. In some rare instances, a clustered media village may replace hotel accommodation. For example, at the Guangzhou 2010 Asian Games, media were accommodated within a custom built media village, located next to the MMC. This village was also close to the athletes' village and technical official village.

According to the IOC, at least 10 per cent of accommodation should be within walking distance of the MMC or IBC at an Olympic Games and media accommodation must provide minimum standards such as:

- 24-hour catering;
- parking;
- laundry; and
- room amenities such as bathroom, kettle, minibar, phone and internet access.

A dedicated transport network is also often available for accredited media and rights holding broadcasters at major sport events, which is provided in the form of a free service that acts as a link between the main media centre and international broadcaster centre with competition venues, athletes' village, official media accommodation and airport. It is important that the transport service meets the demands of the media, and as such the timing of the service and its likely demand should be taken into consideration when planning the network and frequency. Where possible, the transportation network should operate from bubble to bubble, meaning that the accredited media should only require security screening at the point of departure and arrive within secure confines at the arrival destination.

## STAFFING

Staffing for media operations varies at each event depending on the services, workspaces and capacity. For example, it may be possible for one person to manage media operations at a state championship; however, a world championships would require a team of managers, coordinators and volunteers. Typically, a head of media operations oversees the various functions at a major event, while each venue will have a dedicated venue-based media operations manager. Within each venue, a supervisor and team of volunteers will manage the various media workspaces including the venue media centre, mixed zone, press conference room, tribune and photo positions. Along with venue specific staff, other roles at a major event include rate card manager, media transportation manager, news service manager, along with editors and writers, and photo manager. Additional volunteers may assist with the distribution of scoring, timing and results documents in the tribunes, organize journalists in the mixed zone and provide help and assistance to media in each workspace. It is important to ensure venues, workspaces and services are well staffed to ensure an effective and successful media operations.

## SUMMARY

This chapter has included an overview of all the elements necessary to service the media at a major sporting event, including accreditation, tribunes, mixed zones, media conferences, media centres, accommodation, rate cards and media transportation, as well as the specific needs of photographers at an event. This chapter illustrates that servicing the media at a major event requires detailed planning and execution, and is paramount to the success of the overall event.

## REVIEW QUESTIONS AND EXERCISES

1 Why is media operations an important component in delivering a major sports event?
2 Think about a state championship, a national championships and a world championship, and work out a strategy for determining how many journalists you might need to accredit. How are they different?
3 Why would you include a headshot on an accreditation pass?
4 What controls would you put in place to manage access to the various media spaces at a major event or Games?
5 What facilities and services would an international journalist require at a main media centre?
6 Why is it important to have the media tribune, mixed zone, venue media centre and press conference room in close proximity?
7 A high-profile athlete has entered the mixed zone. What media commitments are they expected to fulfil? How is it managed?
8 How do mixed zones and media conferences differ for the media?
9 As a member of the media, what kind of information do you think you would need to access from a news service?
10 Pick your favourite sport and identify the best photo positions. In particular, think about what element of the sport is most attractive to photographers, and how many might be able to fit in a certain area.

## FURTHER READING

Billings, A. C. (2008) *Olympic Media: Inside the Biggest Show on Television*. New York: Routledge.

Gratton, R. (1999) Managing the media. In R. I. Cashman and A. Hughes (eds) *Staging the Olympics: The Event and Its Impact* (121–131). Sydney: University of New South Wales Press.

MacNeill, M. (1996) Networks: Producing Olympic ice hockey for a national television audience. *Sociology of Sport Journal, 13* (2), 103–124.

Miah, A. and Jones, J. (2012) The Olympic movement's new media revolution: Monetization, Open Media and Intellectual Property. In H. J. Lenskyj and S. Wagg (eds). *The Palgrave Handbook of Olympic Studies* (274–288). Basingstoke: Palgrave Macmillan.

Rivenburgh, N. (2002) The Olympic Games: Twenty-first century challenges as a global media event. *Culture, Sport, Society, 5* (3), 32.

Slater, J. (1998, October) Changing partners: The relationship between the mass media and the Olympic Games. Paper presented at the fourth international symposium for Olympic research (49–69). London, ON: University of Western Ontario.

Solberg, H. A. and Gratton, C. (2013) Broadcasting the Olympics. In S. Frawley and D. Adair (eds) *Managing the Olympics* (147–164). Basingstoke: Palgrave Macmillan.

## RELEVANT WEBSITES

FIFA – www.fifa.com
International Olympic Committee – www.olympic.org
International Triathlon Union – www.triathlon.org
Olympic Broadcasting – http://m.olympic.org/mobile/olympic-broadcasting

## CASE STUDY

### Major event photographers

*A picture says a thousand words.* If the classic adage is anything to go by, the importance of sport photographers can't be overestimated in the planning and execution of media operations at major events. As the eyes of the world, photographers capture the colour, drama and emotion of the event – distributing their pictures worldwide to the leading websites, newspapers and publications. One of these photographers is Delly Carr, the founder of Sportshoot, who has photographed six Olympics (2000, 2004, 2008, 2010, 2012, 2014), seven Commonwealth Games (1994, 1998, 2002, 2006, 2008, 2010, 2014) and two FIFA World Cups (2006, 2010) (Carr, 2014). This case study is based on an interview with Carr conducted by the author, which explored the role of photographers within major sport events.

> *Carr*: Photographers are more important nowadays, more than ever due to the way that images are being used with the addition of social media, such as Facebook, Instagram and Twitter. There are now so many photos, but I think a good photographer will have a photo that rises above the clutter. Photographs are a powerful tool, the old cliché that they tell a thousand words is completely true. As well as getting the message across to all the people that follow sport, images are used in other ways, which is marketing, sponsorship, even technical reviews. At an event, the role of the photographer is to give a visual of how the thing was put together. As well as to visually show sponsors what they are sponsoring, getting the message across, and the marketing power too, it's started with sports memorabilia but it's gone further than that now.

Photographers require particular attention during major sport events, as they have additional requirements in order to fulfil their responsibilities regardless of whether they are filing for a local newspaper at the venue or for an international agency from the main media centre. Along with basic journalistic needs, such as a desk, chair, power and internet, photographers need additional equipment, such as multiple camera bodies and lenses, computers and a monopod, and access to dedicated and uninterrupted photo locations, known as photo pools. These photo pools are

identified and planned for prior to the events to ensure that photographers have access to locations to capture the best images – this may include at the finish line, court side, on the back of a motorcycle for road events, in a boat for sea events or high above in a gantry for a bird's eye view.

> *Carr*: My preferred photo position when I scout for a location really does depend on why I'm there and what the client has asked of me. In triathlon they want me to tell stories, so I look for those stories. That could be where we are actually at, or where I feel something will happen. It will be sports specific. For football, the primo position would be down in the corner on the side where their bench will be . . . so if a team scores a goal, and if you watch the World Cup, a player will turn towards the side where their bench is, run through that corner and then towards their bench; 99 times out of 100, that will be the arc. So, you want the best position for a camera in football, it's in that corner. The player will be celebrating and jumping. That's the best way to hedge your bets.

The evolution of digital photography has dramatically changed the way photographers operate at major sport events, with rolls of film being replaced by hi-speed network cabling, memory cards and picture editing software. A standalone photographer must attend, photograph, edit and file their own pictures, often within minutes of the event and often multiple times a day from numerous venues. Delly Carr explains how the evolution has significantly changed his job over the last decade as print and media deadlines have shifted towards the need for immediacy. No longer is sending pictures by courier around the world a standard practice for a sports photographer, instead media now expect images to be accessible during competition.

> *Carr*: The workflow after an event has changed completely with the digital revolution. We used to go to the pub after an event and that's not the case now. We are doing stuff three to four hours afterwards, and that's down to social media and the objectives of your employer. Sporting events have worked out who is of value and who is not, so there aren't as many photographers at an event – they are much stricter on accreditation now. You just can't walk in unless you have a valid reason to be there. So that allows more space for photographers and a bit more access and a bit more comfort. But the number one change is just how the workflow has evolved. We used to have to wait two to three days to get our film processed and that's not the case anymore. Now it's instant, our images can go from camera to the internet to an office in London in an instant, whereas once upon a time you would have someone pick up the film at halftime or at full-time, drive them to the office and process the print they want and then run it through the media. During the Sydney 2000 Olympics, when I photographed the triathlon, my local camera

lab opened up for me because I was a good customer, even though it was a Saturday or Sunday, so they had a guy there who had the machines running, he did all the films that night, I picked them up the next morning and then there was an army of friends of mine who got all them all packaged up into Fedex envelopes to send to all the magazines around the world. Now I can get one picture and send it to everyone within minutes. It's a totally new medium.

International photo agencies, such as Getty Images, Reuters and Associated Media, have dedicated photo positions at venues with a LAN network, which means that pictures are sent to photo editors, often located at the main media centre, within seconds and published online within minutes.

*Carr*: I've got a feeling the future of sports photography will be a lot more involved in social media. I think it will happen that the camera and the computer will become one and we can all do it in one place. They are already building attachments that transmit Wi-Fi on cameras so you can send directly from the camera and there are compacts that do that too. You can update Facebook straight from the camera.

## CASE STUDY QUESTIONS

1 Why are photographers so important at international sports events?
2 Why is it important for photo positions to be sport specific?
3 What kind of extra provisions from the media operations team at a major sport event do photographers need that journalists might not?
4 What do you think the future of sports photography might be?

CHAPTER 13

# Managing crises, scandals and reputations

## Not all publicity is good

## OVERVIEW

This chapter examines crises and scandals. It highlights their impact on sport organizations, as well as discusses the strategies available to sport media professionals to manage the image and reputation of a sport organization or athlete during these events. In particular, this chapter investigates the most important stages in the media management of a crisis or scandal and provides guidelines for how to steer the crisis management process. The prevalence of crises and scandals within professional sport, coupled with the competitive nature of the media market, means that effective media management is essential to ensure the credibility and profitability of an organization or athlete is maintained.

## LEARNING OUTCOMES

After completing this chapter, the reader should be able to:

- describe what crises and scandals are in terms of their impact on a sport organization;
- identify the types of crises that might beset a sport organization and distinguish between sporadic and systemic crises;
- establish a crisis media management process within a sport organization; and
- apply a set of media management guidelines at a time of crisis or scandal within a sport organization.

## INTRODUCTION

The saying that 'any publicity is good publicity' assumes that creating any amount of public awareness is worth the consequences. In the case of sport though, bad publicity can ruin careers and severely damage organizations. Artist Andy Warhol claimed that in the future everyone would be world famous for 15 minutes and, in a world saturated by

media, this means that bad publicity is likely to be the only publicity that some people receive. Professional sport organizations and their employees, however, are subject to intense media and public interest, which often means that they are the recipients of bad publicity and are portrayed in the court of public opinion in a negative light. Bad publicity, which results from crises and scandals at one end of the spectrum and from accidents and minor misdemeanours at the other, is therefore to be avoided because of its potential negative impacts.

Importantly, managing a crisis, scandal or reputation is not about making sure procedures are in place to 'clean up the mess' as quickly as possible (Pearson *et al.*, 1997). Nor is it about implementing practices and tactics that will limit the amount of information available to the media in order to protect employees that have been negligent or have transgressed boundaries governed by social values and norms. Rather, as Pearson *et al.* (1997: 52) have noted, 'crisis management is a mindset and process that, on a daily basis, drives a company's decisions and actions'. As such, this chapter is a starting point for the implementation of broader management processes that contribute to media management practices and organizational culture. Furthermore, framing crisis and scandal management within the context of media management is useful because sport organizations often recognize that their public profile makes them a natural target by the media when things go wrong.

## CRISES AND SCANDALS

Crises have 'become front-page material – a key word in the vocabulary of official and everyday speech' (Keane, 1984: 10). From a cursory glance at media headlines it is clear that the term is frequently used and abused. In both official and everyday speech, 'crisis' is used to signify a broad range of traumatic happenings – from wars and acts of terrorism to athletes who have suffered career-threatening injuries, taken drugs or committed sexual indiscretions.

As a result, there is much debate and confusion as to what constitutes a crisis. The academic definition refers to a threat to a system or organization (Offe, 1984). The threat implies change, and the change must be significant, to the point that the system or organization will undergo an irrevocable transformation. Based on this understanding, examples in the sporting context might include the relocation of a club to another city, province or state, the merger of two clubs, or the collapse of a league due to financial insolvency. In each of these instances, the crisis would result in transformative change.

In the main, however, this academic definition does not reflect common usage, especially in the hyper-commercialized media coverage of sport. In this context, 'crisis' primarily refers to a problem that a club, league, association or individual is experiencing, albeit a serious one, which typically has the potential to cause a negative impact or, at the very least, negative publicity for the individual or organization. In short, a crisis in this respect is likely to transform the functional into the dysfunctional, often at a moment's notice.

Derived from the Greek *krisis*, in its most literal form, the term 'crisis' means decision. At its core, a crisis event is a decisive or critical turning point, a moment of rupture. If the

everyday workings of an organization are perceived as continuous, relatively stable and normal, then crises are moments of discontinuity, in which the threat of change necessarily defines them as abnormal. By their very nature, crises are the antithesis of the status quo. Crises are often ambiguous (where the link between cause and effect can be unclear), have a low probability of occurring (but a high impact or consequence), require an immediate response, are often a surprise to the members of the organization and require a decision that will have positive or negative results (Pearson and Clair, 1998).

Like crises, scandals also threaten the status quo and relative stability of sport organizations. Rowe (2000) suggested that sport scandals are an integral feature of the contemporary media landscape that require serious attention, rather than be dismissed simply as the work of tabloid or gutter journalism (McKay *et al.*, 2000). Both crises and scandals result in disruption. While a crisis is able to cause disruption without media coverage, a scandal's disruption is fuelled, by definition, by the attention of the media. In fact, it is more accurate to adopt the term 'media scandal', as the two are inextricably linked.

Although the two terms are often used as synonyms by the sport media, it is useful to separate them. Crises typically relate to institutional, systemic and widespread dysfunction or to an event or incident that occurs outside the control of a sport organization, such as an act of terrorism or a lightning strike. By contrast, scandals more often relate to individual instances of personal impropriety. The terms are confused by their usage, such as the way in which the media refer to a spate of injuries suffered by a team as a crisis. In this situation, the term scandal is not appropriate because no impropriety has taken place. The severity of the situation does not really warrant the description of crisis, particularly given that the same nomenclature might also be used for a stadium collapse or similar calamity; however, hyperbole is a common feature of media descriptions. Whatever the context, it is clear that scandals almost always relate to the actions of individuals and more often than not involve sex, money, power, corruption and incompetence.

Lull and Hinerman (1997) identified a range of scandal criteria. The first is that the act or actions transgress social norms; a scandal cannot occur without transgressing social norms. These acts or actions are carried out by specific people and their transgressions reflect the extent of their desires and personal interests. Through the media scandal these individuals are identified and held accountable for actions that are demonstrated to be intentional and reckless. Scandals are widely circulated via the media, are constructed as a story for audience consumption and typically inspire widespread interest and discussion. In turn, the public profile and intense interest in sport stars make sport scandals particularly attractive to the media and decidedly volatile for sport organizations. Sport news is already subject to significant audience consumption, which makes the sport scandal a complementary product. For instance, consider the global interest in the murder trial of South African triple Paralympian, Oscar Pistorius, known to many around the world as 'Blade Runner'. Importantly, in the case of a major scandal or crisis, the promotional and protective elements of the sport media nexus discussed earlier are often abandoned.

Even the broad definitions of scandal and crisis referred to above can be obscured and complicated by the media's account of an incident. Ben Johnson testing positive to steroids at the Seoul 1988 Olympics, former South African cricket captain Hansie

Cronje's involvement in match fixing, and even the introduction of a bounty on opposing players by NFL New Orleans Saints coaches, have all been described in the media as scandals because of the moral boundaries that were transgressed. In these cases the actual incident is referred to as a crisis because of the immediate severity, yet a broader crisis – performance-enhancing drug detection and use, the payment of players and the regulation of sport betting and the win at all costs mentality of professional sport – is most often at the heart of significant media coverage. In this respect the incident acts as a touchstone for systemic problems within sport and its organizations. Whether it is a crisis or scandal that generates negative publicity, each has the potential to adversely affect, and, in some instances, irrevocably destroy, the reputations of individuals and organizations alike.

## CRISIS AND SCANDAL IMPACT

In order to understand their impact, it is useful to classify crises into four distinct categories: internal, external, sporadic and systemic. Internal crises are limited to the internal workings of the organization and have no impact on the general public. These crises require management, planning and effective and efficient internal processes, but very rarely require media management because they are of little interest to the media or the public, are dealt with quickly or are of limited consequence beyond the organization.

External crises, on the other hand, have an impact beyond the boundaries of the organization. External crises are defined by the interest of both the general public and the media and require significant media management because of the negative impact they can have on an organization. The distinction between internal and external crises is important because when a crisis becomes public, its impact, as well as the course the crisis might take, is partly out of the control of the organization. An internal crisis, although it may involve stakeholders outside the organization, should be able to be managed satisfactorily through internal processes; external crises, such as scandals, are controlled in part by the media. The media will not only report on external crises, but will also create the context in which the general public is able to understand and interpret them.

Sporadic crises occur without warning, and are typically isolated and unique. An example of a sporadic crisis might be a light plane carrying tourists on a joy flight crashing into a baseball stadium or football field, injuring players and spectators as a result. The plane crash is in all likelihood a one-off event and will occur with little or no warning. Furthermore, although the team or league running the event at the stadium should have a crisis management or emergency response plan, a light plane crash is not likely to be high on the list of things that might go wrong. The sporadic crisis will hopefully only have to be dealt with once, if ever. On the other hand, the systemic crisis is like an organizational disease. If the sporadic crisis is akin to a small child getting a broken arm from a freak accident that was no fault of his or her own, the systemic crisis is akin to a middle-aged man or woman being diagnosed with lung cancer as a result of a sustained nicotine habit.

The systemic crisis is the most dangerous for a sport organization because not only is it difficult to remedy, but the media is also likely to feed off the story for weeks, months and, in the worst cases, for years. Unlike the sporadic crisis, which occurs suddenly and

## IN PRACTICE 13.1

### Image repair: Phelps and Owens

Many scandals in sport that receive media coverage are often due to moral transgressions such as infidelity or cheating (such as Tiger Woods), but are also the result of criminal offences such as drink driving, illicit drugs, domestic violence and sexual assault. In these criminal cases, sport organizations and individual athletes must follow due process and often lines of communication should and will be dictated by a legal team in conjunction with the sports organization or individual athlete. However, where a moral transgression occurs, immediate and clever communication can help restore the sport organization's or individual athlete's reputation and image. Benoit's (1995) image restoration theory encompasses five strategies: denial, evading responsibility, reducing offensiveness, corrective action, and mortification (admitting fault and asking for forgiveness). There are various examples of how each of the five image repair strategies have been used in the aftermath of sport scandals, two of which are examined below.

Walsh and McAllister-Spooner (2011) explored Michael Phelps' response in the wake of a British tabloid printing a photo of him smoking marijuana, in particular looking at the statement he issued and the subsequent statements from USA Swimming, sponsors and other stakeholders. The statement made by Michael Phelps was:

> I engaged in behavior which was regrettable and demonstrated bad judgment . . . I acted in a youthful and inappropriate way, not in a manner that people have come to expect from me. For this, I am sorry. I promise my fans and the public – it will not happen again.

Walsh and McAllister-Spooner (2011:157) contended that his strategy worked to restore his image; his statement was well received by his sponsors and organizations, and the media all but dismissed the transgression as a 'boys will be boys' scenario. In the end Phelps' sponsors and governing organizations not only supported the swimmer, but also bolstered his image.

One instance where this was not well received was in the case of the NFL's Terrell Owens. Brazeal (2008: 147) presented the case of when the Philadelphia Eagles deactivated Owens, who had become 'sullen with the press, belligerent with the coaching staff, and publicly critical of his team and quarterback', after failed attempts to renegotiate his contract. Owens and his manager staged a press conference. Owens spoke first and used the strategies of mortification and bolstering, such as:

> And I think the mentality that I have, my greatest strength can also be my greatest weakness. I'm a fighter . . . I've always been and I'll always be. I fight for what I think is right. In doing so, I alienated a lot of my fans and my teammates.
>
> (Brazeal, 2008: 147)

Brazeal argued that Owens used an admirable quality to justify his behaviour, 'arguing that this quality that makes him an excellent athlete sometimes leads to friction with others' (Brazeal, 2008: 147). But it was his manager Drew Rosenhaus who failed to follow the image repair strategy and instead launched attacks against the club and media, and even when trying to engage in image repair strategies – appeared aggressive and arrogant.

Ultimately Brazeal (2008) stated that although both men painted Owens as the victim, they failed to acknowledge that Owens was responsible, and neither discussed any corrective action Owens planned to take in order to prevent future conflicts. Ultimately, their rhetoric demonstrated a complete failure to understand the culture of team sport, which demands unity, commitment, and sacrifice, and failed to earn Owens' reinstatement.

This small snapshot of image repair examples shows how language and its delivery can help repair an image and reputation tarnished, or in some cases, make it worse. Overall, an apology is often a simple but effective strategy to help restore a reputation, but it must be genuine in its delivery. However, it is important to note that this may dependent on context. Brown (2014) rightly established that the case will likely depend on whether it is a criminal or noncriminal situation, where the criminal proceedings are likely to prohibit any type of apology.

Sources: Brazeal (2008); Walsh and McAllister-Spooner (2011); Brown (2014).

without warning, the systemic crisis has grown and festered over time, usually as a result of organizational inadequacy, such as corruption, illegal activity or manifestly inappropriate culture and procedures. An example might be of a league underpaying its players over an extended period of time, as a percentage of total revenue, therefore making it more profitable for the players to bet on matches, which may encourage the match-fixing of games for betting profit. Initially, when a story 'breaks' about an athlete or organization attempting to fix the result of a contest, the crisis might appear to be sporadic, a one-off event, in which a key individual is represented in the media coverage as a 'bad seed'. However, further examination might reveal that corruption and match fixing is widespread throughout the organization and perhaps is a common practice. This chronic and long-term problem within the sport represents a systemic crisis.

Once these crisis categories or types are combined, it is clear those crises that are sporadic and internal have the lowest impact in the media and with the general public, while crises that are systemic and external have the highest impact.

However, sport scandals are always external. Sport organizations invariably attempt to ensure the actions of their employees are only for internal consumption and analysis. In these instances, moral transgressions may either be hidden, in the hope they are never discovered, or dealt with, through an internal rehabilitation process. But a moral transgression that is internal is not a scandal, for it must be reported by the media in order to generate widespread public interest. Single transgressions, by either an individual or a group, can be considered sporadic within the crisis typology. Depending on the profile of

the people involved, and to what extent moral and social boundaries have been transgressed, the impact may be anywhere between medium and high. Multiple transgressions by an individual or group will mean that the scandal is becoming systemic and the impact will be high. This is particularly the case where a high profile athlete repeatedly transgresses moral boundaries and, in doing so, becomes a regular feature of tabloid journalism.

Despite its relatively humble beginnings, sport is no longer simple. It is typically not just a group of people getting together to engage in play, games or athletic contests on an ad hoc basis. Even in the amateur club environment, sport is governed by a set of regulations that cover a range of issues such as insurance, health and safety and member protection, to name only a few. In the professional context, sport is a complex activity that involves substantial organization. In fact, as the activity becomes more commercial, the level of complexity increases and, as the complexity increases, so too does the risk. Put simply, the bigger the organization or the event, the greater the chance and opportunity that things will go wrong. Similarly, the potential for individual moral transgressions increases as the organization becomes larger and more commercial. In essence, as professional sport organizations and their employees gain greater commercial and cultural influence, there is a greater likelihood that crises and scandals will occur and, as the likelihood increases, so too does the potential impact.

The challenge for sport organizations is to develop and implement processes to limit the damage to the organization. Crisis management and crisis and scandal media management go hand in hand. Without effective and efficient crisis management, media management is difficult, if not a waste of time. Furthermore, media management at a time of crisis or scandal undertaken without any substantive attempts to address, change or remedy the situation is simply an attempt to disguise the problem and ensure the reputation of the organization is maintained, at whatever cost. In short, this is unethical and to be avoided.

In a media-saturated professional sport landscape, protecting a sport organization's reputation and image is becoming increasingly important. Sport organizations, like generic business organizations, need to do more than make a profit or have more wins than losses in order to be considered successful. In order to be successful, sport organizations must operate and behave in ways that conform to social norms and expectations (Galloway and Kwansah-Aidoo, 2005).They must demonstrate that the values of the organization and those of general society are aligned. If the distance between the actions of the sport organization and the values of society is small then the crisis is likewise likely to be small, if it can be considered a crisis at all. On the other hand, if the distance between actions and values is great, then the crisis is likely to be amplified. The degree to which actions and values are aligned in generic business organizations is not always clear, partly because the 'public face' of the business is its products, rather than its people. Sport organizations face distinct challenges because the 'public face' of their business is people, the athletes themselves. This visibility, which is created partly by the nature of the enterprise and partly by the media's involvement, means that the degree of alignment is a constant issue. The visibility also means that small breaches of social and public trust by sport organizations can result in significant short-term crises and scandals.

## CRISIS AND SCANDAL MANAGEMENT

Pearson and Mitroff (1993) identified five phases, or stages, through which almost all crises pass, graphically represented in Figure 13.1. These phases are useful for understanding the place of crisis media management, the way in which a crisis or scandal will develop and how it should be managed. The five phases are: signal detection; preparation and prevention; containment and damage limitation; recovery; and learning. These five phases apply equally well to the management of scandals and, throughout the following discussion, the term crisis will be used to describe both crises and scandals.

### Phase 1: Signal detection

Although sport organizations focus a significant amount of attention on containment and damage limitation, because this is when media attention is at its greatest, the most important phases of the crisis management process are the first two: signal detection, and preparation and prevention. Importantly, in these two phases an organization has the ability to define itself and its actions as proactive, rather than reactive. Furthermore, the sport organization can create an organizational culture that is able to prevent and detect crises, rather than simply manage the media storm when it inevitably hits.

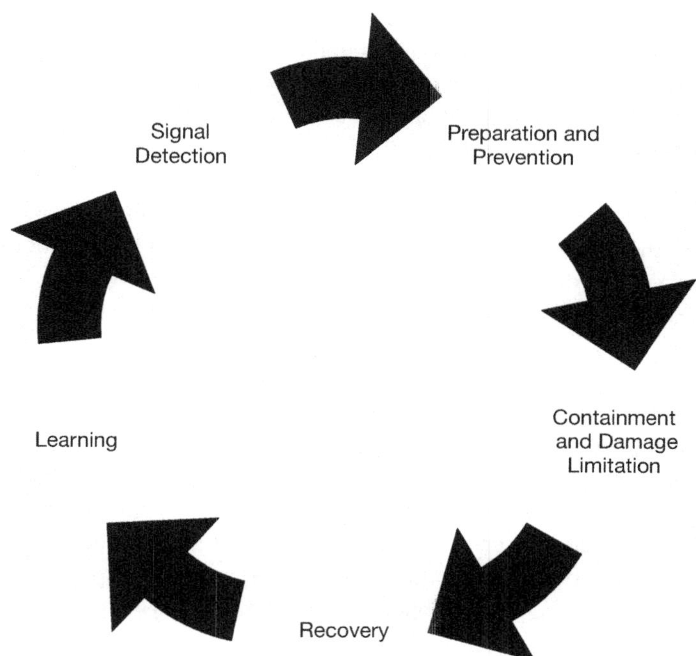


**FIGURE 13.1** Crisis management phases

Pearson and Mitroff (1993) found that crises invariably leave a trail of early warning signs, but that organizations often ignore the signals. Early detection can ensure that a sport organization is aware of a crisis before the media, whereas late or no detection can result in a sport organization being forced to react to media reports and public condemnation. In other words, beginning a crisis management process means cultivating an awareness of the dangers and developing a system that is receptive to the signals. Pearson and Mitroff (1993) found that the most successful organizations were those that established lines of communication within the organization that allowed and encouraged employees to report bad news. Furthermore, these organizations institutionalized the internal scrutiny of their operations to ensure that faults and problems were discovered. For some sport organizations, simply beginning a crisis management process may be sufficient to start a process whereby employees are more aware of potential dangers and are more alert to the signals.

## Phase 2: Preparation and prevention

Planning for a crisis should be an essential part of any sport organization's day to day business. Organizations in which the senior employees believe that the organization is bullet proof and that a crisis will never happen because their team, club or league is run better than its competitors are only tempting fate. Pearson and Mitroff (1993: 59) suggested:

> [This type of thinking] reinforces organizational vulnerability: early warning signals may go undetected or unreported; key internal contacts for resources may remain unaware of needs; critical alliances with external stakeholders may not be made; [and] learning after an incident or a near-miss may not be formalized or disseminated throughout the organization.

In essence, an organizational culture in which an 'it can't happen to us' attitude prevails is likely to cause crises, rather than prevent them. A healthier and more constructive perspective is to acknowledge that bad news is simply an unavoidable consequence of being in the sport business.

Beginning the crisis management planning process is often very difficult, and is frequently met with resistance. Sport organizations are often resistant to change and have difficulty accepting that they might be susceptible to crises. It is essential to begin planning for the occurrence of crisis, but the question is where to start? A useful way to begin is by assessing how ready the organization is to deal with crises. A simple method is to ask the following questions of and within the organization:

- What crises present a risk to our organization and which ones are we susceptible to?
- What is the probability of these crises occurring based on the history of our organization, current personnel, organizational culture, external environment, etc.?
- What is the potential impact of each?
- Are we prepared to deal with each of the crises we have identified?

Asking these questions is an effective method of raising awareness within the organization about the need for crisis management, but it should be noted that they are merely a starting point, not an end in themselves. Furthermore, Pearson *et al.* (1997) suggested that this questioning should occur throughout the organization, because they found that the best prepared organizations have staff at all levels that know where to turn for help and have a clear sense of their own roles and responsibilities. Attempting to brainstorm the crises that the organization might be susceptible to should be a relatively easy process if the organization's employees agree to abandon the phrase 'that will never happen to us'. Table 13.1 provides some examples of crises and scandals that might occur, although this is by no means an exhaustive list.

One of the most important steps in this process is determining the probability of each of the crises occurring based on the history and culture of the organization, which might also be referred to as risk assessment. A common mistake of crisis planning is to develop plans for worst-case scenarios and to be under prepared for crisis events that are more likely to happen (Fallin, 2005). An organization must do both, but also be prepared to prioritize. If the team's players have previously been charged and convicted of driving while drunk or have been charged and convicted of sexual misconduct and these incidents relate to organizational culture, then there is a higher probability that this type of crisis will occur again. Good crisis management planning should recognize and acknowledge that the prevalence of some of these issues indicates a systemic problem, rather than a series of sporadic crises. As such, there should be a crisis management plan in place, but perhaps more importantly, the crisis management process should alert the organization to more substantive problems, such as a poor organizational culture or poor professional

**TABLE 13.1** Sport organization crises and scandals

| *Crisis/Scandal* |
|---|
| Stadium fire |
| Player/coach/administrator death or serious injury (on-field) |
| Player/coach/administrator death or serious injury (off-field) |
| Sexual misconduct |
| Bomb threat |
| Bomb explosion |
| Terrorist attack |
| Drug taking (performance) |
| Drug taking (recreational) |
| Match fixing |
| Spectator injury or death |
| Facility malfunction or collapse |
| Drunk driving |
| Public fighting |

development and training for younger members of the team. If team players are constantly being caught driving while drunk, it is likely that the team has a culture in which excessive alcohol consumption is the norm, rather than the exception. If the organization constantly has to deal with media reports about their players and alcohol consumption then the more systemic problem needs to be addressed.

Likewise, if the facility that the team plays in is old or in need of repair, then the crisis management plan will need to reflect that there is a greater probability of a significant fault and a significant crisis occurring as a result. Often the sheer organizational complexity of the sport and its inherent danger will mean that the crisis potential is high. Motor racing and horse racing are prime examples in this respect, where there is a significant chance of personal injury, for participants, spectators and officials alike.

The final steps in the initial planning process are to assess the potential impact of each of the crises that the organization is most susceptible to, and then assess how prepared the organization is to deal with these crises if they occurred. In assessing how prepared the organization is, it is useful to consider what the organization would do upon hearing the bad news. Is there a process in place to communicate the news to the media? Is there a process in place to communicate the news within the organization? Has a person, or people, been nominated as the organization's spokespeople at a time of crisis? If the answer is 'no' or 'we are not sure' then the organization is not prepared.

Pearson and Mitroff (1993) have noted that a goal of the prevention and preparation phase should not be to eliminate the possibility of all crises. In many professional sport organizations this is a difficult task made impossible by media attention and the prevalence of highly paid young men. Rather, a sport organization should set itself a goal of preventing most crises and scandals, while being prepared to handle those that go undetected or are beyond its control.

A key strategy that will contribute to effective crisis media management is the formulation of a crisis plan. Crisis management plans must be put in writing, but they need not be overly complex. Importantly, a crisis management plan must create protocols that instil confidence in the organization and provide direction at times when chaos may threaten to take over. A crisis management plan for a sport organization might consist of the following elements:

- a title page that contains the title, effective date and the signature of the organization's senior manager;
- a clear and direct policy statement that details how the organization will manage a crisis;
- a list of emergency telephone numbers for essential staff within the organization who will be contacted at a time of crisis;
- a criterion for activation that prioritizes crises and scandals into different levels, depending on their severity and impact on the organization;
- a set of step-by-step procedures that correspond to the crises based on their level of severity;
- a section that describes appropriate media communication at a time of crisis; and
- a set of appendices that may include items such as media release templates, speech guidelines and a media list.

## IN PRACTICE 13.2

### Salt Lake City – citius, altius, corruptus?

Michael Payne, former marketing director of the IOC, described the Salt Lake City 2002 Winter Olympics as a 'catalyst for the most significant reform and change in recent Olympic history' (Payne, 2005). In terms of the performances of athletes, the Salt Lake City Olympics was very successful, with a record 78 events and gold medallists from 18 separate countries; however, prior to the Games it was a completely different story as a widespread and damaging crisis engulfed the IOC. The crisis that beset the 1972 Munich Olympic Games, where terrorists killed 11 Israeli athletes and coaches was a sporadic, one-off event; the Salt Lake City crisis, on the other hand, was systemic, the result of long-term institutional corruption.

In late 1998, a local Salt Lake City television station reported allegations of unethical behaviour by Salt Lake City bid committee members and an IOC delegate, which resulted in the IOC executive board establishing a special commission to investigate the allegations. Media coverage of the allegations and revelations, which lasted throughout 1999, badly damaged the reputation of Salt Lake City and the IOC. Headlines such as 'Olympic vote buying scandal' were juxtaposed with 'Is the Olympic ideal destroyed?' The first action the committee took was to issue an apology to 'the Olympic athletes who have inspired us through the years and whose lives so poignantly embody the Olympic ideals' (Jennings and Sambrook, 2000: 70).

The IOC commission discovered that IOC members were bribed for their votes and that the gifts offered by the Salt Lake City bid committee included cash, overseas trips, educational scholarships and medical treatments, totalling approximately US$1 million in value. As a result, the IOC announced sanctions against some of its members and ultimately expelled six African and South American IOC board members.

The IOC's investigative commission widened its scope to include other Olympic Games, such as those held in Nagano, Atlanta and Sydney and found similar instances of unethical dealings by members of bid committees and the IOC. Indeed, there were even allegations that some IOC members had solicited bribes as far back as Anchorage, Alaska's quest to host the 1992 and 1994 Winter Olympic Games. The decisive move made by the IOC during the Salt Lake City crisis was to establish the investigative commission – which ultimately led to the development of an Ethics Commission. From the moment allegations were levelled at the successful Salt Lake City bid committee, the media were going to rigorously pursue the story. Any attempt to conceal the corruption would have resulted in even more negative publicity. Taking decisive action to expose further corruption seems counterintuitive, but in the long term the establishment of the committee served to indicate that the International Olympic Committee was willing to fix a systemic problem.

In his speech to the 113th session of the IOC, president Jacques Rogge remarked that it was in Salt Lake City that the IOC first learned 'of a profound crisis which nearly destroyed the IOC' and that 'inappropriate structures and human weakness on both sides [the IOC and the bid committee] were the roots of [the] evil'. Rogge also noted that the IOC had reacted decisively to punish its members, set up a commission to

investigate, altered its processes and reformed its structure to improve its transparency and democracy. The process by which a city can bid to host the Olympic Games is now totally different from the one that allowed Salt Lake City to win the rights.

Payne (2005) suggested that the Salt Lake City crisis was a clear breach of public trust, but that the positive side of the crisis was that it illustrated how much both the media and the general public cared about the Olympic Games and its values. Thus, in Payne's (2005) view, the crisis and the institutional reform that followed might have clarified the meaning of the Olympic Games and 'unleashed the power of the Olympic brand'. In this respect it might be said that the IOC, although besieged by the world's media at the time, benefited from the crisis because it led to improved institutional processes – for instance, the IOC has since prohibited any participants betting on the Olympic Games – in a bid to eradicate corrupt practices and people. It also strengthened the resolve of the organization to adhere to the fundamental principles within its own charter, which states that 'Olympism seeks to create a way of life based on the joy found in effort, the educational value of good example and respect for universal fundamental ethical principles'. Despite this resolve, however, corruption still occurs as the IOC's longest-serving member, Joao Havelange, resigned in 2011 just days before he was to face an ethics hearing over multi-million dollar bribery charges, underlining the importance of organizational vigilance regarding systemic crises.

Sources: Payne (2005); Jennings and Sambrook (2010); BBC Sport (2011); www.olympics.org.

## Phase 3: Containment and damage limitation

Sport organization employees face many challenges when a crisis breaks in the media, including the assessment of the crisis and communicating necessary information to stakeholders as quickly as possible. The following communication principles will aid the containment of the crisis or scandal (Patterson, 1993; Helitzer, 1999; Massey, 2001; Ramsey, 2004, Mackey, 2004; Stephens *et al.*, 2005):

- do not ignore the problem, as any delay in your response will worsen the resulting crisis or scandal;
- do not attempt to cover the problem up, as the cover up will become part of the crisis or scandal when the media finally uncover it. Revealing bad news is a way of establishing control, rather than relinquishing it;
- gather all the facts as quickly as possible and try not to comment with only partial knowledge of the crisis or scandal;
- appoint a spokesperson to act as the media liaison for the duration of the crisis. This may be the most senior manager, the media manager or the person most comfortable in front of the media;
- establish a consistent message or story and communicate this with all stakeholders, including the media. It is important that the media do not receive mixed messages which can then be used as a way of elongating the news story;

- explain the steps the organization has or will be taking in order to rectify or manage the problem;
- be accessible throughout the crisis or scandal, in order to build trust with the media and have the organization's point of view recorded; and
- be as truthful as possible throughout the crisis or scandal, as lying will destroy trust with the media and reduce the organization's overall credibility.

### Phase 4: Recovery

Another key challenge of effective crisis management is to return to business as usual as quickly as possible. With intense media and public interest this can often be a difficult task. Recovering from the crisis or scandal is partly about the way in which the organization communicates with the media: a strong and consistent message will help to maintain credibility with a variety of stakeholders. Recovery is also dependent on the strategies that the organization puts in place to deal with the cause of the crisis or scandal.

### Phase 5: Learning

A crisis is often a crucial moment in the development and evolution of an organization. As such, crisis can be used as a unique opportunity for making a diagnosis. In other words, a crisis can be conceptualized as an ideal moment to understand the system as a whole, rather than see it as an isolated event that has occurred outside the boundaries of the organization or system (Morin, 1976). Using the crisis to understand the organization as a whole enables the crisis to be used as a catalyst for improvement. As Augustine (1995: 4) noted, 'almost every crisis contains within itself the seeds of success as well as the roots of failure'. Effective crisis and scandal media management is a process whereby a sport organization is able to demonstrate publicly that it is able to rehabilitate or sever the damaged and rotten roots, propagate the seeds and foster new growth. The five phases of crisis management are part of a loop, as illustrated in Figure 13.1, whereby the learning that occurs during a crisis event can be used to aid detection and improve prevention and preparation. For some sport organizations, the phases of crisis management may begin with a crisis, which then leads to a broader evaluation of the organization's susceptibility and preparedness.

## SUMMARY

This chapter has demonstrated that crises and scandals are events and incidents that sport organizations must be prepared for. Furthermore, it has highlighted that crisis and scandal media management must be an essential part of an organization's long-term media planning, as well as its short-term media strategy. In other words, crisis and scandal media management involves being prepared for something that may never happen, as well as responding decisively and effectively to something that has

happened. How an organization prepares, responds and learns from crises and scandals is equally important. Without planning, an organization leaves itself open to crisis events and scandals being controlled entirely by the media. With sound media management practices in place an organization can reasonably hope to achieve some degree of control and have its side of the story told through the media which will, in turn, limit the damage to the organization. Review questions and exercises are listed below to assist with confirming your knowledge of the core concepts and principles introduced in this chapter.

## REVIEW QUESTIONS AND EXERCISES

1. What is a crisis?
2. What is a scandal?
3. Why is crisis and scandal media management more important for sport organizations than most non-sport organizations?
4. What is the difference between sporadic and systemic crises?
5. What are the five phases of crisis management and in which phase is media management likely to occur?
6. Which phase of the crisis management process is the most important for sport organizations with limited resources (human or financial)?
7. Conduct some preliminary research on a professional sport organization and then prepare a list of crises and scandals to which the organization is susceptible.
8. Which of the crises and scandals you have identified is likely to be reported in the media? Which will have the biggest impact, given the history of the organization?
9. Choose one of the crises or scandals you have identified and write a media release that communicates essential information to the media.
10. What can a sport organization learn by going through a crisis or scandal?

## FURTHER READING

Bernstein, B. (2012) Crisis management and sports in the age of social media: A case study analysis of the Tiger Woods scandal. *The Elon Journal of Undergraduate Research in Communications, 3* (2), 62–75.

Bruce, T. and Tini, T. (2008) Unique crisis response strategies in sports public relations: Rugby league and the case for diversion. *Public Relations Review, 34* (2), 108–115.

Cycling's Greatest Fraud (2013) *National Geographic Channel*, 16 July.

Elliott, D. and Smith, D. (1993) Football stadia disasters in the United Kingdom: Learning from tragedy? *Organization and Environment, 7* (3), 205–229.

Fortunato, J. A. (2008) Restoring a reputation: The Duke University Lacrosse scandal. *Public Relations Review, 34* (2), 116–123.

Gross, M. (2006) 'Not cricket': A 'nexus of silence' over the cricket match-fixing scandal. *Proceedings of the 20th Australian New Zealand Academy of Management (ANZAM) Conference on Management: Pragmatism, Philosophy, Priorities, Central Queensland University, Rockhampton, December 6–9.*

Hamilton, T. (2010) The long hard fall from Mount Olympus: The 2002 Salt Lake City Olympic Games bribery scandal. *Marquette Sports Law Review, 21* (1), 219–240.

Pistorius, O. (2012) *Blade Runner: My story.* London: Random House.

Storm, R. K. and Wagner, U. (2011) The anatomy of the sports scandal: Outset, development and effect. Paper presented at Play the Game 2011, Cologne, Germany.

Trosby, E. (2010) Public relations, football and the management of player transgressions in Australia. *Public Communication Review, 1* (2), 49–66.

# RELEVANT WEBSITES

## Americas

Major League Baseball – www.mlb.com
New Orleans Saints – www.neworleanssaints.com
United States Anti-Doping Agency – www.usada.org

## Australia and South Africa

Australian Sports Anti-Doping Authority – www.asada.gov.au

## Europe

Tour de France – www.letour.fr

## Global

International Cycling Union (UCI) – www.uci.ch
International Olympic Committee – www.olympic.org
International Paralympic Committee – www.paralympic.org
World Anti-Doping Agency – www.wada-ama.org

## CASE STUDY

### Lance Armstrong: 'It wasn't all about the bike'

Athletes have been taking performance-enhancing drugs since the birth of organized sport. Roman gladiators drank herbal infusions before chariot races and the Ancient Olympics were riddled with corruption and doping. Although these Olympians swore to play fair, potions were used to enhance athletic performance and athletes often cheated. Two thousand years later and athletes are still trying to gain an unfair advantage over their rivals. In the early 1900s many athletes, such as Thomas Hicks who won the 1904 Olympic Marathon, turned to a cocktail of alcohol and strychnine to improve performance, while many years later athletes such as Ben Johnson used steroids to gain a similar competitive advantage over rival competitors.

The use of banned drugs in sport (or doping) is considered unethical by most international sport organizations, including the IOC. In the late 1990s, the IOC established the World Anti-Doping Agency (WADA) to promote, coordinate and monitor the fight against drugs in sport. WADA is responsible for the World Anti-Doping Code, adopted by more than 600 sport organizations around the world and implemented by national bodies such as USADA in the United States and ASADA in Australia. In 2013, both parties were in the news as part of their role in implementing WADA's anti-doping programmes: USADA reported that Tyson Gay, a silver medallist at the 2012 London Olympic Games, had tested positive for a banned substance and would not be contesting the World Championships later that year; while ASADA reported that the widespread use of banned drugs in Australian sport and links to organized crime threatened to undermine the integrity of professional sport. Later that year, WADA also welcomed Major League Baseball's punishments in the wake of the Biogenesis scandal that saw New York Yankees slugger Alex Rodriguez suspended for more than a season. Although doping continues to be a problem for many sport organizations worldwide, the issue is perhaps most prevalent in cycling, especially in the annual Tour de France.

One of the reasons that doping has been long associated with the Tour de France is the physically demanding nature of the race and, as a result, there have been allegations of doping in the event since it began in 1903. Until the 1940s, riders relied on alcohol, strychnine, ether and amphetamine use to survive the pain and exhaustion of stages that could last more than 300 kilometres. According to the 1923 winner, Henri Pélissier, drug use was a necessary evil to complete the race: 'It's [the Tour de France] a Calvary. But Christ had only 14 stations of the cross. We have 15. We suffer from start to finish' (Mignon, 2003, p. 230). It took the death of a rider at the 100 kilometre team time trial at the 1960 Rome Olympic Games for authorities to criminalize doping. Performance-enhancing drugs were banned in France in 1965 and the Tour began testing for these substances in 1966; however, it wasn't until the death of British rider, Tom Simpson, who collapsed on the steep slopes of Mount Ventoux, that the spectre of amphetamine use really hit home. During the 1970s, cyclists used steroids in a bid to improve recovery; when these drugs became

detectable in the 1990s, riders turned to erythropoietin, or EPO, a drug that increases red-cell production, the use of which came to a head in the 1998 Tour de France.

In July 1998, French Customs intercepted Willy Voet, the physiotherapist for the Festina Tour de France team, with a car full of illegal drugs, including EPO, growth hormones, testosterone and amphetamines, on the Belgian border. The team was thrown off the tour, doctors were arrested, and nine riders were taken into custody, having admitted to doping under medical supervision. The trial and the enquiries brought to light a system that many teams and, in hindsight, many riders, including Marco Pantani, Erik Zabel, Floyd Landis, Alberto Contador and Lance Armstrong, had adopted over the years.

Although American Lance Armstrong retired from the sport with a record-setting seven Tour de France titles and inspired many in his successful battle against testicular cancer, allegations of drug use hounded the cyclist from the start of his comeback from testicular cancer and first victory in 1999 through to his retirement. Armstrong was eventually found to be 'cycling's greatest fraud' and given a lifetime ban for his involvement in 'the most sophisticated, professionalised and successful doping program that sport has ever seen' (Benammar, 2013). The impact of Armstrong's final admission, in an interview with US TV host Oprah Winfrey, was startling, particularly given how vigorously he had defended his innocence since allegations first appeared.

During his first title run in 1999, French newspapers reported that Armstrong had tested positive for the banned substance cortisone. Armstrong denied any wrongdoing and, upon further investigation, it was found that he had been using a medicated skin cream that contained anti-inflammatory and pain-killing drugs to treat saddle sores. Although these drugs are banned unless prescribed for health reasons, the matter was put to rest when the American's camp presented the International Cycling Union (UCI) with a back-dated prescription for the medication and Armstrong went on to claim his maiden Tour de France for the US Postal Service team. A year later, Armstrong won his second Tour de France and went on to take bronze at the 2000 Sydney Olympic Games. A Nike commercial hit the airwaves, with Armstrong advocating an apparently non-doping message: 'Everybody wants to know what I am on. What am I on? I'm on my bike . . . six hours a day. What are you on?'. In November 2000, the US Postal Service team was again at the centre of controversy when a French television station aired footage of management disposing of rubbish bags in a suspicious manner. The bags were found to contain quantities of medical products, including Actovegin, a product derived from calves' blood that, while not on the UCI banned list, could have blood-boosting effects and so should fall under the banned category of 'manipulation of a rider's blood'. The team claimed that none of its riders used Actovegin and, based on analysis of the team's blood and urine samples, French authorities could not prove otherwise.

Right before Armstrong began his 2004 campaign – a campaign that culminated in an unprecedented sixth Tour de France title – fresh allegations surfaced in *L.A. Confidentiel: Les secrets de Lance Armstrong* (Ballester and Walsh, 2004'. The book includes witness testimonies alleging that Armstrong had admitted to the use of growth hormone, cortisone, EPO, steroids and testosterone and had even taken steps

to disguise needle marks. Armstrong sued for defamation and won US$1 million in an out-of-court settlement from the UK's *The Sunday Times*. Under oath, Armstrong continued to deny doping, yet the rumours persisted and he took out his seventh Tour de France in 2005. On the podium, he remained defiant and lashed out at his critics: 'I'll say to the people who don't believe in cycling, the cynics and the sceptics. I'm sorry for you. I'm sorry that you can't dream big. I'm sorry you don't believe in miracles . . . You should believe in these athletes, and you should believe in these people' (Gallagher, 2009). A month later Armstrong was again trying to defuse doping allegations as *L'Equipe* reported that the American had tested positive for EPO. French anti-doping authorities had urine samples from the 1999 Tour de France and were now able to test for the drug's presence. The Armstrong camp called the allegations a 'witch hunt', the UCI ruled that the samples were tested strictly for research purposes, and Armstrong was again cleared of doping allegations and retired.

While Lance Armstrong enjoyed retirement, stories of drug use continued to surface among former US Postal Service team riders, notably Roberto Heras, Franke Andreu, Tyler Hamilton and Floyd Landis. Landis had won the 2006 Tour de France before a positive drug test saw him eventually stripped of the yellow jersey. Four years later, during the Tour of California, Landis sent an email to USA Cycling to 'blow the whistle' on Armstrong's alleged doping activities, including multiple blood transfusions and bribery of UCI officials. The federal investigation continued for two years before the case was closed, but Lance Armstrong's respite did not last for long.

In May 2011, Tyler Hamilton told CBS 60 Minutes that he and Armstrong had taken EPO during the 1999–2001 Tours de France, while other former teammates said they had seen Armstrong take banned substances, including EPO. A year later Lance Armstrong was charged with doping and the trafficking of drugs by USADA. The federal agency banned the seven-time Tour de France winner from competition, alleging that he had used, distributed and administered EPO, blood transfusions, testosterone, corticosteroids and masking agents to engage in 'a massive doping conspiracy from 1998–2011'. In response, Armstrong continued to deny doping and filed a lawsuit against USADA:

> [to fight charges] motivated by spite and advanced through testimony bought and paid for by promises of anonymity and immunity . . . [and] are at odds with our ideals of fairness and fair play [as] I have never doped, and, unlike many of my accusers, I have competed as an endurance athlete for 25 years with no spike in performance, passed more than 500 drug tests and never failed one.

On 20 August 2012 Armstrong's lawsuit against USADA was dismissed and he declined to publicly fight any further doping accusations. In a personal statement released on his LIVESTRONG website, Armstrong explained that:

> I have been dealing with claims that I cheated and had an unfair advantage in winning my seven Tours since 1999. Over the past three years, I have been subjected to a two-year federal criminal investigation followed by

> Travis Tygart's [CEO, USADA] unconstitutional witch hunt. The toll this has taken on my family, and my work for our foundation and on me leads me to where I am today – finished with this nonsense . . . Regardless of what Travis Tygart says, there is zero physical evidence to support his outlandish and heinous claims. I know who won those seven Tours, my teammates know who won those seven Tours, and everyone I competed against knows who won those seven Tours . . . There were no shortcuts, there was no special treatment. The same courses, the same rules.

As a result of the more than 1,000 pages of evidence, and Armstrong's decision to 'give up the fight', in October 2012 USADA stripped the cyclist of his Tour de France medals. The UCI upheld USADA's lifetime ban and expunged his results since 1998. According to UCI President Pat McQuaid, 'Lance Armstrong has no place in cycling. He deserves to be forgotten'. After years of denials, his fall from grace was finally complete when he admitted to Oprah Winfrey and millions of viewers around the world that he had doped throughout the course of his career. As such, the Texan who had given hope to cancer survivors and graced the sports pages for nearly 20 years, left a multi-million dollar business empire and legacy in ruin: he stood down from his LIVESTRONG charity, reportedly lost US$75 million in sponsorship deals from the likes of Nike, Oakley and Anheuser-Busch, is facing court to repay millions of dollars in prize and sponsorship money and the IOC has asked him to return the bronze medal he won at Sydney 2000. At the same time, the sport itself is at a crossroads as sponsors are suing the UCI or are withdrawing their support for professional cycling as a result of being associated with a sport 'tarnished' by the ongoing doping scandals. According to Tyler Hamilton, a cyclist who played a major role in the unmasking of Lance Armstrong, the only way the sport can move forward is to offer cyclists an amnesty and the chance to 'come clean'. In a post-script to the story, the UCI reported that extensive drug testing of more than 600 blood and urine samples during the 2013 Tour de France confirmed that no riders had tested positive for doping at that year's event.

## CASE STUDY QUESTIONS

1 Both crises and scandals threaten the relative stability of a sport organization; however, sport scandals have become an integral feature of the contemporary media landscape. Lance Armstrong was given a lifetime ban for violating the sport's doping code and found to be 'cycling's greatest fraud'. Identify the four crisis categories and evaluate the potential impact of this incident.

2 Pearson and Mitroff (1993) identified five phases through which almost all crises pass and these can be used to implement crisis media management. Discuss these five phases or stages in the context of the case of Lance Armstrong and the International Cycling Union (UCI).

3 Player transgressions have cost athletes such as Tiger Woods and Lance Armstrong lucrative endorsement deals in recent years. Nike terminated its support of Lance Armstrong yet stuck by the golfing star after he was caught cheating on his wife. Why do you think Nike decided to terminate its relationship with Armstrong and not Woods?

4 Despite constant allegations of doping throughout his career, Lance Armstrong's final admission of doping guilt shocked his many supporters and fans worldwide, because he had denied it so forcefully for so long. Do you think Armstrong's admission would have been better accepted if he had done it earlier in the process?

Sources: Mignon (2003); Makitalo (2012); Benammar (2013); Benson (2013); *Cycling's Greatest Fraud* (National Geographic, 2013).

# References


ABC (2012) *Media Watch*. Retrieved 19 November 2013, from www.olympic.org/news/new-app-brings-olympic-athletes-closer-together/214014.

AFL (2012) *AFL Annual Report 2012*. Retrieved 5 March 2015, from www.afl.com.au/staticfile/AFL%20Tenant/AFL/Files/AFL%20Annual%20Report%202012_web.pdf.

Anderson, W. B. (2003) Crafting the national pastime's image: The history of Major League Baseball public relations. *Journalism and Communication Monographs, 5* (6), 7–43.

Andrews, D. L. (2003) Sport and the transnationalizing media corporation. *The Journal of Media Economics, 16* (4), 235–251.

ANZ Championship (2014) ANZ Championship Media Guide. *ANZ Championship*. Retrieved 19 September 2014, from http://anz-championship.com/Statistics/Media-Guide.

AP (2010) Turner wins NCAA digital rights. *ESPN College Sports*. Retrieved 31 October 2012, from http://sports.espn.go.com/ncaa/news/story?id=5599491.

App, S. (2013) Beyond the selfie: Is Snapchat the next frontier for sports franchises? *Sport Techie*. Retrieved 14 May 2014, from www.sporttechie.com/2013/12/13/beyond-the-selfie-is-snapchat-the-next-frontier-for-sports-franchises/.

Arts Council (n.d). Cultural Olympiad and London 2012 Festival. *What We Do*. Retrieved 18 January 2014, from www.artscouncil.org.uk/what-we-do/arts-council-initiatives/cultural-olympiad/.

ASAP Sports (2011a) Caroline Wozniacki Press Conference (1). *ASAP Sports*. Retrieved 19 September 2013, from www.asapsports.com/show_interview.php?id=68673.

ASAP Sports (2011b) Caroline Wozniacki Press Conference (2). *ASAP Sports*. Retrieved 19 September 2013, from www.asapsports.com/show_interview.php?id=68648.

ASAP Sports (2011c) Caroline Wozniacki Press Conference (3). *ASAP Sports*. Retrieved 19 September 2013, from www.asapsports.com/show_interview.php?id=68647.

ASAP Sports (2012) Caroline Wozniacki Press Conference (4). *ASAP Sports*. Retrieved 19 September 2013, from www.asapsports.com/show_interview.php?id=77213.

ASAP Sports (2013) Nascar Media Conference. *ASAP Sports*. Retrieved 19 November 2013, from www.asapsports.com/show_conference.php?id=94490.

Ashtari, O. (2013) The Super Tweets of #SB47. Retrieved 14 February 2014, from https://blog.twitter.com/2013/the-super-tweets-of-sb47.

ATP World Tour (2014) Hutchins named as Queens Tournament Director. *APT World Tour*. Retrieved 19 November 2014, from www.atpworldtour.com/News/Tennis/2014/03/10/Hutchins-Named-Queens-Tournament-Director.aspx.

Augustine, N. (1995) Managing the crisis you tried to prevent. In *Harvard Business Review on Crisis Management* (1–31). Boston, MA: Harvard Business School Press.

Australian Broadcasting Authority (2001) Investigation into events on the anti-siphoning list. Sydney: Australian Broadcasting Authority.

Baer, J. (2013) Behind the curtain of a sports social media giant. Convince and convert. Retrieved 2 February 2014, from www.convinceandconvert.com/social-pros-podcast/behind-the-curtain-of-a-sports-social-media-giant/.

Ball, P. (1992) Premier League kicks off with Pounds 304m TV deal – Football. *The Times* (London), 19 May.

Ballester, P. and Walsh, D. (2004) *L.A. Confidentiel: Les secrets de Lance Armstrong*. Paris: La Martinière.

Barnett, S. (1990) *Games and Sets: The Changing Face of Sport on Television*. London: BFI Publishing.

Barnett, S. (1995) Sport. In A. Smith (ed.) *Television: An International History* (85–96). Oxford: Oxford University Press.

Barrett, D. (2005) Cash the key to broadcast rights. Foxsports, 30 December.

Battenfield, F. L. (2013) The Culture of Communication in Athletics. In P. M. Pedersen (ed.) *Routledge Handbook of Sport Communication* (441–450). Abingdon: Routledge.

Battenfield, F. L. and Kent, A. (2007) The culture of communication among intercollegiate sport information professionals. *International Journal of Sport Management and Marketing, 2* (3), 236–251.

Bayartsaikhan, K., Danielak, P., Dunst, K., Guibert, J., Luxford, L., Romanossian, R., . . . Seal, K. C. (2007) Market for third screen: A study of market potential of mobile TV and video across the U.S. and selected European countries. *International Journal of Mobile Marketing, 2* (1), 12–27.

BBC Sport (2011) Scandal-hit Olympic city sweeps clean. *BBC Sport*. Retrieved 22 June 2014, from http://news.bbc.co.uk/2/hi/sport/278035.stm.

Benammar, E. (2013) Stuart O'Grady, Lance Armstrong, Marco Pantani, Floyd Landis and Alberto Contador: Cycling's doping scandals. *ABC News*. Retrieved 29 December 2014, from www.abc.net.au/news/2013–07–25/cycling27s-infamous-doping-scandals/4842066.

Benoit, W. L. (1995) *Accounts, Excuses, and Apologies: A Theory of Image Restoration*. Albany, NY: State University of New York Press.

Benson, D. (2013) Lance Armstrong: Exclusive interview. *Cycling News*. Retrieved 26 March 2014, from www.cyclingnews.com/features/lance-armstrong-exclusive-interview-part-1.

Blodget, H. (2012) Don't mean to be alarmist, but the TV business may be starting to collapse. *Business Insider Australia*. Retrieved 22 August 2013, from www.businessinsider.com.au/tv-business-collapse-2012–6.

Boyd, T. (1997) Anatomy of a murder: O.J. and the imperative of sports in cultural studies. In A. Baker and T. Boyd (eds) *Out of Bounds: Sports, Media and the Politics of Identity* (vii–xi). Bloomington, IN: Indiana University Press.

Boyd, D. M. and Ellison, N. B. (2007) Social network sites: Definition, history, and scholarship. *Journal of Computer-Mediated Communication, 13* (1), 210–230.

Boyle, R. and Haynes, R. (2000) *Power Play: Sport, the Media and Popular Culture*. Sydney: Longman.

Boyle, R. and Haynes, R. (2006) The football industry and public relations. In J. L'Etang and M. Pieczka (eds) *Public Relations Critical Debates and Contemporary Practice* (221–241). Mahwah, NJ: Lawrence Erlbaum Associates.

Brazeal, L. (2008) The image repair strategies of Terrell Owens. *Public Relations Review, 34*, 145–150.

Briggs, A. and Burke, P. (2005) *A Social History of the Media: From Gutenberg to the Internet*. Cambridge: Polity.

British Sky Broadcasting (2012) *Annual Report 2012*. Retrieved 17 January 2013, from http://corporate.sky.com/documents/publications-and-reports/2012/annual-report-2012.pdf.

Broom, G. M. (2009) *Cutlip and Center's Effective Public Relations* (10th edn). Upper Saddle River, NJ: Prentice Hall.

Brown, K. A. (2014) Is apology the best policy? An experimental examination of the effectiveness of image repair strategies during criminal and noncriminal athlete transgressions. *Communication and Sport*, 1–20.

Bryant, K. (2013) This is such BS! All the training and sacrifice just flew out the window with one step that I've done millions of times! The frustration is unbearable. (Facebook status update.) *Facebook*. Retrieved 14 February 2014, from www.facebook.com/Kobe/posts/10151563315250419.

Businesswire (2014) CRICKET AUSTRALIA MEDIA ADVISORY: Australian cricketers to test their skills on the Thames. *Businesswire*. Retrieved 19 September 2013, from www.businesswire.com/news/home/20130618006873/en/CRICKET-AUSTRALIA-MEDIA-ADVISORY-Australian-Cricketers-Test.

Byrnes, H. (2010) Shattered Stephanie Rice says sorry over homophobic tweet. *Daily Telegraph*. Retrieved 31 October 2013, from www.dailytelegraph.com.au/shattered-stephanie-rice-says-sorry-over-homophobic-tweet/story-e6freuy9–1225915930831.

Came, B. (1998) Murdoch's Big Play, *Maclean's*, 111, October 19, 56.

Carey, M. and Most, J. (2003) *High Above Courtside: The Lost Memoirs of Johnny Most*. United States: Sports Pub.

Carr, D. (2014) My Nikon life. Retrieved 29 November 2014, from https://mynikonlife.com.au/dellycarr/.

Cave, M. and Crandall, R. (2001) Sports rights and the broadcast industry, *The Economic Journal, 111*, F4–F26.

CBS Sports (2014) www.cbssports.com/.

Chandler, J. (1988) *Television and National Sport: The United States and Britain*. Urbana, IL: University of Illinois Press.

Chenoweth, N. (2005) Lachlan's legacy – $560m lost on Super League. *Australian Financial Review*, 5 August.

Chessell, J. and Holgate, B. (2012) Nine stumps up for NRL. *Australian Financial Review*, 22 August.

CIPR (n.d.) The definition debate. *Chartered Institute of Public Relations*. Retrieved 31 October 2014, from www.cipr.co.uk/content/about-us/about-cipr/about-pr/definition-debate.

Coakley, J. (2003) *Sports in Society: Issues and Controversies*. Maidenhead: McGraw-Hill Education.

Coca-Cola (n.d.) Coca Cola launches 'Move to the Beat'. *News*. Retrieved 19 September 2014, from www.coca-colacompany.com/press-center/press-releases/coca-cola-launches-move-to-the-beat-london-2012-olympic-games-campaign-with-unveiling-of-beat-wall.

Cohen, R. (2013) New Fox Sports network to debut in August. *Yahoo News*. Retrieved 23 February 2014, from http://news.yahoo.com/fox-sports-network-debut-august-190301583–spt.html.

Comcast (2013) 2012 *Annual Report*. Retrieved 30 December 2014, from http://ly.comcast.com/2012annualreview/#&panel1-2.

Competition Commission (1999) British Sky Broadcasting Group plc and Manchester United PLC: A Report on the Proposed Merger.

Consoli, J. (2005) XM Scores Exclusive NHL Deal. *Mediaweek*, 12 September.

Conway, D. (2013) Tom Waterhouse's Reported $50 million NRL Deal 'Exaggerated'. *The Daily Telegraph*. Retrieved, 1 April 2013, from www.dailytelegraph.com.au/sport/nrl/tom-waterhouses-reported-50-million-nrl-deal-exaggerated/story-e6frexnr-1226607665314?nk=330a7649535700a0f8e484369b41e654.

Cooke, A. (1994) *The Economics of Leisure and Sport*. London: Routledge.

CoSida (n.d.). *About CoSida*. Retrieved 18 September 2014, from www.cosida.com/about/general.asp.

Cowan, P. (2014) SBS celebrates World Cup streaming success. *itNews*. Retrieved 26 July 2014, from www.itnews.com.au/News/389514,sbs-maintains-clean-sheet-against-live-streaming-outages.aspx.

Cowie, C. and Williams, M. (1997) The economics of sports rights. *Telecommunications Policy, 21* (7), 619–634.

Cricket Australia (2014) About us. Retrieved 16 February 2014, from http://coaches.cricket.com.au/cricketaustralia/about-us.

Crupi, (2011) Update: NBC bids $4.38 billion for Olympic Gold. No Ebersol, no problem: Lazarus delegation nabs rights through 2020. *Adweek*. Retrieved 18 February 2013, from www.adweek.com/news/television/update-nbc-bids-438-billion-olympic-gold-132319.

Dahlgren, P. (1992) Introduction. In P. Dahlgren and C. Sparks (eds) *Journalism and Popular Culture* (1–23). London: Sage.

Daniels (2014) Instagram announcement of head coach. Retrieved 19 December 2014, from http://instagram.com/p/oMvBUyJE3l/.

Dart, J. (2014) New media, professional sport and political economy. *Journal of Sport and Social Issues, 38* (6), 528–547.

Deloitte (2013) Deloitte Football Money League, 2013. *Sports Business Group*, Manchester UK, January.

Department of Broadband, Communications and Digital Economy (2009) www.dbcde.gov.au [now Department of Communications – www.communications.gov.au].

Duguid, S. (2004) Trading on the global football commodity market. *Media: Asia's Media and Marketing Newspaper, 21*, 21.

Dunne, F. (2011) TV Sports Markets, Sportel Briefing, Monaco, October, *SportBusiness*.

Dwyer, K. (2013) Russell Westbrook, via Twitter, helps a Thunder fan propose to his girlfriend #SheSaidYes. Retrieved 9 February 2014, from http://sports.yahoo.com/blogs/nba-ball-dont-lie/russell-westbrook-via-twitter-helps-thunder-fan-propose-155137481.html.

Eco, U. (1986) Sports chatter. In *Faith in Fakes: Essays* (translated from the Italian by W. Weaver). London: Secker and Warburg.

EFPL (2008) Record revenues for Bundesliga – 2.5 billion euros secured in new media rights deal. *European Professional Football Leagues*. Retrieved 16 May 2012, from www.epfl-europeanleagues.com/dfl_record_revenues.htm.

ESPN (2013) http://espn.go.com/.

European Commission (2003) Commission Decision of 23 July 2003 relating to a Proceeding Pursuant to Article 81 of the EC Treaty and Article 53 of the EEA Agreement (COMP/C.2–37.398—Joint Selling of the Commercial Rights of the UEFA Champions League).

European Commission (2011) Communication from the Commission to the European Parliament, the Council, the European Economic and Social Committee and the Committee of the Regions, 'Developing the European Dimension in Sport', 18 January 2011. Brussels, Belgium.

European Union (2007) Directive 2007/65/EC of the European Parliament and the Council of 11 December 2007 Amending Council Directive 89/552/EEC on the Coordination of Certain Provisions laid down by law, Regulation or Administrative Action in Member States Concerning the Pursuit of Television Broadcasting Activities. Retrieved 1 January 2013, from http://eur-lex.europa.eu/legal-content/EN/TXT/?uri=uriserv:OJ.L_.2007.332.01.0027.01.ENG.

Falcous, M. (1998) TV made it all a new game: Not again!: Rugby League and the case of the 'Superleague'. *Occasional Papers in Football Studies, 1* (1), 4–21.

Fallin, S. (2005) The five most common mistakes in crisis planning – and how to avoid them. *Tactics*, February, 11–12.

Farhi, P. (2014) The rules of the Super Bowl advertising game. *The Washington Post*. Retrieved 19 September 2014, from www.washingtonpost.com/lifestyle/style/the-rules-of-the-super-bowl-ad-game/2014/01/31/6333b7fe-89f3-11e3-a5bd-844629433ba3_story.html.

Favale, D. (2013) Full recap of Kobe Bryant's live tweet session of 81-point game. Bleach Report. Retrieved 14 February 2014, from http://bleacherreport.com/articles/1496690-full-recap-of-kobe-bryants-live-tweet-session-of-81-point-game.

FIBA (2013) www.fiba.com/.

FIFA (2004) *Annual Financial Report*. Retrieved 5 March 2015, from www.fifa.com/aboutfifa/officialdocuments/doclists/financialreport.html.

FIFA (2011) Almost half the world tuned in at home to watch 2010 FIFA World Cup South Africa. *FIFA News*. Retrieved 13 March 2013, from www.fifa.com/newscentre/news/newsid=1473143/.

FIFA (2013) *Annual Report*. Retrieved 5 March 2015, from www.fifa.com/aboutfifa/officialdocuments/doclists/financialreport.htmlFIFA (2014) *Annual Report*.

FIFA (2014) Record breaking downloads for FIFA's World Cup app, *FIFA*. Retrieved 13 May 2015, from www.fifa.com/worldcup/news/y=2014/m=6/news=record-breaking-downloads-for-fifa-s-official-world-cup-app-2382723.html.

Forde, P. (2008) An embodiment of the Olympic ideal, Michael Phelps saved the Games. *ESPN*. Retrieved 14 May 2013, from http://sports.espn.go.com/oly/summer08/columns/story?id=3539324.

Fortunato, J. (2000) Public relations strategies for creating mass media content: A case study of the National Basketball Association. *Public Relations Review, 26* (4), 481–497.

Foster, G., Greyser, S. and Walsh, B. (2006) *The Business of Sports: Text and Cases on Strategy and Management*. London: Thomson South-Western.

Fox Sports (2014) www.foxsports.com.au.

Frier, S. (2014) Facebook and Twitter battle for World Cup bragging rights. *Bloomberg Global Tech*. Retrieved 15 August 2014, from www.bloomberg.com/news/2014–07–30/facebook-and-twitter-battle-for-world-cup-bragging-rights.html.

Frost, L. (2004). Globalisation and the future of indigenous football codes. *Economic Papers, 23* (4), 355–368.

Futterman, M., Schechner, S. and Vranica, S. (2011) NHL the league that runs TV. *Wall Street Journal*. Retrieved 30 December 2014, from www.wsj.com/articles/SB10001424052970204026804577098774037075832.

Gallagher, B. (2009) Top 20 sporting moments of the decade: Lance Armstrong's Seventh Tour de France. *The Telegraph*. Retrieved 30 December 2014, from www.telegraph.co.uk/sport/othersports/cycling/lancearmstrong/6710593/Top-20-sporting-moments-of-the-decade-Lance-Armstrongs-seventh-Tour-de-France.html.

Galloway, C. and Kwansah-Aidoo, K. (2005) Getting to grips with issues management and crisis communication. In C. Galloway and K. Kwansah-Aidoo (eds) *Public Relations Issues and Crisis Management* (1–12). Melbourne: Thomson Social Science Press.

Galtung, J. and Ruge, M. (1981) Structuring and selecting news. In S. Cohen and J. Young (eds) *The Manufacture of News: Social Problems, Deviance and the Mass Media* (52–63). London: Constable [revised edition].

Gandy, O. H. (1982) *Beyond Agenda Setting: Information Subsidies and Public Policy*. Norwood, NJ: Ablex Publishing Company.

Gibbs, C. and Haynes, R. (2013) A phenomenological investigation into how Twitter has changed the nature of sport media relations. *International Journal of Sport Communication, 6*, 393–408.

Gilbert, D. (2010) Letter from Cavaliers' Owner: Dan Gilbert. *ESPN*. Retrieved 18 March 2011, from http://sports.espn.go.com/nba/news/story?id=5365704.

Gilmour, R. (2008) BBC Olympic coverage under threat as IOC rejects bid by Europe's free-to-air stations. *Daily Telegraph*. Retrieved 15 September 2013, from www.telegraph.co.uk/sport/olympics/3544110/BBC-Olympic-coverage-under-threat-as-IOC-rejects-bid-by-Europes-free-to-air-stations-Olympics.html.

Gorse, S., Chadwick, S. and Burton, N. (2010) Entrepreneurship through sports marketing: A case analysis of Red Bull in sport. *Journal of Sponsorship, 3* (4), 348–357.

Gratton, R. (1999) The Media. In R. I. Cashman and A. Hughes (eds) *Staging the Olympics: The Event and Its Impact* (121–131). Sydney: University of New South Wales.

Gray, K. (2011) Twitter athletes: $5 million in 140 characters. *Men's Journal*. Retrieved 23 June 2012, from www.mensjournal.com/magazine/twitter-athletes-5-million-in-140-characters-20131119.

Griffiths, A. (2003) *Digital Television Strategies*. New York: Palgrave Macmillan.

Grigg, A. (2006) Seven wins AFL with $780m bid. *Australian Financial Review*, 6 January.

Guttmann, A. (1978) *From Ritual to Record: The Nature of Modern Sport*. New York: Columbia University Press.

Hagey, K. and Peers, M. (2013) Time Warner opts to spin off all magazines. *The Wall Street Journal*. Retrieved 23 September 2013, from http://online.wsj.com/article/SB10001424127887324128504578344662798168222.html.

Hall, A., Nichols, W., Moynahan, P. and Taylor, J. (2007) *Media Relations in Sport* (2nd edn). Morgantown, WV: Fitness Information Technology.

Hardin, R. and McClung, S. (2002) Collegiate sports information: A profile of the profession. *Public Relations Quarterly*, *47* (2), 35–39.

Harris, N. (2010) Premier League nets £1.4bn TV rights bonanza. *The Independent*. Retrieved 31 October 2013, from www.independent.co.uk/sport/football/premier-league/premier-league-nets-16314bn-tv-rights-bonanza-1925462.html.

Hart, S. (2013) Tom Daley reveals he is in a relationship with a man in frank YouTube video from Olympic diver. *The Telegraph*. Retrieved 14 February 2014, from www.telegraph.co.uk/sport/olympics/diving/10487809/Tom-Daley-reveals-he-is-in-a-relationship-with-a-man-in-frank-YouTube-video-from-Olympic-diver.html.

Harvey, A. (2004) *The Beginnings of a Commercial Sporting Culture in Britain, 1793–1850*. Aldershot: Ashgate.

Healey, N. (2012) Analyst prediction: 800 million Smart TVs by 2017. *Cnet*. Retrieved 30 November 2013, from www.cnet.com/news/analyst-prediction-800-million-smart-tvs-by-2017/.

Helitzer, M. (1999) *The Dream Job: Sports Publicity, Promotion and Marketing*. Ohio: University Sports Press.

Hepworth, A. (2012) Olympic fury over rules for TV sport. *The Australian*. Retrieved 23 December 2012, from www.theaustralian.com.au/media/olympic-fury-over-rules-for-tv-sport/story-e6frg996-1226320796182.

Higgins, J. (2005) TV touch down: Can networks make money on record NFL deal?. *Broadcasting and Cable*, 25 April.

Hoehn, T. and Lancefield, D. (2003) Broadcasting and sport. *Oxford Review of Economic Policy*, *19* (4), 552–568.

Hoehn, T. and Kastrinaki, Z. (2012) Broadcasting and sport: Value drivers of TV right deals in European football. Retrieved 14 April 2013, from www.city.ac.uk/__data/assets/pdf_file/0007/120130/Hoehn_Kastrinaki_Sports_Rights_Feb_2012.pdf.

Horlock, (2013) Sportel Briefing: Top Ten Sports Deals. *Sport Business International*, No 176. Retrieved 30 December 2014, from www.evs.com/sites/default/files/1333378585_20120320-Sportel Briefing.pdf.

Hoye, R., Smith, A., Westerbeek, H., Stewart, B. and Nicholson, M. (2006) *Sport Management: Principles and Application*. London: Elsevier-Butterworth-Heinemann.

Hoye, R., Smith, A., Nicholson, M. and Stewart, B. (2015) *Sport Management: Principles and Applications* (4th edn). London: Routledge.

Hughes, H. (1981) *News and the Human Interest Story*. London: Transaction Books [reprint of the 1940 University of Chicago Press edition].

Hunter, P. (2005) NASCAR popularity running in high gear. *The Toronto Star*, 20 February.

Hutchins, B., and Rowe, D. (2009) From broadcast scarcity to digital plenitude: The changing dynamics of the media sport content economy. *Television and New Media*, *10* (4), 354–370.

Hutchins, B. and Rowe, D. (eds) (2012) *Sport Beyond Television: The Internet, Digital Media and the Rise of Networked Media Sport*. New York: Routledge.

ICC (2013) www.icc-cricket.com/cricket-world-cup.

IOC (2005) *Technical Manual on Media*. IOC. Retrieved 30 December 2014, from www.gamesmonitor.org.uk/files/Technical_Manual_on_Media_Written_and_Photographic.pdf.

IOC (2011) Hello World! IOC President Rogge interacts with Olympic fans live on Chinese microblog. *IOC*. Retrieved 19 September 2012, from www.olympic.org/news/hello-world-ioc-president-rogge-interacts-with-olympic-fans-live-on-chinese-microblog/141405.

IOC (2014) Olympic Broadcasting. *Olympic Org*. Retrieved 28 December 2014, from www.olympic.org/olympic-broadcasting.

IPC (2011) IPC releases social media guidelines for London 2012 Paralympic Games. *IPC*. Retrieved 14 May 2013, from www.paralympic.org/press-release/ipc-releases-socia-media-guidelines-london-2012-paralympic-games.

IPC (2012) London 2012 Paralympics prove to be online success. *IPC*. Retrieved 15 May 2013, from www.paralympic.org/news/london-2012-paralympics-prove-be-online-success.

Iezzi, T. (2012) Most Innovative Companies 2012. Fast Company. Retrieved 28 November 2013, from www.fastcompany.com/3017413/most-innovative-companies-2012/29red-bull-media-house.

Iosifidis, P. and Smith, P. (2011) *The European Television Sports Rights Market: Balancing Culture and Commerce*. Paper presented at the Private Television in Europe, 28–29 Apr 2011, Brussels, Belgium.

James, L. (2014, 11 July). LeBron: I'm coming back to Cleveland. *Sports Illustrated*. Retrieved 19 April 2014, from www.si.com/nba/2014/07/11/lebron-james-cleveland-cavaliers.

Jennings, A. and Sambrook, C. (2000) *The Great Olympic Swindle: When the World Wanted Its Games Back*. London: Simon & Schuster.

Jessop, A. (2012) The secret behind Red Bull's rise as an action sports leader. *Forbes*. Retrieved 31 July 2012, from www.forbes.com/sites/aliciajessop/2012/12/07/the-secret-behind-red-bulls-action-sports-success/.

Jhally, S. (1984) The spectacle of accumulation: Material and cultural factors in the evolution of the sports/media complex. *Insurgent Sociologist, 12* (3), 41–57.

Jhally, S. (1989) Cultural studies and the sports/media complex. In L. Wenner (ed.) *Media, Sports, and Society* (70–95). London: Sage.

Johnston, J. (2012) *Media Relations: Issues and Strategies*. Crows Nest, NSW: Allen & Unwin.

Kahn, J. (2013) Google TV getting rebranded as 'Android TV' for next-generation devices. *9TO5 Google*. Retrieved 30 December 2014, from http://9to5google.com/2013/10/10/report-google-tv-getting-rebranded-as-android-tv-for-next-generation-of-devices/.

Kantar Media (2013) Kantar Media reports Super Bowl spending reached $1.85 billion over the past ten years. *Kantar Media*. Retrieved 19 September 2013, from http://kantarmedia.us/press/kantar-media-reports-super-bowl-spending-reached-185-billion-over-past-ten-years.

Kaplan, A. M. and Haenlein, M. (2010) Users of the world, unite! The challenges and opportunities of social media. *Business Horizons, 53*, 59–68.

Karst, G. (1992) The Cardinals' first publicity man: St Louis' Favourite Sport. *Society of American Baseball Research, 1*, 52–57.

Keane, J. (1984) *Public Life and Late Capitalism: Toward a Socialist Theory of Democracy*. Cambridge: Cambridge University Press.

Kerr, A. K. and Emery, P. R. (2011) The allure of an 'overseas sweetheart': A Liverpool FC brand community. *International Journal of Sport Management and Marketing, 9* (3/4), 201–219.

Kerr, A. K. and Gladden J. M. (2008) Extending the understanding of professional team brand equity to the global marketplace. *International Journal of Sport Management and Marketing, 3* (1/2), 58–77.

Kruger, C. (2013) Blockbuster Tom Waterhouse deal 'not on': Suitor. *Sydney Morning Herald*. 20 March.

LAKings (2012a) To everyone in Canada outside BC, you're welcome. [Tweet]. Retrieved 14 June 2013, from https://twitter.com/LAKings/status/190309931210113025.

LAKings (2012b) @rainnwilson We can give you tickets – if you let us deliver them to you in a bowl of jello. Retrieved 14 June 2013, from https://twitter.com/LAKings/status/202911157374291968.

LAKings (2013) We apologize for the tweets that came from a guest of our organization. They were inappropriate and do not reflect the LA Kings. Retrieved 14 June 2013, from https://twitter.com/lakings/status/337057581489082368.

Laird, S. (2012a) How the L.A. Kings are redefining sports social media. *Mashable*. Retrieved 14 May 2013, from http://mashable.com/2012/05/30/kings-social-media/.

Laird, S. (2012b) L.A. Kings are NHL's Twitter champions too [INFOGRAPHIC]. *Mashable*. Retrieved 14 May 2013, from http://mashable.com/2012/06/15/kings-nhl-twitter-infographic/.

Larmer, B. (2005) The center of the world. *Foreign Policy*, September/October, 66–74.

Larsen, T. and Grice, A. (1999) Murdoch's Man Utd Bid Blocked. *The Independent*. Retrieved 22 September 2012, from www.independent.co.uk/news/murdochs-man-utd-bid-blocked-1086123.html.

Law, A., Harvey, J. and Kemp, S. (2002) The global sport mass media oligopoly. *International Review for the Sociology of Sport, 37* (3–4), 279–302.

Lelyukhin, A. (2013) The impact of EU on sport broadcasting: What does the line of recent ECJ cases signal about? *The International Sports Law Journal, 13* (1–2), 104–131.

Levy, D. (2011) Is watching sports on TV actually better than being at the game? *Bleach Report*. Retrieved 29 December 2014, from http://bleacherreport.com/articles/923563-is-watching-sports-on-tv-actually-better-than-being-at-the-game.

Littlewood, T. B. (1990) *Arch, a Promoter, not a Poet: The Story of Arch Ward*. Ames, IA: Iowa State University Press.

Liverpool FC (2014) LFC Twitter. Retrieved 23 December 2014, from www.liverpoolfc.com/fans/socialmedia/lfc-twitter.

LOCOG (2012) London 2012: App launched for fans to share Olympic experiences. *London24*. Retrieved 25 October 2013, from www.london24.com/news/london_2012_app_launched_for_fans_to_share_olympic_experiences_1_1382069.

Lowes, M. (1997) Sports page: A case study in the manufacture of sports news for the daily press. *Sociology of Sport Journal, 14* (2), 143–159.

Lowes, M. (1999) *Inside the Sports Pages: Work Routines, Professional Ideologies, and the Manufacture of Sports News*. Toronto: University of Toronto Press.

LPGA (2013) Players taking game to new heights at RR Donelly LPGA Founders Cup media day. *LPGA*. Retrieved 19 November 2014, from www.lpga.com/golf/news/2013/2/founders-cup-media-day.aspx.

Lull, J. and Hinerman, S. (1997) The search for scandal. In J. Lull and S. Hinerman (eds) *Media Scandals: Morality and Desire in the Popular Culture Marketplace* (1–32). New York: Columbia University Press.

Lunn, S. (2011) Odds-on for change in sports bets. *The Australian*. Retrieved 23 February 2013, from www.theaustralian.com.au/news/features/odds-on-for-change-in-sports-bets/story-e6frg6z6-1226217630636?nk=330a7649535700a0f8e484369b41e654.

McChesney, R. (1989) Media Made Sport: A History of Sports Coverage in the United States. In L. Wenner (ed.) *Media, Sports and Society* (49–69). Newbury Park, CA: Sage.

McCleneghan, J. S. (1995). The sports information director – no attention, no respect, and a PR practitioner in trouble. *Public Relations Quarterly, 40*, 28–32.

McCoy, J. (1997) Radio sports broadcasting in the United States, Britain and Australia, 1920–1956 and its influence on the Olympic Games. *Journal of Olympic History*, Spring, 20–25.

McDonalds (n.d.) McDonalds unveils sponsorship plans for London 2012. *Media Releases*. Retrieved 20 March 2014, from http://news.mcdonalds.com/Corporate/manual-releases/2011/McDonald-s-Unveils-Sponsorship-Plans-for-London-20.

McGaughey, S. L., and Liesch, P. W. (2002) The global sports–media nexus: Reflections on the 'Super League Saga' in Australia. *Journal of Management Studies, 39* (3), 383–416.

McKay, J., Hutchins, B. and Mikosza, J. (2000) Shame and scandal in the family: Australian media narratives of the IOC/SOCOG Scandal Matrix. *Fifth International Symposium for Olympic Research.*

McManus, J. (2012) New television deal helps French football narrowly avoid financial 'catastrophe'. *Goal.* Retrieved 16 January 2013, from www.goal.com/en/news/1722/french-ligue-1/2012/06/29/3208185/new-television-deal-helps-french-football-narrowly-avoid.

Mackey, S. (2004) Crisis and issues management. In J. Johnston and C. Zawawi (eds) *Public Relations: Theory and Practice.* Crows Nest, NSW: Allen & Unwin.

Magee, K. (2012) Campaign of the year: London 2012 Olympic and Paralympic Games by LOCOG. *PR Week.* Retrieved 30 December 2014, from www.prweek.com/article/1156232/campaign-year-london-2012-olympic-paralympic-games-locog.

Maguire, J. (1993) Globalization, sport development, and the media/sport production complex. *Sport Science Review, 2* (1), 29–47.

Maguire, J. (1999) The global media-sport complex. In J. Maguire (ed.) *Global Sport: Identities, Societies, Civilizations* (144–175) Malden, MA: Polity Press.

Makitalo, G. (2012) A timeline of Lance Armstrong's doping controversy. *My Fit Family.* Retrieved 30 December 2014, from www.myfitfamilyusa.net/group/La.

*Manchester Evening News* (2010) Reds Fans Double. *Manchester Evening News.* Retrieved 26 April 2011, from www.manchestereveningnews.co.uk/sport/football/football-news/reds-fans-double-938963.

Manchester United (2014) Manchester United Google plus front row hangout. Manchester United FC. Retrieved 29 December 2014, from www.manutd.com/en/Fanzone/News-And-Blogs/2014/Feb/Manchester-United-Google-plus-Front-Row-Hangout.aspx.

Massey, J. (2001) Managing organizational legitimacy: Communication strategies for organizations in crisis. *The Journal of Business Communication, 38* (2), 153–183.

Mattos, C. (2012) Broadcasting football rights in Brazil: The case of Globo and 'Club of 13' in the antitrust perspective. *Estudos Econômicos (São Paulo), 42* (2), 337–362.

MEAA (2014) Media entertainment and arts alliance – journalists' code of ethics. Retrieved 16 September 2014, from www.alliance.org.au/code-of-ethics.html.

Meserole, M. (2002) Roone Arledge, created Monday night football. *ESPN Classic.* Retrieved 16 July, 2013, from http://espn.go.com/classic/obit/s/2001/0501/1189828.html.

Michael, E. (2006) *Public Policy: The Competitive Framework.* South Melbourne, Victoria: Oxford University Press.

Mickle, T. (2012) Revamped sales strategy helps IOC boost media rights fees. *SportsBusiness Daily Global Journal.* Retrieved 21 July 2013, from www.sportsbusinessdaily.com/SB-Blogs/Olympics/London-Olympics/2012/08/iocrevenue.aspx.

Mignon, P. (2003) The Tour de France and the doping issue. *International Journal of the History of Sport, 20* (2), 227–245.

Miller, J. A., and Shales, T. (2011). *Those Guys Have All the Fun: Inside the World of ESPN.* New York: Hachette Digital.

Mitchell, A. and Rosenstiel, T. (2012) *The State of the News Media 2012*, Pew Research Centre's Project for Excellence in Journalism. Retrieved 31 October 2013, from www.stateofthemedia.org/2012/overview-4/.

Mitten, M. (2010) *American Needle v. NFL*: U.S. Professional clubs are separate economic threads when jointly marketing intellectual property (19 July 2010). *Marquette Law School Legal Studies Paper No. 10–33.* http://dx.doi.org/10.2139/ssrn.1645364.

Morin, E. (1976) Pour une crisologie. *Communications, 25*, 149–163.

Murillo, E. and Murillo, C. (2005) El Nou Barca. *Edicions* (62), 199–200.

NASCAR (2011) NASCAR, Sprint announce sponsorship extension. NASCAR News. Retrieved 26 January 2013, from www.nascar.com/en_us/news-media/articles/2011/12/03/nascar-sprint-extend-sponsorship-agreement.html.

NASCAR (2013) www.nascar.com/.

National Geographic (2013) *Cycling's Greatest Fraud.* National Geographic documentary, retrieved 29 December 2014, from https://www.youtube.com/watch?v=PgRBxsW26vY.

NBA (2012) *Blue Book: NBA Media Directory 2013–2013.* New York: NBA.

NBA (2013) Player Profile: Kobe Bryant. *NBA.* Retrieved 30 August 2013, from www.nba.com/playerfile/kobe_bryant/.

Neupauer, N. C. (1999) A personality traits study of sports information directors at 'big' vs 'small' programs in the east. *Social Science Journal, 36* (1), 163–172.

New York Yankees (2015) Media Kit. *New York Yankees.* Retrieved 5 March 2015, from http://newyork.yankees.mlb.com/nyy/fan_forum/mediaguide.jsp.

New, B. and Le Grand, J. (1999) Monopoly in sports broadcasting. *Policy Studies, 20* (1), 23–36.

News Corporation (2005) *Annual Report.*

News Corporation (2013) *Annual Report.*

New York Yankees (2014) Media Kit. *New York Yankees.* Retrieved 19 March 2014, from http://newyork.yankees.mlb.com/nyy/fan_forum/mediaguide.jsp.

Nielsen (2012) State of the Media: 2012 Year in Sports. *Nielsen Reports.* Retrieved 21 August 2013, from www.nielsen.com/us/en/insights/reports/2013/state-of-the-media–2012-year-in-sports.html.

NHL (2013) Collective bargaining agreement between the National Hockey League and the National Hockey League Players' Association. *NHL.* Retrieved 29 December, 2014, from www.nhl.com/nhl/en/v3/ext/CBA2012/NHL_NHLPA_2013_CBA.pdf.

NRL (2012) Billion dollar deal secures game's future. *NRL.* Retrieved 30 December 2014, from www.nrl.com/billion-dollar-deal-secures-games-future/tabid/10874/newsid/69393/default.aspx.

NRL (2013) Fans to get ultimate digital experience. *NRL.* Retrieved 27 April 2013, from www.nrl.com/fans-to-get-ultimate-digital-experience/tabid/10874/newsid/70510/default.aspx.

Offe, C. (1984) 'Crises of crisis management': Elements of a political crisis theory. In J. Keane (ed.) *Contradictions of the Welfare State* (35–65). Cambridge, MA: MIT Press.

O'Halloran, J. (2012) BSkyB to 'tighten belt' after EPL football rights deal. *Satellite Card Sharing.* Retrieved 1 April 2013, from www.satellitecardsharing.com/bskyb-to-tighten-belt-after-epl-football-rights-deal/.

Oldenburg, R. (2001) Introduction. In R. Oldenburg (ed.) *Celebrating the Third Place: Inspiring Stories About the 'Great Good Places' at the Heart of Our Communities,* (1–8). New York: Marlowe & Company.

Olympic.org (n.d). London 2012 Torch Relay. *News.* Retrieved 17 January 2014, from www.olympic.org/news/london-2012-olympic-torch-relay.

Oriard, M. (1993) *Reading Football.* Chapel Hill, NC: University of North Carolina.

Otto, T. (2013) Cricket Australia fines David Warner $5750 over Twitter rant. *Daily Telegraph.* Retrieved 26 May 2013, from www.dailytelegraph.com.au/sport/cricket/cricket-australia-fines-david-warner-5750-over-twitter-rant/story-fni2fnmo-1226648382977.

Owen, D. (2014) Bumper 2014 forecast for value of premium sports broadcasting rights. *Inside the Games.* Retrieved 17 February 2014, from www.insidethegames.biz/news/1017695-bumper-2014-forecast-for-value-of-premium-sports-broadcasting-rights.

Patterson, B. (1993) Crises impact on reputation management. *Public Relations Journal,* November, 47–48.

Payne, M. (2005) As time goes by. . . . *Sport Business International,* 1 March.

Pearce, L. (2014) Thomas Berdych taking the tweet approach. *Sydney Morning Herald.* Retrieved 19 September 2014, from www.smh.com.au/sport/tennis/tomas-berdych-taking-the-tweet-approach-20140109–30kge.html.

Pearson, C. and Clair, J. (1998) Reframing crisis management. *Academy of Management Review, 23* (1), 59–76.

Pearson, C., Clair, J., Misra, S. and Mitroff, I. (1997) Managing the unthinkable. *Organizational Dynamics*, Autumn, 51–64.

Pearson, C. and Mitroff, I. (1993) From crisis prone to crisis prepared: A framework for crisis management. *Academy of Management Executive, 7* (1), 48–59.

Pedersen, P. M., Miloch, K. S. and Laucella, P. C. (2007) *Strategic Sport Communication*. Champaign, IL: Human Kinetics.

Perform (2012) *Global Sports Media Consumption Report 2012*. London: TV Sports Markets.

PGA (2014) Media Guide. *PGA*. Retrieved 9 March 2014, from www.pgamediaguide.com/.

Phillips, M. (1996) *An Illusory Image: A Report on the Media Coverage and Portrayal of Women's Sport in Australia*. Canberra: Australian Sports Commission.

Pickert, K. (2009) A brief history of the X Games. *Time*. Retrieved 31 October 2012, from http://content.time.com/time/nation/article/0,8599,1873166,00.html.

Poor, N. (2006) Playing internet curveball with traditional media gatekeepers: Pitcher Curt Schilling and Boston Red Sox fans. *Convergence: The International Journal of Research into New Media Technologies, 12* (1), 41–53.

Portet, X. and Ortiz, R. (2008) Corporate communication in a global sports media complex: The case study of FC Barcelona. In R.A. Oglesby and M. G. Adams (eds) *Business Research Yearbook: Global Business Perspectives* (Vol. XV, 389–394). Beltsville, MD: International Academy of Business Disciplines.

Productivity Commission (2000) *Broadcasting Inquiry Report*. Canberra: Commonwealth of Australia.

PWC (2012) Business model transformation the key to success. *PWC*. Retrieved 22 April 2013, from www.pwc.com.au/media-centre/2012/entertainment-media-outlook-jul12.htm.

Rader, B. (1984) *In Its Own Image: How Television Has Transformed Sports*. New York: Free Press.

Ramsey, R. (2004) Responding to a crisis. *Supervision, 65* (10), 6–7.

Rao, V. (2008) *Facebook Applications and Playful Mood: The Construction of Facebook as a Third Place*. Paper presented at the 12th International Conference on Entertainment and Media in the Ubiquitous Era, Mindtrek 2008, Tampere, Finland, October 7–9.

Rasmussen, B. (2010) *Sport Junkies Rejoice: The Birth of ESPN*. Hartsdale, NY: CreateSpace Independent Publishing Platform.

Raynovoich, S. (2014) New England Patriots content chief talks social, video, analytics. *CMS Wire*. Retrieved 19 December 2014, from www.cmswire.com/cms/customer-experience/new-england-patriots-content-chief-talks-social-video-analytics-024113.php.

Read, B. and Honeysett, S. (2005) Gallop secures $500m TV deal. *The Australian*, 2 July.

Real, M. (1998) MediaSport: Technology and the Commodification of Postmodern Sport. In L. Wenner (ed.) *MediaSport* (14–26). London: Routledge.

Red Bull (2013) www.redbull.com/au/en.

Rios, M. (2012) Euro 2012 Recap. Retrieved 14 February 2013, from https://blog.twitter.com/2012/euro-2012-recap.

Rodrigues, J. (2012) Premier League Football at 20: 1992, the start of a whole new ball game. *The Guardian*, 2 February. Retrieved 17 May 2013, from www.theguardian.com/football/from-the-archive-blog/2012/feb/02/20-years-premier-league-football-1992.

Rosner, S. (2010). Team ownership could fade with Comcast-NBC universal deal. *SportsBusiness Daily Global Journal*. Retrieved 23 March 2013, from www.sportsbusinessdaily.com/Journal/Issues/2010/03/20100301/Opinion/Team-Ownership-Could-Fade-With-Comcast-NBC-Universal-Deal.aspx.

Rotunno, T. (2013) Budweiser unveils its Super Bowl ad lineup. *Global Post*. Retrieved 14 February 2013, from www.globalpost.com/dispatch/news/business/companies/130111/budweiser-unveils-football-super-bowl-ad-lineup.

Rowe, D. (1997) Rugby League in Australia: The Super League saga. *Journal of Sport and Social Issues, 21* (2), 221–226.

Rowe, D. (1999) *Sport, Culture and the Media: The Unruly Trinity*. Buckingham: Open University Press.

Rowe, D. (2000) Let the media games begin. *Australian Quarterly: Journal of Contemporary Analysis,* June–July, 21–23.

Ryan, N. (2013) Hendrick social media plan could be prototype. *USA Today*. Retrieved 23 July 2014, from www.usatoday.com/story/sports/nascar/2013/08/14/hendrick-motorsports-social-media-reddit-dale-earnhardt-jr-twitter/2657983/.

Salkin, A., and Jurovaty, M. (2013) *2013 Patriots Media Guide*. New England, USA: New England Patriots. Retrieved 23 July 2014, from http://patriots.1stroundmediagroup.com/.

Sandy, R., Sloane, P. and Rosentraub, M. (2004) *The Economics of Sport: An International Perspective*. New York: Palgrave Macmillan.

Savage, P. and Savage, O. (2009) *Mobile Apps for Sport: Exploiting New Mobile Media Opportunities*. London: SportBusiness Group.

Saward, J. (2013) Some ruminations on TV rights. Joeblogsf1: The real stories from inside the F1 paddock. Retrieved 17 October 2013, from http://joesaward.wordpress.com/2013/01/07/some-ruminations-on-tv-rights/.

Sawers, P. (2013) MUTV is now 100 per cent owned by Manchester United, after BSkyB sells its one-third stake. *The Nextweb*. Retrieved 30 December 2014, from http://thenextweb.com/media/2013/01/22/mutv-is-now-100-owned-by-manchester-united-after-bskyb-sells-its-one-third-stake/.

SBS (2014) Media Release: SBS's FIFA World Cup multi-platform broadcast a success with TV audiences up 15 per cent on 2010's Final. *SBS*. Retrieved 14 August 2014, from www.sbs.com.au/aboutus/news-media-releases/view/id/904/h/MEDIA-RELEASE-SBS-S-FIFA-WORLD-CUP-MULTI-PLATFORM-BROADCAST-A-SUCCESS-WITH-TV-AUDIENCES-UP-15-ON-2010-S-FINAL.

Scherer, J. and Jackson, S.J. (2008) Producing allblacks.com: Cultural intermediaries and the policing of electronic spaces of sporting consumption. *Sociology of Sport Journal, 25*, 187–205.

Schudson, M. (1978) *Discovering The News: A Social History of American Newspapers*. New York: Basic Books.

Scot Johns, R. (2011) Latest iPad sales figures, Scot's blog, Adventures of an Independent Author. Retrieved 17 August 2014, from http://authoradventures.blogspot.com.au/2011/01/latest-ipad-sales-figures.html.

Sha, B.-L. (2011) 2010 Practice analysis: Professional competencies and work categories in public relations today. *Public Relations Review, 37* (3), 187–196.

Silkstone, D. (2010) Western Sydney, Gold Coast so ho-hum as AFL chases slice of China market. *The Age*. Retrieved 17 August 2012, from www.theage.com.au/afl/afl-news/western-sydney-gold-coast-so-hohum-as-afl-chases-slice-of-china-market-20100728–10w3h.html.

Simpson, C. (2014) SBS's 2014 FIFA World Cup broadcast, by the numbers. *Gizmodo*. Retrieved 17 August 2014, from www.gizmodo.com.au/2014/07/sbs-fifa-world-cup-2014-broadcast-by-the-numbers/.

Soccerex (2011) Barcelona President calls for La Liga change. *Soccerex*. Retrieved 31 December 2012, from www.soccerex.com/industry-news/barcelona-president-calls-for-la-liga-change/.

Soccerex (2013) Latin American leagues register big rise in broadcast revenues. *Soccerex*. Retrieved 22 October 2013, from www.soccerex.com/industry-news/latin-american-leagues-register-big-rise-in-broadcast-revenues/.

Solis, B. (2012) Inside look at how the Boston Celtics win in social media. *Brian Solis*. Retrieved 29 June 2014, from www.briansolis.com/2012/06/inside-look-how-the-boston-celtics-win-in-social-media/.

Soukup, C. (2006) Computer-mediated communication as a virtual third place: Building Oldenburg's great good places on the World Wide Web. *New Media and Society, 8* (3), 421–440.

Speers, D. (2009) Sky News Interview with Rupert Murdoch, Retrieved 15 September 2014, from www.youtube.com/watch?v=M7GkJqRv3BI.

Spits, S. (2012) Greek athlete expelled over racist tweet. *The Age*. Retrieved 14 March 2014, from www.theage.com.au/olympics/news-london-2012/greek-athlete-expelled-over-racist-tweet-20120726–22rm7.html.

Sports Business (2012) News Corp completes move for EPSN star sports. *Sports Business Insider*. Retrieved 19 December 2014, from http://sportsbusinessinsider.com.au/international-news/news-corp-completes-move-for-espn-star-sports/.

Sports Business (2013) Sports Business Insider. Retrieved 30 December 2014, from http://sportsbusinessinsider.com.au/.

Stapleton, R. (2005) Australian TV football rights battle royal in prospect. *Sport Business International*, 1 April.

Stephens, K., Malone, P. and Bailey, C. (2005) Communicating with stakeholders during a crisis. *Journal of Business Communication*, *42* (4), 390–419.

Stevenson, S. (2003) C_Schilling1966 has entered the room: What happens when a Red Sox pitcher 'logs on?' *Slate*. Retrieved 19 September 2012, from http://slate.msn.com/id/2091927/.

Stewart, B. (1995) 'I heard it on the radio, I saw it on the television': The commercial and cultural development of Australian first class cricket: 1946–1985. Unpublished Doctoral Thesis, La Trobe University, Melbourne, Australia.

Stewart, B., Nicholson, M., Smith, A. and Westerbeek, H. (2004) *Australian Sport: Better By Design? The Evolution of Australian Sport Policy*. London: Routledge.

Stoldt, G. C. (2000) Current and ideal organizational roles of NCAA Division I-A sports information professionals. *Cyber-Journal of Sport Marketing*. Retrieved 23 February 2013, from http://fulltext.ausport.gov.au/fulltext/2000/cjsm/v4n1/stoldt41.htm.

Stoldt, G. C. (2013) College athletics communications: Evolution of the field. In P. M. Pedersen (ed.) *Routledge Handbook of Sport Communication* (482–491), Abingdon: Routledge.

Stoldt, G. C., Dittmore, S. and Branvold, S. (2012) *Sport Public Relations: Managing Stakeholder Communication*. Champaign, IL: Human Kinetics.

Strange, A. (2012) Yahoo Sports, NBC sports team up for web content. *PCMag*. Retrieved 16 January 2013, from www.pcmag.com/article2/0,2817,2413019,00.asp.

Straubhaar, J. and LaRose, S. (2008) *Media Now: Understanding Media, Culture, and Technology, 2008 Update*. Belmont, CA: Thompson Learning.

Sundheim, M. (2013) Guy behind the guy: Breaking in. *Carolina Hurricanes*. Retrieved 13 May 2014, from http://hurricanes.nhl.com/club/news.htm?id=680068.

*The Telegraph*. (2011) London 2012 Olympics: Full 'London Prepares' test event schedule for summer 2011. *The Telegraph*. Retrieved 18 April 2014, from www.telegraph.co.uk/sport/olympics/8498150/London-2012-Olympics-full-London-Prepares-test-event-schedule-for-Summer-2011.html.

Theberge, N. and Cronk, A. (1986) Work routines in newspaper sports departments and the coverage of women's sports. *Sociology of Sport Journal*, *3*, 195–203.

Time Warner (2001) America Online and Time Warner complete merger to create AOL Time Warner. *Time Warner*. Retrieved 27 September 2013 from www.timewarner.com/newsroom/press-releases/2001/01/11/america-online-and-time-warner-complete-merger-to-create-aol-time.

Time Warner (2013) *Annual Report*. Retrieved 5 March 2015, from http://ir.timewarner.com/phoenix.zhtml?c=70972&p=irol-reportsannual.

Toft, T. (2003) Football: Joint selling of media rights. *European Commission Competition Policy Newsletter*, *3* (Autumn), 47–52.

Tonazzi, A. (2003) Competition policy and the commercialization of sport broadcasting rights: The decision of the Italian Competition Authority. *International Journal of the Economics of Business*, *10* (1), 17–34.

Tour de France (2014) Le Tour de France Media Kit. Retrieved 17 March 2014, from www.letour.fr/le-tour/2013/docs/communiques/_TDF_20121024_Press_kit.pdf.

Tourdownunder (2014) *Santos Tour Down Under media kit.* Retrieved 17 March 2014, from www.tourdownunder.com.au/documents/gallery-and-media/2014-media-kit.pdf.

Turk, J. V. (1985) Information subsidies and influence. *Public Relations Review, 11* (3), 10–25.

Turner, G. and Cunningham, S. (2002) *The Media and Communications in Australia.* Crows Nest, NSW: Allen & Unwin.

Turner, P. and Cusumano, S. (2000). Virtual advertising: Legal implications for sport. *Sport Management Review, 3* (1), 47–70.

Tymson, C. and Lazar, P. (2002) *The New Australian and New Zealand Public Relations Manual.* Chatswood, NSW: Tymson Communications.

UEFA (2011) *Annual Report.* Retrieved 5 March 2015, from www.uefa.org/documentlibrary/aboutuefa/.

UEFA (2012) *Annual Report.* Retrieved 5 March 2015, fom www.uefa.org/documentlibrary/aboutuefa/.

UFC (2013) www.ufc.com.

Vivendi (2013) *Annual Report.* Retrieved 5 March 2015, from www.vivendi.com/.../20140415_annual_report_doc_de_ref_2013_en.pdf.

Wallace, F. (1960) *Knute Rockne.* Garden City, NY: Doubleday & Company.

Walsh, J. and McAllister-Spooner, S. (2011). Analysis of the image repair discourse in the Michael Phelps controversy. *Public Relations Review, 37,* 157–162.

Walt Disney Company (2005) *Annual Report.*

Walt Disney Company (2012) *Annual Report.*

Walt Disney Company (2013) *Annual Report.* Retrieved 5 March 2015, from http://thewaltdisneycompany.com/investors/financial-information/annual-report.

Ward, R. (2012) TV Boomers: All NBL games to be streamed live. *Sydney Morning Herald.* Retrieved 22 January 2013, from www.smh.com.au/sport/basketball/tv-boomers-all-nbl-games-to-be-streamed-live-20120828–24xju.html.

Warren, A. (2010) SANZAR lands rich rugby broadcast deal. *Wide World of Sports.* Retrieved 19 June 2012, from http://wwos.ninemsn.com.au/article.aspx?id=1043394&rss=yes.

Warner, M. (2012) The World from Berlin: 'Sky is playing a dangerous game'. *Spiegel Online International.* Retrieved 31 December 2012, from www.spiegel.de/international/german-press-review-of-bundesliga-sky-deutschland-broadcast-tv-rights-a-828301.html.

Wenner, L. (ed.) (1998) *MediaSport.* London: Routledge.

Whannel, G. (1992) *Fields in Vision: Television Sport and Cultural Transformation.* London: Routledge.

Whitcomb, D. (2013, 25 September). Tennis star Novak Djokovic announces engagement to girlfriend. *Reuters.* Retrieved 19 September 2014, from www.reuters.com/article/2013/09/26/us-djokovic-idUSBRE98O1BV20130926.

White, T. (2005) *Broadcast News Writing, Reporting, and Producing* (4th edn). London: Elsevier.

White, D. (2012) TV executives must look outside the box. *Australian Financial Review.* 22 October. Retrieved 5 March 2015, from www.afr.com/p/national/tv_executives_must_look_outside_eztBA3WQxHG4wTNGW0UFMM.

White, A. and Davidson, D. (2012) Why winner Gyngell feels like a loser. *The Australian,* 22 August.

Whiteside, E. and Hardin, M. (2010) Public relations and sports: Work force demographics in the intersection of two gendered industries. *Journal of Sports Media, 5* (1), 21–52.

Wilcox, D. (2008) *Public Relations Writing and Media Techniques* (5th edn). Boston, MA: Allyn & Bacon.

Wilcox, D., Ault, P., Agee, W. and Cameron, G. (2000) *Public Relations: Strategies and Tactics.* New York: Longman.

Wiley, R. (2002) Arledge's World Flowed with Ideas. *Page 2.* Retrieved 27 March, 2013 from http://espn.go.com/page2/s/wiley/021209.html.

Williams, J. (1994) The local and the global in English soccer and the rise of satellite television. *Sociology of Sport Journal, 11*, 376–397.

Willoughby, K. A. and Mancini, C. (2003) The inaugural (and only) season of the Xtreme Football League: A case study in sports entertainment. *International Journal of Sports Marketing and Sponsorship, 5*, 227–235.

Wilson, B. (2009) Can sport still net winning TV deals? *BBC News*. Retrieved 24 May 2013, from http://news.bbc.co.uk/2/hi/business/8026393.stm.

World Rugby (2011) IRB Strategic Plan. Retrieved 22 June 2012, from www.worldrugby.org/strategic-plan.

WTA (2010) A day in the life of the tour (communications). Retrieved 28 July 2013, from www.wtatennis.com/news/article/1952999/title/a-day-in-the-life-of-the-tour.

WTA (2013) www.wtatennis.com/.

Wyshynski, G. (2012) Inside the Los Angeles Kings Twitter feed, social media sensation of NHL playoffs. *Yahoo*. Retrieved 25 June 2013, from http://sports.yahoo.com/blogs/nhl-puck-daddy/inside-los-angeles-kings-twitter-feed-social-media-225509441.html.

Yanity, M. (2013) Publishing for paydirt: A case study of an athletic department writer. *International Journal of Sport Communication, 6*, 478–489.

YouTube (2012) Call Me Maybe – 2012 USA Olympic Swimming Team. Retrieved 18 March, 2013, from www.youtube.com/watch?v=YPIA7mpm1wU.

YouTube (2014) About YouTube. Retrieved 23 December 2014, from www.youtube.com/yt/about/.

Zeidler, S. and Richwine, L. (2013) CBS scores record local ad sales for Super Bowl. Reuters. Retrieved 19 May 2013, from www.reuters.com/article/2013/01/25/superbowl-ads-idUSL1N0AQ0AZ20130125.

Zoch, L. M. and Molleda, J. C. (2006) Building a theoretical model of media relations using framing, information subsidies, and agenda-building. In C. H. Botan and V. Hazleton (eds) *Public Relations Theory II* (247–272). Mahwah, NJ: Lawrence Erlbaum Associates.

# Index


ABC 20–22
access 129–131, 153, 220–222, 249
accommodation 257–258
accreditation 170–171, 247–249
advertisements 31–32, 70–71, 86–90, 107–108, 166–168
advisory 193–194
AFL 77, 109–110, 129–130, 135
agenda 147, 238–239
Al Jazeera 50
Anderson, W.B. 146
ANZ 195
Apple 29, 31
apps 28–29
Arledge, R. 22
Armstrong, L. 280–282
ASP 57–58
athletes 12, 72, 221–222, 234–237, 253–254
Atlanta Games 245–246
audience 70–71, 75, 83, 86–90, 190–191
Augustine, N. 276
Australia 73, 77, 90, 107–112, 129, 147
Austria 105

Barnett, S. 21–22
Barrett, D. 130–131
basketball 56
Battenfield, F.L. 152
BBC 20
beat system 126–127
Belgium 105–106
Benoit, W.L. 267
Berdych, T. 221–222
Bertelsmann 50
betting 90, 111–112
Bewkes, J. 48
Boyd, D.M. 222
Boyd, T. 9
Boyle, R. 19, 21
brand awareness 70
Brazeal, L. 267–268
Brazil 114–115
briefing 208
Briggs, A. 5
broadcast rights 23, 70–73, 249; buying 75–80, 82–83; revenue 86–90; selling 73–75, 80–81, 83–86, 103–104; value 81; *see also* regulation
Bryant, K. 222–223
BSkyB 101–102
Burke, P. 5

Canada 148
Case, S. 48
Cave, M. 112
CBS 20, 50, 88
CCTV 113–114
change 12–15
China 74–75, 113–114, 230
circuits 59, 61, 85–86
Coe, S. 29
collective selling *see* joint selling
Comcast 45–46
commercialization 13, 23, 68–71, 98–99, 220; *see also* advertisements; broadcast rights; regulations
communication 5–6, 50–51, 128, 183–184; advisory 193–194; corporate 149; crisis 275–276; fact sheets 191–193, 211; media guides 184, 194–196, 198–200; release 184–191, 196; *see also* interactions
competition 78, 80, 166; *see also* regulation
competitive sport 4–5
conference 136–137, 202–207, 254–256
consumer 26–27, 29, 51–52, 70–72
containment 275–276
content 51–52, 72–73, 219–220, 231–234, 238–239
convergence 13–14, 27, 48, 100
corporations 14, 149; *see also* advertisements; media organizations; sport organizations

coverage 12, 74, 165–168, 176–177; conferences 202–207; exposure 86–90; goals 168–170; interviews 207–213; media grids 174–176; media list 170–173; opportunities 173–174; release 190–191
Crandall, R. 112
cricket 56, 58
Cricket Australia 168–169, 193–194
crisis 149, 263–266, 270–274; impact 266, 268–269
Cronk, A. 127
culture 9–10, 87–88, 102–103

Daniels, L. 86
*The Decision* 175
Deloitte Football Money League 93–97
digital media *see* internet; social media
digital television 30–32
Disney 27, 29, 46–47, 49, 65–66, 82, 87; *see also* ESPN
distribution 50–52, 191
doping 279–282

Eisner, M. 66
elite sport 4–5
Ellison, N.B. 222
entertainment 44
equipment 257
ESPN 29, 46–47, 59, 64–67, 78, 82
Europe 81, 83–84, 93–97, 103–107, 118–122
events 58–59, 72, 191–193, 244–247; accreditation 247–249; conference 254–256; media 207–209; media centre 250–251, 256; mixed zone 253–254; news service 256–257; photographers 260–262; rate card 257; staff 257–258; tribunes 251, 253
exposure *see* coverage

F1 61
Facebook 224–225
fact sheets 191–193, 211
Farmer, S. 139–141
FCC 113
Fenway Sports Group 50–51
FIBA 56
FIFA 53–54, 85
financial solvency 74
Fininvest 50
flow chart *see* media grid
follow up 196
football 35–38, 53–56, 81, 93–97, 114; NFL 21, 23, 59, 76, 88, 112–113, 219; UEFA 54–55, 81, 104, 118–122
Fortunato, J. 147

FOX 60
France 121

Galtung, J. 190
gambling *see* betting
Gandy, O.H. 150–151
Germany 50, 106, 118–119
Gibbs, C. 153
globalization 9–10, 14–15, 21, 23, 25–26, 230–231
Globo 50, 114–115
goals 168–170
golf 59
Google 31, 45, 227–228
government intervention *see* regulation
Gratton, R. 245–246
grid 174, 176
guides 184, 194–196, 198–200

Haenlein, M. 30
Hardin, M. 152
Hardin, R. 152–153
hashtags 229–230
Haynes, R. 19, 21, 153
HD *see* digital television
Hearst, W.R. 19
Heggie, S. 158–162
Helitzer, M. 173
Hinerman, S. 265
Hoehn, T. 99
HR *see* management
Hulu 31
Hutchins, B. 31, 72

IBC 251
ICC 56, 58
identity 10, 103
ideology 11
Iger, R. 46
image 267–268
information 13, 44, 176; media release 185–186; off the record 136, 213; subsidies 150–151
Instagram 227
integration 52–53
interactions 170–173, 201–202; conferences 202–207; interviews 208–213; media events 207–208
internet 25–27, 72–73, 86, 128–129; *see also* digital television; social media
interpretation 11
intervention *see* regulation
interviews 132–135, 139–144, 207–213; etiquette 214–217; public relations 156–162
investment *see* broadcast rights; sponsorship

IOC 58–59, 83–85, 256, 274–275
IPC 235–237
IRB 169
Ireland 106
issues management *see* crisis
Italy 50, 106, 119–120
ITV 50

Jackson, S.J. 153–154
James, L. 175
joint selling 103–104, 112–113, 118–122
journalists 125–126, 131–137, 149–151, 153–154; access 129–131; beat system 126–127; marginalization 127–128; *see also* interviews

Kaplan, A.M. 30
Karst, E. 146–147
Kent, A. 152

LA Kings 241–243
Lancefield, D. 99
LaRose, S. 184
Law, A. 46
Lazarus, M. 49
learning 276
list *see* media list
Littlewood, T.B. 146
Lowes, M. 127, 148
LPGA 209
Lull, J. 265

McAllister-Spooner, S. 267
McChesney, R. 17–18
McCleneghan, J.S. 152
McClung, S. 152–153
McHugh, H. 146–147
magazines 18
Malthouse, M. 129–130
management 11–12, 129–130; crisis 234–237, 269–274; events 244–251, 253–258; public relations 149, 152–153; *see also* communication; interactions
Manchester City 128
Manchester United 13, 29, 51, 93, 95–96, 101–102, 128; 'Front Row' competition 228, 230; MUTV 72–73, 238
Marconi, G. 19
marketing *see* advertisements
markets 74–76, 80–81, 83–84, 99–100, 231; *see also* regulation
mass communication *see* communication
MEAA 132
media 5–6, 50–53; advisory 193–194; centre 250–251, 256; conference 136–137, 202–207; events 207–209; guides 184, 194–196, 198–200; relations 149–154; release 184–191, 196; *see also* interactions; journalists; sport media
media communications *see* communications
media organizations 14, 43–50, 70; *see also* broadcast rights 72, 75–80, 82–83
media planning 173–174, 176–177, 179–182; crisis 271–273; goals 168–170; grid 174, 176; list 170–173; social media 231–237
Mitroff, I. 270–271, 273
Mitten, M. 112–113
mixed zone 253–254
MMA 60
MNF 22
mobile technology 27–29, 86, 90
modification 23
Molleda, J.C. 150
money *see* commercialization
motor sport 61
MUFC 29, 51
Murdoch, R. 25, 35–38, 47–48
Murillo, C. 26
Murillo, E. 26
Murtagh, I. 141–144
MUTV 72–73, 128, 238–239

narrative 9–10
NASCAR 61, 85–86, 89, 206
national leagues 55–56
NBA 56, 74–75, 82, 147–148
NBC 20, 46, 76, 78
NBL 73
Netherlands 121–122
networks 222–224, 229–230
Neupauer, N.C. 152
*New York World* 19
News Corporation 9, 35–38, 47–49, 66, 76, 82, 86
news release 184–191, 196
news service 256–257
newspapers 18–20, 25
nexus 7–8
NFL 21, 23, 59, 76, 88, 112–113, 219
NRL 77, 90

Oldenburg, R. 30
Olympic Games 58–59, 83–85, 179–182, 244–247, 255–256, 274–275
online content *see* internet; social media
operations *see* events
organizations *see* media organizations; sport organizations
Oriard, M. 19
Owens, T. 267–268
ownership 14

Paralympics 235–237
partnerships 49
pay television 23–25, 35–38, 89, 100, 104–105
Payne, M. 274–275
Pearson, C. 264, 270–273
perception 11
personal relations *see* interactions
personnel *see* events; journalists
PGA 195–196
Phelps, M. 255, 267
photographers 260–262
planning *see* events; media planning
player management *see* athletes; management
Poor, N. 221
Porter, W. 18
press: conference 136–137; kits 184, 194–196, 198–200; operations 245–246; release 184–191, 196
print media 18–20, 25
products 51–52, 71–72
professionalism 11–12, 72, 269
profits 44, 70, 86–90; *see also* commercialization
promotion 52–53, 166–168; *see also* advertisements; coverage; media planning
public relations 148–150, 152–154; history 146–148; information 150–151; practitioners 152–153, 156–162
Pulitzer, J. 19
Puskas, T. 19

radio 19–20, 86
Rasmussen, B. 64, 67
rate card 257
Real, M. 10
recovery 276
Red Bull 78–79, 90
Reddit 237–238
regulation 99–103; Australia 107–112; Brazil 114–115; China 113–114; Europe 103–107; US 112–113
release 184–191, 196
reputation *see* crisis
return on investment 44, 70, 86–90
rights *see* broadcast rights
risk management 234–237, 241–243; *see also* crisis
Roberts, B. 45
Rockne, K. 146
Rogers Communications 50
Rogge, J. 274–275
Rosner, S. 51
Rowe, D. 10, 31, 72, 265
Rozelle, P. 21
rugby 36–37, 77
Ruge, M. 190

Salt Lake City 274–275
SANZAR 86
saturation 8–10
scandal 265–266, 270–274; impact 266, 268–269
Scherer, J. 153–154
Schilling, C. 221
segmentation 80–81, 171–172
Sha, B.-L. 149
SID 152–153
signal detection 270–271
Sina Weibo 230
Snapchat 237–238
social media 29–30, 218, 237–239; access 128–129, 153, 220–222; content 219–220, 231–234; Facebook 224–225; globalization 230–231; Google+ 227–228; Instagram 227; networks 222–224, 229–230; risk 234–237, 241–243; YouTube 228–229; *see also* Twitter
Solis, B. 231–232
solvency 74
sources 127, 136
Spain 120–121
sponsorship 70–71, 89–90, 234
sport 3–5
sport media 7–8, 10–15, 43–44, 61; digital television 30–32; internet 25–27; mobile technology 27–29; print 17–19; radio 19–20; saturation 8–10; social media 29–30; television 21–25; *see also* events; media; regulation
sport organizations 43–44, 53–58, 70–72; broadcast rights 73–75, 80–81, 83–86; crisis 263–266, 268–274; *see also* communications; interactions
sporting circuits 59, 61, 85–86
Srabian, B. 232–233
staffing 257–258
Stern, D. 74–75
Stevenson, S. 221
Stoldt, G.C. 152
strategy 168–169, 177, 231–237; *see also* media planning
Straubhaar, J. 184
Super Bowl 59, 88
surfing 57–59
symbiosis 17–18

Tate, C. 147
technology 13–14, 184
telecoms providers 29, 31, 45, 72, 167–168

television 8–9, 21–23, 70–73, 100; digital 30–32; pack 151; pay 23–25, 35–38, 89, 104–105; *see also* broadcast rights; regulation
Television Without Frontiers Directive 104–105
Telstra 90
tennis 59
Tesla, N. 19
texts 10–11
Theberge, N. 127
Time Warner 48, 83
Tour de France 198–200, 279–282
transcript 151
transgressions *see* scandal
transport 257–258
triathlon 252
tribunes 251, 253
Turk, J.V. 151
Twenty-first Century Fox 47–48
Twitter 153, 221–222, 225–227, 241–243
Tyson, E. 156–158

UEFA 54–55, 81, 104, 118–122
UFC 60
UK 18, 20–21, 30; football 81, 119, 147; journalists 132; Olympics 179–182; regulation 101–102, 106–107
US 18–21, 83–85; journalists 129, 132; PR 146–147, 152–153; regulation 112–113
USA Swimming 167

venue media centre 250–251
video release 196
Vivendi 49, 83

Wallace, F. 146
Walsh, J. 267
Walt Disney Company *see* Disney
Ward, A. 146
Warhol, A. 263–264
Whannel, G. 21
Whiteside, E. 152
Wilcox, D. 203
World Cup, FIFA 54
Wozniacki, C. 214–217
WRC 61

X Games 59, 66–67, 78
XFL football 76, 78

Yanity, M. 154
YouTube 45, 228–229

Zoch, L.M. 150

Made in the USA
Coppell, TX
11 January 2022

First published 2007
by Routledge

This edition published 2015
by Routledge
2 Park Square, Milton Park, Abingdon, Oxon OX14 4RN

and by Routledge
711 Third Avenue, New York, NY 10017

*Routledge is an imprint of the Taylor & Francis Group, an informa business*



*British Library Cataloguing-in-Publication Data*
A catalogue record for this book is available from the British Library

*Library of Congress Cataloging in Publication Data*
Nicholson, Matthew.
Sport and the media: managing the nexus/Matthew Nicholson, Anthony Kerr and Merryn Sherwood.
pages cm
Includes bibliographical references and index.
1. Mass media and sports. 2. Sports – Marketing. 3. Sports – Economic aspects. I. Title.
GV742.N54 2015
796.06'88 – dc23
2014048552

ISBN: 978-0-415-83981-5 (hbk)
ISBN: 978-0-415-83982-2 (pbk)
ISBN: 978-1-315-77642-2 (ebk)

Typeset in Berling and Futura
by Florence Production Ltd, Stoodleigh, Devon, UK

# Sport and the Media

## Managing the nexus

SECOND EDITION

**Matthew Nicholson, Anthony Kerr and Merryn Sherwood**

Routledge
Taylor & Francis Group
LONDON AND NEW YORK

## Sport Management Series

Series Editor: Russell Hoye, La Trobe University, Australia

This **Sport Management Series** has been providing a range of texts for core subjects in undergraduate sport business and management courses around the world for more than ten years. These textbooks are considered essential resources for academics, students and managers seeking an international perspective on the management of the complex world of sport.

Many millions of people around the globe are employed in sport organizations in areas as diverse as event management, broadcasting, venue management, marketing, professional sport, community and collegiate sport, and coaching as well as in allied industries such as sporting equipment manufacturing, sporting footwear and apparel, and retail.

At the elite level, sport has moved from being an amateur pastime to one of the world's most significant industries. The growth and professionalization of sport has driven changes in the consumption and production of sport and in the management of sporting organizations at all levels.

Managing sport organizations at the start of the twenty-first century involves the application of techniques and strategies evident in leading business, government and nonprofit organizations. This series explains these concepts and applies them to the diverse global sport industry.

To support their use by academics, each text is supported by current case studies, targeted study questions, further reading lists, links to relevant web-based resources, and supplementary online materials such as case study questions and classroom presentation aids.

Available in this series:

**Sport and Policy**
*Russell Hoye, Matthew Nicholson and Barrie Houlihan*

**Sports Economics**
*Paul Downward, Alistair Dawson and Trudo Dejonghe*

**Sport Governance**
*Russell Hoye and Graham Cuskelly*

**Sport Funding and Finance**
(Second edition)
*Bob Stewart*

**Managing People in Sport Organizations**
A strategic human resource management perspective (Second edition)
*Tracy Taylor, Alison Doherty and Peter McGraw*

**Introduction to Sport Marketing**
(Second edition)
*Aaron C.T. Smith and Bob Stewart*

**Sport Management**
Principles and applications
(Fourth edition)
*Russell Hoye, Aaron C.T. Smith, Matthew Nicholson and Bob Stewart*

**Sport and the Media**
Managing the Nexus (Second edition)
*Matthew Nicholson, Anthony Kerr and Merryn Sherwood*

# Sport and the Media

Successful media relations and a sound communication strategy are essential for all sport organizations. Any successful manager working in sport must have a clear understanding of how the media works, as well as the practical skills to manage the communication process. Now in a fully revised and updated second edition, *Sport and the Media: Managing the nexus* is still the only textbook to combine in-depth analysis of the rapidly developing sport media industry with a clear and straightforward guide to practical sport media management skills.

The book explains the commercial relationships that exist between key media and sport organizations and how to apply a range of tools and strategies to promote the achievements of sport organizations. This updated edition includes a wider range of international examples and cases, as well as four completely new chapters covering new and social media, managing the media at major sports events, the work of the sports journalist, and the role of the sport media manager. The book's online resources have also been updated, with new lecture slides and teaching notes providing a complete package for instructors.

*Sport and the Media* is an essential textbook for any degree level course on sport and the media, sport media management or sport communication, and invaluable reading for any sport media or sport management practitioner looking to improve their professional skills.

Additional resources for instructors are available for this book at www.routledge.com/9780415839822.

**Matthew Nicholson** is an Associate Professor within the Centre for Sport and Social Impact at La Trobe University, Australia. Matthew's research interests include the social impact of sport, the capacity of the community sport sector, increasing participation in sport and physical activity, the sport media nexus and efficacy of government policy. Matthew is the author and editor of a wide range of books, including *Sport Management: Principles and Applications*, *Participation in Sport*, *Sport and Policy: Issues and Analysis* and *Sport and Social Capital*.

**Anthony Kerr** is a Lecturer in the Department of Management and Marketing at La Trobe University, Australia. He has designed and delivered a wide range of subjects in sport business and marketing and his research interests focus on brand equity and professional football, especially the contribution that foreign fans ('satellite supporters') can make to an organization's bottom line in a global marketplace. He has been recognized for excellence in teaching and has a proven track record in marketing, sponsorship and media relations for sport organizations worldwide, and has worked with some of the world's most famous brands: Nike, AT&T Wireless, SEGA, TimeWarner and the UK Super League.

**Merryn Sherwood** is a former award-winning newspaper journalist, who has worked in the media space at major events including the Vancouver 2010 Winter Olympic Games, Singapore Youth Olympic 2010 Games, Delhi 2010 Commonwealth Games, the 2011 Rugby World Cup and the Australian Open. Since 2011 she has worked as a media contractor for the International Triathlon Union, including driving the ITU's social media channels at the London 2012 Olympic Games and editing *Mind, Body, Soul – 25 Years of the International Triathlon Union*, a limited edition book release to celebrate 25 years of the ITU's history. She is currently undertaking a PhD that explores the roles of communications and media relations staff within Australian sports organizations at La Trobe University, where she also teaches in the sport management programme.

est Air Force in history." Skeptics were quick to note that the navy already has the fewest ships since 1916, that the types of ships now and then are quite different, that counting ships is hardly a measure of military might, that today's navy is larger than the next thirteen combined, and that across-the-board spending cuts would leave the Pentagon with as much money, adjusted for inflation, as it had in 2007, when there were few complaints about money for defense.

Panetta's cry is widely seen as a bargaining stance: the defense budget almost surely will be cut more in any deficit-reduction compromising, forcing the Pentagon to pare its long wish list. "We do not have and probably never will have enough money to buy all the things we could effectively use," military strategist Bernard Brodie said–in 1959. It's still true.

The bulk of the Pentagon's budget goes for three big items: personnel, operations and maintenance, and buying weapons. A close look at a couple of choices illuminates where the money goes, just how much this stuff costs, and why cutting the defense budget is so contentious.

Some of the decisions are too complex for ordinary civilians to understand. Others can be stated simply, such as: How many big aircraft carriers does the navy need to keep America safe? The price tag on these ships is staggering. The navy estimates each aircraft carrier costs in excess of $11 billion, more than Medicare spends annually on knee, hip, and shoulder joint replacements for nearly seven hundred thousand elderly. Aircraft carriers are expensive even in death: it costs about

$2 billion to decommission a carrier, including removing and storing two nuclear reactors.

The navy now has eleven big carriers, the oldest launched fifty years ago. The current plan is to replace one every five years with a new one–bigger, better, and much more expensive. The existing Nimitz class carriers are the largest warships in the world. The navy calls them "4.5 acres of mobile, sovereign U.S. territory." The new carriers will be about one-fifth of a mile long, capable of launching seventy-five aircraft from a flight deck almost as large as a football field. Partly because shipbuilding creates so many jobs and partly because aircraft carriers are such a symbol of military might, Congress, by law, requires the navy to maintain eleven carriers. It has, however, okayed a temporary plan to sail only ten carriers between the retirement of USS *Enterprise* in 2013 and the commissioning of the first of the new ones, USS *Gerald R. Ford*, in late 2015.

The more carriers, of course, the greater the navy's global reach and the greater the nation's capacity to send aircraft anywhere, even when no conveniently located nation is willing to offer a land base. The nagging question is this: Are aircraft carriers obsolete? Pearl Harbor, where so many U.S. planes were destroyed on the tarmac, demonstrated the strategic value of aircraft carriers, but that was sixty years ago. Today, the Chinese–now seen as the biggest potential maritime threat–are developing missiles that could render the modern carrier as vulnerable as the battleships at Pearl Harbor were.

"The need to project power across the oceans will never

go away," then defense secretary Robert Gates said in a 2010 speech. "But consider the massive over-match the U.S. already enjoys. Consider, too, the growing anti-ship capabilities of adversaries. Do we really need eleven carrier strike groups for another thirty years when no other country has more than one?" Some naval strategists suggest smaller, more flexible, amphibious ships carrying unmanned aircraft will be more valuable.

One money-saving option would be to retire an existing carrier ahead of time, reducing the carrier fleet to ten. Decommissioning rather than refueling the twenty-year-old USS *George Washington* in 2016 would save $7 billion over ten years, the CBO estimates, if the navy also cut its workforce by the 5,600 sailors who now man the ship. Obama reportedly rejected this option during internal budget negotiations. "The president feels strongly that, if we're going to have a presence in the Pacific, cutting a carrier would undercut the message," Panetta said, adding that savings elsewhere in the navy budget made room for the carrier. But when Congress eyes further cuts in the defense budget, as it is likely to do at some point, the need for an eleventh carrier will be reexamined.

The Pentagon is more than an armada, though. It's also among the world's largest employers, with all that implies. In May 2010, Gates marked the sixty-fifth anniversary of the Allied victory in Europe with a speech at the Dwight D. Eisenhower Presidential Library in Abilene, Kansas. He spoke not about General Eisenhower's battlefield victories but about President Eisenhower's frustrations with the defense budget, which Gates clearly shared. Some of their concerns were similar. Both were frustrated at the military's insatiable appetite for new weapons. Some of their concerns were different. Eisenhower complained that it took the army fifty years to get rid of horses. Gates complained, "Health care costs are eating the Defense Department alive." Eisenhower would have been stunned.

When Gates spoke, the Defense Department was spending as much on health care–about $50 billion–as on the war in Iraq. The tab has risen since; in 2011 it came to $54 billion. Health care consumes about 10 percent of the defense budget (excluding the costs of Iraq and Afghanistan). One big reason: Tricare, the military health insurance program created in 1995, is significantly more generous than insurance offered to other employees. Yet, every attempt by the White House or Pentagon to curb the benefits, Gates said, "meets with a furious response from the Congress and veterans groups. The proposals routinely die an ignominious death on Capitol Hill"–even though none of the changes would affect active-duty military or wounded warriors in the care of the Veterans Administration's health system.

Why does Tricare survive unscathed? Mostly because of the enormous political power of veterans' groups. "They've always been very strong, and when you've been in ten years of war, the veterans get that much more leverage," Panetta said recently. The rising cost of wages, health insurance, and retirement–"if it keeps growing on the path that it's on now"–

will "eat away at our ability to provide the training, the equipment, and all the other things that are basic to our defense," he said.

Few outsiders appreciate how generous Tricare is. About 15 percent of enlisted men and women and 50 percent of officers stay in the military the twenty years needed to qualify for health insurance after they "retire," often in their forties. The annual premium was set at $460 a year per family in 1995, and for those who signed up before October 1, 2011, it hasn't changed since. For personnel who enrolled after that, the premium has been boosted–to a still-bargain price of $520. For similar coverage, federal civilian workers pay around $5,000 a year. "Try to change . . . that, and you get 'You're not a patriot,' " says Alan Simpson, the retired Republican senator who cochaired a deficit-reduction panel with Erskine Bowles. Obama's latest budget, though, proposes significant premium increases over the next five years, bigger ones for those with bigger pensions.

The health plan is so generous that most of those who retire from the military and take other jobs turn down their new employers' insurance because Tricare is a much better deal. Among them is Francis Brady, a retired marine lieutenant colonel in his early fifties who was earning six figures at the consulting firm Booz Allen when he was interviewed by the *New York Times* in 2010. Tricare, he said, is "so cheap compared to what Booz Allen has. . . . [It's] phenomenal." So it's no surprise that a growing share of military retirees and their families are signing up for the government coverage instead of the insurance offered by their new employers.

Later, when military retirees reach age sixty-five and become eligible for Medicare, a program called Tricare for Life picks up the tab for insurance to cover things that Medicare doesn't. Other Americans pay around $2,100 a year for such policies. Tricare for Life "is costing us $11 billion a year in the defense budget . . . basically enough to buy a new [aircraft] carrier every year," says Todd Harrison, a budget analyst at the Center for Strategic and Budgetary Assessments, a defense think tank.

## FROM DIRT DAM SAFETY TO LANDING ON MARS

Much of what Americans think of as "the government" is the remaining 18 percent of federal spending that Congress appropriates annually for a hodgepodge of domestic programs. This money, $566 billion last year, goes for salaries of everyone from the president to the cooks in federal prisons. It aids inner-city schools in Chicago, subsidizes housing for the poor in Omaha, inspects meatpacking plants in Chino, California, and operates air-traffic control towers outside Atlanta. Most of what can be considered an investment in future productivity or economic growth falls in this bucket: bridges, broadband networks, research at the National Institutes of Health, prekindergarten classes for poor kids, and on and on. This is called "non-defense *discretionary* spending" because it's subject to annual congressional votes, unlike "mandatory" Social Security or Medicare benefits. In recent years, it has been swollen by Obama's fiscal stimulus. Last year, Congress passed a law that sets spending for the next ten years, yet another attempt to tie its hands and keep increases on these expenditures below the rate of inflation over time. While it's easy to argue that somewhere in this half trillion dollars a year are examples of government excess, this new austerity inevitably will limit funding for programs valued by someone, no matter if they have huge profiles and big budgets (the National Aeronautics and Space Administration) or are virtually unknown (the National Dam Safety Program).

The United States' biggest dams–among them, Hoover on the Nevada/Arizona border, Oroville in California, and Mossyrock in Washington State–are owned by the federal government or by big government-run utilities. But 65 percent of dams in the United States are privately owned, nearly all of them small earthen structures built years ago; most of the rest are owned by state and local governments. With all the demands on the federal budget, the safety of these lesser dams might be seen as one thing Washington could leave to the states, and indeed every state but one (Alabama) has a law regulating dam safety. But according to the American Society of Civil Engineers, "Many state dam safety programs do not have sufficient resources, funding, or staff to conduct dam safety inspections, to take appropriate enforcement actions, or to ensure proper construction by reviewing plans and performing construction inspections." South Dakota, for example, has only three dam inspectors–one for every 782 dams. In Iowa, it's one for every 1,674 dams. When these dams do fail, the results can be devastating.

A 1972 dam collapse in West Virginia claimed 125 lives. Another–in Idaho, in 1976–resulted in eleven deaths. The following year, thirty-nine people died when a dam failed in Jimmy Carter's home state of Georgia, prompting the new president and Congress to step in to protect people and property downstream. The Army Corps of Engineers was told to build what's now the National Inventory of Dams (84,134 at last count, 17 percent of them deemed very hazardous). And thus was born the National Dam Safety Program, eventually reorganized into the Federal Emergency Management Agency, which now lives within the sprawling Department of Homeland Security.

The program–which officially coordinates the Interagency Committee on Dam Safety–employs just three people and operated last year with a budget of only $8.9 million. Most of that gets spread around the states to pay for inspectors who check the dams and are supposed to get owners to prepare emergency evacuation plans and fix dangerous conditions. In budgeting, the more an office spends, the more advocates it has, which ought to make the minuscule National Dam Safety Program ripe for plucking. But it has a protective political edge: no one wants to argue that the country would be better off letting unsafe dams deteriorate further. Besides, protecting the nation's infrastructure–including bridges, dams, and levees–became sacrosanct after 9/11. And so the National Dam Safety Program, like hundreds of similar federal backwaters, soldiers on. In the early 1990s, Susan Tanaka, who is now research director at the Peter G. Peterson Foundation, says she tried to kill the program when she worked at the Office of Management and Budget. "Most of the dams are on private property and pose no threat to public safety," she reasoned. "The program is too small to do much and it didn't seem a national priority." She failed. "It was too small for anyone to care about," she says today. All those "too smalls" add up, though.

## TO THE MOON, BUT NOT TO MARS?

NASA is as famous as the National Dam Safety Program is obscure, and a heck of a lot bigger. Created in 1958 to explore space separately from the military, the agency was not yet three years old when it was asked by John F. Kennedy to put a man on the moon before the end of the decade–and it did. At its peak in the mid-1960s, NASA accounted for more than 4 percent of all federal spending. Today, the agency spends, adjusted for inflation, about half what it did then and its budget represents about 0.5 percent of all federal spending. It's still a substantial sum: $18.5 billion last year, roughly the size of the entire budget of the state of Iowa.

Polls suggest the public remains enthusiastic about spending money to explore space. A 2011 Pew Research Center poll found 58 percent deemed it "essential" for the United States "to continue to be a world leader in space exploration." In a Gallup poll taken on the fortieth anniversary of the 1969 moon landing, an identical 58 percent said the space program has brought enough benefits to justify its costs. Presidents of both parties and many members of Congress offer lofty rhetoric about it. In 2004, George W. Bush directed NASA to focus on returning humans to the moon by 2020, and then sending them to Mars and "worlds beyond." Before the end of the decade, though, it became clear that fulfilling these missions would cost far more than either the White House or Congress was prepared to spend. Obama scrapped the return trip to the moon but promised to come up with enough money so humans could orbit Mars by 2030 and land there in his lifetime. "Space exploration is not a luxury," he said in a speech at the Kennedy Space Center in Florida. "It's not an afterthought in America's quest for a brighter future–it is an essential part of that quest."

In that speech, delivered on Tax Day, April 15, 2010, Obama raised the pregnant question for a debt-burdened government: "Why spend money on NASA at all? Why spend money solving problems in space when we don't lack for problems to solve here on the ground? We have massive structural deficits that have to be closed in the coming years." But that is "a false choice," he insisted. "For pennies on the dollar, the space program has improved our lives, advanced our society, strengthened our economy, and inspired generations of Americans." Not to mention creating jobs. NASA administrator Charles Bolden noted as he unveiled the agency's budget in 2012: "Every dollar spent on space exploration is spent here on Earth."

Still, Congress has been squeezing NASA's budget–by $250 million in 2011, or 1.2 percent less than the year before. For 2012, Congress pared another $685 million, or 3.7 percent. And in February 2012, Obama proposed shaving $59 million from NASA's overall budget in fiscal year 2013 to make room for other spending under the congressionally imposed cap. That still left room for, among other things, the 2018 launch of the increasingly expensive James Webb Space Telescope, with its mirror twenty-one feet in diameter and a sun shield as large as a tennis court; education and administration (more than $600 million a year); and the U.S. share of the International Space Station ($3 billion a year).

But Obama's "false choice," it turned out, was a real one. Over objections from some at NASA, the White House proposed a 20 percent–$300 million–cut in the budget for planetary science, ending U.S. participation in a European venture to send an unmanned explorer to Mars. That prompted the resignation of the head of NASA's science mission, Ed Weiler. "The Mars program is one of the crown jewels of NASA," Weiler says. "In what irrational, Homer Simpson world would we single it out for cuts?"

NASA administrator Bolden's explanation: "We could not afford the path we were on." He insisted, though, that the United States remains intent on exploring Mars.

Nearly all of the belt-tightening in the federal budget in the past year and a half has been focused on these last two pieces of the pie, defense and annually appropriated domestic programs. But that won't be nearly enough to bring the deficit and national debt down to sustainable levels; hence the focus on Medicare, Medicaid, and Social Security–and on taxes, the subject of the next chapter.

## CHAPTER 4

# WHERE THE MONEY COMES FROM

Taxing the people to raise money for the government has ancient roots. In Genesis, Joseph decreed that one-fifth of every farmer's crop should go to Pharaoh. Large parts of the Rosetta Stone, carved around 200 B.C., detail a tax exemption for priests. In the seventeenth century, Britain's Charles I relied on "forced loans" from landowners, who weren't repaid. In the eighteenth century, England and Scotland taxed windows; the rich had more of them than the poor. Peter the Great taxed beards in czarist Russia. In 1799, Britain, no longer collecting taxes from its former colonies in America, imposed an income tax to finance a war against France.

Today the U.S. federal government gets money primarily in two ways: it taxes and it borrows–a lot of each. Last year, it collected $2.3 trillion in taxes, fees, and other revenues–about $19,400 per household–and borrowed another $1.1 trillion, or $9,300 per household, committing future generations to tax themselves to pay that back.

Today, most federal tax revenues come from the income

tax on individuals (47 percent last year) and the payroll tax on employers and employees (36 percent).

It wasn't always this way.

Until the Civil War, the U.S. government relied almost exclusively on tariffs on imported goods, a practice that provoked conflict between Northern manufacturers who favored tariffs to keep imports out and Southern farmers who did not. An income tax was imposed during the Civil War, but proved so unpopular that it died in 1872. In its place, the government imposed taxes on alcohol and tobacco that accounted for 43 percent of all federal revenue by 1900. Repeated attempts to revive the income tax were thwarted when the Supreme Court declared it unconstitutional in 1895. But the Sixteenth Amendment to the Constitution changed that. Less than eight months after it was ratified in February 1913, Congress enacted an income tax. It was this new source of tax revenue that made Prohibition possible six years later. "After the income tax was passed, reformers realized there was a replacement for the revenue that came from taxing alcohol, and they started to push for a constitutional amendment," according to Daniel Okrent, author of a history of Prohibition.

Initially, the income tax hit only the rich, those with incomes above $20,000, the equivalent of $450,000 in today's dollars. The top marginal tax rate, the slice of each additional dollar of income the government took from the very best off, was 7 percent on earnings over $500,000, equivalent to $11 million today. The need for money to fight World War II democratized the income tax. "Because of the need for a lot of revenue fast, personal income taxation was expanded dramatically during World War II . . . transforming what had been a 'class tax' into a 'mass tax,'" economists Joel Slemrod and Jon Bakija wrote in *Taxing Ourselves: A Citizen's Guide to the Great Debate over Tax Reform*.

In the years since, tax rates have risen and fallen in intervening years almost as much as hemlines. The top marginal rate hit an astounding 92 percent in the 1950s, though few actually paid that because there were so many ways to avoid it and so much reason to do so. Ronald Reagan's landmark Tax Reform Act of 1986 brought it down to 28 percent by eliminating deductions, exemptions, and tax shelters, which is known as broadening the tax base. Today's top marginal rate, 35 percent, applies to couples with taxable income (that is, after deductions and credits) of $338,350 and up. Obama wants to raise the rate; Republicans want to lower it.

The payroll tax–levied on wages but not capital gains, interest, or dividends–was imposed in 1937 to finance Social Security. It was expanded in 1965 to help fund Medicare and enlarged in 1983 to shore up Social Security. Before Medicare was born, the payroll tax accounted for only about one-sixth of all federal revenue. Today, it accounts for more than one-third.

In contrast, the tax on corporate profits, born in 1909, is a shrinking share of federal revenue. In the early 1950s, more than 30 percent of federal revenues came from the corporate income tax. Last year, revenues accounted for an unusually

**The Changing Tax Mix**

The individual income tax is a mainstay for the federal government. Payroll taxes have grown in importance, while corporate income taxes have shrunk.

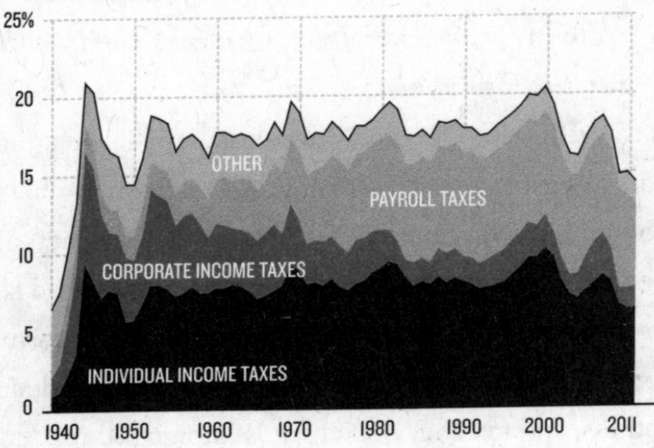


Source: White House Office of Management and Budget

low 7.9 percent, but as the economy returns to normal, it is projected under the current tax code to account for about 12 percent of federal revenues over the next few years.

Why such a declining share? In part, because Congress has offered corporations all sorts of tax breaks. And, in part, because businesses have exploited loopholes or shifted profits overseas or legally organized themselves into entities that aren't subject to the corporate tax. (That last factor is a big one: in 1980, 22 percent of all U.S. business profits were booked by outfits organized so they didn't pay corporate taxes, though their owners–like partners in a law firm–paid individual income taxes on the profits. In 2008, 73 percent of all business profits were in entities that didn't pay corporate taxes.)

With competition from abroad to attract businesses increasingly stiff, most economists and many politicians challenge the wisdom of relying more heavily on corporate taxes. Both the White House and congressional Republicans were flirting with corporate tax reform in early 2012, but both were talking about rearranging the burden among businesses, not raising more money from corporations.

The federal government's only explicit tax on wealth–the estate tax levied on the money that the wealthy leave when they die–was an important source of revenue in the 1930s but has been on the wane ever since. Last year, it accounted for much less than 1 percent of revenues. Unlike most other developed countries, the United States at the federal level doesn't rely on broad sales taxes on consumer spending, such as the value-added tax common abroad.

This book focuses on the federal government, but Americans pay state and local taxes, too. For every $1 the federal government raised in 2011, state and local governments collected another 58 cents from sales, property, income, and other taxes. That measure recently has been distorted by the federal government's ability to cut taxes and run deficits during a recession; most states can't do that. But even before the recession, the weight of state and local taxes rose from 44 cents for every $1 of federal taxes in 2001 to 49 cents in 2007. Of course, the burden varies widely by state. State and local governments in New York take about 15 percent of personal income, while in Missouri they take about 9 percent.

## WHO MAKES THESE DAMN TAX LAWS ANYHOW?

Details of tax laws–more than almost anything else Congress does–are largely the province of congressional and Treasury staff tax experts and battalions of well-paid lobbyists. Particularly the lobbyists. At last count, more than 12,500 people were registered as lobbyists in Washington, all trying to influence the government, many of them toiling over an obscure piece of the tax code that matters to a handful of companies.

Among them is Jon Talisman. He is a balding tax lawyer and accountant who would never be cast as a flashy lobbyist in a Hollywood drama about money and politics. But he is both typical and highly successful, regularly named one of the two or three dozen most influential lobbyists in Washington. Talisman spent eight years as a tax lawyer in private practice, six as a congressional staffer, and another four years as a top tax official in the Treasury during the Clinton administration, much of that time waging war against tax shelters. In 2000, he turned to lobbying because, he says, "Gore lost and I got fired."

He formed Capitol Tax Partners, a firm that, like most others, deliberately mixes tax experts who once worked for Democrats with others who had worked for Republicans. The firm's client list includes brand-name companies like Delta Airlines, Federal Express, JPMorgan Chase, Time Warner, and 3M that pay retainers of between $10,000 and $20,000 a month. Talisman's office in a modern building at 101 Constitution Avenue is triangular in shape. The placement of the conference table in front of a large window tells clients they've come to the right place: Talisman sits with his back to the window. The client sits on the other side. Over Talisman's shoulder, perfectly framed in the window, is the U.S. Capitol building.

The job of getting or protecting tax breaks for companies is harder than it used to be, Talisman says. One reason is the overwhelming size of looming federal budget deficits. "Everybody understands that deficits make everything in the tax arena harder," he says. "Tax reform"–the always popular, always politically treacherous goal of making the tax code simpler and smarter–"is really difficult when you can't throw money at it. Losers always squeak louder than winners cheer," he says. Another reason is the passing of the day when there was bipartisan cooperation to fix glaring problems in the tax code–outdated provisions, conflicting requirements, abused loopholes, sections that had been challenged by the courts. "You didn't worry about whether it raised revenue or lost revenue," he recalled. "Today, if it raises revenue, it's a tax increase. And if it loses revenue, it's a special-interest provision." And either one makes it controversial.

## RESISTING TAXES: FROM LADY GODIVA TO GROVER NORQUIST

Taxes are never popular, and resistance is perennial, sometimes successful. According to eleventh-century legend, Lady Godiva repeatedly begged her husband, Leofric, to lift heavy taxes he had imposed on the people of Coventry. He relented on one condition: that she ride naked on horseback through the streets. After demanding that everyone stay inside behind closed windows and doors, Godiva took her famous ride, and Leofric kept his promise. (A fellow named Tom, the story goes, cut a hole in his shutters to watch her–the original "Peeping Tom.") The Boston Tea Party of 1773 was a reaction to the British tax on imported tea. The American Revolution was fought, in part, over colonists' anger at "taxation without representation." In 1794, in what was known as the Whiskey Rebellion, Pennsylvania farmers attacked federal agents trying to collect a tax on whiskey. The insurrection was forcibly quashed by George Washington, but populist anger at taxes has been a recurring theme in American politics ever since.

In today's Washington, one cannot talk about taxes without mentioning Grover Norquist, a round-faced Harvard MBA with a closely cropped beard who has been a Republican activist since he volunteered for Nixon's 1968 campaign at age twelve. Norquist, fifty-five, has had a single mission since Ronald Reagan recruited him from the staff of the U.S. Chamber of Commerce in 1985 to build an organization to push for tax reform–i.e., to fight increases in tax rates. Nearly thirty years ago, Norquist's Americans for Tax Reform asked members of Congress to sign "the pledge" that they'll oppose any tax increases. "It's very difficult to lie when you write it down," Norquist says.

Norquist has helped brand the Republican Party as the antitax party. Republicans who violate his pledge, he says, are as damaging to the image as reports of rat heads in Coke bottles would be to the Coca-Cola brand, he says. His organization raised more than $13 million in 2010, according to its latest available IRS filings.

Norquist is not subtle. He keeps a miniature bathtub on his desk, a reference to a 2001 NPR interview in which he famously declared: "I don't want to abolish government. I simply want to reduce it to the size where I can drag it into the bathroom and drown it in the bathtub." He is funny, though, the runner-up in a Washington's funniest celebrity contest. (A sample: "I'm drinking bourbon neat. No water. I never drink water. Dick Cheney tortures with it." Another, coming from the father of two: "The person who came up with the phrase 'sleeps like a baby' was an eighth-century eunuch who had never seen a baby, and had certainly never seen one try to sleep.")

Norquist insists the no-tax-increases pledge is made to voters, not to him, but he has become the arbiter of what policies would or wouldn't violate the promise. That has made him a huge obstacle for those of both parties who see no way to bring the deficit under control except by raising taxes *and* cutting spending. Among them is Tom Coburn, a fiercely independent, conservative Republican senator from Oklahoma who began as a manager in the family manufacturing business, then went to medical school and became a family doctor and obstetrician. After six years in the House, Coburn left in 2001, keeping a vow to serve no more than three terms. But he came back to Congress as a senator four years later and lately has been among a bipartisan band–dubbed the Gang of Six–trying to fashion a package of tax increases and spending cuts to reduce the deficit. When he successfully pushed to eliminate a tax break for ethanol, Norquist accused him of having "lied his way into office" because the resulting increase in revenues wasn't used to reduce other taxes. "Which pledge is most important," Coburn asked on *Meet the Press*, "the pledge to uphold your oath to the Constitution of the United States or a pledge from a special interest group who claims to speak for all of American conservatives when in fact they really don't?"

## WHO PAYS? HOW MUCH?

In the high-volume debate over taxes, facts about basic issues–who pays? how much? who doesn't?–often get lost, twisted, or distorted. Perhaps the most salient and overlooked fact is this one: *for most Americans, federal taxes have not risen over the past couple of decades.*

Over the last thirty years, the U.S. tax collector has sliced

### The Tax Bite

The share of income paid in federal taxes of all kinds by Americans at the bottom and in the middle of the income distribution has fallen steadily over the past thirty years. For those in the top fifth and for the now-famous 1 percent, the average tax rate has bounced around, but is lower today than it was thirty years ago.

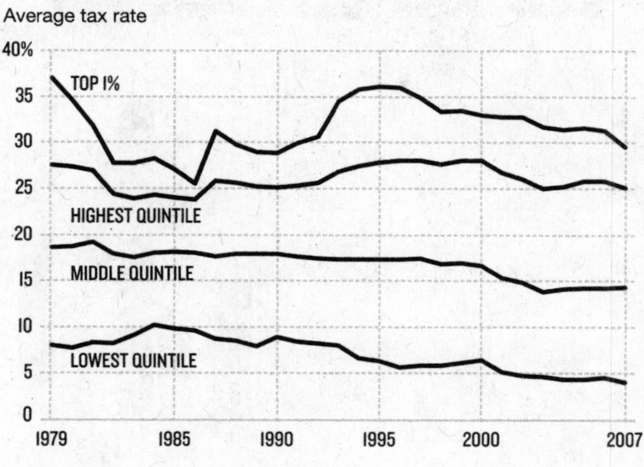


Source: Congressional Budget Office

for itself a share of the national economic pie of about 18 percent of the GDP, which is the broadest way to measure the tax burden. The government's take hit 19.6 percent in 1981 as Ronald Reagan was arriving in Washington, fell in subsequent years due to tax-cutting and recessions, and peaked at 20.6 percent in 2006 as George W. Bush was running for president, which was one of the forces that drove his tax-cut proposals. Before the Great Recession arrived in 2007, taxes as a share of GDP were hovering around 18.5 percent. Lately, the tax take has been unusually low–15.4 percent of GDP last year. That's the consequence of the very weak economy and tax cuts

### The Rich Make More and Pay More

The best-paid Americans get a far bigger slice of the national income than those at the bottom, and they pay more taxes. The bottom fifth got 3.7% of all the income in 2011 and paid only 0.2% of all federal taxes. The 1 percent, in contrast, got 16.8% of the income and paid 25.6% of the taxes.

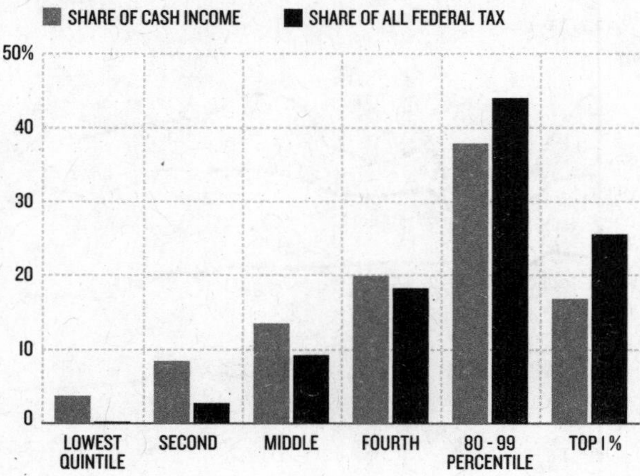


Source: Tax Policy Center

enacted in response. The CBO projects that if current policies persist–that is, even if all the Bush tax cuts are renewed beyond December 31, 2012–revenues will rise gradually, returning to the 18 percent of GDP average in 2017.

For ordinary Americans, the tax take as a percentage of GDP is hard to comprehend. Their question is simpler: how much of my paycheck does the government take? That answer depends on how much money they make and whether their income derives from wages or more lightly taxed profits from trading stocks or other capital gains.

Although many taxpaying Americans suspect otherwise,

the share of the income that most of them have been paying to Washington has been coming down over the past few decades.

Consider taxpayers on the middle rungs of the ladder: the 60 percent of households whose incomes put them neither in the top fifth nor the bottom fifth–the ones with incomes these days between $16,800 and $103,500 a year. Their federal *income* taxes fell, on average, from about 8 percent of their income in 1979 to around 4 percent in 2007, according to the latest CBO estimates.

Then add the payroll tax, generally split between employer and employee, which has been taking a bigger and bigger bite. The payroll tax is a big deal. In 2011, about 40 percent of all households paid more in the *employee* share of the payroll tax than they paid in federal income taxes. Combining the *employee* and *employer* shares of taxes (because the employer share comes out of the wages they would otherwise pay and because the self-employed pay both halves themselves), over 60 percent of households paid more in payroll than income taxes.

The payroll tax rate has more than doubled over the past fifty years, and the ceiling on the wages to which it applies has risen with inflation. But because wages for the best-paid workers have been rising faster than those of other workers, the tax hit a shrinking fraction of all wages paid in the economy. The current tax rate is 15.3 percent–12.4 percent for Social Security (on wages up to $110,100 in 2012) and another 2.9 percent for Medicare (without any wage ceiling). At Obama's urging, Congress has for the past couple of years declared a temporary 2-percentage-point tax holiday for workers. That is likely to disappear as the economy recovers. Beginning in 2013, Obama's health reform law, the Affordable Care Act, imposes an additional 0.9% Medicare payroll tax on wages over $200,000 for individuals and over $250,000 for couples, and adds a new 3.8 percent tax on their investment income.

A full tax accounting has to include not only income and payroll taxes, but taxes imposed on corporations that eventually are passed along to consumers, workers, and shareholders. Add them in and, by the CBO's reckoning, that middle 60 percent of taxpayers paid about 19 percent of their income in federal taxes of all kinds, direct and indirect, in 1979. In 2007, it was down to 15 percent. In 2011, according to separate estimates by the Tax Policy Center, it was down to 13 percent.

No one enjoys paying taxes, but public opinion polls suggest the attitude toward taxes is more complex than the rhetoric of antitax politicians sometimes suggests. In fact, recent surveys find fewer Americans complaining about the size of their federal tax bill. In December 2011, for instance, the Pew Research Center asked: "Considering what you get from the federal government, do you think you pay more than your fair share of taxes, less than your fair share or about the right amount?" Some 52 percent answered "the right amount," significantly more than the 41 percent who gave the same answer in March 2003 shortly after Bush cut taxes significantly. Pew's polls are no fluke. Gallup's shows a similar trend.

For a lot of Americans, the issue isn't the size of their tax bill, but whether the tax code is–in their minds–"fair." As Pew puts it, "The focus of the public's frustration is not how much they themselves pay, but rather the impression that wealthy people are not paying their fair share." In the December 2011 Pew poll, 55 percent said the U.S. tax system isn't fair.

## TAX RETURNS: FROM NIXON TO ROMNEY

This off-again, on-again "fairness" issue surfaced early in the 2012 Republican presidential primaries when Mitt Romney, reluctantly, released his 104-page tax return. "Tax returns of the rich and famous have a way of highlighting important policy issues that often get ignored in public debate," tax columnist Joseph J. Thorndike said at the time. Indeed.

Romney's return revealed that he and his wife had income of $20.9 million in 2011 and paid $3.2 million in federal income and payroll taxes. In other words, they paid about 15 percent of their gross take (that is, before deductions) in federal income and payroll taxes, much less than the typical upper-income taxpayer. Romney's income was largely from capital gains (taxed at a lower rate than wages), and his taxes were reduced by big deductible charitable contributions, mainly to the Mormon Church.

The controversy over Romney's taxes was nothing compared to the one that erupted over Richard Nixon's during the Watergate scandal. On November 17, 1973, four hundred newspaper editors gathered at Walt Disney World for a televised question-and-answer session with the president. Nixon was tense. He had been reelected, but his presidency was on the rocks. He joked that if Air Force One went down, Congress "wouldn't have to impeach." The joke drew laughs, but the editors pressed him about the Watergate break-in and subsequent cover-up as well as a less-remembered scandal: his taxes.

The *Wall Street Journal* had reported that the president's handwritten tax returns (fewer than twenty pages each) revealed that he had paid just $5,100 in combined federal income taxes for 1970, 1971, and 1972 on income that totaled $795,000. His 1970 tax bill was only $792. It would have been zero if not for the alternative minimum tax enacted in 1969 over Nixon's objections, to make sure no one got so many deductions and credits that he or she came close to avoiding taxes altogether. The new tax followed testimony by the Treasury secretary that 155 households with incomes above $200,000 in 1967 (about $1.4 million in today's dollars) hadn't paid any income taxes. Tax historians speculate that Nixon's $792 bill in 1970 may have been made him the first AMT taxpayer.

It was during questioning about all this that Nixon uttered the famous words: "I'm not a crook. I've earned everything I've got." That was true, but he had cheated on his taxes. He took a questionable $576,000 deduction for donating his vice presidential papers to the government, though the transfer documents were later found to have been backdated. He overdid the home-office deductions for his San Clemente, California, house, claiming it was his primary residence even though he was living in the White House, and then, to top matters off, he didn't pay state taxes in California despite alleging that he was living there. After audits by the IRS and, because the Nixon White House had so undermined the credibility of the IRS, audits by the staff of the congressional Joint Committee on Taxation, Nixon ultimately agreed to pay $465,000 in back taxes for those years. No surprise, every president since Nixon has released his tax returns voluntarily. Nixon's successor, Gerald Ford, reported paying more than $95,000 in federal income taxes in 1975 on gross income of $252,000, a 38 percent tax rate.

The flap over Nixon's taxes, largely forgotten today, focused public attention at the time on the "fairness" of the tax code–who should be asked to pay how much–and the capacity of the best off to find ways to reduce their taxes. That debate has been revived lately for reasons beyond Romney's tax returns: the gap between winners and losers in the U.S. economy has been widening substantially. Underlying the debate over how much to tax the rich is a fundamental disagreement about how hard the government should use the tax code to resist that tendency. Obama would raise taxes on those with incomes above $250,000: "Those who have done well, including me, should pay our fair share in taxes to contribute to the nation that made our success possible," he argued. Romney objected. His counterargument: "You know, there was a time in this country that we didn't celebrate attacking people based on their success and when we didn't go after people because they were successful."

It is important to understand the starting point. Today's tax code does take more from the rich than from the middle class and the poor. The political issues are whether the rich, whose share of national income has been growing, should pay even more and whether making them do so would have undesirable side effects on the economy. Here's where things stand today, based on estimates covering all federal taxes–income, payroll, and corporate–produced by the Tax Policy Center:

- The bottom 40 percent of Americans, whose gross incomes were below $33,500, got 12 percent of the income in 2011 and paid 3 percent of all federal taxes.
- The middle class, the 40 percent of Americans with incomes between $33,500 and $103,000, got 33 percent of the income and paid 27 percent of the taxes
- The best-off 20 percent, whose incomes range upward from $103,000, got 55 percent of the income and paid 70 percent of the taxes.

That last group includes some really well-off people, of course. Zooming in on them, the Tax Policy Center estimates:

- Those famously branded "the 1%" by the Occupy Wall Street protesters, the ones with incomes above $533,000 in 2011, got 17 percent of the income and paid 26 percent of the taxes.

- The top-top tier, the 0.1%, the 120,000 taxpayers with incomes above $2.2 million—think Goldman Sachs partners, Microsoft's Bill Gates, the megastars of sports and music—got 8 percent of all the income in 2011 (which, by the way, is four times the size of the slice the top 0.1% got thirty years earlier). They paid 13 percent of all federal taxes.

And then there are the Fortunate Four Hundred. For years, Congress has required the IRS to report each year on the income taxes paid by the four hundred taxpayers with the highest incomes without identifying them. The snapshot for 2008, the latest available, is illuminating. To make the list, one had to have income in that one year of $110 million; the average for the group was above $270 million, down from the boom year of 2007 but more than comfortable. The ranks of the Fortunate Four Hundred aren't stable: people move in and out; about one hundred of them have made the list more than once in the seventeen years for which the IRS reports the data.

As a group, these four hundred taxpayers paid 18.1 percent of their gross income in taxes. "The very rich not only made lots more money, they made it in a very different way," Roberton Williams of the Tax Policy Center observed. Nearly 60 percent of their gross income in 2008 came from capital gains, nearly all of it taxed at a 15 percent rate. Only 8 percent of their income came from wages taxed at a marginal rate of 35 percent. In contrast, the rest of the population got only

5 percent of its income from capital gains and 72 percent from wages.

Over the years, under both Republican and Democratic presidents, the tax burden on those at the bottom of the pyramid has been steadily lightened. One big reason is the earned income tax credit, created by Senator Russell Long, the Louisiana Democrat who, in 1975, was seeking an alternative to spending more on welfare. The EITC is a bonus the government pays the working poor, reducing the taxes they would otherwise owe or, depending on their circumstances, giving them cash. After food stamps, the EITC is now the federal government's biggest antipoverty program, worth nearly $60 billion in 2011 to 27 million households, more than one in every five households.

## "SPENDING THROUGH THE TAX CODE"

For ordinary Americans, there's the money you take in and the money you spend. The federal budget doesn't work that way. No discussion of taxes can avoid the money that the government doesn't collect because of some provision of the tax code, a deduction or a credit or an exclusion or an exemption. In response to years of calls to control "spending" and "smaller government," Congress and presidents have discovered something simple: giving people a tax break–a credit, a loophole, a deduction–makes them happy without increasing government "spending" and can accomplish the same objective. Practically and economically, there's no difference between getting $1,000 in cash from the government and getting a $1,000 voucher that you can use to reduce your taxes. Either results in a federal budget deficit that's $1,000 bigger than it would have been had the tax break not been created. But the first is called "spending" (boos, hisses) and the second is called "a tax cut" (applause, cheers). The first is formally recorded on the budget books as an outflow of money. The second doesn't show up in the outflow and inflow accounting. It is revenue that wasn't collected. By the same logic, the Earned Income Tax Credit is a way for the government to spend money–in this case, giving money to low-wage workers–without counting it as spending.

The late tax economist David Bradford once joked that Congress could wipe out the defense budget and replace it with a Weapons Supply Tax Credit. Arms makers, he said, would be allowed to save enough money on taxes to cover whatever the government would have paid them. Then the government would announce that through "targeted tax relief," taxes had been slashed without jeopardizing national security or increasing the deficit. But nothing would have changed: the same labor, energy, and materials would have been taken by the government to make the weapons.

It's no longer a joke.

These "tax expenditures," as they're called in Washington patois, add up to a lot of money. There's a credit for adopting a child, another for investing in biomass generation of electricity, and the popular deduction for home-mortgage interest. More than 60 percent of all federal subsidies for energy are routed through the tax system rather than through direct spending. Put all these together, and they added up to $1.1 trillion in forgone revenue in 2011, the Treasury calculates. That's enormous, given that the total revenues of the U.S. government that year were $2.3 trillion.

Erskine Bowles calls them "backdoor spending through the tax code." He told (yet another) congressional deficit-reduction committee last year, "It is just spending by another name. It's somebody's social policy." The deficit-reduction commission he cochaired recommended doing away with most of them, and using the money to lower tax rates and reduce the deficit.

The Tax Reform Act of 1986 stripped away many barnacles from the tax code, wiping out tax shelters, raising taxes on businesses, and using the money to lower individual income tax rates. The barnacles grew back, though. Today, about 10 percent of the spending through tax-code savings goes to businesses and 90 percent to individuals, notably the provisions that allow workers to get health insurance from employers without paying taxes on that as wages ($184.5 billion in 2012) and homeowners to deduct mortgage interest ($98.6 billion). If all the tax expenditures in the *corporate* tax code were wiped out, which will never happen, the tax rate on big companies could fall from 35 percent to 28 percent and raise the same amount of money.

The saga of a tax break known as Section 1031 for its place in the tax code shows how entrenched these are. If you sell a share of Microsoft stock at a profit, you owe capital gains taxes even if you immediately put the proceeds into shares of Google. But if you swap one office building for another, and play by 1031 rules, that's considered "a like-kind exchange," and you can defer–or, if you're clever, avoid–capital gains taxes. "All real estate, in particular, is considered 'like-kind,' allowing a retiring farmer from the Midwest to swap farm land for a Florida apartment building or a right to pump water tax-free," the Congressional Research Service has said. The revenues lost through this one provision were about $2.5 billion in 2011. It's relatively small, but illustrative.

Like so many tax breaks, this one began long ago for reasons that have little to do with its current size. It popped up in 1921 when the income tax was in its youth, to allow investors to avoid taxes when swapping property without a "readily realizable market value." In 1934, the tax-writing House Ways and Means Committee explained, "If all exchanges were to be made taxable, it would be necessary to evaluate the property received in exchange in thousands of horse trades." Over the years, it has been tweaked and the definition of "like-kind" shrunk, stretched, and reinterpreted.

Today, one can swap a dental office for a vacation property and avoid taxes, if you structure the deal the right way. One can trade horses, cattle, hogs, mules, donkeys, sheep, goats, and other animals owned for investment, breeding, or sporting, advises Andy Gustafson, a 1031 broker, but not chickens, turkeys, pigeons, fish, frogs, or reptiles. But you can't trade a bull for a milk cow and avoid taxes: "Livestock of different sexes," the IRS cautions, "are not like-kind properties."

In 1935, the federal Board of Tax Appeals, a precursor of the federal Tax Court, approved the use of middlemen in the transactions, which made like-kind exchanges far more practical. Then in a court case that reverberated for decades, T. J. Starker and his son and daughter-in-law traded 1,843 acres of Oregon timberland to Crown Zellerbach Corp. in 1967 for a promise to get property (or cash) of equal value five years later.

It was, the Starkers argued, a like-kind exchange with lag, so they said they didn't owe capital gains taxes on the deal in 1967. The Internal Revenue Service disagreed, arguing that waiting five years to make the exchange broke the law. The matter went to court. Twelve years later, a federal appeals court sided with the Starkers, establishing that an exchange didn't have to be simultaneous to qualify for the tax break. Congress later narrowed the window to 180 days.

The result is an industry of middlemen devoted to helping people find property to buy and sell, and matching the transactions in ways that the IRS considers like-kind. One twelve-year-old outfit, Accruit LLC of Denver, secured a patent in 2008 on its method of matching buyers and sellers to assure that their exchanges comply with the tax rules. (In September 2011, Congress said no more patents could be issued for "any strategy for reducing, avoiding or deferring tax liability.")

There are even "reverse exchanges" where–as one 1031 broker describes it on its website–"you can make a new purchase prior to selling the current asset, allowing you to continue generating revenue from your original asset."

Real estate, cable television, and other industries argue that if investors had to pay capital gains taxes, they wouldn't swap one property for another even when the trade made sense, such as for consolidating adjacent cable franchises. Perhaps. But consider this example Accruit posted on its website: Joe and Marilynn Croydon (not their real names) collected and restored vintage cars. A buyer was interested in several of their Formula 1 race cars to the tune of $2.5 million. "After going through countless part orders, mechanic expenses and original purchase prices," the couple figured they would turn a $1.97 million profit–which at the current capital gains tax rate on collectibles meant a tax bill of $552,440. Their accountant recommended a 1031 exchange, and the couple began looking for other cars to buy with the proceeds of the sale.

Eventually they found four of them–a 2008 Lamborghini Reventon ($1.2 million), a 1969 Yenko Camaro ($180,000), a 1981 BMW M1 ($133,500), and a 1933 Duesenberg Model J ($1 million). That more than covered the $2.5 million proceeds. They didn't have to pay the $542,400 in capital gains taxes immediately. And with smart accountants and careful planning, a tax deferred can become a tax never paid. Accruit said in its account that the gains might escape taxation altogether if the cars were bequeathed to the Croydon children.

The tax code has few defenders these days. It's criticized for being too complicated and too onerous, for pushing companies overseas and rewarding them for going abroad, for discouraging saving and restraining growth. In concept, tax reform is popular. But ultimately reforming the tax code turns on some big, contentious issues. Will Congress actually force *anyone* to surrender a cherished provision of the tax code? Will it raise anyone's taxes, even if only to come up with the money to lower taxes for everyone else? Can Republicans and Democrats resolve their standoff over whether the tax code should bring more money to the Treasury in the future than the unreformed tax code would?

CHAPTER 5

# WHY THIS CAN'T GO ON FOREVER

Although it is said that the most important things in life cannot be measured, American presidents are judged in real time by numbers, particularly when it comes to the economy. There's the unemployment rate, the one economic statistic everyone instantly understands. And the price of gasoline, the largest price tag on anything sold in the entire country. And the stock market, an instant barometer of the mood of the business and investing class.

Then there's the budget, the national credit card bill. By that metric, where did the United States stand in the fourth year of Barack Obama's presidency? Four years older, and deeper in debt. "We're driving seventy miles an hour toward a cliff," says Bob Reischauer, the former CBO director. "And when we reach that cliff will be determined by events over which we have very little control. The path we're on can't go on for fifteen years. Whether it can go on for two, three, four years, I have no idea."

In Washington, where no one seems to agree on anything these days, substantial agreement actually exists on this assertion. Problem is, there's next to no agreement on *what* to do about it and *when*.

The debate over how to steer the budget has produced a multiact Washington drama for the past couple of years. Act One was the rush to rescue a collapsing economy in 2009 with fiscal stimulus, and the bitterness over bank bailouts. Act Two featured tension among Obama's brainy, big-ego economic advisers about whether to pump more money into the economy and when to shift to worrying about deficits. In Act Three, a procession of bipartisan blue-ribbon groups assembled to seek compromise, none of which forged a consensus broad enough to produce action. Act Four involved a confidence-shaking showdown in August 2011 between the White House and congressional Republicans over raising the ceiling on federal borrowing. And then came Act Five, the legislation that emerged from the showdown that threatens deep, across-the-board spending cuts at the beginning of 2013 unless some deficit-reducing alternative passes before then. In classical tragedy, this is known as the denouement. In Washington, it could be just farce.

Each episode had political consequences, ripples that almost surely will influence the outcome of the 2012 presidential and congressional elections. But in the midst of the political jockeying and brinkmanship, the relevant *economic* consequences of the past four years can be summed up in two fiscal facts. Everything else is pretty much detail.

The first fiscal fact is this:

**Obama inherited a collapsing economy. He used substantial fiscal muscle that, with a significant assist from the Federal Reserve, helped arrest that collapse.**

A running argument among Obama advisers early in the administration–one that has continued in the after-action books–involves whether the Obama fiscal stimulus *should* or, given political realities, *could* have been bigger than the $787 billion initially approved by Congress in February 2009. There were unending debates about whether the mix of spending increases and tax cuts in that package was optimal: Too much in tax cuts or too little? Too much spending that went instantly into consumers' hands or too much on "shovel-ready" construction projects that took years to launch? The 2012 presidential campaign has homed in on whether the fiscal stimulus did any good at all. Barack Obama said it helped save the United States from repeating the Great Depression. Mitt Romney called it a failure that amounted to "throwing $800 billion out the window."

The fiscal response was big by the standards of history, but then so was the recession. The first shots were fired by what are known in budgetspeak as "automatic stabilizers," the built-in features of the budget that resulted in more spending (because more people were unemployed or eligible for food stamps, for instance) and lower tax receipts (because fewer people had income on which to pay taxes). These added up to well over $300 billion a year for 2009, 2010, and 2011, CBO estimated. Then came the Obama fiscal stimulus–or, as he prefers, "the Recovery Act." CBO's latest price tag on that: $831 billion over a few years, more than initially estimated because the economy was worse, so more were eligible for aid. And then, with the economy still languishing, came the $100-billion-a-year payroll tax holiday for 2011 and 2012, temporarily reducing the payroll taxes workers pay by 2 percentage points.

The argument that such massive spending had *no* impact on the economy at all hasn't much merit. It isn't possible to throw that much money out of the window without someone getting a job and someone spending more than he or she otherwise would. Even Obama critic Douglas Holtz-Eakin, a former McCain adviser who now heads his own center-right think tank, allows, "No one would argue that the stimulus has done nothing." (Never mind that Republican candidates routinely argue just that.)

Yet it's easy to understand why many ordinary citizens see the stimulus as a failure, given how poorly the economy did after the money began to flow. Gauging the impact, measuring the bang for the billions of bucks, requires an exercise with which economists are comfortable and the public isn't–comparing today's economic conditions to what they would have been without the spending increases and tax cuts. "Suppose a patient has been in a terrible accident and has massive internal bleeding," Christina Romer of the University of California at Berkeley told a League of Women Voters audience in August 2011, a year after leaving her post as chair of Obama's White House Council of Economic Advisers. "After life-saving surgery to stop the bleeding, the patient is likely to still feel pretty awful. . . . But that doesn't mean the surgery didn't work. . . . Without the surgery the patient would have died. Well, the same is true of the economy back in 2008 and 2009."

Economists like Romer who believe that fiscal stimulus is a potent weapon against unusually severe recessions use economic models and rules of thumb that kick out big beneficial impacts. Witness Harvard's Larry Summers, adviser to Clinton and Obama: "Do you really believe if we had done nothing in response to the crisis in 2008, it would have been a good idea?" But other economists have less faith in fiscal potency, and they produce models that reveal smaller impacts–or even none at all. Witness Stanford's John Taylor, adviser to both Bushes: "They [tax cuts and spending increases of stimulus] wither and they don't give you a lasting recovery," he said. "It goes away and we are even weaker than before."

Though the debate over the efficacy of fiscal stimulus will go on, the consensus among *economists* is that the spending and tax cuts did more than a little good. A February 2012 survey of forty of the biggest names in academic economics ("the world's best economics department," the organizers at the University of Chicago Booth School of Business call it), for instance, found near-unanimity on one point: 90 percent said that unemployment was lower in 2010 than it would have been had there been no stimulus.

Bob Reischauer, seventy, is with the consensus. The physically towering economist, son of prominent Japan scholar Edwin Reischauer, is one of the wise men of budgeting in Washington. Recently retired as head of the Urban Institute think tank, he spent his entire career at CBO–he was one of Alice Rivlin's lieutenants in the agency's infancy–and at Democratic-leaning think tanks in Washington. Reischauer's influence is amplified by his unusual combination of hard-nosed political realism with trenchant economic insight and by reporters' affection for his pithy sound bites. "I'm a believer that Obama saved us from a world depression," he said. "And the American people give him zero credit for that–99 percent of the population has no appreciation for what kind of threat it was." That's an overstatement: the public has warmed to the stimulus as time has passed and the economy has perked up. In a February 2012 Pew poll, 61 percent said it was "mostly good" for the economy, substantially more than the 38 percent who voiced approval two years earlier.

Whatever the merits, that money has been borrowed, and it has been spent–which leads to the second fact:

**To rescue the economy, Obama piled more government debt on top of the debt that he inherited. He has yet to sell the public or Congress on a credible plan to avoid unsustainable increases in debt in the future.**

On the day Obama took the oath of office, January 20, 2009, the U.S. government owed $6.3 trillion to others–$6,307,310,739,681.66 to be precise, according to the Treasury's "Debt to the Penny" website. That works out to $54,000 per household or 45 percent of GDP, the yardstick that measures the debt against the size of the whole U.S. economy.

On February 13, 2012, when Obama sent his budget to Congress, the government owed $10.6 trillion–$10,596,768,009,341.49. That's $90,000 per household, or nearly 70 percent of GDP, higher than at any time in the past sixty years.

The real problem lies ahead, as Reischauer suggested with his car-at-the-cliff analogy. Obama said as much the day his February 2012 budget was released: "[T]ruth is we're going to have to make some tough choices in order to put this country back on a more sustainable fiscal path. By reducing our deficit in the long term, what that allows us to do is to invest in the things that will help grow our economy right now. We can't cut back on those things that are important for us to grow. We can't just cut our way into growth. We can cut back on the things that we don't need, but we also have to make sure that everyone is paying their fair share for the things that we do need."

But Obama's latest budget showed that even if Congress accepted every one of his money-saving and tax-increasing proposals and even if his health care law worked as hoped and even if the economy steadily improved, the government would still need to borrow another $4 trillion over the next four years, and the ratio of debt to GDP would keep climbing. And that *doesn't* count trillions more in unfunded promises to pay benefits in the future, which are not formally recorded on the government's books.

## ABOUT THE NATIONAL DEBT

For most of recent American history, most U.S. government borrowing was domestic–the Liberty Bonds sold during World War I, War Bonds sold during World War II, the savings bonds that generations of grandparents gave at graduation time, the U.S. Treasury bonds held in Americans' trust accounts and pension funds. "We owe it to ourselves" was the comforting mantra. No longer. Back in 1955, when the federal debt was much smaller, less than 5 percent was held by foreigners. Foreign holdings began to climb in 1970 and surged in the 2000s. Today, foreign governments and private investors hold nearly half of all the U.S. government debt outstanding. A big chunk of this lending is from China and Japan. They have been big

**The National Debt**

The federal government's debt, measured against the size of the economy, the gross domestic product, has risen to levels that haven't been seen in more than half a century and will keep rising if current policies are pursued.

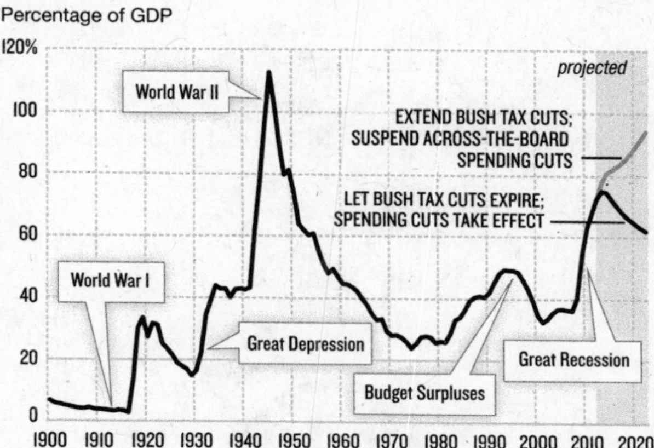


Source: White House Office of Management and Budget

savers, so they have a lot of money to lend to foreigners. And they export a lot more to the United States (when dollars flow into China) than they import (when dollars flow out of China), which leaves them with a growing stockpile of dollars that has to be invested somewhere. The U.S. Treasury bond is still the safest place to put them.

Right now, all this federal government borrowing isn't a problem. While Washington has borrowed heavily over the past few years, consumer and business borrowing has been subdued. Measured as a percentage of GDP, borrowing by the U.S. economy as a whole–not only the federal government but also state and local governments, businesses, and households–

## Foreign Debt

A growing fraction of the federal government's borrowing is from abroad, much of it from China and Japan.

HELD BY AMERICANS

HELD BY FOREIGNERS

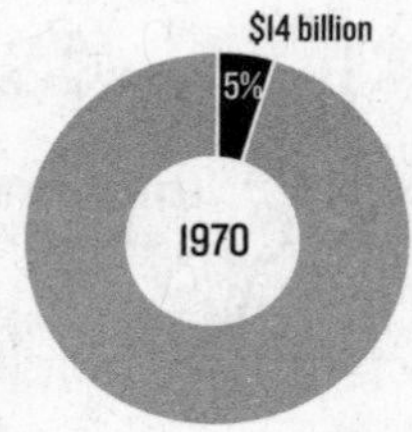


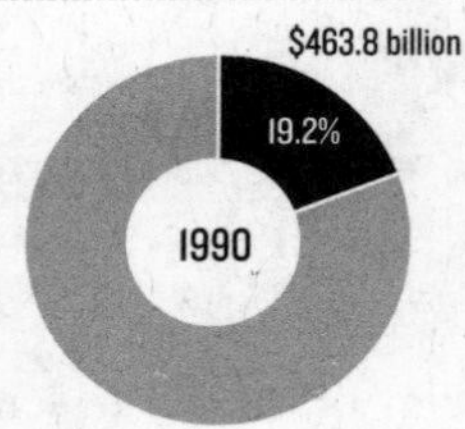


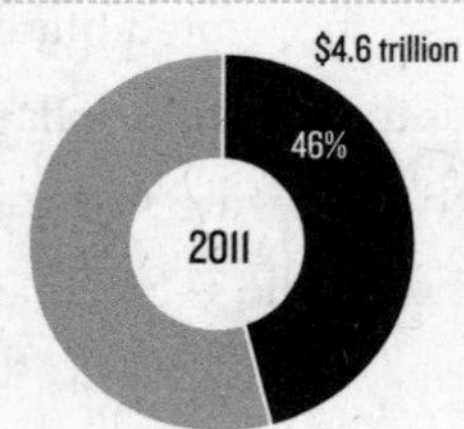


Source: Treasury, White House Office of Management and Budget

peaked in early 2009 and has been falling since. As Massachusetts Institute of Technology economist Simon Johnson and his co-blogger James Kwak put it in their new book, *White House Burning*: "If the Treasury Department never had to pay interest (and could always borrow as it needed), the national debt would not matter very much."

But the federal government does have to pay interest. Even though the U.S. Treasury borrows more cheaply than almost anyone else on the planet, the U.S. government paid $230 billion in net interest last year, more than triple the $64 billion it spent on all nondefense research and development, from medical research to space exploration. And that's with interest rates at extraordinarily low levels. When rates return to normal, perhaps around 5 percent, each additional $1 trillion in debt will add $50 billion a year to the government's annual interest payments.

And even the mighty U.S. government cannot assume it will always be able to borrow whatever it needs cheaply. The fact that the Chinese, in particular, hold so much of the federal debt–about 25 percent of the debt held by foreigners, according to the U.S. Treasury–conjures up a lot of angst, and that doesn't count the Chinese holdings of debt of Fannie Mae and Freddie Mac, the mortgage lenders backed by the U.S. government. The worry is either that the Chinese will yank all their money out at once (not likely, given that doing so would tank the U.S. economy and with it their investments and exports) or that the reserves give the Chinese leverage over U.S. economic and foreign policies. (They do.) But even if the United States were borrowing from reliable allies, the more borrowed from abroad, the bigger the share of future Americans' income that goes overseas to pay interest and principal.

For all the rhetoric from politicians of both parties about the dangers of debt and deficits, in the end, little was actually done about it in 2011 or 2012. "Kicking the can down the road" became an almost daily mantra in the press, and an accurate one.

One piece of recent legislation took direct aim at the deficit: the Budget Control Act. The law was passed in August 2011 in order to persuade reluctant members of Congress to take the politically unpopular step of voting to raise the ceiling on the federal debt, a bizarre practice in which Congress votes once to spend money and then votes again later to pay the credit card bill when it arrives. Essentially trying to tie its own hands–as it did from 1990 to 2002–Congress set hard ceilings for each of the next ten years on the 40 percent of spending that it appropriates annually, the panoply of domestic and defense items from aircraft carriers to the National Dam Safety Program described in chapter 3 but not Social Security or Medicare or other benefit programs. The caps allow this spending to rise about 2 percent a year, not enough to keep up with expected inflation, which in the world of budgeting is considered a cut of $1 trillion over ten years. If, and it's a big if, the caps hold, spending on everything outside of Social Security, major health programs, and interest would come in below 8 percent of GDP in 2022, lower than at any time in the past forty years.

Congress then took one more step. It pointed a gun at itself (or, if you listen to Panetta, at the Pentagon budget) by mandating further across-the-board defense and domestic spending cuts beginning in January 2013–unless Congress and the president agree on an alternative way to bring projected deficits down by an additional $1.2 trillion over the next ten years. This self-imposed deadline could prompt a significant attack on the deficit some time after the November 2012 elections. Or Congress and the president could undo it, kicking the can down the road again.

## WHERE ARE WE NOW?

Each January, the Congressional Budget Office attempts to show where the fiscal ship is headed before Congress tries to steer it with changes to taxes and spending. One telling measure of how contentious budget politics have become is the increasing difficulty of getting agreement even on this starting point, known in Washington as "the baseline." (When there's talk in the newspapers of a $500 billion, ten-year deficit-reduction package, that means some combination of taxes and spending cuts is projected to reduce future deficits by $500 billion from some baseline.)

Crafting baselines has never been easy: they rest on forecasts of everything from the stock market to the number of elderly hips that will be replaced, and those forecasts are certain to be wrong. Understanding baselines hasn't been easy either: if it takes a 4 percent increase in Medicare spending to provide the same services next year as this year, then baseline accounting says that a 3 percent increase in Medicare spending is a 1 percent *cut*. And if that isn't enough to give you a headache, the baseline-making task has grown tougher lately because Congress and presidents have stamped expiration dates on many costly tax and spending programs, and then repeatedly extended them. So should the baseline assume that Medicare spending will go down because the law says doctors' fees will be slashed? Or should it assume that Congress will, as it has to date, waive the fee cuts? Ultimately, what matters is where Congress and the president end up, not where they start. But defining the starting point and crafting the baseline are important to the politics and public perceptions of the budget–they're used by one side to magnify the size of the spending cuts or tax changes proposed by the other side–and politics and perceptions have a lot to do with what actually happens.

Pretending that Congress will let taxes rise and spending fall sharply at the start of 2013 can provide a dangerously misleading picture of the course on which the federal government is set. So the CBO has crafted an alternative. It projects future spending, taxes, and deficits if Congress extends all the Bush tax cuts for everyone at year-end, continues to adjust the pesky alternative minimum tax so it doesn't reach ever deeper into the middle class, and continues to waive the provision in a

1997 deficit-reduction law that would cut Medicare doctor fees. Not everyone likes this approach, but it's a useful road map to where the budget is heading without a course correction.

What does it show? "The good news is that the improving economy will reduce the deficit as a share of GDP considerably over the next few years," said Doug Elmendorf, the current CBO director. As more people get jobs, more tax receipts will flow into the Treasury and spending on unemployment compensation and the like will come down. "The bad news," he continued, "is that the improvement will still leave the deficit so large that, if we maintain our current spending and tax policies, debt will continue to rise sharply, relative to GDP."

In this steady-as-she-goes scenario, spending driven by the aging of the population and rising health costs climbs faster than revenues. A lot faster. Deficits of $1 trillion or more would be the norm, and the national debt would approach 100 percent of GDP within a decade–and climb still higher in the years after that.

No one *really* knows how much the U.S. government can borrow before global investors get uneasy and begin to demand higher interest rates. The national debt exceeded 100 percent of GDP during World War II and then came down as the economy sprinted. But history suggests that debt of that level is in the danger zone. Think Argentina, circa 2001. Think Greece, circa 2012.

"If a country has not balanced its long-run budget when the long run arrives, then the market balances its budget for it–and does so in a way that nobody in the country likes," Brad DeLong, a Berkeley economist and blogger, and a former Clinton adviser, has written. Then he added, drily, "[T]he long run seems to vary between three years and 200 years, depending."

The 2012 election campaign has produced a lot of talk about taxes, spending, and deficits, much of it less than useful in understanding the choices the country faces. Basically, there are three poles in the debate.

The first says: The deficit is a problem. But not now, especially when there is still so much unemployment. The poster boy: Paul Krugman, a Princeton University economist and *New York Times* columnist.

The second says: The deficit is a problem. And the solution is to shrink the government and cut taxes. The poster boy: Paul Ryan, the Republican congressman from Wisconsin and chairman of the House Budget Committee.

The third says: The deficit is a big problem. In fact, it is the "transcendent threat to our economic future." The poster boy: Peter G. Peterson, an octogenarian who is spending a large part of his considerable fortune to warn about the five-alarm fiscal fire ahead.

## IT'S UNEMPLOYMENT, STUPID

Paul Krugman is not and probably never will be a policy maker. But he is formidably armed with a Nobel Prize, a perch on the op-ed page of the *New York Times*, and a very sharp pen. Drawn to economics initially by a set of Isaac Asimov's science-fiction novels in which social scientists save the world, Krugman earned his Ph.D. at MIT and won the American Economic Association's prize for the most accomplished economist under forty. Krugman's most noteworthy academic work focuses on international trade and economic geography. Outside the profession, he began to make his mark as a polemicist about twenty years ago and has been writing twice a week for the *Times* since 1999, while blogging in between columns.

Krugman's world is black-and-white: There are good guys and bad guys, smart guys and dumb ones, truth tellers and liars–and most of the bad guys are Republicans. His columns, speeches, and books often offer more ammunition than argument, bolstering those who agree with him rather than changing the minds of those who don't. But compared to other economists and to many policy makers, Krugman saw early how big a blow the economy had suffered. As a result, he advocated for far more fiscal and monetary stimulus than Obama eventually got Congress to approve and Fed chairman Ben Bernanke got his colleagues to pursue. Keynes was right, he shouted. Take his advice.

Rahm Emanuel, Obama's first chief of staff, once dismissed Krugman as economically brilliant and politically naive. "How many bills has he passed?" he asked. To which Krugman replied, "The question is why Obama didn't ask for what the economy needed, then bargain from there."

Krugman's attitude toward the deficit is *fuggedaboutit.* "Premature deficit reduction," he has said, risks "diverting attention from the more immediately urgent task of reducing unemployment." Shouldn't we worry that the rest of the world won't keep lending the U.S. government more money? No, Krugman said. The interest rates that the bond market is charging on long-term loans to the U.S. government suggest that investors aren't worrying about that prospect, so why should the U.S. government? Europe, in his view, provided an instructive case study of misguided fiscal austerity. Countries like Greece that were forced to cut spending aggressively to reduce borrowing strangled their economies and choked off the very growth that would allow them to pay off future debts.

"If we had slashed spending to ward off the invisible bond vigilantes . . . we'd be emulating Europe, and hence emulating Europe's failure," he wrote. We were wise, and we'd be wiser still if we gave the economy another dose of stimulus, he argued.

## IT'S SPENDING, STUPID

After Republicans took control of the House, Paul Ryan became chairman of the House Budget Committee, and the most prominent Republican voice on budget matters. His fiscal script, called "A Path to Prosperity," outlined unprecedented changes to the federal budget. Social Security was left alone, but he proposed big changes in the health programs. Federal spending on Medicaid's long-term care coverage would be capped and turned over to the states. Those who turn sixty-five after 2022 would be offered vouchers to buy something resembling today's fee-for-service Medicare or private insurance; to save money, each voucher would be worth less than the CBO currently projects health insurance for the elderly will cost. The notion was that the constraints on spending–"reform," Ryan called it–would force the health care system to get more efficient. Critics said they simply shifted the costs onto the beneficiaries. But that was just a start. Ryan also proposed shrinking the rest of the federal government. Spending on everything outside Social Security, the health insurance programs, and interest would go from 12 percent of GDP in 2010 to 6 percent by 2022, he said, though the outline didn't specify what would be cut.

Unlike the deficit-*über-alles* crowd, Ryan said he wanted to cut taxes, too. Although he didn't offer details–budget resolutions generally don't–he called for lower tax rates for both households and corporations. Backed by economists at the conservative Heritage Foundation (and without the endorsement of the CBO), Ryan predicted a resulting surge in economic growth that would produce enough revenues to reduce future deficits and bring down the debt.

"You shouldn't put yourself in a position of trying to feed ever-higher spending with higher revenues, because you'll never catch up," he argued. His framework rejected what he called the "shared scarcity mentality" of "ever-higher taxes and bureaucratically rationed health care."

Krugman described Ryan's plan as "a strange combination of cruelty and insanely wishful thinking." House Republicans voted for it, but many were uneasy, believing that the far-reaching changes to Medicare (which were altered in the 2012 iteration of the Ryan plan) made them an easy mark for Democrats on the campaign trail.

But Ryan was looking beyond the next election: "I believe the way to make change is to shift the political center of gravity as best you can, by putting ideas out there, solutions out there, and surviving the gauntlet of demagoguery you'll inevitably receive," he said.

## IT'S THE DEFICIT, STUPID

If there's a chart or PowerPoint slide that shows a volcano-like explosion of spending or deficits in the future, chances are it was made by, paid for, or inspired by Pete Peterson, age eighty-six, the modern incarnation of an Old Testament prophet roaming the country and the airwaves to lament the profligacy of his times. "My daughter jokes that when I do pass on, it will be at my desk with my head huddled over a speech explaining why the Social Security trust fund is an insolvent oxymoron," he wrote in his memoir. "I hope she's right and that it has lots of PowerPoint charts."

His mission: to generate enough alarm about deficits so politicians cut spending and raise taxes–and soon. Peterson is "the godfather of this whole effort of trying to bring sanity to our nation's finances," said Erskine Bowles, who chaired a deficit-reduction commission that Obama appointed.

Pete Peterson is the son of a Greek immigrant who ran a café in Kearney, Nebraska, that was, Peterson allows, known less for its food than for being open 24/7 for twenty-five uninterrupted years. He hopscotched through corporate America, getting rich along the way. Between stints as chief executive of Bell & Howell and of Lehman Brothers, he served as Nixon's secretary of commerce. In 1985, Peterson cofounded Blackstone Group, a private equity firm, a venture that made him and his partner, Steve Schwarzman, *really* rich.

As Peterson tells it from his office on the forty-eighth floor of a Manhattan office tower with a spectacular view of the New York skyline, his intense focus on the dangers of deficits dates to the early 1980s. He and his wife, his third, were trying to buy a house in East Hampton on Long Island from a friend who was playing hard to get. To win her favor, Peterson agreed to speak at the inaugural forum of a group she was forming, the Women's Economic Round Table. She accepted on the condition that he talk about Ronald Reagan's budget. Peterson had voted for Reagan, assuming him to be both a social and a fiscal conservative, but the homework he did for the speech convinced him otherwise. In March 1981, just two months after Reagan took office, Peterson stunned the White House and Reagan's many fans on Wall Street by condemning his tax cuts as "too much of an all-or-nothing gamble, too much of a high-wire act." The problem, he told the women's roundtable in 1981, was "a growing systemic inability to control mandated [benefit] spending programs." He has been making the same point in speeches, magazine essays, and books for the past thirty years. (And he got the house.)

When Blackstone sold shares to the public in 2007, Peterson cashed out to the tune of $1.85 billion. "I did not want to finish life as the retired CEO playing golf five times a week," he said. He had financed antideficit campaigns before. In 2008, he went big time, creating the Peter G. Peterson Foundation to "engage the American people and our leaders in confronting what I consider to be the greatest challenge before us as a nation: our unsustainable long-term national debt" and endowing it with *$1 billion.*

Peterson's foundation has bankrolled what might be called the deficit-industrial complex, a set of overlapping organizations with a shared goal of rallying the public–and especially the business and political elite–to reduce the deficit before financial Armageddon arrives. In 2011, the foundation gave $3.1 million to an outfit formed by a passionate deficit warrior, David Walker, a former head of the Government Accountability Office and also an ex–chief executive of the Peterson Foundation; $1.5 million to the Concord Coalition, a group Peterson helped form in the 1990s that, among other things, runs a roving "fiscal wake-up tour" to get the public alarmed; more than $500,000 to the Committee for a Responsible Federal Budget, a nonpartisan Washington group that presses the case for deficit reduction; and $200,000 each to six think tanks of differing political persuasions to craft deficit-reduction plans of their own. The foundation has financed an eighty-five-minute documentary on the dangers of debt, called *I.O.U.S.A.* It has run a national advertising campaign around a fictional presidential candidate named "Hugh Jidette." (Say it quickly three times.) Because Pete Peterson likes them, the foundation also produces a steady stream of scary and colorful charts.

The message is simple and consistent: the United States must slay the deficit dragon before it kills the United States. The actual belt-tightening should be delayed until the economy has recovered, but it must be done if the nation is to make the investments needed to restore the American dream of rising living standards.

"On our current course, we are headed toward an unthinkable situation in which the federal government spends more than four times as much on interest as it spends on education, R&D, and infrastructure, combined," Pete Peterson has said. "This effectively would mean spending much more on our past than we do on our future... robbing future generations of the opportunities we have enjoyed." And in contrast to Paul Ryan–and current Republican orthodoxy–Peterson has long argued that tax increases are essential, inevitable, *and* wise. "Unlike some of my Wall Street colleagues," Peterson wrote in the *Atlantic* back in October 1993 and has repeated frequently ever since, "I see absolutely nothing wrong with imposing higher tax burdens on the wealthiest in our society."

## A TWO-FISTED FISCAL POLICY

Inside the White House, the banner for doing more, much more, to help the economy than Obama and Congress did was carried by Christina Romer, the Berkeley economist and chair of the Council of Economic Advisers. The CEA is an unusual cog in the economic-policy-making apparatus. Created by Congress in 1946, the three-member council of economists, usually drawn from academia, controls nothing. Its sole task is to give the president "objective economic advice and analysis." Its influence varies from administration to administration, and its fiscal advice over the years is a history of the evolution of economists' thinking about budgets.

Romer is a numbers-crunching bleeding heart. "The first recession I really remember was that in 1981–82," she once said. "That recession was personal." In 1983, her father lost his engineering job at a chemical company. "I vividly remember the phone call where he told me that he had 'been sacked.' He was careful to say that I shouldn't worry about my wedding, which was scheduled for that summer. There was money put aside for that." Her father later found a lower-paying, though stable, job overseeing subway car rehabilitation in Philadelphia.

Romer drew unwelcome notoriety early in the administration when she and a colleague predicted in January 2009 that, without any stimulus, the unemployment rate would reach 9 percent but an $800 billion dose of fiscal adrenaline would keep it from rising above 8 percent. As later revisions to government data revealed, the economy was in much worse shape at that moment than the Obama team realized. Still, unemployment peaked at 10 percent in October 2009, and Republicans have never let her forget the flawed prediction.

Romer shared Krugman's frustration that the government wasn't doing more to bring down unemployment–and still does. "The evidence is stronger than it has ever been that fiscal policy matters–that fiscal stimulus helps the economy add jobs and that reducing the budget deficit lowers growth, at least in the near term," she said after leaving the White House. In the early days of the Obama administration, she saw a case for a much bigger fiscal stimulus (as much as $1.8 trillion) than the new president eventually proposed. She believes the economy would be better today if Obama had secured another big dose of stimulus in late 2009.

But she doesn't share Krugman's conviction that the deficit can be safely ignored for now, especially in the wake of the tumult in Europe over governments that can't pay their debts. In fact, the *only* way, in her view, to get more stimulus now is to package it with a credible set of deficit-reducing measures that would take effect later when the economy was stronger. "We don't have to reduce the deficit immediately. In fact, we can increase it temporarily, as we need to, to help create jobs," she has said. "But to reassure financial markets (and ourselves) that we will be solvent over the long haul, we need to pass a plan as soon as possible for reducing the deficit gradually over time."

Although less emphatic in public, Fed chairman Bernanke takes a similar view. He is wary about prescribing fiscal policy to members of Congress, who like to remind him that decisions on taxes and spending are their turf, not his. But when pressed at a February 2012 hearing in the House, he endorsed what he called "a two-handed plan"–one that coupled increased spending on infrastructure or education or tax cuts while simultaneously addressing "the long-term necessity of making fiscal policy sustainable.... You need to think about those two things together."

Alas, thinking about "two things together" is not Congress's strength. In their rhetoric for much of the past couple of years, both Congress and the president have rushed to one side (extend the Bush income tax cuts, continue payroll tax holidays, cut corporate tax rates) and then to the other (raise taxes on the rich, close tax loopholes, cap annually appropriated spending, slow the growth in Medicare spending). Obama's latest budget has elements of both: a proposal, for instance, for a new tax break to encourage employers to hire (would increase the deficit by $14 billion in the first year) and a proposal to limit the tax deductions for upper-income taxpayers (would reduce the deficit by $27 billion in the first year). Republicans promptly chastised him for seeking to raise taxes and cut spending on Medicare, and then complained he wasn't doing anything about the deficit.

## THE TRUTH TELLER

Romer and Ryan, Krugman and Peterson are full-throated advocates with clear and loudly stated views on what the government should and shouldn't do differently. In contrast, Doug Elmendorf, director of the CBO, is more of a national truth teller, trying to make the public and the politicians understand choices they cannot evade while at the same time not hurting his–and the CBO's–credibility by taking sides. The *Washington Examiner* once dubbed him "a geek with guts." At a time when almost every fact about the federal budget is the subject of fierce debate, Elmendorf's measured voice can be hard to hear, but some people do listen. When he called a press briefing on the agency's annual economic and budget outlook in January 2012, he drew ten television cameras to record his carefully calibrated words.

Slim and bespectacled, Elmendorf could play a college professor on TV. "A quiet man who thinks carefully about everything," the *New York Times* once said of him. Indeed, he deliberately chose a baseball game for one of his first dates with his future wife. "You want to be sure there's something going on to fill the lull in the conversation but not like a movie where you can't talk," he explained.

Elmendorf's academic pedigree is impeccable: Princeton, 1983; Harvard Ph.D., 1989. The advisers for his dissertation–"Fiscal Policy and Financial Markets"–were Martin Feldstein and Greg Mankiw, top economic advisers, respectively, to Reagan and George W. Bush, and Larry Summers, top economic adviser to Clinton and Obama. After five years helping to teach the big introductory economics course at Harvard, Elmendorf came to Washington in the mid-1990s to work at the CBO. "Starting about then," he said, "I thought being CBO director would be a very good job." But first he went to work on the staff of the Federal Reserve Board, with a couple of breaks to work on the staffs of the White House Council of Economic Advisers and the Clinton Treasury. Elmendorf left government in 2007 for the Brookings Institution think tank but came back in 2009 when the congressional leadership–then all Democrats–picked him to run the CBO, succeeding Peter Orszag, who went to the White House to be Obama's budget director.

At congressional hearings, Elmendorf is like the referee in a food fight. With calm dispassionate words and charts, he tries to give his bosses in Congress a reality check. Members of Congress cross-examine Elmendorf as if he were an expert witness in a murder trial, laboring to get him to support the questioner's point of view. (Senator Kent Conrad, a Democrat from North Dakota, at a February 2012 hearing: "Why wouldn't one conclude from what you've said here that the best policy in the short term would be to extend tax cuts, at least some significant part of the tax cuts, and defer some of the spending cuts . . . several years, but right now agree to a plan that will raise revenue and cut spending so that at the end of the 10 years we've dramatically reduced deficits and reduced the growth of debt?")

Elmendorf tries just as hard to be sure Congress understands the daunting dimensions of the deficit and the alternative ways to reduce it while avoiding taking sides in the partisan debate, particularly over taxes. ("I don't want to speak to a specific combination of policies that the Congress might choose to extend or let expire," he told Conrad. "But on your general point, I think agreement about how the country's budget will be put on a sustainable path would be a good thing for the economy in the short run because it would give people some confidence that they knew where policies were headed, which is very hard to have in the current environment.")

Elmendorf, in short, is a good guide to the fiscal landscape. His tour begins with a couple of observations.

One is a demographic fact. "We cannot go back to the tax and spending policies of the past because the number of people sixty-five or older will increase by one-third between 2012 and 2022," Elmendorf says. As more baby boomers cross the threshold for collecting Social Security or being covered by Medicare, spending on those programs will rise. And even hard-core spending cutters willing to talk about paring Social Security or Medicare or raising the eligibility age propose exempting those who have already turned fifty-five.

The other is a political fact that sums up the entire budget dilemma in a single sentence. "The country faces a fundamental disconnect between the services the people expect the government to provide, particularly in the form of benefits for older Americans, and the tax revenues that people are willing to send to the government to finance those services," he has said.

The CBO's traditional role is to take budget plans that the president and members of Congress devise and put numbers on them: what would the course of spending and taxes and deficits be if they were enacted. To that end, it also produces a Chinese menu of deficit-reducing options from which Congress can choose.

But none of that seemed to be penetrating the political debate. So Elmendorf tried a different tack. He started by projecting today's tax and spending policies ten years out, the baseline referred to earlier. That would put the budget deficit in 2022 above $1 trillion and rising. By then, the U.S. government would be borrowing so much that the national debt, as a percentage of the GDP, would be dangerously high (over 90 percent) and still rising.

Then he asked: What would have to happen to avoid that outcome, to bring the spending and revenue lines close enough together so that the national debt would at least stop climbing, as a percentage of GDP? His answer: spending cuts or tax increases or a combination of the two that add up to $750 billion a year by 2022. Even in Washington that's a big number.

What would it take to get to that goal? Remember, the starting point for the exercise is that Congress sticks to the caps it has set on annually appropriated defense and domestic spending. "The country," Elmendorf pointed out, "is [already] on track to substantially reduce the role of most federal activities, relative to the size of the economy." Perhaps Congress will squeeze more out of defense between now and 2022, depending on the state of the world. But it's a good bet that what it saves in defense, it'll end up spending on domestic programs–highways or job training or disaster relief or something.

So say Congress decided to get really serious about the deficit by looking at spending on the big benefit programs that today account for 40 percent of all federal outlays: Social Security and the growing Medicare and Medicaid budgets. Say it raised the age at which the elderly become eligible for Medicare to sixty-seven (from sixty-five) and the age at which they're eligible for full Social Security benefits to seventy (from sixty-seven). Say it shifted to a less generous formula for setting Social Security benefits and adjusting them for inflation. Say it boosted the premiums that the elderly on Medicare pay for their coverage and made them pay more of their health care bills out of pocket. And say it limited increases in federal spending for Medicaid, the joint state-federal health insurance program for the poor, so the tab rose no faster than the pace at which private sector wages rise.

Any one of those would be a very big deal. But if Congress did all that, it would be saving about $250 billion annually by 2022. That's a big number to be sure, but here's the rub: all those measures combined would save only a third of what's needed to reach Elmendorf's budget nirvana goal. If *all* the weight is put on the big entitlement programs–Social Security, Medicare, and Medicaid–they would need to be cut by 25 percent to put the budget on a sustainable course by 2022.

Which is why the conversation inevitably turns to raising taxes alongside cutting spending.

Elmendorf's starting point for the exercise is that all the tax cuts that Bush instigated and Obama continued are extended at the end of the year. Say Congress took Obama's advice and let income tax rates on the over-$250,000-a-year crowd rise to pre-Bush levels. That would bring in between $100 billion and $150 billion in 2020. Say it also eliminated the federal income tax deductions for mortgage interest and state and local taxes, changes that would raise taxes on many more people. That would yield another $180 billion. Both would be huge changes, and they, too, would get Congress only about one-third of the way toward the goal. If Social

Security, Medicare, and Medicaid were shielded altogether, then taxes would have to be raised by about one-sixth. That's a big tax increase.

Put all the spending cuts and the tax increases on this shopping list into the deficit-reduction basket, and there still would not be enough money to bring the deficit to sustainable levels by 2022. Elmendorf's list of options is hardly exhaustive: if Congress let *all* the Bush tax cuts expire, raising the taxes of almost everyone who pays income taxes, it would, by CBO estimates, come close to hitting the target. But the point is clear: small changes will *not* suffice.

That's not to say that the nation's fiscal problem is unsolvable. The proliferation of reports by bipartisan commissions illustrates the mix of significant, but manageable, policies that could arrest the rise in the federal debt over the next decade. Most of them raise some taxes by eliminating deductions, credits, loopholes, and exemptions; cut the defense budget; restrain spending on health and other benefits; and spread the pain widely while trying to shield the poorest Americans. Yet the polarization of the American political system has left it, so far, unable to choose between Barack Obama's approach to reducing the deficit or Paul Ryan's. Neither side has enough votes to prevail, and neither is willing to compromise on some amalgam that might spread the pain and that both can live with. This is the crux of the issue: the deficit widens, the debt grows, the interest burden gets heavier, the voices grow even more shrill as the budget burden is passed to future generations, and nothing gets done.

"I used to tell the students that we are either governed by leadership or crisis," Leon Panetta said in a recent interview. "And I always thought that if leadership wasn't there, then ultimately you rely on crisis to drive decisions. In the last few years, my biggest concern is that crisis doesn't seem to drive decisions either. So there goes my theory."

# NOTES

### CHAPTER 1: SPENDING $400 MILLION AN HOUR

16 "broken promises": Paul Ryan press release, February 13, 2012. http://budget.house.gov/News/DocumentSingle.aspx?DocumentID=280066

16 "I have a soft spot": Interview, Jack Lew.

17 "The purpose of power": Tim Weiner, "Old-Time Democrat Tries to Weave a Budget Tapestry," Public Lives, *New York Times*, November 8, 1999. http://www.nytimes.com/1999/11/08/us/public-lives-old-time-democrat-tries-to-weave-a-budget-tapestry.html

17 Eleven days after: "Paul Ryan: Rebel Without a Pause," *Wisconsin Policy Research Institute,* July 2010. http://www.wpri.org/WIInterest/Vol19No2/Schneider19.2p2.html

18 "I do believe": Jennifer Rubin, "Making the Case for Free Markets and Profit," washingtonpost.com, January 12, 2012. http://www.washingtonpost.com/blogs/right-turn/post/making-the-case-for-free-markets-and-profit/2012/01/11/gIQAX9zVrP_blog.html

18 "It cost me": Ezra Klein, "Rep. Paul Ryan: Rationing Happens Today! The Question Is Who Will Do It?,"

washingtonpost.com, February 2, 2010. http://voices.washingtonpost.com/ezra-klein/2010/02/rep_paul_ryan_rationing_happen.html

18 One liberal group: Paul Ryan Wheelchair Commercial, The Agenda Project, May 17, 2011. http://www.politifact.com/truth-o-meter/statements/2011/may/25/agenda-project/throw-granny-cliff-ad-says-paul-ryan-plan-would-pr/

19 "Byrd droppings": Mary Agnes Carey, "How the Senate Will Tackle Health Care Reform," *Kaiser Health News,* March 21, 2010. http://www.kaiserhealthnews.org/Stories/2010/March/22/Senate-health-bill-whats-next.aspx

19 CHIMPS: Jim Monke, "Reductions in Mandatory Agriculture Program Spending," Congressional Research Service (Washington, D.C.: May 19, 2010). http://www.nationalaglawcenter.org/assets/crs/R41245.pdf

19 As humor columnist: David Wessel, "Deficit Dilemma: How to Dig Out," *Wall Street Journal,* October 15, 2009, A2. http://online.wsj.com/article/SB125554787267585505.html

21 "In 2009, for the first time": Interview, Eugene Steuerle.

21 The United States spends: http://milexdata.sipri.org/files/?file=SIPRI+milex+data+1988–2010.xls

22 Yet in a CNN poll: CNN Opinion Research Poll, March 11–13, 2011. http://i2.cdn.turner.com/cnn/2011/images/03/31/rel4m.pdf

22 Wages and benefits: Office of Management and Budget, *Fiscal Year 2013 Analytical Perspectives* (Washington, D.C.: Government Printing Office, 2012), Table 11–4.

22 4.4 million workers: Ibid., Table 11–3.

22 Where does the rest of the money go?: Office of Management and Budget, *Historical Tables* (Washington, D.C.:

Government Printing Office, 2012), Tables 11–3, 12–1. http://www.whitehouse.gov/omb/budget/Historicals

23 "It's the things:" Interview.

23 The heart of federal health care spending: Congressional Budget Office, *Long-Term Budget Outlook* (Washington, D.C.: Government Printing Office, 2012), Figure B-1. http://www.cbo.gov/doc.cfm?index=12212

24 The Medicare prescription drug benefit: David Wessel, "Tallying the Toll of Terrorism on the Economy from 9/11," *Wall Street Journal*, September 1, 2011, A2.

24 "You can't fix": Interview at WSJ CEO Council.

24 wiped out $7 trillion: http://www.newyorkfed.org/research/staff_reports/sr482.pdf

25 "At one point": http://cybercemetery.unt.edu/archive/cop/20110401232213/http:/cop.senate.gov/documents/cop-031611-report.pdf

25 only $470 billion: U.S. Department of Treasury, "Troubled Asset Relief Program (TARP)–Monthly Report to Congress," April 10, 2012. http://www.treasury.gov/initiatives/financial-stability/briefing-room/reports/105/Documents105/March%2012%Report/%2010%20Congress.pdf

26 As of December 2011: Federal Housing Financing Agency, *Conservator's Report on the Enterprises Financial Condition, Fourth Quarter 2011.* http://www.fhfa.gov/webfiles/23879/Conservator%27sReport4Q201141212F.pdf

27 for families in the very middle: Congressional Budget Office, "Trends in Federal Tax Revenues and Rates," December 2, 2010, 2. http://www.cbo.gov/publication/21938

27 Nearly half of American households: Rachel M. Johnson et al., "Why Some Tax Units Pay No Income Tax," Tax Policy Center, July 27, 2011. http://www.taxpolicycenter.org/publications/url.cfm?ID=1001547

28 less than a third of the populace: Bureau of the Census, "Income, Poverty, and Health Insurance Coverage in the United States: 2010," September 2011, 23. http://www.census.gov/prod/2011pubs/p60-239.pdf

28 government at all levels: Organization for Economic Cooperation and Development, *Revenue Statistics 2011* (Paris: OECD Publishing, 2011), 19.

28 All these tax breaks: Office of Management and Budget, *Fiscal Year 2013 Analytical Perspectives,* "Estimates of Total Income Tax Expenditures for Fiscal Years 2011–2017," Table 17–1.

30 U.S. government borrowed: Office of Management and Budget, *Historical Tables,* Table 8–1.

32 "A lot of us": Interview, Erskine Bowles.

## CHAPTER 2: HOW WE GOT HERE

33 "This country cannot": Leon E. Panetta, Speech at the Commonwealth Club of California, October 23, 2009. http://www.5min.com/Video/CIA-Director-Calls-Deficit-a-Threat-to-National-Security-516897448

34 "a dangerous experiment": Testimony, Leon E. Panetta, Senate Committee on Government Affairs, January 11, 1993. http://www.archive.org/stream/nominationofleon00unit/nominationofleon00unit_djvu.txt

35 "I've become very eclectic": Interview, Leon Panetta.

35 A natural politician: "The Defense Secretary: Leon Panetta," *60 Minutes,* January 29, 2012. http://www.cbsnews.com/8301-18560_162-57367997/the-defense-secretary-an-interview-with-leon-panetta/?tag=contentMain;cbsCarousel

37 Every week: 2011 Annual Report of the Boards of Trust-

ees of the Federal Hospital Insurance and Federal Supplementary Medical Insurance Trust Funds, May 11, 2011, 51. https://www.cms.gov/ReportsTrustFunds/downloads/tr2011.pdf

37 Back then, the entire output: Louis Johnston and Samuel H. Williamson, "What Was the U.S. GDP Then?," MeasuringWorth, 2011. http://www.measuringworth.com/usgdp/

38 Until Congress created: *United States Government Manual,* 1945. http://www.ibiblio.org/hyperwar/ATO/USGM/Executive.html

38 "The first requirement": Herbert Stein, *The Fiscal Revolution in America: Policy in Pursuit of Reality* (Washington, D.C.: American Enterprise Institute Press, 1996), 33.

38 About 70 percent: Office of Management and Budget, *Historical Tables* (Washington, D.C., Government Printing Office, 2012), 7.

38 "The federal budget": Stein, *Fiscal Revolution in America,* 14.

38 "Too often": Quoted in Stein, 44.

39 "Spending," Stein wrote: Ibid., 54.

39 Largely because of: Bureau of the Census, "District of Columbia–Race and Hispanic Origin: 1800 to 1990," Table 23. http://www.census.gov/population/www/documentation/twps0056/tab23.pdf

40 In a move with: Philip R. Dame and Bernard H. Martin, *The Evolution of OMB* (Washington, D.C.: privately published, 2009), 9. Also see Franklin D. Roosevelt, Exec. Order No. 8248: Reorganizing the Executive Office of the President, September 8, 1939. http://www.presidency.ucsb.edu/ws/index.php?pid=15808#ixzz1maeq2AWc

40 "Never again": Stein, 54.

41 "In three short years": Governor Mitch Daniels's Republican response to the 2012 State of the Union, January 24, 2012. http://www.speaker.gov/News/DocumentSingle.aspx?DocumentID=276315

41 "From the mid-1930s": Interview.

42 "My dad used to": "The Defense Secretary," *60 Minutes,* transcript, 2. http://www.cbsnews.com/8301-18560_162-57367997/the-defense-secretary-an-interview-with-leon-panetta/?tag=contentMain;cbsCarousel

42 "I had read about": Leon Panetta Interview, Conversations with History, Institute of International Studies, UC Berkeley, May 22, 2000, 243. http://globetrotter.berkeley.edu/people/Panetta/panetta-con2.html

43 Frank Lichtenberg estimates: Frank R. Lichtenberg, "The Effects of Medicare on Health Care Utilization and Outcomes," January 2002. http://www.nber.org/chapters/c9857.pdf

44 It's a living laboratory: David Wessel, "Medicare Cures: Easy to Prescribe, Tricky to Predict," *Wall Street Journal,* June 30, 2003, A1.

44 "the man who blew": Leon E. Panetta and Peter Gall, *Bring Us Together: The Nixon Team and the Civil Rights Retreat* (New York: J. B. Lippincott Co., 1971). http://www.amazon.com/Bring-together-Nixon-rights-retreat/dp/B000CKH9Q

45 Congress hasn't finished: Gregory Korte, "Congress Looks at Ways to Fix Budget Process," *USA Today,* October 4, 2011. http://www.usatoday.com/news/washington/story/2011-10-03/congress-examines-budget-process/50647934/1

45 But in a city riddled: David Wessel, "Man Who Wounded Health Care Effort Could Also Save It," *Wall Street Jour-*

*nal*, July 23, 2009, A4. http://online.wsj.com/article/SB124829913479973605.html

46 "who can grasp": Philip G. Joyce, *The Congressional Budget Office: Honest Numbers, Power and Policymaking* (Washington, D.C.: Georgetown University Press, 2011), 20, 388.

46 "Congress would have a bill": Ibid., 20.

46 "on the explicit grounds": Hali J. Edison, "An Interview with Alice Rivlin." http://www.cswep.org/rivlin.htm

47 "schmoozy": Peter Suderman, "The Gatekeeper," *Reason,* January 2010. http://reason.com/archives/2009/12/08/the-gatekeeper/singlepage

47 "Elmendorf . . . is the stone-faced banker": RJ Eskow, "Elmendor vs. Orszag: A 'Teachable Moment' . . . for Geeks and Nerds," July 28, 2009. http://www.huffing tonpost.com/rj-eskow/elmendorf-vs-orszag-a-tea_b_246672.html

48 "In the end, everyone": Interview, Douglas Holtz-Eakin.

48 "To a degree": Allen Schick, *The Federal Budget: Politics, Policy, Process* (Washington, D.C.: The Brookings Institution, 2000), 19–20.

48 for the first time: George Hager and Eric Pianin, *Mirage: Why Neither Democrats nor Republicans Can Balance the Budget, End the Deficit, and Satisfy the Public* (New York: Times Books/Henry Holt, 1997), 97.

49 "Well, you know": Ronald Reagan, quoted in Bruce Bartlett, " 'Starve the Beast': Origins and Development of a Budgetary Metaphor," *The Independent Review,* Summer 2007, 11. http://www.independent.org/pdf/tir/tir_12_01_01_bartlett.pdf

49 "If you insisted": David Stockman, *The Triumph of Politics* (New York: Harper & Row, 1986), 53.

50 "Two Santa Claus Theory": See Jude Wanniski, "Taxes and a Two-Santa Theory," *National Observer,* March 6, 1976. http://capitalgainsandgames.com/blog/bruce-bartlett/1701/jude-wanniski-taxes-and-two-santa-theory.

51 "At that point": Interview, Leon Panetta.

51 The Reagan tax cut was gigantic: Office of Tax Analysis, "Revenue Effects of Major Tax Bills–Updated Tables for All 2010 Bills." http://www.treasury.gov/resource-center/tax-policy/Documents/OTA-Rev-Effects-1940-present-6-6-2011.pdf

51 "If the American political system": Richard Darman, *Who's in Control? Polar Politics and the Sensible Center* (New York: Simon & Schuster, 1996), 79.

51 "$200 billion a year": Steven R. Weisman, "Budget Tie-up: Reagan at the Crossroads," *New York Times,* April 20, 1983.

52 the budget deficit averaged: Office of Management and Budget, *Historical Tables* (Washington, D.C.: Government Printing Office, 2012), Table 1.2.

52 "A significant tax cut": http://globetrotter.berkeley.edu/people/Panetta/panetta-con0.html

52 "the six most destructive words": Colin MacKenzie, "How Bush Blew It," *Globe and Mail,* November 4, 1992, A1.

53 "a borrow, bailout, and buy-out binger": Leon Panetta, speech to the National Press Club, January 17, 1989, in *Congressional Record,* January 20, 1989.

53 "Both Democrats and Republicans": http://globetrotter.berkeley.edu/people/Panetta/panetta-con0.html

54 "The American people": "Budget Plan Nears Vote in House," *Chicago Tribune,* October 28. 1990, C17.

54 The vote tally: http://www.govtrack.us/congress/vote.xpd?vote=h1990-528

55 "For Democrats": Interview, Leon Panetta.

55 "undermined": Andrew Rosenthal, "The 1992 Campaign: Breaking Tax Pledge Hurt His Credibility, President Tells ABC." *New York Times,* June 26, 1992. http://www.nytimes.com/1992/06/26/us/the-1992-campaign-breaking-tax-pledge-hurt-his-credibility-president-tells-abc.html

55 "The record shows": http://www.thefiscaltimes.com/Articles/2010/06/25/A-Budget-Deal-That-Did-Reduce-the-Deficit.aspx#page1

56 "The Soviet Union": Interview, Robert Reischauer.

56 "I think the most dangerous threat": Craig Whitlock, "Former Deficit Hawk Leon Panetta Now Fights Budget Cuts as Defense Secretary," *Washington Post,* November 3, 2011. http://www.washingtonpost.com/world/national-security/leon-panettas-mind-meld/2011/10/26/gIQAhtU4iM_story.html

57 "We talked": "Conversations with History," Institute of International Studies, University of California, Berkeley, 2000. http://globetrotter.berkeley.edu/people/Panetta/panetta-con0.html

58 The deficit came down even faster: http://www.cbo.gov/ftpdocs/103xx/doc10392/1993_09_14reischauertestimony.pdf

58 In 1995, the IRS counted: David Wessel, "The Wealth Factor: Again, the Rich Get Richer, but This Time They Pay More Taxes–Their Deductions Are Cut, and That Pesky Levy for Medicare Adds Up–a Big Break on Capital Gains," *Wall Street Journal,* April 2, 1998, A1.

58 "You know . . . does it really hurt": U.S. House of Representatives, Committee on the Budget, *Hearings on President Clinton's Fiscal Year 1995 Budget Proposal,* February 4,

1994, serial no. 103–18 (Washington, D.C.: Government Printing Office, 1994), 42, 45.

59 "In the time that I've been in Washington": http://www.pbs.org/newshour/bb/white_house/january97/panetta_1-17.html.

60 "We know big government": State of the Union address, January 23, 1996. http://clinton4.nara.gov/WH/New/other/sotu.html

60 "Leon [Panetta] and John Kasich": Interview, Jack Lew.

61 "Gingrich wanted to do it": http://www.usnews.com/news/politics/articles/2008/05/29/the-pact-between-bill-clinton-and-newt-gingrich

61 "Why would we go back": Interview, Grover Norquist.

62 "[T]he highly desirable": Testimony of Alan Greenspan, Senate Budget Committee, January 25, 2001.

62 "a feeding frenzy": Alan Greeenspan, *The Age of Turbulence: Adventures in a New World* (New York: Penguin Press, 2007).

62 "misjudged the emotions": Ibid., 222.

62 "policies that could": Testimony of Alan Greenspan, Senate Budget Committee, January 25, 2001.

64 *$3.3 trillion:* http://www.cbo.gov/ftpdocs/121xx/doc12187/ChangesBaselineProjections.pdf

64 the government spent more: http://cboblog.cbo.gov/?p=3058

66 "The era of big government": David Wessel, "Capital: Small-Government Rhetoric Gets Filed Away," *Wall Street Journal,* September 8, 2005, A2.

66 In 2011, it was 5 percent: Office of Management and Budget, *Historical Tables,* Tables 8.2 and 8.4.

67 By 2010, the *annual* tab: https://www.cms.gov/ReportsTrustFunds/downloads/tr2011.pdf, 9, 34.

67 "[A]fter Democrats": "Remarks by the President on Fiscal Policy," April 13, 2011. http://www.whitehouse.gov/the-press-office/2011/04/13/remarks-president-fiscal-policy

68 "would never again permit": http://www.scribd.com/doc/18757758/Pa-Nett-at-Ask-Force-Testimony-October-2007

## CHAPTER 3: WHERE THE MONEY GOES

69 The *instructions*: White House, "Preparation, Submission, and Execution of the Budget." http://www.whitehouse.gov/omb/circulars_a11_current_year_a11_toc

69 The Department of Homeland Security's: "U.S. Department of Homeland Security Annual Performance Report: Fiscal Years 2011–2013." http://www.dhs.gov/xlibrary/assets/mgmt/dhs-congressional-budget-justification-fy2013.pdf

70 The typical respondent: CNN Opinion Research Poll, March 11–13, 2011. http://i2.cdn.turner.com/cnn/2011/images/03/31/rel4m.pdf

70 a 2008 Cornell University: Suzanne Mettler, "Reconstituting the Submerged State: The Challenges of Social Policy Reform in the Obama Era." *Perspective on Politics* 8, no. 3 (September 2010): 809. http://government.arts.cornell.edu/assets/faculty/docs/mettler/submergedstat_mettler.pdf

71 When Gallup asked: Jeffrey M. Jones, "Americans Say Federal Gov't Wastes over Half of Every Dollar," September 19, 2011. http://www.gallup.com/poll/149543/americans-say-federal-gov-wastes-half-every-dollar.aspx

71 unused wireless devices: Office of Management and Budget, "Cuts, Consolidations and Savings," 144. http://www.whitehouse.gov/sites/default/files/omb/budget/fy2013/assets/ccs.pdf

71 the *Washington Post* identified: David S. Fallis, Scott Higham, and Kimberly Kindy, "Congressional Earmarks Sometimes Used to Fund Projects Near Lawmakers' Properties," *Washington Post,* February 6, 2012. http://www.washingtonpost.com/investigations/2012/01/12/gIQA97HGvQ_story.html?hpid=z1

71 Social Security Administration: Office of Management and Budget, "Cuts, Consolidations and Savings," 150. http://www.whitehouse.gov/sites/default/files/omb/budget/fy2013/assets/ccs.pdf

71 "Reducing the deficit": Interview, Stan Collender.

72 "My goal was": Interview, Rob Portman.

76 "It is the aging": House Budget Committee, The Congressional Budget Office's Budget and Economic Outlook Hearing, February 1, 2012.

76 Between 1999 and 2009: : Agency for Healthcare Research and Quality, H-CUPnet. http://hcupnet.ahrq.gov/

76 In 2009, Medicare spent: Government Accountability Office, *Medicare: Lack of Price Transparency May Hamper Hospitals' Ability to Be Prudent Purchasers of Implantable Medical Devices* (Washington, D.C.: January 2012).

78 Under the new system: Congressional Budget Office, "Reducing the Deficit: Spending and Revenue Options," March 2011, 55. http://www.cbo.gov/ftpdocs/120xx/doc12085/03-10-ReducingTheDeficit.pdf. See also Medicare Payment Advisory Commission, "Health Care Spending and the Medicare Program," June 2011, 167. http://www

.medpac.gov/documents/Jun11DataBookEntireReport .pdf

79 The White House budget office: Office of Management and Budget, *Fiscal Year 2013 Budget,* 227.

81 "When Republicans seized": Michael Grunwald, "Why Our Farm Policy Is Failing," *Time,* November 7, 2007. http://www.time.com/time/magazine/article/0,9171,1680139,00.html

81 "an entitlement tied": Dan Morgan, "The Farm Bill and Beyond" (Washington, D.C.: The German Marshall Fund, 2010), 13. http://209.200.80.89/publications/article.cfm?id=781&parent_type=P

81 Half of the direct: Office of Management and Budget, *Fiscal Year 2013 Budget,* 28. http://www.whitehouse.gov/sites/default/files/omb/budget/fy2013/assets/cutting .pdf

82 the first congressional district: Environmental Working Group, 2011 Farm Subsidy Database. http://farm .ewg.org/progdetail.php?fips=00000&progcodeotal _dp&page=district®ionname heUnitedStates

82 half of the money: Ibid.

82 "no longer defensible": Office of Management and Budget, "Cuts, Consolidations and Savings," 29. http://www .whitehouse.gov/sites/default/files/omb/budget/fy2013/assets/ccs.pdf

82 "Everybody needs to share": http://www.kansas.com/2011/06/14/1891504/payments-to-farmers-likely-to .html

82 tab to the taxpayer: Office of Management and Budget, *Fiscal Year 2013 Budget* (Washington, D.C.,: Government Printing Office, 2012), 28.

83 "the food-stamp president": Damian Paletta, "Campaign Renews Scrutiny of Growing Food-Stamp Program," wsj .com, January 17, 2012. http://blogs.wsj.com/economics/ 2012/01/17/campaign-renews-scrutiny-of-growing -food-stamp-program/

83 "wants us to become": Interview, Fox News, January 16, 2012. http://www.foxnews.com/on-air/hannity/2012/ 01/17/romney-sticks-story-super-pac-ads-post-sc-debate-interview

83 as of December 2011: USDA, "Supplemental Nutrition Assistance Program." http://www.fns.usda.gov/pd/ 34SNAPmonthly.htm

84 "We got a picture": Jerry Hagstrom, "From Farm to Table," *Government Executive,* September 1, 1998. http:// www.govexec.com/features/0998/0998s4s2.htm

84 "the food stamp program": "The Safety Net: A History of Food Stamps Use and Policy," nytimes.com, February 11, 2010. http://www.nytimes.com/interactive/2010/ 02/11/us/FOODSTAMPS.html

85 "relentless": Interview, Paul Ryan.

85 more than 80 percent: CNN/ORC Poll, September 23–25, 2011. http://www.pollingreport.com/social.htm; "Public Wants Change in Entitlements, Not Change in Benefits," Pew Research Center, July 7, 2011. http:// www.people-press.org/2011/07/07/section-5-views-of -social-security/

86 In contrast to: Social Security Administration, "Vote Tallies: 1935 Social Security Act." http://www.ssa.gov/ history/tally.html

86 "You cannot keep": Michael Lind, "Is Social Security a Ponzi Scheme?," nytimes.com, September 9, 2011.

http://www.nytimes.com/roomfordebate/2011/09/09/is-social-security-a-ponzi-scheme

87 The number of taxpaying: http://www.socialsecurity.gov/OACT/TR/2011/lr4b2.html

87 if nothing is done: http://www.ssa.gov/oact/TRSUM/index.html

87 Nearly 55 million people: http://www.ssa.gov/pressoffice/basicfact.htm

88 Most who draw benefits: http://www.socialsecurity.gov/policy/docs/quickfacts/stat_snapshot/index.html?qs

88 But nearly half: http://www.socialsecurity.gov/policy/docs/statcomps/income_pop55/

88 "I feel like": Interview, Martha Soderberg.

90 "[A]fter 10 years": Letter from Leon Panetta to John McCain, November 14, 2011. http://www.scribd.com/doc/72831635/Panetta-McCain-Graham-Ltr

91 Skeptics were quick to note: Lawrence Korb, "The Real Effects of Sequestration on Defense Spending," *Huffington Post,* November 17, 2011. http://www.huffingtonpost.com/lawrence-korb/sequestration-defense-spending_b_1100484.html

91 "We do not have": Bernard Brodie, *Strategy in the Missle Age* (Santa Monica, Calif.: Rand Corp., 1959), 359–61. Quoted in Todd Harrison, "$trategy in a Year of Fiscal Uncertainty," Center for Strategic and Budgetary Assessments, February 2012.

91 Aircraft carriers are expensive: Congressional Budget Office, "Reducing the Deficit: Spending and Revenue Options," March 2010, 90. http://www.cbo.gov/ftpdocs/120xx/doc12085/03-10-ReducingTheDeficit.pdf

91 The navy calls them: Julian Barnes and Nathan Hodge,

"The New Arms Race: China Takes Aim at U.S. Naval Might," *Wall Street Journal,* January 4, 2012.

92 The new carriers: U.S. Navy Fact File: Aircraft Carriers. http://www.navy.mil/navydata/fact_display.asp?cid=4200&tid=200&ct=4

92 "The need to project": Remarks as delivered by Secretary of Defense Robert M. Gates, May 3, 2010. http://www.defense.gov/speeches/speech.aspx?speechid=1460

93 Obama reportedly rejected: http://www.nytimes.com/2012/01/05/us/in-new-strategy-panetta-plans-even-smaller-army.html?_r=1

93 "The president feels": Interview, Leon Panetta.

93 In May 2010: Remarks as delivered by Secretary of Defense Robert Gates, Dwight D. Eisenhower Presidential Library, May 8, 2010. http://www.defense.gov/speeches/speech.aspx?speechid=1467

94 as on the war in Iraq: http://www.fas.org/sgp/crs/natsec/RL33110.pdf

94 Health care consumes: Lawrence Korb et al., *Restoring Tricare: Ensuring the Long Term Viability of the Military Health Care System* (Washington, D.C.: Center for American Progress, March 2010). http://www.americanprogress.org/issues/2011/02/pdf/tricare.pdf

94 "meets with a furious": Remarks by Gates. http://www.defense.gov/speeches/speech.aspx?speechid=1467

94 "They've always been very strong": Interview, Leon Panetta.

95 Few outsiders appreciate: Congressional Budget Office, "Reducing the Deficit: Spending and Revenue Options," 80. http://www.cbo.gov/ftpdocs/120xx/doc12085/03-10-ReducingTheDeficit.pdf

95 "Try to change": Belinda Luscombe, "Ten Questions for Alan Simpson," *Time,* August 8, 2011. http://www.time.com/time/magazine/article/0,9171,2084567,00.html

95 Obama's latest budget: Karen Parish, " 'Budget Request Preserves Troop Health Benefits,' Official Says," Department of Defense, February 14, 2012. http://www.defense.gov/news/newsarticle.aspx?id=67190

95 The health plan is so generous: http://www.cbo.gov/sites/default/files/cbofiles/attachments/GrahamLetter021712.pdf

95 "so cheap": Elisabeth Bumiller and Thom Shanker, "Gates Seeing to Contain Military Costs," *New York Times,* November 28, 2010.

96 "costing us $11 billion": Quoted in Amanda Palleschi, "Budget Request Includes TRICARE Cut, Military Retirement Details," *Government Executive,* February 13, 2012. http://www.govexec.com/defense/2012/02/budget-request-includes-tricare-cut-military-retirement-details/41193/print/

97 But 65 percent: Association for State Dam Safety Officials, "Dam Owners." http://damsafety.org/community/owners/?p=e9a03866-a7b1-469a-83d8-27122057751a

97 "Many state dam safety programs": American Society of Civil Engineers, "America's Infrastructure Report Card." http://www.infrastructurereportcard.org/fact-sheet/dams

98 South Dakota: Association of State Dam Safety Officials, "2010 Statistics on State Dam Safety Regulation," November 2011.http://www.damsafety.org/media/Documents/STATE_INFO/State%20Performance%20Data/2010_StateStats.pdf

98 A 1972 dam collapse: Association of State Dam Safety Officials, "Dam Failures, Dam Incidents." http://www.damsafety.org/media/Documents/STATE_INFO/State%20Performance%20Data/2010_StateStats.pdf

98 The Army Corps of Engineers: Army Corps of Engineers, "Dams by Hazard Potential." http://geo.usace.army.mil/pgis/f?p=397:5:3537652343623686::NO

98 And thus was born: Association of State Dam Safety Officials, "National Dam Safety Program Act of 2006." http://www.damsafety.org/media/Documents/Legislative%20Handouts/2007-08/National%20Dam%20Safety%20Program%20Act%2006.pdf

100 A 2011 Pew: Pew Research Center poll, June 15–19, 2011. http://www.people-press.org/files/legacy-questionnaires/June11%20space%20topline%20for%20release.pdf

100 Gallup poll: Gallup Inc., "Majority of Americans Say Space Program Costs Justified," July 17, 2009. http://www.gallup.com/poll/121736/majority-americans-say-space-program-costs-justified.asp

100 "Space exploration": Barack Obama, "On Space Exploration in the 21st Century," April 15, 2010. http://www.nasa.gov/news/media/trans/obama_ksc_trans.html

101 "Every dollar": Charles Bolden, NASA budget briefing, February 13, 2012. Video is at http://www.c-span.org/Events/NASA-Fiscal-Year-2013-Budget-Briefing/10737428275/

101 "The Mars program": Yudhijit Bhattacharjee, "Ed Weiler Says He Quit NASA Over Cuts to Mars Program," *Science Insider,* February 9, 2012. http://news.sciencemag.org/scienceinsider/2012/02/ed-weiler-says-he-quit-nasa-over.html

102 "We could not": Charles Bolden, NASA budget briefing,

February 13, 2012. Video is at http://www.c-span.org/Events/NASA-Fiscal-Year-2013-Budget-Briefing/10737428275/

## CHAPTER 4: WHERE THE MONEY COMES FROM

103 Joseph decreed: Genesis 47:26.

103 Large parts of the Rosetta Stone: Rosetta Stone translation by R. S. Simpson, Griffith Institute, Oxford University. http://www.britishmuseum.org/explore/highlights/article_index/r/the_rosetta_stone_translation.aspx

103 In the eighteenth century: W. R. Ward, "The Administration of the Window and Assessed Taxes, 1696–1798," *English Historical Review* 68 (1952): 522–42. http://www.buildinghistory.org/taxation.shtml

103 Peter the Great taxed: *Modern History Sourcebook: Peter the Great and the Rise of Russia, 1682–1725,* Fordham University. http://www.fordham.edu/halsall/mod/petergreat.asp

103 In 1779, Britain: "A Tax to Beat Napoleon," HM Revenue and Customs. http://www.hmrc.gov.uk/history/taxhis1.htm

104 "After the income tax": Quoted in Daniel Gross, "A Look Back at America's Time of Temperance," *Newsweek,* June 6, 2010. http://www.thedailybeast.com/newsweek/2010/06/01/a-look-back-at-america-s-time-of-temperance.html

104 Initially, the income tax: Michael J. Graetz, *The U.S. Income Tax: What It Is, How It Got That Way, and Where We Go from Here* (New York: W. W. Norton, 1997), 16. Also see Bruce Bartlett, *The Benefit and the Burden: Tax Reform–Why We Need It and What It Will Take* (New York: Simon & Schuster, 2012), 249; and Tax Foundation, "Fed-

eral Individual Income Tax Rates History." http://www.taxfoundation.org/files/fed_individual_rate_history_nominal&adjusted-20110909.pdf

105 "Because of the need": Joel Slemrod and Jon Bakija, *Taxing Ourselves: A Citizen's Guide to the Great Debate over Tax Reform* (Cambridge, Mass.: MIT Press, 1996), 23.

105 In contrast: Corporation Income Tax Brackets and Rates, 1909–2002. http://www.irs.gov/pub/irs-soi/02corate.pdf

105 In the early 1950s: Bartlett, *Benefit and Burden,* 3–12.

106 That last factor: U.S. Treasury, "The President's Framework for Corporate Tax Reform," February 2012, 8. http://www.treasury.gov/resource-center/tax-policy/Documents/The-Presidents-Framework-for-Business-Tax-Reform-02-22-2012.pdf

107 For every $1: U.S. Census Bureau, "Quarterly Summary of State and Local Tax Revenue." http://www.census.gov/govs/qtax/

108 State and local governments: Tax Policy Center, "State and Local Tax Revenue as a Percentage of Personal Income, 1977–2009." http://www.taxpolicycenter.org/taxfacts/displayafact.cfm?Docid=511

108 At last count: Center for Responsive Politics, "Lobbying Database." http://www.opensecrets.org/lobby/

108 "Gore lost": Interview, Jon Talisman.

111 "It's very difficult": Interview, Grover Norquist.

111 Republicans who violate: "The Pledge: Grover Norquist's Hold on the GOP," *60 Minutes,* November 20, 2011. http://www.cbsnews.com/8301-18560_162-57327816/the-pledge-grover-norquists-hold-on-the-gop/

111 "I don't want to abolish": "Profile: Political Activist Grover Norquist," *Morning Edition,* NPR, May 25, 2001.

http://www.npr.org/templates/story/story.php?storyId=1123439

111 He is funny: "Funniest Celebrity in Washington," September 30, 2009. http://www.youtube.com/watch?v=WWs0wAuNPY8

112 When he successfully: Bernie Becker, "Vote to End Ethanol Subsidies Revives Coburn-Norquist Tax Revenue Battle," *The Hill,* June 11, 2011. http://thehill.com/blogs/on-the-money/domestic-taxes/165891-ethanol-subsidies-revive-coburn-norquist-battle

112 "Which pledge is": *Meet the Press* transcript, April 24, 2011. http://www.msnbc.msn.com/id/42703787/ns/meet_the_press-transcripts/t/meet-press-transcript-april/; also see Philip Klein, "A Brief History of the Coburn-Norquist Tax Spat and Why It Matters," *Washington Examiner,* April 25, 2011. http://washingtonexaminer.com/blogs/beltway-confidential/2011/04/brief-history-coburn-norquist-tax-spat-and-why-it-matters#ixzz1l9502EUR

115 Their federal *income* taxes: http://www.cbo.gov/sites/default/files/cbofiles/attachments/10-25-HouseholdIncome.pdf

115 In 2011, about 40 percent: Tax Policy Center, "Distribution of Tax Units That Pay More in Payroll Taxes Than Individual Income Taxes, by Cash Income Percentile, Current Law, 2011," June 17, 2011. http://www.taxpolicycenter.org/numbers/displayatab.cfm?Docid=3073&DocTypeID=2

116 separate estimates by the Tax Policy Center: Personal communication, Tax Policy Center.

116 In December 2011: "Tax System Seen as Unfair, in Need

of Overhaul," Pew Research Center, December 20, 2011. http://www.people-press.org/2011/12/20/tax-system-seen-as-unfair-in-need-of-overhaul/; also see Gallup Poll, "Taxes," http://www.gallup.com/poll/1714/taxes.aspx

117 "Tax returns of the rich": Joseph J. Thorndike, "The Lessons of Mitt Romney's Tax Returns": CNN.com, January 26, 2012. http://money.cnn.com/2012/01/26/news/economy/romney_tax_returns/index.htm

117 Romney's return revealed: Tax History Project, "Presidential Tax Returns." http://taxhistory.tax.org/www/website.nsf/Web/PresidentialTaxReturns?OpenDocument

117 (taxed at a lower rate than wages): Tax Policy Center, "Average Effective Federal Tax Rates by Cash Income Percentiles, 2011 Baseline: Current Law," February 8, 2012. http://www.taxpolicycenter.org/numbers/displayatab.cfm?Docid=3277

117 newspaper editors: "Question-and-Answer Session at the Annual Convention of the Associated Press Managing Editors Association, Orlando, Florida," November 17, 1973. http://www.presidency.ucsb.edu/ws/index.php?pid=4046&st=associated+press&st1=#axzz1td0m7mRJ

118 testimony by the Treasury secretary: Joseph W. Barr, "Statement of Hon. Joseph W. Barr, Secretary of the Treasury," in U.S. Congress, Joint Economic Committee, *Hearings on the 1969 Economic Report of the President, pt. 1, 91st Cong., 1st sess., January 17* (Washington, D.C.: Government Printing Office, 1969), 4–98. Also see Graetz, *U.S. Income Tax,* 113.

118 first AMT taxpayer: William D. Samons, "President Nixon's Troublesome Tax Returns," April 11, 2005. http://www.taxhistory.org/thp/readings.nsf/cf7c9c870b600

b9585256df80075b9dd/f8723e3606cd79ec85256ff6006f82c3?OpenDocument

119 Nixon's successor: Ibid.

119 "Those who have done well": "Remarks by the President on Economic Growth and Deficit Reduction," Rose Garden, September 19, 2011. http://www.whitehouse.gov/the-press-office/2011/09/19/remarks-president-economic-growth-and-deficit-reduction

119 "You know, there was": Mitt Romney at Iowa State Fair, transcript, August 11, 2011.

120 Here's where things stand today: Tax Policy Center, "Share of Taxes Paid by Filing Status and Demographics, Under Current Law, by Cash Income Percentile, 2011," February 2, 2012. http://www.taxpolicycenter.org/numbers/displayatab.cfm?Docid=3271

121 size of the slice: http://g-mond.parisschoolofeconomics.eu/topincomes

121 The snapshot for 2008: Internal Revenue Service, "The 400 Individual Income Tax Returns Reporting the Highest Adjusted Gross Incomes Each Year, 1992–2008." http://www.irs.gov/pub/irs-soi/08intop400.pdf

121 "The very rich": http://taxvox.taxpolicycenter.org/2011/05/12/the-very-rich-really-are-different/

121 Nearly 60 percent of their gross income: http://www.irs.gov/pub/irs-soi/08intop400.pdf

122 After food stamps: Internal Revenue Service, "Earned Income Tax Credit Statistics." http://www.eitc.irs.gov/central/eitcstats/

123 Weapons Supply Tax Credit: Edward Kleinbard, "The Congress Within the Congress: How Tax Expenditures Distort Our Budget and Our Political Processes," *Ohio*

*Northern Law Review* 6, no. 2 (2010): 1–30. http://web law.usc.edu/assets/docs/contribute/Kleinbard%20 ONU%20proofs%20Final.pdf

123 These "tax expenditures": Office of Management and Budget, *Fiscal Year 2013 Analytical Perspectives,* "Estimates of Total Income Tax Expenditures for Fiscal Years 2011–2017," Table 17–1. http://www.whitehouse.gov/sites/default/files/omb/budget/fy2013/assets/spec.pdf

124 $2.3 trillion: Kleinbard, "The Congress Within the Congress," 26.

124 "It is just spending": Joint Select Committee on Deficit Reduction, *Hearing: Overview of Previous Debt Proposals,* November 1, 2011. http://www.c-span.org/Events/Super-Committee-Looks-at-Past-Debt-Proposals/10737425140-1/

124 about 10 percent of the spending: Office of Management and Budget, *Fiscal Year 2013 Analytical Perspectives,* Table 17-1. http://www.whitehouse.gov/sites/default/files/omb/budget/fy2013/assets/spec.pdf

124 If all the tax expenditures: Joint Committee on Taxation, memo, October 27, 2011. http://www.novoco.com/hottopics/resource_files/jct-memo_tax-expenditure-repeal_102711.pdf

125 "All real estate": Congressional Research Service, "Tax Expenditures" (Washington, D.C.: Government Printing Office, 2007), 336. http://www.gpo.gov/fdsys/pkg/CPRT-109SPRT31188/pdf/CPRT-109SPRT31188.pdf

125 The revenues lost: http://www.budget.senate.gov/democratic/index.cfm/files/serve?File_id=8a03a030-3ba8-4835-a67b-9c4033c03ec4, p. 425.

125 "readily realizable market value": http://www.exeter1031.com/history_section_1031.aspx

125 "If all exchanges": Quoted in Boris I. Bittker and Lawrence Lokken, *Federal Taxation of Income, Gifts and Trusts, 3d ed.* (Valhalla, N.Y: Warren, Gorham & Lamont, 2000), Section 44.2.1, p. 564.

125 one can swap a dental office: Atlas 1031 Exchange LLC, "The 1031 Exchange Blog: Medical, Dental and Veterinary Practice 1031 Exchange." http://www.atlas1031.com/blog/1031-exchange/bid/41380/Medical-Dental-and-Veterinary-Practice-1031-Exchange

125 One can trade horses: Atlas 1031 Exchange LLC, "The 1031 Exchange Blog: Livestock Eligible for 1031 Exchange." http://www.atlas1031.com/blog/1031-exchange/bid/37086/Livestock-Eligible-for-1031-Exchange

126 "Livestock of different sexes": Internal Revenue Service, "Like-Kind Exchanges–Real Estate Tax Tips," February 17, 2012. http://www.irs.gov/businesses/small/industries/article/0,,id=98491,00.html

126 "any strategy for reducing": "HR. 1249: An Act to Amend Title 35, United States Code, to Provide for Patent Reform," January 5, 2011, 44. http://www.uspto.gov/aia_implementation/bills-112hr1249enr.pdf

127 "you can make": http://accruit.com/accruit-1031-single-like-kind-exchanges/

127 Joe and Marilynn Croydon: Sam Smith, "Case Study: 1031 Exchanges and Vintage Motorcars," Accruit.com. http://accruit.com/case-study-1031-exchanges-and-vintage-motorcars/

## CHAPTER 5: WHY THIS CAN'T GO ON FOREVER

129 "We're driving": Interview, Robert Reischauer.

131 "throwing $800 billion out the window": "Romney Cam-

paigns in New Hampshire," Money, CNN.com. http://www.thebostonchannel.com/r/29327664/detail.html

132 CBO's latest price tag: Congressional Budget Office, *The Budget and Economic Outlook: Fiscal Years 2012 to 2022* (Washington, D.C.: Government Printing Office, January 2012), 9. http://www.cbo.gov/publication/42905

132 "No one would": David Weigel, "Douglas Holtz-Eakin: 'No One Would Argue That the Stimulus Has Done Nothing,' " *Washington Independent,* August 9, 2009. http://washingtonindependent.com/54312/douglas-holtz-eakin-no-one-would-argue-that-the-stimulus-has-done-nothing

133 "Suppose a patient": Christina D. Romer, "The Economy: Where Are We and What Should We Do?," League of Women Voters Annual Community Luncheon, August 18, 2011. http://www.econ.berkeley.edu/~cromer/The%20Economy%20Where%20Are%20We%20and%20What%20Should%20We%20Do.pdf

133 Harvard's Larry Summers . . . Stanford's John Taylor: Amanda E. McGowen, "Summers Debates Fiscal Policies," *Harvard Crimson,* February 29, 2012. http://www.thecrimson.com/article/2012/2/29/Summers-Debates-Fiscal-Policies/

134 A February 2012 survey: IGM Forum, "Economic Stimulus," posted February 15, 2012. http://www.igmchicago.org/igm-economic-experts-panel/poll-results?SurveyID=SV_cw5O9LNJL1oz4Xi

134 "I'm a believer": Interview, Robert Reischauer.

134 In a February 2012 Pew poll: Pew Research Center for the People & The Press, "February 2012 Political Survey," February 8–12, 2012. http://www.people-press.org/files/legacy-questionnaires/2-23-12%20Topline.pdf

135 "Debt to the Penny": "Debt to the Penny–and Who Owns It." http://www.savingsbonds.gov/NP/NPGateway

135 "[T]ruth is": "Remarks by the President on the Budget," February 13, 2012. http://www.whitehouse.gov/the-press-office/2012/02/13/remarks-president-budget

136 Back in 1955: Office of Management and Budget, *Fiscal Year 2013 Analytical Perspectives,* "Federal Borrowing and Debt," 81.

137 Measured as a percentage: David Wessel, "What's Going on with Debt in the U.S.," wsj.com, January 23, 2012. http://blogs.wsj.com/economics/2012/01/23/whats-going-on-with-debt-in-u-s/

139 "If the Treasury": Simon Johnson and James Kwak, *White House Burning: The Founding Fathers, Our National Debt and Why It Matters to You* (New York: Pantheon Books, 2012), p. 123.

139 more than triple: Office of Management and Budget, *Fiscal Year 2013 Historical Tables,* Table 9–7. http://www.whitehouse.gov/omb/budget/Historicals

140 Budget Control Act: http://cbo.gov/publication/42214

143 "The good news": Interview, Doug Elmendorf.

143 "If a country": J. Bradford DeLong, "Budgeting and Macro Policy: A Primer," February 2, 2012, 12. http://delong.typepad.com/20120221-budgeting-and-macro-policy-a-primer.pdf

144 "transcendent threat": Peter G. Peterson remarks, May 15, 2012. http://www.pgpf.org/Issues/Fiscal-Outlook/2012/05/051512-FS-Pete-Remarks.aspx

145 Drawn to economics: Interview with Paul Krugman, nobelprize.org, December 6, 2008. http://www.nobelprize.org/mediaplayer/index.php?id=1049

145 "How many bills": Ryan Lizza, "Letter from Washing-

ton: The Gatekeeper," *New Yorker*, March 2, 2009. http://www.newyorker.com/reporting/2009/03/02/090302fa_fact_lizza?currentPage=all

145 "The question is": Jane Hamsher, "Krugman Responds to Rahm Emanuel," Firedoglake.com, February 22, 2009. http://firedoglake.com/2009/02/22/krugman-responds-to-rahm-emanuel/

146 "Premature deficit reduction": Paul Krugman, "Notes on Deleveraging," *The Conscience of a Liberal*, January 22, 2012. http://krugman.blogs.nytimes.com/2012/01/22/notes-on-deleveraging/

147 "You shouldn't put": Interview, Paul Ryan.

148 "a strange combination": Paul Krugman, "Paul Ryan's Multiple Unicorns," *The Conscience of a Liberal*, April 6, 2001. http://krugman.blogs.nytimes.com/2011/04/06/PAUL-RYANS-MULTIPLE-UNICORNS/

148 "I believe the way": Interview, Paul Ryan.

148 "My daughter jokes": Peter G. Peterson, *The Education of an American Dreamer* (New York: Hachette Book Group, 2009), p 347.

149 "the godfather": Alan Feuer, "Peter G. Peterson's Last Anti-Debt Campaign," *New York Times*, April 10, 2011, MB1. http://www.nytimes.com/2011/04/10/nyregion/10peterson.html?pagewanted=all

150 "too much of an all-or-nothing": Leonard Silk, "Political Costs of Reagan Cuts," *New York Times*, March 20, 1981.

150 "a growing systemic inability": Peter G. Peterson, "Spending Limits," *New York Times*, July 23, 1981.

150 "playing golf": Interview, Peter Peterson.

150 "engage the American people": Peter G. Peterson Foun-

dation, "Q&A with Pete Peterson," October 7, 2011. http://www.pgpf.org/Issues/Fiscal-Outlook/2011/06/QA-with-Peter-Peterson.aspx?p=1

151 "On our current course": "A Letter from Peter G. Peterson to the Super Committee," November 2, 2011. http://www.pgpf.org/Issues/Fiscal-Outlook/2011/11/110211_Letter-to-Super-Committee.aspx

152 "Unlike some of my Wall Street": Peter G. Peterson, "Facing Up," *The Atlantic,* October 1993. http://www.theatlantic.com/past/politics/budget/facingf.htm

152 "objective economic advice": Robert Stanley Herren, "Council of Economic Advisers," EH.net, Encyclopedia. http://eh.net/encyclopedia/article/herren.cea

152 "The first recession": Christina D. Romer, "Not My Father's Recession: The Extraordinary Challenges and Policy Responses of the First Twenty Months of the Obama Administration," National Press Club, September 1, 2010. http://www.whitehouse.gov/sites/default/files/microsites/100901-National-Press-Club.pdf

153 "The evidence is stronger": Christina D. Romer, "What Do We Know About the Effects of Fiscal Policy? Separating Evidence from Ideology," Hamilton College, November 7, 2011. http://www.econ.berkeley.edu/~cromer/Written%20Version%20of%20Effects%20of%20Fiscal%20Policy.pdf

154 "We don't have to": Christina Romer, "The Economy: Where Are We and What Should We Do," League of Women Voters Annual Community Luncheon, August 18, 2011. http://elsa.berkeley.edu/~cromer/The%20Economy%20Where%20Are%20We%20and%20What%20Should%20We%20Do.pdf

154 "a two-handed plan": Ben Bernanke at House Committee on Financial Services, February 29, 2012.

155 "a geek with guts": Sheryl Gay Stolberg, "Capital Holds Breath as He Crunches Numbers," *New York Times,* November 17, 2009.

155 "A quiet man": Ibid.

156 "You want to be sure": Interview, Doug Elmendorf.

157 "Why wouldn't one conclude": "The Budget and Economic Outlook: Fiscal Years 2012–2022," Hearing of the Senate Budget Committee, February 2, 2012.

157 "I don't want to speak": Ibid.

157 "We cannot go back": Interview, Doug Elmendorf.

158 "The country faces": David Wessel, "The Federal Deficit Mess in a Single Sentence," wsj.com, November 11, 2009. http://blogs.wsj.com/washwire/2009/11/11/the-federal-deficit-mess-in-a-single-sentence/

159 "The country": Interview, Douglas Elmendorf.

162 "I used to tell the students": Interview, Leon Panetta.

# BIBLIOGRAPHY

In addition to the publications and websites of the White House Office of Management and Budget, the Congressional Budget Office, the Tax Policy Center, the Committee for a Responsible Federal Budget, the Bipartisan Policy Center, the Center on Budget and Policy Priorities, and the Peter G. Peterson Foundation, the following books provided valuable context and explanation.


Bartlett, Bruce. *The Benefit and the Burden: Tax Reform–Why We Need It and What It Will Take.* New York: Simon & Schuster, 2012.

Dame, Philip R., and Bernard H. Martin. *The Evolution of OMB.* Privately published, Washington, D.C., 2009.

Darman, Richard. *Who's in Control? Polar Politics and the Sensible Center.* New York: Simon & Schuster, 1996.

Graetz, Michael J. *The U.S. Income Tax: What It Is, How It Got That Way, and Where We Go from Here.* New York: W. W. Norton, 1997.

Hager, George, and Eric Pianin. *Mirage: Why Neither Demo-*

*crats nor Republicans Can Balance the Budget, End the Deficit, and Satisfy the Public.* New York: Times Books, 1997.

Johnson, Simon, and James Kwak. *White House Burning: The Founding Fathers, Our National Debt, and Why It Matters to You.* New York: Pantheon Books, 2012.

Joyce, Philip G. *The Congressional Budget Office: Honest Numbers, Power, and Policymaking.* Washington, D.C.: Georgetown University Press, 2011.

Panetta, Leon, and Peter Gall. *Bring Us Together: The Nixon Team and the Civil Rights Retreat.* New York: J. B. Lippincott Co., 1971.

Peterson, Peter G. *The Education of an American Dreamer: How a Son of Greek Immigrants Learned His Way from a Nebraska Diner to Washington, Wall Street, and Beyond.* New York: Hachette Book Group, 2009.

Scheiber, Noam. *The Escape Artists: How Obama's Team Fumbled the Recovery.* New York: Simon & Schuster, 2012.

Schick, Allen. *The Federal Budget: Politics, Policy, Process.* Washington, D.C.: The Brookings Institution, 2000.

Slemrod, Joel, and Jon Bakija. *Taxing Ourselves: A Citizen's Guide to the Great Debate over Tax Reform.* Cambridge, Mass.: MIT Press, 1996.

Stein, Herbert. *The Fiscal Revolution in America: Policy in Pursuit of Reality.* Washington, D.C.: American Enterprise Institute Press, 1996.

Stockman, David A. *The Triumph of Politics: Why the Reagan Revolution Failed.* New York: Harper & Row, 1986.

# ACKNOWLEDGMENTS

In a sense, I have been working on this book for the twenty-five years I've been an economics reporter in Washington, a pursuit that depends in part on the willingness of budget experts in and out of government to field reporters' questions and offer instruction. Among those on whom I have relied over the years and to whom I turned in researching this book were Barry Anderson, Ken Baer, Steve Bell, Stanley Collander, Robert Greenstein, Bill Hoagland, James Horney, Robert Reischauer, Gene Sperling, Douglas Holtz-Eakin, Douglas Elmendorf, Donald Marron, Todd Harrison, Allen Schick, Eugene Steuerle, Conor Sweeney, Susan Tanaka, Eric Toder–and several others who prefer not to be named. Among the reporters on the budget beat whose thorough work I consulted for perspective and detail were Naftali Bendavid, Jackie Calmes, Nathan Hodge, Janet Hook, Ryan Lizza, Lori Montgomery, Dan Morgan, Damian Paletta, Eric Pianin, David Rogers, and Noam Scheiber.

# ACKNOWLEDGMENTS

My agent, Raphael Sagalyn, sparked this book, and was a constant and valued counselor from start to finish. Howard and Nathan Means were extremely efficient and perceptive editors, helpful on matters large and small. Roger Scholl at Crown Books was an enthusiastic supporter, offering his advice at key moments. Able copy editor Maureen Clark fixed broken sentences and caught careless errors. Veteran budget reporters Jackie Calmes of the *New York Times* and Janet Hook of the *Wall Street Journal* generously read the manuscript and offered suggestions. Nelson Hsu turned my ideas into clear and attractive charts. Benjamin Grazda, Spencer Wright, and Lois Parshley were agile and conscientious research assistants. The Woodrow Wilson Center for International Scholars provided a quiet place to work and resourceful librarians. The editors of the *Wall Street Journal,* which remains the best place to practice daily journalism, granted me a leave without which this book would not have been possible. Any mistakes are my responsibility alone.

Book-writing is hard on spouses. This book is no exception. My wife, Naomi, put up with my absence, crabbiness, and sleepless nights without complaint, and I love her for that and for many other reasons.

# INDEX

Affordable Care Act, 116
Afghanistan war, 21, 63, 64, 66, 89, 90
aircraft carriers, 91–93
alcohol taxes, 104, 110
Americans for Tax Reform, 111–12
automaker bailouts, 25, 26, 130
autopilot spending, 20–21, 48–49, 74, 150

bailouts, 24–26, 130
Bakija, Jon, 105
balanced budgets, 37–38, 40, 49
  online budget games, 69–70
bank bailouts, 24–26, 130
Barry, Dave, 19
Bartlett, Bruce, 55–56
benefit programs, 22–23, 30, 34, 68, 73. See also *specific programs*
  as autopilot spending, 20–21, 48–49, 74, 150
  future growth and spending, 86, 87, 102, 157–58, 159–60
  pay-as-you-go rule, 56
Bernanke, Ben, 145, 154
big government, 39–40, 60, 111
Blackstone Group, 149, 150
Boehner, John, 14
Bolden, Charles, 101, 102
borrowing, 31. *See also* government borrowing
Bowles, Erskine, 32, 60, 95, 124, 149
Bradford, David, 123
Brady, Francis, 95
Brodie, Bernard, 91
Brookings Institution, 46, 156
Budget Control Act, 140–41
budget deficits. *See* deficit *entries*
budget future, 161–62. *See also* deficit reduction
  CBO forecast, 141–44, 158
  Elmendorf on, 143, 156–61
  Obama on, 135
budget games, 69–70

budget history, 35–68
  1930s–1940s, 34, 37–40
  1960s–1970s, 34, 43–48
  1980s, 48–52
  1990s, 52–62
  overview, 35–37
  2000s, 61–68
budget surpluses, 34, 38, 55, 61–68
Buffett, Warren, 88
Bureau of the Budget, 38, 40
Bush, George H. W., 51, 52, 53, 55
  1990 budget deal, 53–56, 61, 66
  tax increases, 34, 53–54
Bush, George W., 25, 40, 55, 100
  food stamp expansion, 83
  tax cuts, 62, 63, 64, 66, 114, 116, 154, 161

Califano, Joseph, 42
capital gains taxes, 121–22, 125–27
Capitol Tax Partners, 108–9
Carter, Jimmy, 47, 52, 98
CBO. *See* Congressional Budget Office
CEA, 152, 156
Cheney, Dick, 57
China, 29, 92, 136–37, 139–40
Clinton, Bill, 16, 32, 57, 59–61
  budget surpluses, 34, 55, 61–68
  deficit-reduction efforts, 57–60
  health care plan, 47
  welfare reform, 84
Coburn, Tom, 112
Collender, Stan, 71
Committee for a Responsible Federal Budget, 67, 151
Concord Coalition, 151
Congress and Congressional budget process, 13–14, 17, 20, 38, 43, 45, 81
  CBO establishment, 45–48
  conflict and dysfunction, 45, 48, 53, 61, 161–62
  current budget debate, 140–41, 154–55, 156–57
  1990 budget deal, 53–56, 61, 66
  no-tax-increase pledge, 111–12
Congressional Budget Act, 45, 48
Congressional Budget Office (CBO), 24, 41, 45–48, 63–65, 134
  current debate and, 141–44, 156–61
Conrad, Kent, 62, 67, 157
corporate taxes, 105–7, 116, 124
Council of Economic Advisers, 152, 156
Crippen, Dan, 63

dam safety program, 97–99
Daniels, Mitch, 41
Darman, Richard, 51, 54, 55
defense spending, 21–22, 35, 56, 74, 89–96
  for health care, 94–96

Iraq and Afghanistan wars, 21, 63, 64, 66, 89, 90
military equipment, 90–93
1940s, 41
1980s, 52, 66, 89, 90
overviews, 73, 90
deficit reduction, 102, 112, 124, 140–41. *See also* spending cuts; tax increases
Bernanke's views, 154
Clinton-era efforts, 57–60
Elmendorf's views, 159–61
Krugman's views, 144, 146
Obama on, 135–36
Peterson's views, 144, 148–52
public suggestions, 72, 74
Romer's views, 154
Ryan's views, 18, 61, 85, 144, 146–48
deficits, 19, 62. *See also* deficit reduction; federal debt; government borrowing
current, 25, 30–31, 41, 63–65
future, 31–32, 129, 158
past, 51–55
DeLong, Brad, 143–44
discretionary spending, 96–97. See also *specific programs*
Dole, Bob, 84

Earned Income Tax Credit, 122, 123
economic conditions, 63–64. *See also* Great Recession; recession/depression
in Europe, 146, 153–54
future, 143
Eisenhower, Dwight D., 93–94
Elmendorf, Douglas, 47, 63, 76, 143, 155–61
Emanuel, Rahm, 145
entitlements. *See* benefits programs
Eskow, RJ, 47
estate tax, 107
European economic conditions, 146, 153–54

Fannie Mae, 26, 139
farm subsidies, 80–82
federal debt, 56–57, 62, 64, 136–40. *See also* government borrowing
current status, 65, 135–36
debt ceiling vote, 140–41
foreign debt, 29, 30, 31–32, 136–40
future, 136, 143, 158
interest on, 30, 33, 73, 139–40, 146
overviews, 137, 138
federal employees, 22–23, 94–96
Federal Reserve Board, 38, 40, 55, 62, 145, 156
Feldstein, Martin, 156
financial crisis. *See also* Great Recession
TARP program and bailouts, 24–26, 65, 130
*The Fiscal Revolution in America* (Stein), 37, 38, 39, 40

fiscal stimulus, 65, 83, 97, 130, 131–34, 145–46, 153–54
food stamps, 23, 70, 82–85
Ford, Gerald, 119
foreign aid, 21–22
foreign countries
  European economic conditions, 146, 153–54
  military spending, 21
  taxes in, 27–28
  U.S. investments, 29, 30, 31–32, 136–40
Fortunate Four Hundred, 121–22
Freddie Mac, 26, 139
Freedom to Farm Act, 81
Friedlander, Robert, 13

gas prices, 129
Gates, Robert, 92–93, 93–94
General Motors bailout, 25, 26
Gingrich, Newt, 54, 59, 60–61, 83
gold standard, 38
Gore, Al, 58
government bonds, 31–32, 64, 136, 137
government borrowing, 21, 29–30, 31, 65, 103, 135–40. *See also* federal debt
  future, 136, 143, 158
government shutdowns, 20, 48, 59
government size, 38, 39–40, 60, 66, 111
Great Depression, 37, 38–40, 83–84
Great Recession, 24–25, 41, 63, 64, 83. *See also* financial crisis; unemployment
  Obama stimulus, 65, 83, 97, 130, 131–34, 145–46, 153
  revenues and, 29–30, 36, 113–14
  spending and, 31, 36
Great Society, 34, 43–44
Greece, 146
Greenspan, Alan, 62
Grunwald, Michael, 81
Gustafson, Andy, 126

Harrison, Todd, 96
health care costs, 18, 23–24, 76, 77, 143
health care reform, 47, 116
health care spending, 23–24, 74–79, 94–96, 147. *See also* Medicaid; Medicare
  future, 55, 75–76, 143
health insurance, 43, 94–96, 124. *See also* Medicaid; Medicare
Heritage Foundation, 147
hip replacements, 76–77
Holtz-Eakin, Douglas, 47, 48, 132
homeland security spending, 64–65, 66, 71, 85
home mortgage tax deduction, 124
Hoover, Herbert, 38, 40, 80
House Budget Committee, 17. *See also* Ryan, Paul

Huelskamp, Tim, 82
humanitarian aid, 22

income, taxes and, 113, 114, 120–21
income taxes, 27–28, 54, 103–5, 106, 112–17, 121–22. *See also* tax *entries*
  corporate, 105–7, 116, 124
  state and local, 107–8
interest
  on federal debt, 30, 33, 73, 139–40, 146
  home mortgage tax deduction, 124
Iraq war, 21, 63, 64, 66, 89, 90

Japan, 136–37
Johnson, Lyndon B., 34, 43–44, 52
Johnson, Simon, 139

Kasich, John, 60
Kennedy, John F., 52, 99
Keynes, John Maynard, 40, 145
Krugman, Paul, 144–46, 148, 153, 155
Kuchel, Thomas, 42–43, 44
Kwak, James, 139

Lew, Jack, 15, 16–17, 23, 60, 61
Lewinsky, Monica, 61
Lichtenberg, Frank, 43–44
like-kind exchanges, 125–27
lobbyists, 108–9
local taxes, 27, 107–8
Long, Russell, 122

Mankiw, Greg, 156
Margolies-Mezvinsky, Marjorie, 58
McGovern, George, 84
Medicaid, 16–17, 43, 77–78
Medicaid spending, 22–23, 44, 55, 73, 76, 147, 160
Medicare, 37, 43–44, 75, 96
  prescription drug expansion, 56, 63, 65, 66–67, 78–79
  Ryan's proposals, 147, 148
Medicare spending, 22–23, 44, 73, 76–77
  future, 76, 154, 158, 159–60
  1990s, 55, 58, 60
Medicare tax, 27, 105, 115, 116
middle class tax burden, 27, 113, 115–16, 120
military spending. *See* defense spending
Mitchell, George, 53
Morgan, Dan, 81
Moynihan, Daniel Patrick, 49
Muskie, Edmund, 46, 47

NASA, 97, 99–102
National Dam Safety Program, 97–99
national debt. *See* federal debt

New Deal, 34, 37–40
9/11 attacks, 65–66
Nixon, Richard, and Nixon administration, 44, 45–46, 52, 117–19, 149
Norquist, Grover, 61, 110–12

Obama, Barack, 40, 67, 83, 100–101, 135–36
  tax cuts, 64, 115–16
  tax increase proposal, 119, 160
Obama administration. *See also* 2013 budget
  budget policy debate, 130, 154–55
  deficit growth, 135–36
  fiscal stimulus, 65, 83, 97, 130, 131–34, 145–46, 153
  health care reform, 47, 116
  staff and advisers, 35, 153, 156
Office of Management and Budget, 15
Okrent, Daniel, 104
OMB, 15
online budget games, 69
Organization for Economic Cooperation and Development, 28
Orszag, Peter, 16, 47, 156

Panetta, Leon, 33–35, 42–43, 44, 52, 55, 67–68
  as Clinton budget director, 57, 58–59, 60, 89–90
  in Congress, 49, 51, 52–53, 54, 56–57, 89–90
  as Secretary of Defense, 35, 90–91, 162
"A Path to Prosperity" (Ryan), 146–47
Paulson, Hank, 25
pay-as-you-go rule, 56
payroll taxes, 27, 104, 105, 106, 115, 154
Penner, Rudy, 47
Perot, Ross, 57
Perry, Rick, 86
Peterson, Peter G., 144, 148–52, 155
Portman, Rob, 72, 74–75
Powell, Colin, 57
prescription drug coverage
  Medicaid, 77–78
  Medicare, 56, 63, 65, 66–67, 78–79
Prohibition, 104
public opinion
  on the budget, 19–20, 22, 70–72
  Peterson deficit-awareness efforts, 149, 150–52
  on Social Security, 85–86
  on the space program, 100
  on the stimulus, 132–33, 134
  on taxes, 110–11, 116–17, 128, 158

Reagan, Ronald, 49, 52, 84, 110
  defense spending, 52, 66, 89, 90

fiscal policies, 34, 49–52, 149–50
real estate exchanges, 125–27
recession/depression, 40, 55, 63–64, 65, 152–53. *See also* economic conditions; Great Depression; Great Recession
Reischauer, Robert, 41, 46, 47, 56, 129, 134
revenues, 36, 103, 113–14. *See also* government borrowing; tax *entries*
Rivlin, Alice, 46–47, 57, 134
Romer, Christina, 133, 152–54, 155
Romney, Mitt, 83, 117, 119, 131
Roosevelt, Franklin Delano, 34, 37–40, 41, 43, 80
Rostenkowski, Dan, 51
Rubin, Robert, 57, 62
Ryan, Paul, 15–16, 17–19, 61, 85, 144, 152, 155

safety net, 18, 83, 88–89. *See also* Medicaid; Medicare; Social Security
sales taxes, 107
Schick, Allen, 48, 66
Section 1031 exchanges, 125–27
Securities and Exchange Commission, 40
September 11 attacks, 65–66
Simpson, Alan, 95
Slemrod, Joel, 105
Snowe, Olympia, 58
Social Security, 18–19, 41, 60–61, 85–89, 147
Social Security spending, 23, 73, 85
  future, 86, 87, 157–58, 159
Social Security tax, 27, 105, 115
Soderberg, Martha, 88–89
Soviet Union, 56
space program, 99–102
spending, 69–102. *See also specific programs*
  mandatory, 20–21, 48–49, 74, 150
  overviews, 36, 73
  in the past, 36, 39, 40, 43, 49, 50, 52
  waste, 71–72
spending caps, 56, 58, 97, 140–41
spending cuts. *See also* deficit reduction; *specific programs*
  1990s, 54, 56, 58, 60, 66
Standard & Poors credit rating, 31
Starker, T. J., 126
state taxes, 27, 107–8
Stein, Herbert, 37, 38, 39, 40
Steuerle, Eugene, 21
stimulus, 65, 83, 97, 130, 131–34, 145–46, 153–54
Stockman, David, 49–50, 51
stock market, 129
Summers, Larry, 133, 156
surpluses, 34, 38, 55, 61–68

Talisman, Jon, 108–9
Tanaka, Susan, 99
tariffs, 104, 110

TARP, 24, 25–26, 65
tax breaks, 27, 28–29, 105, 122–28, 154–55, 160
 for corporations, 106–7, 124
 lobbyists, 108–9
tax cuts, 123, 147, 154–55
 Bush Jr. tax cuts, 62, 63, 64, 66, 114, 116, 154, 161
 Clinton era, 57, 60
 Obama tax cut, 64, 115–16, 154
 pay-as-you-go rule, 56
 Reagan tax cuts, 34, 49, 51–52
taxes, 103–28
 corporate, 105–7, 116, 124
 individual, 26–28, 112–17
 overview, 103–8
 payroll taxes, 27, 104, 106, 115, 154
 political wrangling, 28–29, 109, 119, 141, 161
 public opinion, 110–11, 116–17, 128, 158
 recent debate, 154–55
 tax lobbying, 108–9
 wealthy Americans, 54, 58, 104, 113, 114, 116, 117–22
tax increases, 111–12, 119, 152, 155, 160–61
 no-increase pledge, 111–12
 in the past, 34, 38, 52, 53–54, 58, 61
*Taxing Ourselves* (Slemrod and Bakija), 105
Tax Policy Center, 27, 120–21
tax reform, 29, 109, 128, 160
 corporate, 107, 124
Tax Reform Act of 1986, 54, 105, 124
Taylor, John, 133
Thorndike, Joseph J., 117
Tricare, 94–96
Troubled Asset Relief Program, 24, 25–26, 65
Truman, Harry, 43
2012 presidential campaign, 82–83, 117, 119, 131, 144
2013 budget, 13, 16, 69, 82, 101, 135–36, 154–55
 defense spending, 90, 95

U.S. Treasury bonds, 31–32, 64, 136, 137
unemployment, 129, 143, 144–46, 153
unemployment benefits, 30, 143

Walker, David, 150–51
Walters, Barbara, 55
Wanniski, Jude, 50
wealthy Americans
 estate tax, 107
 tax burden, 54, 58, 104, 113, 114, 116, 117–22
Weiler, Ed, 101
welfare and welfare reform, 84
Whiskey Rebellion, 110
*White House Burning* (Johnson and Kwak), 139
Williams, Roberton, 121
Wirthlin, Richard, 52
World War II, 41, 84, 90, 104–5

# ABOUT THE AUTHOR

David Wessel is economics editor for the *Wall Street Journal* and writes the Capital column (wsj.com/capital), a weekly look at the economy and forces shaping living standards around the world. He appears frequently on National Public Radio's *Morning Edition* and on WETA's *Washington Week.* He tweets actively at www.twitter.com/davidmwessel.

Previously, Wessel was deputy bureau chief of the *Wall Street Journal*'s Washington bureau. He joined the *Wall Street Journal* in 1984 in Boston, and moved to Washington in 1987. In 1999 and 2000 he served as the newspaper's Berlin bureau chief. He previously worked for the *Boston Globe,* as well as the *Hartford Courant* and the *Middleton Press* in Connecticut.

Wessel has shared two Pulitzer Prizes, one for *Boston Globe* stories in 1983 on the persistence of racism in Boston and the other for stories in the *Wall Street Journal* in 2002 on corporate wrongdoing.

His book *In Fed We Trust: Ben Bernanke's War on the Great Panic* was selected by the *New York Times* as one of the 100 Notable Books of 2008. He is also the coauthor, with *Wall Street Journal* reporter Bob Davis, of *Prosperity,* a 1998 book on the American middle class.

A product of the New Haven, Connecticut, public schools and a 1975 graduate of Haverford College, he was a Knight Bagehot fellow in business and economic journalism at Columbia University in 1980–1981. Wessel and his wife, Naomi Karp, have two children, Julia and Ben. His website is www.davidwessel.net.